Action and Conviction
in Early Modern
Europe

E. HARRIS HARBISON, 1907-1964

# Action and Conviction in Early Modern Europe

*Essays in Memory of E. H. Harbison*

*Editors*

THEODORE K. RABB
JERROLD E. SEIGEL

PRINCETON UNIVERSITY PRESS
PRINCETON, NEW JERSEY
1969

This book has been composed in
Granjon type.


Printed in the United States of America
by Princeton University Press, Princeton, New Jersey


*Publication of this book has been
aided by a grant from the Rollins Fund of the
Department of History, Princeton University*

# E. HARRIS HARBISON

E. Harris Harbison—known to his friends and colleagues as "Jinks"—was born in Sewickley, Pennsylvania, on April 28, 1907. He graduated from Princeton in 1928, took his Ph.D. at Harvard under Roger Bigelow Merriman, and returned to Princeton as Instructor in History in 1933. He remained at Princeton for the rest of his life. In 1949 he became Henry Charles Lea Professor of History, a post he held until his death on July 13, 1964.

To fill in the outline of his life would be to list the many honors he received (and refused) and the many students and colleagues whose spirits he enlightened with his thoughtful sympathy, his warm understanding, and his superb wit. These qualities will not be forgotten. Their memory is already enshrined in the E. Harris Harbison Awards for Distinguished Teaching, presented every year by the Danforth Foundation. And the contributors to the present volume hope this book will help keep Jinks Harbison's memory and influence alive—especially among those who share his interest and carry on his work in late medieval and early modern European history.

Professional historians, like all men, commit themselves to a variety of tasks whose demands are not always equally well met. Scholarship does not necessarily go hand in hand with teaching, and the reconciliation of both these pursuits with the deepest-felt needs of an individual human being is rare indeed. Few men are able to combine teaching, scholarship, and personal conviction so that each grows out of the others. E. Harris Harbison was one of the few. The organic harmony of his life was the fundamental reason for the unique position he occupied in his university and in his profession, and for the genuine inspiration he gave—and still gives—to his students.

Near the end of his life Jinks Harbison told of having once been jokingly dubbed "the departmental Christian," and it is from his faith and the humanity of his attitude toward it that any understanding of the man must begin. We cannot presume to describe the inner character of this faith, but we can try to suggest the ways—profound yet unobtrusive—in which it informed his teaching and his scholarship.

Traditional as it was, Jinks Harbison's Christian commitment was also humanistic in the best sense. We cannot do better than to quote one of his own descriptions of the relationship between faith and his calling:

The Christian who is also a historian, then, will be known neither by any fully-rounded "philosophy of history" which is the necessary outcome of his Christian belief, nor by the amount of time he spends talking or writing about Christianity. He will be known by *his attitude toward history*, the quality of his concern about it, the sense of reverence and responsibility with which he approaches his subject.

Rejecting both dogmatism and skepticism, he approached history and life with a firm belief in human possibilities and an uncompromising recognition of human inadequacies which together illuminated all his work as teacher and scholar. The humanity of his outlook ensured that his influence would extend to colleagues and students who had spiritual commitments different from his own. And the profundity of his faith helped to establish that organic relationship between personal conviction, teaching, and scholarship which was his hallmark.

His teaching was characterized by a continual concern for the underlying meaning of history, and by a ceaseless effort to reveal the relevance of his scholarly knowledge to his own life and to that of his students. While never allowing himself to present secular history as a witness to the truth of Christianity, he succeeded in conveying to his students "the quality of his concern about it." The quality of his concern merged with the quality of his mind to produce one of the most loved and respected teachers in the history of his university, known for his sympathetic interest in students and his rigorous criticism of sloppy thinking. Asked for the secret of the famous Harbison preceptorials, a recent Princeton senior could only reply, "He always asks the right questions." He was not afraid to raise the "big" questions, as his essays on "Divine Providence and Human History" or "Freedom in Western Thought" demonstrated. But even when dealing with such themes he employed humor, not only to sharpen his insights but also to suggest his own limitations and those of scholarly inquiry in general. In these ways he resembled the Erasmus whom he once described (commenting on *The Praise of Folly*) as follows:

These are light-hearted words with serious undertones, the words of a man who takes his calling seriously and himself lightly. . . . Erasmus knew his calling as a Christian scholar to be serious and important, but he also knew the presumption in it, the presumption that taints all human aspirations and must often amuse a loving God. In a word, he believed that intellectuals are both necessary and ridiculous. This is the meaning . . . of Huizinga's remark that "Only when humor illuminated Erasmus' mind did it become truly profound."

The same spirit animated his own scholarship. In his most mature and characteristic work he sought reflective understanding rather than novel interpretation. Writing of Machiavelli's career as a Florentine diplomat, he pointed out that the author of *The Prince* was "generally second in command on any given legation, not first—which suggests that his bosses valued his brains above his judgment." To Jinks Harbison good judgment was as important as analytic insight. Deeply imbued with a sense of the complexity of history, he continually reminded us that "there are no simple solutions."

His concentration on the Age of Reformation was the natural outcome of his abiding concerns. Within this historical period he turned his attention to two connected problems, which had also been of major importance to the Christian humanists with whom he felt a close bond: the relations between conduct and reflection, and between outer morality and inner conviction. He dealt with the first of these problems in his first book (based on his doctoral dissertation), *Rival Ambassadors at the Court of Queen Mary,* which received the Herbert Baxter Adams Prize of the American Historical Association in 1942. His later writings, including his general survey of *The Age of Reformation,* and especially *The Christian Scholar in the Age of the Reformation* and the essays collected in the volume *Christianity and History,* showed his mind at work on the questions which touched him most deeply. In these works he discussed the situation of the Christian who is also a scholar, and sought to reveal how a complementary relationship between genuine scholarship and real belief could be formed. Perhaps the best introduction to Jinks Harbison's conception of this relationship was furnished by his own description of the attitude which a teacher or writer of history should take toward such a figure as Luther.

It may be suggested, without any intent to blaspheme, that the best professional historian's ideal here is theoretically the same as the Christian's: to see Luther as nearly as possible as his own Lord saw him, in all his weakness and strength, his compromises and triumphs, his freedom and his compulsion, so that in the resulting judgment justice is perfectly tempered with mercy. As a matter of fact, close and persistent study of Luther and his whole age by professional historians has brought us closer at least to the possibility of such a judgment than was conceivable a century ago, simply because we knew too little then. Mere knowledge is no guarantee of sound judgment of men and movements, either in historical study or in ordinary Christian living, but it is often the beginning of true understanding. The kind of judgment the best historians strive for is not so far as some may think from the kind of judgment the truest followers of Christ have striven for.

These are the words of a man who was true to his students and his scholarship by being true to himself.

The present collection of essays cannot claim to embody the vision of history which Jinks Harbison pursued. The authors are diverse: some are separated from the man whose memory they honor by conviction, others by circumstance. Yet, as the table of contents will show, these essays by students and friends are unified by the effort to treat problems which were at the center of Jinks Harbison's own concerns and which, in many cases, the contributors to this memorial volume learned to understand through him. In particular, the questions raised here are those referred to above: the relationship between conduct and reflection, and between outer morality and inner conviction. The essays in the first part of the book, "Faith, Reason, and the World of Action," all deal with the ways in which political activity (in the largest sense) from the later Middle Ages through the seventeenth century was influenced by religious and intellectual conviction. The papers in Part Two, "Christians, Scholars, and the World of Thought," treat questions of intellectual history, and show the ways in which the movement of ideas during the same period was shaped by the diverse forces of social change, political controversy, religious commitment, and methodological preconception. Taken together, the two parts reveal the interplay between thought and action, society and reflection.

While it is obvious that the preparation of a volume of this kind requires the assistance of many people, a few special words of thanks must be said. The task could not have been brought to completion without the sympathetic cooperation of all the contributors. They met deadlines and endured the editors' suggestions with grace and good humor; and their advice on many matters was invaluable. To those who agreed to change the subject of their essays in order to enhance the unity of the volume as a whole, a special word of thanks is due. Throughout the preparation of the book, the editors' task was lightened by the encouragement and counsel of Joseph R. Strayer. Miss R. Miriam Brokaw, Associate Director of the Princeton University Press, helped to shape the collection through her understanding of the problems of assembling scholarly symposia. Publication has been aided by a generous grant from the Department of History, Princeton University.

# CONTENTS

xi

# PART ONE
## FAITH, REASON, AND THE WORLD OF ACTION

# FRANCE: THE HOLY LAND, THE CHOSEN PEOPLE, AND THE MOST CHRISTIAN KING

### JOSEPH R. STRAYER

TWO turning points are obvious in the development of the modern state in Western Europe. The first was a shift in loyalties. As long as loyalties (and obedience) were hopelessly divided between ecclesiastical and secular authorities, and as long as the fraction of loyalty which went to secular authority was still further divided among local lords, provincial rulers, and kings, it was hard to frame a concept of the state and almost impossible to make the concept a reality. Only when primary (though not exclusive) loyalty went to one secular authority could the state come into existence.

The other turning point was closely related to the first. A state must have a certain permanence, and it must have this permanence in geography as well as in time. A state must have authority not only over such people as choose to give loyalty to its head but over all people who live within certain boundaries. Early kings were kings of peoples, not of regions. A king of the Goths was king of the Goths whether they were settled on the shores of the Baltic, the Black Sea, or the Bay of Biscay. A king of the Franks was king of the Franks whether he ruled east or west of the Rhine. Kingship was like kinship, primarily personal and only incidentally territorial. A kingdom was composed of people who recognized a certain royal family as *their* royal family, just as a kin-group was composed of people who recognized the founders of a certain family as their common ancestors.

A state could not be based on such uncertain foundations. In the thirteenth century there were, in the heart of what we would now call France, men who denied that they belonged to the kingdom of France or that they owed any service to its ruler.[1] The king and his agents,

---

[1] See, e.g., the part of the record of the great lawsuit over royal and episcopal rights in Gévaudan, published by the Société d'Agriculture, Sciences, et Arts de la Lozère under the title *Mémoire relatif au paréage de 1307*, ed. A. Maisonobe (Mende, 1896). The bishop of Mende asserted his independence throughout the process: e.g., p. 522, "non erat memoria mortalium quod aliquis Gaballitani Episcopus recognovisset se regis Francie fidelem vel subditum aut episcopatum de regno Francie esse." The nobles of Gévaudan went even further and said that the bishop was "rex in Gaballitano" (Archives Départementales, Lozère, G872, foll. 38ᵛ-40).

quite rightly, viewed these assertions as a threat to their new concepts of government. They insisted that the kingdom was a geographical unit and that within certain boundaries the king had final authority.[2] The concept of the kingdom as a territorial entity was essential in solving the problem of divided loyalties.

Brute power and administrative skill were necessary factors in establishing both loyalty to a single authority and acceptance of the idea that the single authority controlled all men and all lands within fixed limits. There was no point in being loyal to local lords who could be crushed by a stronger ruler. There was more reason to accept the assertion of central authority in regions where it had never existed if accepting central authority meant increased security and better government. But, although power and administrative skill were necessary factors, they were not sufficient by themselves. A state based on power alone has a poor chance for survival. A state built on improved administrative techniques is not apt to gain undying popularity. People soon take the benefits of the new techniques for granted and regret the cost, both in money and in the loss of local privileges. They find that the new techniques may only create new problems—long and expensive foreign wars instead of short, cheap, local wars, financial extortion by bureaucrats instead of by barons. The best administration creates only a tepid loyalty, and very few administrations remained at their best during the Middle Ages.

In short, real loyalty is based neither on fear nor on self-interest. There has to be genuine respect, admiration, and, if possible, love for the object of loyalty. This sort of attitude is not always easy to achieve, and, unfortunately, in Western Europe the state emerged at a time when it was difficult to have respect and admiration for any man or any institution. In some regions the problem was never really solved— hence, the chaotic condition of parts of Germany and Italy after 1300. In France the problem was solved, not completely, but well enough so

---

[2] One of the strongest statements appears in the Gévaudan case, p. 521. Since the bishop is "intra fines regni, erat imperio predicti domini regis subjectus." The king can take any property within the realm for the common welfare, "cum omnia que sunt intra fines regni sui sint domini regis. . . ." The king is "imperator in regno suo et imperare possit terre et mari, et omnes populi regni sui ejus regantur imperio. . . ." The bishop's lawyers answered this last assertion very much in the fashion of Hotspur: "Porro utrum dominus rex sit imperator in regno suo vel non, et utrum possit imperare terre et mari et elementis et si obtemperarent ipsa elementa si eisdem imperaret, responsio advocato regio relinquatur . . ." (p. 532).

that the French state could survive the disasters of the fourteenth and fifteenth centuries.

One peculiar aspect of the problem in France was that the transfer of loyalty to the king and the definition of the kingdom as a territorial unit took place almost simultaneously, culminating in the reign of Philip the Fair. England had had clearly defined boundaries for generations, and it was equally clear, at least by the end of the twelfth century, that all authority within those boundaries came directly or indirectly from the king. But the thirteenth century Capetians had to invent the France which they claimed to rule. They had to make men proud of the country as well as loyal to the king; they had to expand the idea of France to make it match the expansion of their own power.[3]

Some excellent things have been said about the "religion of monarchy" in France, often by Germans who have looked on the early growth of French nationalism with some envy.[4] These works touch on the concomitant theme of France as a favored land filled with superior people, but they do not give it quite the importance it should have. A religion without followers would be an idle dream; a most Christian king ruling over the heathen or infidel might become a martyred saint but scarcely a power in European politics. It was the union of the two ideas of the sacred king and the holy country which speeded the emergence of the French state at the end of the thirteenth century.

It is scarcely necessary to mention the development of the beliefs which made the king a sacred ruler: the coronation oil brought down from heaven, the healing of the scrofulous, the possession of the relics of Charlemagne, the Crusade tradition. All this has been discussed with great learning by Bloch and by Schramm. Only one point needs to be stressed: the holiness of the king reflects credit on his kingdom. As Guillaume le Breton puts it, "because our king is more worthy

[3] This paragraph was written before the appearance of the stimulating article by Charles T. Wood, "*Regnum Francie,* a Problem in Capetian Administrative Usage," *Traditio,* XXIII (1967), 117-147.

[4] P. E. Schramm, *Der König von Frankreich* (Weimar, 1939); Helene Wieruszowski, *Vom Imperium zum nationalen Königtum* (Munich/Berlin, 1933); K. Wenck, *Philipp der Schöne von Frankreich* (Marburg, 1905); H. Finke, *Weltimperialismus und nationale Regungen im späteren Mittelalter* (Freiburg/Leipzig, 1916); F. Kern, *Die Anfänge der französischen Ausdehnungspolitik* (Tübingen, 1910); H. Kämpf, *Pierre Dubois und die geistigen Grundlagen des französischen Nationalbewusstseins um 1300* (Leipzig/Berlin, 1935). The basic book in French is Marc Bloch, *Les rois thaumaturges* (Strasbourg, 1924).

than any other king, the greater excellence of our kingdom is made clear."[5] Another closely associated idea is that the holy and pious king reigns over an especially devout kingdom. For example, the protest on behalf of the king to the Pope in 1245 calls Louis IX a "most Christian prince" and then goes on to speak of the "kingdom of the Franks, where men are accustomed to be most devout."[6] Primat expressed the same idea a generation later when he said that the faith was held more fervently in France than in any other land.[7] He added that one reason for this devoutness was that "la fonteine de clergie" flourished at Paris and that chivalry and scholarship worked together for good.[8] Guillaume de Nangis tied all these ideas together when he used the fleur de lis, a symbol of royal holiness, as a symbol of the preeminence of France. In his interpretation the three petals of the flower represent faith, learning, and military power; France is illustrious for all three, and these virtues flourish more abundantly in France than in other kingdoms.[9]

It is clear that by the middle of the thirteenth century the ideas of the unique position of the French king[10] and the special devotion of his kingdom to the true faith were generally accepted. Neither had yet been fully tested in the work of building a state, however. Louis IX, in extending his authority, relied more on his own reputation for decency, justice, and determination than on theories of sacred kingship. There were several vigorous arguments between him and the Church, but none of these controversies went so far that a man had to choose between loyalty to the king and loyalty to the Pope. He went

[5] ". . . quo major nostri patet excellentia regni dignior ut vere rex noster rege sit omni" (*Oeuvres de Rigord et de Guillaume le Breton*, ed. H. F. Delaborde [Paris, 1885] II, 21, lines 345-346).

[6] ". . . regnum Francorum, ubi solebant homines esse devotissimi" (Mathew Paris, *Chronica majora*, Rolls Series [London, 1882] VI, 99, 100).

[7] *Les grandes chroniques de France*, ed. J. Viard (Paris, 1920-    ) I, 5 ("la foi . . . fust plus fervement et plus droitment tenue que en nule autre terre . . .").

[8] *Ibid.*, pp. 5-6.

[9] *Recueil des historiens des Gaulles et de la France* (Paris, 1738-    ), XX, 320 ("Jesus Christus voluit tribus predictis gratiis, scilicet fide, sapientia, et militia specialius quam cetera regna regnum Francie sua gratia illustrare. . . . Quasi dicerunt toti mundo: fides, sapientia et militie titulus abundantius quam regnis ceteris sunt regno nostro. . . .").

[10] Even the Englishman Mathew Paris admits this uniqueness, *Chronica Majora*, V, 480: "rex Francorum qui terrestrium rex regum est, tam propter eius coelestum iniunctionem, tum propter sui potestatem et militie eminentiam"; and, 606, "rex Francorum regum censetur dignissimus."

further in forcing a choice between loyalties in secular affairs; in many parts of the realm it was made clear that loyalty to the king took precedence over loyalty to a great lord. This obligation, however, was stressed especially in the region of fully developed feudalism. In parts of the South, and especially in the ecclesiastical lordships, men could doubt for another generation whether they were bound to the king in any way.

Louis also made a start—but only a start—in defining the territorial limits of his kingdom. The treaty with England made it clear that Aquitaine was part of the kingdom, and the treaty with Aragon cancelled French claims to Roussillon and Catalonia in return for Aragonese renunciation of suzerainty over parts of Languedoc. But very little was done to define the long eastern frontier with the Empire, and the status of southern prelates, such as the bishops of Mende and Viviers, was left in doubt. Even in the settlements which were reached with England and Aragon, Louis thought more in terms of feudal and family relationships than in terms of fixing the boundaries of a sovereign state.

In short, although Louis did a great deal to strengthen loyalty to the monarchy and made some attempt to define the boundaries of his kingdom, he never pushed either process to its ultimate limits. No emergency which required such an effort arose in his reign, and Louis by character and training preferred compromise to sweeping assertions of royal authority. Louis's successor, Philip the Bold, did little more than his father. By asserting his right to the lands of Alfonse of Poitiers, Philip strengthened his position in the South, especially in forcing the Count of Foix to recognize royal suzerainty. But this was only a partial success; the Count of Foix in the next reign tried once more to gain a wide measure of autonomy, and in the campaign which led to the surrender of the Castle of Foix the southern bishops denied that they owed military service to the king.[11]

Philip the Fair was in a very different position. For the first time in almost a century the king of France had to wage a long, dangerous, and expensive war. For the first time in two centuries a French king found himself involved in a bitter controversy with the Pope. The test could no longer be avoided. Philip had to demand men and money from all parts of his kingdom. He had to assert that all people living within certain boundaries were "in regno et de regno" (in the kingdom

---

[11] *Histoire Générale de Languedoc*, Privat edition (Toulouse, 1872-1904), X, *preuves*, cols. 111-115.

and part of the kingdom) and, hence, were required to aid in the defense of the kingdom. He had to insist that loyalty to king and kingdom took precedence over all other loyalties, including loyalty to the Pope and to the Church.

Philip did not, of course, succeed completely in making these claims effective. He had to compromise in many cases. He received less money than he wanted, and he had to leave more power in the hands of some bishops and barons than he would have liked. The amazing thing is that he succeeded as well as he did and that his success did not require, to any significant degree, the use of force. Every part of what he considered to be the kingdom of France contributed men and money to his campaigns. Every part of the kingdom supported him in his controversy with Boniface VIII. There was, naturally, opposition to his policies, but the opposition usually took the form of legal protests and could be handled by political manipulation or decisions of the royal courts. Only at the very end of the reign, when both king and people were weary after years of crisis, were there serious rebellions. The concessions made by Philip and by his successor show how little inclination the government had to use force to put down internal opposition. The relative moderation of the demands of the rebels shows how successful Philip had been in gaining acceptance for his basic doctrines. The baronial leaders admitted that defense of the kingdom took primacy over all other loyalties and privileges. Their chief goal was to limit the consequences of this principle.

If Philip did not rely on force, then he must have relied on persuasion and propaganda. This fact has long been realized, and I do not propose to repeat the analysis of documents which are already well known. I do want to stress two points: first, that the propaganda was effective in all parts of the realm and, second, that it glorified the kingdom fully as much as it did the king. The basic theme ran something like this: the kings of France have always been pillars and defenders of the faith; the people of France are devout and pious; the kingdom of France is so specially favored by God that it is the most important part of the Church. (As one recent German writer put it, "God couldn't get along without France.")[12] Therefore, any attack on the rights of the king or the independence and integrity of his kingdom is an attack on the faith. Conversely, any steps taken by the king

[12] Friedrich Sieburg, *Gott in Frankreich* (Frankfurt-am-Main, 1932), p. 56. See also the excellent discussion of this topic in Wieruszowski, *Vom Imperium zum nationalen Königtum*, pp. 146-150.

to defend and strengthen his kingdom are for the good of the faith and the benefit of Christendom.

The first of these propositions needs little discussion, but a few special points may be made. Although Valois was quite right in saying that the title "rex Christianissimus" was not a monopoly of French kings at this time[13] and that it was seldom used by the popes of the late thirteenth century,[14] it should be noted that the phrase appeared in almost every type of royal propaganda. It is not surprising that Nogaret and Dubois spoke constantly of the most Christian king of France,[15] but so did the prelates of France writing to Boniface VIII in 1302[16] and the masters of theology of Paris discussing the arrest of the Templars.[17] Moreover, writers who had no special reason to call the king "most Christian" did so as if it were common form: for example, the provincial Council of Sens in 1292[18] and a rather pro-papal crusade propagandist.[19] Counting references proves nothing, but I have a strong impression that Philip was called "rex Christianissimus" more often than his father and grandfather had been and that this was not a purely accidental occurrence.

As for the other phrases describing the king's piety, his zeal for the faith, his responsibilities as "champion of the faith and defender of the Church,"[20] they are too numerous and too well known to list. We

---

[13] Noel Valois, "Le roi très chrétien," in Baudrillart, *La France Chrétienne dans l'Histoire* (Paris, 1896), pp. 319-320.

[14] *Ibid.*, p. 322.

[15] P. Dupuy, *Histoire du differend d'entre le pape Boniface VIII et Philippe le Bel* (Paris, 1655), pp. 45, 242, 326, 358; Pierre Dubois, *Summaria brevis*, ed. Hellmut Kämpf (Leipzig, 1936) p. 26; Pierre Dubois, *De recuperatione terre sancte*, ed. Ch. V. Langlois (Paris, 1891), p. 100; Robert Holtzmann, *Wilhelm von Nogaret* (Freiburg-im-Breisgau, 1898), pp. 257, 275.

[16] Dupuy, p. 67.

[17] G. Lizerand, *Le dossier de l'affaire des templiers* (Paris, 1923), p. 62.

[18] Georges Digard, *Philippe le Bel et le Saint-Siège* (Paris, 1936), p. 281.

[19] Wenck, *Philipp der Schöne*, p. 18. It might be added that the popes occasionally used the phrase; e.g., Nicolas IV in 1289, asking Philip to ease pressure on the Church of Lyon, spoke of him as a "princeps Christianissimus" and told him that through honoring the Church "locum magnum obtines inter ceteros catholicos principes orbis terre" (P. Bonnassieux, *De la réunion de Lyon à la France* [Lyon, 1875], p. 45). In the bull *Ausculta fili*, Boniface VIII managed to use the term as a rebuke in comparing Philip to "progenitores tui, Christianissimi principes" (Dupuy, *Histoire du differend*, p. 52).

[20] Dupuy, p. 102. See also pp. 297, 517, and Lizerand, *Le dossier*, p. 127. A variant of this idea is that the royal house of France was always "veritatis directrix ac ecclesie auxiliatrix" (see Dupuy, pp. 124, 297).

might note, however, the remarkable sermons of the Dominican Guillaume de Sauqueville,[21] in which he says that the "heir of France" is, like Christ, "the son of David"[22] and that "Christ, the king of the Franks [the free or the French: the word has both meanings in the text], used and uses in His two comings two banners," the fleur de lis and the war banner which is "entirely blood colored." "The sign of the first coming of Christ was the lily of virginity . . . but at His second coming, to war on sinners, he will carry the blood-red banner." So the first banner signifies the mercy of the king, but the second marks his wrath.[23] If the king of France is a type of Christ and if, as Guillaume implies, the kingdom of France is a type of the heavenly kingdom,[24] then resistance to the king and attacks on the kingdom are obviously sinful.

One immediate deduction from this doctrine would be the right of the king to require money for defense of the realm. This argument was, in fact, especially effective with the clergy. In 1294 Cluny made a grant to the king as "the leader . . . of the cause of God and the Church and the fighter for all of Christendom."[25] About the same time the bishops of Brittany, the prelates of the province of Lyon, and the order of Prémontré all praised the faith and orthodoxy of the French kings in making their grants.[26] Philip gave the idea a somewhat dif-

[21] N. Valois, in *Histoire littéraire*, XXXIV, 298ff., gave a general account of Guillaume's life and work but said nothing about the sermons praising the king. H. Kämpf, *Pierre Dubois*, printed the sermon "Osanna filio David" on pp. 112-114. The most thorough study was made by Hildegard Coester in a typewritten thesis (Frankfurt, 1935/36) entitled "Der Königskult in Frankreich um 1300 im Spiegel von Dominikanerpredigten." The late Professor Kantorowicz, who directed the thesis, was kind enough to let me use his copy. Unfortunately, this copy could not be found among his papers after his death. I therefore quote directly from the manuscript in the Bibliothèque Nationale, but it was Miss Coester's work which called this manuscript to my attention.

[22] Bibliothèque Nationale, ms. lat. 16495, fol. 97.

[23] *Ibid.*, fol. 101 ("Modo rex Francorum Christus in duplo adventu suo usus est et utetur duplici vexillo. . . . Signum enim adventus sui primi fuit flos vel lilium virginitatis . . . set vexillum adventus secundi, quando veniet contra adversarios ac peccatores debellandum erit totum coloris sanguinei. . . . Primum vexillum non indicabit furorem sed pacem et mansuetudinem regis. . . . Sed secundum vexillum sanguineum ab eo indicabit furorem regium . . .").

[24] *Ibid.*, foll. 97ᵛ, 101. See the discussion of these texts below, pp. 14-15.

[25] ". . . prosecutor . . . cause Dei et ecclesie, et totius Christianitatis athleta" (Archives Nationales [henceforth cited as A.N.], J259, no. 3; printed in part in Bruel, *Chartes de Cluny*, VI).

[26] A.N., J1035, nos. 36, 37, 39.

ferent turn—and incidentally showed the close connection between the holiness of the king and the sanctity of the kingdom—when he asked the clergy of Tours for a double tenth in 1305. He told them that they owed "spiritual and temporal aid to preserve, defend and guard the unity of this realm . . . a venerable part of the Holy Church of God." He went on to say that they should not value their goods above the welfare of the people—"since it is for this welfare that Jesus Christ . . . exposed himself to death"—and that failure to pay would be to violate a "sacred ministry."[27]

Almost equal emphasis was placed on the piety and orthodoxy of the French people, a proposition which may seem a little strange, considering the vast number of heretics in France in the twelfth and thirteenth centuries. Yet, as far as I can find, the claim was never seriously challenged; perhaps the zeal of the royal family covered the sins of the people. Nogaret spoke of the Gallican nation, a nation "well known to be most Christian,"[28] and the so-called *Remonstrances du peuple de France* claimed that "la pueble du royaume de France . . . ha esté et sera par la grace de Dieu devost et obeissant a seinte Yglise plus que nul autre."[29] Dubois praised the right reason, constancy, and firmness of the French, in which they excelled all other nations,[30] and, as we shall see, Clement V called the French a chosen people.[31]

Both the merits of its kings and the devoutness of its people made France a holy land, and much of the praise of the kingdom was actually praise of either the rulers or their subjects. Philip himself said in 1308 that the kingdom was blessed by the firmness of its belief in Christ,[32] and he repeated the idea in a letter of 1312 to Henry VII: "Jesus Christ, the Most High, finds in this realm, more than in any other part of the world, a sure foundation for the holy faith and the Christian religion and the deepest devotion to Himself and His vicars and ministers, since He has noticed that He is loved, feared and honored in this country above all others."[33] Dubois, also, spoke of the

---

[27] ". . . auxilium spiritualiter et temporaliter ad conservationem, deffensionem, et custodiam unitatis ipsius regni . . . pars venerabilis ecclesie sancte Dei"; "hec enim est salus pro quam Jesus Christus . . . morti se ipsum exposuit" (A.N., J350, no. 5).

[28] Dupuy, *Histoire du differend*, p. 335.

[29] Lizerand, *Le dossier*, p. 84.

[30] Dubois, *Summaria brevis*, pp. 12, 21.

[31] See below, p. 15.

[32] G. Picot, *Documents relatifs aux Etats-Généraux* (Paris, 1901), p. 487.

[33] "Altissimus Jhesus Christus in regno ipso pre ceteris partibus mundi sancti

habitual devotion of the kingdom of the French, greater than that of other kingdoms,"[34] and an appeal to the king to carry on the case against Boniface VIII condemned attacks on the honor and liberty of "the most Christian . . . king of France and his most devout and most Christian kingdom."[35]

An effective variant on this theme was the idea that the kingdom was an essential or even principal part of the Church and that, therefore, to injure France was to weaken the Church. Very early in the reign, while Philip was still on reasonably good terms with the Papacy, he said that to lessen his "status" would hurt the French and perhaps the universal Church.[36] Again and again during the struggle with Boniface, Nogaret spoke of France as "a venerable part" of the Church, as "the chief and most noble member of the Church," or even as the "principal pillar supporting the Roman Church and the Catholic faith."[37] Thus, Nogaret could argue that in defending his fatherland, as he was bound to do,[38] he was actually working for the salvation of the Church.[39]

Even more, the kingdom had been blessed by God with wisdom and justice as well as piety. It was therefore flourishing, prosperous, and deservedly preeminent in the world. Dubois's remarks on this subject

---

fidei et religionis christiane stabile fundamentum reperiens sibique et eius vicariis et ministris summam devocionem considerans sicut se in eo pre ceteris amari, timori, et honorari conspexit" (Wenck, *Philipp der Schöne*, p. 72; from *Monumenta Germaniae historica, Constitutiones et acta publica imperatorum*, IV, no. 811).

[34] Dubois, *Summaria brevis*, p. 26, "solita devocio regni Francorum pre ceteris regnis."

[35] Holtzmann, *Wilhelm von Nogaret*, p. 257. Boniface himself in *Etsi de statu* spoke of the "Christianissimi regni Francie."

[36] Digard, *Philippe le Bel et le Saint-Siège*, II, 250 (about Sept., 1289).

[37] Dupuy, *Histoire du différend*, pp. 241, 309, 325; Holtzmann, *Wilhelm von Nogaret*, p. 275. See esp. Dupuy, p. 241; France is a "venerabilem partem ecclesie sancte Dei, ac principalem columnam sustentionis ecclesie Romane, doctrine sacre pagine et fidei Catholice splendore lucens. . . ."

[38] Dupuy, p. 309, "quisque teneatur patriam suam defendere," see also pp. 310, 312.

[39] Dupuy, p. 250; Nogaret says he acted with righteous zeal to defend the faith, the Church, and the kingdom "agonizando pro iustitia, pro Romana Ecclesia, pro Republica . . . ac pro sua patria . . . ac pro suo domino Rege Francie. . . ." See also Holtzmann, *Wilhelm von Nogaret*, p. 268. There is an excellent discussion of this material in E. H. Kantorowicz, *The King's Two Bodies* (Princeton, 1957), pp. 249-259.

are well known[40] but have often been dismissed as the exaggerations of an obscure pamphleteer who was seeking to attract attention.[41] But, as we have seen, some of this glorification of France dates back to a period long before Dubois wrote,[42] and some of the most fervent praise of France comes from a letter written by Philip at a time (ca. 1289-1290) when neither Dubois, Nogaret, or any of the other extremists could have influenced him. Philip said that all Christians agreed that no other kingdom abounded in "such peace, such regard for justice, such prosperity, such happiness."[43] He went on to claim that even Jews and Saracens admitted that France was more prosperous than any other kingdom in the world, a prosperity based on "a highly developed regard for justice, from which in turn, by the grace of God, has come the fullness of our peace."[44]

It is not surprising that Nogaret spoke of France as a kingdom "which God established to endure forever," strong in arms and firm in faith. But in the same place he refers to an old theme, that the kingdom has the singular privilege "that there the source of wisdom and knowledge shines and flourishes among the learned";[45] this kingdom, blessed by God, surpasses all other kingdoms in faith, justice, respect for the freedom of the Church, and other virtues. Strongest of all is

[40] Dubois, *Summaria brevis*, pp. 11, 12, 21, and *De recuperatione*, pp. 128, 129, 139.

[41] There is some danger that, after being overrated, Dubois is now being underrated. He is important, not because he influenced policy, but because he represented the views of the hundreds of officials who worked for the king throughout France. The *Summaria brevis*, especially, is not a patriotic tract; it is a lawyer's brief suggesting ways of curbing the power of ecclesiastical courts. I have studied the careers of several hundred lawyers who worked for the king in this period; most of them, and especially the procurators (the position Dubois held) would have agreed with Dubois's main line of argument. See n. 43.

[42] See above, and also Kantorowicz, *The King's Two Bodies*, pp. 237-238.

[43] Digard, *Philippe le Bel et le Saint-Siège*, II, 269. Note that this document is an emphatic statement of the supremacy of royal justice over the claims of the Church of Chartres to exemption. Cf. p. 249: "nullum et nullius judicis territorium . . . infra fines regni nostri exemptum a nostra jurisdictione recognoscimus . . . nec recognoscere proponimus in futurum." In other words, praise of France as a land of piety, peace, and plenty is used to justify sweeping assertions of royal power, especially in the field of justice. This is Dubois's formula long before Dubois wrote; the idea came to him from higher authority, and by the time he composed his pamphlet it was already a commonplace in the royal court.

[44] ". . . ex matura observacione justicie ex qua observacione Deo summe grata provenit habundantia nostre pacis" (*ibid.*, p. 274).

[45] Dupuy, *Histoire du differend*, p. 326. See above, p. 6.

the assertion that "God . . . chose it as his own, special kingdom,"[46] or, in another document, that "the kingdom of France was chosen by the Lord and blessed above all other kingdoms of the world."[47] This claim is echoed, a little more modestly, in 1312 in the letter Philip sent to Henry VII (which Nogaret might well have helped compose). Because France is firm in the faith, and loves and honors Jesus Christ, "He determined that it should be honored above all other kingdoms and principalities by a certain unique and distinctive eminence."[48]

Guillaume de Sauqueville was a much less lucid writer than Nogaret, perhaps because some of his comparisons would have seemed too bold if he had stated them explicitly. But the way in which he plays with the word France is striking. First France comes from "freedom . . . because the heirs of France are not subject to the Empire." The Empire is evil (in a bad pun he derives "empire" from "en pire"), and to be free of the Empire is to be free of sin. When St. Nicholas freed himself from worldliness by fasting, he was "part of the kingdom, not of the Empire." Spiritually, "no kingdom is Frank or free except the kingdom of heaven," or, as he put it later, "properly speaking no kingdom should be called the Frank [French] kingdom except the kingdom of Christ."[49] This remark is followed by the passage in which Christ is said to use the fleur de lis and the oriflamme as his banners. Now, Guillaume certainly does not say that the kingdom of France *is* the heavenly kingdom; but he does imply that there is some resemblance between them, and those who heard (rather than read) his sermons might have been a little confused about how close the resemblance was. Even if Guillaume were only making a series of learned puns, they were puns which could have been made only about France. And since the first pun ("France comes from freedom because France is free of the Empire") would have seemed true and sensible

[46] "Deus . . . tanquam sibi peculiare regnum illud eleget" (Dupuy, p. 384).

[47] ". . . regnum Francie a domine electum et benedictum pre ceteris regnis mundi" (Lizerand, *Le dossier*, p. 116).

[48] ". . . sic ipsum pre ceteris regnis et principatibus singulari quadam eminencio prerogativa disposuit honorari" (Wenck, *Philipp der Schöne*, p. 72, from *M.G.H.*, *Constitutiones et acta publica imperatorum*, IV, no. 811).

[49] ". . . franchyse . . . quia heredes Francie non subiciuntur imperio"; "nullum regnum est Francie seu liberum nisi regnum celorum"; "proprie loquendo nullum regnum debet vocari regnum Francie nisi solum regnum Christi" (Bibliothèque Nationale, ms lat., foll. 97, 97ᵛ, 101). See Kämpf, *Pierre Dubois*, pp. 112-113, and Kantorowicz, *The King's Two Bodies*, pp. 238, 255.

to most Frenchmen, the last pun ("the Frank or free kingdom is the kingdom of heaven") may have seemed equally true.

It may appear that men like Nogaret, Dubois, and Guillaume de Sauqueville took such extreme positions that their assertions have little importance. But these were not lonely zealots working for hopeless causes like Ramon Lull (who, incidentally, agreed with the French propagandists on the virtues of Philip the Fair).[50] They were all responsible men, even if their degree of responsibility varied from that of a minister of state to that of a court preacher to that of a provincial procurator. The really surprising thing is how well such different men agreed and how clearly they were reflecting the common opinion of many Frenchmen. Clement V may have been weak, but he was not foolish, and, when he was trying to end the wretched business of the accusations against Boniface VIII, he found it expedient to use most of the ideas, and even the phrases, which we have been discussing. The bull *rex glorie* gave papal sanction to the concept of the holy kingdom and the chosen people: "The King of Glory formed different kingdoms within the circuit of this world and established governments for diverse peoples according to differences of language and race. Among those, like the people of Israel . . . , the kingdom of France, as a peculiar people chosen by the Lord to carry out the orders of Heaven, is distinguished by marks of special honor and grace."[51]

After this endorsement little more needed to be done. The publicists of the reign of Charles V repeated, and perhaps sharpened, the old themes, but they added nothing new. Within another generation a peasant girl from the very fringes of the kingdom believed as firmly

[50] Wenck, *Philipp der Schöne*, pp. 11-12, quoting Lull's *Liber natalis*: "Philippus rex Francie in quo, pre ceteris mundis rectoribus, singulariter pollent hodie justitia, veritas, fides, charitas, recta spes . . . humilitas et devotio et christiana religio . . . cum ipse sit pugil ecclesie et defensor fidei christiane . . . ."

[51] "Rex glorie . . . in huius orbis orbita diversa regna constituit, diversorum populorum regimina secundum divisiones linguarum et gentium stabilivit, inter quos sicut israeliticus populus . . . sic regnum Francie in peculiarem populum electus a Domino in executione mandatorum celestium specialis honoris et gratie titulis insignitur" (*Registrum Clementis Papae V* [Rome, 1885-1892], no. 7501). Gregory IX had said almost as much in 1239: "Dei filius . . . diversa regna constituit, inter quae, sicut tribus Juda inter filios patriarchae ad specialis benedictionis dona suscipitur, sic regnum Franciae prae caeteris terrarum populis praerogativa honoris et gratiae insignitur." L. Gautier quoted this letter in *La chevalerie* (Paris, 1895), pp. 64-65, n. 2. I could not find it in the Register of Gregory IX.

in the sacred king and his holy kingdom as she did in God and the saints.[52] Like her better educated predecessors, she was sure that God needed France.

This was the great good fortune of the French kings and their people. In the difficult task of rearranging basic loyalties to concentrate them on king and kingdom, they could avoid, to a very large degree, any feeling of contradiction between their duties to the Church and their duties to the state. The most Christian king ruled a chosen people who lived in a kingdom which was the principal support and eternal defender of the faith. Loyalty to France was bound to be loyalty to the Church, even if the Church occasionally doubted it. As Kantorowicz has shown, all governments of the period were trying to develop a "political theology" which transferred religious symbols and slogans to the political sphere. It was easier for the French to do this than for any other government because the transfer started early and was largely completed by the end of the thirteenth century.

For the same reason, the French, earlier than any other continental kingdom, solved the problem of the "mosaic" state—that is, a state put together out of provinces which had strongly autonomous cultural, legal, and institutional traditions. These local loyalties could not be eradicated, but they could be subordinated to a higher loyalty to king and kingdom. No local lord, however ancient his lineage, could be compared to the king, heir of Charlemagne, anointed by heaven, worker of miracles. The king could be accepted as a symbol of unity because, as Guillaume de Sauqueville pointed out, he was a type of Christ. And the unity which he symbolized, the unity of the kingdom of France, could be accepted because France was a symbol of the kingdom of heaven. In France the religion of nationalism grew early and easily out of the religion of monarchy, and, although neither the degree of French unity nor the depth of French nationalism should be exaggerated, both were strong enough to give France a clear advantage over her neighbors for many centuries.

[52] J. Quicherat, *Procès de condamnation et de rehabilitation de Jeanne d'Arc* (Paris, 1841-1849) V, 127 ("Tous ceulx qui guerroient audit saint royaume de France, guerroient contre le roy Jhesus . . .").

# THE RENAISSANCE MONARCHY AS SEEN
# BY ERASMUS, MORE, SEYSSEL,
# AND MACHIAVELLI*

J . R U S S E L L   M A J O R

FOR a long time it was commonplace to find the origins of the modern state in the "New Monarchies" of the Renaissance. It was argued that the Renaissance monarchs, aided by a rising middle class and the growth of nationalism, created absolute, centralized states in which they governed with the aid of large bureaucracies and in which they stifled all opposition with armies plentifully supplied with artillery.

Recently, nearly every aspect of this interpretation has been challenged. The typical Renaissance monarchy, in the view of the present writer, was dynastic, not national; decentralized, not centralized; and constitutional, not absolute, in that there were laws, customs, and institutions which checked the authority of the ruler. The dominant class was the aristocracy, not the middle class, and the monarchy itself was inherently weak because neither the bureaucracy nor the army was large or loyal enough to insure orderly government without a wide measure of popular support. To secure this support, kings rewarded their most important subjects with titles, positions, land, and economic opportunities; held representative assemblies and enlarged meetings of their councils to explain their policies and to become better acquainted with the problems of their subjects; and traveled about the countryside to obtain firsthand knowledge of local conditions and to maintain closer contact with the people.[1]

The above interpretation has been developed from the study of society and institutions, especially those of France, but to date little effort has been made to relate it to contemporary political thought. This essay is intended to fill partially this gap by briefly exploring

* I should like to express my appreciation to Professor J. H. Hexter of Yale University for reading and criticizing this article while in manuscript form.

[1] For short essays by various historians and a selected bibliography, see Arthur J. Slavin, *The "New Monarchies" and Representative Assemblies—Medieval Constitutionalism or Modern Absolutism?* (Boston, 1964). In addition to the essay included in this work, I have outlined my conception of the Renaissance monarchy in *Representative Institutions in Renaissance France, 1421-1559* (Madison, Wis., 1960), pp. 3-20, and in "The French Renaissance Monarchy as seen through the Estates General," *Studies in the Renaissance*, IX (1962), 113-125.

books by Erasmus, More, Seyssel, and Machiavelli written between 1513 and 1517. Neither the choice of authors nor the choice of works has been entirely arbitrary. The period 1513-1517 comes after the Renaissance monarchies had become fully established but before the Protestant Reformation had created new political and religious issues. The authors selected provide a cross section of opinion in that they differed in their country of origin, education, and experience. Erasmus was a citizen of the Holy Roman Empire who had been educated as a theologian and humanist. More was an Englishman who coupled law with a humanistic background. Seyssel was a Savoyard who, because he spent most of his adult life in the service of the French king, may be considered as representing France; he had been trained in Roman and canon law but was also interested in humanistic activities. Machiavelli was the product of an Italian city-state who had been educated more as a man of affairs than as a scholar. Both Machiavelli and Seyssel wrote their principal works after long years of experience in government, while More wrote *Utopia* just before he embarked on a distinguished public career. Erasmus never had practical political experience.

A man whose interests were as narrowly centered on Christian morality and good literature as Erasmus's was not likely to be a penetrating observer of the political scene. His writings, including the book-length *Education of a Christian Prince*, are full of the pious platitudes so common in the "mirror of princes" literature. He knew little about the problems of government, and even the political views he derived from his study of antiquity came more from equally inexperienced moral philosophers or early Christian teachers than from the politically minded Roman historians to whom Machiavelli owed so much. Erasmus's conception of what was and what ought to be was deeply influenced by his residence in the Low Countries, the Rhineland cities, France, England, and Italy; by his personal contacts with kings, emperors, popes, ministers, bishops, scholars, and less exalted persons in many walks of life; and by the basic precepts of Christian humanism. Under such circumstances the value of his writings lies less in their originality than in the manner in which they reflect the scholar's attitude in that age.[2]

[2] Essays on Erasmus's political and social thought may be found in Augustin Renaudet, *Études Erasmiennes* (Paris, 1939), pp. 65-121, and in the introduction of Lester K. Born's translation of *The Education of a Christian Prince* (New York, 1936). The quotations below are taken from the Born translation, except

Erasmus admitted that "it is the consensus of nearly all wise-thinking men that the best form [of government] is monarchy. . . . If a prince be found who is complete in all good qualities," he added, "then pure and absolute monarchy is the thing. (If that could only be! I fear it is too great a thing even to hope for.) If an average prince (as the affairs of men go now) is found, it will be better to have a limited monarchy checked and lessened by aristocracy and democracy. Then there is no chance for tyranny to creep in, but just as the elements balance each other, so will the Commonwealth hold together under similar control. If a prince has the interests of the Commonwealth at heart, his power is not checked on this account, . . . but rather helped. If his attitude is otherwise, however, it is expedient that the state break and turn aside the violence of a single man."[3]

Thus Erasmus's conception of a monarchy was essentially contractual. The good prince, he felt, should not only recognize the rights of towns and provinces but should also convoke representative assemblies to consent to taxes and to advise on laws and ordinances. By doing so, he would increase his authority because he would have secured the support of the people. And, like his subjects, the prince should obey the laws he had made.

Although *The Education of a Christian Prince* was intended for the future emperor Charles V, Erasmus did not hesitate to point out that "even the greatest dominions prospered without a prince; for example, the republics of Rome and Athens. But a prince cannot exist without a commonwealth. . . . What is that which alone makes a prince, if it is not the consent of his subjects?"[4]

Such a state was not an unattainable Utopia. In Erasmus's view, it actually existed in the Netherlands and elsewhere. If in later years he strayed from this ideal, it was not in the direction of absolute monarchy, for even his limited trust in princes waned; rather, he increasingly admired the republican institutions of the Swiss cantons.

Erasmus recognized the dynastic character of the monarchies of his day, but he bitterly regretted that this situation existed and counseled princes to confine their marriage alliances within the limits of their own kingdoms. Part of his objection came from his sympathy for brides "who are sometimes sent away into remote places to [marry] men who

---

that, where he translated *res publica* and *patria* as "state," I have used "commonwealth" and "fatherland," respectively.

[3] Born, pp. 173-174.

[4] *Ibid.*, p. 233.

have no similarity of language, appearance, character, or habits, just as if they were being abandoned to exile."[5] But he also argued that foreign marriages weakened that close bond that should exist between the royal family and the people, because "it could hardly be expected that the fatherland would whole-heartedly recognize children born of such alliances, or that such children would be lastingly devoted to the fatherland."[6] Furthermore, foreign marriages are "the cause of making wars more frequent and more atrocious; for while one kingdom is allied to another through marriage, whenever anyone is offended he uses his right of relationship to stir up the others."[7]

Erasmus also noted the dominant position of the European aristocracy, although once more he was not pleased with what he saw. "Nature created all men equal," he declared.[8] "I should not strip the well-born of their honors if they follow in the footsteps of their forefathers and excel in those qualities which first created nobility. But if we see so many today who are soft from indolence, effeminate through sensual pleasures, with no knowledge of any useful vocation, . . . I ask you, why should this class of persons be placed on a higher level than the shoemaker or the farmer?"[9] Among the charges Erasmus leveled against the nobility was that those of their number "who are more lavish than their private means allow, when the opportunity is presented, stir up war in order to replenish their resources at home even by the plunder of their peoples."[10]

One should not expect Erasmus and his fellow observers to have referred to the Renaissance monarchs as being inherently weak, for in spite of their lack of power these rulers were much stronger than their fifteenth-century predecessors. Erasmus, however, did hold that a king's strength depended less on his army and bureaucracy than on whether he had won the love of the people. "He does not lose his prerogatives, who rules as a Christian should," he declared. "The following arguments will make that clear. First, those are not really yours whom you oppress in slavery. . . . But they are really yours who yield obedience to you willingly and of their own accord. Secondly, when you hold people bound to you through fear, you do not possess them even half. You have their physical bodies, but their spirits are estranged from you. But when Christian love unites the people and their prince, then everything is yours that your position demands, for a good prince

[5] *Ibid.*, p. 243.    [6] *Ibid.*, p. 242.    [7] *Ibid.*    [8] *Ibid.*, p. 177.
[9] *Ibid.*, p. 226.    [10] *Ibid.*, p. 252.

does not demand anything for which service to his country does not call."[11] In short, "the king rejoices in the freedom of his people; the tyrant strives to be feared, the king to be loved."[12]

To win the love of his people the prince must be worthy of their love. He should make every effort to get to know his kingdom. "This knowledge is best gained from [a study of] geography and history and from frequent visits through his provinces and cities. Let him first be eager to learn the location of his districts and cities, with their beginnings, their nature, institutions, customs, laws, annals, and privileges. No one can heal the body until he is thoroughly conversant with it. . . . Next, the prince should love the land over which he rules just as a farmer loves the fields of his ancestors or as a good man feels affection toward his household."[13] He should reside in his kingdom, for "nothing so alienates the affections of his people from a prince as for him to take great pleasure in living abroad, because then they seem to be neglected by him to whom they wish to be most important."[14]

The prince himself should be kindly, clement, and courteous and should choose ministers with similar virtues. He must make every effort to increase the prosperity of his people and to avoid taxation by governing honestly, living frugally, and avoiding wars. Were taxes to become necessary, the rich, not the poor, should bear the brunt of the burden. A prince should not shut himself up in a palace, like the Persian kings, but ought to travel about to see and be seen by the people. On public occasions "the prince should not be extravagant or lavish, but splendid. . . . In those matters which pertain to him as an individual, he should be more frugal and moderate. . . ."[15] In this manner foreigners and subjects were to be impressed on great occasions, but the prince ought normally to live a simple life in order to avoid expense and to maintain contact with his people.

It is not surprising that More's evaluation of the Renaissance state and society was essentially the same as that of his friend, Erasmus. Yet the medicine he prescribed in *Utopia* was much more potent.

More's *Utopia* is divided into two books. The first consists of a dialogue between three persons in which a somewhat exaggerated picture of the evils of European, and especially English, society is drawn. The second consists of Raphael Hythlodaye's account of life on the island of Utopia, a country whose size and geographical location near

[11] *Ibid.*, pp. 179-180.    [12] *Ibid.*, p. 164.    [13] *Ibid.*, p. 205.
[14] *Ibid.*, p. 208.    [15] *Ibid.*, p. 247.

?. a continent were similar to England's but whose institutions and social structure were almost the exact opposites.[16]

In the first book More leaves no doubt that he recognized the dynastic nature of the European states, a situation he decries because wars have resulted from conflicting dynastic claims. Even when dynastic wars are successful, further difficulties result—a point More makes by having Hythlodaye tell a story about the Anchorians who lived on the mainland to the southeast of Utopia. "Once upon a time they had gone to war to win for their king another kingdom to which he claimed to be the rightful heir by virtue of an old tie by marriage. After they had secured it, they saw they would have no less trouble over keeping it than they had suffered in obtaining it. The seeds of rebellion from within or of invasion from without were always springing up in the people thus acquired. They realized they would have to fight constantly for them or against them and to keep an army in continual readiness. In the meantime they were being plundered, their money was being taken out of the country, they were shedding their blood for the little glory of someone else, peace was no more secure than before, their morals at home were being corrupted by war, the lust for robbery was becoming second nature, criminal recklessness was emboldened by killings in war, and the laws were held in contempt—all because the king, being distracted with the charge of two kingdoms, could not properly attend to either."[17] As a result, the Anchorians finally insisted that their king give his new kingdom to a friend "who," Hythlodaye remarked pointedly, "was driven out soon afterwards."[18] In Utopia itself there were no dynastic problems because the cities were presided over by elective, not hereditary, princes.

Equally clear was More's recognition of the predominance of the European aristocracy, which derived much of its power from bastard feudalism and used its position to provoke wars and to exploit the poor. "Now there is the great number of noblemen who not only live idly themselves like drones on the labors of others, as for instance the tenants of their estates whom they fleece to the utmost by increasing

---

[16] For the genesis of *Utopia*, see J. H. Hexter, *More's Utopia: The Biography of an Idea* (Princeton, 1952). For a description of the government of Utopia, see Marie Delcourt, "Le Pouvoir du roi dans l'Utopia," *Mélanges offerts à M. Abel Lefranc* (Paris, 1936), pp. 101-112.

[17] This and other quotations are from Edward Surtz's translation of *Utopia* (New Haven, 1964), pp. 42-43.

[18] *Ibid.*, p. 43.

the returns, . . . but who also carry about with them a huge crowd of idle attendants who have never learned a trade for a livelihood."[19] These idle retainers are permitted to rob the countryside in the vain hope that they will prove useful as soldiers in time of war. English "noblemen, gentlemen, and even some holy abbots . . . leave no ground to be tilled, they enclose every bit of land for pasture; they pull down houses and destroy towns, leaving only the church to pen the sheep in."[20] Because of their behavior, More placed neither an aristocracy of birth nor an aristocracy of wealth in Utopia and saw to it that society there was predominantly urban rather than rural.

More recognized that a constitutional and legal structure existed in the European states, but he thought that rulers were often encouraged by their advisors to abuse their positions. In describing the methods that were used to obtain money, More unconsciously revealed the inherent weakness of the European monarchs. Instead of raising taxes, as a strong king would logically do if he wanted additional funds, these Renaissance rulers were often advised to alter the quantity of precious metal in the currency, to have make-believe wars as a pretext to raise money, to fine persons for breaking "old and moth-eaten laws, annulled by long non-enforcement, which no one remembers being made and therefore everyone has transgressed,"[21] and to take other stopgap measures. The crown's reliance on popular support is revealed when Hythlodaye suggests "that these counsels are both dishonorable and dangerous for the king, whose very safety, not merely his honor, rests on the people's resources rather than his own."[22]

It might be argued that More's decision to give Utopia a decentralized government consisting of semi-autonomous city-states was a reaction against the centralizing efforts of the Renaissance monarchs. It is more likely, however, that Utopia's city-state structure was borrowed from the much admired ancient Greeks. More does not accuse the Renaissance monarchs of centralizing their states in Book One of *Utopia*; indeed, in Book Two he gives the Utopian government the right to transfer children from one family to another and to regulate the lives of the people to a degree that no Renaissance king would have dared imitate. In this respect, at least, More's criticism of the European monarchies was that they governed too little, not too much. On the whole, the picture he painted of the Europe of his day was done in the same colors that Erasmus had used in his work. The writings of

---

[19] *Ibid.*, p. 21.     [20] *Ibid.*, pp. 24-25.     [21] *Ibid.*, p. 44.
[22] *Ibid.*, p. 45.

both point to the need to revise the traditional interpretation of the Renaissance monarchy.

Claude de Seyssel was the illegitimate offspring of a distinguished Savoyard family.[23] After a brief period on the law faculty at Turin, he entered the service of the Duke of Savoy and, later, of Louis XII of France. He participated in numerous diplomatic missions, helped organize the French government in the newly conquered duchy of Milan, and was made Bishop of Marseilles as a reward for his services. After the death of Louis XII in January 1515, he wrote *La Monarchie de France* to show the new king, Francis I, why France was the best-ordered monarchy and how this monarchy "could be preserved and increased."

In Seyssel's opinion, the French monarchy owed its superiority to kingship being hereditary in the male line, to three reins that checked royal authority, and to the harmony that existed between the social classes. The three reins were religion, justice, and *la police*. Since the French were Christians, it was necessary for the kings of France to be good Christians also in order to have "the love and complete obedience of the people. . . ."[24] Almost by definition, a Christian king could do nothing tyrannical. Justice was a check because it was administered by judges of *Parlement* and other sovereign courts who were appointed for life and could not be removed by the king. *La police* consisted of the basic laws, ordinances, and customs which had been kept for such a long time that kings did not attempt to change them. There were three social classes: the nobles, who were primarily a military order; the *peuple gras*, consisting of merchants, important public officials, and lawyers; and the *peuple menu*, consisting of farmers, craftsmen, and minor officials. Harmony between these classes was facilitated by the relative ease with which an able man could rise from one class to another, a situation which removed much of the desire of one class to conspire against the other two. In Seyssel's view, the clergy was not a separate estate because its members came from all three classes, a circumstance which also contributed to greater social harmony and mobility.[25]

[23] For the life of Seyssel, see Alberto Caviglia, "Claudio di Seyssel," *Miscellanea di Storia Italiana*, 3rd ser., XXIII (1928). For a study of his political thought, see William F. Church, *Constitutional Thought in Sixteenth-Century France* (Cambridge, Mass., 1941), pp. 22-42.

[24] Claude de Seyssel, *La Monarchie de France*, ed. J. Poujol (Paris, 1961), p. 117. For the three reins, see esp. pp. 112-119, and pp. 143-166.

[25] *Ibid.*, pp. 120-128.

The bulk of *La Monarchie de France* was devoted to showing how the kingdom "could be preserved and increased." Here, even more clearly than in the brief description of France itself, support may be found for this writer's interpretation of the Renaissance monarchy. Its dynastic character was assumed. Wars of conquest were to be undertaken only if the justice of the cause could be sustained "before God and before the world."[26] Although Seyssel gave no specific examples, one may rest assured that dynastic claims were the most likely type to be placed on the approved list. The three reins on royal authority were specifically designed to provide a constitutional check, but the king was told that he must support them "to secure the conservation and augmentation of the state."[27] The nobles were recognized as constituting the preeminent estate, but instead of counseling their destruction Seyssel advised the king to help maintain their position, although he was to take care that they "did not become too insolent."[28] Decentralization was assured by Seyssel's insistence not only that the customs and privileges of French provinces and social classes be preserved but also that the same consideration be extended to newly acquired territories. Only after the affection of new subjects had been won were they to be drawn slowly and gently toward "the manners and laws of the Prince, so that they would forget their old ones and dwell better with the other subjects of the said Prince...."[29]

The inherent weaknesses in the monarchy and the need of the prince to win popular support are everywhere apparent. For Seyssel, the strength of the kingdom was determined by the wealth, unity, and obedience of the people, the quality of the army, and the fortifications of cities, towns, and castles—all of which "depend on good counsel and government."[30] To secure this good counsel and government, the French kings had small, medium, and large councils to consult. Seyssel did not mention the Estates General or, more surprisingly, the provincial estates, but he pointed out that "it is sometimes expedient to summon a small number of people from the principal cities and towns of the kingdom."[31] In addition, the king was advised to visit all his provinces, including those on the frontier, "in order to see and hear . . . how the people are governed and how officials conduct themselves, . . . giving ready audience and prompt judgment to subjects who come with complaints."[32] In this manner Seyssel preserved the consultative nature of the monarchy, although he

[26] *Ibid.*, p. 204.  [27] *Ibid.*, pp. 142-143.  [28] *Ibid.*, p. 156.
[29] *Ibid.*, p. 217.  [30] *Ibid.*, p. 167.  [31] *Ibid.*, p. 136.  [32] *Ibid.*, p. 168.

assigned little or no role to representative institutions. The need to instill harmony between social classes, to provide justice, to keep taxes
low, and to promote prosperity were all advocated, not only as a moral
duty but also as a means of winning popular support. On the other
hand, Seyssel devoted many pages to the problem of how to control the
army, whose loyalty could not be counted on and whose services were
evidently designed to be used against a foreign enemy, not against the
liberties and privileges of the people.[33] No more than Erasmus and
More did he envisage a centralized, absolute, national, bourgeois
monarchy.

But can the same be said of Machiavelli? Surely the man who has
been accused of writing a textbook for tyrants and praised for devising a plan to achieve the "unity of his Italian motherland,"[34] the man
who has been acclaimed as the founder of *raison d'état* and the father
of political science—surely this man must have anticipated the modern
state. There is, of course, a vast literature that says he did, but our
suspicions are aroused by Professor J. H. Hexter's discovery that, although Machiavelli no longer used *lo stato* to mean a "state of mind"
or a social class, he did not employ the term to mean a dynamic living
organism in whose service men should live and die. Rather, *lo stato*
nearly always found itself in the position of being the subject of a passive verb or the object of an active one. Hence, to Machiavelli, "*lo stato*
is not a matrix of values, a body politic; it is an instrument of exploitation, the mechanism the prince uses to get what he wants. . . ."[35] True,
the Florentine had abandoned the medieval definitions of *lo stato*; yet
he did not adopt the modern one. Between the Middle Ages and
modernity lay the Renaissance, an age that was indebted to its parent
and contributed to its child, but also an autonomous age in which the
state in theory and in fact can be classified as being neither medieval
nor modern.

It has often been pointed out that the organization of *The Prince*[36]
resembled the "mirror of princes" literature, but it has not been sufficiently stressed that, in spite of different moral overtones, the author's
conception of the nature of the state was similar to that of Seyssel,

[33] *Ibid.*, pp. 169-187.

[34] A phrase used by Pasquale Villari.

[35] J. H. Hexter, "The Loom of Language and the Fabric of Imperatives: The
Case of *Il Principe* and *Utopia*," *American Historical Review*, LXIX (1964), 958.

[36] In view of the numerous editions of *The Prince*, references will be made to
the pertinent chapter. With one or two minor changes, I have quoted from the
translation of Luigi Ricci, as revised by E.R.P. Vincent.

26

Erasmus, and More. Machiavelli opened *The Prince* in the customary manner by defining the different types of states. Monarchies, which he alone planned to treat in this work, "are either hereditary in which the rulers have been for many years of the same family, or else they are of recent foundation. The newly founded ones are either entirely new, as was Milan to Francesco Sforza," or else they are mixed, consisting of an hereditary state like Spain and a newly acquired one like Naples.[37] "The difficulty of maintaining hereditary states accustomed to a reigning family is far less than in new monarchies; for it is sufficient not to transgress ancestral usages, and to adapt one's self to unforeseen circumstances. . . . In as much as the legitimate prince has less cause and less necessity to give offence, it is only natural that he should be more loved. . . ."[38]

It was to new and mixed monarchies, however, that Machiavelli devoted most of his attention, because their problems were most pertinent in Italy. Military might was not enough to hold a new territory, for, "however strong your armies may be, you will always need the favour of the inhabitants to take possession of a province."[39] It is easy to win this favor if the newly annexed inhabitants have "the same nationality and language." To possess them securely it is necessary to "bear in mind two things: the one, that the blood of their old rulers be extinct; the other, to make no alteration either in their laws or in their taxes. . . ."[40]

"But when dominions are acquired in a province differing in language, laws, and customs, the difficulties to be overcome are great, and it requires good fortune as well as great industry to retain them; one of the best and most certain means of doing so would be for the new ruler to take up his residence there. . . . Being on the spot, disorders can be seen as they rise and can quickly be remedied. . . . Besides which, the province is not despoiled by your officials, the subjects being able to obtain satisfaction by direct recourse to their prince, and wishing to be loyal they have more reason to love him, and should they be otherwise inclined they will have greater cause to fear him."[41] Another method of holding a newly acquired state is to plant colonies in it, but garrisons are useless because the cost of maintaining them will "consume all the revenues of that state, . . . so that the acquisition will result in a loss, besides giving much greater offence, since it injures every one in that state. . . ."[42]

[37] Ch. I.    [38] Ch. II.    [39] Ch. III.    [40] *Ibid.*
[41] *Ibid.*    [42] *Ibid.*

In view of the stress he had placed on the difficulty of holding newly acquired territories, Machiavelli felt it necessary to devote the next chapter to explaining why Alexander the Great and his successors had been able to hold so much of Asia. "Kingdoms," he declared, "have been governed in two ways: either by a prince and his servants, . . . or by a prince and by barons, who hold their positions not by favour of the ruler but by antiquity of blood."[43]

"Examples of these two kinds of government in our own time are those of the Turk and the King of France. All the Turkish monarchy is governed by one ruler, the others are his servants, and dividing his kingdom into 'sangiacates,' he sends to them various administrators, and changes or recalls them at his pleasure. But the King of France is surrounded by a large number of ancient nobles, recognized as such by their subjects, and loved by them; they have their prerogatives, of which the king cannot deprive them without danger to himself. Whoever now considers these two states will see that it would be difficult to acquire the state of the Turk; but having conquered it, it would be very easy to hold it. In many respects, on the other hand, it would be easier to conquer the kingdom of France, but there would be great difficulty in holding it."[44]

For Machiavelli, then, the dominant class in France—and, by implication, in most other Western European monarchies—was the nobility. Bureaucratic government, so often associated with the Renaissance monarchies, he found in the ancient kingdom of Darius and the Ottoman empire of his day. One need only read the first four chapters of *The Prince* to see that Machiavelli recognized the importance of dynasticism and unconsciously accepted the inherent weakness of monarchs that made it advisable for them to win support by leaving laws and taxes as they were, respecting the privileges of the aristocracy, and making themselves available to their subjects. These basic presumptions underlie the remainder of *The Prince* and all of his relevant political writings.

So much has been written concerning Machiavelli's recommendations that a prince disregard moral laws that this topic must be investigated further. In the first place, it should be pointed out that Machiavelli recognized that it was advantageous for a ruler to govern within a basic institutional framework, because he would lose popular support if he did otherwise.[45]

[43] *Ibid.*, ch. IV.      [44] *Ibid.*
[45] *Ibid.*, chs. II and XII. In *The Discourses* Machiavelli warned princes to

"I conclude, therefore, that a prince need trouble little about conspiracies when the people are well disposed, but when they are hostile and hold him in hatred, then he must fear everything and everybody. Well-ordered states and wise princes have studied diligently not to drive the nobles to desperation, and to satisfy the populace and keep it contented, for this is one of the most important matters that a prince has to deal with."

"Among the kingdoms that are well ordered and governed in our time is France, and there we find numberless good institutions on which depend the liberty and security of the king; of these the chief is the *parlement* and its authority, because he who established that kingdom . . . [recognized the need for] a third judge that, without direct charge of the king, kept in check the great and favoured the lesser people. Nor could any better or more prudent measure have been adopted, nor better precaution for the safety of the king and the kingdom."[46]

It is true that a prince must be prepared to lie and deceive, "for how we live is so far removed from how we ought to live, that he who abandons what is done for what ought to be done, will rather learn to bring about his own ruin than his preservation." Nevertheless, mindful of the prince's need for popular support, Machiavelli added that "he should be prudent enough to avoid the scandal of those vices which would lose him the state. . . ."[47]

Even a man who acquires a state through villainy "must arrange to commit all his cruelties at once, so as not to have to recur to them every day, and so as to be able, by not making fresh changes, to reassure people and win them over by benefiting them."[48] It is true that, if a choice has to be made, "it is much safer to be feared than loved"; nevertheless, "every prince must desire to be considered merciful and not cruel."[49]

Machiavelli advised that "a prudent ruler ought not to keep faith when by so doing it would be against his interest, and when the reasons which made him bind himself no longer exist." But, aware of the

---

remember "that they begin to lose their state from the moment when they begin to disregard the laws and ancient customs under which the people have lived contented for a length of time" (Bk. III, ch. V).

[46] *The Prince*, ch. XIX. For other comparable statements concerning the role of law in France, see also *The Discourses*, Bk. I, chs. XVI, XIX, LV, LVIII, and Bk. III, ch. I.

[47] *The Prince*, ch. XV.   [48] *Ibid.*, ch. VIII.   [49] *Ibid.*, ch. XVII.

need of the prince to have popular support, he added that "it is well to seem merciful, faithful, humane, sincere, religious, and also to be so. . . ."[50] "The prince," in short, "must . . . avoid those things which will make him hated or despised. . . ."[51]

On a more positive side, Machiavelli suggested that the prince "ought, at convenient seasons of the year, to keep the people occupied with festivals and shows; and as every city is divided either into guilds or into classes, he ought to pay attention to all these groups, mingle with them from time to time, and give them an example of his humanity and munificence, always upholding, however, the majesty of his dignity, which must never be allowed to fail in anything whatever."[52]

Machiavelli's preference for native troops over mercenaries has often been commented upon, but it should be equally stressed that his evaluation was based on the presumption that the former would be more loyal, a loyalty that could be ensured only if the prince had won the support of his subjects. "Fortresses may or may not be useful according to the times; . . . a prince who fears his own people more than foreigners ought to build fortresses, but he who has greater fear of foreigners than his own people ought to do without them. . . . Therefore the best fortress is to be found in the love of the people, for although you may have fortresses they will not save you if you are hated by the people."[53]

The chief difference between Machiavelli's and Erasmus's contributions to the "mirror of princes" literature lies in the fact that the former advised the prince to commit immoral acts in case of necessity while the latter never abandoned the Christian code; but many of their underlying presumptions concerning the nature of the Renaissance monarchy were essentially the same.

Of the characteristics so long associated with the Renaissance monarchy, only one, nationalism, seems to have really played an important role in the thought of any of our four thinkers, and among them it is most apparent in Machiavelli. Yet, even in regard to the Italian, one must be cautious. Most contemporary scholars have abandoned the theory that Machiavelli sought a prince who would unite Italy and form a territorial monarchy like those in the North. Rather, they interpret the last chapter of *The Prince* as a call for a temporary alliance between the various Italian states to drive out the foreigners.[54] Na-

---

[50] *Ibid.*, ch. XVIII.      [51] *Ibid.*, ch. XIX.      [52] *Ibid.*, ch. XXI.

[53] *Ibid.*, ch. XX.

[54] See, e.g., Felix Gilbert, *Machiavelli and Guicciardini: Politics and History*

tionalism, for Machiavelli, was essentially a negative force that provoked cooperation against the outsider, rather than a positive force that would bring unity to long-separated kingdoms, duchies, and provinces. Although Machiavelli saw that it was easier for a prince to acquire and hold a province in which his language was spoken, he never suggested that a prince should try to conquer only those lands where his tongue was used or that he should attempt to unite all his fellow nationals in one state.

The medieval concept of the Empire had died, and even the cosmopolitan Erasmus avoided publishing an edition of Dante's *De Monarchia* when requested to do so by Charles V's great chancellor, Gattinara.[55] But our four observers were equally far removed from seeing in nationalism the cohesive force that it became in the nineteenth century. They were men of the Renaissance, and the dynastic, decentralized, constitutional, aristocratic monarchy, as they saw it, was neither medieval nor modern: it was the monarchy of the Renaissance, a monarchy whose power rested neither on its army nor on its bureaucracy but on the degree of support it received from the people.

---

*in Sixteenth-Century Florence* (Princeton, 1965), pp. 182-184; 325-326. Allan Gilbert, however, still holds to the older view. See his translation of *Machiavelli: The Chief Works and Others* (Durham, 1965), I, 8-9.

[55] Renaudet, *Études Erasmiennes*, pp. 95-97.

# A MATTER OF CONSCIENCE

LACEY BALDWIN SMITH

"CONSCIENCE," so the medieval saying goes, "is a pretty theory to carry to church, but he that pursueth it in fair market or shop may die a beggar." The advice may be sound business, but the rule proved inadequate when Henry VIII carried conscience into every capital of Europe and thereby set all Christendom by the ears. On the grounds of conscience the King justified his "Great Matter" and dared risk his immortal soul by violating the sacred instincts of the Christian world.

Historians, from the start,[1] have been reluctant to accept Henry's motive at its face value. They have refused to believe that a great spoiled brute of a sovereign, carefully schooled in the adage that "three may keep counsel if two be away," could have been seriously touched by the small voice of conscience. For a monarch such as Henry there must have been a more physical and political explanation for his determination to rid himself of Catherine of Aragon; statecraft or sex, or some combination of the two, not piety, it is said, were the driving impulses behind the mask of conscience.

The "continuation of the succession" and "inordinate carnal love" were doubtless factors;[2] yet to accept politics and lust as the central motives behind the divorce is to read into the sixteenth century dangerously modern standards of thought. The political situation was precarious but not incapable of resolution. The Princess Mary could have been married to her first cousin, James V of Scotland, thereby achieving what we are so often told was the vision of Henry's Scottish policy: the creation of Great Britain.[3] Henry could have adopted any one of the ingenious, if tawdry, expedients offered by a Pope desperately anxious to find any solution short of divorce. His Holiness had made known his willingness to sanction royal bigamy, to permit adultery by legitimizing any children of the King and Anne Boleyn,

[1] George Cavendish, *Thomas Wolsey late Cardinal, his Life and Death*, ed. Roger Lockyer (London, 1962), p. 22.

[2] M. St. Clare Byrne, *The Letters of King Henry VIII* (London, 1936), p. 62; Cavendish, *Thomas Wolsey*, p. 111.

[3] Garrett Mattingly, *Catherine of Aragon* (Boston, 1941), p. 246. Mattingly says "forward-looking men in both countries were eager for it; in 1524 the Scottish envoys would have been glad to arrange it, and in 1527 his alliance with France put it again in Henry's reach. He did not consider it."

or to bless the marriage of Henry's bastard, the Duke of Richmond, with the Princess Mary.[4] Public opinion, if Erasmus accurately reflected it, obviously preferred that the English monarch "should take two Junos rather than put away one."[5]

There was another way out of the King's difficulties—carnal as well as political—which was so obvious that it is extraordinary that it was never whispered abroad: Catherine could have been quietly murdered in her bed, and no one would have been the wiser. Had Henry really been a Machiavellian monster willing to sacrifice all upon the altar of his dynasty or his lust, his easiest course would have been to take a page from his ancestor's book and utilize the poisoner.[6] This was to be his daughter's preferred method of resolving the riddle of what to do with Mary of Scotland,[7] and Henry himself sanctioned the murder of Cardinal David Beaton, though he wisely refused to put it in writing.[8] He knew full well that his subjects were sufficient realists to accept the argument that "it is no murder in a King to end another's life to save his own," for, "if you fail, the state doth whole default, the realm is rent in twain in such a loss."[9]

Yet Henry would have no murder, no papal dispensation, and no Scottish marriage. His representative in Rome in September of 1530 dismissed the Pope's proposition that the King take two wives on the ground that he "did not know whether it would satisfy [his] Majesty's conscience,"[10] and nowhere is there any hint that the easy way out—quietly to do away with Catherine—was ever considered. Instead, Henry stood squarely on conscience, writing the Emperor Charles that he could not "quiet his conscience remaining longer with the Queen, whom, for her nobleness of blood and other virtues, he had loved entirely as his wife, until he saw that their union was forbidden in Scripture"; and he pointedly asked the Emperor whether Charles

---

[4] A. F. Pollard, *Henry VIII* (London, 1934), pp. 184, 206.

[5] *Opus Epistolarum Des. Erasmi Roterodami*, ed. P. S. Allen et al., 12 vols. (Oxford, 1906-1958), VII, Ep. 2040 (to John Vives, 2 Sept. 1528), 471.

[6] Henry had a number of extraordinarily vicious ancestors: Bernabo Visconti of Milan on his father's side, and Peter the Cruel of Castile on his mother's.

[7] J. E. Neale, *Elizabeth I and her Parliaments*, 2 vols. (London, 1953-1957), II, 139-140.

[8] Byrne, *Letters of Henry VIII*, p. 349.

[9] Robert Greene, *James the Fourth*, printed in Alexander Dyce, *The Dramatic and Poetical Works of Robert Greene and George Peele* (London, 1861), p. 211.

[10] *Letters and Papers, Foreign and Domestic, of the Reign of Henry VIII*, ed. J. S. Brewer et al., 21 vols. in 33 parts (London, 1862-1910), IV, no. 6627.

"would wilfully destroy his soul" by refusing to support the dissolution of such an unlawful marriage.[11]

Henry was unwilling to contemplate murder, but he was ready to commit what his contemporaries held to be a far greater crime: to risk his soul by defying the Pope and to cut off his kingdom from salvation. His soul alone would pay the ultimate price if he was wrong and the Christian-Catholic world was right. The sixteenth century accepted as a fact that kings, in their estate as God's lieutenants on earth, were "judged more severely in proportion to the great power entrusted" to them. "For if God do extremely punish men of base estate and of low degree ... how severely will He punish kings and princes. . . ."[12] Lesser men—Cromwell, Gardiner, Cranmer, and the like—could always justify their actions by the Erastian creed that the prince must be obeyed at all costs, but Henry could hide behind no such sophistry. Eventually he was bound to render account to God. Emotionally, politically, and spiritually, the defiance of Rome took extraordinary nerve, and not even the anti-clerical and humanistic currents of the century or the fervent support of a small coterie of admirers could conceal the fact that most of the Christian world was convinced that "the King will hang in Hell one day."

It is clear that Henry appreciated the spiritual danger of his actions, for he shied away from schism as long as he could. The two people who knew him best—his wife and his chief minister—thought that he would never risk his chances of paradise.[13] All his actions up to the very threshold of the break with Rome were those of a man wavering on the brink, fearful of taking the final, irrevocable step. As late as 31 March 1533, Henry was still telling Chapuys, the Imperial ambassador, that, if the Pope would "do his pleasure in this affair," he would be willing to reconsider the matter.[14] Yet the fact remains that, when the chips were down and his bluff—if it was a bluff—was called, his will alone gave legality to the Royal Supremacy and his soul alone would be held accountable in the final judgment.

[11] *Ibid.*, IV, 6111; VI, 775.

[12] Franklin Le Van Baumer, *The Early Tudor Theory of Kingship* (New Haven, 1940), p. 207, n. 48; J. G. Nichols, *Literary Remains of King Edward VI*, 2 vols. (Roxburghe Club, 1857), I, clix-clx.

[13] Mattingly, *Catherine of Aragon*, pp. 304, 311; G. R. Elton, "King or Minister? the Man Behind the Henrician Reformation," *History*, XXXIX (Oct. 1954), 221-232.

[14] *Calendar of State Papers, Spanish*, ed. G. A. Bergenroth et al., 13 vols. (London, 1862-1954), IV, no. 1057, 626.

Possibly, the King's willingness to accept spiritual responsibility was evidence of Satanic pride; possibly, the narrow closet and polished walls of insensate egotism gave him the strength to defy world opinion, historic authority, and God's Word. Rebellion presumably took no great courage, for pride inured his heart to fear or remorse; conscience was dead, and in its place was nothing but the criminal's greed and the instinct for survival. Such a diagnosis, however, is more a matter of opinion than of evidence, and it is important to record that Henry did not seek to justify his actions on the grounds of political expediency or to hide behind statistics. He was right, he said, "not because so many say it, but because he, being learned, knoweth the matter to be right."[15] He appealed to the essential individualism of the Christian faith: "Though the law of every man's conscience be but a private court, yet it is the highest and supreme court for judgment or justice."[16] Although his subjects were offered no such liberty of conscience, the King, as a man apart, took his stand as Luther and Calvin had done, on his nearness to God and the voice of inner conviction, not on the multitude of his supporters or the justification of statecraft. His conviction gave him the spiritual enthusiasm and the "inhibition-quenching fury" to do what he knew was right. If historians are ready to dignify Luther's will by calling it conscience, then possibly it is time to take Henry's scruple seriously, to dismiss it no longer as evidence of a proud and willful man, and to canvass the inward reaches of the King's soul. As Chesterton said, it may be wise for a landlady to investigate her boarder's income, but it is even more revealing to know his approach to God.[17] On these grounds, then, the historian should view Henry's conscience in terms of the whole man and place it within the context of the religious psychology of his day and the habits of his mind.

Theory is one thing, execution another. How, indeed, can the historian sound the inner reaches of a mind devoid of speculative thinking and reach down to what William James calls the "experiences of individual men in their solitude, so far as they apprehend themselves to stand in relation to whatever they may consider the divine"?[18] For a Calvin, a Luther, or a Loyola, the inner profile of the man is revealed

[15] *Letters and Papers*, VI, no. 775.

[16] Byrne, *Letters of Henry VIII*, p. 86.

[17] Gilbert K. Chesterton, *Heretics* (New York, 1919), p. 15.

[18] William James, *The Varieties of Religious Experience*, Mentor pap. edn. (New York, 1958), pp. 42, 45, 379.

a hundred times over both in action and in writing, but Henry was a great, blundering Prometheus who accepted without question the subliminal assumptions of his age as being so self-evident that they needed neither defense nor articulation. Since formal evidence is lacking, then, imagination must suffice as we move about in the most obscure regions of mind and soul: the inherited structure of Henry's faith, his relationship to God, his attitude toward sin, his constant desire to shift blame to others, and the ritualistic nature of his religion. The details are fuzzy and the evidence difficult to assess, but the final picture of the King's inner personality should emerge clearly enough: an image very different from the corporeal man but no less monstrous.

Henry's faith was the product of countless generations and centuries of belief; it came to him ready-made, and he received it fully sanctioned and guaranteed by the weight of an authority which was not only fifteen hundred years old but was built into the mentality of his day. The doctrine of authority—of Christ's life, death, and redemption of mankind, of Peter's possession of the keys to the kingdom of heaven, of God's Word revealed in Scripture, of glosses on commentaries penned by Church Fathers, of historic custom and time-honored privilege, of father over child, of husband over wife, of priest over layman, of king over subject—was awe-inspiring in the hierarchic harmony of its parts, with power ascending from level to level and ultimate authority residing in the Godhead who was the capstone of the entire system. In heaven, so the Homily of 1547 informed the Tudor reader, there were archangels, angels, saints, and martyrs; likewise, on earth "every degree of people, in their vocation, calling, and office, hath appointed to them, their duty and order."[19]

To sustain such a complex and perfectly balanced scheme of things, the aim of medieval and Tudor religious education was severely catechetical: to drill the mind in habits of piety and duty. Happiness and religious contentment consisted in the simple arithmetical computation of balancing acts of righteousness and obedience against those of sinfulness and willful rebellion. The Church was at pains to insist that a Christian's worth must be judged solely in terms of the simple calculation of pluses and minuses recorded during his life. Each soul was warned to keep constantly in mind that the end of life is not death but the eternity of heaven or hell. If, at the final reckoning, a Christian cared to be numbered among the saved, he must choose on earth the society of the righteous. Nothing was more central to the teaching of

[19] Quoted in Van Baumer, *Early Tudor Theory of Kingship*, p. 104.

the medieval Church than the prick of conscience, for only a clean conscience could secure the Christian from the torments of hell; and it was regularly reiterated that "the poor man in his hut, wealthy in conscience, sleeps safer upon earth than the rich man in his gold and purple."[20] Henry was speaking no more than what he and his generation believed when he said during the divorce trial that "every Christian man knoweth what pain and what inquietness he suffereth that hath a conscience grieved. . . ."[21]

We know next to nothing about Henry's formal religious education except that the final product was a conventionally religious sovereign who had read his Proverbs with their moral enjoinder to give obedience to father, magistrate, and God, had studied diligently the works of Thomas Aquinas, and had been drilled by John Skelton in a healthy respect for stern piety and in a fear of the seven deadly sins which no amount of humanistic laughter or Renaissance anti-clericalism could dispel.[22] In the oft-quoted observation of the Venetian ambassador, it was early noted that Henry had been thoroughly indoctrinated in orthodox religious habits, for he was "very religious; heard three masses daily when he hunted, and sometimes five on other days," besides regularly attending vespers and compline.[23] The King's zeal for religion is undeniable and only to be expected in a civilization which viewed God as the measure of creation and which insisted upon a ubiquitous and intimate deity "who understandeth the bottom of your heart." The sixteenth century did not doubt that God spoke to man and man to God. Consequently, Henry's conception of his deity and the abode of heaven are crucial to the study of the man, for "the gods we stand by are the gods we need and can use, the gods whose demands on us are reinforcements of our demands on ourselves and on one another."[24]

[20] G. R. Owst, *Literature and Pulpit in Medieval England* (Oxford, 1961), pp. 293, 571; Ray C. Petry, *Christian Eschatology and Social Thought* (New York, 1956), p. 301.

[21] Edward Hall, *The Union of the Two Noble and Illustre Families of Lancastre and Yorke* (London, 1548), fol. clxxii.

[22] Edward Lord Herbert of Cherbury, *England under Henry VIII* (London, 1870), p. 199; Pollard, *Henry VIII*, pp. 20-24; G. G. Coulton, *Medieval Panorama*, Meridian pap. edn. (New York, 1955), p. 698; F. M. Salter, "Skelton's *Speculum Principis*," *Speculum*, IX (Jan., 1934), 27-29; H. Maynard Smith, *Pre-Reformation England* (London, 1938), p. 507.

[23] *Calendar of State Papers, Venetian*, ed. Rawdon Brown et al., 38 vols. (London, 1864-1940), II, no. 1287, 559.

[24] James, *Religious Experience*, p. 259.

Heaven and hell were clearly mapped societies. Both were reflections of man's organizational mind—heaven being the state of exquisite order, hell that of perfect disorder—and both are symbolic representations of man's life on earth. Hell was the place where soft couches turned into beds "more grievous and hard than all the nails and pikes in the world," where loving embraces became the hugs of loathsome devils, and the great retinues of kings and princes became a legion of worms and demons which tormented the sinner's body.[25] Conversely, heaven was a bright and beautiful city, "the hereditary stronghold of the Eternal King," and, though God himself had become an indescribable spiritual essence, the heavenly host who inhabited the spacious halls, fields of joy, and green meadows filled with flowers and sweet odors were a highly corporeal and active lot. At one time, paradise had been populated with God's faithful vassals, who practiced to perfection the virtues and ideals of medieval feudalism; by 1500, the residents of heaven were somewhat less feudally oriented, but they remained firmly patriarchal and monarchical. God was king of kings, with all the attributes of human sovereignty, for the sixteenth-century mind could not conceive of a deity without the heavy cruelty of "retributive justice" by which to prove his omnipotence.[26]

The King's relation to this spiritual world and his position as a potential citizen of the kingdom of God were unique, and it is important to consider them in seeking to understand the operation of his conscience. Henry was not a normal man but a sovereign by divine right, which posed all sorts of difficulties when it came to his participation in the eternal joys of a heavenly society in which all men were kings. Rich and poor alike believed in the reality of paradise, but with this distinction: the poor understandably assumed that God preferred their rustic virtues and would reward their humble ways, punishing the rich, blessing the downtrodden; the rich, on the other hand, argued that in paradise all men were equal but that some men were more equal than others. But the whole of Tudor society knew that "In my Father's house are many mansions" and that heaven, where peace reigned eternal, could not possibly be without "degree, order and true proportion." A special level of kingliness had to be reserved for God's lieutenants on earth, for, said Thomas Aquinas, kings have a heavier duty than other

---

[25] Owst, *Literature and Pulpit*, p. 294, quoting from Bromyard's "Gloria."

[26] Petry, *Christian Eschatology*, p. 347; H. R. Patch, *The Other World* (Cambridge, Mass., 1950), pp. 112-113, 316.

men and, therefore, can expect a greater reward and "receive a high degree of heavenly happiness."[27]

Henry's association with heaven is difficult to assess. He was certainly aware of his own divinity and the divine trappings of his regal office. As a young man he had dreamed of an imperial crown equal in dignity to that of the Holy Roman Emperor, and he took seriously the tale of the mythical hero, King Arthur, and his own descent from the Emperor Constantine.[28] At Henry's coronation God had been asked to bestow on him "the dew of heaven and the fatness of the earth, and the plenty of the corn and wine." The King's scepter was a magical staff; the canopy over his throne was the symbolic shield protecting his kingdom; and he had been anointed with the holy oil found by Richard II and said to have been used by Edward the Confessor.[29] As Bishop Stephen Gardiner pointed out, kings were a breed apart, for God had set princes on their thrones "as representours of his Image unto men"; therefore, they must be accepted as being "in the supreme and most high room, and to excel among all other human creatures. ..."[30] When Henry, the "head, and so the soul of us all," announced that he prayed "for you my members, that God may light you with His grace," he was simply reiterating the obvious—his special relationship with the deity.[31]

Although there is no way of proving what Henry thought about heaven and the ultimate reckoning with his Master, it may not be too far off to assume a direct and anthropomorphic picture. If monarchs were in fact God's viceroys in this world, the assumption is, of course, that God was a captain: hence, Henry's relationship to his deity was that of a lesser commander to his general. If Henry's concept of heaven in any way reflected the views of his own generation, which judged paradise by the standards of earth and translated human society into the afterlife, then his heaven must have been replete with Christ as king of kings, the holy family dressed in the height of Tudor fashion, a

[27] Petry, *Christian Eschatology*, pp. 282-283, 344-345.

[28] R. Koebner, " 'The Imperial Crown of This Realm': Henry VIII, Constantine The Great and Polydore Vergil," *Bulletin of the Institute of Historical Research*, XXVI (May 1953), 30-32, 36-48.

[29] Margaret A. Murray, *The Divine King in England* (London, 1954), pp. 179-185.

[30] Stephen Gardiner, *De Vera Obedientia*, ed. Pierre Janelle (Cambridge, England, 1930), p. 89.

[31] Philip Hughes, *The Reformation in England*, 3 vols. (London, 1950-1954), I, 22, n. 1.

divine court with musicians, jesters, and servants, and a privy chamber in which Henry Tudor knelt, neatly balancing subservience with a due appreciation of his own importance. He acknowledged his allegiance but at the same time claimed God as his ally.

That Henry's contemporaries viewed divine-right kings in this fashion is clear from Hans Springinklee's woodcut of the Emperor Maximilian entering heaven. Christ stands at the portal in his regal garb; at his feet kneels the Emperor, his own insignia properly set aside but his dress every bit the equal of Christ's and quite putting to shame the attire of his heavenly sponsors. A woodcut from the Cranmer Bible of 1539 approaches the problem from a slightly different perspective and portrays Henry's own close association with the deity. The King is shown sitting in his majesty, and above is God, bestowing upon him divine wisdom. As God's vicar on earth, Henry presents the Word to his spiritual and temporal lords, who in turn transmit the truth as revealed by the King to the laity who dutifully sing, not God's praise, but "Vivat Rex."

In an age which was perfectly clear about the geography of heaven and hell and the joys and torments awaiting the eternal traveler, Henry's dealings with his divine overlord were central to his role as monarch and to the tenderness of his conscience. The special claim he had, as God's faithful vassal, to a secure and prominent abode in paradise carried with it weighty obligations and dire consequences. Doubtless "the spirit of God," as Henry boasted, brought freedom,[32] but the free man is the responsible man, and the King knew well what he owed his deity. His authority stemmed from on high, and he was determined to do his duty lest he be branded "an unprofitable servant and an untrue officer."[33] In part, that duty was to demand of his subjects the same obedience which he offered to God, and to do unto his people as he would have God do unto him: to punish sin, root out evil, and reward charity, concord, and obedience. But duty involved far more than the strict discipline of the magistrate; it behooved Henry, as a Christian king, to keep his spirit free of the taint of sin. Possibly he spoke no more than the truth when he exclaimed at the divorce trial: "Think you, my lords, that these words touch not my body and soul; think you that these doings do not daily and hourly trouble my conscience and vex my spirits . . . ?"[34]

[32] *Letters and Papers*, IV, no. 6111.
[33] Byrne, *Letters of Henry VIII*, p. 421.
[34] Hall, *Union of Lancastre and Yorke*, fol. clxxx.

Kaiser Maximilian before Christ. Woodcut by Hans Springinklee from Ludwig von Baldass, *Der Künstlerkreis Kaiser Maximilians* (Wien, 1923), plate 100.

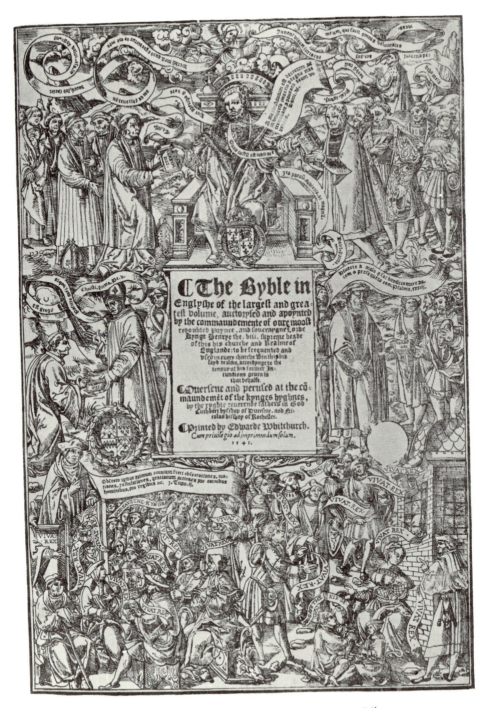

Frontispiece from the Cranmer Bible of 1541. Newberry Library.

In any study of conscience, especially that of a divine-right monarch, it is important not only to reconstruct the inherited and intuitive structure of a man's faith but also to cut through the thick hide of convention and ask what was his understanding of, and reaction to, sin and evil. The frame of Henry's thinking is clear: he belonged firmly in the camp of William James's "healthy-minded man," whose "contentment with the finite encases him like a lobster-shell and shields him from all morbid repining at his distance from the Infinite."[35] The contented man, such as Henry, settles his score with evil by declining to admit his association with it; he is an activist who strikes a blow for righteousness and disdains to spend his days dwelling upon evil, especially when confession and absolution exist to wipe the slate clean of old debts and past trespasses. For these happy few, evil is merely a "mal-adjustment with *things*, a wrong correspondence of one's life with the environment," and sin may be cured simply by rectifying the balance.[36] Henry is the picture of healthy-mindedness. The wonderful vigor, the boundless energy, the warm admiration of all men, the knowledge that the world was his oyster, the simple faith that obedience and piety were sure antidotes to sin, and, above all, the conviction that heaven had reserved a special place of honor for the anointed king: all these understandably produced the firm belief that "God's in his Heaven, all's right with the world." A feeling of precariousness, the stench of the sepulcher, an awareness of discord, a fear of not meriting the fatness of the earth and the serenity of salvation— in a word, a sense that something is wrong with man and nature— never penetrated the coarse skin of Henry's sanguinity or disturbed the neat and cosy tidiness of his cosmic consciousness.

Evil and sin for the King were real enough, but they always remained outside him and were either to be avoided or to be exorcised. Henry was a faithful follower of the policy noted by William James: "We divert our attention from disease and death as much as we can; and the slaughter houses and indecencies without end on which our life is founded are huddled out of sight and never mentioned. . . ."[37] No one was more anxious than the King to escape sickness, and, when plague and death approached, he fled—partly from fear, partly on the time-honored premise, "out of sight, out of mind." When evil

[35] James, *Religious Experience*, p. 87.

[36] *Ibid.*, pp. 83, 112-113, 116-117.

[37] *Ibid.*, p. 85; Walter H. Clark, *The Psychology of Religion* (New York, 1958), p. 156.

41

could not be willed out of existence, when he found it in those so close to him that he could not ignore it, then he pulverized it, thereby striking a blow for God and doing his spirit no end of good. During the very year that Henry's conscience became articulate and public, he lectured his sister Margaret on the "inevitable damnation" awaiting the adulteress. His sister had obtained a divorce from her second husband on the highly questionable grounds that the Earl of Angus had been involved in a pre-contract and on the even more extraordinary claim that her first husband, James IV of Scotland, had not been killed at Flodden Field but was still living at the time of her second marriage. Not only were Henry's notions of decency outraged by such flummery, but he warned Margaret "what charge of conscience, what grudge and fretting, yea, what danger of damnation" she would bring upon her soul unless she, "as in conscience ye are bound under peril of God's everlasting indignation," relinquished "the adulterer's company with him that is not nor may not be of right your husband. . . ."[38] When evil could not be bullied or ignored, and when it entered his own life, Henry translated it into one of the most normal and universal of human reactions: he saw sin in terms of personal persecution. Why has this happened to me? What have I done to deserve ill fortune, sickness, and frustration? How have I erred to warrant God's wrath?

The King's healthy-mindedness was doubtless a reflection of the happy knowledge that heaven smiles upon earth, but operating in him were two qualities peculiar to a spoiled and conventional-thinking monarch: a tendency to place the blame for failure, misfortune, and evil outside himself, thereby throwing up immense walls to protect the inner man from the suggestion that sin lies within; and the firm conviction that God can be coaxed by prayer or ritual into granting the wishes of men.

Throughout the divorce crisis Henry was clearly seeking to protect his tender conscience; it was necessary to his peace of mind that he rule out the possibility that God could be angry because of any innate sinfulness in himself. Both healthy-mindedness and his position as God's viceroy on earth precluded that possibility. Therefore, evil had to lie elsewhere—in a misapplication of the mechanics of living. His dynasty was barren, his wife old and infertile, because he had inadvertently broken God's commandment and thereby incurred divine wrath. He had unconsciously sinned. Yet to make this admission

[38] Byrne, *Letters of Henry VIII*, p. 68.

was not the same as acknowledging the source of sinfulness to lie within himself. Obey God's laws, renounce the marriage, and follow in the path of duty and piety, and all would go as "merry as a marriage bell again."

Ten years later, when Henry was having further matrimonial troubles, he reacted in exactly the same way. He completely dissociated himself from any responsibility for the failure of his marriage to Anne of Cleves, blaming Cromwell for the decision, and, when his fifth wife, Catherine Howard, proved her treason and cuckolded her royal spouse, Henry, as the Spanish ambassador noted, "took to tears regretting his ill luck in meeting such ill-conditioned wives, and blaming his Council for this last mischief."[39]

The King's approach to his divorce and the extraordinary persistence with which he harkened to the inner voice of conscience, not to mention his efforts to blame others, are explicable only in terms of the overpowering sense of ritual which pervaded most sixteenth-century religious thought and which was strengthened in Henry by his conviction that the source of sin must derive from some malfunction within the system, not from himself. There are three positions, it has been said, in which man can stand in association with whatever he considers to be his God: "moral, physical or ritual."[40] Certainly the last is the most common and instinctive of the three, for the essence of primitive religious consciousness is the desire, not to know God or to understand him, but to use him, "sometimes as meat-purveyor, sometimes as moral support, sometimes as friend, sometimes as an object of love," but most of the time as a source of power.[41] A deity who does not concern himself with the immediate wellbeing of his believers, who fails to give them victory in war, to answer their prayers, or to cure hoof-and-mouth disease in their cattle, isn't much of a god. Henry's God, it is true, could not be coerced, but he could be entreated; he had long since ceased to react to burnt offerings or the sacrifice of the first born, but there remained a tacit understanding that the deity could, and did, interfere in the affairs of man, and that he did so on the basis of a *quid pro quo*. Passionate supplication in prayer, flattering promises about going on a pilgrimage or crusade, sharp attention to ceremonial detail, and, above all, absolute obedience to God's laws could assure the scrupulous worshiper the good things of life.[42]

---

[39] *Letters and Papers*, XVI, no. 1426.    [40] James, *Religious Experience*, p. 42.
[41] *Ibid.*, p. 382.
[42] George B. Vetter, *Magic and Religion* (New York, 1958), p. 166.

The sixteenth century expected a great deal of God. The youthful Henry grew up in a world which was convinced of the efficacy of papal excommunications directed against traitors. When Cornishmen rose up against Henry VII, the Pope received "much praise" for calling down the vengeance of heaven, whereby "all who eat grain garnered since the rebellion, or drink beer brewed with this year's crops, die as if they had taken poison, and hence it is publicly reported that the King is under the protection of God eternal."[43] His father's contemporary, Louis XI of France, expected an even greater return for his piety. After having lavishly endowed chapels for the benefit of the Virgin, he was outraged when told that the English were once again invading his kingdom, and he cried: "Ah, Holy Mary; even now, when I have given thee fourteen hundred crowns, thou hast done nothing for me."[44] Religion as the magical power by which to influence a heavenly world populated with singularly militant and interfering, not to say vengeful, personalities was by no means a Catholic monopoly. As the peasant burned a candle to Saint Clement to protect his house from fire and to Saint Apollonia to cure a toothache, so young Protestant Edward VI in 1552 calmly informed his physicians, when they assured him that his friend and tutor John Cheke would die, that their prediction was unwarranted: "He will not die at this time, for this morning I begged his life from God in my prayers, and obtained it."[45]

Religion, in the hands of both educated and illiterate, Protestants and Catholics, tended to become a form of magic, and Henry was neither worse nor better than his contemporaries. During the first year of his marriage, his Queen was delivered of a stillborn child, and Catherine wrote her father pointing out that the calamity was surely the will of God and that she planned to propitiate His anger by giving one of her richest headdresses to the Franciscan Friars.[46] A year later another child was born, alive but sickly, and Henry went on a secret and barefoot pilgrimage to ensure the baby's recovery.[47] Saint Cuthbert's hand was perceived at Flodden Field in July of 1513, when an English army routed a Scottish force, killing 10,000 men, and it was

[43] *Calendar of State Papers, Venetian*, I, no. 751, 261.

[44] Orville W. Mosher, *Louis XI as He Appears in History and in Literature* (Toulouse, 1925), pp. 63, 128-130; Paul M. Kendall, "Louis XI: the Legend and Man," *History Today*, XI (Aug. 1961), 520.

[45] Owst, *Literature and Pulpit*, p. 147; Nichols, *Literary Remains of Edward VI*, p. clix.

[46] *Calendar of State Papers, Spanish*, II, no. 43, 38.

[47] Theodore Maynard, *Henry VIII* (Milwaukee, 1949), p. 38.

avowed that the defeat had been inflicted by the outraged saint because James IV had plundered his church. Queen Catherine preferred to acknowledge only God's interference in this instance; she wrote Henry that "this matter is so marvelous that it seemeth to be God's doing alone" and that she trusted "the King shall remember to thank Him for it. . . ." Henry not only agreed with his wife and did as she bid, but he also assured the Pope that, as God had given "Saul power to slay 1,000 and David strength to kill 10,000," so He had made Henry strong.[48] As late as May of 1521, the King was planning a pilgrimage in gratitude for his recovery from a serious fever, and twenty years later, in 1543, he ordered prayers and public processions for more temperate weather during a particularly rainy summer.[49] Each of these cases is an example of a cause-and-effect approach to religion, a ritualistic and ceremonial performance in which the deity is assumed to take delight in "tapers and tinsel, costume and mumbling and mummery."[50] When the words and actions of the formula have been performed to perfection, then it behooves God to fulfill his side of the bargain and bestow power, wealth, and peace of mind upon His devoted followers.[51]

There is little doubt that Henry was a ritualist. On Good Fridays he dutifully crept to the cross and served the priest at mass, "his own person kneeling on his Grace's knees"; he scrupulously received "holy bread and holy water every Sunday" and daily used "all other laudable ceremonies."[52] His reverence for the sacrament of the mass, it was reported late in his reign, "was always most profound." When it was

---

[48] *Letters and Papers,* I, nos. 4461, 4462; Henry Ellis, *Original Letters, Illustrative of English History,* 11 vols. (London, 1824, 1827, 1846), I, 90; *Calendar of State Papers, Spanish,* II, no. 141, 165.

[49] *Letters and Papers,* III, no. 1293; XVIII (2), no. 66.

[50] James, *Religious Experience,* p. 259.

[51] Before passing judgment on the sixteenth century, it might be well to take a look at our own society. Probe the mind of a twentieth-century man and it is not difficult to discover the conception of religion as magic. For instance, 42% of a group of undergraduates, when asked why they prayed, confessed that prayer "was a kind of magical technique to be used in case of need." A nineteen-year-old student said, "Well, usually before a test I pray to the Lord if He couldn't help me in some way. . . ." Or again, there is the case of the "Washington hostess who found herself coming down with a bad cold on the morning of an important reception. Having telephoned a 'Kansas City prayer center' at 11:00 A.M., she found herself sufficiently recovered to greet the guests at 2:00 P.M.!" (Clark, *Psychology of Religion,* pp. 135, 311.)

[52] *Letters and Papers,* XIV(1), no. 967.

suggested that, because of "his weakness and infirmity," he did not have to "adore the body of Our Saviour" on his knees but could "make his communion sitting in a chair," he answered: if "I lay not only flat on the ground, yea, and put myself under the ground, yet in so doing I should not think that I have reverence sufficient unto His blessed sacrament. . . ."[53] In early life he was fascinated by the strict ritual surrounding jousts, state functions, and religious pageants; as he grew older, the same attention and methodical thinking-out of copious detail was directed toward military matters.[54] This same expert dexterity was also applied to theology and religion. Luther branded him a "glossator, colouring everything with glosses and with illusions," a victim not merely of his love of minutiae but of his early training in scholastic thinking, with its heavy insistence upon historic authority.[55] Campeggio, the Papal Legate, was kinder; he said that the King had "so diligently studied this matter [of the divorce] that I believe in this case he knows more than a great theologian or jurist."[56]

Henry was not only a ritualist but also a high priest, who knew every word of the incantation, every gesture of the ceremony, and every rule of the commandment. It has been said of ritual that it "attaches itself to the basic activities and events of life, which are naturally those that affect the emotions most deeply—eating, drinking, intercourse, birth and death." It tends also to be repetitive, pedantic, and precise, and, "when some detail is omitted, worry and a sense of impending danger follow."[57] Of all the sources of the Christian faith, and of all the books used in shaping Henry's mind, Leviticus is without question the most ritualistic. It is, in effect, a catalogue of taboos and prohibitions, a listing of the ferocious retributions in store for those who dare to disobey. It offers the basic explanation of Christian causation in history—for it is written: "I am the Lord Your God" and, "If Ye will not harken unto me and will not do all these commandments," then will I do this unto you: "I will even appoint over you terror, consumption, and the burning ague, . . . and ye shall sow your seed in vain. . . . And I will set my face against you, and ye shall be slain before your enemies. . . . And I will break the pride of your power; and I will make your

---

[53] British Museum, Hargrave MSS 311, fol. 124.

[54] Byrne, *Letters of Henry VIII*, pp. 122, 353-391, 426-427.

[55] Erwin Doernberg, *Henry VIII and Luther* (London, 1961), p. 118.

[56] *Letters and Papers*, IV, no. 4858.

[57] Mortimer Ostow and Ben-Ami Scharfstein, *The Need to Believe; the Psychology of Religion* (New York, 1954), p. 85.

heaven as iron, and your earth as brass. And your strength shall be spent in vain; for your land shall not yield her increase, neither shall the trees of the land yield their fruits. And if ye walk contrary unto me, and will not hearken unto me; I will bring seven times more plagues upon you according to your sins." Henry knew his God as a "consuming fire, ever a jealous God"; therefore, it was absolutely essential not to commit any of those things "which are forbidden to be done by the commandments of the Lord," for, even though "he wist it not," yet was "he guilty, and shall bear his iniquity."[58]

Firm in his knowledge of the nature of the deity and walking in the shadow of the fear of his Lord, Henry became something of a spiritual hypochondriac. No one was more careful of his soul's welfare than the King, no one more scrupulous in his exact conformity to the prescribed religious formula of the day. He was constantly testifying to "his zeal for the faith" with all the "resources of his mind and body,"[59] for his relationship with his God was sanguine, if elementary: in return for the punctilious fulfillment of his religious obligations, God would reward him with material success and eternal salvation. Very early in life, Henry confessed to the Venetian ambassador the core of his faith, and the crux of the argument of this paper: "Nor do I see that there is any faith in the world, save in me, and therefore God Almighty, who knows this, prospers my affairs."[60] Should God remove his blessings and plague him with misfortune, then it was manifest that somehow, somewhere, he had involuntarily sinned by failing to propitiate the divine wrath. When Catherine of Aragon failed to secure the succession by providing a male heir, Henry searched his conscience for the source of such obvious divine malediction and discovered the cause in Leviticus: "And if a man shall take his brother's wife, it is an unclean thing: he hath uncovered his brother's nakedness; they shall be childless."[61] Though the sin was unconscious, ignorance of God's law was no excuse, for it was clearly stated that he must "make an atonement for him concerning his ignorance wherein he erred . . . and it shall be forgiven him."[62]

It was perfectly obvious to the King that here was the root of the difficulty, and not even the protestations of a wife whom he had once loved and still respected could outweigh the evidence of sin. Catherine's passionate oath that she had come to his bed "a true maid without touch of man" had to be balanced against the fact that God had

---

[58] Lev. 5:17 and 26:14-21.     [59] *Letters and Papers*, III, no. 1297.
[60] *Ibid*., II, no. 3163.     [61] Lev. 20:21.     [62] Lev. 5:18.

not only destroyed all but one girl child of that union but had also punished Henry seven times over. It was plainly written in Deuteronomy for all to read: "I set before you this day a blessing and a curse; a blessing, if ye obey the commandments of the Lord your God . . . and a curse, if ye will not obey. . . ."[63] Everywhere Henry looked there was fearful evidence that the Lord had turned his face against him. It is here, possibly, that we have a clue to the dating of Henry's conscience.

The question of timing has always plagued Tudor historians. The first documented evidence of a divorce justified on the grounds of conscience does not appear until May of 1527, but the issue of a divorce goes back almost a decade. The Queen's last pregnancy was in 1518; the following year Henry proved where the fault of sterility lay by siring a son by his mistress, Elizabeth Blount; and by 1524/25 he had ceased to cohabit with a wife who had reached her fortieth year and was "long past the usual age of childbearing."[64] It is clear that the small voice of conscience did not spring fully armed with the verses of Leviticus from Henry's theological brow. The thought may have been lingering unformed and unexpressed for years before 1527, or it may in fact have been planted by Cardinal Wolsey in the King's unsuspecting and naive mind sometime during the winter of 1526/27.[65] Whatever the inspiration, the fact remains that the year 1524/25 held the most overwhelming evidence of God's displeasure, a series of terrible blows guaranteed to make any monarch wonder why he was being singled out and cursed with ill fortune and bad luck.

In March of 1524 Henry received a bad scare and a dreadful warning. He was jousting with the Duke of Suffolk and entered the lists with the visor of his helmet open. Though the horrified audience shouted to the Duke to hold, Suffolk could neither hear nor see, and his lance struck and shattered against the King's helmet, a fraction of an inch from his exposed face.[66] A year later, while out hawking, Henry had an even narrower escape. In running after his quarry he jumped a ditch, tripped, broke his jumping pole, and fell headfirst into the water, his face stuck firmly in the mud. Panting attendants arrived just in time to save their sovereign from a singularly undignified death by drowning.[67] On top of accidents came diplomatic insult: the Emperor Charles in June of 1525 had the appalling effrontery

---

[63] Deut. 11:26-27.  
[64] Mattingly, *Catherine of Aragon*, p. 235.  
[65] *Ibid.*, p. 242.  
[66] Hall, *Union of Lancastre and Yorke*, fol. cxxiii.  
[67] *Ibid.*, fol. cxl.

to ask to be released from his contract to marry the Princess Mary. A month later the worst plague in a decade descended straight from heaven to chastise the kingdom. Fifty people a day died in London, and not even the King himself was safe; for, no matter how far or fast he fled, death followed, and in January of 1526 two gentlemen of his household died.[68] For the next two years the plague was chronic, and the King was again in fear of the terrible disease. "Fear of death," Professor Pollard has argued, "is fatal to the peace of a guilty conscience, and it might well have made Henry pause in his pursuit after the divorce and Anne Boleyn."[69] The logic, however, is specious; Henry refused to waver, not in defiance of the plague, but because of it. Here was simply further confirmation of God's promise, "I will send the pestilence among you," and further evidence of the pressing need to make atonement by a "sin offering" in the form of a formal dissolution of his marriage.

One further point should be noted in the development of Henry's conscience—his age. It may be significant that the King in 1525 was moving into a period of life when he could no longer take for granted his iron constitution. He was thirty-five in a century which reckoned forty-five as old and fifty-five as hoary. Again, there is no sure evidence, simply suggestive hints. In 1521 he was struck down by a severe fever and complained of sinus pains, and in 1528 his chronic headaches were first recorded.[70] All that can be said with certainty is that, medically speaking, thirty-five was a critical age and that Henry's society was absolutely sure that sickness was a visitation sent by God either as a chastisement or as a warning.

For a pampered monarch resentful of misfortune, regarding it as a personal affliction ordained in heaven, and desperately anxious to deflect God's wrath by his expertise in ritual worship, sickness, plague, accident, and diplomatic defeat were all clearly the wages of sin. It is little wonder, then, that Henry's conscience was so pricked or that he refused to consider shoddy half-measures or immoral substitutes. Atonement had to be made both for the sake of his own soul and for the welfare of his kingdom, for which God and man held him strictly accountable.

The intensity and operation of Henry's conscience can be explained

[68] *Calendar of State Papers, Venetian*, III, nos. 1073, 1187, 1193, 1275, 1294.
[69] Pollard, *Henry VIII*, p. 209.
[70] Frederick Chamberlin, *The Private Character of Henry the Eighth* (New York, 1931), pp. 141-151.

in terms of cultural conditioning and religious psychology, but a final factor remains to be considered: the impulsive and heavy-handed logic which stood behind and sustained the small voice of conscience. We are dealing with a mentality which handled all problems with a degree of immediacy and immoderation which was terrifying, if at times comical. The King's approach to life was refreshingly naive and dangerously impulsive. He rarely appreciated the implications of his actions, thinking only in terms of the immediate effect, and he almost invariably used a battleship to do a rowboat's job.

In one of the earliest clashes between church and state, the Hunne case of 1514, the King proclaimed the doctrine of the Royal Supremacy in its most extravagant form, but it took him twenty-five years to perceive the full implication of his words: "By the ordinance and sufferance of God we are Kings of England, and the Kings of England in time past have never had superior but God only."[71] In 1521 Sir Thomas More had to warn him against overstating the theory of papal authority on the grounds that popes were political figures with whom the King might some day find himself in conflict. "I think it is best therefore that the part be amended, and his authority more lightly touched." Henry, however, would have no such politic half-measure. "Nay, quoth his Grace, that it shall not. We are so much bounden to the See of Rome that we cannot do too much honor to it."[72]

The same tank-like logic, pulverizing tactics, and blindness to consequences were revealed some eighteen years later when those putrefied old oaks, the monasteries, were pulled down. The approach was typically Henrician—simple and without subtlety. The foundations were corrupt and rotten; therefore, they should all, without exception, be destroyed. Once they were nationalized, that was the end of the problem as far as the King was concerned. Henry resolutely closed his mind to Hugh Latimer's argument that "the founding of monasteries argued Purgatory to be: so the pulling of them down argueth it not to be." The King adamantly refused to see the theological implications of his actions, and, when the Bishop wrote that "now it seemeth not convenient" for "the Act of Parliament to preach one thing, and the pulpit another clean contrary," Henry refused to accept any such sophistry and coldly noted down in the margin, "why then do you?"[73]

[71] Arthur Ogle, *The Tragedy of the Lollards' Tower* (Oxford, 1949), p. 153.

[72] William Roper, *Life of More* in *The Utopia of Sir Thomas More including Roper's Life of More* (New York, 1947), p. 255.

[73] John Strype, *Ecclesiastical Memorials Relating Chiefly to Religion*, 3 vols. in 6 parts (Oxford, 1822), I, Pt. II, Appendix XCVIII, 391.

In Henry's mind, if a position was good, it was wholly good—not only right for the moment but for all time—and half-measures were no substitute. On the same logic, if God had saddled you with a middle-aged and barren spouse, then you must ask yourself, what have I done to deserve such a Fate? When you have found the correct solution, no other will do, for that which achieves the immediate purpose of God's blessings and deflects His curses must, by definition, be good. When the Imperial ambassador noted that, "when this King decides on anything he goes the whole length,"[74] he was merely recording a facet of Henry's personality which the King would have been proud to acknowledge. There is no question where he stood: "We have done what became us for the discharge of our conscience and found the truth so manifest that it ought to be allowed on all hands."[75]

It is doubtless true that the conscience of a great leader must almost of necessity be good, for conscience tends to coalesce with will. Certainly Henry never lost his way in the darkness of eternity; he was always free from the melancholy and mental pain that hold life to be an agony until the grave. The circle of his understanding was doubtless small, but he was ready to rest his case on the simple alliance between God and man. As he put it, "God and his conscience were perfectly agreed on that point."[76]

Given the nature of Henry's faith and the operation of his mind, I think we must accept the fact that not only was his conscience real and excessively tender but also that it was a vital factor which prevented him from accepting papal dispensations or stooping to political murder and which led him to risk schism and hell to achieve his purpose—the blessings of God, as measured in terms of material wellbeing, good health, a pleasing wife, a secure dynasty, and diplomatic success.

[74] *Letters and Papers*, XVII, no. 441, 252.
[75] *Ibid.*, VI, no. 775.
[76] *Calendar of State Papers, Spanish*, IV (2), no. 1061, 636.

# JAMES V AND THE SCOTTISH CHURCH,
## 1528-1542

### J. WILSON FERGUSON

JAMES V has long had an ambiguous reputation among historians of the Scottish Reformation. Catholic commentators of the 1560's saw him as a man who had supported the old faith against foreign and domestic enemies; but they also considered that royal control and exploitation left the Church vulnerable to Protestant attacks, and they believed James's demands for clerical reform were hypocritical in the light of his own utilization of corrupt practices.[1] Most early Protestants thought of the King as a persecutor of the saints and a supporter of superstition; yet some of them implied that he had helped the spread of reforming opinions by permitting and encouraging attacks on clerical abuses.[2]

This ambiguity persists in the recent scholarship stimulated by the four hundredth anniversary of the triumph of Scottish Protestantism.[3] One present-day Catholic views James as "a cynical opportunist. For material reasons, he represented himself to the papacy as a staunch upholder of orthodoxy, while obtaining financial favours by a form of blackmail. By his support of anti-clericalism, he attempted to force the clergy into meeting his demands for taxation. . . . Such were his nominations and the effects of his clerical taxation that the traditional description of his policy as pro-clerical is very much a travesty."[4] Another

---

[1] John Leslie, Bishop of Ross, *The History of Scotland from the Death of King James I to the Year 1561*, ed. Thomas Thomson (Edinburgh, 1830), pp. 90-91, 215-216, 226-227, 231-232, 244, 260-262; Quintin Kennedy quoted in Matthew Mahoney, "The Scottish Hierarchy, 1513-1565," *Essays on the Scottish Reformation*, ed. David McRoberts (Glasgow, 1962), pp. 50-51 (hereafter cited as *Essays*).

[2] John Knox, *John Knox's History of the Reformation in Scotland*, ed. William Croft Dickinson (New York, 1950), pp. 21, 26, 28, 30; George Buchanan, *Rerum Scoticorum Historia: The History of Scotland*, tr. and ed. James Aikman (Glasgow, 1829-1830), II, 314; David Calderwood, *The History of the Kirk of Scotland*, ed. Thomas Thomson (Edinburgh, 1842), I, 109, 111, 140-141, 146-148; John Spottiswoode, *History of the Church of Scotland*, ed. Mark Napier (Edinburgh, 1851), I, 140.

[3] For a critical review of many of the more important recent interpretations, see Maurice Lee, "The Scottish Reformation After 400 Years," *Scottish Historical Review*, XLIV (Oct. 1965).

[4] Mahoney, *Essays*, pp. 39, 70.

Catholic writer believes that "it was in this reign that a healthy reform was still possible, no doubt difficult, but there was still time. Church reform was possible only through active cooperation between a determined king and a zealous and competent churchman, both working with papal approval. . . . He found the papacy useful and had no wish to break with it; [but] he was unfitted to collaborate with it in a serious work of practical re-organization and reform which were sorely needed in Scotland."[5] But these historians also recognized that James was personally orthodox and supported the established Church in many ways.[6] Recent Protestant interpreters present James V as "outwardly orthodox"[7] but consider his attachment to the old religion "sordid,"[8] practical rather than ideological, and exploitative. They, too, view his actions as a chief contributing factor to the fatal weakness of Catholicism in the 1550's and 1560's.[9] It may be possible to set James and his policies in a somewhat clearer light by carefully examining his relationships with the Church during the period of his personal rule.

When James made himself King of Scots, in fact as well as in title, through his escape from the custody of the Douglas faction in the spring of 1528, shortly after his sixteenth birthday, his attention was necessarily concentrated on the repression of those elements in Scotland which most seriously threatened his personal power by rebellion and disorder. The long years of his minority, however, had witnessed a general dislocation in many areas of Scottish life and government, and the King began his reign by addressing himself to the solution of pressing problems in financial, administrative, judicial, diplomatic, and religious affairs as soon as the country was sufficiently pacified. That these concerns actively conditioned James's attitude to the Scottish Church and clergy, his relations with the Papacy, and his personal

[5] William James Anderson, "Rome and Scotland, 1513-1564," *Essays*, pp. 469-470. Analogous views are found in *Essays*, pp. 67, 84, 334, 381-382.

[6] J. H. Burns, "The Political Background of the Reformation," *Essays*, p. 6.

[7] John D. Mackie, *A History of Scotland* (Baltimore, 1964), p. 138.

[8] A. M. Renwick, *The Story of the Scottish Reformation* (Grand Rapids, Mich., 1960), p. 33.

[9] Gordon Donaldson, *Scotland: Church and Nation through Sixteen Centuries* (London, 1960), p. 42; John D. Mackie, *A History of the Scottish Reformation* (Edinburgh, 1960), pp. 72, 93, 95-97; William Croft Dickinson, *Scotland from the Earliest Times to 1603* (London, 1961), pp. 299, 308; Gordon Donaldson, *Scotland: James V to James VII* (New York, 1966), p. 54.

religious opinions can be seen in the instructions sent in the spring of 1530 to the Scottish ambassador at Rome.[10]

In these letters the King advocated the promotion of worthy clerics, the reformation of clerical abuses, the preservation of ecclesiastical revenues, and the stubborn maintenance of royal rights in regard to Scottish benefices. James always insisted on this last point, which amounted to royal control of all nominations, and, as his principal secretary remarked, he would "never be turned in the other direction."[11] Several secular concerns, such as the internal security of the realm, were also dealt with in these instructions. But the most significant element was James's determination to make use of the Church, to draw on its resources for his own needs.

One of the most acute needs of the country was financial, and it is in this area that James's dealings with the clergy of his kingdom have been most investigated and criticized.[12] Scotland had always been a poor country, and royal income had seldom been considered adequate by her stronger and more ambitious rulers. This natural poverty, combined with a steady European rise in prices, a constant devaluation of the Scottish pound relative to the currency of other nations, and James's own extravagant tastes, presented his financial officers with acute problems. There were simply not enough feudal dues, mercantile duties, and royal estates—the established sources of regular income. New revenues had to be found. Although several secular expedients were tried, they proved to be either temporary or too slowly realized. The Church, the greatest single repository of wealth in the country, was the source best fitted to supply both immediate and continuing benefits.

The most obvious way of sharing in this wealth would have been to confiscate some of it, but this method had little appeal for James V. He appears to have had a real reverence for Catholic traditions and no wish to destroy the extant ecclesiastical structure. It is also likely that he thought any secularization of church property would be of

---

[10] Scotland, General Register House, *The Letters of James V*, collected and calendared by Robert Kerr Hannay, ed. Denys Hay (Edinburgh, 1954), pp. 174-176 (hereafter cited as *L of J V*).

[11] *Ibid.*, p. 198.

[12] The standard account of this subject is W. Stanford Reid, "Clerical Taxation: The Scottish Alternative to Dissolution of the Monasteries, 1530-1560," *Catholic Historical Review*, XXXIV (1948), 129-153.

greater advantage to the Scottish nobility than to himself.[13] The most persuasive argument, however, may have been that he saw no reason to seize the property of the Church when he could get what he wanted from the clerics by less radical means.[14]

One way in which James sought to tap the wealth of the Church was by establishing royal control over its personnel and over vacant positions. James's frequent representations to Rome in these matters were based on the preservation and extension of traditional Scottish "rights." He was particularly insistent that Scottish benefices go only to Scots whose capabilities he himself had deemed satisfactory.[15] In 1534 the Pope granted officially what had already become standard practice: the King got the right of nomination, within a year of vacancy, to all benefices worth two hundred florins or more. It was also agreed that he might draw the fruits of such benefices for his own use during the period of vacancy.[16]

The direct revenue derived from this concession, because of the uncertainty involved, could not meet royal requirements, but the rights of nomination did provide the King with the indirect assistance of the Church in rewarding his councillors and supporters. Many nominees were adjudged suitable for being the "admirable son of an admirable father," a "familiar" of the King, or the scion of a family which had done good service.[17] James also used benefices to maintain the members of his household staff[18] and some of the great officers of the crown. Robert Cairncross was Treasurer before becoming Abbot of Holyroodhouse, and during four years of royal service William Stewart progressed in rank from canon of Glasgow to Bishop of Aberdeen.[19] This assistance too, however, met only a small part of James's needs.

[13] *Rentale Sancti Andree . . . , 1538-1546*, ed. Robert Kerr Hannay (Edinburgh, 1913), p. xxiii (hereafter cited as *RSA*).

[14] Great Britain, Public Record Office, *Calendar of Letters and Papers, Foreign and Domestic, of the Reign of Henry VIII* (London, 1862-1923), XV, no. 248 (hereafter cited as *L&P*).

[15] *L of J V*, pp. 166-168, 175, 206-207, 209 (among others).

[16] Scotland, General Register House, *Acts of the Lords of Council in Public Affairs*, ed. Robert Kerr Hannay (Edinburgh, 1932), pp. l-lii (hereafter cited as *ALC*).

[17] *L of J V*, pp. 157, 160, 184, 231.

[18] *Ibid.*, p. 155.

[19] Buchanan, *History of Scotland*, II, 300; *L of J V*, pp. 153-159, 185-186, 192-193, 217, 225; John Dowden, *The Bishops of Scotland . . . prior to the Reformation*, ed. J. Maitland Thomson (Glasgow, 1912), pp. 139-140, 225.

The most desirable and satisfactory means of drawing on the wealth of Scottish clerics, at least in royal eyes, was the imposition of a direct tax—a solution which, however, had the disadvantage of being contrary to custom and canon law. Yet, by 1530, James's financial problems were so pressing that he felt he had to try this expedient.[20] The first implementation of this decision occurred the following year, the ostensible basis for the request being an expedition which the King proposed to make to the Western Highlands and Islands in order to restore order. In January 1531 the clergy voted James a "gratitude" of £5,000 "to be raised on all churchmen being beneficed of £100 or above, equally after the rate of their benefices."[21] But only £3,457 was actually raised. James was still trying to collect long afterward, and he was determined to obtain a more stable and regular form of ecclesiastical income.[22]

A Scottish envoy in Rome was instructed to approach Clement VII with the request that the Scottish clergy be required to pay a *permanent* tax of £10,000 per year. The Pope was no little taken aback by this appeal, but he wrote to the Scottish clerics to obtain their opinion and took some steps to relieve James's financial straits on a *temporary* basis. A bull was issued approving civil taxation of the Scottish Church on certain occasions, such as the danger of imminent invasion. As Scotland was now stated to be in such danger, the clergy were ordered to pay three-tenths of all ecclesiastical fruits for three years, two shillings on the pound of the assessed value of their lands.[23]

Shortly afterward, a new proposal was presented at Rome. James declared that the machinery for civil justice had broken down so far as to be practically useless—as, indeed, it had—and that the only real solution would be the establishment of a new permanent civil court. Since such a court would be of immense value to the clergy of Scotland in insuring the enforcement of ecclesiastical discipline and the speedy processing of all disputes involving land and other matters, it was

[20] Reid, "Clerical Taxation," p. 135; for a review of earlier Scottish attempts to tap the wealth of the Church, see the earlier part of Reid's article.

[21] Quoted in *ibid.*, p. 137.

[22] Scotland, Court of Exchequer, *Compota Thesaurariorum Regum Scotorum: The Accounts of the Lord High Treasurer of Scotland* (Edinburgh, 1877-1916), V, 450-458; VI, 64 (hereafter cited as *TA*).

[23] *L of J V*, pp. 173, 174-176; Robert Kerr Hannay, "A Study in Reformation History," *Scottish Historical Review*, XXIII (1925), 20-22; Robert Kerr Hannay, "On the Foundation of the College of Justice," *Scottish Historical Review*, XV (1917), 36.

urged that they should pay for it. The royal finances, it was explained, could not bear the expense. A *regular, annual* contribution of £10,000 was suggested, a figure which just happened to be identical with that refused as a tax. Clement agreed with the reasonableness of this request, and on 13 September 1531 a bull was published granting such a contribution.[24]

The reaction of the Scottish churchmen to this bull can well be imagined, for the imposition of such a subsidy on top of the three-tenths already levied meant that they would owe the King almost eight shillings on the pound of assessed value. They could not actually re-fuse to obey a papal bull, but a strong opposition formed, and negotia-tions were opened with the King. James accepted the bull as the signal to establish the court, known officially as the College of Justice, and he proceeded to regard and call the old Court of Session, which was in fact one element in the Lords of Council, the College (about May 1532). Two advantages resulted from this move: James could now pay some of his councillors, and the dissident clerics were faced with an accomplished fact.[25]

A settlement was reached during the course of 1532. The clergy agreed to turn over to the College of Justice enough vacant benefices to bring in an annual sum of about £1,400, which was reckoned its true cost, and James was to receive a donation of £72,000 during the next four years, which he could use as he wished.[26] He renounced in return all claim to a permanent, yearly £10,000. A papal bull was issued in confirmation of this compromise.[27] In addition to his financial con-cession, the King undertook to protect the security of the Church in Scotland, and the Estates of the Realm duly enacted a law forbidding the future passage of any anti-papal legislation.[28] At the same time,

[24] Reid, "Clerical Taxation," p. 139; Great Britain, Public Record Office, *Calendar of Milanese Papers* (London, 1912), no. 853.

[25] Reid, p. 140.

[26] That he could so use it is clearly recognized in a royal letter of 16 June 1532 (*ALC*, p. 379).

[27] Reid, pp. 140-141; Hannay, "Foundation," pp. 39, 41; Hannay, "Study," pp. 23-35; *L&P*, V, no. 1286; Robert Keith, *History of the Affairs of Church and State in Scotland* (Edinburgh, 1845), I, Appendix; *A Diurnal of Remarkable Occurrents that have Passed Within the Country of Scotland from the Death of King James the Fourth till the Year 1575*, ed. Thomas Thomson (Edinburgh, 1833), p. 15 (hereafter cited as *Diurnal*).

[28] *ALC*, p. 379; Great Britain, Record Commission, *The Acts of the Parlia-ments of Scotland* (Edinburgh, 1814-1844), II, 335 (hereafter cited as *APS*).

action was taken to enforce ecclesiastical censures. There is some evidence, too, that interest in the prevention or suppression of heresy was increasing. So happy was James with this apparent release from financial anemia that a newly arrived papal legate was reportedly denied nothing.[29]

James V now appears to have believed that his financial and judicial problems had been solved in a satisfactory way. But the realization of the fruits of clerical taxation was more difficult than the King expected; therefore, further recourse was had to special assessments. One of these, intended to pay for a small body of mercenary troops to resist English raids, was levied on both prelates and burghs in 1532-1533.[30] Another suitable occasion was not found until 1535, when the Estates voted £6,000, payable by both laymen and clerics, for the financing of royal marriage negotiations.[31] This enactment apparently had little result, for the royal treasurer's accounts for 1535 included receipts from only a few bishops and abbots, totaling about £454. By 1537 only £170 more had been collected, all from clerics.[32] Such a minimal response may explain why there was no additional attempt at taxation of this sort.

The most important difficulty blocking full implementation of the compromise worked out with church leaders in 1532 was that it still had to be ratified by the Scottish clergy as a whole. Although the King treated the grants made as due, payment could reasonably be delayed. In the period of the middle thirties, therefore, any successful ingathering of church revenue depended on the good will of the clerics themselves. Such good will apparently was present in 1532-1533, the result of clerical antagonism to English pressures on Scotland, the efforts of the papal nuncio, and James's defense of the established church against domestic critics; for approximately £16,440 was collected from the three-tenths granted in face of the threat of English invasion and from the Great Tax, as the 1532 compromise was known.[33] Collections soon fell off, however, reaching about £7,605 in 1543.[34] The drop seems to have been due partly to the payment of the three-tenths in full by some, partly to a growing antagonism between the King and the Archbishop of St. Andrews, and partly to clerical resentment at

[29] *L&P*, V, no. 1110.

[30] *ALC*, pp. 391-392, 394, 399, 406.

[31] *APS*, II, 342-343; Scotland, Exchequer, *Rotuli Scaccarii Regum Scotorum: The Exchequer Rolls of Scotland* (Edinburgh, 1878-1908), XVI, xlii.

[32] *TA*, VI, 245, 296.      [33] *Ibid.*, pp. 143-150.      [34] *Ibid.*, pp. 227-231.

having to bear the major cost of the secular administration. Many of those assessed may have been unable to pay as a result of past taxation and the destruction of church lands and buildings during English raids on the southeast. In any case, the whole machinery of government was near collapse from lack of funds by the end of 1535.[35] Both James and his clergy, however, mistrusted the religious and diplomatic policies of Henry VIII, and the King of Scots reasserted his claims on the spiritual estate.[36]

A convention of the Provincial Council of the Scottish Church had been ordered at the session of Parliament in 1535,[37] and it met in March 1536. After some pointed royal remarks about needed reforms, the Council ratified the compromise of 1532.[38] The collection of funds from churchmen thereafter became increasingly effective. By 1537 the various ecclesiastical assessments seem to have been combined, and about £10,000 was received during 1536-1537.[39] Legal actions against delinquents, including some of the leading prelates, were also fairly successful.[40]

During the same period James continued to profit from the Church indirectly. In March 1535 he received a papal bull designed to enable him "to bear the more easily the burdens incurred for the good government of his subjects" by extending his right of appropriating the temporalities of vacant benefices to include all prelacies.[41] More substantial and regular was the income from the acquisition *in commendam* of the principal (that is, the richest) abbeys in Scotland for royal bastards, a procedure novel for James but practiced by his father and grandfather.[42] The youth of these appointees meant that the fruits of their abbeys came directly into the royal treasury. According to Bishop Leslie, these revenues were of greater profit to the King "than the whole revenue of the crown."[43] Not only did this tactic swell his

---

[35] An account of this situation is in Reid, "Clerical Taxation," pp. 141-143.

[36] See, e.g., Scotland, General Register House, *Registrum Secreti Sigilli Regum Scotorum: The Register of the Privy Seal of Scotland* (Edinburgh, 1908-    ), II, no. 1923 (hereafter cited as *RPS*).

[37] *APS*, II, 342.

[38] *ALC*, p. 503; Reid, pp. 142-143.

[39] *TA*, VI, 296, 359-362.

[40] *ALC*, pp. 488, 491, 498, 503.

[41] *Ibid.*, p. 466; *L of J V*, p. 285.

[42] Details of the commendations of these infants may be found in *L of J V*, pp. 235, 279, 287, 342-343, 345, 348, 356-358, 399-400, 423, 425-427, 433; *ALC*, pp. 441, 466; and Dowden, *Bishops of Scotland*, pp. 172, 225, 373.

[43] Leslie, *History of Scotland*, pp. 154-155.

purse, but it also enabled James to provide handsomely for the futures of his illegitimate children.

Between 1538 and 1540 direct income from the Church was assigned to the Master of Works to pay for the King's architectural plans. Although the collection of arrears proved quite difficult, many legal actions being necessary to overcome clerical resistance, it may truthfully be said that the churchmen underwrote the notable improvements made to the palaces at Linlithgow, Falkland, Holyrood, and Stirling.[44]

Further financial demands were made on the Scottish Church in 1540. The details of this request are not clear (one source states that the money was sought for the crown prince),[45] but there is evidence that the effective motive for compliance was an implied royal threat to move closer to England in diplomacy and religion.[46] The Scottish prelates did promise a contribution of £5,000, to be paid by 1 August 1541, but they required that their action be confirmed by the Pope.[47] This condition enabled them to delay payment, and, apparently, they hoped it might enable them to avoid contributing altogether.[48] The records of the diocese of St. Andrews indicate that there was, indeed, reluctance in yielding up this "free offering"; Cardinal Beaton himself, by now the chief royal minister and advisor, was delinquent in his payment until early 1542.[49] Others might have been expected to delay longer, but such procrastination could not be permanent; for James knew from experience the extent of his power over the Scottish Church, and the churchmen were actually forced by events "to stake their fortunes in an effort to direct the policy of the crown."[50]

During the latter part of James's reign revenues from ecclesiastical sources played a much smaller role than previously in the total finan-

[44] Reid, "Clerical Taxation," p. 144; *ALC*, pp. 490, 491-492, 493, 502, 504, 509, 515; Scotland, Public Record Office, *Accounts of the Masters of Works for Building and Repairing Royal Palaces and Castles*, ed. Henry M. Paton (Edinburgh, 1957), pp. xiv-xv.

[45] *L&P*, XVI, no. 990.5.

[46] Buchanan, *History of Scotland*, II, 318; *L of J V*, pp. 724-725; Sir John Herkless and Robert Kerr Hannay, *The Archbishops of St. Andrews* (London, 1907-1909), IV, 63 (hereafter cited as *Archbishops*).

[47] *L&P*, XVI, no. 990.5; *St. Andrews Formulare, 1514-1546*, ed. Gordon Donaldson (Edinburgh, 1941, 1944), no. 410 (hereafter cited as *Formulare*).

[48] *L of J V*, pp. 724-725; *L&P*, XVI, nos. 990.5, 1178, 1288.

[49] *Formulare*, no. 410; *RSA*, p. 126.

[50] *RSA*, p. xvii.

cial manipulations of the King and his chief fiscal officers. This change seems to have been partly the result of a large increase in revenues from other areas; perhaps it was also a consequence of the realization that even the resources of the Church were limited and that church-men had many other heavy expenses. James always wished only to profit from the Church, not to destroy it.

In the area of finance, then, James V diverted some of the wealth of the Scottish Church to the support of both his administrative neces-sities and his pleasures, a maneuver made possible mainly by the pre-carious international position of Catholicism and his own much ad-vertised orthodoxy.

He also employed the Church and churchmen to help solve other difficulties. One such problem, noted above, was the central dispensa-tion of civil justice. It is undoubtedly true, as the leading historian of the new court has remarked, that the "endowment of the Session and the erection of the College of Justice . . . were the incidental results of an astute diplomacy which . . . succeeded in exploiting the Church for the benefit of [James's] treasury, and found in the need of an as-siduous civil court, in which the Churchmen were largely interested, a useful pretext for ecclesiastical contribution."[51] Nevertheless, the in-stitution of judicial reform was no sudden innovation. That the exac-tion of clerical funds took this form was not accidental: it reflected the King's abiding passion for law and order, in the establishment of which he often took a personal part.[52]

When James actually inaugurated the College of Justice, it was de-termined that seven of the fifteen members, including the president, should be clerics.[53] Further efficient development of this court was undermined, however, by the non-payment of the assessments which were to support it and by the employment of the judges in other business.[54]

The Scottish clerics thus played vital, if somewhat unwilling, roles in James V's solutions to financial and judicial problems. They were no less prominent in the solution of another difficulty which faced

---

[51] *ALC*, pp. xxxvi-xxxvii.

[52] See, e.g., *L&P*, IV, no. 5706; *ALC*, pp. 306, 309-311, 440, 445; Buchanan, *History of Scotland*, II, 309; *Exerpta e Libris Domicilii Domini Jacobi Quinti Regis Scotorum, 1525-1533* (Edinburgh, 1836), Appendix, pp. 26, 32 (hereafter cited as *Libris*).

[53] *APS*, II, 335-336; *ALC*, p. xxxviii.

[54] See *ALC*, pp. xxxix ff.

the young King—the establishment of an adequate, efficient, and loyal administration.

After having made various shifts and temporary expedients during the first establishment of his personal power, most of which worked well only when he was exercising personal supervision, James came to rely on minor members of the landowning class (called "lairds" in Scotland) for local administration.[55] In the central government the King first relied on personal friends and servants from the days of his minority.[56] As the situation became more settled, however, a new pattern began to emerge. Men were sought who had the ability and training to serve well, who would be able to devote most of their time, who would be unable to use their position to create personal power rivaling that of their sovereign, and who could afford royal appointments.

Several classes failed to produce appropriate individuals in significant numbers. Neither the greater nor the lesser nobility had the talent, training, or time for extensive service,[57] and James's experiences made him wary of giving any of the nobles great power. The common people, though of great and continuing concern to the King, lacked the necessary education; nor did James have either the money or the time to train potential talent. The merchants were often able men, but they were seldom interested in becoming royal officials.[58]

Some recruiting for the royal administration did take place among the lairds and the tangential members of aristocratic families (bastards, younger sons, members of cadet branches), many of whom possessed the necessary qualifications. But the chief source of the kind of person the King required was the Church, the only Scottish institution in which talent could be fostered, trained, and adequately rewarded regardless of its origins.[59] Only a cleric could completely meet James's standards. For these men were trained and experienced in such various fields as law, finance, and diplomacy; they were often

---

[55] Buchanan, *History of Scotland*, II, 306; *ALC*, pp. 281, 382, 383.

[56] *ALC*, pp. 277, 281, 290, 294; *L&P*, V, nos. 4457, 4531; David Edward Easson, *Gavin Dunbar—Chancellor of Scotland, Archbishop of Glasgow* (Edinburgh, 1947), pp. 37, 98.

[57] *L&P*, XV, no. 248.

[58] Perhaps because of the unfortunate experiences of Robert Barton; see W. Stanford Reid, *Skipper From Leith: Robert Barton of Overbarnton* (Philadelphia, 1962), pp. 224-242.

[59] Easson, p. 38; W. S. Forbes-Leith, *Pre-Reformation Scholars in Scotland* (Glasgow, 1915) gives a rather thorough exposition of the talents of the Scottish clergy.

supported by ecclesiastical stipends and were thus independent of the scanty royal income; and their ambitions for preferment and promotion were largely non-secular. This last point was especially attractive to the King, for it was very difficult for a cleric to establish great hereditary power of a sort which might threaten the royal position. In view of their peculiar fitness, it is not surprising that James wrote to Clement VII in 1530 that "at present" he found it "advisable frequently to select his chancellor, treasurer, and other councillors from the ecclesiastical estate."[60]

Parallel to this use of churchmen as administrators was James's policy of turning administrators into clerics by persistently using his influence to secure benefices as rewards for his lay officials.[61]

The general composition of the royal administration continued to follow the pattern established by 1530. Important national offices were held by churchmen, lairds, and very minor nobles. When a change of officials was made, the choice seems to have continued to fall on those qualified and available.[62] During the years 1533-1538, however, continuity of tenure in positions was more remarkable than any changes, and the King's belief that he had found an efficient and loyal body of servants was attested by his willingness to leave the nation in their hands while he sought pleasure and a wife in France (1536-1537).

The chief administrative development in the last years of James's life was the emergence of David Beaton, who was successively and concurrently Abbot, Bishop, Archbishop, and Cardinal, as the principal royal advisor. Beaton came from a clerical family (his uncle was Archbishop of St. Andrews), but his most rapid advancement came after his demonstration of diplomatic skill in the negotiations for James's two French marriages. The King came to consider him "invaluable," claimed that "it would be difficult . . . to manage without him," and exerted great influence for his promotions.[63]

It is evident, then, that James V relied on the clergy of his realm in several important ways. They were a chief source of revenue; they staffed and underwrote both the chief civil court and the central administration to a large extent; and the most influential royal advisor had come from their ranks. This reliance was to some extent based on

[60] *L of J V*, p. 184. See also *ibid.*, p. 203; *ALC*, p. 321; Knox, *History of the Reformation*, II, Appendix 2.

[61] See above, p. 55, and *L of J V*, p. 374.

[62] The case of the post of treasurer is discussed in *TA*, VI, xi-xiii.

[63] *L of J V*, p. 296; *L&P*, XII(1), nos. 647, 923. The best account of Beaton's whole career may be found in *Archbishops*, IV.

necessity, but it may also have been part of a deliberate plan to create a counterweight to the traditional and decentralizing power of the Scottish nobility. Even if James did not pursue such a policy consciously, his actions had this effect.[64]

The cooperation which existed between the King of Scots and his churchmen was reinforced by the situation which he faced in foreign affairs, and the choices which he made in this field solidified it. Scotland had been a country of little interest and even less importance to most medieval Europeans, who regarded it as a savage, impoverished, and sparsely populated outpost on the fringes of civilization. Whenever England became a factor in continental affairs, however, Scotland acquired some strategic value as a possible base for attack on her southern neighbor and as a potential distraction or diversion of English strength and attention. Such considerations led to a sporadic and seldom effective alliance between Scotland and France. England, which had never entirely renounced the ambitions of Edward I to rule Scotland, was considered the "old enemy," mutual irritation being maintained by the incessant unruliness of those who lived on the Anglo-Scottish borders. These factors were intensified by the personal rivalries of Charles V, Francis I, and Henry VIII, but they developed their highest significance only after Henry's break with the Papacy.

James V's firm commitment to the old ways in religion combined with his country's geographical position to make his adherence a principal factor in the possible success of any of the many projects aimed at the overthrow of his uncle and the reunion of England with Christendom. Such plans had frequently been mentioned in marriage negotiations with Imperial interests, and Charles V's envoy in London had been assured by one of his Scottish counterparts that, in spite of the provisions of an Anglo-Scottish peace treaty of 1534, the Scots

---

[64] There is no record of James's own attitude, but the tendency of his policy was recognized by contemporaries and by modern commentators. See, e.g., Buchanan, *History of Scotland*, II, 318-320, 324; Leslie, *History of Scotland*, p. 167; and Mackie, *History of Scotland*, p. 136. It is worth noting, though, that the King was not prepared to replace overmighty barons with overmighty clerics, as the experiences of James Beaton, Archbishop of St. Andrews, revealed. See *Archbishops*, III, 191 ff.; *ALC*, pp. 370, 389, 400-401; *L of J V*, pp. 242-244, 251-252, 292-293; Great Britain, Public Record Office, *Calendar of State Papers, Spanish* (London, 1882-1916), V(1), no. 7; and Scotland, General Register House, *The Hamilton Papers: Letters and Papers Illustrating the Political Relations of England and Scotland in the 16th Century*, ed. Joseph Bain (Edinburgh, 1890-1892), I, no. 8.

would always be ready to join in any anti-English crusade sanctioned by the Holy See.[65]

It was only after James's first French marriage in 1537, however—a union which sealed his commitment to the French and Catholic interests and which had been negotiated by David Beaton[66]—that the Scots were subjected to considerable papal pressure on this point. While still in France with his bride, James was presented with the sword and cap which were blessed by the Pope each Christmas Eve and presented to a Christian prince. In his covering letter the Pope left no doubt about the purpose of the gift. Asking that James think of the mystic and spiritual significance of the objects, he nevertheless prayed that the King, "so often vainly solicited to defile his realm with heresies from across his borders, may have blessing from on high, God strengthening his right hand with the sword, and covering his head with the cap . . . that he may defend the church and the faith against those for whom justice and the judgement of God are made ready."[67]

James's response was dutiful and respectful, but he refused to commit himself to any action against England except in the most general terms.[68] James V, indeed, always resisted any suggestions of unilateral action against the heretics to the south. Still, no one doubted that, if the Pope were to succeed in persuading Charles V and Francis I to unite in action against Henry VIII, the Scots would join in the assault. Scottish participation was even considered essential for the success of such a venture.[69]

The King of England was as aware as his enemies were of the importance of the position of James, and between 1534 and 1538 he attempted to convert his nephew to the Henrician view. Some of the arguments advanced by several English ambassadors might have been expected to have had great appeal for James, containing as they did vindications of royal authority against foreign encroachments and suggestions for the curbing of overmighty subjects and for the filling of the treasury. But since these ends could only be achieved by an anti-papal revolution like that of England, James remained cool. He always replied that he valued his uncle's good will but could not

[65] *L&P*, VII, nos. 214, 662.

[66] The most thorough account of all aspects of James's marriages is in Edmond Bapst, *Les Mariages de Jacques V* (Paris, 1889).

[67] *L of J V*, p. 328; *L&P*, XII(1), nos. 414, 443.

[68] *L&P*, XII(1), nos. 463, 647, 923. See also *L&P*, XI, nos. 473, 1119, 1183, 1194, and *L of J V*, pp. 311-312, for similar responses in 1536.

[69] *L&P*, XII(2), no. 1162; XIV(1), nos. 27, 51; *L of J V*, pp. 361, 420.

in good conscience depart from the traditional responsibilities of a Christian king "towards God and Holy Church."[70]

Henry's irritation at these rebuffs was aggravated by James's evasive treatment of proposals for a royal meeting,[71] his French marriages,[72] his acceptance of the papal cap and sword,[73] and the shelter given in Scotland to religious refugees whom the English considered traitors.[74] By 1538 Anglo-Scottish relations were marked by acute mutual annoyance and distrust, emotions heightened by English apprehensions that the Scots might seize any favorable opportunity to undertake a pro-French and pro-papal invasion.[75]

In spite of constant disagreements, however, Henry VIII pursued a policy of conciliation toward the Scots. When some letters taken from a Scottish ship wrecked near Bamborough in 1540 suggested that James might be estranged from the Pope, Sir Ralph Sadler, an experienced diplomat, was sent north to exploit the supposed opportunity to bring Scotland into a friendlier stance.[76] But the results of this embassy, in English eyes, were no more favorable than before. James once again revealed himself to be firmly set in his solutions to domestic problems, and he made it perfectly clear that he was not going to imitate Henry's policy in either religion or statecraft. The King of England could not, therefore, accept without reservations the gracious words and fervent protestations of friendship which his nephew freely offered.[77]

James recognized the need for peace with England and was prepared to go far to avoid open conflict, but he was committed also to

[70] A typical embassy was that of William Barlow in 1535. See *L&P*, IX, nos. 730, 959; X, nos. 141, 190, 427; *Hamilton Papers*, I, nos. 22, 23.

[71] *L&P*, IX, nos. 256, 257; X, nos. 142, 482, 483, 601, 699, 728, 729, 740, 809, 810, 863, 928; XI, no. 656; *Calendar, Spanish*, V(2), no. 61; *Hamilton Papers*, I, nos. 26, 28-30; *L of J V*, pp. 316-317, 320-321.

[72] *L&P*, XII(1), nos. 445, 762; XIII(1), nos. 56, 273, 994.

[73] *L&P*, XII(1), no. 665.

[74] *TA*, VI, 310; VII, 258; *L of J V*, p. 366; *Hamilton Papers*, I, nos. 38, 40; *L&P*, XII(1), nos. 1043, 1094; XII(2), nos. 559, 590, 666, 1076; XIV(1), nos. 455, 481, 538, 625.

[75] *L&P*, XII(2), no. 1285; XIII(2), nos. 26, 776, 1162.

[76] *L&P*, XIV(2), no. 724.3; XV, nos. 25, 40, 136, 191, 248, 249, 279; *L of J V*, pp. 382-383; *TA*, VII, 289. A recent account of the background and substance of this embassy may be found in Arthur Joseph Slavin, *Politics and Profit* (Cambridge, England, 1966), pp. 68-93.

[77] For examples, see *L of J V*, pp. 417-418, 421; *L&P*, XV, no. 432; XVI, nos. 2, 356, 373, 426, 499, 502, 612, 766, 1034.2.

the retention of traditional theology and papal supremacy. Since it would have required the destruction of at least the latter of these commitments to reassure the English monarch, relations between the realms could not but deteriorate. Sadler's mission failed in its primary objective, the establishment of Anglo-Scottish amity on a firm base, and this failure had consequences not only in renewed tension between the realms but within Scotland itself. As English pressures advanced from diplomatic solicitation to military harassment during 1540-1541, the Scottish clerics grew more anglophobic, and they received more support from James.[78] Yet James continued to seek a diplomatic solution, perhaps because he was not fully aware that Henry had determined on the total subordination of Scotland. In his search for some peaceful solution, the King of Scots seems to have been opposed by his clergy.[79] While the clerical party was correct in its assessment of the issues, James was more practical. There was, in fact, little possibility of successful military action against England, action which would escape serious reprisals.

The King was, however, converted to an offensive policy after a fairly ill-prepared English force raided Scotland and the Scottish army failed to respond effectively, neither pursuing the retreating enemy, nor penetrating English territory (22 October 1542). This decision may have been largely emotional—the nobles had refused his direct orders—but James may also have seen it as a good time to damage English resources and reputation as a preliminary to further negotiations.[80]

Overjoyed at the King's decision and hoping to publish the papal condemnation of Henry VIII in England, the clerical party promised to raise a substantial force using their own resources and, with royal help, teach the English a severe lesson.[81] James and Beaton both wrote

[78] L&P, XVI, nos. 1105, 1115, 1116, 1125, 1126, 1130, 1141, 1143, 1144, 1183, 1208, 1211, 1243, 1405; Leslie, History of Scotland, pp. 160-161.

[79] L&P, XVII, nos. 720, 759, 824, 896, 906, 912, 1025, 1100.2, 1157; Knox, History of the Reformation, I, 31; RSA, p. xxii; Archbishops, IV, 68-69; Easson, Gavin Dunbar, pp. 70, 74-75.

[80] L&P, XVII, nos. 988, 1007, 1013, 1025, 1039, 1100.2, 1100.3, 1117; Buchanan, History of Scotland, II, 322; Leslie, History of Scotland, p. 163; Robert Lindsay of Pitscottie, The History and Chronicles of Scotland, ed. Aeneas J.G. Mackay (Edinburgh, 1899-1911), I, 400-403; Knox, I, 32-33; Diurnal, p. 24; RSA, pp. 139-140.

[81] L&P, XVII, nos. 1117, 1124, 1136.1, 1140, 1157; RSA, p. 140; Archbishops, IV, 75; Easson, p. 76; Buchanan, II, 322; Knox, I, 33-35.

to Rome to supplement this private arrangement with an additional levy on the whole Church in Scotland, a request which was granted in January.[82]

By that time, however, this Scottish expeditionary force had already been raised, had invaded Cumberland, and had been ignominiously routed by a much smaller English party in the swamps of the Solway. Shortly afterward, James V died. Legend has it that he died of a broken heart and that his failure was the result of his dependence on, and support of, the old faith in Scotland.[83]

That James used and defended the established Church is plain, but confusion has arisen over his attitudes and actions in connection with the growing agitation for religious reform. Such confusion, however, seems to be mainly the product of a failure among Scottish writers, beginning with John Knox, to distinguish between two sorts of reform movements. One, whose chief European spokesmen were men such as Erasmus and Thomas More, sought the amendment of the lives of the clergy and a return of church practices to the strict standards of canon law. The culmination of this movement was the Council of Trent. The other (Protestant) movement sought not only moral but theological reform (or innovation) and ended in the establishment of non-Catholic communions. Although these agitations often overlapped and many men passed from one to the other, the distinction was manifest in this period, and it clarifies the role of the King of Scots.[84]

As early as 1530, James was writing to the Pope about irregularities and abuses within the Scottish Church; subsequent correspondence reiterated charges of innovations, ignorance, luxury, perjury, secularism, unworthiness, neglect of divine offices, immorality, and lack of discipline.[85] Royal antagonism to such abuses was also expressed through legislation and direct exhortation of the churchmen. At the Provincial Council of 1536 the King demanded that the clergy abandon mortuary dues and so reform the tithe system that every husbandman would pay a fixed, regular sum, "suchlike as he pays to his landlord." If these changes were not made, James threatened, he would compel churchmen to grant long leases of church lands at the old

---

[82] *L of J V*, pp. 444-445; *L&P*, XVIII(1), no. 31.

[83] A popular account of these events may be found in Albert Makinson, "Solway Moss and the Death of James V," *History Today*, X (1960), 106-115.

[84] Some notice is beginning to be taken of this distinction; see, e.g., Mackie, *History of Scotland*, pp. 147-150.

[85] *L of J V*, pp. 174-176, 187, 339.

rents, thus imposing upon them a serious loss.[86] In 1541 the Estates, which were under complete royal control, passed an act for the "reforming of churches and churchmen" which censured neglect of divine service, dishonesty, and deficiencies in wit, knowledge, and manners. Such behavior, it was stated, explained why both the Church and its servants were held in contempt. Although the act carried no penalties for disobedience, "the King's Grace" exhorted and prayed all churchmen of whatever degree to remedy this situation by reforming themselves and their subordinates in their relationship to God and man and by repairing the churches under their supervision. If any were negligent or disobedient to their superiors in this matter, James promised to "find remedy therefore at the Pope's Holiness."[87]

The most famous of the King's expressions of disenchantment with ecclesiastical practices, however, were connected with his patronage of writers who held the clergy up to ridicule. George Buchanan related that, when James was annoyed with the Conventual Franciscans, whom he suspected of being involved in some plots against him, he commissioned a literary attack on them. The resultant *Palinodia* was a strong indictment, and it angered its victims; but the King was not satisfied and requested a further exposé, "which should not only prick the skin, but should probe the vitals." The fruit of this second effort was the *Franciscanus*, wherein the friars were pictured as those ruined in purse, ignorant, diseased in mind and body, as law breakers, exhausted gamblers, and voluptuaries. This attack satisfied James. The Franciscans, however, were so thoroughly aroused that, when they got the opportunity (in 1539), they forced the author to flee the country.[88]

Buchanan's work might be dismissed as the product of political rather than religious passion, but this can hardly have been a factor in the royal support of David Lindsay, who had been James's companion and tutor in infancy. In two poems of 1528-1530, aimed in part at gaining their author a good position in the household, Lindsay argued the need for reformation of clerical practices.[89] He must have believed

---

[86] *L&P*, X, no. 536; *Statua Ecclesiae Scoticanae*, ed. Joseph Robertson (Edinburgh, 1866), I, cxxxvi-cxxxvii (hereafter cited as *Statua*).

[87] *APS*, II, 370.

[88] Buchanan, *History of Scotland*, II, 317; George Buchanan, *The Franciscan Friar, etc.*, ed. and tr. George Provand (Glasgow, 1809); P. Hume Brown, *George Buchanan* (Edinburgh, 1890), pp. 92-95.

[89] David Lindsay, *The Works of Sir David Lindsay of the Mount*, ed. Douglas Hamer (Edinburgh, 1931-1936), I, 40-90; IV, xvi-xviii; *Statua*, I, cxxxvii.

that such sentiments would prove agreeable. On 6 January 1540, more-over, James V was an approving spectator at the first performance of Lindsay's *Ane Satyre of the Thrie Estaitis.*

There is no extant text of this first version of the play, but a summary of its main features was prepared for the English authorities by a Scot sympathetic to Henry's ecclesiastical policies. According to this abridg-ment, the chief character, Poor Man, after hearing complaints of abuses and oppressions in many areas of Scottish life, praises James for the restoration of law and order. He adds, however, that one thing "which pertained as well to his charge" has not yet been done. When asked what this is, Poor Man launches into "a long narration" about the collection of mortuary dues, the harrying of the poor by consistory law, "and of many other abusings by the spiritual[ity] and the church. . . ." Poor Man is at once rebuked by Bishop, who commands him to be silent on pain of death. Encouraged by Man of Arms, however, Poor Man proceeds to denounce the unchastity of the clergy and the expedients employed in the marriages of their children. Attacks on "the great superfluous rents that pertained to the church by reason of overmuch temporal land given them . . ." and on the lives of those in cloisters and monasteries follow. The denunciation is completed by an exposition of the true office of a bishop, based on the New Testament. All these charges are proved by both Poor Man and Experience. Bishop objects, but is outvoted by Man of Arms and Burgess; the vote is ratified by King.[90]

James, it was reported, was so moved by this presentation that he called on the ecclesiastics who were present to reform their manner of living. If they did not, he said, he would send six of the proudest of them to his uncle in England. As he had ordered them, he added, so would he order all the rest. The same observer also stated that royal enthusiasm for clerical reform was so great that the King contemplated removing all churchmen from positions of authority under him.[91]

It is possible to dismiss such expressions of desire for a purer religious life and clerical reformation[92] as temporary passions which were in-effective because of James's own political commitments and his ex-ploitation of ecclesiastical abuses. In 1539, for example, the King even opposed a reform which had already been instituted at Rome and sup-ported the continued holding of incompatible benefices by two of his lay officials.[93]

---

[90] Lindsay, II, 2-6; *L&P*, XV, no. 114.  [91] *L&P*, XV, no. 114.
[92] See also *ALC*, pp. 481-482.  [93] *L of J V*, p. 374.

Where the correction of malpractices did not directly affect his own financial and political interests, however, James V did carry on a forceful and consistent campaign for the implementation of his reforming sentiments. He was, for example, a resolute champion of the Observant Franciscans and the Sisters of St. Catherine of Siena, generally recognized as the most pious religious orders in Scotland.[94] A frequent advocate of monastic reform, he urged the highest authorities of both the Cistercians and the Carmelites to send officials to purge their Scottish houses of abuses.[95] In 1529 he secured the appointment without fees of a bishop for the diocese of the Isles, vacant for sixteen years, and secured the necessary financing until the collection of the regular episcopal dues could recommence.[96] Even royal control of the temporalities of vacant prelacies was sometimes used to endow those for whom full provision to the office was intended.[97]

Yet no matter how sincere James's desire for reform might have been, it is clear that his solutions of non-religious problems, which claimed his first attention, involved him so deeply in the extant system, with all its corruptions, that he would have had to reconstruct most aspects of Scottish life in order to purify the Church. This he was never secure enough to do.

None of James's reform activities, however, contains any indication that he either understood or approved of the theological revolution which was spreading throughout Europe at this time. He always showed himself, in fact, to be thoroughly opposed to anything that touched on heresy.

Lutheran opinions had become known in Scotland shortly after their first appearance on the continent, presumably through the Scottish merchant and intellectual communities. An Act of the Estates was passed in 1525 against importation or exposition of these opinions, and, just before the escape of James from the Douglases, Patrick Hamilton, an avowedly Lutheran teacher, was burned at St. Andrews. There were, however, no further prosecutions during the first part of James V's personal rule.[98]

Although the King always proclaimed himself a great opponent of heresy in his letters, these asseverations were usually connected with

---

[94] *Ibid.*, pp. 213, 231, 232-233; *Libris*, Appendix, p. 20.

[95] *L of J V*, pp. 187, 339.

[96] *Ibid.*, pp. 162-163, 209; Dowden, *Bishops of Scotland*, pp. 291-292.

[97] *RPS*, II, nos. 2736, 3974, 4028.

[98] *APS*, II, 295; Knox, *History of the Reformation*, II, Appendix 1; Mackie, *History of the Scottish Reformation*, pp. 91-94.

requests for papal favors.[99] The real test of James's opinions must be sought in the role he played in the trials of accused Lutherans. One series of trials took place in 1533-1534, shortly after papal approval of the chief clerical taxation. The strong connections between the two sorts of opposition to the established Church, as well as James's attitude, may be seen in the case of David Straton.

Straton was a landowner who had first come to the attention of church authorities when he refused to pay a tithe of the fish caught by his servants. He ordered them instead, as a protest against such exactions, to cast the tenth fish back into the sea. When he ignored the process of cursing brought against him for this action, he was accused of heresy, whereupon he began "to frequent the company of such as were godly," notably John Erskine of Dun, later a Protestant leader. Straton refused to admit any error at his trial upon being confronted with the original charge of withholding tithes, in spite of great efforts by the King to get him to do so. Having been judged guilty and condemned to the fire, Straton asked James for mercy, "which he would willingly have granted to him," but the episcopal judges stated that the royal "hands were bound in that case, and that he had no grace to give to such as by their law were condemned." This evaluation the King was forced to accept, and Straton was executed on 27 August 1534.[100] James's continuing interest in the case was attested by the gift, eleven months later, of Straton's escheated goods to his widow and brother.[101]

The other Scot to be executed for heresy in this period, a priest named Norman Gourlay, was apparently considered a relapsed heretic, and the only details of his crimes reported were that he had been in Scandinavia and that he had been married. He also, according to one source, proved impervious to royal pleadings that he abjure and escape death.[102] Others who were examined at the same time were apparently more willing to take the advice of their earthly king, for they did abjure and save their lives, though not their goods.[103]

The cases of the sister and brother of Patrick Hamilton continue

[99] *L of J V*, pp. 161, 163, 174, 183, 231, 276, 307; *ALC*, p. 423; *L&P*, XII(1), no. 804.

[100] Knox, I, 24-25; Lindsay of Pitscottie, *History and Chronicles*, I, 349-350; Buchanan, *History of Scotland*, II, 311; Leslie, *History of Scotland*, p. 149; *Diurnal*, p. 19.

[101] *RPS*, II, no. 1736.

[102] Knox, I, 24-25; *Diurnal*, pp. 18-19; Leslie, p. 149; Lindsay of Pitscottie, I, 350; Alexander R. MacEwen, *A History of the Church in Scotland* (London, 1913, 1918), p. 454.

[103] *Diurnal*, p. 18; Knox, I, 24.

and extend this pattern. Examined at Holyrood before the King, Catherine Hamilton secured her release by clever and evasive answers. James Hamilton escaped by following royal advice, according to one report.[104] No doubt his case was the more desperate, for he was condemned *in absentia* as a relapsed heretic who held that God alone, and no saints, should be adored. He was also accused of keeping prohibited books in the vernacular, of being doubtful of purgatory and the efficacy of prayers for the dead, and of using the *Pater Noster* in Scots. Because of his non-appearance, his fate was left to the secular power, and his goods were escheated to the crown.[105] Whether or not the King "showed signs of goodwill towards the accused," he was not so moved as to refrain from using Hamilton's escheated property for royal purposes.[106] Early in 1536, moreover, James wrote to the Pope condemning Hamilton as a relapsed heretic and "an outstanding supporter of Lutheranism," the occasion being a report that Hamilton was going to Rome to secure a papal pardon in order to be able to return home. "If the Pope permits this he cannot expect strong loyalty in Scotland, nor will James make further efforts to avert or stamp out the plague." In a covering letter to the Cardinal of Ravenna, Protector of Scottish affairs at Rome, the King remarked that "neither regard for ancestral faith, very many royal warnings, a sense of shame, the consequent humiliation, nor the punishment of his brother in his very presence sufficed to recall Hamilton from his unhappy course." James also pointed out that "restoration to country and status are in the king's hands" alone.[107] These remarks reveal not only James's opposition to heresy but also his concern for his prerogatives and his exasperation at Hamilton's obstinacy. But this was not yet the final word on the matter. Writing from Rouen on 29 March 1537, James presented the Pope with a somewhat different version of Hamilton's case and situation. Hamilton, the King claimed, "was led by youthful pliability and inexperience to depart from the ways of his fathers. Called to answer, he willingly abjured all his heresy and professed a will to conduct himself as an orthodox person. A few years later he was again charged on suspicion, and he left the realm. Because of his contumacy he was judged as a suspect to have relapsed to the abjured opinions. He now gives the king unmistakable tokens of repentance; and James is therefore all the readier to supplicate the pope on his behalf for Christ's abounding clemency, provided that he is found to exhibit that evidence

---

[104] MacEwen, p. 453; *Archbishops*, III, 210.
[105] *L of J V*, pp. 274-275; *Diurnal*, p. 19; Leslie, p. 150.
[106] *RPS*, II, nos. 1585, 1928.          [107] *L of J V*, pp. 307-308.

of a better and constant mind which for many important reasons he seems to show before the king." This petition was to have effect in spite of any previous letters.[108]

In all these cases, the King's distaste for severe penalties and his concern for reconversion of the heretic—attitudes apparently at times connected with political considerations and his own sense of discontent with clerical actions—were evident. He could, however, be relentless in the pursuit of heretics when such factors played no part. This stringency was manifest in several cases, the most notable of which was that of James Melville, an Observant Franciscan, whose crypto-Lutheranism got him into repeated trouble with both sacred and secular authorities.[109] Yet James's continuing reputation for clemency and fair dealing was attested by four men from Ayr who fled to England in March 1537. Stating that they were "cumbered" at home for the opinion that the Bishop of Rome should not be called Pope and for having a New Testament in English, they proposed to remain at Carlisle until the King returned from France. They would, they said, "abide the law before him; otherwise they fear to have no justice."[110]

The next serious prosecutions for heresy began in 1538. The gap in the period of repression may be accounted for in three ways: the King and his officers were absorbed with problems outside Scotland; the actions of 1534 were apparently thorough enough to drive the chief advocates of new theologies underground or out of the country; and 1538 marks the full emergence of the influence of David Beaton. If the Cardinal, whose elevation had been partially justified and sanctioned by the necessity of preventing the spread of English opinions,[111] was responsible for the rigorous inquisition of heretical professors (as there seems little reason to doubt),[112] he was not unsupported by the power of his royal master. The importance of the role played by James in opposing heterodoxy was recognized by contemporaries[113] and is revealed in his correspondence[114] and in his actions.

---

[108] *Ibid.*, p. 330.

[109] *Ibid.*, pp. 137-138, 275-276, 287, 315-316; *ALC*, p. 426; Hugh Watt, "The Three James Melvilles," *Records of the Scottish Church History Society*, III (1929), 102-109. For similar cases, see *ALC*, pp. 371-372, 426-428, 437.

[110] *L&P*, XII(1), no. 703.

[111] *L&P*, XIII(2), no. 1136; XIV(1), no. 36; *L of J V*, p. 361.

[112] *Formulare*, II, xiv; Easson, *Gavin Dunbar*, pp. 66-67, 97; Knox, *History of the Reformation*, I, 27-28; *Archbishops*, IV, 31ff.

[113] *L&P*, XVI(1), no. 585; *L of J V*, p. 417; Knox, I, 28.

[114] *L of J V*, pp. 405, 410, 422.

The King made a special trip to be present at the burning of five heretics on 1 March 1539[115] and was an approving spectator in May 1540 at the trial *in absentia* of a man who had been one of his favorites.[116] Yet this apparent rigor should be balanced against the fact that, in many cases, the goods escheated after conviction of heresy were regranted to the heretic himself or to his family for a very reasonable sum, or even *gratis*. Occasionally, such grants were accompanied by the complete legal rehabilitation of the individual involved.[117]

Final evidence for James V's continuing concern for the repression of heresy may be found in some enactments of his parliaments, acts which could have been little more than expressions of royal wishes. In 1535 the possession and discussion of heretical books and opinions were restricted to scholars, and the anti-Lutheran act of 1525 was reaffirmed.[118] In 1540 it was ordered that the Scottish Church be maintained and defended in all those privileges and liberties it had enjoyed in the past.[119] This endorsement of the traditional ecclesiastical order was followed in the spring by a series of nine acts directed against such specific novelties of practice and belief as anti-sacramentalism, the denial of papal supremacy, private discussions of the Scriptures, and the destruction of holy images. At the same time, a system of rewards was established for information about heretics and their activities.[120]

These last acts go far beyond anything necessary merely as a sop to clerical feeling or as an inducement for papal favors. The generalized law of 1540 would have been enough for such purposes. Although the King did use his position as a supporter of the old Church in both domestic and international affairs as a lever to work his will with clerical authorities at Rome and in Scotland, his belief in the traditional system appears to have been more than expedient and his detestation of innovations sincere. Moreover, the policy of repression with mercy that he followed, although it did not solve the real issues involved in the anti-clerical and anti-Catholic agitation, does seem to have been successful in keeping the situation under control. It was not until after his death that the Protestantization of Scotland began in earnest.

---

[115] Henry Ellis, "Observations upon a Household Book of King James the Fifth of Scotland—from September 14th 1538 to September 13th 1539," *Archaeologia*, XXII (1829), 7.

[116] *L&P*, XV, no. 714.

[117] See, e.g., *RPS*, II, nos. 2648, 2952, 3396.

[118] *APS*, II, 341.    [119] *Ibid*., p. 358.    [120] *Ibid*., pp. 370-371.

James V thus appears to have been very thoroughly a man of his time. Though not personally ascetic, he nevertheless seems to have believed sincerely in the faith of his fathers and the established religious order. He refused to abandon the one and hoped for the purification of the other. To expect him to have placed the reform of the Church before the solution of his immediate problems (solvency, centralization, independence), however, is unrealistic: necessities, for him, were stronger than ideals.

The significance of James's reign for the Scottish Church is harder to establish. His taxation does not seem to have destroyed the resources of the clergy generally, though individuals may have been ruined.[121] One phenomenon which has received widespread attention is the setting of church lands in feufarm, a long-term fixed lease which raised immediate cash but entailed eventual losses in an inflationary period. Most ecclesiastical feufarm charters, however, date from the period after James's death.[122] Nor can this king be blamed for the long-standing involvement of the Scottish Church in politics, an involvement often held to have resulted in neglect of spiritual responsibilities. James V seems to have left the Church pretty much as he found it.

If James did little to change the old Church, he also did not eradicate the incipient movement for reform. His reluctance to be an ecclesiastical executioner and his personal sympathies may have contributed to the spread of both theological and moral criticism, even though a greater factor was the proximity of England and Scandinavia. Still, in assessing the causes of the triumph of Protestantism in Scotland, the actions and policies of James V must be assigned a relatively minor place.

[121] See Dickinson, *Scotland*, p. 299, for a concurring opinion.
[122] *RSA*, pp. xxvii-xxix; Reid, "Clerical Taxation," p. 152.

# UTOPIA AND GENEVA

## J. H. HEXTER

LIKE many of the noblest men of the early decades of the sixteenth century, Thomas More was deeply concerned with the
problem of bringing about a fundamental spiritual change in
Europe. But in *Utopia* he did not suggest a strategy for achieving that
change. Rather, he revealed two daunting obstacles which any such
strategy must encounter and had but little chance to overcome: first,
the inability of reformers to serve with good conscience as advisors
to the rulers of Europe; and second, the fundamental character of
Europe's institutions, especially its institutions of property. Scarcely a
decade after More's death, a Christian humanist reformer in some
ways very unlike More, in others somewhat like him, obliterated the
first obstacle, circumvented the second, and established in a town in
the heart of Europe a Hagnapolis—a holy community almost as austere
as Utopia. That reformer wrought mightily for almost two decades,
his successors for several more, and by the end of the sixteenth century
the town had become under resolute pressure "peaceful, well-ordered,
pious, literate, learned, poised, cultured, when before it was nothing
but a big uncivilized village."[1] The transformed "village" was Geneva;
the reformer was John Calvin.

The curious similarities between Utopia and Geneva have been un-
duly obscured by the undeniable differences between More and Calvin, between the Roman Catholic martyr and the hero of the Reformation. Calvin, of course, wrought under limitations with which More did
not have to concern himself, and Calvin's materials were considerably
more intractable. More worked with pens and paper, Calvin with men
and a social order. It is easier to impress one's aspirations with pens on
paper than with men on a social order; men are more balky, a social
order less readily receptive to new imprints. Consequently, compared
with some of Utopia's iron ordinances, the law of Calvin's Geneva
was mild. Idle pastimes and evil resorts, prohibited in Utopia,[2] were

---

[1] Émile Doumergue, *Jean Calvin, les hommes et les choses de son temps*, 7
vols. (Lausanne / Neuilly-sur-Seine, 1899-1927), VI, 116, quoting H. Bordier,
*L'école historique de Jérome Bolsec*, p. 15.

[2] Thomas More, *Utopia*, ed. Edward Surtz, Yale Edition of the Selected Works
of St. Thomas More, II (New Haven, 1964), 69-71, 82-83 (hereafter cited as Y.S.);
Thomas More, *Utopia*, ed. Edward Surtz and J. H. Hexter, Yale Edition of the
Complete Works of St. Thomas More, IV (New Haven, 1965), 127, 129, 147
(hereafter cited as Y.C.).

regulated in Geneva. In the Swiss city no law reduced to bondage a citizen who twice left town without permission, as Utopia's law did;[3] nor was criminal intent punished as heavily as criminal act,[4] as it was on More's blessed island. And, real flesh being somewhat harder to tame than paper flesh, the Utopian penalty for adultery—bondage for the first offense, death for the second[5]—was, despite Calvin, too stern for Calvin's Geneva, where the reformer's own sister-in-law and step-daughter so offended[6] and where, as late as 1556, a citizen reckoned that rigorous proceedings against adulterers and fornicators might cost the town half its population. Unlike King Utopus, Calvin did not fall heir to what every radical reformer dreams of—a submissive and ductile people like the conquered Utopians. Only slowly and with frequent setbacks was he gradually able to mold the tough, late medieval institutions of the Genevan urban patriciate into something closer to his heart's, and therefore (as he saw it) to God's desire.

Granted all the differences, the similarity both in detail and in spirit between Utopia and Geneva is nevertheless noteworthy, even when the instruments and institutions for working out the details and for maintaining the spirit diverge. This similarity is evident in the rules of More's "best ordered commonwealth" and of Calvin's New Jerusalem with respect to dress, leisure, and privacy. Consider the apparently trivial matter of costume. Sumptuary legislation dealing with dress was an old medieval story. But in the Middle Ages the purpose of such legislation was to maintain social hierarchy—in effect, to maintain the status value of aristocratic, conspicuous consumption by denying bourgeois crows the right to noble peacock feathers.[7] Utopia and Geneva, too, had rules about what the inhabitants might wear, but they differed markedly, and in a similar way, from the medieval rules. In Utopia plainness of dress was so much a matter of course and good custom that a Utopian, seeing a finely decked-out ambassador from another land, mistook him for the ambassador's fool.[8] The Utopians wore plain, undyed grey garments;[9] and when,

[3] Y.S., p. 82; Y.C., p. 147.    [4] Y.S., p. 112; Y.C., p. 193.
[5] Y.S., p. 112; Y.C., p. 191.
[6] John T. McNeill, *The History and Character of Calvinism* (New York, 1957), p. 189.
[7] The first general English statute regulating apparel was 33 E III c. 8-15. For the history of such regulation, see Frances E. Baldwin, *Sumptuary Legislation and Personal Regulation in England*, Johns Hopkins University Studies in Historical and Political Science, vol. 44, no. 1 (Baltimore, 1926).
[8] Y.S., p. 88; Y.C., p. 155.    [9] Y.S., p. 74; Y.C., pp. 133-135.

some weeks after he had sent his book to Erasmus to have it printed, More dreamed of being a prince in Utopia, he imagined himself wearing the habit of Franciscan grey that was standard there.[10] For a Utopian there was nothing else to wear; the law allowed no finery, not so much as variety in the color of men's clothing, even to the magistrates. Similarly, and at considerable risk, on the rather odd issue of slashed breeches for the local soldiery, Calvin faced down the chief of the citizen militia, who was also the spearhead of the patrician opposition to the reformer.[11] Geneva's law and Utopia's were much alike; Calvin's attitudes and More's stood squarely and precisely opposed in purpose to medieval sumptuary legislation and precisely identical to each other. The Utopians despised men who felt that the more splendidly they dressed, the higher was the honor due them.[12] Or, as Calvin succinctly put it, slashed breeches, like other unnecessary adornments, ministered to pride. Therefore, "it is against God and of the devil, and a disorder such as ought not to be tolerated at any price."[13]

As on the matter of dress, so on the question of leisure, the views of More and Calvin were much alike. In both Utopia and Geneva mere idleness lay under a ban.[14] The aristocratic-courtly conception of a pastime as something to fend off *accidia,* or boredom, was offensive to both More and Calvin. Time is God's gift to men, not to be destroyed, but to be used to glorify Him through righteous, useful doing in the world, whether with hands or with mind. In both Utopia and Geneva the courtly pastime is replaced by the scholar's recreation, that respite which does not kill time but saves it by renewing a man's energies for the activity or study to follow.[15]

As with dress and leisure, so with privacy. In Utopia, with its extended families,[16] multiple-unit houses without locks on the doors,[17] and common meals,[18] privacy had little place. Nor was this an accident. The open and common way of life in Utopia was designed to maintain a common standard of conduct, to foster a common ethic. In the ecclesiastical ordinances for his New Jerusalem, Calvin created a new kind

---

[10] *Opus Epistolarum Des. Erasmi Roterodami*, ed. P. S. Allen et al., 12 vols. (Oxford, 1906-1958), II, 414; Thomas More, *Selected Letters*, ed. Elizabeth F. Rogers (New Haven, 1961), p. 85.

[11] Eugène Choisy, *La Théocratie à Genève au temps de Calvin* (Geneva, n.d.), p. 90.

[12] Y.S., p. 95; Y.C., p. 167.

[13] Choisy, p. 90.    [14] Y.S., pp. 82-83; Y.C., p. 147.

[15] Y.S., p. 70; Y.C., 127-129.    [16] Y.S., pp. 75-76; Y.C., pp. 135-137.

[17] Y.S., p. 65; Y.C., p. 121.    [18] Y.S., p. 79; Y.C., p. 141.

of church officer whose authority over morals obliterated the customary line between private affairs and public life almost as effectively as Utopian institutions did. The lay elders had the duty "*to watch over the life of everyone,* to admonish in a friendly way those who fell short or led ill-ordered lives." Such elders were to be chosen for every section of the city, "*in order to have an eye everywhere.*"[19] In a startling way Calvin's language echoes More's description of Utopia. There, too men have no "license to waste time nor pretext to evade work, . . . no lurking hole . . . being under the eyes of all."[20]

By making sin very public indeed, Calvin succeeded in achieving some of the ends of Utopian society without resorting to Utopian means—community of property, destruction of the market, abolition of money. As a very practical man with a series of very knotty problems to solve in his relentless drive to create in Geneva a model Christian commonwealth, Calvin did not consider means as far beyond his reach as the Utopian social order was. He had a system, however, which in a measure served the same purpose. And that system is curiously prefigured in detail in *Utopia* itself. Describing the Utopian clergy, Hythlodaeus says that they

> are censors of morals. It is counted a great disgrace for a man to be summoned or rebuked by them as not being of upright life. It is their function to give advice and admonition, but to check and punish offenders belongs to the governor and the other civil officials. The priests, however, do exclude from divine services individuals whom they find to be unusually bad. There is almost no punishment which is more dreaded: they incur very great disgrace and are tortured by a secret fear of religion. Even their bodies will not long go scot free. If they do not demonstrate to the priests their speedy repentance, they are seized and punished by the senate for their impiety.[21]

It was precisely such a refurbished and sharpened instrument of ecclesiastical discipline that Calvin established in Geneva. The institution he created to suit his purpose was the Consistory, the assembly of ministers and lay elders. The weapon was excommunication, with restoration to the holy community contingent on public repentance.

[19] B. J. Kidd, *Documents Illustrative of the Continental Reformation* (Oxford, 1911), p. 595. (Italics mine.)
[20] Y.S., p. 83; Y.C., p. 147.
[21] Y.S., pp. 139-140; Y.C., pp. 227-229.

And the cutting edge was condemnation to exile by the civil magistrates of those who long failed to repent. Using its disciplinary power, the Consistory "intervened to re-establish peace and union in families, to recall individuals to their duty; it took in hand ... reforms favorable to the weak and the lesser folk, it summoned and censured the lazy and the idle, over-hard fathers and creditors; it was pitiless to usurers, monopolists and engrossers. It combatted the coarse manners of the age, the brutality of men."[22] Thus the expression of brotherhood was achieved, not through community of property, but by the spiritual communion of those who shared in the holy sacrament of the Lord's Supper and by the exclusion from it of the unworthy. Through the disciplinary instrument provided by the Lord's Supper, too, the Reformed Church at Geneva was able to express the profound leveling implicit in the Calvinist sense of God's majesty and man's depravity and in Calvin's doctrine of the calling. So worthless and shriveled was sinful man beside the greatness of God that the scale of earthly rank was as nothing to Him or to the ministers of His Word. To those entrusted with earthly authority who glorified God by earnest service in their calling, praise was due, as it was to all men who served God well; to men who did otherwise, whatever their rank, censure was due. Accordingly, with no respect of person or station, the Consistory brought to book the big folk of the city—councillors, the wife of the captain-general, the city treasurer, his wife and his mother, the wife of Calvin's own brother.[23] Thus, by means less than Utopian, Calvin came close to achieving in his City of Saints an equality of austere men not unlike that found in More's Hagnapolis.

Moreover, like Utopia, Geneva was dedicated not only to education but to the principle that sound education helps to make righteous citizens. That it was is not surprising, since Calvin was an admirer of Erasmus and, more than Luther, perhaps even more than Zwingli, a Christian humanist. In his inaugural address at the founding of the Academy of Geneva, Theodore Béza, the first rector, chosen by Calvin, spoke to the students who, "instructed in the *true religion* and *the knowledge of good literature*, have come in order to *work for the glory of God*."[24] It would be hard to find in so few phrases a more perfect expression of the religious aspiration which the Utopian commonwealth reflected.

[22] Choisy, *La Théocratie à Genève*, pp. 244-245.
[23] McNeill, *Calvinism*, pp. 165-166.
[24] Choisy, pp. 212-213. (Italics mine.)

Except of course that the religion Béza called true, and loved, More, had he known it, would surely have called false, and hated. Between Utopia and Geneva, between More in 1516 and Calvin, after all, lies the thundering torrent of religious revolution. All the better reason then, lest we lose our bearings in a flood that destroyed many landmarks, for us to recognize continuities, however unexpected, indeed however unlikely, they may seem at first glance. Those continuities exist as elements in a vast stratum of events—the Christian Revival, a stratum that stretched across to both sides of that conspicuous historical watershed, the year 1517. The part which preceded 1517 has been called the Pre-Reformation and the Religious Revival. Part of what followed 1517 has been called the Protestant Reformation (or, simply, the Reformation), the Protestant Revolt, or the Protestant Revolution; the other part, the Catholic Reformation, the Catholic Counter-Reformation, or the Catholic Counter-Revolution. And this may not be an exhaustive inventory of the current nomenclature. To add yet another name to the many already in use may seem a supererogatory contribution to an already more than adequate confusion. The addition, however, may be warranted because historians have no single covering phrase to describe the intensification of religious sentiment and concern that began long before 1517 and extended long afterward, that in its full span had room for Ximenes and Savonarola, Luther and Loyola, the Reformed Churches and the Jesuits, John of Leyden and Pope Paul IV, Thomas Cranmer and Edmund Campion, and Michael Servetus. Only if amid the upheavals of the following century we discern the continuity provided by the Christian Revival can we find clues to render intelligible some of the varieties of human conduct during the Age of Reformation, varieties otherwise hard to understand. They become intelligible as partial consummations of some of the durable aspirations of that Revival. It thus may seem improbable that the nearest men came in the sixteenth century to realizing More's dream of a sober, disciplined commonwealth, ruled in its daily life by the teaching of Christ, was the Calvinist capital at Geneva. But it is a fact, and, unless we grasp that fact, it is hard to explain a considerable group of other facts about the history of Europe in the sixteenth century.

Of these facts the most significant is the survival and resilience of Protestantism in the century after the death of Luther. In the generation between the posting of the ninety-five theses on indulgences and Luther's death, the religious movement that took his name had lost most of its momentum in the heart of Europe and advanced only

82

in murky struggles in the backward northlands—Scandinavia and the Baltic regions. Toward the end of that same generation the Roman Church began to rally its forces of defense and soon launched a counter-attack. When Mary Tudor became Queen of England in 1553, there was not a single great Protestant realm in Europe, only a few low-grade German and northern principalities whose princes were all too likely to make a deal and return to the Roman obedience if the going got rough, as it looked to be doing. Yet, for better or worse, Protestantism was still very much alive and kicking in 1600; it did not fold up in face of the Catholic Counter-Revolution. And that it did not do so was unmistakably the result of the initiative of the followers of Calvin.

What were the resources of the Calvinists that enabled them to resist the Catholic counter-attack so effectively? No doubt they had a certain amount of luck, but no more than their share, and in almost all the more obvious equipage of combat they were absurdly deficient, compared with their Catholic adversaries. Their military resources were trivial. The other side had all the best generals—the Duke of Guise, Alva, Parma—and by far the best soldiers, the Spanish tercios, as well as *most* of the soldiers. Since the Calvinists did not control the political apparatus in a single important European state, their military recruiting was always hand-to-mouth. And, of course, compared to the enemy, they were bone poor. Even when Elizabeth was dragged kicking and screaming into Europe's religious wars, the gross financial resources available to the Calvinists came far short of those commanded by the Pope, the Catholic League, and Philip II. Before the half-hearted accession of Elizabeth to support of their cause, the Calvinists had been *gueux* indeed—Sea Beggars, Land Beggars, beggars in every way. And, finally, the Calvinists were enormously outnumbered. At a very rough guess, there were from ten to thirty Catholics for every Calvinist, and perhaps even more.

Under such adverse circumstances, how were the Calvinists able not only to hold their own but to enjoy a more secure position in 1600 than they had held in 1564 at Calvin's death? Part of the answer is suggested by a letter sent in the 1560's from a Catholic *gouverneur*, or stadholder of a province in the Netherlands to his masters in Brussels. With something between petulance and patience, he explains to the council in Brussels why he is not enthusiastically uprooting heresy in his territory, as ordered. Unfortunately, he observes, all the ablest people in the province are heretics—which makes matters difficult. The heretics in question were, of course, Calvinists. Any explanation of the

83

survival of Protestantism that leaves out of account what the stadholder was pointing to, however unprecisely, is deficient. Most students of the sixteenth century would probably agree with this rephrasing of his insight: in the later sixteenth century, compared with other religious creeds, Calvinism had a very high proportion of adherents who combined keen intelligence with deep dedication and zeal, and among such adherents was a high proportion of laymen.

This insight suggests that Calvinism somehow drew on a reservoir of talents that had hitherto remained untapped. The reservoir consisted of men of a kind that had begun to come to the fore in the Christian Revival. This kind of man was well-read in classical literature, deeply pious, convinced that there was a hideous gap between what Christ demanded of Christians and the way professed Christians lived, and sure that to narrow that gap was part of the duty of a true Christian. The difficulty for such a man lay in the fact that, though he believed himself called by God to action, he did not find in the world he lived in any channels into which he could pour forth his energies in the conviction that he was making the full and right use of the talents God had given him. Drawn to the monastic life by its theoretical rigor and discipline, by the renunciation of avarice and sloth and pride which it demanded, he was repelled by the actualities of that life in his time—the rules relaxed, the monks resistant to reform, study at a halt, an existence marked by idleness and tedium instead of learning and labor. And though taking the vows of an order did not necessarily prevent a man from working for God's kingdom on earth, still, by subjecting his freedom of action to a religious superior of dubious zeal, it well might do so. Nor, outside Italy, did the universities offer great attraction, since in the main they were still devoted to the old learning, which to such a man was not merely old but bad. Rightly or wrongly, like More, this kind of man found the scholastic questions which were the formal basis of that learning empty and stultifying. What drove him was zeal for the Christian commonwealth, the desire to employ as instruments to draw men toward the *regnum Christi* such powers as God gave him. Consequently, as More observed, he did not regard it as the pinnacle of human achievement and godly doing to "squat with the monks," in the ill-warranted belief that "to reside forever in the same spot like a clam or sponge, to cling eternally to the same rock is the last word in sanctity."[25]

[25] Thomas More, *The Correspondence of Sir Thomas More*, ed. Elizabeth F. Rogers (Princeton, 1947), p. 201; More, *Selected Letters*, p. 137.

Of course, some men of the Christian Revival did go to the cloister and some to the schools, but probably not without qualms of conscience and the sense that they had left half their work behind them in a world in which they belonged.

There was another way to go—the way of the court. "Mere" humanists, proficients in the classical languages with little Christian concern and no commitment to reform, paddled merrily—and some, indeed, wallowed—in courtly pleasure and courtly rackets, hitherto mainly the perquisites of the legists and the military élite. But to the men most deeply engaged by the religious resurgence there was bound to be about the courts of most Renaissance princes the stench of a moral pigsty, rather than the odor of sanctity. Of course, the man at the very heart of the resurgence, Erasmus, became a councilor to his native ruler, Charles, Prince of Castile and, among other things, Count of Holland. But Erasmus's councilorship was what in academic circles today would be called a "prestige appointment," with a concomitant absence of responsibilities. Erasmus received the post, as he put it, with "my liberty reserved by the vote of the Council."[26] The terms were, indeed, such as any man might have found gratifying— no duties and a regular stipend. But Erasmus was unique. Such a tidy and sanitary arrangement was not offered to lesser men; they had to get right down into the courtly muck. The better the man, the worse his lot at court; it was not a place for one with a demanding conscience. Others with such a moral constitution had learned the same lesson before the Renaissance, and more were to do so afterward. In earlier centuries medieval authors, quite unaffected by deep religious feelings, had produced a considerable literature on the falseness of court life and recommended retreat to the country to avoid its pitfalls.[27] Some men touched by the Christian Revival doubtless pursued this course; but it, too, had its frustrations—the frustrations of village Hampdens or mute inglorious Miltons ready to serve the Christian commonwealth with all their heart, all their soul, and all their mind, but finding nothing in their rustic retirement to engage even half their talents. Christian reformers were not endowed with either the temperament or the intricate egoism of Michel de Montaigne.

From the 1540's on, a number of men whose response to their his-

[26] Erasmus, *Opus Epistolarum*, II, 204.

[27] E.g., Alain Chartier, *Tractatus de vita curiali*, written about 1427 and early translated into French as *Le curial*. G. R. Owst, *Literature and Pulpit in Medieval England* (Cambridge, England, 1933), pp. 310-311.

torical milieu was similar to the one that inspired *Utopia* found in Calvin's Geneva the resolution in action of dilemmas that More resolved only in imagination in his well-ordered commonwealth. They poured into the Savoyard town in thousands from France, from the Netherlands, from Italy, from Spain, from Germany, from England, and from Scotland. And there they believed they found what they sought: "the most perfect *school of Christ* that ever was in the earth since the days of the apostles,"[28] "the miracle of the whole world" where men of many nations "being coupled with the only yoke of Christ . . . live . . . lovingly and friendly, and monks, laymen, and nuns . . . dwell together like a spiritual and Christian congregation."[29] What gave Geneva its magnetic attraction for men who had felt the impulse toward a Christian Revival John Knox explained very succinctly. Christ was truly preached in other places, "but manners and religion to be so sincerely reformed, I have not yet seen in any other place."[30] It was the "manners . . . sincerely reformed" that drew monks and nuns from their cloisters, well-to-do laymen from town and country, "to live in poverty"[31] in Geneva in enjoyment of "the holy discipline." In the Middle Ages successive waves of religious fervor, the impulse toward dedication, toward living wholly for God and by His rule, flowed into new or revitalized forms of monastic life and an *ausserweltliche Askese*, an otherworldly asceticism. In the sixteenth century, as a consequence of the holy discipline in Geneva, many of those waves flowed into the *innerweltliche Askese* of a City of Saints.[32] The layman official in the councils or Consistory of Geneva had no need to feel the compunction which afflicted Hythlodaeus and the author of *Utopia* over a life spent in serving the wicked appetites of vainglorious princes. He could find fulfillment in the austere joy of ruling in a holy commonwealth, in a realization, partial at least, of More's dream of being a prince in Utopia.

In the later sixteenth century this emancipation from scruple of pious Calvinist laymen, which brought the full range of their abilities into action in the political arena, spread from Geneva to the lands where Calvinism penetrated, especially to France, the Netherlands, England, and Scotland. It was able to spread because Geneva remained an exam-

[28] John Knox, quoted in McNeill, *Calvinism*, p. 178.
[29] John Bale, quoted in McNeill, pp. 178-179.
[30] John Knox, quoted in McNeill, p. 178.
[31] John Bale, quoted in McNeill, pp. 178-179.
[32] Max Weber, *The Protestant Ethic and the Spirit of Capitalism*, tr. T. Parsons (London, 1930), pp. 95-128; Ernst Troeltsch, *The Social Teaching of the Christian Churches*, 1 vol. in 2, tr. O. Wyon (New York, 1931), pp. 602-617.

ple to Calvin's followers of how a community could be transformed by the holy discipline. In France Calvinist laymen provided zealous support for Henry of Navarre, in the Netherlands for William of Orange, and in England for Elizabeth. Henry eventually became a Roman Catholic. William, baptized as a Roman Catholic, raised as a Lutheran in his nonage, and living as a Roman Catholic thereafter, did not become a Calvinist until 1573, when he was forty—with what degree of conviction it is hard to know. And Elizabeth never made any bones about her opposition to the Genevan Church order. Yet men touched by the Calvinist aspiration to see that God's will, as they conceived it, was done on earth could serve Henry and William and Elizabeth, because God not only walked in mysterious ways but occasionally chose rather odd instruments, His wonders to perform; and again, as they saw it, Henry and William and Elizabeth were clearly such instruments. Through them the society of saints might yet bring Christ's kingdom on earth. Thus able and religious laymen, among whom Francis Walsingham, Philippe de Mornay, and St. Aldegonde are perhaps the most eminent, men who might have turned away from political action under other circumstances, provided invaluable aid to their princes during Europe's religious civil wars in the later sixteenth century.[33]

Most remarkable was a cluster of Elizabeth's councillors—Mildmay, Sadler, Knollys, Wilson, Walsingham. They brought to the Queen's service a sobriety, honesty, and zeal not common in princely courts, accompanied by a continuing and unpunished personal alliance with the elements in the country intent on subverting her too-worldly religious settlement. This almost accidental materialization in More's country of a situation in which men similar to him, not in creed but in moral temper, were drawn toward the service of their ruler did not last. Even before the accession of the Stuarts, the curious symbiosis had broken down. Lay religious zeal gradually went out of the court when Archbishop Whitgift won his struggle against the Puritans. The dilemmas of *Utopia* reasserted themselves again—the dilemma of the intellectual in a bureaucracy, the dilemma of a Christian servant of worldly power, the dilemma of the prophet and the Prince.[34]

[33] Whether and how the post-Tridentine forms of Roman Catholic piety affected the service and servants of Catholic rulers during the Counter-Reformation are interesting questions, to which, unfortunately through ignorance, the author is unable even to suggest answers.

[34] For an attempt to explore these dilemmas, see J. H. Hexter, *More's UTOPIA: The Biography of an Idea*, Harper Torchbook edn. (New York, 1965), pp. 111-138; Y.C., pp. lxxxi-xcii.

Those dilemmas were in the cards for men with their hearts and minds set on the attainment of the Christian commonwealth, on having God's will done on earth as it is in heaven, who tried to reach that goal through service in the courts of Renaissance princes. Indeed, More had already well read those cards in 1516, when he wrote *Utopia*.

> "At court . . . one must openly approve the worst counsels and subscribe to the most ruinous decrees. He would be counted a spy and almost a traitor, who gives only faint praise to evil counsels. Moreover there is no chance for you to do any good because you are brought among colleagues who would easily corrupt even the best men before being reformed themselves. By their evil companionship either you will be seduced yourself or, keeping your own integrity and innocence, you will be made a screen for the wickedness and folly of others."[37]

The conjuncture of the aims and aspirations of zealous Calvinists directed toward the *regnum Christi* with the aims and aspirations of rulers with eyes hard fixed on the earthly kingdom was both fortuitous and short.

For a while, however, Calvin's Geneva and international Calvinism provided psychic fulfillment for a number of men steeped in the spirit of Christian humanism. And the curious similarities of Utopia and Geneva help us understand how this could have been. Yet, as we have seen, in one most important matter Utopia was not at all like Geneva. Calvin tried to infuse into all citizens a sense of their obligation to serve God and do His will unremittingly, and to this end he forced a remodeling of the Church in doctrine, government, and discipline. But it was the Church alone that he sought directly to remodel. In Geneva, and wherever else Calvinists planted a Reformed Church, they accepted in the main the existing structure of rules about property and power. They sought to permeate that structure with the spirit of the holy community generated by the Church. More, too, recognized how essential it was that good teaching permeate the structure of society. But not for a moment in *Utopia* does he accept the notion that merely by good teaching (or good preaching), or even by ecclesiastical discipline and censure, can a corrupt commonwealth be transformed into a good one. Such a transformation is only possible through a transmutation of the *forma reipublicae*, the structure of

[85] Y.S., pp. 51-52; Y.C., p. 103.

the commonwealth,[36] of the *maximum totius institutiones fundamentum*, the principal foundation of the whole structure, of the *vitae instituta*, the institutions of life, of the *reipublicae fundamenta*, of the foundations of the commonwealth.[37] For these sixteenth-century Latin phrases the nearest present-day English equivalent is "the social order," and the nearest present-day English equivalent for the transformation More wrote about is "social revolution."[38]

[36] Y.S., pp. 146-147; Y.C., pp. 236-237.

[37] Y.S., p. 151; Y.C., pp. 244-245.

[38] For successive attempts to deal with the special peculiarities of More's radicalism, see J. H. Hexter, "Thomas More: on the Margins of Modernity," *Journal of British Studies*, I (1961), 20-37; Y.C., Introduction, pp. cv-cxxiv; "Claude de Seyssel and Normal Politics in the Age of Machiavelli," *Art, Science, and History in the Renaissance*, ed. Charles Singleton (Baltimore, 1967).

# RELIGION AND
# POLITICS IN THE THOUGHT OF
# GASPARO CONTARINI

## FELIX GILBERT

STEPPING from the gates of his palace[1] in Venice, Gasparo Contarini was immediately drawn into the teeming life of the city in whose triumphant history his ancestors had played a leading part since earliest times. But from the rear of his palace Contarini could see across the lagoons the Camaldolese monastery of San Michele with the white dome of its recently built church and, beyond San Michele, the dark cypresses of Murano. These islands were the refuge of those who rejected the value of worldly activity and believed that man's only concern ought to be the salvation of his soul.

These were the two worlds in which Contarini lived. On the one hand, he had a political career which led him to high positions in the Venetian government. And his political interests found literary expression in his famous treatise on the institutions of the Venetian republic.[2] On the other hand, he was an intellectual who wrote extensively on philosophical, moral, and theological issues. And the religious bent of his intellectual concerns brought him, at the end of his life, from Venice to Rome where he became a member of the College of Cardinals and a guiding spirit in the last great attempt to bring the Lutherans back into the fold of the Church.

Much has been written about Gasparo Contarini.[3] His treatise on

---

[1] In the section of Cannareggio, on the Fondamenta Contarini no. 3539, one sees the "bella facciata cinquecentesca del Pal. Contarini del Zaffo, fatto costruire dal card. Gaspare Contarini" (*Venezia e Dintorni—Guida d'Italia del Touring Club Italiano*); the palace is now seat of the "Centro Giovanni XXIII." The church of San Michele was built between 1469 and 1478.

[2] *De magistratibus et republica Venetorum* (first published in Paris, 1543).

[3] Franz Dittrich, *Regesten und Briefe des Kardinals Gasparo Contarini* (Braunsberg, 1881), and *Gasparo Contarini, eine Monographie* (Braunsberg, 1885), remain basic for all modern research, despite incompleteness of facts and the intellectual naïveté of the author. Bibliographies, listing later literature, may be found in Hanns Rueckert, *Die theologische Entwicklung Gasparo Contarinis*, Arbeiten zur Kirchengeschichte, vol. VI (Bonn, 1926); Hermann Hackert, *Die Staatsschrift Gasparo Contarinis und die politischen Verhaeltnisse Venedigs im 16. Jahrhundert*, Heidelberger Abhandlungen zur mittleren und neueren Geschichte, vol. LXIX (Heidelberg, 1940). See also the article on Contarini in the *Enciclopedia Cattolica* (Città del Vaticano, 1950). I shall refer to special studies relevant to the particular problem under investigation at the appropriate places.

Venice has had a great influence on the development of constitutional thinking, and its importance for later political thought has been frequently analyzed.[4] Contarini's theological position and his activities as a church reformer have been of crucial interest to students of the Reformation period.[5] But those who have written on Contarini's views about Venetian politics seem only vaguely aware that he was also a religious thinker, whereas those who have investigated Contarini's role in the confessional struggle have given little or no attention to his earlier career as a Venetian statesman.[6] This partitioning of Contarini's life seems contradictory to what we know about human nature.[7] Thus we are justified in looking for the intellectual bond which explains the road Contarini traveled from Venetian statesman to reforming Cardinal.

## I

Gasparo Contarini was the eldest son of his parents, and as such he was expected to take an active part in business and politics; but his remarkable intellectual gifts—that, at least, is the report of his biographers[8]—became evident at such an early age that he was permitted to devote himself to a life of study. In 1502 Gasparo's father died, and Gasparo, then a student at the university in Padua, went back to Venice. As soon as he had ordered the affairs of his family and set up his brothers in their careers, however, he returned to Padua. This episode is revealing because it shows that, despite his scholarly inclinations,

[4] See, e.g., Zera S. Fink, *The Classical Republicans* (Evanston, 1945), pp. 37-40.

[5] See Hanns Rueckert, *Die Entwicklung Contarinis*, and, more recently, Hubert Jedin, "Gasparo Contarini e il contributo Veneziano alla Riforma Cattolica," *La Civiltà Veneziana del Rinascimento*, Centro di Cultura e Civiltà della Fondazione Giorgio Cini (Firenze, 1958), pp. 105-124.

[6] Indicative is the article "Gasparo Contarini" in the *Enciclopedia Italiana,* which concentrates on his activities as Cardinal, not mentioning his book on the Venetian republic.

[7] There is a reason why, in former years, students have concerned themselves only with particular and partial aspects of Contarini's life and mind. A fuller understanding of Contarini has become possible only in recent years when a fortunate find brought to light a number of revealing personal letters written by Contarini during a critical period of his life. See n. 13.

[8] Sixteenth-century biographies of Contarini are those by Giovanni della Casa and Lodovico Beccadelli. Both authors knew Contarini well, Beccadelli having been Contarini's secretary. Casa's life of Contarini was published as an introduction to Contarini, *Opera* (Paris, 1571); Beccadelli's biography of Contarini can be found in his *Monumenti di Varia Letteratura* (Bologna, 1799), vol. I, Pt. 2. For a survey of early writings on Contarini, see Dittrich, *Regesten*, pp. 1-7.

Contarini was very much aware of the obligations involved in being a member of his family and a Venetian patrician. Contarini's years of study in Padua ended in 1509, when the war of the League of Cambrai forced a closing of the university. Contarini returned to Venice with a high reputation as a philosopher, even though he had not yet published anything. That he had made a great impression among the intellectuals of Padua is indicated by the fact that the university's most brilliant and audacious teacher, Pomponazzi, dedicated a treatise to him.[9]

The war which forced Contarini's return to Venice brought about a serious crisis in his native city.[10] In a few weeks Venice lost her possessions on the *terra firma*, and, although the situation soon improved, the war continued and Venice could begin to feel safe only in 1515. Venetian nobles were deprived of remunerative administrative positions on the *terra firma*. The Venetian government was in desperate financial straits and had to take recourse to the imposition of new taxes and to forced loans; payments from the Monte ceased. For those able to pay, admission to the Great Council was eased. The Venetians who had prided themselves on their role as protagonists of Christianity against the Turks turned to the Sultan for help; and, in order to separate the Pope from the anti-Venetian alliance, they conceded their claims to be free from papal interference in ecclesiastical affairs.

This reversal of Venetian fortunes made an immense impression. To the Neapolitan Tristano Caracciolo, the unexpected collapse of the Venetian empire, of "this miracle of wisdom and strength," was a striking example of "God's providence" and demonstrated "that we ought never to cease to fear God."[11] To the Venetians themselves, their fall from the heights of power meant the destruction of a historical image which had grown slowly throughout the centuries: the image of Venice as a perfect political society, of the God-willed expansion of

---

[9] Pomponazzi's treatise *De reactione*, dated Bologna, 13 July 1515, was dedicated to Gasparo Contarini. The sentence about Contarini in this dedication runs as follows: "Verum cum te ab ineunte aetate fedissimam adulationem tam acriter detestari meminerim nihilque apud te antiquius aut sanctius aut magis venerandum esse cognoverim quam justitiam et veritatem ideo tuum judicium subire non dubitavi."

[10] For a survey of the situation, see Heinrich Kretschmayr, *Geschichte von Venedig* (Gotha, 1920), II, 395-448.

[11] Muratori, *Rerum Italicarum Scriptores*, new edn. (Bologna, 1934), XXII, 101 (". . . et prudentiae et virium miraculum . . .") and 103-104 (". . . ut nunquam timere Deum desistamus . . ."), from Caracciolo's "De Varietate Fortunae."

the Venetian empire, of the excellence of Venetian institutions that guaranteed internal stability and safety from external enemies.[12] The impact of this blow was the greater because in the previous decades Venetians had begun to question whether Venice was not defecting from its old, true traditions. Warnings had been uttered against over-indulgence in luxury and pleasure; and laws had been issued to stem the spread of corruption in government. To many Venetians this time of troubles appeared as divine punishment for the sin of surrender to worldly concerns.

When Contarini returned to Venice in 1509, he came in close contact with a group of young Venetian nobles who had felt repelled by the materialistic atmosphere of Venetian political and social life and had withdrawn to Murano and San Michele to contemplate in isolation the salvation of their souls. Like Contarini, they came from Venice's oldest and most distinguished patrician families: Giustiniani, Quirini, Canale. Paolo Canale had just begun to acquire literary fame when he suddenly decided to become a Camaldolese monk on San Michele; his early death strongly reinforced the belief his friends had in the vanity of worldly ambitions and aims. Tomaso Giustiniani, the strong-est personality in this circle, had traveled in 1507 to the Holy Land where he intended to remain as an eremite for the rest of his life. Be-fore leaving Venice he gave his villa on Murano to Quirini and other friends, stipulating that they remain unmarried. However, Giustiniani found conditions in Palestine unsuited to his plans to withdraw from the world, and, when Contarini came to Venice in 1509, Giustiniani was back in Murano. Shortly afterward, in December 1510, Giustiniani discovered in the mountain wilderness above Arezzo a Camaldolese monastery; here were the surroundings which he believed would per-mit him to lead the life of an eremite undisturbed by the troubles of the world. Nine months later Vincenzo Quirini followed Giustiniani to Camaldoli. Quirini's decision provoked tremendous excitement, be-cause shortly before he had been entrusted with important diplomatic tasks by the Venetian government and he seemed to stand at the be-ginning of a brilliant political career. Even as monks Giustiniani and Quirini kept in contact with their Venetian friends, and it is from Contarini's correspondence with Father Paolo and Father Pietro, as

---

[12] On the origin and the development of the Venetian "myth," see my article, "The Venetian Constitution in Florentine Political Thought," in *Renaissance Florence*, ed. Nicolai Rubinstein (London, 1968).

Giustiniani and Quirini were now called, that we can gain insight into Contarini's aims, intellectual interests, and spiritual struggles.[13]

Contarini never intended to follow the example of Giustiniani and Quirini and become a monk.[14] In the first letter which Contarini wrote to Giustiniani in Camaldoli, he stated: "I shall not say, lest I deceive

[13] Giustiniani and Quirini, and their relations to Contarini, have been treated in a number of important articles by Hubert Jedin: "Ein Turmerlebnis des jungen Contarini," *Historisches Jahrbuch*, LXX (1951), 115-130; "Vincenzo Quirini und Pietro Bembo," *Miscellanea Giovanni Mercati*, IV (Città del Vaticano, 1946), 407-424; and, most of all, "Contarini und Camaldoli," *Archivio Italiano per la Storia della Pietà*, II (1952), 53-117. In the last-mentioned article, Jedin published thirty letters of Contarini to Giustiniani and Quirini from the years 1511 to 1523; this important find has shed quite new light on Contarini's development. However, these letters must be read in connection with the letters of Giustiniani and Quirini to Contarini and other Venetian friends, published in *Annales Camaldulenses* (Venice, 1773), VIII, Appendix, 447-595. Important material on Giustiniani and Quirini is contained also in J. Schnitzer, *Peter Delfin, General des Camaldulenserordens* (Munich, 1926). After the completion of this manuscript the article by Innocenzo Cervelli, "Storiografia e problemi intorno alla vita religiosa e spirituale a Venezia nella prima metà del '500," *Studi Veneziani*, VIII, 1966 (Firenze, 1967), pp. 447-476, was published. Pp. 455-466 present a perceptive analysis of Contarini's relations to Giustiniani and Quirini.

[14] This is the point on which I differ from Jedin. Jedin starts from the assumption that Contarini had decided to become a monk and that he abandoned this plan only after, in a severe religious crisis, he had arrived at a "new" concept of the "justification through faith" which constituted an "innere Affinität" with Luther. Thus, according to Jedin, Contarini underwent a "conversion" which determined his entire life and in relation to which all other issues and problems were of secondary importance, almost irrelevant. It must be fully acknowledged that Jedin's discovery of Contarini's correspondence with Giustiniani and Quirini is of fundamental importance for an understanding of Contarini's thought. And it is very comprehensible that Jedin, who was interested chiefly in Contarini from the point of view of his contribution to church reform, tied the interpretation of his new material to the formula on "justification" to which Contarini agreed at the Diet of Ratisbon in 1541. Nevertheless, Jedin's assumption that Contarini intended to become a monk is erroneous. It cannot be reconciled with Contarini's repeated declaration that he was not suited to a monastic life. Although Contarini was certainly concerned with the problem of the salvation of his soul, this problem was integrated with the wider problem of the general relation between Christianity and secular activities. For this reason it is necessary to give in the following an analysis of the correspondence of Contarini with Giustiniani and Quirini even though Jedin, in his above-mentioned articles, "Ein Turmerlebnis" and "Contarini und Camaldoli," has outlined the contents of this exchange. Fine observations about the exchange between Contarini and Giustiniani can be found in the article by Heinz Mackensen, "Contarini's Theological Role at Ratisbon

you, that I am coming to keep you company. Such good thoughts are not in me."[15] There was no doubt in Contarini's mind that he was unsuited for life in a monastery, or as an eremite. He might sometimes regret that he would never achieve that peaceful and quiet life which his friends enjoyed; but he had no illusions that, in this respect, he was different from them.[16]

Contarini had ambivalent feelings toward those who withdrew from the world and concentrated exclusively on their own salvation. Contarini revealed these feelings when, after a few months in the hermitage, Quirini fell ill and had to go to Florence. For a while it seemed possible that Quirini might not return to Camaldoli, especially since his family found itself in financial difficulties. Contarini urged his friend to regard this illness as a sign from God and as an opportunity to reconsider his decision. The fulfillment of one's duties to one's family and to one's city, Contarini wrote to Quirini, were also sacred obligations. Giustiniani then reproached Contarini vehemently for attempting to divert Quirini from his religious calling, and Quirini did return to Camaldoli.[17] Yet Contarini stuck to his views: when, in 1514, Quirini hesitated to accept the Cardinal's hat offered him by Pope Leo X, Contarini, in order to persuade Quirini to submit to the Pope's wishes, used arguments very similar to those he had used a few years before. Quirini, he said, ought to examine whether it would not be egoism and self-love if he placed the concern for the salvation of his

---

in 1541," *Archiv für Reformationsgeschichte*, LI (1960), 36-56, but the author is too much influenced by Jedin's misleading point of departure. When I quote passages which Mackensen cited, I have sometimes used his English rendering.

[15] Contarini to Giustiniani, 1 Feb. 1511: ". . . Non dico però, aziò non ve inganate, de venir a farve compagnia: non è in mi sì boni pensieri. . . ." (Jedin, "Contarini und Camaldoli," p. 62). See also p. 65: ". . . io, a chi non è dato una minima parte di core a fare quello fate vui. . . ."

[16] Contarini to Giustiniani, Nov. 1515: "[on becoming 'frate'] A me non solum non dilecta ma genera horrore un tal pensiero. Nè a me per niente pare che una tal perfectione di viver convenga a la infermità et debellezza de l'animo mio." (*Ibid.*, p. 106.)

[17] See Contarini's letters to Quirini, 26 Dec. 1511 (*ibid.*, pp. 72-76, and *Annales Camaldulenses*, pp. 539-543); this second letter, written in Latin, is much sharper than the letter in Italian printed by Jedin. Jedin suggests that the letter in Latin was not sent. In Giustiniani's letter to Contarini and Niccolò Tiepolo in *Annales Camaldulenses*, pp. 544-550, Giustiniani called Contarini and Tiepolo, because of their attempt to dissuade Quirini from entering the order, "anticristi, satanani, istrumenti del Diavolo."

soul above service to others and work for the wellbeing of all Christianity.[18] In Contarini's view, man was a social being and withdrawal from the world was unnatural.[19]

This does not mean that Contarini condemned those who, like Giustiniani and Quirini, broke with the world. On the contrary, he admired them greatly; such men were higher human beings who were attempting to raise themselves above human limitations. However, this course was possible and permissible only for a select few.[20] It was not the appropriate road for the great majority of people. There was value, too, in remaining in the world and in the fulfillment of man's duty toward his neighbor. Contarini was not willing to say that one way of life was of intrinsically greater value than another: "Although the contemplative life is nobler than the active life, nevertheless the active life in which man helps others in their spiritual struggles has greater merits."[21]

The difference between Contarini and his Camaldolese friends should not be reduced, however, to the simple formula of the contrast between *vita activa* and *vita contemplativa*, between action and thought. The passage just quoted indicates that Contarini regarded the assistance which man could lend to others in their striving for spiritual perfection as the chief justification for remaining in the world. There is no reason to doubt that from his earliest years Contarini was a person of deep religiosity. But the crisis which the war of the League of Cambrai brought about in Venice, together with the intimacy which developed between him and the group around Giustiniani and Quirini, certainly served to place religious problems into the center of his thought. In discussions with Giustiniani and Quirini he arrived at the decision to devote himself, after the termination of his philosophical

[18] Contarini to Quirini, 13 June 1514 (Jedin, "Contarini und Camaldoli," 94-96).

[19] "Il viver solitario non è natural a l'homo, el quale la natura ha fato animal sociabile, ma bisogna che colui che vuol metersi a tal vita sia de una perfection excendente quasi la condition humana, tal che non cun li sensi ma solum cun lo intellecto viva" (*ibid.*, p. 73).

[20] "La vita de Religiosi, presertim de quelli Heremiti era una vita de homeni perfectissimi, a la qual perfection pochissimi pervengono . . ." (*ibid.*, p. 81).

[21] "Ben sapete melgio di me che, benchè la vita contemplativa sia più nobile de la activa, pur la vita activa, la qual versa nel' adiuvar el proximo ne la vita spiritual, è più meritoria" (*ibid.*, p. 69). This, of course, is a modification of a traditional formula.

studies, to the study of theology for the rest of his life.[22] Thus Contarini and his Camaldolese friends were agreed that concern for the salvation of one's soul ought to be man's supreme interest. But Contarini did not share the convictions of his friends that there was only one sure way to obtain salvation, namely, withdrawal from the world. Contarini believed it could be attained also by remaining within the world.[23]

In theological terms, the problem which faced Contarini was that of man's justification before God. The great issue which in later years was to be a stumbling block to Contarini's efforts to reconcile the Lutherans with the Church emerged early as a central theme in his religious thinking.

When, in 1511, Giustiniani wrote Contarini from Camaldoli that, despite "having left the world for the love of Christ and leading an ascetic life," he did not feel confident of his salvation, Contarini was deeply disturbed about what his own fate might be.[24] But he could also report to Giustiniani that in the Easter week, through the counsel of a wise priest, his worries and troubles had been lifted. He had realized that man could never expiate his sins by his own efforts. God had shown through the sacrifice of His Son that He was willing to proceed with charity toward man. What could be expected from man was only to meet God's forbearance with Faith, Hope, and Charity. "Now I shall sleep securely, although in the midst of the city, although I have not paid off the debt I had contracted, since I have such a Payer of my debt. Truly, I shall sleep and wake as securely as if I had spent all the time of my life in the hermitage, with the intention of never letting this support go.... Vivamus ergo laeti, ut ex hoc timore liberati, in laetitia serviamus illi omnibus diebus nostris."[27]

---

[22] "Et è venuto el tempo che, secundo lo antiquo mio desiderio, son per darme tuto a la Scritura Sacra . . ." (*ibid.*, p. 75).

[23] "Ma non essendo nè via de solitudine, nè via de Religion certa, ne etiam la vita civil certa di perditione, ma in tutte essendo modo di pervenir a salute et a perdition . . ." (*ibid.*, p. 70).

[24] Contarini to Giustiniani, 24 April 1511: "Tamen, da l'altra parte vedendo quel che vui ditte di buon core, che, dapoi lassato tuto el mondo per amor di Christo, et dapoi fati una vita così austera, non restati però di temer che i peccati vostri commessi per il passato non siano di tal sorte che non siate per farze conveniente penitentia in questo avanzo di la vostra vita, in el qual pensier et in el qual timor ve vedo assai continuato . . ." (*ibid.*, p. 63).

[25] "Non dormirò adonque io securo, benchè sia in mezo la città, benchè non

Yet this was not a problem which could be solved once and for all. A year later fears and anxieties again arose in Contarini's mind, this time even more intensely. He had completed his philosophical studies, and the time had come to turn to theology. But, he wrote, "I have begun to hate studying and what once was my delight, the reading of the Holy Bible, now fills me with ennui."[26] In this spiritual crisis, as in the one of the preceding year, Contarini arrived at the solution that man with his own forces is unable to work his salvation, that he must trust God's love that is proved by Christ's death. This trust in God's abundant love had now reinforced his conviction that man has the right to live in the world and for the world. God could never demand from man more than what is appropriate to the nature which God had given him. Contarini thought that he had deceived himself when formerly he had believed himself to be one of the elect who, by virtue of their intellectual gifts and the earnestness of their efforts, might be granted security and peace.[27] He was not, as he had formerly supposed, a man superior to others; on the contrary, he was one of the lowliest creatures. Nature had not fitted him to live the life of a religious, so he would spend his life in the world according to the status in which he had been placed by God. And because God had given him this place, this way of life would not separate him from God. He would keep up the hope that one day God might help him to arrive at a deeper understanding of divine wisdom and at a fuller realization of His peace. But this was only a remote hope. Contarini was aware that his life would be full of uncertainties: sometimes he might believe he could rise to heaven; sometimes he might feel himself to be

---

satisfaci al debito che ho contracto, havendo io tal pagatore del mio debito? Veramente dormirò et vegierò cusì securo come se tuto el tempo di la vita mia fosse stado ne l'Heremo, con proposito di non mi lassar mai da tal apozo." (From the same letter of 24 April 1511, *ibid.*, p. 64.)

[26] Contarini to Giustiniani and Quirini, 17 July 1512: "Me son venuti in odio li studii, et quella sol cosa che a l'altra volta mi ralegrava, cioè la lection de la Scriptura Sacra, hora me da grande molestia" (*ibid.*, p. 87).

[27] The above is a summary of Contarini's letter to Giustiniani, 20 April 1513 (*ibid.*, pp. 89-90). See esp. p. 89: "Hor cognosco che io son homo non solum separato dal vulgo, come io me credeva, immo, il più infimo del vulgo; et vivome in questa sorte di vita humile et bassa ... In questo mezzo viverò in questa humilità, sempre sperando." See also p. 97: "[God] dispone le cose nostre humane et le action de' diversi homeni a diversi gradi, de li quali algun sono altissimi, alguni mediocri, et algun bassi, le quali però tuti, quando che con animo humile sono acceptati, resultano et in bene di coloro che li acceptano et etiam in bene de l'universo. . . ."

as low as brute animals. Life in the world is a constant struggle. Contarini used the same image which others, concerned with the renewal of true Christianity, employed when they taught that man, whatever he did and wherever he was, could serve God. The life of a Christian is like that of a knight.[28]

Contarini's letters to Giustiniani and Quirini were written on an abstract and theoretical level. Contarini himself said that, in these letters, he did not want to discuss at length the "particular causes" which had shaped his views.[29] Nevertheless, Contarini did mention activities and used arguments which permit some insight into the more practical considerations and social pressures which influenced his thinking. Clearly, the duties a man owes to his family weighed heavily in Contarini's mind; and he was aware that abandoning a political career might be taken as a sign of despairing of the future of Venice.[30] Moreover, the correspondence testifies to the extent to which Contarini felt himself to be a member of a scholarly community. Besides the circle around Giustiniani and Quirini, he had many friends in intellectual life, particularly among the professors and humanists of Padua.[31]

Giustiniani and Quirini, although highly educated and sophisticated men fully cognizant of the intellectual trends of their time, regarded intellectual activities as basically futile. After Giustiniani had arrived in Camaldoli, he wrote his Venetian friends a long and detailed report about his voyage into the wilderness.[32] With evident satisfaction, Giustiniani mentioned that he had met a priest whose sermons had made little impact as long as he had occupied himself with modern theological writings and interpretations but whose preaching had become effective as soon as he had gone to the true sources, the Bible and the Church Fathers. Giustiniani's views emerge still more clearly in a letter which he wrote after the death of Marcantonio della Torre, a scholar

---

[28] Contarini to Giustiniani, 28 June 1515: "Io non so essere homo, ma, da uno certo fervore trasportato, vorrei in un momento ascendere sopra i cieli, nè molto dapoi cascho nel modo de' bruti animali, quasi disperando di consequire quello termine il quale me avevo io proposto ne l'animo. . . . Nui qui semo in via, et nostro officio è non cercare di havere la nostra quiete dequi, nè vivendo potere pertingere a quella la quale aspectiamo. . . ." (*Ibid.*, 102.) "La vita de l'huomo in terra è una continua militia" (p. 109).

[29] "Le cause particulare . . ." (*ibid.*, p. 89).

[30] See esp. the letter to Quirini, *Annales Camaldulenses*, pp. 539-543.

[31] Friends and scholars mentioned in these letters are: Trifone Gabriele, Giovanni Baptista Egnazio, Alberto Carpi, Niccolò Dolfin, Baptista della Torre.

[32] *Annales Camaldulenses*, pp. 467-496.

and a common friend of his and Contarini's. The scholarly works to which della Torre had devoted his life—"dialectical arguments, philosophical disputes, mathematics and medicine, Greek, Latin, and Tuscan"—would be of no use in heaven, where "without rational arguments one will know all truth."[33]

Contarini did not share Giustiniani's contempt for humanism and philosophy. Like many of his contemporaries, Contarini believed that a simple man could have insights which to the ordinary secular mind might appear foolish but which in reality were an expression of divine wisdom.[34] Contarini had reservations about the unlimited enthusiasm of many of his contemporaries for the classics. He was sure that a full understanding of the Bible and of the Church Fathers required acquaintance with the languages in which these works had been written. Knowledge of Hebrew, Greek, and Latin helped to foster a true Christian spirit. And the establishment of correct texts was a worthwhile and necessary undertaking.[35] But, whereas in the rest of Europe interest in classical studies came about simultaneously with interest in church reform, in Italy humanist studies had flowered long before religious reform became urgent. Thus, like Giustiniani and Quirini, Contarini regarded the passionate fascination of Italians with all aspects of the pagan world with distrust. The titillating eroticism of the classical poets seemed to him morally dangerous. Nevertheless—and here he deviated from Giustiniani and Quirini—his views about the value of pagan authors were ambiguous. Contarini's interest in ancient thought and classical studies was more pronounced than his correspondence with Giustiniani and Quirini suggests. Even these letters, however, give us some glimpse into his involvement in humanistic studies. They testify to his intimacy with Trifone Gabriele, the friend

---

[33] "Forse in quella celeste patria . . . bisognan dialettici argomenti, o filosofiche dispute, o matematiche discipline, o arte di medicina, forse o Greco, o Latino, o Tosco ivi si ragiona?" (*Annales Camaldulenses*, p. 552). See also Giustiniani's letter on the erroneously reported death of Egnazio (pp. 589-594). For a more detailed discussion of Giustiniani's and Quirini's intellectual development, see my article, "Cristianesimo, umanesimo e la bolla 'Apostolici Regiminis' del 1513," *Rivista Storica Italiana*, LXXIX (1967), 976-990, esp. 983-986.

[34] In the correspondence with Giustiniani, Contarini's views on this issue are reflected in a particular concern for the views of a recluse, living separate from the other Camaldolensians.

[35] "Leggo etiam quel de Republica di Platone, el qual hora è stato impresso ne la sua lingua. Ricevo utilità et da le cose da quel eccellente homo scripte et etiam de la lingua. . . ." (Jedin, "Contarini und Camaldoli, p. 93.)

of Bembo and the translator of Horace; and they show Contarini's interest in the progress of the work of his friend Egnazio, who wrote about the outstanding men of Venetian history in the pattern of Valerius Maximus.[36] In one letter Contarini described the great impression which Francesco da Diacceto, the Florentine Neo-Platonist philosopher, had made on him.[37] Contarini mentioned that immediately upon its publication he studied the Greek Plato edition which Aldus was publishing and frequently in these letters he expressed his immense admiration for Plato.[38] Contarini was convinced of the value of philosophical studies, and he justified this position against the opposition of Giustiniani and Quirini. He admitted that the pagan philosophers could not have known the highest truth; still, he argued, the knowledge which can be obtained by means of man's "natural light" is of value. For the "natural light" is "a great gift of God."[39] Philosophy has its function even if it does not lead to absolute wisdom.

Against the persuasions of Father Paolo and Father Piero, Gasparo maintained his right to remain in the world, to be a Contarini, a Venetian patrician, a humanist and a philosopher—that emerges from an analysis of Contarini's correspondence with his Camaldolese friends. Yet the fundamental religious problem in which he became involved through his friendship with Giustiniani and Quirini left a sharp imprint on his mind; from then on, life assumed a new aspect for him. He had become deeply convinced that all secular activities had to be placed in a Christian framework and that social life had to be ordered in such a way that man would be ready to receive what only God could give—the salvation of man's soul.

## I I

After arriving at some settlement of his spiritual crisis, Contarini felt free to devote himself to politics and literary work. In 1515 Contarini was for the first time a candidate for public office; in February 1518 he was elected to his first government position, the beginning of a brilliant career in the service of the Venetian republic. It was also in

---

[36] Egnazio's work is mentioned *ibid.*, p. 78. It was published, under the title *De exemplis Illustrium virorum Venetae civitatis atque aliarum gentium*, in 1554.

[37] See Contarini's letters to Giustiniani of 30 May and 9 June 1515; in the latter, see the joking remark: "Non più venetiano ma thoscano mi posso senza dubio chiamare" (*ibid.*, p. 101).

[38] See above, n. 36.

[39] ". . . di quella moralità, la qual li philosophi hanno visto con el lume naturale, el qual è etiam dono grande di Dio, mi debba contentare . . ." (*ibid.*, p. 77).

1515 that Contarini embarked upon a period of intense literary productivity. His book against Pomponazzi's treatise *De immortalitate animae* and a work entitled *De officio episcopi* were completed in 1516 and 1517. A second book against Pomponazzi followed in 1518. Then, between 1522 and 1526, during his diplomatic mission to Charles V, Contarini composed his chief philosophical study, the *Compendium primae philosophiae*, as well as the main sections of his treatise *De magistratibus et republica Venetorum*. The *Compendium* was corrected and revised in 1526/27, and the book on Venice was completed only after 1531.[40] Nevertheless, in their basic features, all his more important and extended works were written or conceived and drafted in the decade between 1516 and 1526.

Because these works originated close to each other, it is not astonishing that their ideas are interrelated.[41] Contarini frequently referred from one to the other; indeed, they represent the application of the same general system of thought to different aspects of life and nature. Moreover, one can also observe that the ideas at which he had arrived in the course of his exchange with Giustiniani and Quirini were basic elements of his philosophical writings.

Contarini was not a thinker of great originality. He explained his methods in his chief philosophical work, the *Compendium primae philosophiae*. He presented what he had learned about a particular problem from the study of other authors and then added the results of his own reflections.[42] Contarini was a slow and careful reader. But he had a prodigious memory, so that he was able to reproduce the statements of other authors almost word for word. He was eclectic, too, and referred in his writings to a large number of philosophical authors: Aristotle, St. Augustine, St. Thomas, Plato, Plotinus, Themistius, Duns Scotus, Averroes, Avicenna, Dionysius Areopagita. The indiscriminate manner in which he cited the most diverse authors provides no secure basis for establishing the particular philosophical school to which he belonged. It is evident, however, that Contarini's philo-

[40] For the date of the composition of Contarini's treatise on Venice, see my article, "The Date of the Composition of Contarini's and Giannotti's Books on Venice," *Studies in the Renaissance*, XIV (1967), 172-184. I shall quote Contarini's works from their first edition in Contarini, *Opera* (Paris, 1571); I shall give the titles of the various works, but the page indications will refer to this volume, in which they were collected.

[41] In *Compendium*, p. 170, Contarini refers to his writing against Pomponazzi; in *De elementis*, p. 8, to the *Compendium*.

[42] *Compendium*, p. 95. See also Beccadelli's "Vita," *Monumenti*, pp. 41-46.

sophical point of departure was Aristotelian, as was appropriate for one who had studied in Padua. But Contarini was also a careful student of Plato and Neo-Platonism, and he was inclined to tie the phenomena described by Aristotle into an interconnected structure emanating from a spiritual center. On purely theological issues this approach was comparable with the views of St. Thomas, whose authority Contarini regarded as supreme. But in its more general aspects Contarini's philosophical thought was similar in many respects to that of Avicenna, with whom he agreed on particular problems, like the role of imagination or the influence of celestial bodies. Hence, there is reason for characterizing him as an Avicennist Aristotelian.[43]

Contarini's first and, in his own lifetime, most widely circulated work was his polemical treatise against Pomponazzi's *De immortalitate animae*.[44] Contarini differed from Pomponazzi on two basic points: the relation of faith to reason and the connection between the spiritual and the material world.

Pomponazzi's treatise had raised fundamental questions about the relation between faith and reason because, in Pomponazzi's opinion, it was impossible to provide valid proof of the immortality of the soul on the basis of rational argument. However, the immortality of the soul as a doctrine of the Church had to be accepted by faith. Contarini argued against this separation of faith and reason. On the one hand, such separation seemed to him conducive to overestimating the power of reason. Man might be inclined to believe that "the natural light must suffice him in everything" and that what could not be explained by reason did not exist. "We believe that this is a very dangerous philosophy which might instill in man's mind the pestilential and harm-

[43] This is the view of Carlo Giacon, "L'Aristotelismo Avicennistico di Gaspare Contarini," *Atti del XII Congresso Internazionale di Filosofia, IX* (Firenze, 1960), 109-119, and my reading of Contarini is along the same lines. Rueckert, *Die Entwicklung Contarinis*, overestimates the influence of Aquinas because he limits himself to a consideration of Contarini's late theological works, in which Contarini consciously tried to emphasize the connection of his views with those of Aquinas; but, actually, the philosophical basis of Contarini's views is much broader. It might be mentioned that, just at the time when Contarini was studying at Padua, Avicenna's works were printed in Venice.

[44] On Pomponazzi, in general, see John Herman Randall, *The School of Padua* (Padova, 1961), pp. 69-115, and Paul Oskar Kristeller, *Eight Philosophers of the Italian Renaissance* (Stanford, 1964), pp. 72-90 (with bibliography). For a survey of the dispute aroused by Pomponazzi's thesis on the immortality of the soul, see Etienne Gilson, "Autour de Pomponazzi," *Archives d'Histoire Doctrinale et Littéraire du Moyen Age*, vol. XXVIII (1961).

ful poison of unbelief and impiety."[45] On the other hand, Pomponazzi's thesis about the relation of faith to reason seemed to Contarini to devalue reason. Reason is a gift of God. Thus, the "natural light" of reason cannot be contrary to the supranatural light; it is only less perfect.[46] In his *Compendium primae philosophiae* Contarini gave these ideas about the value of reason a still more positive form. Reason provides the criterion through which man can avoid the traps of speculative fantasies; in purifying man's mind from depraved emotions, reason prepares him for entering the realm of the divine, because—and here Contarini quoted Plato—"the impure cannot touch the pure."[47] Nevertheless, "human intellect by its nature cannot go beyond certain limits in providing knowledge."[48] Reason leads to God but cannot reveal anything about the divine world. Reason can show that man's soul is immortal, but it cannot show what happens to the soul after man's death.

In Contarini's views about the character and the role of reason his differences with Pomponazzi about the connection between the spiritual and material world are implicit. Pomponazzi maintained that the functioning of man's intellect is dependent on sensory perceptions which man, as part of the material world, receives from it. Thus, the end of man's bodily existence implies the end of his spiritual life, at least according to rational considerations. For Contarini, the relation is the reverse. The spiritual world is independent of the material world, and the phenomena of the material world assume shape and distinctive character only when and insofar as they are permeated by the spiritual world. The spiritual world gives form to matter.[49] In the

[45] "Hocque putamus esse vere philosophari, hancque philosophiam quae suum nescit defectum, perfectionem animi esse censemus. Illam vero quae putat lumen naturale sibi debere in omnibus sufficere, negatque scientiam eius inchoatam quia nequit pertingere ad perfectam: putamus nos esse philosophiam admodum periculosam et quae instillare animo possit pestiferum et nocivum infidelitatis impietatisque venenum." (*De immortalitate animae*, p. 231.)

[46] ". . . lumen supernaturale non esse contrarium lumini naturali . . ." (*ibid.*, p. 229). See also p. 194.

[47] "Non tamen quivis eius supremae scientiae erit auditor idoneus, neque mentis aciem poterit fingere in tam immensa luce: nisi prius caeteris scientiis fuerit imbutus atque pravis purgatur affectibus. Nam impuro purum tangere non licet, ut inquit Plato." (*Compendium*, p. 99).

[48] "Ea enim est natura intellectus humani, ut certos terminos in cognitione rerum non egrediatur" (*ibid.*, p. 157).

[49] "Formae materiales sint mortales. Formae vero immateriales sunt immortales et incorruptibiles." (*De immortalitate animae*, p. 185).

104

context of the problem of the immortality of the soul, this means that every human represents a convergence of spiritual and material factors and that the spiritual factors do not necessarily disappear when the body dies. Again, these ideas are developed at greater length and more systematically in Contarini's *Compendium primae philosophiae*. There he stated that "nothing among the things of this world is of simple substance but everything consists of two parts, one form, one matter. Form gives to everything its aim and its particular nature."[50] Contarini saw the universe as a great hierarchy, and the *Compendium* gives an outline of Contarini's views on the order of the universe. The source of all spiritual forces is God, the pure spirit; below Him are those beings that have a primarily spiritual nature, like the angels; next come the celestial bodies and then the human beings, which exist at the place where spiritual forces and material factors are in balance; and finally, below man come those bodies which are weighted toward matter: animals, plants, metals, the elements. Clearly, this is a strictly graduated hierarchical structure.[51] The feeling that an ordered world meant a hierarchically organized world was extremely strong in Contarini and permeated his entire thinking. In discussing in his book *De officio episcopi* the support which ought to be given to the poor, he emphasized that poor members of the nobility ought to be assisted before all others.[52] Nevertheless, because every being and every thing receives its particular existence from the imprint of an ideal form on matter, not only is each being placed in relation to higher and lower things but each has its own particular function: to divest itself as far as possible of matter and to realize its own ideal form, to reach perfection.[53] Full perfection is not obtainable for beings and things of this world because, as long as they exist in the world, they remain bound to matter. But striving toward perfection is possible for everyone because the world is God's creation and an outflow of His spirit. "All nature, whatever it may be, is good and can never abandon the appetite for

[50] "Nulla in rebus hisce, quae infra limam agitantur, substantia simplex est, sed omnis ex duabus partibus constat, quarum alteram dicimus formam, alteram vero materiam: forma actus, perfectio, ac propria uniuscuiusque rei natura est" (*Compendium*, p. 169).

[51] *Ibid.*, p. 171.

[52] "Omnibus vero in hoc officio anteferendi sunt illi, quibus nobili genere ortis paupertas ignominiae essere solet neque mercenarias artes exercere sine calumnia querunt" (*De officio episcopi*, p. 430).

[53] *Compendium*, p. 123.

good."[54] Evil is not a force by itself but something negative—inability to overcome matter.

This entire system comes sharply into focus in Contarini's attitude toward the problem of the relation between *vita activa* and *vita contemplativa*. "Nobody can doubt or fail to comprehend that the contemplative life must be preferred to practical and active work."[55] Contemplation seeks a vision of the divine world. Yet the achievement of a direct contact with God is not a question of knowledge: a simple good man can come nearer to God than a learned man. In any case, closeness to God is possible only for a select few, and even they can never arrive at complete knowledge of God. "For such secrets, words and concepts fail and they must be venerated in holy silence."[56] Because man remains bound to matter, a full entering into the spiritual world is not possible for him. Contarini formulated this view most strongly in a small treatise which was directly devoted to the question whether "the speculative sciences are nobler and more perfect than the moral virtues."[57] Abstractly Contarini felt that science stands above moral virtue because action must be directed and intellect gives the direction. But, if man cannot have both, then he should choose moral virtue. "Moral virtue and active life is appropriate to man. The contemplative life is beyond man."[58] This view of the relation between contemplative and active life is entirely consonant with the concept of a graduated hierarchy which dominated Contarini's ideas about the universe. "Before man can obtain full perfection he must reach an imperfect one."[59] It is not possible to leave the level of existence into which things have been placed and to leap into a higher or different level. Thus, Contarini rejected the possibility of arriving at truth

[54] "Omnem naturam, quatenus esse habet, bonam esse, neque omnino ab appetitu boni recedere posse: quamvis fortasse a potiori bono ad inferius retrocedat, fieri tamen nequit, ut omnino ab appetitu boni destituatur neve ipsa quodpiam bonum non sit . . . huic respondemus malum non esse in rebus veluti naturam, sed tamquam privationem quandam . . ." (*ibid.*, p. 127).

[55] "Nulli namque dubium aut incompertum esse potest, quin contemplativae disciplinae factivis artibus atque activis sint praeferendae" (*ibid.*, p. 98).

[56] "Arcanum namque ipsius, cum verba ac capitationes deficiant, sacro silentio est venerandum" (*ibid.*, 142).

[57] "Quali sono più nobili e perfette: le scientie speculative over le virtù morali?" *Quattro Lettere di Monsig. Gasparo Contarino* (Firenze, 1558).

[58] "La virtù morale e la vita attiva è propria all'huomo, la contemplativa sopra l'huomo" (*ibid.*, p. 38).

[59] ". . . priusquam absolutam obtineat, obtinere inchoatam . . ." (*De officio episcopi*, p. 410).

through magic and astronomy, because those who practice these arts believe or pretend that they have direct contact with purely spiritual beings, like demons, to which man, by his nature, simply cannot have any access.[60] Nevertheless, Contarini's emphasis on the value of the *vita activa* was not merely the result of theoretical considerations; it had an undertone of emotion and was the result of personal experience. For Contarini, pure thinking, pure contemplation, was something cold and dead. For instance, he mentioned that a statue by Praxiteles may be perfectly beautiful but remains unsatisfactory because it lacks the warmth of life.[61] Or, he said that friends have served him as "living books," that he has learned more from them than from the study of what has been written or printed.[62] It was possible for Contarini to consider his personal inclination toward the *vita activa* as philosophically justifiable and justified because love has a central place in his theoretical system and love must express itself in actions toward fellow men. Because God forms the source from which the spiritual forces flow out to imprint their form on the material world, all that exists has an innate tendency toward the good. This means that "the foremost and primary motive power of man's rational will is love because good and love are connected. Good is the object of love."[63] But, for anyone who is inspired by love for the good, it would be contradictory to look down upon others and to reserve the good for himself. On the contrary, he would want to impart good to all who are receptive, for, by the good and through the love which he imparts, he will awaken a response and arouse a desire for perfection and for the good in those who are lacking in love. Theoretical speculations and moral philosophy were inextricably tied together in Contarini's philosophical system.

Thus, for Contarini, the treatment of problems of the social order was combined with philosophical discussion, and, vice versa, philosophical discussion issued frequently into consideration of social and

---

[60] *Ibid.*, p. 424.

[61] *Ibid.*, p. 411.

[62] ". . . multa namque plerumque ab amicis, veluti ex vivis libris decerpimus" (*ibid.*, p. 420).

[63] "Superiores vero vicissim amant inferiores et suae bonitatis ratione ac naturae. Appetitus vero huius primus motus ac praecipuus est amor, cuius objectum est bonum. Non enim est boni invidere, ac intra se bona sua continere sed effundere ac effluere. Nam intellectum quemcumque sequitur intellectualis appetitus, qui in ratione est et a philosophis voluntas nominatur." (*Compendium*, p. 163).

political problems. This point is clearly illustrated by Contarini's early work *De officio episcopi*.[64] Only its last part provides what a book with such a title can be expected to contain. There Contarini inveighed against the luxury of the princes of the church, the frequent absences of bishops from their diocese, the use of churches for business negotiations or political discussions, the superstitious veneration of *reliquiae* and the exaggerated adornment of chapels; he urged a bishop to have a simple but dignified household, to study Christian and not profane authors, to preach, to take a personal interest in the moral wellbeing of the people of his diocese, and to use his income for the support of the poor. Thus, like many of his most distinguished contemporaries, Contarini demanded a reform of the Church, and his ideas are close to those which his friends Giustiniani and Quirini formulated in the *Libellus ad Leonem X*,[65] which has been called "the most comprehensive and most radical of all reform programs since the conciliar period."[66] It seems likely that Contarini knew this work of his Camaldolese friends. He certainly discussed its ideas with them.

Contarini's outline of the functions of a bishop is preceded by a discussion of the personal qualities which a bishop ought to possess. And this part, in turn, is preceded by a section which places the entire problem in a philosophical context. Contarini began by emphasizing that, although perfection cannot be reached by man, the striving for perfection is implied in man's rational nature. On certain levels of human existence this struggle for perfection can be conducted with man's natural faculties. On a higher level this striving requires divine assistance. The goal to which man aims with his innate forces is less worthy than that for which he struggles with God's help. Yet the striving for perfection on the lower level represents the necessary preparation for the striving for perfection on the higher level. The application of these theoretical statements to the concrete issue with which Contarini was concerned is that man lives in two societies: in a political organization and in a Christian world, the latter being ranked above the former. These societies must be organized in such a way that they are directed toward perfection, that they permit an approach to the realization of

[64] See Hubert Jedin, "Das Bischofsideal der Katholischen Reformation," *Kirche des Glaubens: Kirche der Geschichte*, II (Freiburg, 1966), 84-86.

[65] Printed in *Annales Camaldulenses* (Venice, 1773), IX, 613-719. For an early testimony of Contarini's interest in church reform, see my article "Contarini on Savonarola: An Unknown Document of 1516," *Archiv für Reformationsgeschichte*, LIX (1968).

[66] Hubert Jedin, *Geschichte des Konzils von Trient* (Freiburg, 1951), I, 103

the ideal by which they were formed. According to Contarini, it is inherent in the concept of society that it has both rulers and those who are ruled. A society must be organized in such a way that it places the right ruler in control. And the ruler himself must possess qualities which make him fit to rule. He must have an image of the idea toward which the life of society ought to be directed, and his own conduct must provide an example of a life directed toward this perfection.[67] Thus, in accordance with his idea of establishing the ruler not only as the organizer of society but also as a pattern for the moral conduct of its members, Contarini embarked on a long discussion of the qualities demanded of a bishop. It was in accordance, also, with his view of a graduated hierarchy, in which the Christian society stands on the base of the political society, that he discussed first the virtues required of a member of political society and then the particular Christian virtues a bishop needs. "Someone might object that so far we seem to describe a citizen rather than a bishop. Our answer is that a bishop should not lack in the moral and social virtues although they do not belong to him alone but also to others. They are the foundations; without them those which are peculiar to a bishop and properly his would necessarily collapse."[68]

This somewhat more extended discussion of *De officio episcopi* seems appropriate because this book discloses some fundamental ideas of Contarini's thinking. Despite the evidently eclectic character of his philosophy, it was permeated by one assumption which was very much his own and which represented a result of his exchange of ideas with Giustiniani and Quirini. This assumption was that behind every existence and every status there is an idea which is an outgrowth of the divine spirit and which man, by his own innate goodness, is drawn to realize. Thus, every activity, if it is moving in the direction of perfection, is hallowed. Furthermore, Contarini saw a close connection between political organization and the Church. The political society may stand lower than the Christian community in the universal hier-

[67] "Postremo, ut inquit Plato, praefectus civitatis talem in urbe institutionem facit, qualem prius in animi sui Republicae gesserat" (*De officio episcopi*, p. 402).

[68] "Reprehendet aliquis fortasse diligentiam hac in parte nostram quod potius civilem virum, quam Episcopum erudire videar. Cui responsum velim, morales ac civiles virtutes, quamvis non ita episcopi sint, ut aliis quoque non conveniant, quemadmodum nonnullae aliae, de quibus infra dicturi sumus non tamen ab episcopo putandum est alienas esse quin potius fundamenta sunt quaedam, quibus sublatis, caeterae quoque Episcopo peculiares et propriae ruant necesse est." (*Ibid.*, p. 406).

archy; nevertheless, the right political organization is the necessary basis on which to prepare for the development of the life of the Church. This interconnection is strikingly formulated in a sentence of *De officio episcopi* dealing with heresy: "It removes not only the foundations of faith but it also undermines the foundation of any government."[69]

## III

We can now turn to Contarini's *De magistratibus et republica Venetorum*.[70] It should be clear that Contarini's interest in politics was inseparable from his philosophical and religious concerns; the problems of social organization formed an integral and essential part of his philosophical system. Politics was, for him, a subordinate branch of philosophy and, as such, had a moral purpose: to teach how man's virtues could be developed in society and through society. Contarini's book on Venice was intended to demonstrate the importance of a right social order for man's striving toward a higher life. This basic theme is clearly stated in the first book of the work. Man, Contarini explained, is a social being and must live together with others for material reasons. But, because men need each others' help and assistance, their living together serves also to develop their innate inclination toward the good. Thus, from the outset the purpose of social life is not only to secure man's material existence but to lead him to a good and blissful life.

This view of the nature and aim of political organization gives to Venice its particular importance. People admire Venice because of its wealth and the splendor of its houses, because of its situation, which provides security from external enemies, because of the extension of its empire, because of its commercial importance, which brings into

[69] "Nulla enim capitalior pestis, nec quae facilius atheismo fenestram patefaciat quam haeresis est, quae fundamenta fidei cum tollat, etiam omnem Reipublicae statum subito evertit" (*ibid.*, p. 425).

[70] The one modern study devoted exclusively to Contarini's treatise on Venice is the book by Hackert already cited (n. 3). The author provides a useful survey of Venetian political institutions at the beginning of the sixteenth century, but, since he does not recognize the consciously idealizing tendency of Contarini's treatise, he accuses Contarini of hypocrisy; in short, Hackert misses the point of Contarini's treatise. Cogent remarks on the idealizing character of Contarini's treatise can be found in Fink, *Classical Republicans*, pp. 39-40. It is interesting that the first French translation of Contarini's work, published in Lyon in 1557, bears the title: *La police et gouvernement de Venise, exemplaire pour le jourd'hui à toutes autres. . . .*

the city peoples and goods from all corners of the world. Contarini was enough of a Venetian patriot to admit that these facets of Venetian life were marvelous. Nevertheless, he stated, these were not the things for which Venice ought to be admired: "There is one more thing in this city which far exceeds all those things we have spoken of. That is not only my opinion but also the opinion of all those who do not believe that a city is walls and houses only, but think that a city is primarily constituted by the assemblage and the order of the people who live in it and deserves the name of a republic only if its aim and organization enables man to lead a blissful life."[71] "No state has existed which possesses institutions and laws equally apt to lead to a good and blissful life."[72] The Venetian constitution is better suited to approach a realization of the moral purpose of political society than any other. That is why, Contarini believed, Venice needed to be studied and to become better known.

Contarini was proud of the excellence of the Venetian institutions; with the knowledge with which his position as a Venetian noble and his experiences as a Venetian politician had equipped him, he was able to describe with precision and in detail the political procedures in Venice which for many decades had aroused astonishment and admiration in the minds of foreigners. Although some reports of the manner in which a doge was elected or the Venetian councils deliberated had been provided in previous writings,[73] Contarini's account of these transactions was far superior to anything written previously. This disclosure of the arcana of Venetian politics constituted the chief attraction of Contarini's book in subsequent centuries. However, Contarini was not only better informed than previous writers; his basic approach was different. In earlier discussions of the Venetian form of government, the thesis that Venice was an ideal state had been mainly a label that justified the attention given to this subject. In Contarini's mind, on the other hand, the idea of what a republic was or ought to be was primary, and a description of the working of Venetian politics

[71] "Verum aliud quiddam est in hac civitate, quod longe omnium praestantissimum censuerim ego; mecumque omnes qui civitatem non tantum moenia et domos esse putant, sed existimant civium conventum et ordinem potissimum hoc sibi nomen vendicare: reipublicae scilicet ratio et forma, ex qua beata vita hominibus contingit" (*De Magistratibus et Republica Venetorum*, Bk. I, in Contarini, *Opera*, p. 263).

[72] ". . . nulla tamen fuit, quae institutione ac legibus ad bene beateque vivendum idoneis, cum hac nostra conferri potest . . ." (*ibid.*).

[73] See my article, mentioned above, n. 12.

111

seemed to him a worthy undertaking because—and insofar as—it approached this idea.

Contarini's attempt to place Venetian politics *sub specie* of a permanent, divinely inspired idea determined the distinctive character of this work and goes far to explain its weaknesses and its strength. His treatise is an idealization because it emphasizes only those aspects of Venetian political life which help to explain how governments can lead people to perfection. War and power politics are almost entirely omitted. Venice undertook military action only when it was attacked, and even then its citizens avoided bearing arms.[74] These aspects of politics must be minimized because nothing can be gained for the moral purposes of society by involvement in war. The need to eliminate force in relations between states was Contarini's deepest conviction. In all his diplomatic missions he pursued constantly and tenaciously the aim of the establishment of peace among the Christian powers. And it was his good fortune that in the times of his political service this aim coincided with the interests of the Venetian government.[75]

But the internal organization of Venice, also, was presented by Contarini as having come about from wise deliberation and general agreement rather than from clashes and conflicts among the groups of society. For instance, annals and histories of Venice available to Contarini[76] offered enough material to show clearly that the Great Council was the product of conflicts arising from efforts to limit the power of the dukes and to secure control for a wealthy aristocracy. For Contarini, however, the Great Council owed its origin to prudent discussions and harmonious agreements among the citizens about the best government. This was the manner in which Contarini thought that men ought to proceed in forming a political organization. His treatise was intended to show how men ought to act in politics rather than how they did act. Like so many political treatises of his time, it was a normative treatment. Yet this approach constituted its strength. Because, in Contarini's view, social life was meant to serve man's development toward the spiritual world, his point of departure was a concern for the welfare of all human beings living together in a community rather than the efficiency of that community's institutions. His view

---

[74] ". . . respuit communis hominum sensus, officia bellica, quibus caedes ac mortalium detrimenta inprimis procurantur . . ." (*De magistratibus*, p. 264).

[75] Contarini's role in the conclusion of the Peace in Bologna in 1529 was usually regarded as his greatest political contribution.

[76] He mentions, e.g., Bernardo Giustiniani's *De origine urbis Venetiarum*, which is a much more realistic work. See below, n. 77.

extended beyond the discussion of government machinery and of prescriptions for the behavior of rulers to embrace the entire body of society. For instance, he included in his discussion of Venice the organization of the fraternities and guilds of the craftsmen and artisans, who, from a political point of view, were ruled and not rulers; mention of them was usually omitted from writings on politics. In focusing on those elements which were related to a philosophical concept of society, he presented Venice as an idea rather than a concrete reality. Probably it was just this aspect of the treatise which obtained for it a significant place in the political thought of the following centuries.

Although a close connection existed between Contarini's treatise on Venice and his philosophical and religious thought, one still may ask whether there was a particular occasion which stimulated him to take up this subject.

At the end of the fifteenth century Bernardo Giustiniani, an old Venetian noble who had had a distinguished political career, composed a Life of San Marco.[77] At the beginning of this work Giustiniani explained that he was led to the undertaking because the saint seemed to have become almost forgotten; many, to Giustiniani's horror, did not seem to know any longer where he was buried and what Venice owed to its patron saint.[78] Giustiniani was deeply concerned that the new intellectual interests and activities of the time were corroding the old beliefs, customs, and traditions which had made Venice great. Giustiniani's concern was the more striking because he had been a prominent patron of humanists.

The defeat which Venice suffered in its war against the League of Cambrai intensified the doubts of those who feared that the Venetians, seduced by new philosophies and greater material prosperity, had deviated from the ideals of their ancestors and lost their old virtues. In these years Egnazio, a Venetian scholar, began to write a book in which he compared the great figures of Venetian history with those of the ancient world and tried to demonstrate that the heroes of Venetian history had cultivated the same simple virtues which the great men of

[77] Bernardi Justiniani (Bernardo Giustiniani), *De Divi Marci Evangelistae Vita, translatione, et sepulturae loco*, was printed as an appendix to Giustiniani's *De origine* . . . at Leyden in 1725. Bernardo Giustiniani was no close relation to Tomaso Giustiniani.

[78] "Quod agendum illa etiam res me non mediocriter commovebat, qui isse in oblivionem mihi sanctus videbatur. Ut plerique de nostris etiam (quod nefas dictu existimabam) dubitarent, an corpus illud sanctissimum, nunc etiam in templo sibi dicato situm perseveraret. Eam rem ex memoria pene omnium excidisse, non potui non aegre ferre." (*Ibid.*, p. 171.)

the ancient world had possessed. It is interesting that Egnazio referred to Bernardo Giustiniani as an example which everyone should hold before himself "like an oracle."[79] Clearly, Egnazio's book was intended to be an appeal to return to the old virtues and customs of Venetian life. Egnazio was a close friend of Contarini's;[80] Contarini's treatise on Venice also belongs within this context—hope that Venice could be saved by returning to its traditions. Like the Church, which needed renewal through a return to the spirit of its beginnings, Venice too needed reform by means of a return to the ideas expressed in the myth of its past.

But was there still another and more particular stimulus for the composition of this work on Venice? There is an incident in Contarini's life which raises an intriguing question. He began to write his treatise on the Venetian government during his diplomatic mission to Charles V. In the beginning of his work Contarini mentioned that information about Venice ought to be particularly welcome to foreigners who had no opportunity of knowing about the excellent and almost perfect political order which Venice had achieved.[81] Certainly, Contarini must have met on this mission many foreigners who, Contarini might have thought, were in need of information about Venice. Yet among them there was one whose lack of knowledge he might have particularly regretted. In Bruges, on 18 August 1521, he invited for dinner "a very learned English gentleman named Master Thomas More."[82] This characterization suggests that Contarini was well aware

[79] "Ille enim Graecis, latinisque literis instructissimus variis amplisque magistratibus et legationibus a repub. ornatus, sic ab omnibus excipiebatur, ut numen quoddam in homine latere crederetur. Quare et procurator creatus, tanta bonitate humanitateque in omnes usus est, ut adhuc exemplum illius veluti oraculum, ab omnibus preferatur: scripsit ille summa diligentia et fide Venetas res pluribus libris, quos ut proposuerat ad suam usque aetatem absolvere non potuit. Scripsit etiam de divi Marci corpore Venetias translato libros duos. . . ." (Joannis Baptistae Egnatii, *De exemplis Illustrium Virorum Venetae civitatis atque aliarum gentium* [Venice, 1554], p. 70.)

[80] See above, n. 37.

[81] "Quam ob rem putavi ego exteris hominibus rem minime ingratum atque inutilem me facturum, si tam praeclarae Reipublicae institutionem literis mandarem, quem praesertim nullum his temporibus videam ex quamplurimis doctissimis viris, qui multum ingenio, eruditione rerum omnium, ac eloquentia valent, hanc rem literis illustravisse . . ." (*De magistratibus*, p. 264).

[82] *Calendar of State Papers*, ed. Rawdon Brown, III (London, 1869), p. 163. More and Contarini must have met again in London the same year when More, on behalf of the City of London, welcomed Charles V in whose suite Contarini

of the intellectual importance of his English guest. E. H. Harbison has described More as "a deeply devoted Christian and a scholar in all his instincts, but one who was called early to a busy and exhausting career as a lawyer and public official. The strong streak of Christian piety in him almost led him to become a Carthusian monk."[83] It would not be wrong to describe Contarini in almost the same way. One cannot help wondering whether Contarini's meeting with a man of such similar sympathies might not have stimulated the Venetian to the writing of a work which could show that, in order to find a place which can lead its citizens to a good and happy life, one need not travel as far as Utopia.


The biographies of Contarini which were written soon after his death[84] have somewhat the character of hagiography. They show him dying like a martyr, crushed by the burdens of his religious duties. And these writings have played their role in creating the view that only in the last period of his existence, in the years of his cardinalate, had Contarini arrived at the appropriate setting for his life. His previous political activities seemed of subordinate interest, a side issue rather than a central factor in his life. But there are some other contemporary portraits of Contarini composed when he had just been made a Cardinal.[85] They appear to give the picture of a very different person, a man involved in every worthwhile concern of his time: a philosopher, a scholar, a political thinker, a successful diplomat, and a devoted servant

---

had come to England. It is strange that no attention seems ever to have been given to the encounter between More and Contarini.

[83] E. H. Harbison, *Christianity and History* (Princeton, 1964), p. 228.

[84] See above, n. 8.

[85] Victor Trincarellus, in the dedication of his edition of Themistius's *Opera omnia* (Aldus, 1533) to Contarini, emphasizes that Contarini was a combination of statesman and philosopher. Michaeli Baroccii's "Oratio in laudem Gaspari Contareni" (never printed, in *Biblioteca Correr*, MS. Cic. 2903), though written after Contarini's appointment as Cardinal, praises chiefly his political efforts for peace and his patriotism, reflected in his book on Venice. In Joannis Pieri Valeriani Bellunenis's dialogue, *Contarenus seu de Literatorum infelicitate*, Contarini is a main speaker and appears chiefly as a humanist and diplomat of peace. Contarini is a speaker in Sperone Speroni's dialogue "Della vita attiva et contemplativa" (*Dialoghi* [Venice, 1596], I, 184), but I cannot find that the views which Speroni puts in Contarini's mouth have much to do with his real opinions.

of his republic, highly respected and admired because of the selfless-ness with which he strove in all these activities for the realization of the common good. These characterizations suggest, more correctly than the later biographies, that Contarini possessed a view of life which saw fulfillment "in the midst of the city." If Contarini is seen in this way, the famous scene of 21 May 1534 in the Venetian Great Council[86] gains full poignancy: the message was brought of Contarini's appoint-ment to the cardinalate; most members applauded, old Alvise Mocenigo fiercely shouted, "These priests have robbed us of the best gentleman this city has," and Contarini himself, stunned and uncom-prehending, could say only, "Why Cardinal? I am a councillor of the government of Venice."

[86] The most detailed report is that by Beccadelli: ". . . Che Cardinale? Io son Consegliero della Signoria di Venetia . . ." (*Monumenti*, p. 21).

# SIR RICHARD MAITLAND
## OF LETHINGTON: A CHRISTIAN LAIRD
## IN THE AGE OF REFORMATION

MAURICE LEE, JR.

THE name of Sir Richard Maitland of Lethington has echoed very faintly down the corridors of time for two reasons. He is remembered as a poet and, more importantly, as a collector and preserver of the poetry of others. Sir Richard was one of the first of Scotland's antiquaries, and as such he rendered a priceless service to the literary historians. Secondly, he is known as the father of two famous sons. The elder, William Maitland of Lethington, "Secretary Maitland," is familiar to all those who have even a passing acquaintance with the melancholy story of Mary Queen of Scots. The achievements and talents of the younger brother John, Lord Thirlestane, chancellor and political mentor to the young James VI, were less spectacular, if more lasting.[1] Richard Maitland ought also to be remembered in another capacity, as a Christian gentleman who lived in the Age of Reformation and whose reactions to that age are extremely interesting because they shed a good deal of light, at least indirectly, on the nature of that Reformation in Scotland.

The traditional view of the Scottish Reformation—a view which can be largely attributed to the florid eloquence of John Knox—is that in the 1550's and 1560's Scotland was the scene of a vigorous clash of ideologies and personalities, which led to almost continous violence: the Wars of the Congregation in 1559-1560, which resulted in the overturn of the old Church; the upheavals and spectacular murders of Mary's reign; and, finally, another civil war after the assassination of the Regent Moray, a war which at last came to an end in 1573 with the triumph of the Protestant faction. No one can deny the existence of these wars and murders and of ideological conflict, too. But the amount of violence has been exaggerated—far fewer people were killed in Scotland in the sixteenth century for either religious or political reasons than in "stable" and "civilized" England—and so, too, has the catastrophic nature of the events of 1560. Professor Gordon Donaldson, the author of the most recent full-scale study of the

---

[1] The standard biography of William Maitland is E. Russell's *Maitland of Lethington* (London, 1912). For John Maitland, see M. Lee, Jr., *John Maitland of Thirlestane and the Foundation of the Stewart Despotism in Scotland* (Princeton, 1959).

Scottish Reformation, puts the point this way: "The Scottish reformation ... was at once less precipitate and less radical than is often believed. From many points of view the year 1560, the conventional date of the Scottish reformation, is not very significant, and must have been much less definitive in the eyes of contemporaries than it has come to be in the text books. Many changes had already taken place before 1560; contemporaries might have been hard put to it to define exactly what changes, if any, had been legally and constitutionally made in 1560; and after 1560 offices and emoluments remained substantially in the hands of those who had enjoyed them before."[2]

The poetry of Richard Maitland stands as a remarkable commentary on the general accuracy of Professor Donaldson's opinion. But it does more than that; it also suggests an explanation of why the Scottish Reformation assumed the character and took the course it did, and is therefore of considerable significance as a source. That his poetry has been overlooked is attributable in part to its lack of literary value. None of it is great, and a good deal of it is not particularly original: Maitland wrote on a number of the same subjects as William Dunbar, whose poetry he had collected and whom he obviously greatly admired. But his verse, though ordinary as poetry, has the supreme advantage of being both topical and strictly contemporary; it was written from the late 1550's to the early 1570's, the crucial years in which the Reformation—whatever it was—took place.

Maitland was born in 1496, of an Anglo-Norman family of lairds who dwelt in the Lowlands south and east of Edinburgh. The Maitlands were a rising family: Sir Richard's mother was the daughter of Lord Seton, and his only sister married Lord Somerville. His father was killed at Flodden. After taking formal possession of his inheritance young Richard seems to have gone to France to complete his education by being trained in the law. In due course he returned, but his career was anything but spectacular; he was evidently not interested in becoming an active politician. In fact, we hear very little of him until he was well over fifty and his son William was beginning his rapid rise to power. In the 1550's Sir Richard was frequently employed as a commissioner in negotiations with England over border matters. He took no active part in the Wars of the Congregation, but, unlike William, now Secretary, he remained loyal to the Queen Regent—or so it is reasonable to conclude from the lines in his poem of welcome to Mary Queen of Scots on her return to her native land: "Madame, I was true servant to thy mother, / And in her favour stood

[2] Gordon Donaldson, *The Scottish Reformation* (Cambridge, 1960), p. 74.

aye thankfully."³ The Queen rewarded him by making him a member of the College of Justice, the highest Scottish court, and in December 1562 she appointed him Keeper of the Privy Seal, in spite of the fact that he was now totally blind. These favors, of course, were attributable less to the deeds of the father than to the merits of the son, who now shared with the Earl of Moray the position of chief advisor to Mary. And as the fortunes of the Secretary rose and fell, so did those of Sir Richard. Favors rained upon the family in the 1560's, but disaster issued from the Secretary's losing choice in the confused struggles that followed the assassination of Moray in 1570. One blow after another fell on the old man. His sons were forfeited; the youngest, Thomas, died in Italy in 1572 at the early age of twenty-seven; a year later, with the fall of Edinburgh castle, the spectacular career of the Secretary came to its unhappy end. No legal action was taken against Sir Richard, but his property was seized, on the pretext that it had really belonged to the Secretary. All this was the doing of the Regent Morton; it was not until Morton's loss of power in the late 1570's that the Maitland family fortunes were restored, thanks to the abilities of Sir Richard's one remaining son, John. The family property was returned, and in 1581 John joined his father on the bench. Three years later advancing age prompted Sir Richard to resign from the College of Justice. As a mark of favor, he was allowed to nominate his successor; his choice, not surprisingly, fell on his son's closest political associate at the moment, Sir Lewis Bellenden, the Justice-clerk. In 1586 Sir Richard died, aged ninety.

Maitland's career thus spanned the most crucial years of the Scottish Reformation. He was fully grown when Lutheran ideas first came to Scotland; he played host to George Wishart just before the martyr's capture;⁴ he died two years before the Armada, just as his son John, now Secretary to the young James VI, was hammering out that compromise between crown and kirk which was to enable James to get control of kirk and aristocracy alike in the 1590's.

³ "Of the Quenis arryvale in Scotland," ed. W. A. Craigie, *The Maitland Folio Manuscript*, Scottish Text Society publication (Edinburgh, 1919), I, 35. The poetry quoted in this essay has been "translated" into modern English in the interest of intelligibility. Spellings have been modernized, punctuation supplied, and Scots words anglicized. The rendering has been kept as literal as possible. An occasional Scots word has been retained for the sake of the meter or the rhyme; in these cases the English equivalent is supplied in parentheses.

⁴ *John Knox's History of the Reformation in Scotland*, ed. W. C. Dickinson (New York, 1950), I, 67. Knox describes Maitland as "ever civil, albeit not persuaded in religion."

Yet the Reformation receives surprisingly little mention in Maitland's poetry. It was not that he lacked concern for religious matters; on the contrary, Maitland was a good Christian, in the sense that he accepted the Christian ethic and lived by it as best he could. The evidence indicates that he became a Protestant out of disgust at the worldliness and corruption of the ancient Church, and not because he held any strong opinions on the questions of justification by faith and predestination. His was the piety of the simple man, for whom Christianity was a way of living rather than a matter of intellectual commitment to a theological doctrine. The guidance provided by Scripture was, for him, all that was necessary:

> To read or hear the holy writ,
> True knowledge shall I get in it:
> How I shall have me at all hours
> Both to my God and my neighbors,
> Instructing me to patiently
> My trouble bear,
> Sin to repent with true intent
> While I am here.
>
> Since in this earth I find no rest,
> Rejoice in God I think it best,
> Who, in this life, give me his grace,
> Then bring me to that resting place
> Where joy and gloir [glory] are evermore,
> Peace and concord.
> To that same joy do me convey,
> Jesus our Lord.[5]

Maitland was not an indifferent man, then, yet he never became an enthusiast for either side. From the beginning he was critical of corruption in the clergy. In a poem written before the Wars of the Congregation he prays that God will

> ... take away the ignorance
> Of churchmen that vices haunt,
> And lead us a-rear,
> That both good life and cunning want[lack],
> Now in to this new year.[6]

[5] "Pleasouris of Aige," *Folio*, I, 336-337.
[6] "On the New Yeir," *ibid.*, p. 25.

During the war he prayed for religious concord; he wanted to see an end to heresy, but he was not prepared to commit himself by declaring who the heretics were:

> God make us quit of all heresy
> And put us once into the right way,
> And in thy law we so instructed be
> That we be not beguiled every day.
> One sayeth this, another sayeth nay:
> That we know not to whom we should adhere.
> Christ send to us one rule to keep for aye
> Without discord now in to this new year.[7]

Only once did Maitland devote an entire poem to the disputes between Protestants and Catholics, a poem written in 1570 and called, appropriately enough, "On the Miseries of the Tyme." The miseries were "Pest, poverty, and most unkindly war." Both sides, in Maitland's view, were equally responsible for this unhappy situation. As for the Catholics, he chided,

> Some time the priests thought that they did well
> When that they made their beards and shaved their crown,
> Used round caps and gowns to their health
> And mass and matins said in their fashion,
> Though that all vices reigned in their person:
> Lechery, gluttony, vain glory, and avarice,
> With sword and fire for zeal of Religion
> Of Christian people oft made sacrifice.

The Protestants were no better:

> Now are Protestants risen among us
> Saying they will make Reformation.
> But yet as now more vices never reigned,
> As pride, envy, false dissimulation,
> Deceit, adultery, and fornication,
> Theft, robbery, slaughter, oppression of the poor,
> Of policy plain alteration.
> Of wrongful gear now no man taketh care.

[7] "Of the Assemblie of the Congregatioun," *ibid.*, p. 33.

They think it well that they the Pope do call
The Antichrist, and Mass idolatry,
And then eat flesh upon the Fridays all:
That they serve God right then accordingly,
Though in all things they live most wickedly.
But God commanded us his law to keep,
First honor him, and then have charity
With our neighbor, and for our sins to weep.

Both sides, Maitland concluded, had transgressed God's laws and should be held equally accountable for Scotland's troubles.[8] What emerges most clearly from this poetic assessment is that Maitland was not interested in religious controversy as such. What did concern him, and very deeply, were the moral, political, and social consequences of the religious strife which the Reformation had brought to Scotland. Although he apparently had no driving urge for an active public career for himself and occasionally seemed a bit baffled by the political ambitions of his sons, there can be no doubt about the depth of his interest in the public weal. This patriotism, in the best sense of that much misused word, runs through most of his verse and shows itself in a good many different ways. The less elevated forms were there; for example, Maitland obviously disliked foreign influence in Scotland. The Wars of the Congregation were deplorable in themselves, he felt, but worse still was the foreign intervention which would inevitably result:

> I cannot sing for the vexation
> Of Frenchmen and the Congregation
> That has made trouble in this nation
> And many bare biging [building].
>> In this new year I see but war,
>> No cause to sing.
>> In this new year I see but war,
>> No cause there is to sing.
> I have no will to sing or dance
> For fear of England and of France.
> God send them sorrow and mischance
> Because of their coming.[9]

[8] *Ibid.*, pp. 40-42.
[9] "On the New Yeir," ed. W. A. Craigie, *The Maitland Quarto Manuscript*, Scottish Text Society publication (Edinburgh, 1920), p. 13b.

His opinions on this score did not change over the years. During the civil wars of the 1570's, in a moving plea to both sides to settle their differences, he urged the King's faction to

> Think on the words King Edward spoke to Bruce:
> Have we naught else to do
> But win a realm for you?

And to the Queen's partisans, who thought of asking France to send troops, Maitland warned,

> Remember how they pleased you before.
>
> .   .   .   .   .   .   .   .   .   .   .
>
> Ere you were of them quit
> You had enough ado.[10]

What he wanted was that Scotland be let alone—that she be allowed to go her way in isolation without interference from any quarter:

> I pray God I hear tell
> We agree among ourselves,
> And then that all this whole country
> Of France and England both were free,
> With them no more to mell [meddle].[11]

What gave France and England their opportunity to intervene, of course, was the political confusion and strife which accompanied the religious revolution. Maitland never ceased to inveigh against this aspect of the Reformation. It was in fact this, and not the question of the idolatry of the Mass, which concerned him. The burden of a great deal of his poetry is contained in the first two lines of "Aganis the Divisioun of the Lordis": "O living lord, that made both heaven and hell,/ From us expel this cruel civil war."[12]

The title of this poem is significant. Maitland held both Catholics and Protestants responsible for Scotland's troubles. But within each faction the real culprits were the aristocratic leaders, who ought to have had the weal of the country at heart but who had completely lost sight of the common good. In fact, in Maitland's view, the blame for Scotland's unhappy state rested almost exclusively with the aristocracy. As the poem just cited says,

[10] "Of Unione amangis the Lordis," *Folio*, I, 310.
[11] "Aganis the Weiris," *ibid.*, p. 307.
[12] *Ibid.*, p. 303.

What is the cause of all this great confusion,
But the division of lords most potent
In land and rent. . . .[13]

Worse still, for many of these men, religious zeal or political principles
were mere pretexts for the pursuit of ancient feuds or for simple
greed. During the struggles of the 1570's between the partisans of the
infant James VI and the deposed Queen Mary, Maitland put the point
this way:

Some have dissembled, yet proud in their conceit,
But others spy out well enough their gait [way].
Neither for king's nor queen's authority
They strive, but for particularity,
That cannot be content
With their own land and rent
As their fathers were before,
Unless they fill their hands
With other men's lands,
Gear, victual, and store.[14]

The ravages of the civil war descended on Maitland himself, but he
made very little of his own losses in his verse. In fact, one is inclined
to wonder whether he would have mentioned them at all if it had not
been for the fact that one of his properties was the barony of Blyth,
which gave him a chance for an obvious play on words:

Blind man, be blithe, though you be wronged,
Though Blyth be plundered, take no melancholy.
Thou shalt be blithe when they shall be hanged
That have despoiled Blyth so maliciously.[15]

Again and again he returned to the theme of the ruin the war was
causing and the responsibility of the nobility for its continuance. All
of these poems ended with a plea for peace and concord. The following is typical:

I pray to him that is lord of lords:
Bring all our lords to one perfect concord,
And with thy grace their spirits all inspire,
Among them kindle of charity the fire,

[13] *Ibid.*, p. 304.
[14] "Of Unione amangis the Lordis," *ibid.*, p. 311.
[15] "The blind Baronis comfort," *ibid.*, p. 43.

All rumor and envy
And faults passed by,
To be forgotten clean,
That justice' execution
For wickedness' punition
May on this land be seen.[16]

Maitland came gradually to realize that the chief sufferers from the civil war were the common people. During the Wars of the Congregation he evidently did not consider their plight very serious; his remarks were conventional and not very deeply felt.

God grant His grace to the inferiors
Of this poor realm, their quarrel to consider,
And to obey their superiors,
So that our head and lieges do confidder [confederate]
In peace and love for to remain together.
Then were we quit of all the men of war,
That all true folk from Berwick to Baquhidder
May live in rest unrobbed in this new year.[17]

Ten years later it was a different story. Maitland then showed far more concern about the disasters which had overtaken his social inferiors:

It is a pity to hear tell
How the poor commons of this land
From wrong cannot defend themselves
From reif [robbery] and spulze [despoiling] by some band
    Of soldiers of some side,
    That none dare walk nor ride
For troubling of some wicked hand.
I know not how this realm shall stand
    And scoundrels walk so wide.[18]

Maitland even devoted a whole poem to the subject: "Aganis Oppressioun of the Commounis."[19] The ordinary man was in a very bad way, Maitland said, but the civil war was not altogether to blame. Landlords had become much more oppressive. Rents had risen, and evictions for non-payment had naturally increased. "Teinds" (tithes) that formerly

[16] "Of Unione amangis the Lordis," *ibid.*, p. 312.
[17] "Of the Assemblie of the Congregatioun," *ibid.*, p. 33.
[18] "Aganis the Weiris," *ibid.*, p. 305.
[19] *Ibid.*, pp. 331-332.

125

were enjoyed by tenants had been appropriated by the landlords, especially those on the lands of the Catholic Church which had "come in great temporal men's hands"—one of the undesirable features of the Reformation. But nowhere did Maitland suggest that the remedy for this situation lay in the hands of the oppressed. The lords, he said, must open their eyes to the situation and, for their own good, improve the lot of the ordinary man: "Rich commons are right profitable / When they to serve their lord are able."

Maitland was not an advocate of social reform; it never occurred to him to question the existing social structure. In fact, if anything, he attributed to that structure a fixity and permanence which it no longer possessed by the later sixteenth century. Henry Killigrew was overstating the case in his oft-quoted remark that the great nobles' power was in decay.[20] But it is certainly true that, relatively, their power was very much less than it had been a hundred years earlier. Maitland was not aware of this decline; he repeatedly blamed the aristocracy for all of Scotland's troubles, which he felt would be ended if only the lords would agree among themselves.

The reforms that Maitland did favor, therefore, were primarily administrative, and to achieve them he called upon the powers that be. As might be expected from one of his profession, improvement in the administration of justice was dear to him. In a singularly graceless poem he made several concrete proposals for reform.[21] The chief problem, as he saw it, was the excessive amount of time it took to get a case tried. This delay was extremely expensive for the rich; and, as for the rest,

> The poor folk say that they for lack of spending
> Must leave the law, it is so long in ending.
> Long process them to poverty hath brought.

To remedy this situation Maitland proposed an increase in both the number and the quality of the senators of the College of Justice and— what was perhaps a reflection on the honesty of some of his colleagues —an increase in their stipends. The present fees, he said, were not paid regularly and fully. Even if they were, they would not be adequate, since "What cost one pound before now costs three." Maitland

[20] Nov. 11, 1572, Killigrew to Burghley, ed. W. K. Boyd, *Calendar of State Papers Relating to Scotland and Mary Queen of Scots*, IV (Edinburgh, 1905), 432.

[21] "Complaint aganis the lang Law-sutes," *Folio*, I, 429-431.

suggested that the money for the increased stipends could be obtained from the property of the old Church. Unfortunately such a solution was not politically feasible; the aristocrats who had laid hands on so much of that property were too powerful to be compelled to loosen their grasp.

Nowhere else in his poetry did Maitland attempt to deal with any comparable administrative problem; nowhere else did he make any precise proposals for reform. For, in fact, Richard Maitland was not fundamentally a reformer. He was, after all, already an old man before he began to write: he seems not to have started writing poetry before he reached sixty, although he doubtless began his activities as a collector of other people's verse much earlier.

Through his poetry there runs a very strong streak of nostalgia. It is backward-looking verse, the product of a man who had seen happier days in his youth, when he could stand apart from the political strife in which his aspiring sons were now involving him.

> Where is the blitheness that hath been
> Both in town and country seen
> Among lords and ladies schein [fair],
> Dancing, singing, game and play.
> But now I know not what they mean.
> All merriness is worn away.[22]

In every respect things had been better in our fathers' day, Maitland reminisced, both in trivial things, such as ladies' dress and behavior:

> Some will spend more, as I hear say,
> On drugs and spices in one day
> Than would their mothers in a year.[23]

and in serious matters:

> Treason is the most shameful thing
> That may in any country reign,
>     And should be hated most:
> But now in this unhappy time,
> So many smitten with that crime
>     That few dare others trust.[24]

[22] "Satire on the Age," *ibid.*, p. 37.
[23] "Satire on the Toun Ladyes," *ibid.*, p. 299.
[24] "Aganis Tressoun," *ibid.*, p. 333.

Men's characters had decayed. There was "Na Kyndnes at Court without Siller": the cash nexus had replaced the old ties of kinship.[25] Men were false, greedy, and ungrateful:

> This world so false is, and unstable,
> Of greediness insatiable,
> In all estates such doubleness,
> To find true friends few are able,
> For kept is no old kindness.[26]

The prevailing vice was greed:

> For greediness now guideth all estates,
> Instructing them with covetous conceits,
> Saying to some, why do you lack this land,
> This tack, this farm, that lies so near at hand?
> It for to get I can find twenty gaits [ways].[27]

Sometimes Maitland's sense of the times being out of joint led him to despair:

> There was one Judas in that time
> For silver did his master sell.
> But now are smitten with that crime
> A thousand more than I can tell
> That do within this country dwell,
> Would sell their souls, as I ween,
> For gear unto the devil of hell,
> In this worst world that e'er was seen.[28]

Usually, however, his mood was much more calm and resigned. Being gloomy, he judged, did no good:

> Let us be blithe and glad,
> My friends all, I pray:
> To be pensive and sad,
> Nothing it help us may.[29]

He was even able to joke, albeit a bit wryly, about his losses in the wars; recompense, he felt, would be granted him in heaven. He wrote

[25] *Ibid.*, pp. 335-336.
[26] "On the Warldis Ingratitude," *Quarto*, p. 82b.
[27] "Advyce to Kyndnes," *Folio*, I, 315.
[28] "On Gude Friday," *Quarto*, p. 22b.
[29] "Advyce to lesom Mirriness," *Folio*, I, 320.

charmingly of old age, warning old men against playing the gallant. As for himself, he said, he was no longer up to engaging in amorous pursuits:

> The fairest wench in all this town,
> Though I had her in her best gown,
>    Right bravely braild [arrayed],
> With her I might not play the loon,
>    I am so old.[30]

It was only natural, in view of this conservative, backward-looking attitude, that Maitland should have put very little stock in the possibilities of useful political action in the direction of reform, especially on the part of people such as himself, who were not members of the aristocracy. He had no objection to his sons' making careers for themselves at court, and he wrote a Polonius-like poem about how they should behave there: "The Laird of Lethingtounis Counsale to his Sone Beand in the Court."[31] It is full of the usual platitudes: keep good company, watch your tongue, tell the truth, avoid flattery and gambling and pride, be loyal to the prince. No one could take exception to this guidance. But there follows one piece of advice which well summarizes Maitland's attitude toward political activity, advice which none of his sons would heed:

> Beware in giving of a high counsel
> In matters great and doubtful specially,
> Which by the working of the world may fail,
> Though it seem never so apparently.
> Behold the world's instability
> That never still within one state doth bide,
> But changeth aye, as do the moon and sea.
> He ruleth well, that well in court can guide.

Here speaks the cautious man, the man afraid to take chances, to accept responsibility. The "world's instability" was so great that positive action or advice would inevitably lead to trouble. Much better would it be for one to do nothing, to say nothing, to let others take responsibility; then, if things went badly, one could not be held accountable. Perhaps, under certain circumstances, this could be considered sound advice. His sons, however, refused to accept it, funda-

---

[30] "Solace in Age," *ibid.*, p. 330.
[31] *Ibid.*, pp. 21-24.

mentally because they did not agree with their father that "To govern all and rule be not our bent." They firmly believed that it was.

The image that emerges from Maitland's self-portrait is that of the conservative *politique*—if one may use that word to describe such a reluctant politician. His principal concerns in public life were with social peace, the preservation of the traditional ordering of society, and the popular welfare. His views were conventional—commonplace, if you will—and, as often as not, were expressed in a commonplace way. The essential point to make about them, however, is that they were not the views of a man passionately concerned about religion. Maitland was pious enough, but he did not believe that religious controversy should be allowed to disrupt the public peace. He, like Erasmus, deplored the fact that the apple of discord had been thrown into the world, although, unlike Erasmus, he placed most of the responsibility on the old Church for its failure to reform itself, rather than on the Protestants.

Maitland's views are significant in two respects. First, they influenced—they could not help but influence—the political attitudes of his sons. Both William and John Maitland rose to the highest offices in the state. Both were extremely able men. Burghley, no mean judge, called William "the flower of the wits of Scotland" and John "the wisest man in Scotland." Both were *politiques* through and through, William so much so that he took too lightly the influence which religious considerations might have on the ordinary man and made several serious political miscalculations as a result. John was equally a *politique*, although, warned by his brother's mistakes, he took much more account of the kirk and did his best to win its support for his efforts to strengthen the authority of the crown. The careers of both men demonstrate over and over again that in their general political outlook they were true sons of their father.

The similarity of Richard Maitland's views to those of his sons is obvious and easy to measure. It is much more difficult to be precise about what his opinions show about the nature of the Scottish Reformation, because the evidence is so largely negative. What Maitland did not say is more significant than what he did say. His belief that Christianity is primarily a matter of ethics and his lack of concern with religious issues as such confirm the views of Professor Donaldson which were quoted at the beginning of this essay. They also suggest that, in common with most revolutions, the religious upheaval in Scotland was brought about by a minority and opposed by a minority,

130

that the majority of people were not concerned with the issues which were dear to the hearts of John Knox and Ninian Winzet. The era of the Reformation, in Scotland as in England, was not a religious-minded age. The succeeding age, the era of the Counter-Reformation, of Puritan and Jesuit, certainly was. But in the Scotland of John Knox the Covenanting mentality simply did not exist, save in Knox himself and some few who thought like him—and that is one reason why Knox, in his *History*, saved some of his most deeply felt criticism for those whom he regarded as backsliding Protestants, like the Earl of Moray.

It is this widespread apathy respecting matters of theological difference and church organization which gives the Scottish Reformation its peculiar character. It helps to explain many things: the continuity which Professor Donaldson stresses; the relatively small numbers of people engaged on each side in the Wars of the Congregation;[32] the tergiversations of people like Châtelherault, who was far more concerned with the welfare of the house of Hamilton than with the welfare of whatever religion he was professing at any given time; the willingness of a patently sincere Protestant like Moray to allow the Queen to have her Mass. It also helps to explain a good deal of Mary's outlook and policy, including her belief that she could get away with marrying Bothwell by Protestant rites. The existence of this apathy has been overlooked in the past by most scholars, because the history of this period was written in the first instance by religious partisans like Knox and David Calderwood and because we, as historians, have fallen victim to our own clichés, to those sweeping generalizations which we like to use in the opening paragraphs of chapters of textbooks or in the first (or last) five minutes of an undergraduate lecture. Thus we tell our classes—and, indeed, we believe—that medieval Europe was "primarily a religious community" and that the transition to modern times was marked by a "process of secularization," to quote a well-known textbook.[33] This assertion is no doubt true—up to a point. Insofar as it suggests, however, that the process of secularization was a steady and irreversible affair, it is misleading. It has made us assume that, because the men of the Counter-Reformation were

[32] This point is stressed by W. L. Mathieson, *Politics and Religion: A Study in Scottish History from the Reformation to the Revolution* (Glasgow, 1902), I, 67-70; he, too, suggests widespread apathy as the explanation.

[33] R. R. Palmer, *A History of the Modern World*, 2nd edn. (New York, 1956), p. 44.

131

preoccupied with religious questions, the men of the Reformation must have been so too. But this conclusion does not necessarily follow. Charles V, Thomas Cromwell, Paul III, for example—how closely do they resemble Philip II, Francis Walsingham, Pius V? So it was in Scotland: the age of Mary and Moray and Knox was not the age of Alexander Henderson and Johnston of Warriston.

Now it may well be objected that this essay has done precisely what its author has just been complaining of, that it has constructed a sweeping generalization about the religious apathy of the period of the 1550's and 1560's in Scotland on the flimsiest scaffolding, the writings of one man, who may not even have been typical of his class. Certainly Maitland's avocation of writing and collecting poetry was atypical, nor is there any way of showing how many lairds shared his views. Nevertheless, an examination of the poetical satires that were turned out on broadsheets during this period suggests that Maitland's habit of viewing the Reformation in non-religious terms was widely shared by ethically minded men like himself, as well as by those who, like the Regent Morton, were a good deal less concerned with living a Christian life. In the outburst of poetical indignation which followed upon the murder of Moray, for example, the political motivations and consequences of the deed were the aspects of the affair that received the most stress.[34] What is put forward in this essay is nothing more than the most tentative kind of hypothesis, which has been brought to mind by a reading of Sir Richard Maitland's poetry. Far more work needs to be done before this hypothesis can be either substantiated or disproved. But it does not appear to do violence to the facts, which point, the more the Age of Reformation is studied, to the conclusion that everywhere, not just in England, politics was the decisive force. Henry VIII and his entourage were not unique in their time.

[34] *Satirical Poems of the Time of the Reformation*, ed. J. Cranstoun, Scottish Text Society publication (Edinburgh, 1891), I, nos. 12-23.

# THE PURITANS AND
# THE CONVOCATION OF 1563

A. J. CARLSON

T HE history of the Convocation of 1563 has never been written. Nor in all likelihood will the full story of the first important meeting of Elizabethan clergy after the 1559 settlement ever be told. The reasons are many. Some historians still have trouble with its date, confusing old style 1562 with new style 1563.[1] Students of Anglican doctrine have examined every aspect of the Thirty-nine Articles, the Second Book of Homilies, and the various catechisms— all of which emerged from these sessions; but their efforts too often have saddled this meeting with an aura of unanimity that was in fact not always present. The forty or so members of the Puritan "choir," who, as Professor Neale has shown, were busily engaged in undermining government bills in the Commons of 1563,[2] had their counterparts in the lower house of Convocation. Within a week of Convocation's opening, St. Mary's chapel in St. Paul's Cathedral rang with the demands of sixty-three clergymen for further reform in the Elizabethan Church.[3] Unfortunately, the extent of their demands is difficult to determine since the lower-house journal, kept by its clerk, William

[1] The sessions ran from 11 January until 14 April 1563. Yet historians from John Strype, *Annals of the Reformation . . . in the Church of England during Queen Elizabeth's Happy Reign* (Oxford, 1824), I, Bk. I, 470ff., to Christopher Hill, *Society and Puritanism in Pre-Revolutionary England* (London, 1964), p. 34, continue to cite the date as 1562. J. C. Bary, in his recent commemorative essay, "The Convocation of 1563," *History Today*, XIII (July 1963), 490-501, corrects the date but does not go beyond Strype on basic issues. The Petyt MSS at Inner Temple, London, are invaluable for any discussion of this Convocation. I am grateful to the librarian for permission to examine vols. 538/36, 538/38, 538/47 for use in the preparation of this article.
[2] J. E. Neale, *Elizabeth I and her Parliaments, 1559-1581* (London, 1963), I, 90-92.
[3] Petyt MS 538/47 foll. 581-584, endorsed as "The requests & petitions of the clergy in the lower house of convocation." The petition is an example of the complexity of Puritan convocation activity, as it is signed by Puritans and some non-Puritans. The early pro-Puritan James Calfhill, who held proxies from London and Oxford, signed twice for emphasis, scrawling "Jacobus Calfhyll" boldly in one column and cramping "Jas. Calfhill pro. cler. Ox." in another (fol. 584). Strype correctly lists Calfhill as having signed twice (*Annals*, I, Bk. I, 512).

133

Saye, was destroyed in the Great Fire of 1666.[4] In any event, these demands, as we shall see, formed the basis for the vigorous reform plans of thirty-four Puritan clergy in the lower house.[5] These plans ultimately failed, as the Puritan clergy lost their first encounter with the Elizabethan establishment. Yet their failure is less significant than the fact that it is in these sessions of 1563 that one is first able to see the issues and personalities which within two years were to coalesce into a Puritan party. The early members of this party were in both houses of the 1563 Convocation, and it is here that we shall find the bishops and preachers who warrant the label "Fathers of English Puritanism."

The term "English Puritanism" probably never has been defined satisfactorily, for it defies inclusive definition. In its earliest stage, Puritanism represented a religion of individual conscience reacting within the circumstances of Tudor conformity; for its Calvinist—or, better, Reformed—protagonists, this reaction took the form of pitting one's individual sense of Christian liberty against one's respect for the royal establishment. These two highly charged terms, conscience and

[4] An abstract of the upper-house journal kept by its clerk, John Incent, fortunately survived. This "Act in Superiore Domo Convocationis, Annis 1562 . . ." somehow made its way into the papers of Charles Battely, a seventeenth-century receiver for Westminster. Battely was the younger brother of Nicholas Battely, Vicar of Bekesbourn. The latter provided Strype with much Canterbury material. See Cambridge University, Baumgartner MSS, 3/24-63. None of Strype's correspondents were able to find evidence that the missing lower-house journal survived the 1666 fire. The upper-house abstract is printed in E. Gibson, *Synodus Anglicana* (Oxford, 1854), pp. 146-163, and with notes in E. Cardwell, *Synodalia* (Oxford, 1842), II, 495-527. Thomas Bennet, *An Essay on the Thirty Nine Articles of Religion* (London, 1715), p. 166, suggests that it came from a bundle of papers Archbishop Laud turned over to the "ravenous claws" of Prynne in 1637 and that it may have originally belonged to Archbishop Parker. Although it occasionally abbreviates names, dates, etc., this journal allows us to reconstruct episcopal activities and, by inference, to form some opinion of the doings in the lower house as well.

[5] Petyt MS 538/47 foll. 576-577. These are the radical seven articles proposed according to the endorsement "by ye Dean of Powles and others," thereby linking the Dean of St. Paul's, Alexander Nowell, directly to the Puritan cause, along with such notorious Puritans as Thomas Sampson, Robert Crowley, and Percival Wilburne. Strype's copyist missed the signatures of John Pedder, Dean of Worcester, and the rabid Puritan Thomas Cole, Archdeacon of Essex (fol. 577); Strype thus recorded only thirty-two names (*Annals*, I, Bk. I, 501-502), whereas actually there were thirty-four. Barry wondered about this confusion ("Convocation," p. 497) but deferred to Strype's authority.

liberty, both of which betokened a renewed sense of individualism, occur repeatedly within the literature of early Puritanism. And it is not difficult to understand why these first Puritans suddenly ran head-long into trouble with their conformist-minded Queen. Yet these same terms designate Puritanism as a part of the "mainstream of Prot-estant thought."[6] The emergence of Puritanism, however, involved a relatively small number of Englishmen who, in the course of their Protestant development, underwent a common set of experiences which helped to fashion their sense of *religionis puritatem*.

At the universities—most notably Cambridge, but also at Oxford—the first tests came during Edward VI's reign. Here, where small num-bers of Englishmen were debating the validity of the sacrament or the character of the new prayer books, a common sense of purpose arose among those of "the godly who were hated for religion's sake."[7] Largely from those who earned vilification as Edwardian "gospellers of the house" would emerge those who were to suffer equal vilifica-tion as Elizabethan Puritans.

A second set of early Puritan experiences came with the Marian exile, which involved some eight hundred English laymen and clergy-men and their families. No Englishman who lived through the Marian exile returned to England after 1558 completely unchanged: he had seen the continental Reformed church in action. Thus, for example, when the vigorous Oxford don, John Parkhurst of Magdalen, returned to England from exile in Zurich and reluctantly accepted the bishopric of Norwich, his first act was to set up a "conference," that is, a classis, on the Zwinglian model.[8] More important even than the later effects of the exile—the impact of which has always been disputed—was the lingering sense of common persecution which existed among those who had spent the Marian years along the upper Rhine or in the Swiss mountains.

[6] A. G. Dickens, *The English Reformation* (New York, 1964), p. 315.

[7] Cambridge University, Baker MS, Mm 1.42 (Baker 31), fol. 12, dated "1550." The quotation is from a petition drawn up by ten of the fellows of Magdalen College, Oxford, against their president, Dr. Oglethorp; four of these fellows— John Mullins, Walther Bower, Michael Reniger, and Arthur Saul—were active Puritans in the 1563 Convocation.

[8] See John Day's edition of *Iniunctions exhibited by John* [Parkhurst] . . . *in his first visitacion beginning the second date of Maye* . . . [1561], STC 10286. Not only did Parkhurst order a conference every Tuesday to produce a literate, preaching ministry, but he also was the first to enforce the use of Bullinger's *A hundred sermons upon the apocalips* (London, 1561). See *Zurich Letters* (Cambridge, 1842-1845), I, no. 42.

When Anthony Gilby wrote some twelve years after his return against episcopal enforcement of the Act of Uniformity, he upbraided "the bold Lordlie Bishoppes, who nowe for the dreggs and patches of Poperie, despise their fellow ministers: and persecute those same persons, whom of late they loved as brethren, and bore Christes Cross with them, in the late persecutions."[9] Despite his bitterness toward the bishops and his chagrin over the failure of the 1572 Parliament to act in favor of the Puritans, Gilby still could recall "Divers of the Bishops that now bee, [who] did once love and cherish their brethren. . . ." For this tough-minded Puritan, the early trials and exile of Elizabethan Protestants had forged a common sense of purpose. The Convocation of 1563 was to determine the direction this purpose would have to take.

There was yet a third common experience which English Protestants shared in the early months of the 1560's—fear aroused by the failure of the new Queen to deal vigorously with the remnants of popery in their midst. Despite the Protestant excesses of the Visitation of 1559, England was still largely a Catholic country during the early 1560's, and the Protestants who were to become Puritans were dissatisfied. That fiery spokesman of Edwardian Protestantism, John Bale, recorded in 1561 his chagrin at the "stynkynge mystes of popish traditions" which still remained in Canterbury. Bale recalled vividly how Protestant ministers were scorned as "paulers" by a mob, which included "some of the aldermen of the city."[10]

Common intellectual experience, persecution at home or abroad, fear of existing circumstances—these, then, were the threads which knit early Puritan-minded Protestants together. The ultimate aim of these men would be to restyle the English Church on the reformed model of Zurich or Geneva. As conformists, or Presbyterians, their method would be from within; as nonconformists, or Separatists, from without. But aims and methods were to come later. The initial division occurred during the Convocation of 1563.

[9] *A Pleasaunt Dialogue Between a Souldior of Barwicke, and an English Chaplaine* (n.p., 1581), sig. A8. STC 11888. Although Gilby dates the preface to this interesting tract "x of May 1566," the context suggests events of 1572.

[10] Lambeth Palace Library, Selden MS 2001, "Bales Boke of obedience," fol. ii[v]. This unique MS volume is part of the recently acquired Selden MSS. See E.G.W. Bill, "Records of the Church of England recently recovered by Lambeth Palace Library," *Journal of the Society of Archivists*, III (April 1961), 24-26. I am grateful to Mr. Bill, the librarian at Lambeth Palace, for permission to examine the Selden MSS for use in the preparation of this article.

Writs were issued on 27 November 1562 to convene the Convocation of Canterbury at St. Paul's Cathedral on 11 January.[11] They were sent out none too soon, for Puritan bishops and lesser clergy alike had long looked forward to the approaching joint sessions of Parliament and Convocation, when the theological nature of the new Elizabethan Church might be spelled out in detail.[12] Ever since the Queen tried to halt further Protestant activities within the chancel,[13] the Puritans had been preparing to confront her with the consequences of the 1559 settlement. Perhaps in response to her efforts to stem the Protestant tide one Puritan, in arguing "why the Communion should not be ministered at the alter," adroitly reminded the Queen that she "hathe hitherto declared [herself] verie lothe to breake evil laws established by parliamente, tyll they were repealed by like authorite."[14] No one knew the limits of this authority better than Archbishop Parker, and in anticipation of the approaching convocation he had drafted an amended version of the Edwardian Forty-two Articles to serve as a guide for a new doctrinal statement.[15] Furthermore, he authorized a series of recommendations, entitled "Certain articles in substance desered to be granted by the queen's majesty," designed to augment his visitation reforms of 1560.

[11] British Museum, Lansdowne MS 1031 foll. 32-32^v (a copy of Parker's writ of mandamus to Grindal). See also John Strype, *The History of the Life and Acts of . . . Edmund Grindal . . .* (Oxford, 1821), Bk. I, pp. 99-100.

[12] *Zurich Letters*, I, no. 46 (28 April 1562). Bishop Parkhurst wrote Bullinger, "Religion is the same state among us as heretofore; a state, I say, not altogether to be thought lightly of. But I hope for an improvement at the approaching convocation."

[13] *Parker Correspondence* (Cambridge, 1853), no. 94 (22 Jan. 1560/61): the Queen's famous "further order" letter to Parker.

[14] Lambeth Palace, Selden MS 2002/18 foll. 107-109. This interesting undated MS falls in the period of 1560-1563 and reflects the early Puritans' desire for "a godly reformacion" in the Reformed tradition, which had already replaced altars with tables, and a desire that they "not be inforced to retourne vnto suche ordinances and devices of man not commanded in goodes word." From the beginning the Puritans had hoped that they would not be required to accept the 1559 settlement.

[15] Corpus Christi College MS 121/26 foll. 233-251. This is the "red leaded draft" copy. Its moderate tone is well defined by C. Hardwick, *History of the Articles of Religion* (London, 1895), pp. 122-130: "it is most important to observe that Parker and his friends, instead of drawing hints from 'Swiss' confessions, which were high in favour with the Marian exiles, had recourse to a series of Articles of 'Saxon' origin [Württemberg Confession, 1552], particularly distinguished by the moderation of their tone."

These twelve articles, lost in an endless sea of suggested reforms, have received scant attention;[16] yet they bear witness to the wide range of reforms Parker anticipated. Foremost was the need for a uniform book of articles drawn from Jewel's *Apology*, followed by an elimination of "imperfections" in the service book.[17] The Archbishop's next concern was with a series of proposed administrative reforms: to invoke "penalties" for nonattendance at church, to reform episcopal courts, increase clerical stipends, redress social morals, and eliminate pluralism. These strictures drew no comment from Edmund Grindal, the Puritan Bishop of London, to whom Parker evidently had submitted the reform suggestions in advance of Convocation.[18] But the mild-mannered Grindal did have second thoughts about drawing unnecessary attention to unpaid benefices.[19] More significantly, the Bishop's anti-Catholicism was evident as he urged seizure of the ecclesiastical livings of English Catholics who fled overseas. And against the Archbishop's proposal for a single prescribed apparel Grindal wrote in the

[16] Two copies are at the Inner Temple, Petyt MS 538/47 foll. 450-453 and foll. 522-525; an additional copy is at Lambeth Palace, Selden MS 2002, no. 3, foll. 17-18. Strype reprints them as the work of "a secretary of the archbishop's," amended by "the archbishop's hand" and "in some places by bishop Grindal" (*Annals*, I, Bk. I, 522-524).

[17] He also sought to reduce the rites and ceremonies of the Church "to edification" and to "godly purity and simplicity." Apparently the Puritans were not the only purists.

[18] Recently, John F.H. New, *Anglican and Puritan* . . . (Stanford, 1964), p. 106, has sought to dismiss Grindal's Puritanism as a matter of sympathy for prophesying groups in 1577, arguing instead that his was an "Anglican" character. No one who has followed Grindal's activities as Bishop of London, however, should deny his Puritanism, especially in light of the following facts: that in attendance at his first ordination in 1559-1560 were twenty-three exiles, including John Foxe, Roger Kelke, and Percival Wilburne (see A. P. Kup, "An Account of the Returned Exiled of 1553-1558 . . . ," Ph.D. diss. [St. Andrews University, 1953], pp. 109ff.); that, while William Whittingham was chaplain at Newhaven in 1563, he supported the chaplain's Puritan activities; and that later he used John Foxe, James Calfhill, John Philpott, and Christopher Golman—all Puritans in 1564—to settle a split within the Dutch congregation in London (see my study, "The Bishops and the Queen: A Study of 'Puritan' Episcopal Activity in early Elizabethan England, 1558-1566," Ph.D. diss. [Princeton University, 1962], pp. 175-177 and 227-233). All these facts bear witness to Grindal's basic Puritan sympathies from the beginning of his career as an Elizabethan bishop. See A. G. Dickens' verdict on Grindal as a "Puritan" (*Reformation*, p. 315).

[19] The articles had noted: the right to hospitality might be kept if the fruits of the benefices "were truly paid." In reply Grindal said, "Consideretur melius."

margin: "Having differences, although not altogether the form used in popish time."[20] Thus, even before Parker arrived in London for Convocation, he must have known that the Puritans would oppose rigorous conformity in external matters.

Although both Convocation and Parliament were slated to begin on 11 January, the opening was delayed two days (as in 1559) owing to the Queen's indisposition.[21] On the 12th the bishops trooped down to Westminster in the full regalia of the royal procession for the opening of Parliament. And not until the 13th did Parker's well-laid plans for his formal arrival, reception, and initial service at St. Paul's have a chance to be put into effect.[22] One wonders about the mood of the twenty-two assembled prelates as they donned their robes in the vestry of St. Paul's and took their places in the stalls of the choir.[23] For many, this was their first chance to exchange notes since becoming bishops. Some doubtless were concerned with their own private bills about to be introduced in Parliament.[24] But all of them were surely conscious of the warning concerning religious reforms made the previous day in the Lord Keeper's "State of the Realm" address.[25] "All men's Eyes be fixed on those who be in Authority," Bacon had said, "for as the Head is, even so is the Foot." Whether the bishops appreciated the analogy or not, they understood his point—some even relished it—that "many Ceremonies . . . are either left undone, or forgotten"; and they

[20] In the Lambeth Palace copy, Selden MS 2002, no. 3, fol. 17ᵛ, Grindal's marginalia are vigorously crossed out by a later hand.

[21] Bacon told the Commons that the Queen was "somewhat sick of a Styche" (*Journals of the House of Commons* . . . [London, 1800], I, 62). See Neale, *Parliament*, I, 92. The clerks of the two houses of Convocation did meet on 11 January, however, to receive proxies. See Gibson, *Synodus*, p. 146.

[22] Gibson, *Synodus*, pp. 164-165, reprints the Archbishop's projected itinerary from the landing at St. Paul's wharf to the English service and Latin sermon in the cathedral through his own oration in the chapter house.

[23] Nineteen of the bishops of Canterbury were present; Oxford and Bristol were vacant, Cheyney holding Bristol in commendam with Gloucester; Kitchin of Landaff sent his proxy. Three of the four York bishops also were present for the House of Lords; Best of Carlisle sent his proxy. The latter complained to Cecil of his impoverished state. British Museum Lansdowne MS 6/48 fol. 123, dated 14 April 1563, from the "poore citie of Carlill."

[24] Bills involving the bishops of Durham, Ely, and Exeter were all introduced during these sessions. None of them received favorable action. *Journal of the House of Lords* (1832-1836), I, 580-619.

[25] Sir Simonds D'Ewes, *A Compleat Journal of the Votes . . . of the House of Lords and House of Commons . . . of Queen Elizabeth . . .* (London, 1693), p. 60.

were personally touched by his frank warning that officers might be appointed "in every Diocese" to amend the "faults . . . as well of the Heads, as the Ministers thereof." Thus were lighted the official flares cautioning gradual reform.

If any such broad hints were necessary, Archbishop Parker brought them up next day in his provincial address following the opening of Convocation. He pointed out to his assembled brethren the opportunity that lay before them to reform the English Church and the need to match their sovereign in furthering reformation.[26] While on the one hand the Archbishop was making a frank appeal for generosity when it came time to consider clerical subsidy, he was on the other hand also very anxious that "matters in the English Church" be well ordered.[27]

This concern explains why he took so much care in preparing the amended manuscript edition of the Forty-two Articles, which, on the whole, Convocation adopted. If the Archbishop had been able to manage Convocation in other matters as well as William Cecil managed the House of Commons, events might have gone differently. As it turned out, the Puritans in both houses of Convocation were preparing nothing less than a liturgical revolution.

Following the Archbishop's address, the clergy of the lower house adjourned to St. Mary's chapel, where they chose the Dean of St. Paul's, Alexander Nowell, as their prolocutor. The Dean's reputation for preaching tactless sermons is well known.[28] Yet this mildly Puritan trait did not prevent Parker from describing Nowell as a man grave in doctrine and experience; nor did it evoke any objections from the bishops, who confirmed his election unanimously on the 16th.[29]

[26] Cardwell, *Synodalia*, II, 501.

[27] *Loc. cit.* (". . . per quam, inter alia, opportunitatem reformandarum rerum in ecclesia Anglicana jam oblatam esse aperuit . . ."). See C. Hardwick, *Articles*, p. 126. Parker, with Bishops Cox and Guest, drafted the "amplifications" of the 1553 articles with "anxiety to check the progress of new forms of error. . . ." Although Hardwick deals primarily with continental Anabaptist errors, there is reason to suspect that Parker and the two bishops regarded some of the exiles' liturgical views with equal concern.

[28] Neale, *Parliament*, I, 92-95, and R. Churton, *Life of Alexander Nowell* (Oxford, 1809), p. 84. Both take note of Nowell's *faux pas* in preaching a "radical" sermon before Parliament opened, speaking against "pride of apparel" as the Queen sat in furred ermine and crimson velvet. British Museum Egerton MS 2035 fol. 164ᵛ, preserves a portion of the sermon, emphasizing what must have been the Puritan theme as the lower house convened: "Discipline ought now speedily to be restored. . . ."

[29] Cardwell, *Synodalia*, II, 501, 504. Nowell was led before the bishops by the Marian Gabriel Goodman, Dean of Westminster, and the strong Puritan

Thereupon began a series of events in both the Commons and Convocation that were hardly coincidental.

It was also on the 16th that a member of the Commons moved consideration by the House of "the Succession Question."[30] The Queen's brush with death in October had revived English fears that Elizabeth might be the last of the Tudors, and Parliament was determined to do something about it. As if this were not a sufficiently explosive issue, on the 19th the Commons took up a bill dealing with sheriffs and justices. Both of these actions in the lower house of Parliament, as Neale has shown,[31] tampered with the royal prerogative and were anathema to the Queen; and each was dealt with in "her own fashion."

Yet on the same day, as the bishops were about to begin their modification of the Forty-two Articles, Nowell and a delegation of six others appeared before the upper house with a series of reform articles —the work, apparently, of a lower-house committee.[32] Again, care must be taken not to confuse the numerous reform plans set before the bishops.[33] Subsequent events in both the Commons and Convocation indicate that these "diversas schedas" were the twenty-one articles of the "Petition for Discipline," signed by sixty-three members of the parochial clergy.[34] In fact, this petition drew attention to the impor-

---

Thomas Sampson, Dean of Church of Christ, Oxford (the "Acta" errs in naming Sampson "decanus Exon"). Thus Parker maintained the middle way.

[30] Strype identifies the member of Commons as the "Mayor of Windsor" (*Annals*, I, Bk. I, 439). If Strype is correct, this must have been Richard Gallys or Gales (ca. 1506-1564). I owe this identification to Miss Norah Fuidge, University of London.

[31] Neale, *Parliament*, I, 121-122.

[32] Cardwell, *Synodalia*, II, 507-508: ". . . exhibuerant quasdam diversas schedas de rebus reformandis per eos respective excogitat. et in scriptis redact. Quae quidem schedae de communi consensu traditae sunt quibusdam viris gravioribus et doctoribus de coetu dictae domus inferioris ad hoc electis perspiciend. et considerand."

[33] On the 16th Parker had urged his colleagues to present all matters of diocesan reform on the 19th (Cardwell, *Articles*, p. 505). Strype, *Annals*, I, Bk. II, 562-568, reprints Corpus Christi College MS 121/27 foll. 257-354, a long series of fifty-one articles dealing largely with external abuses. Barry "Convocation," p. 500, associates these with the later "Book of Discipline."

[34] Petyt MS 538/47 foll. 581-584; reprinted in Strype, *Annals*, I, Bk. I, 507-512. Nor must these twenty-one articles be regarded solely as the work of Puritan clergymen. Nineteen of those who signed this petition would ultimately vote against the Puritans later. Yet only six of the forty-five clergymen who favored later Puritan reforms failed to sign this one. Thus, for the Puritans, the petition became the first step.

tance of the "book of articles," that is, the eventual Thirty-nine, mentioned in nine of the petition's items requiring the entire clergy, laity, or any who enjoyed spiritual promotion, plus those in the universities, to bear allegiance to these same articles or suffer the consequences. It was for that reason the real precursor of the radically extended requirements of the second Supremacy Act that came from the Commons a month later. Thus the lower house cleverly took Parker's desire for a book of articles and turned it into the first test of loyalty to the new religion.

Other hints also mark this petition as a preview of more radical Puritan demands yet to come.[35] Opposition was expressed to private baptism, godparents, and the "Idolatrous mass"; all roods or images used "superstitiously" were to be "utterly destroyed"; and fellows in college were to preach at least twice a year or leave the universities. Most ambitious of all, however, was the eighteenth recommendation that the bishop's ordinary be allowed to summon before him both "ecclesiastical persons [and] any lay persons" that he suspected "concerning religion" and to use the proposed articles as the basis for his examination. The Spanish ambassador was not far off the mark when he later noted, "It looks as if they wanted to mimic the Spanish inquisition. . . ."[36] For this was precisely the impression that the Puritans wished to create. Protestants generally, and Puritans in particular, were deeply distressed at the government's failure to act against Catholics. This joint statement thus represented the unqualified aim of the lower house to harry the Papists from the land. It also suggests another reason why the Queen spoke of "restless heads" when she addressed a committee from the Commons on the 29th.[37]

It is impossible to gauge the immediate effect of this petition on the upper house. The episcopal "Acta Superiore" for the next four sessions has them meeting at Westminster, where they often convened on alternate Parliament days, but their discussion is cloaked in the useful phrase, "secretam quandam communicationem." We may be certain, however, that most of the discussion centered on the Thirty-nine Articles. For on the 29th the clerk entered the fact that "quibusdam

---

[35] Canon Dixon also placed these twenty-one articles prior to the crucial vote on the seven and six articles. See R. W. Dixon, *History of the Church of England* (Oxford, 1902), V, 388.

[36] *Calendar . . . State Papers . . . Simancas, Vol. I, Elizabeth, 1558-1567* (London, 1892), no. 212 (15 Feb. 1563).

[37] Neale, *Parliament*, I, 108.

articulis orthodoxae" had received the unanimous approval of the assembled bishops.[38]

The missing lower-house journal would be helpful here in determining how the obstreperous Puritans took to Parker's editing of the Forty-two Articles. Their kindred spirits in the Commons had already caused quite a stir. They had presented a petition on the 29th urging the Queen to marry, and it had been politely but firmly turned down. Some of the courage and enthusiasm it had taken to face the Queen may well have infected the Convocation clergy: if the Commons could withhold subsidy to urge royal marriage, the lower-house members reasoned, perhaps they might do the same thing with the draft of the Thirty-nine Articles to force liturgical reform.

Some such scheme propelled Nowell and six others, with the "libellum de doctrina," back to the bishops on 5 February, to whom they announced that not all of their house had been willing to subscribe.[39] Thereupon the bishops ordered that unanimous consent be obtained by the next session (10 February). This session came and went, however, with Nowell able to report only that "all have not yet subscribed."[40]

Bishop Grindal would recall the following summer, "I think not one that was present refused to subscribe the Articles as they were first offered to the qu[een's] Ma[jesty]."[41] Grindal's recollection, however, is in error. Although the upper-house journal did omit further mention of the Thirty-nine Articles, a careful collation of surviving manuscript copies, allowing for duplications of signatures, suggests that only ninety-one separate names were actually affixed to Arch-

[38] Cardwell, *Synodalia*, II, 511. Different MSS have omitted the names of Bishops Barlow, Sandys, Scambler, Guest, and Cheyney from the unanimous roll. Probably all but Cheyney did subscribe. Cf. Hardwick, *Articles*, p. 123, and Bennet, *Essay*, p. 183.

[39] *Ibid.*, p. 514 (". . . asseruit . . . qui hactenus articulis dicti libelli non subscripserunt"). This "book of doctrine" (MS Thirty-nine Articles) should not be confused with the "librum de disciplina," which was the reconsideration of the 1552 *Reformatio Legum* of Cranmer. The canons had been sent to a committee of bishops on 29 January and were approved by Convocation on 26 February; however, the canons were never allowed to emerge from Convocation.

[40] *Ibid.*, p. 516.

[41] British Museum, Lansdowne MS 6/59 foll. 145-145ᵛ. Grindal did qualify this statement by mentioning "no nott D. Whyte off Oxforde." However, he was also wrong here, for Thomas White of New College, Oxford, and Archdeacon of Berkshire did sign Parker's draft copy. Strype, *Annals*, I, Bk. I, 488-490, reprints the signature.

bishop Parker's "red leaded" draft copy.[42] And a comparison of these names with other extant manuscripts of Convocation sources reveals that, at most, there probably were never more than ninety-nine members present during the entire session of the lower house of Convocation. Together, these analyses indicate that perhaps eight members failed to sign the 1563 version of the Thirty-nine Articles.[43] The members of the lower house, in other words, were hardly unanimous in their support of the Articles. Furthermore, the delay in obtaining the signatures suggests that what the Puritans actually were doing was attempting to buy time as they sought to bargain for changes in ceremonial rites. For during the next week (13-19 February) Puritan elements in the lower house made their final effort to reform the Elizabethan Church from within.

Again, one cannot help but be impressed with the continuity of events between the Commons and Convocation. From the opening debates on the government's Subsidy Bill (6 February), there had been Puritan scruples in the Commons about the oath affixed to its preamble.[44] These debates served only to heighten the fervor of the Puritans to strengthen the government's new Supremacy Bill, which received its first reading on Saturday, 13 February.[45] Its title on entry was

[42] Corpus Christi College MS 121/26 foll. 251-260, and British Museum, Egerton MS 2035 foll. 103ᵛ-105ᵛ. Strype's reprint lists the fourteen duplications, totaling 105 signatures, including two for Thomas Bolt of Chichester but omitting one signature for John Price from St. Asaph. Bennet, *Essay*, pp. 192-197, corrects these errors but also includes two proxy names, Henry Squire of Berwick and "Mri. Smith" of Landaff, while ignoring William Luson, who was present (Petyt MS 530/47 foll. 575). These errors reduce the total to our ninety-one.

[43] The collation of signatures was done using the Egerton MS copy of the Thirty-nine Articles and the extant Puritan petitions in Petyt MSS 548/47 foll. 575-576 and fol. 588. These eight absentees include the Puritans, Thomas Bacon, William Burton, John Ellis, and the prolocutor, Alexander Nowell; one unknown, Thomas Richley of Peterborough; and three non-Puritans, Thomas Hewett, John Warner, and William Luson. Petyt MS 548/47 fol. 588 lists those absent from the later crucial vote, totaling twenty-four names; however, only thirteen signed the Articles, a fact which suggests that as many as eight of these never attended any sessions, among them the Puritans William Turner, Dean of Wells, and George Carew, Dean of Windsor and Bristol.

[44] *Commons Journal*, I, 65, 10 Feb., "Divers Arguments upon the Bill of Subsidy, and the Oath therein"; 13 Feb., "Arguments touching the Oath of the Assessors in the Subsidy."

[45] *Commons Journal*, I, 64-65. Professor Neale does not include in his discussion of the 1563 Parliament (*Parliament*, I, 85-128) mention of a typical Puritan touch: on 30 January a by-law was inserted into the journal, stating "that every

simply "the Bill against those that extol the Power of the Bishop of Rome, and refuse the Oath of Allegiance." When it returned from a committee headed by Francis Knollys on the 16th, however, the clerk described it as "I, *nova*: the new Bill for *Punishment* of those that shall extol the Bishop of Rome, or refuse to take the Oath" (italics mine). The additional word and the final text of 5 Eliz. c. 1 bear witness to the ferocity of the Commons' anti-Catholicism: now all Elizabethan officials in any way dependent upon the state—those in holy orders, universities, schoolmasters, lawyers, law officers, councillors, and all members of Parliament except the peers—were required to take the oath of supremacy to the Queen or suffer premunire on the first offense and death for high treason on the second.[46] A partial explanation for the severity of this new Commons' Supremacy Bill and the rapidity with which it reached the floor for debate, we believe, involves the events that transpired in the lower house of Convocation during the same week.

On Saturday, 13 February, the same day that the Puritans in the Commons were debating exclusion of any oath in the Subsidy Bill, their brethren in Convocation were also locked in heated debate.[47] Discussion apparently turned on a series of seven articles that had been presented to the house by a group of thirty-four members headed by Nowell, the prolocutor.[48] The character and purpose of these articles

---

of the House that cometh after the Prayer, which shall be at Eight of the Clock, shall pay 4d. to the poor Men's Box."

[46] I Eliz. c. 1, the Supremacy Act, applied only to ecclesiastical officials and royal officers, including justices; punishment for refusal involved (1) loss of office, (2) premunire, and (3) death.

[47] Bishop Burnet later claimed to have "had in my Hands the Original Journal of the Lower House of Convocation" (Gilbert Burnet, *A Sermon Preached before the House of Convocations on the 31st of January 1688* . . . [London, 1689]). Yet his own *History of the Reformation of the Church of England* (ed. Nares, [London, 1830], IV, 574-575) reprints only Petyt MS 538/47 excerpts, giving an accurate account of the "publicae Disputationes fieri" that led to the crucial vote on the 13th and listing both the disputants and the order of votes.

[48] Petyt MS 538/47 foll. 576-577, reprinted in Strype, *Annals*, I, Bk. I, 500-502. See n. 5 for the two missing names in Strype. These thirty-four included six cathedral deans (of St. Paul's; Christ Church, Oxford; Litchfield; Hereford; Worcester; and Exeter) and thirteen archdeacons. The group breaks down into thirteen non-exiles and twenty-one exiles (eleven from Frankfort, including the missing Pedder and Cole; five from Geneva; four from Strasbourg; one from Aarau). This analysis demonstrates that the so-called Genevan influence was in the minority.

is quite clear: psalm-singing by the congregation was to replace organs; only ministers were to baptize, without the sign of the cross; superstitious kneeling was to be left an indifferent matter; cope and surplice were to be "taken away"; no prescribed ministerial dress was to be legally compelled; the proposed 33rd Article, directed against those who opposed public religious orders, was to be "mitigated"; and all superstitious holy days were to be ended, that men might treat them as any other working day. In effect, this Puritan petition from the lower house called for a complete overhaul of the moderate 1559 Act of Uniformity.

There is little wonder that debates grew hot and that the list of disputants was long.[49] When all had been heard, the seven Puritan articles had become six, and their order had been somewhat changed.[50] Abrogation of holy days now topped the list. A new article, requiring ministers to read the service facing the people, was inserted. The sign of the cross was still to be omitted at baptism. Superstitious kneeling was now to be avoided by a fine piece of Puritan casuistry, "for age, sickness, and sundry other infirmities." The surplice was to suffice as service habit. And organs were to be removed. Debate had evidently removed any mention of the ominous opposition to the 33rd Article against *publicum ordinem ecclesiae*. It had shown, too, that the Puri-

---

[49] Burnet, *History*, IV, 575, lists the thirteen "Disputatores" but fails to indicate which side they took. By comparing their later voting record on the Puritan six articles (above), the following breakdown is possible: "Decanus Wygorn" (John Pedder), intransigent Puritan, supported both sets of Puritan articles and, therefore, must have favored them here; "Mr. Byckley" (Thomas Bickley), chaplain to Archbishop Parker, who opposed the Puritan six articles, must have opposed them in this debate; "Archd. 'Covent'" (Thomas Lever), signed both Puritan articles; "Mr. Nebyson" (Stephen Nevyson), Proctor of Canterbury, supported the Puritan articles; "Mr. Pullen" (John Pullain), Archdeacon of Colchester, supported both Puritan articles; "Mr. Cotterell" (John Cotterel), Archdeacon of Wells, opposed the Puritan six articles; "Mr. John Waker" (John Walker), Proctor of Suffolk, supported both Puritan articles; "Mr. Laur. Neuell" (Laurence Nowell), Dean of Lichfield, supported both Puritan articles; "Mr. Talphill [sic]" (James Calfhill), Proctor of London, supported both Puritan articles; "Mr. Crowley" (Robert Crowley), Archdeacon of Hereford, supported the Puritan articles; "Mr. Tremain" (Richard Tremain), Treasurer of Exeter Cathedral, supported both Puritan articles; "Mr. Hewet" (Thomas Hewet), Precentor of St. David's, opposed the Puritan articles; "Decanus Eliens" (Andrew Perne), opposed the Puritan articles. Thus nine Puritans rose to favor the seven articles, whereas only four spoke in opposition. Burnet's view, "multis affirmantibus illos a se non probari," is not confirmed by the debate.

[50] Strype, *Annals*, I, Bk. I, 502-503.

tans apparently were willing to accept the surplice, although they resisted any other "comely garment or habit."

On this basis, traditionally on the afternoon of the 13th, the crucial vote on these six Puritan articles was taken in the lower house of Convocation. Whether it was done orally or by division is unknown. Some slight variations in the voting lists also exist.[51] But whatever the voting procedure, the tension must have been enormous.

One might ask what difference it made, after all, how Convocation voted. In 1559 a lower house still dominated by the Marian Catholic clergy had voted unanimously against any religious changes, and the Elizabethan government had ignored them completely.[52] The difference in 1563, however, came with three new sets of circumstances. First, the Queen—whether she liked it or not—was a publicly proclaimed Protestant. Her clergy, also, were now ostensibly all Protestant. It would have been extremely impolitic to have allowed any open break to develop in the English Protestant façade, especially since the Council of Trent was in session at the time (18 January 1562 to 4 December 1563). Second, the Puritans in Convocation knew that the House of Commons contained men of the same "religion of conscience" as themselves. Unlike the gathering in 1559, Convocation was now moving with the religious tide of the future, not against it. Third, the Puritans thought that they could win. Their iconoclasm in the cathedrals during the earlier visitations of 1559-1561 had produced no widespread Catholic reaction, and the proposed articles were clearly designed to cleanse the Church of all remaining vestiges of "Popery."

[51] Strype unaccountably gives Thomas Wilson (an undistinguished Frankfort exile and canon of Worcester) two votes (*Annals*, I, Bk. I, 504-505), while Petyt MS 538/47 foll. 575-576 clearly records only one; on the other hand, he assigns Thomas Godwin (chaplain to Bishop Bullingham of Lincoln) only one vote, while Petyt MS, *loc. cit.*, gives him two votes. Burnet's list (*History*, IV, 575) is correct for Wilson and Godwin but errs with Richard Tremain (Treasurer of Exeter Cathedral and a member of an important Dorset family), assigning him two votes, which would have given the Puritans a tie. Petyt MS is ambiguous (fol. 575), as the copyist gave Tremain one vote and then slashed through it with a second. Tremain had but one vote. Barry, "Convocation," p. 499, notices the difference but remarks: "I have no doubt that Strype is correct in his version." Such, however, is not the case.

[52] Burnet, *History*, III, 455, takes this view when he concludes: "It is not to be imagined, but if the affirmative vote had prevailed, that it could not be intended to have any other effect, but to make an address to the parliament to alter the book in those particulars." For the 1559 Convocation, see Philip Hughes, *The Reformation in England* (London, 1954), III, 22.

The debates had produced numerous Puritan supporters; moreover, the fatal optimism that allowed the Puritans to regard the Queen as their own Deborah deluded them into believing that, once Convocation affirmed their view, she would accept their reforms.

And so a vote was taken on the six Puritan articles. The tally of the popular vote revealed forty-five members for, and thirty-five against, the articles; but this was only half of the story. Convocation represented all provincial clergymen of Canterbury, whose representation totaled 144 votes, and those who held the proxies of the approximately forty-five absent clergymen made the real difference. The forty-three Puritans could muster between them only fifteen proxies,[53] whereas their thirty-five opponents amassed a total of twenty-four proxies.[54] Thus the final count was fifty-nine opposed to the Puritan reforms, fifty-eight in favor of them. By the slim margin of one proxy vote, the Puritans had failed to carry the lower house. Unless reform plans were now to be given up completely, the Puritans' only hope lay with the upper house of Convocation, among those Puritan bishops who would be inclined to listen and to press for reform.

Despite later Puritan gibes at "Lordlie Bishops" or "Proud Prelates," it is not always recalled that Puritan conscience initially had no qualms about Puritan ministers accepting episcopal office. Even Anthony Gilby, "the puritan pope of Ashby-de-la-Zouch,"[55] wrote much later: ". . . in the cleare light of the Gospell, God will have Bishoppes or Ministers that shalbe discerned from the people by doctrine and conversacion, and not by garments of straunge fashion."[56] And the Elizabethan Bishop of Durham, James Pilkington, wrote shortly after taking office that the chief work of a bishop was the "raising up of men's sinful clogged conscience. . . ."[57] Even the Puritan exiles, Withers and

---

[53] Petyt MS 538/47 foll. 575-576 reveals the group to have been composed of twenty-three exiles and twenty non-exiles. The former had a total of five proxies (four from Frankfort, one from Strasbourg).

[54] Petyt MS 538/47 fol. 576 records that among this number there was only one French exile (Thomas Bickley), the remaining thirty-four being non-exiles. This analysis indicates that the conservative Marian holdovers controlled sixteen of the proxies and thus were really responsible for the Puritans' defeat. Twenty-seven potential voters were absent, however, including four who had signed the Puritan seven articles—Thomas Cole, Gregory Dodd, John Mullins, and Richard Rogers.

[55] Harry Porter, *Reformation and Reaction in Tudor Cambridge* (Cambridge, 1958), p. 88.

[56] *A Pleasaunt Dialogue*, sig. A8ᵛ.

[57] *The Works of James Pilkington*, ed. J. Scholefield for the Parker Society (Cambridge, 1842), p. 492.

Barthelot, who fled England to Geneva in 1566, wrote of the assistance which they had received from some bishops during that year of final crisis.[58] Thus we should not be surprised that voices were raised in the upper house among those Puritan bishops who supported the cause of their brethren in the lower house.

During these climactic days in the lower houses of Parliament and Convocation, the name of Edwin Sandys, Bishop of Worcester, appears prominently in Incent's account of episcopal activity in the upper house. Sandys presided at the Friday morning session (12 February) that preceded the Saturday afternoon debate and vote on the six Puritan articles; and, when Archbishop Parker was absent on the 15th, Sandys and Nicolas Bullingham of Lincoln made a "thorough examination" of the proposed clerical subsidy.[59] It is likely that on these two occasions Sandys presented two proposals for further reform in the Elizabethan Church, which manifest the sheer audacity of at least one Puritan bishop.

The first proposal was very short, consisting of only three terse articles.[60] The last article, recalling the memory of Henry VIII and Edward VI, urged the appointment of "ecclesiastical orders and rules," that is, a revival of the 1552 Canons.[61] But the first two articles—advocating the elimination of private baptism, especially its ministration by women and the "blot[ting] out" of baptismal "crossing [of] the infant's forehead" as superstitious—constituted major points in the Puritan reform offensive in the lower house. They appeared in both the seven-article petition and the six-article reduction of the 13th. Their presence in Sandys's proposal underscores the Puritan desire to press for reform in the upper house and also suggests a possible chronological link between reform drafts in both houses.

Sandys's second proposal, a series of seven recommendations,[62] was concerned mainly with episcopal administration reforms.[63] Sandys

[58] *Zurich Letters*, II, no. 58 (dated "Aug. 1567"). They urged Bullinger to write letters "to the bishops of Norwich [John Parkhurst], Worcester [Edwin Sandys], and Durham [James Pilkington]" to thank them for episcopal encouragement in "the purification of the churches."

[59] Cardwell, *Synodalia*, II, 516-517.

[60] Petyt MS 538/47 fol. 531.

[61] Wilkins, *Concilia Magnae Britannicae . . .* (London, 1735-1737), IV, 238-239, dates Sandys's articles "after the matters of doctrine [i.e., the Thirty-nine Articles] were thus despatched." This reference dates Sandys's proposal before 26 February. See n. 39.

[62] Petyt MS 538/47 fol. 531ᵛ, reprinted in Wilkins, *Concilia*, IV, 240.

[63] Convocation was urgently concerned with financial matters from 13 Feb-

urged strongly that a bishop or dean be permitted to lease or grant advowsons only "for his own time." However, when Sandys came to local reforms, his Puritan inclinations were unmistakable: all clergy, he advised, should catechize "every Sunday according to the injunction on that behalf";[64] common swearers should be banished from the communion; none should be beneficed save those learned in "sound religion"; and the learned candidate for the ministry should be admitted only with "the consent of six learned ministers, who shall all lay their hands upon his head at his admission." Sandys seemed to be proposing something that would look very much like ordination by a Swiss presbytery.

Unfortunately, we cannot be certain how Sandys's proposals were received by his episcopal colleagues. There was considerable absenteeism from the House of Lords after 11 February, which perhaps indicates zealous attention to provincial matters.[65] Bishops Pilkington and Horne were the only prelates outside Convocation listed as having preached publicly during this period. They joined other known Puritan sympathizers in delivering "godly sermons" at Paul's Cross and elsewhere.[66] Although their sermons have not survived, they doubtless joined part of a chorus lamenting lack of reform; or at least they may have warned of the fate awaiting English Protestants if Catholicism should return.[67]

---

ruary until the final acceptance of the clerical subsidy (6s. per £) on the 24th. On the 19th the bishops directed the lower house to answer a series of questions on benefices, dilapidations, etc. The clerk, Incent, apparently went down to the lower house and took the answers verbatim. Cardwell, *Synodalia*, II, 518-519.

[64] Article 44 of the royal injunction of 1559 specifies the catechism for "every second Sunday."

[65] D'Ewes, *Journal*, p. 67, indicates that the Lords often adjourned on Convocation days. But it is also clear from the spotty attendance record kept by the clerk of Lords (*Lords Journal*, I, 580-619), that Archbishop Young of York and Bishop Bentham of Lichfield left London after 11 February. Barlow of Chichester—true to his Henrician indoctrination in statecraft—did not miss a session until 1 April; and Downham of Chester missed only three sittings during the entire 1563 session.

[66] *The Diary of Henry Machyn . . .* , ed. J. G. Nichols for the Camden Society (London, 1848), vol. 48, pp. 299-305. When we take note of the other known Puritans preaching at this time—e.g., Thomas Cole and John Salisbury—it is clear how completely Reformed clergy dominated London pulpits in 1563. See Miller Maclure, *The Paul's Cross Sermons, 1534-1642* (Toronto, 1958), pp. 56-57.

[67] Machyn, *loc. cit.* Horne took up a collection for Huguenot refugees on the 12th.

One voice of protest against these Puritan reforms was raised in the upper house. A paper by William Alley, Bishop of Exeter, has survived, which may have been a direct rejoinder to Sandys's proposals.[68] Its vigorous tone is suggestive of the tensions in the upper house that paralleled the Puritan heat in the lower one.

The paper is quite long, its eleven articles arranged as though for a convocation address. The proposals fall naturally into two categories: two concerned with the prevalence of dissent and nine involving matters of clerical and lay discipline. The first two concern us here, for they bear testimony to the kinds of bitter discontent then rampant in England. Alley's first sentence spoke of a need for "one kind of doctrine" against those who "inveigh one against the other" in scriptural or *adiaphorous* matters.[69] The Bishop spoke here from the depths of his own experience at Exeter; he told in particular of the "great invectives" hurled by preachers "in my diocese" at each other over the doctrine of Christ's descent into hell.[70] Alley became quite explicit as he noted, rather contemptuously, the symbolic view of this doctrine held by "Erasmus and the Germans, and especially upon the authority of Mr. Calvin and Mr. Bullinger," comparing this view with the universal consent to the literal acceptance of the doctrine by many Latin and Greek Fathers "by a space of 1100 years."[71]

---

[68] Petyt MS 438/47 foll. 448-449ᵛ, reprinted in Strype, *Annals*, I, Bk. I, 518-522.

[69] Alley used the argument in reverse in *Ptokomoseion or the Poore Mans Librarie* . . . (London, 1565), a series of lectures given at St. Paul's in 1560. There he chided the Catholics for calling the new Elizabethan religion heresy: "Heresy unto them is, if a man swarue one fote, from their accustomed opinions" (p. 22). Alley's views changed after he had accepted the mantle of authority.

[70] C. H. Garrett, *The Marian Exiles* . . . (Cambridge, 1938), pp. 311-312, notes Alley's difficulties with his treasurer, Richard Tremaine, "a strong Puritan" who allowed an unlicensed "young man" to preach offensive doctrine among the Cornishmen, causing "a flood of mischief." Alley also had fallen heir to a long-standing struggle between town and cathedral, which dated from the fifteenth century. See M. E. Curtis, "Some Dispute between the City and Cathedral Authorities of Exeter," *History of Exeter Research Monograph No. 5* (Manchester, 1932).

[71] See Hardwick, *Articles*, p. 135, for a discussion of this doctrine's connection with Article 3 of the Thirty-nine Articles, and see J. Calvin, *Institutes* . . . , ed. J. T. McNeill (Philadelphia, 1960), I, 512-514, for notes on Calvin's adoption of the views of Aquinas and Erasmus. For Calvin, the descent meant symbolically "that Christ was put in place of evil doers as surety and pledge . . . as the price of our redemption . . ." (*Institutes*, II, xiv, 10).

Having described the tragic consequences of allowing such erroneous Reformed dissension to continue, Alley then proceeded to answer those preachers who "murmur, spurn, kick, and very sharply inveigh" against required ecclesiastical vestments.[72] Alley's reply to the Puritans' seven and six articles, as well as to Grindal's earlier scruples about uniform attire, soon became the stock episcopal response to Puritan attacks against vestments. Although he admitted that the shape of the cap was an indifferent matter, he insisted that uniformity of dress had been "made politic by the prescribed order of the prince" and that any variation was both "odious and scandalous."

This appeal to royal—and parliamentary—authority for the establishment of one uniform English faith was from the very beginning the answer of loyal Elizabethan bishops to their Puritan brethren. In Alley's case, it served to quash all differences of opinion on either delicate theological questions or indifferent ceremonial matters. Yet this position must be compared with Grindal's pre-Convocation appeal for an end to popish apparel, with Sandys's specific proposals against private baptism, superstitious crossing, and the establishment of a presbyterian ordination service, and with the reform oratory of Pilkington and Horne. When such a comparison is made, it is evident that some explosive debates on Puritan dissension over ceremonies must have occupied both the upper and the lower houses of Convocation during the fateful week of 13-19 February.

The Convocation did not end until 14 April.[73] Its long-term effect was great, for this session provided the Elizabethan Church with most of its later literature. The Thirty-nine Articles, the large and small catechisms, the Second Book of Homilies, and the Welsh Prayer Book and Bible—all these had their beginnings in 1563. Yet the immediate effect of these sessions was a legacy of division. Since the Puritans had been turned away from any hope of reforming the English Church from within, they were now forced into devising new ways—especially parliamentary ways—of reforming the church from without.[74] Re-

[72] He noted specifically one London preacher who had boasted of eight sermons "against surplices, rochets, tippets, and caps, counting them not to be perfect that do wear them."

[73] Cardwell, *Synodalia*, II, 527. Parliament had been prorogued on the 10th. D'Ewes, *Journal*, p. 75.

[74] The effect of the 1563 Convocation never faded from the Puritans' minds. Whithers and Barthelot told Bullingham in 1567 (*Zurich Letters*, II, no. 58), that "many things of the greatest advantage of the church, which had been adopted by the last convocation but one, were suppressed, and never saw the light."

formers were now matched against the reform of 1559, and the garb of religious unity woven so carefully in the first Elizabethan Parliament ceased to exist after the second.

Writing a few days after the Convocation had closed, Archbishop Parker lamented the open opposition of his clergy. On the qualities of "my brethren"—that is, the bishops and clergy of Canterbury—Parker wrote to Cecil: "I see some of them to be 'full of cracks, running from this to that,'[75] although indeed the Queen's Majesty may have good cause to be well contented with her choice of most of them, very few expected, amongst whom I count my[self]."

There is little doubt that the self-effacing Parker was reflecting here on the Puritan protagonists in the 1563 Convocation. Even some of these had chosen not to be counted in the final vote on the Puritan reforms, thereby causing the rejection of the reforms by a margin of one vote.[76] Others, particularly the London clergy, returned to their own cures to take up the Puritan cause from the pulpit, a campaign which led directly to the extremities of the 1565-1566 vestment controversy.[77] One such London curate wrote shortly after the end of the Convocation: ". . . I am curate over three thousand and more of God's sheepe, and thereby my Function is not to sleepe, and be sluggish, but to waite on my office to Discharge as I am charged in Teaching and Governing and to exercise myselfe to dooing my duty if I were worthy before the Lord . . . so I must blow the trumpet against ungodliness, or else the Lord will require the blood of the people at my hands. . . ."[78] Unfortunately, for the Puritans, no trumpet part had been scored for the Elizabethan Protestant symphony. And the first sounds of discord raised in the 1563 Convocation would swell to a cacophony of sound after 1566.

---

[75] ". . . pleni rimarum, hac atque illac effluunt. . . ." The phrase is a popular quip from Terence's *Eunuchus. Parker Correspondence*, no. 127 (ca. 14 April).

[76] The vigorous Dean of Exeter, Gregory Dodd, for example, controlled three proxy votes. Had he chosen to be present at the final vote, the Puritans would have won. Episcopal pressure from Bishop Alley may in this instance have been effective.

[77] See J. H. Primus, *The Vestments Controversy* (Kampen, 1960), pp. 71-148.

[78] British Museum, Egerton MS 2350, fol. 67, dated 25 June 1563. The curate is Walter Tempeste of St. Giles-without-Cripplegate. I owe notice of this interesting citation to E.L.C. Mullins, "The Effects of the Marian and Elizabethan Religious Settlements on the Clergy of London," unpublished M.A. thesis (University of London, 1948).

# REFORM AND COUNTER-REFORM:
# THE CASE OF THE SPANISH HERETICS*

PAUL J. HAUBEN

THERE is much to recommend the view that the Catholic Reform and the Counter-Reformation of the sixteenth century were two parts—distinct yet frequently overlapping, even in individual careers[1]—of a broad Catholic Revival.[2] Nevertheless, when one looks at Spanish Catholicism's vehement response to the presence of two apparently Protestant congregations in Seville and Valladolid in 1558, the traditional word Counter-Reformation alone seems to provide the most appropriate description. The autos-da-fé celebrated at Valladolid on 21 May and 8 October 1559 and at Seville on 24 September 1559, 29 December 1560, and 26 April 1562, which collectively extinguished what organized Protestantism had existed in Spain, were clear expressions of the national faith, attended as they were by throngs of persons from all levels of society, including the country's leaders.[3] It is quite possible that Philip II's return home from the Low Countries was hastened by these events, and they may have blinded him temporarily to the far more real danger of heresy in his northern dominions.[4]

Spain (more precisely, Castile) and its Inquisition called these two

* I wish to express my appreciation to the American Philosophical Society for the grant it awarded me in 1965, which freed me from other duties and enabled me to prepare this essay.

[1] E.g., those of Caraffa, Morone, Pole. Delio Cantimori's penetrating essay, "Italy and the Papacy," *New Cambridge Modern History: The Reformation, 1520-1559* (Cambridge, England, 1958), II, ch. VIII, is very enlightening on this point.

[2] Pierre Janelle, *The Catholic Reformation* (Milwaukee, 1949), despite certain shortcomings of interpretation, is historiographically a relatively early work employing this approach.

[3] The standard accounts are in Henry C. Lea, *A History of the Inquisition in Spain* (London/New York, 1907), III, iii; Ernst Schäfer, *Geschichte des spanischen Protestantismus und die Inquisition* (Gütersloh, 1902), 3 vols.; *idem*, "Seville und Valladolid," *Verein für Reformationsgeschichte* (1903), pp. 1-137; M. Menéndez y Pelayo, *Historia de los heterodoxos españoles* (Santander, 1947) III, 391-442, and IV, 76-123.

[4] M. F. Van Lennep, *De Hervorming in Spanje* (Haarlem, 1901), notes that the existence of the congregations was well known to persons like Carranza, then visiting the Low Countries with Philip.

154

congregations Lutheran. But were they really Lutheran? What kind of Reform did their members desire? Or was "the alleged heresy of the little communities . . . merely the pathetic finale to a story of heterodox practices . . . begun many decades before?" Is it true that "twenty years earlier a man like Cazalla [one of the Valladolid leaders] would probably have received little more than a brief penance?"[5] Does one, in fact, "search in vain for a reformed sect following the Lutheran formulas" in these two groups?[6] Students of the problem have increasingly come to think that, far from being Lutheran or

[5] John H. Elliott, *Imperial Spain* (London/New York, 1964), pp. 204, 217. The word "probably" suggests at least some need for caution. The same view is expressed in the other equally fine recent survey of sixteenth-century Spain, John Lynch, *Spain under the Habsburgs* (London, 1964), I, 236-242. Elliott indicates that the conventicles had been in touch with Geneva toward the end, probably through book-smugglers like Hernández (of whom more below). In fact, long after the obiteration of these congregations, translated heretical literature kept pouring into Spain, though to whom it was being sent has never been disclosed. See Eduard Böhmer, "Protestantische Propaganda in Spanien im Anfänge des 17 Jhrds.," *Zeitschrift für Kirchengeschichte*, XVII (1897), 373-390. (The date of this publication suggests a pressing need for new research, although this seems to be a reliable article.) Dr. John Tedeschi of the Newberry Library, Chicago, has told me not only that book-smuggling rings were well organized for making deliveries to Italy (and to Spain as well) but also that we know to whom the materials were sent.

We must also note here that nothing at all points to anything but an assault on native Protestantism, real or imagined. The then Inquisitor-General, Valdés (no relation of Juan Valdés's) clearly had personal motives in having Carranza arrested on charges of "Lutheranism," but, as is well known, this is a matter separate from the Seville-Valladolid affair. Although the autos-da-fé of 1558-1562 appear as the symbol of the Counter-Reformation in its traditional sense—and that they were—they were aimed solely at Protestantism. Erasmism completely and Illuminism for all practical purposes had been destroyed by ca. 1540; nor do I see any reason to suspect that the Inquisition looked upon men like Constantino as mere "Catholic Reformers," even though, in retrospect, most scholars now think they were.

[6] Marcel Bataillon, *Erasme et l'Espagne* (Paris, 1937), p. 751. (The revised two-volume Spanish edition of 1950 does not affect this area.) He came to this conclusion after a careful analysis of extant writings of the congregations' leaders, especially those of Constantino Ponce de la Fuente (of whom more below). See chs. X and XIII. For more recent treatment of Constantino, see William B. Jones, "Constantino Ponce de la Fuente," 2 vols., Ph.D. diss. (Vanderbilt University, 1965); I owe this reference to Professor John E. Longhurst of the University of Kansas. Dr. Jones, now a member of Southwestern University's faculty, has kindly informed me that his interpretation of Constantino and those like him agrees with the one set forth here.

genuinely Protestant at all, these congregations fell into a category best described by the somewhat cumbersome formula, Erasmist-Illuminist-Evangelical Catholic. Marcel Bataillon's great monograph established once and for all the vital role of Erasmism in Castile from Charles V's arrival until the mid-1530's. No such work exists for Illuminism, but several scattered studies make clear the interpenetration of the latter with Erasmism during this period and thereafter.[7] In his remarkable *The Radical Reformation*, George H. Williams has elaborated a religious concept, Evangelical Catholicity, which makes clear how the fusion of certain aspects of Erasmism and mysticism created this third category in Southern Europe.[8] There can be little reason to doubt that "Evangelical Catholics" of the South constituted a vital segment of Catholic Reform—in the broader sense of the term, as used by Janelle and Cantimori—certainly through the 1540's.[9] If the heretics who suffered in the autos-da-fé of 1559-1562 belonged to this current, then the zeal of the Spanish inquisitors suggests something different about the Catholic reform impulse than what we might conclude if the Seville and Valladolid congregations were genuinely Lutheran.

Before we discuss in detail the Spanish situation, it may be useful to glance at a country which has been studied much more in this regard in recent years than Spain—namely, Italy. Although it was the home of the Papacy and likewise a country in which Protestantism was never strongly established, Italy nevertheless provides an interesting contrast to Spain in its treatment of heretical groups. While sixteenth-

[7] Bataillon, chs. IV and IX; Menendez, *Historia*, IV, 210-249; John E. Longhurst, "The *Alumbrados* of Toledo," *Archiv für Reformationsgeschichte*, XLV (1954), 233-252; A. Selke de Sanchez, "Algunos datos nueves sobre los primeros alumbrados," *Bulletin hispanique*, LIV (1952), 125-152; E. Asensio, "El erasmismo y las corrientes espirituales afines," *Revista de la Filología española*, XXXVI (1952), 31-99; and Americo Castro, *Aspectos del vivir hispánico* (Santiago de Chile, 1949), 21-71, are good starting points. It is interesting to note, however, that at least some Spanish Erasmists viewed the Illuminists with alarm. Thus, in 1525, Archbishop Manrique, head of the Inquisition and a fervent admirer of Erasmus, led an attack against the Illuminists. One suspects that the Archbishop and others like him foresaw that they might be bracketed with the latter to their detriment (and later they were). This conflict almost foreshadows the fratricidal Protestant divisions in face of the Catholic counter-attack in Germany later on—or, nearer home, the *conversos'* often ambivalent attitude toward unconverted Jews.

[8] (Philadelphia, 1962), esp. ch. I and pp. 529-544.

[9] See nn. 1 and 8.

century Spain obviously was a single state in a way that fragmented Italy was not, the regional differences marking the former's history should not be overlooked: it was no mere accident that expressions of Catholic zeal appeared in Reconquista-oriented Castile rather than in other parts of Spain.[10] Nonetheless, even in Catalonia it was inconceivable that some local Calvinists could survive quasi-publicly in the way that they could—thanks to the "continual resistance of the local authorities to the interference of the inquisitors"—in Milan.[11] Although parts of Spain occasionally manifested jealousy of inquisitorial power, in general the Inquisition's assault on Protestantism was considered to fall within accepted native traditions, elaborated earlier against Jews, Moors, and the always suspect converts to Christianity from these faiths. In many sections of Italy, on the other hand, the Holy Office was frequently viewed primarily as a jurisdictional-administrative competitor and trespasser.[12]

Cantimori remarks that throughout the Italian peninsula "sympathy with and interest in . . . reform established beyond the Alps penetrated all social levels from the peasant to the prince, . . . the artisan to the professor of law."[13] Of course, one can hardly speak of a mass movement there any more than in Spain, and at first much of this interest seems to have been a blend of naive curiosity and vague hopes of some kind of *aggiornamento*.[14] Even so, Protestantism attracted a much wider range of social groups in Italy than in Spain. As far as I can discover, no prince, professor of law, or, above all, peasant adhered to Protestant heresy in Spain. Thus Protestantism had at least some grass-roots potential in Italy that it never possessed in the Iberian peninsula,

[10] It is also mandatory to note that Erasmism and Illuminism flourished primarily in Castile, as far as we can tell. The whole question of whether Castile was "open" or "closed" from the time of Catholic Kings through the reign of Philip II is explored convincingly in the aforementioned books by Elliott and Lynch.

[11] Cantimori, "Italy and the Papacy," p. 260.

[12] This is made absolutely clear in H. G. Koenigsberger, *Government of Sicily under Philip II of Spain* (New York/London, 1951), ch. VI.

[13] Cantimori, p. 255. To my knowledge, there is virtually no research in this area under way among Spanish historians, whereas in Italy it is quite a respectable field, as the recent collaborative volume, *Ginevra e l'Italia* (Florence, 1959), indicates.

[14] *Ibid.*, p. 256, where he calls this a matter of "individuals rather than groups." However, some of the essays in the cooperative work mentioned in n. 13 suggest, at least occasionally, the reverse.

157

and, consequently, the situation in Spain was distinctly more favorable to the rigid suppression of heresy than it was in this major center of Catholicism.

The Spanish Inquisition, in its highly successful campaign against Erasmists and *alumbrados* earlier in the century, had discovered a most effective procedure when it labeled all the accused as Lutherans.[15] Yet it is difficult to agree that this was merely a cynical device, used to help the prosecution. Though rare, there were a few instances when the charge was obviously sincere,[16] and it must not be dismissed out of hand. For, even when skepticism is justified, as it is with regard to the 1520's and 1530's, the existence of Evangelical Catholics such as Juan Valdés[17] makes problems of definition extremely complicated. Valdés died in 1541 in communion with Rome, but it is absolutely certain that for him to have left Naples for Spain would have meant personal disaster at the Inquisition's hands. Just as his works were used subsequently by Catholics and Protestants alike, so too, his followers ended up in all ranges of the contemporary religious scene, as the mere mention of an Ochino indicates.[18] Of his Neapolitan

[15] See, e.g., Longhurst, "The *Alumbrados*," p. 234, who mentions the case of Juan del Castillo, who "circulated among the Erasmists . . . [was] closely associated with . . . illuminism . . . [and was] burned . . . as a disciple of . . . Luther" in 1535. The same author, in *Luther and the Spanish Inquisition*, New Mexico University Publications in History #5 (1953), studies a similar case which did not end so drastically. In both these cases, and others, the accused could not be considered Lutherans by any stretch of the imagination. Cf. Bataillon, *Erasme et l'Espagne*, ch. IX.

[16] Despite the general accuracy of the thesis in n. 15, see Longhurst, "Luther in Spain," *Proceedings of the American Philosophical Society*, CIII (1959), 75ff. and n. 52, where the case of an Aragonese accused of Lutheranism who apparently deserved the label in 1535-1536 is cited.

[17] Williams' designation is used throughout. The history of the Meaux circle in France during the 1520's, the details of which lie outside the scope of this article, presents some illuminating parallels. With the destruction of the group under conservative Catholic pressure (e.g., the Sorbonne), its members moved to religious positions ranging from Calvinism (Farel) to Rome (Roussel). Henri Daniel-Rops, *The Protestant Reformation*, paperback edn. (New York, 1963), II, 113ff., synthesizes well the researches of Renaudet and others and concludes that these French Christian humanists were also "Evangelicals," in the sense we have been using the term. The similarity of the Meaux reformers to the Southern Europeans, with the exception of the "Nicodemite" tendencies among some of the Italians, is very striking. See nn. 18-20 below.

[18] The literature on Valdés is enormous, and interpretations are unending and opposed. Longhurst, *Erasmus and the Spanish Inquisition*, New Mexico Uni-

circle in the master's lifetime, Cantimori comments: "unlike Renée of Ferrara and her followers Valdés's group had no need to celebrate the Lord's Supper according to the Calvinist rite, nor to avoid hearing Mass. . . ."[19] Calvin called such people Nicodemites, and Catholics like Caraffa not only helped drive men such as Ochino "far from Rome"[20] but themselves must have hewn all the more straitly to "Counter-Reformation," as opposed to "Catholic Reform," Catholicism when they saw before them the histories of the Ochinos.[21] In the face of such varied personal histories, the Inquisition's indiscriminate use of the label "Lutheran" had some point, even when it was far from precise.

The Valdesians suggest a clue to an analysis of the Valladolid and Seville congregations. Perhaps the leaders of the Spanish groups, such as Juan Gil and Constantino Ponce de la Fuente, were originally products of the Erasmist-Illuminist milieu of the 1520's. Both, after all, were educated at Alcalá, the university center of these currents (though also a source of much orthodox Catholicism, as Cardinal Ximenez de Cisneros intended when he founded it). As Bataillon's careful scrutiny has shown, Constantino's writings are especially indicative of such a background.[22] If such a judgment of these men's beliefs has

---

versity Publications in History #1 (1950), p. 95, n. 3, demonstrates the range of opinion. Cf. also n. 8 above. A convenient sampling of Valdés' writings is in vol. XXV of the *Library of Christian Classics: Spiritual and Anabaptist Writers* (London, 1957), ed. G. H. Williams and A. M. Mergal. Williams' introduction here ought to be read as a preface to *The Radical Reformation*.

[19] Cantimori, "Italy and the Papacy," p. 265. He adds (p. 268) that many such people justified their religious flexibility at this time by pointing out that the Council of Trent had either not yet begun or was still debating fundamentals; hence, one was free to "wait" and act in the "Nicodemite" fashion in more or less good conscience. But see n. 20.

[20] *Ibid.*, p. 267.

[21] *Ibid.*, pp. 271ff., sums them up now as "Counter-Reformers in the Spanish style"!

[22] See n. 6. As to what the Sevillans may have read, see the articles by E. Droz, "Notes sur les Impressions genevoises transportées par Hernández," and by George Bonnant, "Note sur quelques ouvrages en langue espagnole imprimées à Genève par Jean Crespin (1557-60)," in *Bibliothèque d'Humanisme et Renaissance*, XXII (1960), 119-132, and XXIV (1962), 50-57, respectively. These works include J. Pérez's *New Testament, Sumario breve de la doctrina Christiana, Psalms of David*, and *Calvinist Catechism* for juveniles (1550 edn.); J. Valdés, *Comentario*; and at least one of Ochino's works. Droz suggests (p. 121) that the *Catechism* may have been translated from the French by refugee Spanish Erasmists at Valence.

any validity, then it may be possible to attribute their persecution to changes in the religious climate of Spain, rather than to any movement toward heresy in their own thinking. One recalls that the middle of the century saw an enormous upsurge in religious militancy, not confined to Spain. Perhaps the argument that in 1528 or 1538 the members of the congregations would have suffered but "brief" penances is correct, and the ferocity of the reaction to them must be attributed to changes in Spain and Europe, not in men like Constantino and their followers.[23]

However, some stubborn details prevent an unqualified acceptance of this interpretation. As the surviving records show, at least several of the Valladolid-Seville people refused to deny their heresy as charged, and these included men who, under considerable duress, implicated others.[24] If they were not really Protestants, or *luteranos*, why did they not deny that they were? The Seville group, which reached out to embrace the nearby Hieronymite monastery of San Isidro del Campo, had had among its members obvious heretics like Cassiodoro de Reina,[25] Juan Pérez de Pineda,[26] Cypriano de Valera,[27] Antonio del Corro,[28] and Julián Hernández.[29] All of these men had left Spain

[23] As nn. 5 and 15 indicate. On the Inquisitor-General's stake in this matter, see Lynch's judicious appraisal, *Spain*, p. 239.

[24] See n. 3.

[25] Part of his career is discussed in the author's "A Spanish Calvinist Church in Elizabethan London, 1559-65," *Church History*, XXXIV (1965), 50-56.

[26] The basic materials on him are in Eduard Böhmer, *Bibliotheca Wiffeniana* (London/Strasbourg, 1874-1904: reprinted, New York, 1962), II, 55-100 (hereafter cited as *BW*), and generous samples of his writings are scattered throughout vols. II, III, VII, XII, and XVIII of Luis Usoz y Rio, *Reformistas antiguos españoles* (Madrid/London, 1847-1880), 22 vols. (This collection is often catalogued under *Obras de los españoles reformados.*) The three-volume *BW* makes extensive use of Usoz y Rio, and the two should be used together.

[27] Usoz y Rio, VI, VIII, contain most of his extant works. Valera finished and revised the Castilian Protestant Bible begun by Pérez and Reina, which is widely used throughout the Hispanic world. For a more recent view, see L. J. Hutton, "The Spanish Heretic," *Church History*, XXVIII (1958), 23-31, and the author's forthcoming "A Note on the Spanish Heretic," in *Hispania Sacra*. The important article by L. Firpo, "La chiesa italiana di Londra nel Cinquecento e i suoi rapporti con Ginevra," in the cooperative volume cited in n. 13, pp. 364ff., sheds new light on Valera from 1570 with respect to Corro (of whom more below).

[28] A biography of Corro forms the major part of my book, *Three Spanish Heretics and the Reformation* (Geneva, 1967). Consult Pt. II on Reina and Valera.

[29] Longhurst's "Julián Hernández, Protestant Martyr," *Bibliothèque d'Humanisme et Renaissance*, XXII (1960), 90-118, is an especially fine piece of work. Hernández's arrest in the fall of 1557, just after his return from abroad, touched

some time after Juan Gil's public abjuration and sentencing in August 1552 and before the discovery and destruction of the conventicles from 1558.[30] Yet others like them may well have remained. There can be no doubt that Pérez and Valera especially were orthodox Calvinists throughout this period. Reina and Corro present another problem altogether; but during this time they, too, were Calvinists, and, even though they moved later to Lutheranism and Anglicanism, respectively, neither ever remotely entertained the notion of returning to Rome. Hernández, the one layman in this quintet, joined the Walloon Lutheran Church of Frankfurt immediately after leaving Seville and appears to have been gravitating toward Calvinism near the end of his life.[31]

These observations suggest that the accuracy of the Inquisition's charge of Lutheranism is a matter worth serious consideration. There is no doubt that in many respects, as Bataillon and others have shown, the Seville-Valladolid congregations typified the Erasmist-Illuminist influences in Spain, which Williams has happily called "Evangelical Catholicism." From this religious position men could move in several violently opposed directions, as the subsequent history of the Valdesians after the master's death demonstrated. Therefore, it seems plausible to conclude that the Seville-Valladolid groups contained a number of real Protestants alongside Evangelicals like Constantino. Apparently, most of the former escaped, whereas most of the latter were caught in the inquisitorial net and were accused of "Lutheranism" in company with some genuine heretics, as the records published by Lea and Schäfer (cited in note 3 above) prove.

Even more indicative of the blanket use of the Inquisition's "Lutheran" label is the fact that, as far as one can tell, the great majority of Spanish Protestants who left Spain were Calvinists. This was even true

---

off the inquiries and other arrests that ended in the liquidation of the congregation.

[30] For the departure of Corro, along with many others, see below. It seems inconceivable that men like Constantino did not hear of the seizure of Hernández and the flight of the Hieronymites. This fact strengthens our belief that they did not consider themselves Protestants and were flabbergasted on being charged as such shortly afterward. Their attitude in turn, accounts for the ease with which they were rounded up. Gil, by the way, died in 1556; he was also called Dr. Egidio. It is safe to say that he would have been executed had he lived longer, for later his bones were disinterred for public burning in the wake of the arrest of Hernández (most recently summarized by Longhurst, "Hernández," 92ff.).

[31] *Ibid.*, 93ff.

of the refugees from the Spanish groups just discussed. A generation earlier the designation "Lutheran" might have been understandable. But with Luther—and Zwingli—long dead, various "left-wing" Protestant groups on the scene,[32] and Anglican and Calvinist churches resurgent, the Inquisition was clearly using a mere catchword. Philip II's diplomats and spies certainly knew otherwise.[33] One can only conclude that, although against Evangelical Catholics "Lutheran" was possibly used as a cynical device, against the full spectrum of heresy it served as a convenient thumbnail description. In retrospect, however, it is clear that "Calvinist" would have been a more appropriate, if still incomplete, designation for these conventicles. Even if a tiny minority of the Seville-Valladolid congregations were real Lutherans,[34] the fact

[32] In 1529 a "Melchior of Württemberg" created a stir in Valencia. Cf. Lea, *Inquisition*, III, 422, and Longhurst, "Luther," 70ff. and n. 27. The latter makes out a tantalizing case for identifying this person as the famous Melchior Hoffman, the Anabaptist preacher.

[33] See, e.g., the very common *calbenistas* used in many reports from France after 1559 in the *Negociaciones con Francia*, 12 vols. to date (Madrid, 1950-    ). On the other hand, at least as late as 1563, Philip II himself was still referring to Protestants generally as Lutherans. See L. P. Gachard, *Correspondance de Marguerite d'Autriche, Duchesse de Parme, avec Philippe II* (Brussels, 1867-1881), II, 468.

[34] Lea, *Inquisition*, III, 444, n. 2, said some time ago that "To the Spaniards of the period all Protestants were Lutherans but, from the relations of the Seville refugees with Geneva, it may be assumed that these were Calvinists." I think that, in fact, it may be assumed that they represented several contemporary religious divisions; Corro, as we shall soon see, had read the Zwinglian Bullinger before being exiled. Given details like this, it seems plausible to assume that initially the congregations represented the several strands in the religious scene; clearly, I have assumed this throughout the essay. It is fair to note, too, that Cazalla and Constantino had traveled to Lutheran Germany as young Catholic preachers in Charles V's entourage much earlier, but absolutely nothing shows a connection between such trips and their later "heresy"; both men were then popular and orthodox Catholics. Of Cazalla, Lynch says (*Spain*, pp. 238ff.) his "travels . . . were probably less important in his religious development than his own processes of thought"—a useful observation. Clearly the bulk of the congregations had no such possibilities for direct contact with Lutheranism, while Calvinist literature was rapidly replacing Lutheran material in heretical book-smuggling in Spain, as elsewhere in Western Europe at this time. Longhurst's article on Hernández illustrates this point well. See also the author's "In Pursuit of Heresy," *Historical Journal*, IX, no. 3 (1966), 275-285, and "Marcus Pérez and Marrano Calvinism in the Dutch Revolt and the Reformation," *Bibliothèque d'Humanisme et Renaissance*, XXIX (1967), 121-132. There are penetrating observations on this subject in Michael Walzer's *Revolution of the Saints* (Cambridge, Mass., 1965), ch. I.

remains that most of the escapees went directly to Geneva rather than to Wittenberg. It is this predominance of Calvinism among Spanish Protestant refugees of the mid-sixteenth century that now requires our attention.

It is possible to exaggerate to the point of distortion the degree of confusion, disunity, lack of direction, and loss of vitality which Lutheranism suffered after its founder's death and felt even more, in certain ways, after Melanchthon's death in 1560. Various circumstances did, after all, give to Calvinism an energy in mid-century which attracted more of the new generation than did the other Protestant faiths.[35] The story of a Spanish Protestant slightly earlier illustrates this very phenomenon. Francisco de Enzinas converted to Lutheranism while a student at Louvain around 1540.[36] His wanderings included a melodramatic escape from an inquisitorial jail at Brussels, visits with Luther and Melanchthon at Wittenberg, with Bucer at Strasbourg, with Bullinger at Zurich, and with Cranmer at Cambridge. In the last year of his life (1552), he made a pilgrimage to Geneva specifically to meet Calvin, and Strasbourg was his final resting place.

The most obvious reason Calvinism attracted heretically inclined Spaniards, however, was simply geographical proximity.[37] Geneva, the Waldensian-Calvinist sections of northwest Italy and southeast France, and the Huguenot bastions of the southwest, such as Navarre-Béarn, were much more accessible than the Lutheran north. Of course, these territories were hardly secure from Catholic attacks. Nonetheless, they were the logical havens for Protestants fleeing Spain.

A summary of the genesis and subsequent travails of Antonio del Corro's Calvinism will perhaps serve as a useful illustration of the difficulties of applying simple labels to the religious figures of the period.[38] Corro was a young member of the aforementioned Hieronymite monastery involved with the Sevillans when he heard of Juan Gil's sentencing in 1552. For undetermined reasons the case aroused his considerable curiosity, and through friends and relations, some of whom seem to have been connected with the local Inquisition, he obtained not only Gil's no longer extant writings but works by Luther, Melanch-

[35] See J. H. Hexter's discussion of why men chose Calvinism during these years in his "Utopia and Geneva" (also in this volume).

[36] The most recent summary of his story is in Longhurst, "Hernández," p. 96, n. 4.

[37] See the author's "In Pursuit of Heresy," cited in n. 34.

[38] Taken from the work cited in n. 28.

thon, and Bullinger. As Corro later recalled,[39] he found Gil's works to be not only not dangerous but positively stimulating; and from Gil he moved on to read the more rewarding fare just mentioned. As far as one can discern, there is absolutely no evidence that Corro had become familiar with Calvin's thought by the late summer or early fall of 1557, when he slipped out of Spain; but whether he had or not cannot be known for sure. From where in Spain he embarked remains unknown (Seville seems a likely enough point of departure), but we do know that he shipped out to Genoa and made his way north to Geneva. This was a rather hazardous and heroic journey for a cloistered monk to undertake; but Corro was not unique, for he was one of a dozen fleeing along various similar devious routes. After a brief bow to Calvin, Corro studied for over a year at the famous Lausanne Academy and then spent the years 1559-1564 at various ministerial posts in the southwest of France—at Bordeaux, Toulouse, the Béarn, the Périgord. Already, with little justification, he was plagued by the shadow of Servetus's radicalism, as well as by occasional hostility from his French colleagues, who resented his attempts to organize a Spanish Calvinist church in the region. Reports of Corro's occasional indiscipline and so-called ambition are not surprising in view of the latter events. From late 1564 through mid-1566 he had the good fortune to be one of Renée of Ferrara's private chaplains at her semi-independent castellany of Montargis. The daily sight of her active, irreproachable Calvinism, combined with an irenicism and humanity even toward Catholic victims of the religious wars' carnage, appears to have crystallized Corro's own development in this direction. Corro overlooked the fact that Renée's unusually high station shielded her from the opprobrium of the orthodox, but it is from this time that one can call Corro a "liberal" Calvinist.[40]

Corro left Renée's service in 1566 in answer to a call from Antwerp for his talents. There he tried to put into action directly the lessons of Montargis. Except for the approval—indeed, the sponsorship—of a small group of like-minded denizens of comparable background,[41] he

---

[39] These remarks are in the 1567 *Letter to the King* (Philip II); a microfilm copy is available at the University of Michigan library.

[40] In 1860 the great Dutch historian, R. Fruin, called Corro an "Evangelical Christian": see his "Het Voorspel van den Tachtigjarigen Oorlog," *De Gids*, N.S., II, no. 1, 417ff.

[41] These were the Calvinists of Marrano background. Corro had been intimate

ran afoul of all concerned. With the collapse of Calvinist hopes in the spring of 1567, he fled to London; there he found himself immediately engaged in a running battle with the local custodians of the true faith of all refugees—the London Strangers' Church of the French and its leadership. Briefly, Corro had compromised himself gravely in their eyes by writing letters to Cassiodoro de Reina during 1563-1564, when Reina was pastor of a London Spanish church. With Reina's flight to the continent that winter following unproven charges of heterodoxy, adultery, and sodomy,[42] the incriminating correspondence was impounded by the French Consistory. In one note Corro, pursuing his eclectic bent for recondite theological books, had asked Reina to procure works for him by persons such as Schwenckfeld. The French were never able to comprehend Corro's claim that he could read where he would without necessarily subscribing to any writer's views and that his right to privacy should be honored, any more than he was able to understand their resentment at his often underhanded tactics and bewildering shifts in defending himself and his notion that he was virtually free of normal consistorial discipline. His efforts to reconstitute Reina's old congregation also helped aggravate matters. Confrontations, hearings, insults, and the like dragged on for years.

Partly through his continental connections, Corro had obtained the patronage of leading Englishmen, such as William Cecil, the Earl of Leicester, and Bishops Parker, Sandys, and Aylmer, among others. Increasingly, as Corro moved toward a formal break with Calvinism, these people helped draw him along the road to Anglicanism. He was theological lecturer from 1571 at the London Inns of Court and from 1578 at Oxford. He ended this part of his career as a prebend of St. Paul's. Once in the Anglican milieu, his "liberal" Calvinist past was dragged out to prevent his obtaining an important degree from Oxford, and this furor disclosed collusion between the Puritans and the

---

with their relations and commercial connections at Bordeaux and Toulouse. William McFadden, *Life and Works of Antonio del Corro*, Ph.D. diss. (Queen's University, Belfast, 1953), chs. VIII-IX and XV-XVIII, has some helpful data on these people; a microfilm copy is in the library of Michigan State University. Though questionable in many of its interpretations, the McFadden thesis is of immense value because of the information it contains, which is based on a great deal of archival work. See, too, my article, "Marcus Pérez and Marrano Calvinism" (cited in n. 34).

[42] See n. 25.

refugee Calvinists in London. Eminent personages, Leicester in particular, intervened directly on Corro's behalf, more often than not successfully.

Throughout these battles Corro found himself frequently accused simultaneously of Unitarianism, Romanism, and other incompatible "isms" of the day. Calvin, interestingly, has left only warm words for Corro, but he died before the storm broke. Beza, Calvin's successor, remained convinced, apparently, that no tactic was too unworthy to use against the Spaniard. Corro's writings, which began in 1567, demonstrate a steady drift away from Calvinist concepts of election, but the other accusations, mainly concerning his supposed tampering with the Trinity, simply do not stand up to scrutiny.[43] One feels that Corro's difficulties can be attributed as much to his abrasive personality as to the shadow of Servetus' radicalism. Both helped to account for the way in which, for example, the French pastors in London jumped at Corro's innocent requests in his letter to the condemned Reina. That Corro could maintain the high regard of so staid a religious figure as Archbishop Parker of Canterbury until the latter's death in 1575 suggests the complexity of the problem of arriving at any final judgment of a man like Corro, or of the shades of religious belief in the period as a whole.

It remains to consider why the public uncovering of a handful of real or presumed Protestants aroused such a furor in Spain. One recalls immediately the national tradition which had so violently rejected native Judaism and Mohammedanism and which had been so effectively resurrected against Erasmism and Illuminism, particularly in the period 1525-1540. The psychological and sociological roots of this unique abhorrence of heresy at home have been most recently and suggestively elucidated by John Elliott.[44] To sixteenth-century Spaniards, statistics were irrelevant in assessing the danger of heresy, the

---

[43] In addition to the work mentioned in n. 39, see his *Letter to the Lutheran Ministers of the Flemish Church of Antwerp, A Theological Dialogue, Tableau de l'Oeuvre de Dieu*, and his "Théobon" letter to Reina. The first two are also on University of Michigan microfilm; the third item is reprinted in C. Sepp, *Geschkiedkundige Nasporigen* (Leiden, 1875), III, 155-174; and the "Théobon" letter is Usoz y Rio, *Reformistas*, XVIII, 59-76.

[44] Elliott, *Imperial Spain*, ch. VI; Lynch, *Spain*, ch. VIII. A. A. Sicroff, *Les Controverses des Statuts de "Pureté de sang" en Espagne du XVᵉ au XVIIᵉ Siècle* (Paris, 1960) is a key monograph on this subject.

inquisitorial records notwithstanding.[45] What impressed the Spanish was not that there were only two Protestant congregations, but that there were *any*. Only forty years before, Luther had been one mere monk challenging Pope and Emperor alike. Now, outside the Iberian peninsula and perhaps Italy, Europe was either engulfed in, or threatened by, the new heresy which, unlike Islam or Judaism, had sprung from within Christendom and, unlike Erasmism or mysticism, was a mass movement, frequently sustained by political power.[46] Indeed, the fact that in Spain (unlike Italy) the adherents of Protestantism were drawn largely from the upper and educated classes further demonstrated the seriousness of the threat and justified the violence of the assault on the conventicles. In this overheated atmosphere Spanish Protestantism's basic weaknesses were overlooked: not one peasant member, no grass-roots organization. In these respects it resembled Erasmism and, to some extent, Illuminism. It is well to keep in mind, however, that the atmosphere of Spain then, as well as the character of most of these Protestants (and "Evangelicals" misnamed *luteranos*), hardly permitted the creation of a revolutionary elite in the fashion of, say, the Dutch Sea Beggars.

Perhaps it is best simply to call the Seville-Valladolid congregations "reformist," in the broadest sixteenth-century sense of the word. Whether the individual members were true heretics like Hernández or Evangelical Catholics like Constantino, they sought to reform all or parts of contemporary Catholicism, as they understood it. Like the followers of Juan Valdés at Naples a generation earlier, they frequently differed on specific issues while sharing a common point of departure. But, after the autos-da-fé of 1558-1562, there could be no more such congregations in Spain. Their fate belatedly and broadly paralleled that of Protestants in Italy after 1541, especially under the regimes of Julius III and Paul IV. For the survivors of the Spanish conventicles and the other Spanish Protestants scattered widely across Western

[45] See n. 3. Lea, *Inquisition*, III, 411, 448ff., was perhaps the first to perceive that the importance of this handful of presumed and real Spanish heretics lay not in their numbers but in the intensity of the reaction of orthodox Spanish, from the authorities on down, and, above all, in the broader ramifications of that reaction for Spain as a whole. Later students, such as Elliott, have eloquently extended this insight, even while questioning the Protestantism of the accused.

[46] For this Spanish sense of embattled isolation in defense of the faith, see Garrett Mattingly's brilliant observations on the Escurial in his classic, *The Armada* (Boston, 1959), ch. VII.

Europe, the Evangelical Catholic alternative was forever destroyed. For them, Catholicism now appeared only as the aggressive and militant Counter-Reformation of the classic Protestant martyrologies.[47] To become reformers, they felt, they would have to leave the Church.[48]

[47] The Spanish one is by R. Gonzalez Montes; the rare books room of the New York Public Library has the 1568 English version by V. Skinner entitled *A Discovery and Playne Declaration of Sundry Subtill Practices of the Holy Inquisition of Spayne*. As students from Böhmer to Longhurst have seen, it is an odd compound of fact and fancy, which, however, has too often been taken at face value. "Gonzalez Montes" very probably was an individual or collective pseudonym.

[48] The second paragraph of n. 5 bears keeping in mind here. It was true, of course, as the role of a Morone under Pius IV showed, that an old "Evangelical Catholic" could more than make his way under the Counter-Reformation, Tridentine Church, and Papacy—provided of course, that he was willing to make certain compromises. Nor did the Church reject every aspect of Catholic Reform, as scholars have been showing in recent years. The Protestants, naturally, viewed this matter in a rather different light.

# FRANCIS BACON
## AND THE REFORM OF SOCIETY

THEODORE K. RABB

URRENT studies of seventeenth-century England commonly portray Francis Bacon as a versatile and far-sighted proponent of reform in many of his country's institutions. His work is pictured as a landmark in the development of radically new ideas, and as a foretaste and inspiration of revolutionary thought. Two of today's most prominent Stuart historians, Hugh Trevor-Roper and Christopher Hill, have viewed him in this light, and both have drawn support from the doyen of modern Stuart historians, S. R. Gardiner. Taking Bacon's popularity in the 1640's and 1650's as a guide, they have stressed his influence on this next generation of reformers of science, and have suggested that his social and political program also prefigured mid-century ideals. At an extreme he has been presented as a man of Puritan inclinations, but even in the mainstream of recent work he appears as a firm advocate of extensive change in English society. This judgment, like that of the revolutionaries who hailed him twenty years after his death, either minimizes or ignores the Lord Chancellor's conservatism.[1]

Scholars who discuss Bacon primarily as a major figure in the history of science or philosophy seem, at first sight, to reinforce the conclusions of these historians of Stuart England. In the realm of learning his wish for wholesale reorganization is unquestioned, and it therefore seems perfectly consistent to expose similar concerns in his treatment of politics and society. Bacon's own writings, however, as well as recent studies of his thought, lend little support to those who make such

---

[1] Gardiner's views can be found in his article on Bacon in *The Dictionary of National Biography*, ed. Sir Leslie Stephen and Sir Sidney Lee, I, (London, 1885), esp. 812, and in the first three volumes of his *History of England . . . 1603-1642* (London, 1883), *passim*. Trevor-Roper's views are in two articles: "Francis Bacon," *Encounter*, XVIII (Feb. 1962), 73-77; and "Three Foreigners and the Philosophy of the English Revolution," *Encounter*, XIV (Feb. 1960), 3-20. The latter has been reprinted in an expanded version in his *Religion, the Reformation, and Social Change* (London, 1967), pp. 237-293. Hill's views are in *Intellectual Origins of the English Revolution* (Oxford, 1965), esp. pp. 85-130, and in *The Century of Revolution, 1603-1714* (Edinburgh, 1961), esp. p. 94. The latter, a textbook widely read in English schools, presents the case for Bacon as the antithesis of the conservatives without hesitation or qualification.

connections, or to those who link him with the Puritan and parliamentary revolutionaries. The literature of the past century has, in fact, concentrated on rather different problems. Only in the last few years have a series of reevaluations raised the question of how Bacon's more general ideas affected his view of society, but this has still been discussed as a matter of secondary importance. If the interpretation offered by historians of Stuart England is to be judged in its proper context, it must be set against the salient features of the historiography of Bacon's philosophy. His interest in society as a stimulus to the advance of science can then be explored, and his treatment of this subject can help disclose his attitude toward change in society at large. This investigation should finally provide a basis, resting on the totality of his thought, which will permit an assessment of the Gardiner—Trevor-Roper—Hill thesis.

A hundred years ago the problems facing historians seemed much simpler. James Spedding opened his final estimation of Bacon, to whom he had devoted a lifetime of study, with a disquisition on the unfairness of Pope's famous line about "the wisest, brightest, meanest of mankind." He forgave Pope, who had been "preaching morality," but he could not forgive other commentators who had accepted the poet's epigram as a just critique. And, indeed, the subject of personal honesty appeared to be the only matter open to serious differences of scholarly opinion. A brilliant but patronizing essay by Macaulay had reiterated the standard condemnation of the defects in Bacon's character, and Spedding was determined to refute these facile accusations. The final pages of his mammoth work consisted primarily of a defense of his hero against the charges of immorality, corruption, and "meanness" which Macaulay had so firmly endorsed. And, by and large, Spedding's arguments, which stressed the prevalence of gifts to public officials in the seventeenth century and the integrity of Bacon's judgment despite his acceptance of gifts, have come to be accepted as a judicious assessment of the morality of a distinguished political career.[2] The one stain on the Lord Chancellor's reputation had

[2] *The Letters and the Life of Francis Bacon*, ed. James Spedding, 7 vols. (London, 1861-1874), VII, 553-577. These volumes are sometimes cited as vols. VIII-XIV of the entire collected works. Here they will be treated as a separate work (henceforth cited as *Letters and Life*), as indeed they were, and references will be to them as vols. I-VII. References to Bacon's other writings will be taken

at last been washed away, the problem had been solved, and his admirers could find no blemish to mar their satisfaction.

But their pleasure was short-lived, for now it was the turn of Bacon's "wisdom" to be questioned. Spedding noted that there had been some criticism of Bacon's philosophy, but on the whole his contribution to knowledge seemed to have remained beyond the reach of his detractors. In the century since Spedding, however, a great deal of attention has been given to Bacon's thought, particularly to his vaunted "method," and its importance in the history of science and philosophy has been challenged with varying degrees of intensity.

The most vehement attack, that of M. R. Cohen, enlarges upon Bacon's well-known failure to make any significant scientific discoveries and adds that his analysis of scientific method was equally sterile. Bacon, argues Cohen, was not a pioneer, he rejected the important advances of his day, and the method he advocated was neither useful nor original.[3] Lesser indictments are returned by H. W. Blunt, who lists a number of Bacon's failings and concludes that he was "masquerading as a new Aristotle," and by R. H. Bowers and F. R. Johnson, both of whom stress Bacon's unacknowledged debt to his predecessors. Johnson sums up the philosopher's fundamental attitude as an "indiscriminate distrust of all systems."[4]

The other side, the defense of Sir Francis's "wisdom," has gained its most impressive support from a series of major reevaluations which have appeared during the last twenty years. The new picture that has emerged differs sharply from the one accepted by Spedding, who progressed hardly at all beyond the founders of the Royal Society and their simple, reverent appreciation of the practical philosophy preached by their guiding light. During the last century Bacon's debt to classical

---

from the full, 15-volume *The Works of Francis Bacon* (henceforth cited as *Works*), ed. James Spedding, R. L. Ellis, and D. D. Heath (Cambridge, 1863). Macaulay's "The Works of Francis Bacon" appeared in *The Edinburgh Review*, CXXXII (1837), 1-104. The most recent comment, Joel Hurstfield's "Political Corruption in Modern England: The Historian's Problem," *History*, LII (1967), 16-34, notes only one instance of corruption in Bacon's career (see 22-23).

[3] M. R. Cohen, "The Myth about Bacon and the Inductive Method," *Scientific Monthly*, XXIII (1926), 504-508.

[4] H. W. Blunt, "Bacon's Method of Science," *Proceedings of the Aristotelian Society*, N.S., vol. IV (1903-1904), 16-31, esp. 31; R. H. Bower, "Bacon's Spider Simile," *Journal of the History of Ideas*, XVII (1956), 133-135; and F. R. Johnson, *Astronomical Thought in Renaissance England* (Baltimore, 1937), pp. 151-299, *passim.*, esp. pp. 245-247 and 297-299.

authors, to a large body of humanist philosophy, to the powerful magical tradition, and to men such as Andreae, Bruno, Campanella, Cardan, Leroy, Palissy, and Telesio has been demonstrated conclusively, even in areas where previously he was considered the generator of new directions in thought, such as his emphasis on observation and induction or his belief in progress.[5] With the influence of his predecessors now established, the assertion of his originality has taken on a new form.

The first major reappraisal came from F. H. Anderson in 1948, and in a recent biography (the best concise account of Bacon's career and thought in light of the latest scholarship) he has condemned earlier writers for their "reckless, uninformed, even at times malevolent" opinions. These commentators, he claims, all fail to realize that they are dealing with a philosopher, not a scientist. To ignore this cardinal fact is to misunderstand the man. Bacon's great contribution was to select and bring together in a systematic body of thought a multitude of ideas from his predecessors. Anderson thus overcomes the reservations of those who deny Bacon's originality because they can discover his views in earlier writers. Also important, according to this analysis, is the fact that Sir Francis devoted his life to a uniquely comprehensive and consistent program for the advancement of learning. And in eight important respects, mainly in the separation of theology and natural science, in the rise of materialism, and in the development of

[5] See Sir Thomas Allbutt, "Palissy, Bacon, and the Revival of Natural Science," *Proceedings of the British Academy* (1913-1914), pp. 233-247; Hans Baron, "The *Querelle* of the Ancients and the Moderns as a Problem for Renaissance Scholarship," *Journal of the History of Ideas*, XX (1959), 3-22; E. D. Blodgett, "Bacon's *New Atlantis* and Campanella's *Civita Solis*: A Study in Relationships," *Publications of the Modern Language Association of America*, XLVI (1931), 763-780; J. B. Bury, *The Idea of Progress* (London, 1920), pp. 50-63; W. L. Gundersheimer, "Louis Leroy's Humanistic Optimism," *Journal of the History of Ideas*, XXIII (1962), 338; C. W. Lemmi, *The Classic Deities in Bacon* (Baltimore, 1933); Lynn Thorndike, "The Attitude of Francis Bacon and Descartes towards Magic and Occult Science," *Science, Medicine and History*, ed. E. A. Underwood, I (London, 1953), 451-454; Pierre Villey, "Montaigne et François Bacon," *Revue de la Renaissance*, XII (1911), 121-158 and 185-203, and XIII (1912), 21-46 and 61-82; V. K. Whitaker, *Francis Bacon's Intellectual Milieu* (Los Angeles, 1962); and, above all, the work of Farrington and Rossi, cited in nn. 7 and 8 below. Chapters IV-VIII of Nell Eurich's *Science in Utopias* (Cambridge, Mass., 1967) have a great deal of information on Bacon's connections with other thinkers. Mrs. Eurich was kind enough to let me see the book in typescript.

induction, Anderson considers his achievements to have been entirely original.[6]

There have been two other major reassessments in the last twenty years. The first, by Benjamin Farrington, diverges significantly from Anderson in that it specifically refutes those scholars interested in the history of philosophy who emphasize logic and systems of thought. Bacon's main aim, according to Farrington, was to make science useful. His ideal was humanitarian, to improve man's lot, and he equated scientific truth with practical utility. This was the theme of all his writings, and only by understanding its central place in his thought can one appreciate his importance and originality.[7] Paolo Rossi's work has provided students of the subject with a remarkably thorough investigation of the context of Bacon's ideas. He has documented exhaustively the influence not only of various Renaissance and six-teenth-century thinkers but also of the strong magical traditions still current in the seventeenth century. With the background established, Rossi is able to conclude that the vital novel concept introduced by Bacon was the belief that science could obtain effective results only through successive and collaborative research. He wanted a unity of language, method, and effort—all for utilitarian ends. As Rossi puts it, "this reform of the concept, practice, and ideals of science is without a doubt the most notable contribution which Bacon made to European culture." However, in contrast to Farrington, he feels that Bacon's ultimate significance lies in the history of philosophy. Sir Francis originally criticized his predecessors' ideas for their lack of practical results, but this criticism developed into an unprecedented wholesale condemnation of earlier thinkers. His wish for a complete revision of the methods and aims of natural philosophy required a rejection of the attitudes which had guided philosophers for centuries.[8]

Regardless of differences in emphasis (and varying opinions about the exact place where Bacon said something new), it is clear that the

[6] F. H. Anderson, *The Philosophy of Francis Bacon* (Chicago, 1948); *Francis Bacon: His Career and His Thought* (Los Angeles, 1962), esp. pp. 3-6 and 318-352.

[7] Benjamin Farrington, *Francis Bacon, Philosopher of Industrial Science* (New York, 1949), esp. pp. 3 and 106-112; "On Misunderstanding the Philosophy of Francis Bacon," *Science, Medicine and History*, ed. E. A. Underwood, I (London, 1953); and *The Philosophy of Francis Bacon* (Liverpool, 1964).

[8] Paolo Rossi, *Francesco Bacone: Dalla Magia alla Scienza* (Bari, 1957), esp. pp. 85-86, 185-194, and 340-341. A translation appeared after this article was completed: *Francis Bacon, From Magic to Science* (London, 1968).

latest interpreters are coming to agree that one of the most fruitful ways to approach Bacon's work is to see him primarily as an *organizer* of science, not as a scientist. Rossi even admits that for this reason there is some justice in William Harvey's jibe that Bacon wrote "philosophy like a Lord Chancellor";[9] and a biography published in 1960 has the title *Francis Bacon, The First Statesman of Science*.[10] Nonetheless, discussions of his "method," or of his wish to change the traditional techniques of philosophical inquiry, still tend to concentrate on his criticisms of earlier systems and his advocacy of progress through induction. Only in the work of Farrington and Rossi has it become fully apparent that the new epistemology was only one part of Bacon's vision of the future. The particular type of reasoning he wanted was, of course, crucial; but equally essential was a very careful organization of effort. His program for reaching truth has to be seen as a whole, because an indispensable element in his reform of ways of thought was a complete overhaul of the system of conducting research. A man must no longer work in isolated splendor; he must become part of a united, collaborative, planned endeavor. Historians of the Royal Society, and of scientific organization in general, have long appreciated the importance of Bacon's stress on this particular point.[11] But now it can be seen that, in his determination to systematize knowledge and to make it more fruitful and more certain of advance, he had a two-part plan. His "method" helped a scientist learn not only *how* to investigate but also *what* to investigate. Central to his program, therefore, was a conception which *per se* has received little scholarly attention, though it revealed an original attitude of major significance: his remarkable view of society, with its vision of nations consciously supporting and regulating intellectual activity for the benefit of mankind. In this day of massive, government-financed research projects, it could be said that Bacon's dream has come true. But even in his own day his hopes for the future were not merely utopian dreams. He was always strictly practical—an inveterate reformer, bursting with proposals for science,

[9] *Ibid.*, p. 341.

[10] J. G. Crowther, *Francis Bacon, The First Statesman of Science* (London, 1960).

[11] The best recent account is Margery Purver's *The Royal Society: Concept and Creation* (Cambridge, Mass., 1967); the first was Thomas Sprat's *The History of the Royal Society of London, for the Improving of Natural Knowledge* (London, 1667).

174

philosophy, politics, and economics. And at the root of his plans was a belief that the attitudes of society and the actions of its most powerful individuals could determine man's achievements.

Bacon's analysis of the obstacles which prevented intellectual advance usually began with the mind itself. The first two of the four "idols" which he considered the chief enemies of progress—idols of the tribe and the cave—represented the psychological and personal shortcomings of individual men. Similarly, in his *Valerius Terminus* he attributed the insufficiency of communication and continuity among researchers to "the internal impediments and clouds in the mind and spirit of man," rather than to "impediments of time and accident."[12] But he went on to emphasize that the other difficulties also had to be overcome. The last two idols—of the market place and the theater— were external blocks, caused by society and its traditions. And in the *Valerius Terminus* he remarked upon the effects of various kinds of government: "monarchies incline wits to profit and pleasure, and commonwealths to glory and vanity." Regardless of the problems, though, he felt that "the period of one age cannot advance men to the furthest point of interpretation of nature, *(except the work should be undertaken with greater helps than can be expected)*," and here he was probably thinking in terms of state support.[13]

His view was most clearly expressed in a significant passage in *The Advancement of Learning* which opened with the statement that "under learned princes and governors there have been ever the best times." He felt that this "felicity of times under learned princes" could best be appreciated by looking at the age between the death of Domitian and the reign of Commodus. In this period there had been "a succession of six princes, all learned or singular favourers and advancers of learning; which age, for temporal respects, was the most happy and flourishing that ever the Roman empire . . . enjoyed."[14] He examined the emperors one by one, reserving particular praise for Trajan, a great "admirer" and "benefactor of learning," who had been "a

[12] *Works*, VIII, 76-86; VI, 47.

[13] *Ibid.*, VIII, 78-79 and 86-98; VI, 73 (italics mine). When Bacon protested in the *Valerius Terminus* that "our purpose is not to stir up men's hopes, but to guide their travels," he stressed that direction from above was essential (*Ibid.*, VI, 52-53). See also n. 22 below.

[14] *Ibid.*, VI, 146-147.

founder of famous libraries, a perpetual advancer of learned men to office, and a familiar converser with learned professors and preceptors, who were noted to have then most credit in court."[15] Adrian had been "the most universal inquirer," a builder of buildings for use, not for glory. Antoninus Pius had been "excellently learned," and Marcus Aurelius had "excelled all the rest in learning."[16] Bacon attributed the golden age to the influence of these rulers and naturally picked Queen Elizabeth as their modern equivalent. She, too, had been learned, had read every day, and had therefore ensured that England would enjoy a "flourishing state of learning, sortable to so excellent a patroness." Her reign had been the perfect example of "the conjunction of learning in the prince with felicity in the people."[17]

In the second book of *The Advancement of Learning* Bacon, practical as ever, examined the means by which such princes could promote the quest for knowledge. The way for them to proceed was "by amplitude of reward, by soundness of direction, and by the conjunction of labours. The first multiplieth endeavour, the second preventeth error, and the third supplieth the frailty of man. But the principal of these is direction."[18] Bacon blithely assumed that kings would indeed perform these functions. The offer of rewards for inventors was one of his favorite practical recommendations, but he also believed in a more far-reaching influence, because he thought that only the ruler could provide the guidance and organization that the advance of science required.[19] Late in life he wrote to Father Fulgentio in Venice about his hopes for the future and told him that, "as for the third part of the Instauration, namely the Natural History, that is plainly a task for a King or Pope, or some college or order; for it cannot be completed, as by rights it should, by the industry of a private individual."[20] He wrote

[15] *Ibid.*, pp. 148-149.

[16] *Ibid.*, pp. 149-152.

[17] *Ibid.*, pp. 152-153. For Bacon's view of history, see L. F. Dean, "Sir Francis Bacon's Theory of Civil History-Writing," *English Literary History*, VIII (1941), 161-183, esp. 177, on the importance Bacon attached to the lessons that could be drawn from historical examples; and G. H. Nadel, "History as Psychology in Francis Bacon's Theory of History," *History and Theory*, V (1966), 275-287.

[18] *Works*, VI, 172. See also the end of n. 44 below.

[19] See n. 22 below.

[20] "Quod ad tertiam partem Instaurationis attinet, Historiam scilicet Naturalem, opus illud est plane regium aut papale, aut alicujus collegii aut ordinis; neque privata industria pro merito perfici potest" (*Letters and Life*, VII, 531).

repeatedly of the need for collaboration, and he was convinced that direction should be given from above. In *The Advancement of Learning* he complained that the actions of kings in previous ages had been "rather matters of magnificence and memory than of progression and proficience, [which had tended] rather to augment the mass of learning in the multitude of learned men than to rectify or raise the sciences themselves."[21] He proceeded, therefore, to enumerate the specific actions that were necessary.

There were three ways to stimulate advances: through places, books, and people. Seats of learning could be helped in four ways: by buildings, endowments, privileges, and ordinances. Books could be made available by the erection of new libraries and support for new editions. And people would be spurred on by advancement, favor, and strong encouragement for existing and new sciences. Bacon wanted the establishment of schools for general arts and sciences to counter excessive specialization—practical studies were all very well, but philosophy, from which everything else was derived, should also be learned. Lecturers deserved better pay, and more instruments and laboratories were needed. Behind these recommendations lay the belief that universities required direction and help from governments and princes in order to reach their full potential. And he gave examples of the reforms that could be introduced, such as the postponement of the teaching of logic, which was usually introduced too early in a child's education. Communication between universities could also be stimulated from above, as could the investigation of areas of learning which were inadequately studied. All of these efforts, he said, "are *opera basilica* [works for a King]."[22]

[21] *Works*, VI, 173. It is clear that Bacon was transforming a panegyric, long a commonplace in literature addressed to monarchs and rulers, into the basis for a concrete plan of action.

[22] *Ibid.*, pp. 172-180. See also VIII, 401-405, where Bacon complained at length that kings did not give sufficient direction to the methods and aims of universities. He stressed "a neglect of consultation in governors of universities, and of visitation in princes or superior persons" concerning curricula (402). When he blamed rulers for the lack of communication and the absence of overall assessments of shortcomings in learning, he added: "The removal of all the defects . . . , except the last [the shortcomings], and of the active part also of the last, which relates to the designation of writers, are truly works for a King; towards which the endeavours and industry of a private man can be but as an image in a crossway, that may point at the way but cannot go it" (405).

Bacon admitted that not enough was known of the effects of temporal circumstances, and he called for research into this subject; but he still felt that "the condition of these times" augured a great age of learning, and he hoped constantly that the royal patronage which was vital for his schemes would be forthcoming.[23] He underlined the point in the *Novum Organum*, where he noted that appropriate governmental patronage had made the efforts of the Egyptians more fruitful than those of the Greeks because the former had "rewarded inventors with divine honours and sacred rites."[24] As he put it, golden ages were "a birth of Time rather than a birth of Wit," and the society, or at least its leaders, could create the right time.[25] He blamed various features of Roman and medieval society for the failure to promote learning, and he stressed that in his own day science not only failed to win rewards but "has not even the advantage of popular applause." Therefore, "it is nothing strange if a thing not held in honour does not prosper."[26] Here again the remedy clearly had to come from above. The task was much too large; and, as he noted elsewhere when discussing the advancement of learning, it had to be accomplished "by public designation and expense, though not by private means and endeavour."[27] His Natural History was "a thing of very great size, and can not be executed without great labour and expense; requiring . . . many people to help, and being . . . a kind of royal work."[28]

The entire thesis was summed up in Bacon's description of his ideal community, the *New Atlantis*, where Solomon's house and its related institutions created the perfect setting for scientific advance. Established and supported by the state, Solomon's house carefully controlled research so as to ensure a constant and rapid flow of discoveries. It was endowed with all the resources it needed: laboratories, museums, instruments, engines, furnaces, factories, lakes, and even orchards. Its leaders were the most respected men in society, and great honors were showered on famous inventors. Under such completely favorable circumstances, learning could flourish unhampered, and remarkable advances ensued. The keynote of the whole system was the creation of the proper environment, and this, in turn, depended on the establishment, in minute detail, of precise guidelines for conduct. Everything had been laid down by King Solamona himself. "Doubting novelties,"

[23] *Ibid.*, VI, 334-338 and 391-392.    [24] *Ibid.*, VIII, 103-105.
[25] *Ibid.*, pp. 109-111.    [26] *Ibid.*, pp. 111 and 127-128.    [27] *Ibid.*, p. 406.
[28] *Ibid.*, p. 353.

he had forbidden strangers to come to the island, or natives to leave, with the solitary exception of the twelve "Merchants of Light" whose job it was to find out periodically what useful discoveries had been made elsewhere. Even the exact function of each researcher had been ordained to be in one of nine distinct categories.[29]

In Bacon's view, therefore, a well-ordered society, regulated by a paternal government, was an essential aid to seekers of knowledge and to those who hoped for "the enlarging of the bounds of Human Empire."[30] He himself turned to his own sovereign, though to no avail. His final appeal, made late in life, was a muted hope that James I would "be aiding to me, in setting men on work for the collecting of a natural and experimental history."[31] But the task, like his reputation, had to be left to future ages.

Bacon's vision of the kind of society that would best promote scientific advance also extended to other activities. He always sought efficiency, and he believed that control for the common good could be exercised over many undertakings by a central regulating agency, either by the government or by institutions specifically created for these tasks. Repeatedly, his practical recommendations for reforms included the suggestion that they be implemented by a special commission or by the action of the government itself. Since he was a chronic proposer of improvements in English society, he came to advocate intervention in a multitude of areas, from the reform of law to reclamation of land. In one memorandum alone he advised the King to set up commissions to being order to a tremendous range of economic and social problems: the cloth trade, the value of money, sales of grain, the growth of industrial enterprises, the distribution of population, road construction, draining the fens, Irish colonization, and national defense. Shortly thereafter he wrote that he favored a commission (which would be more effective than the law) to deal with the poor and even greater centralization, a single treasurer rather than a commission, to supervise royal finances. In line with his usual aims, he asked that strict procedures be laid down for the King's treasury. All of these proposals came from his pen in 1620;[32] at other times he was advocating

[29] *Ibid.*, V, 359-413, esp. 381-384 and 398-413.
[30] *Ibid.*, p. 398.
[31] *Letters and Life*, VII, 130.
[32] *Ibid.*, pp. 71-73 and 85-89. See also *Works*, XII, 127-128 and 197.

direct state control of usury, central surveillance of the licensing of inns, and establishment of a commission to reform England's laws.[33] No other man of his day had so comprehensive a program for the reform of society, and this fact has naturally led historians to look at his plans in light of the political and social revolution that erupted less than twenty years after his death.

Yet it is difficult to draw any simple connections between Bacon and the revolutionaries. In the first place, he considered royal power the best instrument for effecting change. We have already seen the reliance he placed on central action and control. As S. R. Gardiner put it when discussing the dispute between the government and the justices of the peace over the licensing of inns, "the question between the Crown and the justices, so far as it was a political one, was only one phase of the great question between the central government and the local authorities, which at this period meets us at every turn. On which side Bacon's sympathies really lay it is impossible to doubt."[34] And Gardiner's conclusion has been endorsed by virtually everyone who has studied the Lord Chancellor during the last hundred years. Although it has been noted that Bacon did not develop a consistent or complete political theory,[35] there has been general agreement that he strongly supported monarchical power in England and disliked changes in political structure. His career and his writings were committed to a defense of the King's position. He upheld the royal prerogative whenever it was challenged,[36] and, although he firmly approved of Parliament's position in the system of government, he clearly wanted control to remain in James I's hands.[37] One writer has even seen power as the theme of Bacon's writings: a striving for imperialism

[33] *Works*, XII, 218-222; S. R. Gardiner, "On Four Letters from Lord Bacon to Christian IV. King of Denmark," *Archaeologia*, XLI (1867), 219-269, esp. 234-236; and *Letters and Life*, VII, 61-71, 358-364, and 415-419. He even thought that sumptuary regulations should be introduced to help the cloth industry (*Letters and Life*, VII, 74).

[34] Gardiner, "Four Letters from Lord Bacon," p. 236.

[35] E.g., by J. W. Allen, *English Political Thought, 1603-1660*, I: *1603-1644* (London, 1938), 50.

[36] *Ibid.*, pp. 50-62; P. H. Kocher, "Francis Bacon on the Science of Jurisprudence," *Journal of the History of Ideas*, XVIII (1957), 3-26, esp. 16; see also nn. 57 and 65-68 below. One of Bacon's strongest defenses of the prerogative can be found in *Works*, XV, 257-311, on the case *De Rege Inconsulto*.

[37] *Letters and Life*, VII, 289-290; for his suggestions on how to manage a Parliament, see IV, 365-373. Contrast Trevor-Roper, "Francis Bacon," p. 74. See also nn. 39 and 41 below.

and sovereignty over men as well as nature.[38] But most scholars have realized that no simple interpretation is possible. M. A. Judson points out Bacon's occasional inconsistencies but concludes that his ultimate recourse was to the prerogative, which rested on law but transcended law because it came from God. For this reason Bacon was able to argue that it was the King who provided for the general welfare and promoted unity and harmony in the state.[39] G. L. Mosse also stresses Bacon's endorsement of the King's sovereignty and his belief that the King was above the law.[40] The most thorough investigation of Bacon's political and social ideas, that of Hellmut Bock, similarly reiterates the importance given to royal power and to the intervention of the government in society. Bock's main concern is to present Bacon as a "materialist" who supported the King's supremacy and the central administration's far-reaching control because of his pragmatic outlook. This kind of power permitted the most practical and natural solutions of administrative and social difficulties.[41]

The explanations and the emphases may differ, but there has been no doubt about Bacon's commitment to a vigorous central government (led by a dominant monarch in England, though other forms might be possible elsewhere). His position was nowhere formulated fully and clearly, and interpreters have been forced to rely on the overall intention that Bacon seemed to convey. Hence, it is particularly significant that they have agreed so consistently on these particular points. Moreover, their conclusions are reinforced by the fact that the political outlook they have stressed is closely related to Bacon's theory of how learning should be advanced. There is an obvious parallel in his be-

---

[38] Oskar Kraus, *Der Machtgedanke und die Friedensidee in der Philosophie der Engländer Bacon und Bentham* (Leipzig, 1926), pp. 3-31.

[39] M. A. Judson, *The Crisis of the Constitution* (New Brunswick, 1949), esp. pp. 28, 116, 138, 148, and 165-170.

[40] G. L. Mosse, *The Struggle for Sovereignty in England* (East Lansing, 1950), pp. 74-82.

[41] Hellmut Bock, *Staat und Gesellschaft bei Francis Bacon*, Neue Deutsche Forschungen, CXXXVI (Berlin, 1937), esp. 75-115. Bock was interested in Bacon, not as a reformer, but as a thinker whose practical and scientific outlook appeared in all his writings. It is hardly surprising that the view of Bacon as a materialist and imperialist, evident in Bock, should have flourished in Germany at this time. It appeared even more strikingly two years later in Ernst von Hippel's *Bacon und das Staatsdenken des Materialismus*, Schriften der Königsberger Gelehrten Gesellschaft, XV-XVI (Halle, 1939), Heft 3, 97-164, which ended with the assertion that Baconian materialism ruled the world and that it was the task of German materialism to fight this pernicious force (142-164).

lief that both scientific research and politics should be regulated by an active executive force; and he wanted similar intervention in social, colonial, economic, and legal affairs.[42] In his essay "Of the True Greatness of Kingdoms and Estates" he even suggested that kings should act, through "ordinances, constitutions and customs," to create the strong military spirit among their people which was essential for greatness. By this means "it is in the power of princes or estates to add amplitude and greatness to their kingdoms"[43]—an endorsement of royal power that could have had little appeal to the opponents of the King in the 1640's.

The second difficulty that arises when connections are drawn between Bacon and the mid-century revolutionaries concerns his paradoxical ambivalence toward innovation. His belief in an active government might seem to imply an expectation of constant change. But reform, in his view, was a more subtle process. The advance of knowledge certainly required inventions, but in the *Novum Organum* he made an important distinction between changes in learning and transformations in society:

> The introduction of famous discoveries appears to hold by far the first place among human actions; and this was the judgment of the former ages. For to the authors of inventions they awarded divine honours; while to those who did good service in the state (such as founders of cities and empires, legislators, saviours of their country from long endured evils, quellers of tyrannies, and the like) they decreed no higher honours than heroic. And certainly if a man rightly compare the two, he will find that this judgment of antiquity was just. For the benefits of discoveries may extend to the whole race of man, civil benefits only to particular places; the latter last not beyond a few ages, the former through all time. Moreover the reformation of a state in civil matters is seldom brought in without violence and confusion; but discoveries carry blessings with them, and confer benefits without causing harm or sorrow to any.[44]

---

[42] See n. 32 above.

[43] *Works*, XII, 187-188. He clearly felt that in England the task would be primarily the prince's.

[44] *Ibid.*, VIII, 161. See also 127: "Surely there is a great distinction between matters of state and the arts; for the danger from new motion and new light is not the same. In matters of state a change even for the better is distrusted, because it unsettles what is established; these things resting on authority, consent, fame and opinion, not demonstration. But arts and sciences should be like mines,

Yet even in regard to matters of learning Bacon carefully qualified his endorsement of change. He felt compelled to conclude *The Advancement of Learning* with the apology that, where he had revised the opinion of the ancients, he had "done so not from a desire of innovation or mere change, but of change for the better."[45] And, as far as the other elements of society were concerned, he took the view that change was very rarely for the better.

On the question of religious reform he was unequivocal: "the introducing of new doctrines is . . . an affectation of tyranny over the understandings and beliefs of men."[46] He regarded Elizabeth's reformation of religion as the accomplishment of "the most dangerous" of all alterations in a state.[47] He disliked intolerance, and he chided the bishops for their severity toward reformers; but he condemned the Puritans for undermining the position of the bishops, and he opposed the wish for constant reform, because he felt that both good and bad had been lost in the overturn of Catholicism and that now the Church of England was "nearest to apostolic truth."[48] Improvements *within* the existing structure he approved and even encouraged, suggesting, for example, that the King could act to stimulate the training of more preachers to staff undermanned areas.[49] But changes in the structure itself he clearly considered dangerous and undesirable.

A similar distinction prompted his disavowal of innovation in the project which he constantly urged upon the King—reform of the law.

---

where the noise of new works and further advances is heard on every side. But though the matter be so according to right reason, it is not so acted on in practice; and the points above mentioned in the administration and government of learning put a severe restraint upon the advancement of the sciences." The last sentence, incidentally, is another expression of Bacon's belief that proper organization and direction are essential for the progress of learning.

[45] *Ibid.*, IX, 356. Even King Solamona, it might be recalled, was described as "doubting novelties" (see n. 29).

[46] *Ibid.*, V, 164. See also n. 70 below.

[47] *Letters and Life*, I, 126-172. In his work *On the Fortunate Memory of Elizabeth Queen of England*, Bacon noted with approval that the Queen had tried to be moderate in religion and had opposed hasty innovations (*Works*, XI, 453-460). In his *Essays* he stressed that "innovation in religion" and "alteration of laws and customs" were major causes of civil troubles and that the way to keep people happy was not to "meddle with the point of religion, or their customs, or means of life" (*Works*, XII, 127 and 145).

[48] *Letters and Life*, I, 78, 80-82, 84, and 86-94; VI, 31. Bacon felt that attacks on the bishops could be the prelude to attacks on the civil government.

[49] *Ibid.*, IV, 254.

It was certainly no innovation, he argued, if by that term was meant the creation of difficulties for particular people, because the reform was general, not specific, and eased rather than constrained. And it was more a "matter of order and explanation than of alteration," a fundamental difference which he justified by giving examples of previous kings and governments who had acted in this fashion.[50] The significant point was that they had all been codifiers or systematizers, not inventors of new law, and Bacon hoped that his own scheme would merely make the law easier to use. He wished to remove some of the more glaring difficulties and complications, but he left the precepts themselves untouched because he feared "a perilous innovation."[51] Again, he was happy to improve the workings of an institution, to remove obstacles and to promote efficiency, but he had no intention of altering its basic structure or functions. He wanted to regulate, not change.

England's social and political framework Bacon treated in similar fashion. He did have decided opinions about the most desirable social conditions. He thought it important, for example, not to have too large a number of gentry; but he never suggested that the framework of society should be altered by precept from above.[52] His proposals were designed to improve existing conditions: the poor were to be cared for more efficiently, the "confusion of ranks and degrees" was to be avoided, and everything was to be done to preserve a harmonious balance between various groups.[53] For all his interest in the perfectibility of the human state, his specific recommendations tended to be conservative, ordering and streamlining the existing situation in accord with his belief that "the great multiplication of virtues upon human nature resteth upon societies well ordained and disciplined."[54] His suggestions for intervention in economic affairs were also designed to

[50] *Ibid.*, VII, 33 and 65-66. He described his *Maxims of the Law* as "a work without any glory of affected novelty, or of method, or of language, or of quotations and authorities, dedicated only to use" (*Works*, XIV, 184-185). See also n. 47 above and n. 73 below.

[51] *Letters and Life*, VII, 65-67. His hope was to "purge" all "ensnaring" laws. "The more laws we make the more snares we lay to entrap ourselves" (*Letters and Life*, III, 19). "What I shall propound," he stressed, "is not to the matter of the laws, but to the manner of their registry" (*Letters and Life*, VII, 63).

[52] *Works*, IX, 302-304; XII, 179-180.

[53] *Letters and Life*, VII, 73; and Bock, *Staat und Gesellschaft*, pp. 78-81.

[54] *Works*, XII, 215.

remove difficulties or to provide encouragement and guidance from above, but not to bring about radical changes.[55]

Bacon's caution was equally evident in his discussions of the state itself. He stressed that a judge's first task was to take care not "to introduce novelty."[56] When analyzing the position of the Council of Wales in the government of the kingdom, he opposed major reorganization because it would be a "dangerous beginning of innovation."[57] And these specific warnings were directly related to his view that "it is most dangerous in a state to give ear to the least alteration of government."[58] He believed that "fair and moderate courses are ever best in causes of estate."[59] And, within England, true to his advocacy of strong central governments, he firmly opposed change. "In civil government . . . it is a more atrocious thing to deny the power and majesty of the prince, than to slander his reputation."[60] In his own day, he noted, "competition of the crown there is none, nor can be," and, if it should somehow arise, it would have to be mercilessly repressed.[61] In the political as in other spheres he strongly endorsed improvements in the existing framework but opposed a fundamental transformation.

Bacon's careful distinction between useful and dangerous changes was summarized in his essay "Of Innovations," which was devoted to this very subject. His main concern was with the nature of custom, which elsewhere he called "the principal magistrate of man's life."[62] He agreed that customs had to begin with a "first precedent," but he spoke of these as events of the past. The only innovations he envisaged in his own day he compared to medicines—remedies and preventers of "new evils." For "time is the greatest innovator," and good customs constantly deteriorate. "If time stood still," it would always be true that innovations did more harm than good; but time, in fact, "moveth so round, that a froward retention of custom is as turbulent a thing as an innovation." Nevertheless, although reforms and improvements were sometimes necessary, "it were good . . . that men in their innovations would follow the example of time itself; which indeed innovateth greatly, but quietly, and by degrees scarce to be perceived." And he

[55] See nn. 32, 33, and 47 above.

[56] *Works*, XII, 265-266.

[57] *Letters and Life*, III, 380-381. See also *Works*, XV, 119-154, on the King's jurisdiction in the Marches.

[58] *Letters and Life*, VII, 31.      [59] *Ibid.*, p. 192.

[60] *Works*, XIV, 94.      [61] *Letters and Life*, VII, 46.      [62] *Works*, XII, 214.

warned in particular that "it is good also not to try experiments in states . . . and well to beware that it be the reformation that draweth on the change, and not the desire of change that pretendeth the reformation." He concluded with the hope "that the novelty, though it be not rejected, yet be held for a suspect."[63]

The paradox of an obsessive reformer who had serious reservations about reform can be resolved only by emphasizing that Bacon used the term in its sense of restoration and repair. What he rejected were its implications of wholesale renovation, of novelty for its own sake, or of experimentation and disregard for the past. As he put it, even if a "custom . . . be not good, yet at least it is fit."[64] The only area in which he was prepared to accept and support a major new start was in the advancement of learning. Here, too, he expressed cautions,[65] but the failings of preceding ages seemed so great that he was willing to demand a complete revision of methods and aims. The government could organize an entirely new system of research, not only by removing obstacles to the pursuit of truth but also by providing resources and directing investigators into the right paths. The task was so great that assistance would have to come from the state, and new attitudes and institutions would have to be created. But, except for this one undertaking, Bacon was opposed to fundamental transformations of society, however good the apparent reason. The state could act to improve itself, to increase efficiency or solve problems, but the reforms he suggested were never meant to be "innovations."

Three strands can thus be discerned throughout Bacon's scattered discussions of the reform of society. He believed in an active central government, which he called upon to intervene whenever a better ordering of the state was needed. He upheld, at least in England, the

[63] *Ibid.*, pp. 160-161. These views echoed Montaigne, whose essay "Of Custom" roundly condemned innovation: "it is very doubtful whether there can be such evident profit in changing an accepted law . . . as there is harm in disturbing it." Bacon said much the same, though he did not go as far as Montaigne's "I am disgusted with innovation, in whatever disguise." See *The Complete Essays of Montaigne*, tr. D. M. Frame, 3 vols. (Garden City, 1960), I, 117-118. See also Fritz Redlich, "The Role of Innovation in a Quasi-Static World: Francis Bacon and his Successors," *Explorations in Entrepreneurial History*, VII (1954-1955), 12-25, esp. 12-16.

[64] *Works*, XII, 160.

[65] See n. 45 above. And it is worth noting that his reforms were repeatedly justified by reference to ancient wisdom, such as the Egyptian custom of honoring inventors (see n. 24).

supreme controlling power of the King. And, except for the advancement of learning, he opposed "innovations" because he limited the functions and extent of reform to improvements in efficiency or corrections of harmful tendencies: change should come "by degrees scarce to be perceived." In all three cases, serious obstacles are placed in the path of those who cast Bacon in the role of forerunner of the Puritans and parliamentarians of the 1640's and 1650's. It is necessary, therefore, that the links historians have traced between his ideas and the social and political aims of the revolutionaries be examined in light of the basic attitudes which permeated his writings.

In his article on Bacon in *The Dictionary of National Biography*, Gardiner suggested that, if the Lord Chancellor's advice to the King on how to handle Parliament—primarily by exercising firm control— had been accepted, "the evils of the next half-century" would have been averted.[66] He was of the opinion that "the one man who could have guided James safely through the quicksands was Bacon,"[67] who sympathized both with the Commons and with the King. But in his history of the period Gardiner stressed that, for all his respect for Parliament, Bacon's ultimate sympathy lay with the Crown, which was far more likely to be capable of resolute action.[68] And he admitted that Bacon's hope for harmony between the two principal components of the government was doomed to failure and obsolescence because, "clinging to the old forms, he hoped against hope that James would yet win the confidence of the nation, and he shut his eyes to the defects in his character which rendered such a consummation impossible."[69] In other words, the Lord Chancellor's uncompromising adherence to the prime importance of the monarch set him apart from the developments that followed his death. The claim that he might have prevented the upheaval of the mid-century loses its force when it is admitted that the means he would have used directly contradicted a basic aim of the revolutionaries' program: the determination to reduce the powers of the royal prerogative.

More recently, H. R. Trevor-Roper has adopted Gardiner's conclusion, "that if only Bacon's programme had been carried out, England might have escaped the Great Rebellion,"[70] but has reached it by a dif-

---

[66] *Dictionary of National Biography*, I, 812.  [67] Gardiner, *History*, I, 194.
[68] *Ibid.*, II, 191-195; III, 29-30. See also n. 34 above.  [69] *Ibid.*, III, 397.
[70] Trevor-Roper, "Three Foreigners," p. 6, and "Francis Bacon," p. 76. See also

ferent path. For Trevor-Roper, Bacon's importance lay, not in his constitutional proposals, but in his hopes for the reform of society. According to this view, all the evidence, "obvious, inescapable, constant throughout his writings," reveals Sir Francis as the great advocate of decentralization, and thus as the forerunner of an essential driving ambition of the revolutionaries. "All the reforms of the law which would be loudly and angrily demanded by a rebellious people in the 1640's had been lucidly and loyally demanded, a generation before, not by Coke, never by Coke, but always by Bacon."[71] It is difficult, though, to reconcile this interpretation with the parliamentarians' early attack on the very prerogative courts whose powers Bacon so staunchly upheld and Coke so bitterly denounced. Great hostility was certainly shown during the Revolution, as in almost all periods of English history, toward the common lawyers, but Bacon attributed the delays which were the chief complaint of the times to the complications and snares of the law, not to the lawyers. And the revolutionaries' wish for decentralization—such as the plan for county registries[72]—cannot be traced back to any similar intention on the part of the Lord Chancellor. As has been indicated, Bacon wanted to prune and to regularize, to remove whatever was unnecessary or prolix in the law—the discharge "of idle and unprofitable or hurtful matter." But he had no wish for major or rapid change. Efficiency, order, and ease of practice were his principal concerns, and he never suggested that centralization was inimical to these hopes.[73]

---

Hill, *Intellectual Origins*, p. 96, where a similar reference to Gardiner is made. Here the stress on Bacon's liberalism (pp. 96-98), promotion of democracy, and advocacy of advancement by merit, not social standing (p. 112), should be contrasted to what has been said above, especially in the section covered by nn. 32-43. On the "levelling of wits," see Farrington, *Philosopher of Industrial Science*, pp. 115-119. Contrast, too, Bacon's comment that "the parity and equality of ministers is a thing of wonderful great confusion; and so is an ordinary government of synods" (*Letters and Life*, I, 85). His interest in a man's social background was revealed in his comment that Cranfield's cleverness was "more indeed than I could have looked for from a man of his breeding" (*ibid.*, V, 187).

[71] Trevor-Roper, "Three Foreigners," p. 6.

[72] *Ibid.*, p. 17. The aims of the revolutionaries are, of course, peripheral to this paper, which is concerned only with the interpretation of Bacon himself.

[73] See nn. 32, 50, and 51 above. Star Chamber was, to Bacon, "one of the sagest and noblest institutions of this kingdom" (*Works*, XI, 130). The best and most complete discussion of law reform as seen by Bacon and, later, by the revolutionaries is C. R. Niehaus, *The Issue of Law Reform in the Puritan Revolution*,

In education the case is much better. This was the one area where Bacon hoped for a fundamental transformation of methods and aims, and the reformers of the 1640's and 1650's acknowledged his inspiration. But none of his proposals resembled the administrative decentralization, primarily the proliferation of universities, which was suggested during the Great Rebellion. Solomon's house, after all, was a highly centralized institution. One document, however, seems to contain an endorsement of decentralization not only in education but also in charitable foundations and religion: Bacon's "Advice to the King, touching Sutton's estate."

Thomas Sutton, a remarkably successful Elizabethan entrepreneur who had amassed a fortune primarily from coal and moneylending, died in 1611, leaving an enormous endowment with a capital worth of over £100,000 to support an almshouse and a school on the property of the Old Charterhouse in London.[74] Bacon thereupon prepared what W. K. Jordan has called a "really infamous brief in which [he] urged his sovereign to set the will aside."[75] He was Solicitor-General at the time, and Jordan has suggested that his action was not the result of any high-minded motives but was rather an indication that he "was ever ready to bend a great mind to ignoble deeds."[76] Even if one is ready to

---

Ph.D. diss. (Harvard University, 1957). On pp. 38-42, Niehaus presents Bacon in much the same light as he appears in this paper. As for the Great Rebellion, Niehaus concludes, first, that "there was no well-defined philosophy of change to guide the efforts of reformers"; second, that nearly all the proposals were either merely negative or much too radical; third, that law reform was never a separate issue (as it was with Bacon) but was always closely tied to attacks on political abuses; and, fourth, that the reforms were *not* blocked by lawyers (pp. 224-226). See also S. E. Prall, *The Agitation for Law Reform During the Puritan Revolution, 1640-1660* (The Hague, 1966), where Bacon is hardly mentioned but where the various proposals and discussions of the 1640's and 1650's are clearly outlined. Prall notes (p. 27) that by the mid-1640's the royalists were the champions of the common law against Parliament's appeal to a higher "fundamental" law of its own; and he points out (e.g., p. 93) that one theme of the agitation was the wish for simplification rather than innovation. If this be a sign of Bacon's influence, it reveals him as anything but revolutionary.

[74] W. K. Jordan, *The Charities of London, 1480-1660* (London, 1960), pp. 151-153. For a complete biography, see N. R. Shipley, *Thomas Sutton, Tudor-Stuart Moneylender and Philanthropist*, Ph.D. diss. (Harvard University, 1967), esp. pp. 167-215 on the will.

[75] Jordan, *Charities*, pp. 152-153. The brief is in *Letters and Life*, IV, 249-254.

[76] Jordan, *Charities*, p. 152. See also his *Philanthropy in England, 1480-1660* (London, 1959), p. 285, where he speaks of Bacon's "brilliant but servile brief,"

accept Bacon's proposals as the product of deeply felt convictions about the structure of the charitable, educational, and religious institutions of England, and not merely as a means to the end of overturning the will, it can still be suggested that his overriding concern was not decentralization.

There is no denying that Bacon expressed the opinion that "some number of hospitals with complete endowments will do far more good than one hospital of an exorbitant greatness" because by choosing "those towns and places where there is most need . . . the remedy may be distributed as the disease is dispersed." But this proposition and its corollary—that one great institution would invite "a swarm and surcharge of poor"—were the last of his arguments, and he went on immediately to stress that *"chiefly* I rely upon the reason that I touched in the beginning; that in these great hospitals the revenues will draw the use, and not the use the revenues; and so through the mass of their wealth they will swiftly tumble down to a mis-employment."[77]  In other words, it was not so much the centralization itself which was at fault, but the opportunity for "corruption and abuse" that a large concentration of revenue would encourage. Implicitly Bacon was arguing against centralization, but explicitly he was saying that this was the least important of his misgivings about the projected hospital. Moreover, the subject made its appearance remarkably devoid of the fervor and claims for general wisdom that usually accompanied Bacon's hobbyhorses. He suggested decentralization because of the specific characteristics of welfare organizations and because of his belief that a concentration of poor people in one area could have unfortunate results *sui generis*. But he still had no reservations about the centralization of welfare *administration*. In the same document he pointed out that the current shortcomings of homes for the poor were due to the ill-advised policy of leaving supervision in the local areas, in the hands of justices of the peace. He advised, instead, "a settled ordinance, subject to a regular visitation."[78]

With regard to education, Bacon's attack on the will's provision for the establishment of a new school is difficult to relate to the issue of centralization. The subject was not mentioned, and his main conten-

---

though he gives no alternative explanation to replace the ostensible reasons Bacon opposed the will. Neither the Crown nor anyone else would have benefited noticeably from the Solicitor-General's recommendations.

[77] *Letters and Life*, IV, 250-251 (italics mine).          [78] *Ibid.*, p. 252.

tion—that there were already too many schools in England—argues, if anything, that he had the reverse in mind. And this interpretation is confirmed by the alternative that he proposed: endowment of *existing* lectureships at England's two universities. His principal contention, in fact, was that there were *too many* educated people in the country—a notion that has little in common with the forward-looking, let alone revolutionary, thought of the seventeenth century.

Finally, on the religious issue, in opposition to Sutton's intention of "maintaining a preacher," Bacon listed three recommendations. The first was for the creation of "a college for controversies," the second for an effort to help converts from Catholicism, and the third for the encouragement of preachers in neglected "corners in the realm."[79] The last certainly implied a further spread of the Church, but it held no suggestion of local autonomy, and in any case it hardly represented Bacon's principal concerns. It was the *last* of the proposals he mentioned, and there is no reason to believe that he considered it incongruous in light of his usual strong endorsement of the hierarchical structure of the Church of England. Control would still come from the center. Furthermore, it is difficult to regard this recommendation as a strong commitment to decentralization after reading Bacon's introduction to the subject: "Concerning propagation of Religion, I shall in few words set before your Majesty three propositions; none of them devices of mine own, otherwise than that I ever approved them." He may have approved them, but he evidently did not consider them sufficiently important to mention again in his other writings.[80]

When the Revolution came, and with it a remarkable boom in editions of his works,[81] Bacon's ideas gained wide currency. His plans for

[79] *Ibid.*, p. 254.

[80] *Ibid.*, p. 254. See also nn. 46-48 above. Trevor-Roper also sees Bacon as a great advocate of laicization. Sir Francis certainly wished to separate divine and secular learning, but his views on the equality of ministers (cited in n. 70 above) do not suggest that he approved of "lay religion" (though this term is not defined in Trevor-Roper, "Three Foreigners," p. 6). And his wish to have wealth widely spread (stressed also by Hill, *Intellectual Origins*, pp. 97-98) did not preclude his recommendation that the economy be regulated by the central government (see nn. 32 and 33 above). The attempt to perform the same service for Coke and to make him seem a progressive like Bacon has been cogently criticized in Barbara Malament, "The 'Economic Liberalism' of Sir Edward Coke," *Yale Law Journal*, LXXVI (1967), 1321-58.

[81] See Hill, *Intellectual Origins*, pp. 116-117.

the advancement of learning, so long ignored, came to be seen as the best blueprint for progress. Propagated by Comenius, Dury, and Hartlib, his utilitarian and humanitarian outlook gained a considerable following, and the first serious attempts were made to implement his suggestions. Comenius went so far as to say that everything except God could be "numbered, measured, and weighed," for "even miracles may be effected by numbers, measures, and weights."[82] In all the talk of the advancement of learning, Bacon's views reigned supreme, and other parts of his vision of the well-regulated society spilled over into the writings of the 1640's. In Hartlib's utopian Macaria there were central councils performing many of the functions that Bacon had wished to assign to such institutions. They supervised husbandry, fishing, trade by land, trade by sea, and new plantations, while a great council heard general abuses. Commerce was carefully regulated and land rationed.[83] The idea of direction from the center was the same, but the reduction of the importance of the king, the much more active intervention in commerce, and the revolutionary suggestion that land ownership be controlled, placed Hartlib in a posture very different from Bacon's. Hartlib's concern was almost exclusively with the economic well-being of the state, a much narrower focus; and, on the other hand, he was willing to accept, as one of his means, an interference in property rights that Bacon would doubtless have considered a very dangerous innovation.

The famous kingdom of Macaria was brought to public attention very early in the Great Rebellion. Before long there were signs that Bacon's view of society and how it should be reformed was finding few disciples among the radicals, even though his hopes for fruitful results from the advancement of learning were much admired. At first many agreed with him that society should be reformed under direction from the center. A large majority of Englishmen also shrank back before the prospect of unending change, of reform for the sake of reform—the very "innovation" that Bacon had warned against. And the revolutionaries originally sought the same restoration of harmony in society that Sir Francis had always wanted: they demanded a more efficient and responsive government, free from the "idle unprofitable or hurtful matter" that he, too, had condemned. But from the earliest

[82] J. A. Comenius, *A Reformation of Schooles*, tr. S. Hartlib (London, 1642), pp. 27-28.
[83] Samuel Hartlib, *A Description of the Famous Kingdome of Macaria* (London, 1641), p. 3.

days their aims included changes that Bacon never could have approved. The imposition of demands upon the King and the attack on the prerogative courts would have been totally foreign to his basically conservative view of society and the structure of government. And very soon, in the snowballing changes after 1641, there was evidence of attitudes which directly contradicted Bacon's insistence that, except in learning, innovations were always suspect and should be introduced very slowly, if at all.

Notwithstanding his constant advocacy of a multitude of advances and improvements and his belief that society as a whole could determine the achievements of an age, Bacon was reluctant to transform its basic components. Governments could and should intervene to make necessary adjustments, but only in the cause of learning did he support a major overhaul of methods and aims. Although other matters might need attention and even strong direction from a central authority, great caution had to be exercised. The harmony of society and the supremacy of the King had to remain immune from the inroads of innovation. Reformer and pioneer Bacon may have been. And his "wisdom" can hardly be questioned, whether it be seen in a brief essay like "Of Studies" or in a grand dream for the future of mankind. The hyperbole appears when he is called a social revolutionary or an inspiration of revolutionaries, without the qualification that his definition of healthy change was very narrow and often conservative. His name may have been invoked with considerable enthusiasm and little precision by men who chose, in the midst of upheaval, to ignore his position as a leading courtier and his impeachment by the Commons, because they admired his advocacy of the advancement of learning. But to accept their impressions of his thought is to forget how limited were Bacon's own wishes when he turned his attention to the reform of society.

*PART TWO*

CHRISTIANS, SCHOLARS, AND THE
WORLD OF THOUGHT

# THE ICONOGRAPHY OF *TEMPERANTIA* AND THE VIRTUOUSNESS OF TECHNOLOGY

LYNN WHITE, JR.

THE academic "Thirty Years War" which started in 1905 with the publication of Max Weber's *Die protestantische Ethik und der Geist des Kapitalismus*[1] ended in an armistice of exhaustion after the appearance of Amintore Fanfani's *Cattolicesimo e protestantesimo nella formazione storica del capitalismo.*[2] Save for historiographic studies,[3] not much that is new has been said on the subject during recent decades. There is little agreement on conclusions; nevertheless, the increment of this controversy to our historical thinking is considerable. Economic history has become a part of cultural history: this is now a platitude as it once was not. There is a consensus that, when one part of life changes, all the other parts tend to adjust. Specifically, a shift in economic methods and attitudes will probably affect religion, and either change or stasis in patterns of religious thought or emotion may well be felt in economics.[4]

This dull legacy of the debate over Weber's historical sociology began to draw profitable interest in the 1950's when the collapse of colonial empires focused attention on how to achieve economic development in the "emerging" nations. The first impulse was to export from America and Europe forms of organization, agriculture, and industrial production which had proved their worth in the Occident. But quickly it became clear that local attitudes toward labor, thrift, diet, mobility, or

---

[1] *Archiv für Sozialwissenschaft und Sozialpolitik*, XX-XXI (1904-1905); English tr. of rev. edn. (London, 1930).

[2] (Milan, 1934); English tr. (London, 1935).

[3] The most enlightening are those of E. Fischoff, "The Protestant Ethic and the Spirit of Capitalism: The History of a Controversy," *Social Research*, XI (1944), 53-77 (reprinted in R. W. Green, *Protestantism and Capitalism: the Weber Thesis and Its Critics* [Boston, 1959], pp. 107-114) and M. Walzer, "Puritanism as a Revolutionary Ideology," *History and Theory*, III (1963), 59-90. See also W. S. Hudson, "The Weber Thesis Reexamined," *Church History*, XXX (1961), 88-102.

[4] Even Kurt Samuelsson in *Religion and Economic Action* (Stockholm, 1961), the most extreme attack upon Weber's "hypothesis of a connection between Puritanism and capitalism in which religion motivated economics" (p. 153), does not deny occasional interaction between religion and economics.

the desirability of surplus production were critical to the workability of a new economic or technological device. "Variations in the value system can make all the difference, to the extent of success or failure of a development scheme, independent of the material and natural resources."[5] In our time the problem of aiding economically backward areas has become, to a great extent, the humanistic problem of understanding contrasting value patterns.

Our historical thinking thus has been forced back, not to Weber's solution, but rather to Weber's problem: what general cultural factors, including perhaps the religious, account for the remarkably productive Western economic system which we usually call capitalism?

If we are to refresh the aridity which sterilized discussion of this question after the middle 1930's, we must discover new reservoirs of insight; we must plow adjacent fields still uncultivated. Historians traditionally deal with texts, but, since the mutual accommodations between different activities within a culture (for example, religion and economics) seem often to be subliminal rather than intentional, texts may not be our most profitable sources. We must explore nonverbal symbols.

Sometimes visual symbols can tell us the meaning of ambiguous words. The spiritual value of hard work was not, as Weber implied, a Calvinist discovery; on the contrary, it was integral to the Christian ascetic tradition going back through the monks to Jewish roots.[6] Greco-Roman antiquity from Plato's time onward had no respect for labor[7] and no sense of its possible place in the life of the soul. When the classical world became ostensibly Christian, its attitude toward work did not immediately change. In his *Psychomachia*, an allegorical description of the struggle between the Virtues and the Vices for a man's destiny, the devoutly Christian poet Prudentius depicts (lines 629-631) "Metus et Labor et Vis et Scelus et placitae fidei Fraus infitiatrix"

---

[5] Kusum Nair, *Blossoms in the Dust: the Human Element in Indian Development* (London, 1961), p. 191.

[6] L. White, jr., "What Accelerated Technological Progress in the Western Middle Ages?" in *Scientific Change*, ed. A. C. Crombie (New York, 1963), pp. 284-288; German tr., *Technikgeschichte*, XXXII (1965), 214-219.

[7] "The pejorative judgments of ancient writers about labour . . . are too continuous, numerous and unanimous, too wrapped up in discussions of every aspect of ancient life, to be dismissed as empty rhetoric"—M. I. Finley, "Technical Innovation and Economic Progress in the Ancient World," *Economic History Review*, 2nd ser., XVIII (1965), 44.

fleeing before virtuous onslaught. In the standard English translation[8] these Vices appear as "Fear and Suffering and Violence, Crime and Fraud that denies accepted faith." In late Latin *labor* may indeed mean "suffering," although it would be curious to think of this as a Vice. But what it meant to contemporaries in this particular context is indicated by a picture in a tenth-century manuscript of the *Psychomachia*—the earliest extant—which seems to reflect the illustrative scheme of Prudentius's time: *Labor* is shown (Fig. 1) as a man bearing on his shoulders a great burden.[9] The implication is clear that, to Prudentius and his audience, Labor meant Drudgery and that, in their minds, there was a grave moral defect, comparable to Timidity, Violence, or Fraudulence, in any man who toiled physically. The tendency to identify privilege with virtue and deprivation with depravity is endemic to our race, as the twelfth-century neologism *vilain* indicates.[10] But the classical attitude toward labor, which was still dominant in the thinking of Prudentius, could not long survive the Benedictine propaganda that *laborare est orare*, that "work is worship."[11] The so-called bourgeois ethos incorporated the final phase of this tradition of ascetic spirituality.

Liturgics and devotion produce sets of symbols which may be of assistance. The cult of St. Joseph has a curious history.[12] In the Chris-

[8] H. J. Thomson, *Prudentius* (Cambridge, Mass., 1949) I, 322.

[9] R. Stettiner, *Die illustrierten Prudentius-Handschriften* (Berlin, 1905), plate 9, no. 2, from Bibliothèque Nationale, MS lat. 8318, fol. 61ᵛ. A. Katzenellenbogen, *Allegories of the Virtues and Vices in Medieval Art from Early Christian Times to the Thirteenth Century* (New York, 1964), p. 6, believes that the illustrations of this MS rest on classical precedents: *Labor* seems modeled after figures on Trajan's column.

[10] W. von Wartburg, *Französisches etymologisches Wörterbuch*, XIV (Basel, 1961), 453.

[11] The variants in the early Christian ascetic tradition are historically significant. A. de Vogüé, "Travail et alimentation dans les règles de saint Benoît et du Maître," *Revue bénédictine*, LXXIV (1964), 242-251, shows that, whereas the *Regula magistri* encourages monastic labor only in garden agriculture and artisanry, the *Rule* of St. Benedict makes labor in the fields central. If the *Regula magistri* had won the West, the history of European agriculture and reclamation might have been less dynamic.

[12] C. A., "Le développement historique du culte de Saint Joseph," *Revue bénédictine*, XIV (1897), 104-114, 145-155, 203-209; J. Dusserre, "Les origines de la dévotion à Saint Joseph," *Cahiers de Joséphologie*, I (1953), 23-54, 169-196, II (1954), 5-30; see also C. P. Deasy, *St. Joseph in the English Mystery Plays* (Washington, 1937); J. Huizinga, *Waning of the Middle Ages* (London, 1929), pp. 152-153.

tian East he was early the object of a certain veneration, but in the Latin Church nothing was heard of him for many centuries, save in scriptural commentaries. To the popular mind, equipped with a robust sense of humor, he seemed the patron saint of cuckolds; until the very late Middle Ages, "Joseph" was rare as a baptismal name in the West.[18] There were no relics of him, and no churches were dedicated to his honor. By the end of the thirteenth century signs of change appeared, possibly stimulated by contact with the Eastern cult; but devotion to St. Joseph long remained private and inconspicuous. Toward the end of the fourteenth century, however, St. Joseph was being widely discovered. In 1399 the Franciscans adopted his feast on 19 March, and the Dominicans quickly followed their example. It was introduced into the Roman breviary in 1479 and became a commemoration in the entire Roman Catholic Church in 1621. In 1729 St. Joseph's name was inserted in the Litany of the Saints by Benedict XIII; in 1870 Pius IX entitled him Patron of the Universal Church— "a lamentable indication of the vulgar concept of the church held by this Pope," grumbles Friedrich Heiler,[14] whose taste in piety is early medieval; in 1889 Leo XIII announced his preeminent sanctity as second only to that of the Blessed Virgin Mary; and in 1962 John XXIII added his name to the canon of the Mass.

How are we to account for this development? Modern ecclesiastical commentators, dazzled by the riches of devotion now centering about St. Joseph, generally regard it as prime evidence of the Holy Spirit's continuing revelation to the Church and repeat the delighted cry of the toastmaster of the wedding feast at Cana: "But thou hast kept the good wine until now!" Scholars less devout inevitably search for supplementary explanations.

By the early fifteenth century St. Joseph—until recently the complaining, hoodwinked husband, the butt of popular mockery—had been transformed into St. Joseph the strong and kindly *pater familias,* the guardian of the Christ Child and of Our Lady, the hard-working artisan, the patron of carpenters and cabinetmakers. Meyer Schapiro, an art historian whose trade it is to deal with symbols, has noted that the praises which Jean Gerson (d. 1429) lavished upon St. Joseph

---

[18] Nevertheless, U. Chevalier, *Répertoire des sources historiques du moyen âge: Bio-bibliographie,* II (Paris, 1907), 2658-60, lists a few Western cases, especially in the eighth and ninth centuries, the origins of which should be investigated by devotees of the cult.

[14] *Der Katholizismus* (Munich, 1923), p. 192, n. 28.

"anticipate the ascetic Protestant concept of vocation and the religious value of industriousness, and should be taken into account in the problem of the origins of the Protestant ethic and bourgeois morality."[15] The cult of St. Joseph would seem to be one of the ways in which Catholicism, both before and after the Protestant revolt, has tried unconsciously (but probably effectively) to validate middle-class ideals.

One aspect of the "bourgeois" mentality which has escaped discussion by historians is moral approval of technology. Doubtless it has been neglected because Marxists also have considered machines salutary: any bad effect associated with machines was blamed on the social structure, not on the machines themselves. Psychic affirmation of technology is one of the presuppositions of the present world, whether capitalist or communist. Without widespread and intense emotional commitment to machines and gadgets, men of talent would not have put their energies into building the new devices for production, transportation, and communication, which are among the most distinctive features of modern life.

The first symptom of this tendency to identify advanced technology with high morality appeared in the Utrecht Psalter (Utrecht University Library, Aevum med., script. eccles. 484), illuminated near Rheims between 816 and 834. Bruce Spiegelberg of Colby College has pointed out to me the clear implication of fol. 35$^v$ (Fig. 2) decorating Psalm 63 (64). On the right is the Psalmist being blessed by God and protected by an angel and a small band of the righteous. On the left are the evil-doers. Between them lies a pit (of Hell?) or snare (cf. verse 6). The central interest of the picture lies in the sharpening of a sword in each camp (cf. verse 4), but by very different means. The iniquitous are content to employ an old-fashioned whetstone. The virtuous, in spectacular contrast, are using the first known example of the rotary grindstone, and it is being turned by the first mechanical crank to appear outside China.[16] Since the substitution of continuous rotary motion for reciprocating motion was basic to the development of machine design, this illumination marks a great moment in the history of technology. But its psychological content is no less portentous than its purely technological import.

[15] M. Schapiro, "Muscipulus diaboli," *Art Bulletin*, XXVII (1945), 184.
[16] L. White, jr., *Medieval Technology and Social Change* (Oxford, 1962), pp. 110, 169.

Spiegelberg's exegesis of this ninth-century illumination is entirely coherent with the context of the picture. Between ca. A.D. 400 and 1000 the Frankish regions seized the initiative in technology from the more sophisticated peoples of the Near East and with amazing rapidity developed improved methods in agriculture, in warfare, and in industrial production.[17] The Utrecht Psalter, fol. 35$^v$, expresses in symbols a historical fact of great importance, which contemporaries seem never to have put into words.

Moral enthusiasm for engines is peculiar to the West. Before the mechanical clock appeared, the most complex machine was the pipe organ. Although the Byzantines used organs habitually for secular ceremonies, the Eastern clergy consistently banned them from sacred liturgies,[18] maintaining that only the unaccompanied human voice can rival the song of the cherubim in God's praise. But, by 950, Winchester Cathedral was resounding with the music of an organ so vast that it required seventy men to pump its twenty-six bellows,[19] and this became the Western pattern. Although Justinian placed sundials and perhaps a clepsydra in a separate building outside Hagia Sophia,[20] clocks were not admitted inside the shrines of Eastern Christendom: Time could not be permitted to desecrate Eternity. Yet as soon as Western Europeans invented the mechanical escapement in the early fourteenth century, they put astronomical clocks in great numbers not only outside but also inside their churches, less to tell time than to demonstrate visually the orderliness of God's cosmos.[21] Increasingly, the Latin Occident felt spiritually at home with elaborate machines.

The fifteenth-century changes in the representation of the Virtue of Temperance are indicative of a later stage in this evolution. The materials are known somewhat to art historians but have not been used to illuminate developing European attitudes toward technology.

[17] *Ibid., passim.*

[18] Egon Wellesz, *History of Byzantine Music and Hymnography*, 2nd edn. (Oxford, 1961), pp. 105-108, 366; cf. the comments of Jean Perrot, *L'orgue de ses origines hellénistiques à la fin du XIII$^e$ siècle* (Paris, 1965), pp. 211, n. 5, and 215.

[19] *Frithegodi monachi Breviloquium vitae beati Wilfredi, et Wulfstani cantoris Narratio metrica de sancto Swithuno*, ed. A. Campbell (Zurich, 1950), pp. 69-70, lines 141-170.

[20] E. H. Swift, *Hagia Sophia* (New York, 1940), p. 180.

[21] White, *Medieval Technology*, pp. 124-125.

The roots of the new iconography of Temperance lay deep in the thought and piety of earlier generations. Since Christian moral theology has drawn upon conflicting Biblical listings and upon variant philosophical traditions mediated largely by Cicero and Macrobius, it has retained remarkable flexibility, not to say confusion, in its schematizations of the Virtues. However, a normative pattern gradually emerged. The Pauline triad of Faith, Hope, and Charity became the Theological Virtues, for the practice of which divine grace was essential; and St. Augustine explained why St. Paul was correct in considering Charity the greatest of these. By Carolingian times they were often augmented by an old pagan quaternity of "natural," "political," or Cardinal Virtues (so called because they provided the "hinges," *cardines*, of the door to the good life), which could be exercised merely with human faculties: Prudence, Courage, Temperance, and Justice. This scheme suited the needs of craftsmen, who not infrequently had either three or four spaces to ornament.

Temperance, however, must have seemed the most colorless and negative of the Virtues: "Temperance is the soul's stalwart and considered condemnation of all excess," said Hugh of Saint Victor in the early twelfth century,[22] a time when even the saints were full-blooded. The speculative neglect of Temperance is shown by Alain de Lille's infelicitous effort to pair the Cardinal with the Theological Virtues: Justice = Charity; Prudence = Faith; Courage = Hope.[23] Temperance was a wallflower at the scholastic ball.

By the end of the thirteenth century her situation had changed radically for the better, but how this change happened has not been made clear. The medieval literature on ethics is a jungle,[24] through which even the vast labors of Dom Odon Lottin[25] have hacked only narrow tracks. The texts now available do not expose how *Temperantia* was able to climb the hierarchical ladder from the lowest to the highest rung. Some of the evidence indicates controversy still unknown to us. St. Thomas Aquinas discussed "whether Temperance may be the

[22] R. Baron, "À propos des ramifications des vertus au XIIe siècle," *Recherches de théologie ancienne et médiévale*, XXIII (1956), 21.

[23] P. Delhaye, "La vertu et les vertus dans les oeuvres d'Alain de Lille," *Cahiers de civilisation médiéval*, VI (1963), 24.

[24] Cf. Morton W. Bloomfield, "A Preliminary List of Incipits of Latin Works on the Virtues and Vices, Mainly of the Thirteenth, Fourteenth and Fifteenth Centuries," *Traditio*, XI (1955), 259-379.

[25] O. Lottin, *Psychologie et morale aux XIIe et XIIIe siècles*, 6 vols. (Louvain, 1942-1960).

greatest of the Virtues" and concluded "that Justice and Courage are more excellent than Temperance, and that Prudence and the Theological Virtues are even preferable to these."[26] "Yet," as Morton Bloomfield acutely remarks,[27] "it is significant that he felt that this was a proposition to refute. Among some thinkers at least, although who they are I have not been able to discover precisely, temperance must have been given absolute pre-eminence among the cardinal virtues."

Even though new discoveries of scholastic texts may eventually help to explain the rise of Temperance to dominance among the Virtues, one suspects that the process went on less in the world of the Latin-writing clergy than among the vernacular-speaking secular aristocracy, who have left us far fewer written records. As the oral literature designed for that elite achieved sophistication, the poets developed an ethical system focusing on *demesure* as the chief source of human evil and on moderation, *mesure, mâze, misura,* as its countervailing Virtue. In the *Song of Roland*—a masterpiece which survives, we should recall, in a single manuscript—Thurold sings "a hymn to moderation—a hymn which proclaims the essentially temperate climate of the end of the twelfth century."[28] Among the German poets of the thirteenth century "*mâze* is the characteristic virtue of the courts, the touchstone of an aristocratic upbringing."[29] Although no known work in Latin clearly identifies this chivalric Virtue of Measure with Temperance, the Florentine Brunetti Latini, Dante's teacher, writing in the late thirteenth century, tells us that in the popular mind these two had become one: "Here stands Temperance / Whom folk at times / Call Measure."[30]

[26] *Summa theologica*, II, II, qu. 141. a. 8 (Rome, 1899), X, 131. Cf. E. K. Rand, *Cicero in the Courtroom of St. Thomas Aquinas* (Milwaukee, 1946), pp. 50, 108-112.

[27] M. W. Bloomfield, *Piers Plowman as a Fourteenth-Century Apocalypse* (New Brunswick, 1964), p. 137.

[28] F. Whitehead, "Ofermod et demesure," *Cahiers de civilisation médiévale,* III (1960), 117. Whitehead survives the criticisms of G. F. Jones, *The Ethos of the Song of Roland* (Baltimore, 1963), pp. 33-34, 65, n. 75, and 127-128.

[29] Gustav Ehrismann, "Die Grundlagen des ritterlichen Tugendsystems," *Zeitschrift für deutsches Altertum,* LVI (1919), 151. The savage attack of Ernst R. Curtius, *European Literature and the Latin Middle Ages* (New York, 1953), pp. 519-537, upon Ehrismann's views does not affect his treatment of *mâze.*

[30] B. Latini, *Il Tesoretto e il Favolello,* ed. B. Wiese (Strassburg, 1909), Bk. XIV, lines 1284-86 ("Qui sta la Temperanza / Cui la gente talora / Suole chiamar misura").

A second force working to elevate Temperance's speculative status was the revival of Aristotelian ethics, the core of which is the notion that virtue is the golden mean, moderation in all things. There is rumor that a translation of the *Nicomachean Ethics* appeared perhaps as early as the third quarter of the twelfth century.[31] Although in 1215 Robert de Courçon listed the *Ethics* as one of the books subject to lectures at Paris on feast days,[32] I have found no other mention of it earlier than ca. 1220, when the *Summa aurea* of William of Auxerre, one of the most widely read ethical treatises of its time, explicitly credited to Aristotle the idea that "virtue [and not simply temperance] . . . is the mean between the vices."[33] Clearly, *Temperantia*, broadly defined as moderation, fits this definition of virtue better than any other Virtue and would thus tend to become the central Virtue.

That this was William of Auxerre's instinct is shown in his handling of the next *quaestio*: "Whether Virtue is of several sorts." "The question of the different kinds of Virtues is raised, and it is shown that there is only one kind of Virtue . . . a single Virtue is enough to incite all the powers of the spirit and all parts of the body toward the good; therefore other Virtues are needless. Yet it is clear that nothing is needless in the works of nature or of God; therefore there is only one kind of Virtue. For example: a man wills to avoid unclean acts by the Virtue of Temperance, and this is good; therefore the man wills the good for himself by the Virtue of Temperance. But to will good for oneself is to love oneself; therefore the man loves himself by the Virtue of Temperance. Yet he can love himself with no Virtue save Charity; therefore Temperance is Charity."[34] To be sure, William hastens to add that "just in the same way it can be shown that any

[31] J. Minio-Paluello, "Jacobus Veneticus Grecus, Canonist and Translator of Aristotle," *Traditio*, VIII (1952), 279, n. 28.

[32] H. Denifle and A. Chatelain, *Chartularium Universitatis Parisiensis*, I (Paris, 1889), 78.

[33] *Summa aurea in quatuor libros sententiarum* (Paris, 1500; reprint Frankfurt am Main, 1964), Lib. III, tract. 2, cap. 2, qu. 1, fol. 129ʳ.

[34] *Ibid.*: "Utrum virtus habeat plures species." "Queritur de speciebus virtutum, et probatur quod unica est species virtutum . . . unica virtus sufficit ad movendum omnes potentias anime et omnia corporis membra ad bonum; ergo alique virtutes superfluunt. Sed constat quod nichil est superfluum in operibus nature vel dei; ergo unica est species virtuum. Item: temperantia virtute vult homo abstinere ab operibus immundis, et hoc est bonum; ergo temperantia virtute vult homo sibi bonum. Sed velle sibi bonum est diligere se; ergo temperantia virtute diligit homo se. Sed nulla virtute diligit se nisi caritate; ergo temperantia est caritas."

Virtue is really Charity" and agrees with St. Augustine on the primacy of Charity among the Virtues.[35] Nevertheless, no reader could escape the impression that, by selecting Temperance as his example to demonstrate the specific unity of all the Virtues, William was undercutting the traditional dominance of Charity.

The later thirteenth century was saturated with influences stemming from the Aristotelian *Ethics*;[36] before 1267 Brunetto Latini, for example, produced a popular summary of it.[37] By the time he wrote his *Tresor*, aimed at the lay public, the Aristotelian *aurea mediocritas* was combining with chivalric *mesure* to make Temperance the supreme Virtue: "By Temperance a man rules himself, and by Force and Justice he rules others; but it is better to govern yourself than another. . . . The Master [Aristotle] says that all the other Virtues are inferior to Temperance."[38] The fact that neither Aristotle nor any other author known to us had ever said it in just this way makes the misquotation all the more significant for our understanding of the cultural pressures that helped to raise the valuation of Temperance.

A third force working in the same direction was the gradual identification of *Temperantia* with *Sapientia*. In the famous discourse of Wisdom in Proverbs 8:12-16, she says: "I, Wisdom [*sapientia*], dwell in good counsel and abide in learned thoughts. . . . Mine is counsel and equity, mine is prudence [*prudentia*]; mine is strength [*fortitudo*]. By me kings reign . . . and princes decree justice [*justitia*]." Only after the quaternity of the Cardinal Virtues was a recognized pattern in much Christian thinking would it be noticed that Wisdom speaks of Prudence, Courage, and Justice as entities other than herself. Surely, then, she herself must be Temperance. In a manuscript of the later twelfth century produced near Trier, *Sapientia* for the first time appears in place of *Temperantia* in an illumination of Solomon and the Virtues in Proverbs[39] (Fig. 3). But, as Mlle. d'Alverny has shown,[40]

[35] Cf. also *ibid.*, fol. 127ᵛ.

[36] See *L'Éthique à Nicomaque*, tr. and commentary by R. A. Gauthier and J. Y. Jolif (Louvain, 1958), pp. 71-86, for an admirable survey.

[37] *L'ethica d'Aristotele ridotta in compendia da ser Brunetto Latini* (Lyons, 1568).

[38] B. Latini, *Li livres dou tresor*, ed. F. J. Carmody (Berkeley, 1948), Bk. II, chs. 71-72, pp. 248-249 (". . . Li mestres dit desous atemprance sont toutes les vertues").

[39] British Museum, Harley MS 2799, fol. 57ᵛ; cf. George F. Warner, *Illuminated Manuscripts in the British Museum*, III (London, 1903), plate 18.

[40] M. T. D'Alverny, "Le symbolisme de la Sagesse et le Christ de S. Dunstan," *Bodleian Library Record*, V (1956), 232-244.

theologians had long since identified Christ with the allegorical figure of Wisdom. Thus, by the curious medieval process of intellectual agglutination, Temperance became not only Wisdom but also Christ himself. The morality of self-restraint could scarcely achieve more lofty symbolic expression.

Temperance's new position in the European ethos was codified in Heinrich Suso's *Horologium sapientiae*, written about 1334,[41] which for the next two centuries was one of the devotional works most widely read in Northern Europe: nearly two hundred manuscripts of the Latin original survive, not counting fragments, excerpts, and re-workings.[42] It was translated into Dutch in the late fourteenth century, into French in 1389, into Danish and Swedish in the fifteenth century, and seven chapters were put into English and published in 1490;[43] moreover, Suso's *Büchlein der Ewigen Weisheit* is a somewhat altered German version of it. The *Horologium* is a dialogue between the author and *Sapientia*, who is presented as Divine Wisdom and who speaks not only with the voice of Christ the *Logos* but also with that of *Temperantia*, the Virtue who regulates the Christian life.[44]

Obviously a lady like Temperance who had risen so rapidly in the social scale could not be expected to keep her old equipment in her new position. The early iconography of *Temperantia* had been a bit confused, but by the eleventh century normally she was recognized because she held a jug from which she was pouring water into a cup of wine to dilute its potency.[45] And so she continued until the fourteenth century.

By 1359, however, the new concept of Temperance, announced by Brunetto Latini as *misura*, is found in Florentine art: on Andrea Orcagna's tabernacle of Or San Michele she appears holding a pair of

---

[41] There is no firm date: the book is dedicated to Hugo de Vaucemain, Dominican General 1333-1341.

[42] D. Planzer, "Zur Textgeschichte und Textkritik des Horologium sapientiae des sel. Heinrich Seuse," *Divus Thomas* (Freiburg), XII (1934), 130.

[43] J. A. Bizet, *Suso et le déclin de la scolastique* (Paris, 1946), pp. 404-406. Bizet does not mention, and I have not been able to date, an Italian version, *Orologio della sapientia*, which had little distribution and was not published until the edition by Ignazio del Nente (Rome, 1663).

[44] Father Planzer has never produced his long-promised edition of the *Horologium sapientiae*. In addition to the early printings, one may turn to two editions by Joseph Strange (Cologne, 1856 and 1861), to that in the *Bibliotheca mystica sanctorum Ordinis Praedicatorum patrum* (Munich, 1923), or to that of G. Richstätter (Turin, 1929).

[45] Katzenellenbogen, *Allegories*, p. 55.

compasses (Fig. 4).[46] But time as well as space may be measured, and the first hint of the new icon of Temperance which was to become dominant is found at almost the same moment in Siena. In 1337-1340[47] Ambrogio Lorenzetti had decorated the Sala della Pace of the Palazzo Pubblico with frescos which depicted the Cardinal Virtues, including Temperance. Unfortunately, exactly the part of the painting which showed Temperance was destroyed by fire, presumably in the enthusiastic burning of tax records during the riots attending Charles IV's visit to Siena in 1355.[48] Lorenzetti is thought to have died in the plague of 1348; the repair of the fresco was accomplished by an unknown artist. To judge by the costumes, horse-trappings, shapes of beards, etc., in the repainted section, the new artist did not follow Lorenzetti in all details.[49] The figure of Temperance, therefore, cannot be dated before the later 1350's. She is shown holding an object which has sometimes been interpreted as her traditional cup (and may have been such in Lorenzetti's original) but which is, in fact, our earliest picture anywhere of a sandglass[50] (Fig. 5).

The Italian idea of representing Temperance with a timepiece was perhaps brought to Northern Europe by one of the Italian artists active in France and Burgundy at the turn of the fifteenth century.[51]

[46] K. Steinweg, *Andrea Orcagna* (Strassburg, 1929), plate XVII (19). Compasses as a symbol for Temperance may have proved unsuccessful because of higher competition: from about A.D. 1000 a pair of compasses is often held by the Creator God. See L. White, jr., "Eilmer of Malmesbury, an Eleventh-century Aviator," *Technology and Culture*, II (1961), 101-102.

[47] C. Brandi, "Chiarimenti sul 'Buon Governo' di Ambrogio Lorenzetti," *Bollettino d'arte*, 4th ser., XL (1955), 119-123.

[48] For the circumstances, see P. Rossi, "Carlo IV de Lussemburgo e la Repubblica de Siena (1355-1369)," *Bullettino Senese di storia patria*, N.S., I (1930), 13-18.

[49] Brandi, *loc.cit.*

[50] Cf. C. B. Drover, "Sandglass 'Sand,'" *Antiquarian Horology*, III (1960), 62-67. T. Belin, *Les heures de Marguerite de Beaujeu* (Paris, 1925), p. 28, identifies objects in the marginal decorations of this MS (dated 1363 and now Morgan Library MS 754) as sandglasses. I have examined the original and found two of these objects on fol. 21ᵛ, three on fol. 22ʳ, one on fol. 67ᵛ, and one on fol. 80ᵛ. The borders of fols. 20ᵛ-22ᵛ are chiefly decorated with motifs from the textile industry: spinning, carding, weaving. I believe that the supposed sandglasses are, in fact, light wooden frames to be held in the hand for winding yarn into hanks. For the documents on the history of the sandglass (the earliest of which is an Italian poem of 1306-1313), see White, *Medieval Technology*, pp. 165-166.

[51] For such artists, see M. Meiss, "The Exhibitions of French Manuscripts of the

On the other hand, it may have been introduced by the father of the Venetian-born Christine de Pisan. About 1400,[52] at the French court, the latter wrote *L'epître d'Othéa*, a treatise supposedly sent by the Trojan goddess Othea to a young prince for the formation of his character. Christine tells us that Othea represents "the wisdom of woman"[53] and remarks in a note explaining the pictures that "Temperance should be called a goddess likewise. And because our human body is made up of many parts and should be regulated by reason, it may be represented as a clock in which there are several wheels and measures. And just as the clock is worth nothing unless it is regulated, so our human body does not work unless Temperance orders it."[54] Our two earliest manuscripts of *Othéa* (now British Museum, Harley MS 4331, fol. 96ᵛ and Bibliothèque Nationale, MS fr. 606, fol. 2ᵛ), both produced shortly after 1400 at the court and presumably with Christine's advice by a Northern artist with "Italian proclivities,"[55] were embellished with pictures of Temperance adjusting a large mechanical clock (Fig. 6). Such clocks became standard in illustrated *Othéa* manuscripts.[56]

Since Christine was five years old when she left Italy in 1368, we can scarcely ascribe the clock in *Othéa* to her own memories of Italian iconology. But her father, Thomas de Pisan, was a native of Bologna who served Charles V of France as personal physician and astrologer. Men in his business were interested in clocks: the contemporary physician and astronomer at Padua, Giovanni de' Dondi, built the most intricate example of the fourteenth century.[57] Thomas would have known, and would have mentioned, the new Italian representation of Temperance.

---

XIII-XVI Centuries at the Bibliothèque Nationale," *Art Bulletin*, XXXVIII (1956), 193-195.

[52] P.G.C. Campbell, *L'epître d'Othèa: Étude sur les sources de Christine de Pisan* (Paris, 1924), p. 30. We have at least forty-five MSS earlier than the first printing of 1490, and there were five editions (*ibid.*, p. 45). Gianni Mombello, "Per un' edizione critica dell' *Epistre Othea* di Christine de Pizan," *Studi francesci*, no. 24 (1964), pp. 404-408, and no. 25 (1965), p. 12, lists many magnificent MSS (some now lost) of this work which existed in the libraries of nobles in the fifteenth century.

[53] Campbell, p. 31.

[54] Cited from British Museum, Harley MS 4331, and Bibliothèque Nationale, MS fr. 606, by Rosemond Tuve, "Notes on the Virtues and Vices," *Journal of the Warburg and Courtauld Institutes*, XXVI (1963), 289.

[55] Meiss, "Exhibitions," p. 193.      [56] Tuve, "Notes," p. 281.

[57] See White, *Medieval Technology*, pp. 125-126; Giovanni Dondi dall 'Orologio, *Tractatus astrarii*, ed. A. Barzon, E. Morpurgo, et al. (Vatican, 1960).

Both he and his daughter, since they lived at the Parisian court, may well have seen an illumination which is the earliest use of clockwork in Christian symbolism. II Kings 20:1-10 tells of King Hezekiah's dream in which God added fifteen years to his life span and, as a sign, pushed back the shadow on a sundial by ten degrees. In the so-called *Moralized Bible*, illuminated for the court in Paris about 1250, there is a picture of this episode which shows God (in the form of Christ) regulating a complex waterclock with a weight-driven striking-train (Fig. 7).[58] Since at Paris, by the turn of the fourteenth century, Christ, Wisdom, and Temperance were tending to amalgamate (thanks partly to the 1389 French translation of Suso's *Horologium sapientiae*), a person of Christine de Pisan's time and place might well pour a new content into this mid-thirteenth-century form.

Moreover, until the death of Charles V of France in 1380 caused the remarkable group of intellectuals which he had gathered about him to disperse, both Thomas de Pisan and his precocious daughter must have had frequent conversation with Nicole Oresme, the thinker most aware of the religious potential in the symbolism of the new mechanical clocks. Although Oresme was Dean of Rouen until 1377 and thereafter Bishop of Lisieux, as a favorite of Charles V he visited the court often and produced several works at Charles's request, including, in 1370, a French translation of Aristotle's *Nicomachaean Ethics*.[59] Since Thomas de Pisan, likewise a man of scientific interests, was in constant and intimate attendance upon the King from 1368 until 1380,[60] he and Oresme certainly knew each other and exchanged ideas, even though Oresme's opposition to astrologers mixing in political decisions[61] may at times have chilled their relationship. In his *Du ciel* Oresme points out that, to explain celestial mechanics and the revolution of the heavenly spheres, the new physical theory of *vis impressa* is insufficient, since without friction the speed of the spheres would accelerate. Thus, to maintain a constant velocity in the heavenly bodies, God, like a divine clockmaker, devised the equivalent of an escape-

[58] See White, *Medieval Technology*, p. 120.

[59] N. Oresme, *Le livre de éthiques d'Aristote*, ed. A. D. Menut (New York, 1940).

[60] M. J. Pinet, *Christine de Pisan, 1364-1413* (Paris, 1927), p. 9.

[61] C. Jourdain, "Nicolas Oresme et les astrologues de la cour de Charles V," *Revue des questions historiques*, XVIII (1875), 136-159; G. W. Coopland, *Nicole Oresme and the Astrologers: A Study of his Livre de divinacions* (Cambridge, Mass., 1952).

FIG. 1. Bibl. Nat., ms lat. 8318, fol. 61ᵛ

FIG. 2. Utrecht Univ. Lib., Aev. med., script. eccles. 424, fol. 35ᵛ

Fig. 3. Brit. Mus., Harley MS 2799, fol. 57ᵛ

OPPOSITE

*Top*: Fig. 4. Orcagna, *Temperantia*, Or San Michele, Florence

*Bottom*: Fig. 5. *Temperantia*, Palazzo Pubblico, Siena

Fig. 6. Bibl. Nat.,
MS fr. 606, fol. 2ᵛ

Fig. 7. Bodleian Lib., MS 270b, fol. 183ᵛ

FIG. 8. Bibl. Nat., MS fr. 926, fol. 113

FIG. 9. Bibl. Royale, Brussels, MS IV. III, fol. 13ᵛ

FIG. 12. Bibl. Nat., MS fr. 9186, fol. 304ʳ

FIG. 13. Bibl. Municipale, Rouen, MS fr. 927. I 2, fol. 17ᵛ

ment.[62] Such a concept, by analogy, would strengthen the idea of God's moral regulation of man inherent in the use of a clock to symbolize *Temperantia*: macrocosm and human microcosm were always closely associated in medieval minds. One can therefore understand why, about 1400, the originally Italian association of a timepiece with *Temperantia* began, in Northern France and Burgundy, to emerge as a major expression of religious devotion.

When he wrote his *Horologium sapientiae* at Constance about 1334, Suso's title had involved no elaborate clock symbolism. Planzer[63] has suggested that the work was divided into twenty-four chapters simply on analogy with John Cassian's *Collationes*, one of Suso's favorite books, and that perhaps this division suggested the hours on the face of a clock; one of Suso's fellow Dominicans, Berthold Huenlein, wrote a *Horologium devotionis circa vitam Christi* about 1350, saying "I wish to call this little book *The Clock of Devotion* because just as the day has twenty-four hours . . . so this booklet on Christ's life has twenty-four chapters."[64]

Suso is slightly more explicit. In his preface he says that the intention of his *Horologium* is that of an alarm clock—"to waken the torpid from careless sleep to watchful virtue"—and adds: "Hence the present little work tries to expound the Savior's mercy as in a vision, using the metaphor of a fair clock decked with fine wheels, and of a dulcet chime giving forth a sweet and heavenly sound, exalting the hearts of all by its complex beauty." This description gave a hint to illuminators, but, so far as I can discover, none of the fourteenth-century manuscripts of Suso is decorated with a clock. However, a 1406 manuscript of the French translation of 1389 belonging to Marie, daughter of the Duke of Berry, shows one[65] (Fig. 8): through the clock and

[62] White, *Medieval Technology*, pp. 125, 174 as corrected by M. Clagett, "Nichole Oresme and Medieval Scientific Thought," *Proceedings of the American Philosophical Society*, CVIII (1964), 300-302; see also his relevant correction of A. C. Crombie in *Technology and Culture*, VII (1966), 227. Not until Galileo unified celestial and terrestrial mechanics could the Deist notion of the total mechanization of God's creation arise.

[63] D. Planzer, "Gab es eine gekürzte Redaktion des lateinischen Horologium sapientiae des sel. Heinrich Suso?" *Divus Thomas* (Freiburg), XIII (1935), 208, n. 2.

[64] Cited *ibid.*

[65] Bibliothèque Nationale, MS fr. 926, fol. 113; cf. A. Wins, *L'horloge à travers les âges* (Mons, 1924), pp. 168-169. Christine de Pisan was presumably familiar with this French version; indeed she may echo the passage cited above in her

*Sapientia-Temperantia* the Holy Trinity grants grace to Suso, while his Franciscan translator stands on the right.

As with *Othéa*, so in illustrated manuscripts of the French *Horloge de sapience*, pictures of clocks thenceforth became normal.[66] This tradition reached extraordinary complexity slightly before 1450 in the Brussels, Bibliothèque Royale, MS. IV, 111, fol. 13ᵛ (Fig. 9). Here Wisdom in her guise of Temperance converses with the devout author amid the finest exhibition of time-measuring devices surviving from the fifteenth century. Indeed, the flat clock on the table is our first indisputable evidence of a spring-driven, fusee-regulated mechanism.[67] The intricate development of this picture beyond any conceivable requirement of Suso's text indicates subconscious pressures to inflate the clock symbol.

The apotheosis of the clock occurs in Bibliothèque Nationale, MS fr. 455, fol. 9, a copy of the French *Horloge de sapience* (Fig. 10). The owner of the manuscript, Louis de Bruges, Lord of Gruuthuse, stands at the left. Since he is depicted in vigorous middle manhood, wearing the collar of the Golden Fleece which he received in 1461 at about the age of thirty-nine,[68] the illumination may be dated roughly 1461-1465. The earlier allegorical figure of *Sapientia-Temperantia* has vanished. King Solomon, who is cited in the first lines of the text as praising wisdom and who is traditionally regarded as the historical embodiment of godly wisdom, is repairing a complex clock, the tools of his craft scattered at his feet. One of Louis's attendants is already at

---

two dedications of *Othéa* to Louis d'Orlèans and to Charles VI: "Car petite clochette grant voix sonne, / Qui, moult souvent, les plus sages reveille / Et le labour d'estude leur conseille," See Mombello, *Studi francesi*, no. 25 (1965), pp. 3, 5.

[66] Cf. H. Michel, "Some New Documents in the History of Horology," *Antiquarian Horology*, III (1962), 288-291.

[67] H. Michel, "*L'Horloge de sapience* et l'histoire de l'horlogerie," *Physis*, II (1960), 291-298; Eleanor P. Spenser, "*L'Horloge de sapience*: Bruxelles, Bibliothèque Royale, MS IV, 111," *Scriptorium*, XVII (1963), 277-299. The other contents of this MS are largely writings of Jean Gerson. Its first owner was a member of the Gouffier family, but before 1488 it passed into the hands of the Duke of Brittany. A closely related miniature, probably slightly later, is in Vienna, Nationalbibliothek, cod. 2574, fol. 2ʳ; cf. *ibid.*, 299, note and plate 23.

[68] *La Toison d'or: cinque siècles d'art et d'histoire* (Bruges, 1962), p. 37; cf. pp. 111-113. P. Paris, *Les manuscrits françois de la Bibliothèque du Roi, leur histoire*, IV (Paris, 1841), 195, followed by A. Wins, *L'horloge*, pp. 81-82, misinterprets this picture, identifying Solomon as Louis de Bruges and indicating that the wearer of the Golden Fleece is unknown.

prayer; the Lord of Gruuthuse himself is about to clasp his hands in awed devotion before the clock, to which Solomon is pointing. The mechanism has become the icon of the Christian life.

The substitution of the fleshly-historical Solomon for the allegorical-eternal *Temperantia* has shifted the religious focus of the picture from *Temperantia* to the clock itself. But another variation is also significant. In the earlier pictures we see *Sapientia-Temperantia* reaching into the clock to adjust it. This iconography reflects the period when weight-driven clocks required frequent correction, not only because of mechanical crudities but more especially because the length of the hours of day and night varied constantly with the shift of seasons. In the late fourteenth and early fifteenth centuries, however, the increasing accuracy of clocks led, or enabled, Europe to abandon experiential time for abstract time, the cycle of night and day conceived as twenty-four hours of equal length.[69] Thus, in the manuscript of Louis de Bruges, Solomon is *repairing*, not regulating, the clock. Human life no longer adapts the mechanism to its needs; mankind is in some measure shaped by a machine which it adores.

This illumination is psychologically related to the roughly contemporary development of the most bizarre hypertely in the history of Christian iconography. Émile Mâle recoiled from what he considered its "disconcerting lack of taste" and vainly searched the texts of the fifteenth century to discover some explanation of it.[70] Rosemund Tuve[71] likewise suspected the existence of a lost or undiscovered text. The first evidence of the new development is found in 1450 in Bodleian MS Laud 570, fol. 16$^r$ (Fig. 11), a French translation of John of Wales's *Breviloquium de virtutibus* (a copy of *Othéa* is found in the same volume with her clock on fol. 28$^v$).[72] Tuve established the probability that this version was made, if not by Christine herself, at least by someone near her. Yet Tuve's implication that the fantastic symbolism of the Cardi-

---

[69] For an introduction to the literature, see P. Wolff, "Le temps et sa mesure au moyen âge," *Annales: économies, sociétés, civilisations*, XVII (1962), 1141-45; see also J. Le Goff, "Au moyen âge: temps de l'Église et temps du marchand," *ibid.*, XV (1960), 417-433, for an interpretation of this change as part of the class struggle.

[70] É. Mâle, *L'art religieux de la fin du moyen âge en France*, 4th edn. (Paris, 1931), p. 316.

[71] "Notes," pp. 283-289.

[72] See K. Chesney, "Two MSS of Christine de Pisan," *Medium aevum*, I (1932), 35-41; Curt Bühler, "Sir John Fastolf's Manuscripts of the *Epître d'Othéa* and Stephen Scropes' Translation of This Text," *Scriptorium*, III (1949), 123-128.

nal Virtues in Laud 570 goes back to Christine's time is implausible: it is in great contrast to the relative coherence in the symbolism of the first part of the century.

Temperance in Laud 570 is wearing a clock on her head as a hat. In her mouth is a bit and bridle. In her right hand she holds eyeglasses. At her heels are rowel spurs. She stands on a windmill.

In his quest for a key to this set of rebuses Mâle found a French manuscript of ca. 1470 (Bibliothèque Nationale, MS fr. 9186) containing pictures of the Cardinal Virtues equipped as in Laud 570 but with doggerel attached to each.[73] The lines appended to the representation of Temperance (Fig. 12) are our sole contemporary explanation of her trappings:

> He who is mindful of the clock
> Is punctual in all his acts.
> He who bridles his tongue
> Says naught that touches scandal.
> He who puts glasses to his eyes
> Sees better what's around him.
> Spurs show that fear
> Make [sic] the young man mature.
> The mill which sustains our bodies
> Never is immoderate.[74]

Clearly, this is not a program for the illuminator: it is a fumbling effort at the exegesis of an existing iconography. The clock indicates regularity, promptitude, and reliability; the bit, restraint, especially in speech; the eyeglasses, perspicacity; the spurs, maturity; the windmill, steady industriousness. The so-called bourgeois ethic is composed of such elements.

An age which showed such immoderation in representing Temperance would naturally lavish symbolism on all the other Virtues as well. The most astonishing exhibition of this virtuosity came only two years

---

[73] *L'art religieux*, pp. 311-316. The volume contains a French translation of the Pseudo-Senecan treatise on the Virtues, made by Jean de Courtecuisse in 1403 for the Duke of Berry. This MS of ca. 1470 was produced for, or in the circle of, the Duke of Nemours.

[74] "Qui a lorloge soy regarde / En tous ses faicts heure et temps garde. / Qui porte le frain en sa bouche / Chose ne dist qui a mal touche. / Qui lunettes met a ses yeux / Pres lui regarde sen voit mieux. / Esperons monstrent que cremeur [i.e., fear] / Font estre le josne homme meur. / Au moulin qui le corps soutient / Nuls exces faire nappartient."

after the painting of Laud 570. In 1452 the city council of Rouen, to honor the memory of its famous former citizen, Nicole Oresme, ordered a superb copy of his translations of Aristotle to be made.[75] The program of the artist was, as Tuve noted, "deliberately eclectic."[76] Ornamenting Oresme's version of the *Ethics*, the seven Cardinal and Theological Virtues stand in a row (Fig. 13).

Two things should be noted about this picture. First, although, in deference to the scholastic doctrine of the "unity of species" of the Virtues, all are shown in the same size, nevertheless in this rigidly symmetrical composition, produced for a hierarchical society, Temperance stands in the center. The meaning is clear: Temperance is the noblest Virtue. Second, the attributes of the other six Virtues subordinate to Temperance are notably less technological and less recent than hers. Indeed, their equipment would have been entirely familiar to a Roman: Faith holds a codex; Hope has a bee hive, spade, and sickles, stands on a bird cage, and wears a ship on her head; Charity stands on a furnace; Justice has her ancient swords and balance; Prudence holds a mirror and sieve; Courage wears an anvil on her head and stands on a screw press, a Hellenistic invention[77] but the most recent bedecking any Virtue other than Temperance, except perhaps for the codex, which is first mentioned by Martial.[78]

In remarkable contrast, except for the bit, whose origin dates back at least to the second millennium before Christ,[79] all the attributes of Temperance are much more recent. Whereas prick spurs are ancient

[75] A. D. Menut, "The French Version of Aristotle's *Economics* in Rouen, Bibliothèque Municipale, MS 927," *Romance Philology*, IV (1950), 55-62; É. van Moë, "Les 'Éthiques, politiques et économiques d'Aristote,' traduits par Nicole Oresme, manuscrit de la Bibliothèque de la Ville de Rouen," *Les trésors des bibliothèques de France*, III (Paris, 1930), 3-15.

[76] "Notes," p. 287.

[77] Cf. A. G. Drachmann, *Ancient Oil Wells and Presses* (Copenhagen, 1932). In the later fifteenth century even an isolated metallic screw probably signifies *Fortitudo*; cf. the personal emblem of the Burgundian composer Gilles Joye on the frame of his portrait of 1472, in F. van Molle, *Identification d'un portrait de Gilles Joye attribué à Memlinc* (Brussels, 1960), plate 1.

[78] Cf. R. H. Roberts, "The Codex," *Proceedings of the British Academy*, XL (1955), 171-204.

[79] Although the bit is fundamental for the use of horsepower and has changed notably, its history has not been written. For a bibliography, see White, *Medieval Technology*, p. 1, n. 4. The bit is one of the older symbols of Temperance: in a late eighth-century poem, Theodulf of Orleans describes *Moderatio* as wearing head-harness (see Katzenellenbogen, *Allegories*, p. 64, n. 3).

Celtic, the rowel spurs shown in pictures of *Temperantia* originated in the late thirteenth century.[80] Eyeglasses were invented in the Pisa-Lucca region in the 1280's.[81] The mechanical clock was developed in the second quarter of the fourteenth century,[82] in the years when Suso was composing his *Horologium sapientiae*. Although the windmill appeared in the 1180's[83] as a small post-mill, the massive masonry tower-mill shown in our *Temperantia* pictures, in which only the conical top rotates to keep the vanes into the wind, was very recent when this iconographic scheme was contrived: the tower-mill is first found in a miniature of the end of the fourteenth century.[84] Four of the five technological items in the new iconography of Temperance were thus relatively novel when the schema was invented slightly before 1450.

What is the meaning of this development? As has been said, the texts to which these illuminations are attached tell us little. But the images themselves speak clearly. Temperance, once the least esteemed of the Cardinal Virtues, had risen during the thirteenth and fourteenth centuries to the status of the preeminent Virtue, equated with Divine Wisdom and the Second Person of the Trinity. Her essential character had become Measure, and, since we mortals dwell in time rather than eternity, her prime symbol came to be the clock. But then, toward the middle of the fifteenth century, Northern Europe clothed this supreme Virtue not simply with the clock but with the new technology of the later Middle Ages: on her head she wore the most complex mechanism of the era; her feet now rested on the most spectacular power engine of that generation; in her hands she held eyeglasses, the greatest recent boon to the mature literate man. The new icon of Temperance tells us that in Europe, below the level of verbal expression,[85] ma-

---

[80] See H. A. Knorr in *Zeitschrift für historische Waffen und Kostümkunde*, Neue Folge, VII (1940), 30-32. Spurs as a mark of admission to knighthood, i.e., maturity, and hence as a symbol appropriate to Temperance have not been traced back to earlier than the thirteenth, or possibly the twelfth, century (see White, *Medieval Technology*, p. 150).

[81] E. Rosen, "The Invention of Eyeglasses," *Journal of the History of Medicine*, XI (1956), 13-46, 183-218.

[82] White, *Medieval Technology*, p. 124.          [83] *Ibid.*, p. 87.

[84] Bibliothèque Nationale, MS fr. 2810, fol. 260ʳ, reproduced in *Livre des merveilles* (Paris, 1907), I, plate 232; see I, p. 2, for date.

[85] The clarity of intent shown in the Utrecht Psalter miniature (Fig. 2) warns us that at times ideas which did not reach written form were conceptualized. Most of Temperance's attributes were still so novel ca. 1450 that it seems im-

chinery, mechanical power, and salutary devices were taking on an aura of "virtuousness" such as they have never enjoyed in any culture save the Western. About 1450 the novel productive system of Europe, based on natural power, mechanization, and labor-saving invention which has been the backbone of capitalism, received the sanction of religious emotion and moral sensibility. The iconography of Temperance[86] furnishes pointer-readings of pressures not easily identified by other means.

We have been tracing two closely related elements in the growth of what has generally been called the "bourgeois" ethos. The first, the increase in speculative emphasis on Temperance in the thirteenth and

---

probable that those who worked out her new iconography were unconscious of the recent impact of clocks, eyeglasses, and tower-mills on European life. But we have no texts showing such awareness until slightly later, and then they came from Italy rather than from France and Burgundy. By the late thirteenth century the idea of invention as a total enterprise is found in Europe, but it looked to the future without surveying the accomplishments of the past (see White, *Medieval Technology*, 129-134). In the 1350's Petrarch's friend Guglielmo da Pastrango of Verona, in *De originibus rerum* (Venice, 1547), foll. 78ʳ-89ᵛ, lists mythological inventors and inventions harvested from ancient Latin sources, but without medieval materials. Filarete, writing in 1461-1464, in his *Treatise on Architecture*, tr. John R. Spencer (New Haven, 1965), I, 259-269, and II, foll. 151ᵛ-156ᵛ, offers no improvement. The earliest recognition of a device unknown to the ancients which I have seen is ca. 1460, when Roberto Valturio, *De re militari* (Paris, 1532), pp. 217-218, notes that neither Greek nor Latin authors mention stirrups; yet, on pp. 261 and 264, he credits Archimedes with inventing gunpowder artillery. Not until 1499 does Polydore Vergil, *De rerum inventoribus*, Lib. III, cap. 18 (Strassburg, 1606), pp. 203-206, write of "nova inventa," ranging from mechanical clocks, *pyxis nautica*, and bombards to tallow candles.

[86] This iconography remained in use for about a century. As humanistic tastes in art spread from Italy northward, the exuberance of late Gothic symbolism declined, and the Virtues became less encumbered. Yet in 1559-1560 Pieter Breughel the Elder, fighting a rearguard action against neo-classicism, used the full iconography of Temperance, except that he reduced the windmill to a single vane lying flat on the ground (see C. de Tolnay, *The Drawings of Pieter Breughel the Elder* [London, 1952], 74-75). Even with simplified symbolism, Temperance generally continued to hold her clock as identification, and in portraits of the sixteenth century clocks were often included to indicate not merely the affluence of the subject but also his superlative virtue. For example, in Holbein's portrait of the Thomas More family (1527) a clock is placed almost directly over Sir Thomas's head, as though *Temperantia* were wearing her horological hat (see D. Piper, "Holbein the Younger in England," *Journal of the Royal Society of Arts*, CXI [1963], 741-742).

fourteenth centuries, is symptomatic of the growth of lay asceticism, which reached its culmination in the Puritans but which long antedated the Reformation. The second begins about 1334 with the emergence of the clock as the image of this disciplined life, regulated by Divine Wisdom. The clock symbol expanded until, just before 1450, the spiritualization of this one machine was generalized into the new iconography of Temperance, which affirmed the essential goodness of the entire technological enterprise. Obviously, this long development had much to do with the evolution of capitalism. But can it be shown that such attitudes originated among merchants and artisans or that they flourished primarily in non-aristocratic circles?

Lorenzetti's fresco at Siena was repaired at the order of a fairly popular city council, and the Rouen manuscript of Oresme was illuminated at the command of commercially minded authorities. But, as we have seen, most of the manuscripts which display the new iconography of Temperance were made for, and presumably were enjoyed by, the upper nobility of France and Burgundy. One recalls the recent change in scholarly judgment concerning the fabliaux. For decades they were regarded as bourgeois in origin—an expression of thirteenth-century middle-class resentment of aristocratic dominance. Then Per Nykrog[87] took the trouble to find where the fabliaux were written, who paid for the manuscripts which preserve them, and what other writings are contained in those same manuscripts. He concluded that the fabliaux were less a bourgeois literature of protest than an aristocratic burlesque of the more conventional courtly tales.

No student of the later Middle Ages can disregard with impunity the often bitter and bloody class conflicts of that time. But it is impetuous to assume any invariable relationship between social structures and value structures, at least in periods of such rapid change as the span from the eleventh through the sixteenth centuries. The eagerness of successful burghers to ape the nobility has long stocked our theater with comic figures. On the other hand, it is axiomatic among historians of revolutions that the thinkers who produce revolutionary ideologies often come from the class which will be most damaged by radical change. The ideal of the rationally regulated life, which Weber rightly stressed as basic for the pattern of capitalist activity, has one of its main roots in the chivalric concept of *mesure*, which, indeed, long retained its earlier knightly trapping. Edmund Spenser, an ardent Puritan who

[87] P. Nykrog, *Les fabliaux* (Copenhagen, 1957), pp. 227-241.

was the scion of an impoverished noble family and spent all his life in the world of aristocrats, surely reflects the ethos of most Elizabethans—whether bourgeois or blue-blooded—when, having treated Holiness, Man's duty to God, in the first book of *The Faerie Queene*, he devotes the second book to Temperance, Man's duty to know and rule himself.[88] Historically viewed, "bourgeois" morality is neither the product nor the mark of one social stratum or of one religious persuasion: it is a phase of the slowly changing ideals of Western culture as a whole. Similarly, the conviction that mechanism is a buttress rather than a denial of the human spirit was fostered not only by artisans, engineers, and industrialists but also by bishops, Dominican mystics, courtly poets, and the illuminators of manuscripts for princesses and dukes. The late medieval affirmation that technological advance is morally benign was effectively unanimous. It remains an axiom of the modern West, and not simply of the bourgeoisie.

[88] Jean R. Purpus's *The Moral Philosophy of Book II of Spenser's Faerie Queene*, Ph.D. diss. (University of California, Los Angeles, 1946), lamentably remains unpublished because of the author's premature death. Better than anyone else, she gathers (pp. 32-51) the materials showing that, in Elizabethan thinking, Temperance was—to quote Barnabe Barnes, *Foure Bookes of Offices* (London, 1606), p. 19—"the moderator and guide of her three sister virtues."

# FLORENCE AND ITS UNIVERSITY,
## 1348-1434*

GENE A. BRUCKER

O N 29 August 1348 the Florentine Signoria authorized the establishment of a *studium generale* "in civil and canon law, in medicine, in philosophy and the other sciences." Members of this Signoria, the survivors of the Black Death, were preoccupied with the immediate problems of restoring life and order to a city which had lost between one-third and one-half of its population. They possessed an unusual measure of faith and vision, which enabled them to look beyond the chaos of the moment and to proclaim that "from the study of the sciences, the city of Florence will receive an increase in honors and a full measure of wealth, and the citizens, and particularly the guildsmen, will prosper...."[1]

In later decades these twin goals of honor and utility were frequently articulated in communal legislation pertaining to the Studio. For in the minds of its founders and supporters was a vision of a renowned

* Research in Italian archives for this article was made possible by fellowships granted by the Guggenheim Foundation and the American Council of Learned Societies. To both institutions the author expresses his gratitude. This brief account, limited to some institutional aspects of Florentine higher education in the late Trecento and early Quattrocento, does not pretend to exhaust the sub-ject. In particular, the role played by the Studio in Florentine intellectual life in these years deserves more intensive study.

[1] This decree of 29 August 1348 is printed in *Statuti della Università e Studio fiorentino dell'anno MCCCLXXXVII seguiti da un'appendice di documenti dal MCCCXX al MCCCCLXXII*, ed. A. Gherardi, *Documenti di storia italiana*, VII (Florence, 1881), 111-113. This was not a provision, approved by the communal councils, but a simple decree by the Signoria and its advisory colleges. A more comprehensive provision, approving the Studio's establishment, was passed by the councils on 18-19 December 1348 (*ibid.*, pp. 113-114). On the foundation and early history of the Studio, see Matteo Villani, *Cronica*, ed. Dragommani (Florence, 1846), I, ch. 8; VII, ch. 90; IX, ch. 58. The provision of 1321 first establishing a *studium generale* is in *Statuti*, pp. 107-110. For a description of this *studium*, and of *studia* in Florentine monasteries, see R. Davidsohn, *Geschichte von Florenz* (Berlin, 1896-1927), IV, Pt. 3, 122-128 and 142-147; also C. T. Davis, "Education in Dante's Florence," *Speculum*, XL (1965), 420-429. The most recent survey of European universities in the late Middle Ages, with bibliography, is E. Delaruelle, *L'Église au temps du Grand Schisme et de la crise conciliare (1378-1449)*, *Histoire de l'Église*, vol. 14 (Paris, 1962-1964), pp. 459-486.

220

institution of higher learning, rivaling the great universities of Padua and Bologna. But these high expectations were never realized. In a report submitted to the Signoria in March 1429 the governors of the Studio candidly admitted that their institution was less than first-rate. The city of Florence, they stated, had been endowed by God with abundant wealth, liberty, and power. Only one element was missing: "the study of the exalted disciplines, in which every perfection of civil life, every light and splendor of things human and divine, is truly placed." "It grieves us sorely," the governors concluded, "that this glorious republic, which has surpassed the rest of Italy and earlier centuries in beauty and splendor, should be surpassed in this one respect by some of our neighboring cities, which in every other way are inferior to us."[2]

This essay will consider the rare phenomenon of Florentine failure. In the contest for academic supremacy the odds strongly favored Bologna and Padua, European centers of higher learning for two centuries. Perhaps in this most conservative of human activities the upstart school could never have overtaken its rivals. But Florence's efforts to achieve distinction in this sphere were hampered by internal disagreement over the value of the Studio. And since the university was a public institution, entirely dependent upon communal subsidy, its fortunes were directly influenced by political vicissitudes.

The provision of December 1348 which ratified the Studio's foundation did not receive the unanimous approval of the communal councillors; nearly one-fourth cast negative votes. This opposition, which varied in size according to circumstances, persisted throughout the university's history, until the school was transferred from Florence to Pisa in 1473. A provision of 1354 authorizing certain Studio expenditures for building repairs and land purchase was opposed by only 25 of 272 councillors who cast their ballots. But an enactment of 1413, which reopened the school after a six-year suspension, barely obtained the required majority of two-thirds in the councils (280 pro, 109 con). Even the 1373 law establishing a lectureship in Dante studies, which must have received general public support, was opposed by 26 councillors who begrudged the public expenditure of 50 florins for this purpose.[3]

Why did some citizens vote against the Studio's foundation and its subsidy? Opinions about the school are rarely articulated in com-

---

[2] *Statuti*, pp. 210-211.

[3] The voting statistics are recorded *ibid.*, pp. 125, 186, 162.

munal sources, but the fragments of extant evidence suggest that some Florentines were convinced that the university was not worth its cost. In November 1365 one of the advisory colleges, the twelve *buon'uomini*, counseled the Signoria "to find out how many students are [in residence] in Florence, and if they conclude that the expenditures for the Studio are useful, then these should be authorized." Seventy years later, in 1432, another advisory group argued that the handful of students matriculated in the university did not justify its support.[4] Men from patrician families may have been more favorably disposed to the Studio than artisans from the lower guilds, who could not hope to send their sons to the university. But the popular government of 1378-1382 was no more hostile to the Studio than the "oligarchic" regime which controlled the city after 1382. The size of the university's budget depended more upon the regime's fiscal situation at a given moment than upon the composition of the ruling group.

The vicissitudes of the Studio, its alternating periods of prosperity and stagnation, can thus be charted from the pattern of its subsidy. In 1350 the commune voted to grant 1,500 florins annually to the school. Seven years later this sum was increased to 2,000 florins; the university was sharing in the general prosperity which the city enjoyed after the great pestilence. In August 1362 the commune authorized an increment of 1,200 florins in the budget,[5] but the outbreak of the Pisan war cast a long shadow over the university and its future. It survived through the war, although part of its revenue was diverted to military needs. The Pisan conflict had scarcely been terminated, however, when one advisory college asked the Signoria in October 1364 to decide whether "it is useful to have a Studio." Similar reservations about the institution's utility were expressed a year later, when a collegiate spokesman demanded that the new governors "should so perform [their duties] that the expected advantages will ensue."[6] When, in November 1367, the Signoria was considering the Studio's fate, its two advisory colleges offered contradictory opinions. The sixteen

[4] For these statements, see *Archivio di Stato di Firenze* (henceforth cited as ASF), *Consulte e Pratiche* (henceforth cited as CP), 7 fol. 66ʳ, 26 Nov. 1365; *Statuti*, p. 247.

[5] *Statuti*, pp. 121, 128-130, 138. At present gold prices the florin was worth approximately $4, but its purchasing power was much greater. Throughout this period a large house rented for 10-15 fl. annually.

[6] CP, 7, foll. 9ʳ, 60ʳ, 1 Oct. 1364 and early Nov. 1365. In late November another collegiate group questioned the Studio's utility; see above, n. 4.

*gonfalonieri* favored the suspension of the university's activities but did not advocate its permanent suppression. The twelve *buon'uomini* on the other hand, rallied strongly to the school's defense: "May the Studio flourish, and let it be preserved as it stands!"[7] Opinions were likewise divided in the spring of 1369, when the city was again on the verge of war. The *gonfalonieri* proposed that the activities of the school be suspended for three or four years, but once again the *buon'uomini* rallied to its defense.[8] The issue was still being debated in the autumn of 1370, when Florence was at war with Milan. But the opinions expressed at that time were generally favorable to the Studio, although proposals were made to cut its budget to 800 florins annually.[9]

The Studio survived the crises of the late 1370's: the war with the Papacy and the interdict which kept both professors and students away from the city; and the Ciompi revolution and its aftermath of social and political turmoil. Thereafter, the subsidence of internal disorder and foreign dangers contributed to a revival of the school's fortunes. The decade following the reform of 1387 was perhaps the most prosperous in the institution's history. In July 1385 the budget was increased to 2,000 florins and, two years later, to 3,000 florins, the largest income enjoyed by the university since its foundation.[10] But such prosperity did not endure. The burdens of the war with Giangaleazzo Visconti forced the commune to reduce the Studio's income to 2,000 florins in 1396. Six years later this figure was again halved, and for three years the school subsisted on a minimal revenue of 1,000 florins. Peace with Milan was finally concluded in 1404, and in the following year the budget was raised to 2,000 florins.[11] This revival in the school's income and fortunes, however, was only temporary. From

[7] *CP*, 9, fol. 9ᵛ. The spokesmen for the two opposing viewpoints were leaders of the rival Albizzi and Ricci factions: Uguccione de' Ricci for the *gonfalonieri* and Michele Castellani for the *buon'uomini*. On partisan conflict in this period, see G. Brucker, *Florentine Politics and Society, 1343-1378* (Princeton, 1962), ch. 5.

[8] *CP*, 10, fol. 86ʳ, 20 March 1369. The colleges which expressed these opposing views on the Studio did not differ significantly in social composition (*ASF, Tratte,* 191, foll. 51ʳ-52ʳ; 214, foll. 19ʳ-20ᵛ).

[9] *CP*, 11, foll. 24ᵛ, 105ʳ, 107ʳ.          [10] *Statuti*, pp. 163, 165.

[11] These budgetary alterations are documented *ibid.*, pp. 178-179, 184. The commune's expenditures on the Studio during the war years are also recorded regularly in *ASF, Camera del Comune, Uscita,* 304 (July 1396) through 337 (Jan. 1403).

1407 until 1413 the doors of the Studio were closed, and the community of scholars was dispersed.[12]

When the Studio was reopened in the autumn of 1413, it received a subsidy of 1,500 florins, and shortly thereafter this amount was doubled.[13] But the university enjoyed this munificence for only five years before the budget was again under attack from fiscal conservatives. Although Florence was enjoying great prosperity in 1420, a provision reducing the Studio's revenue to 1,500 florins was approved by the councils in that year.[14] In 1422 the subsidy was again cut to 600 florins, and in the midst of the long and exhausting war with Milan a fiscal commission placed a ceiling of 200 florins on expenditures for the Studio.[15] This derisory allotment marked the nadir of communal financing for its university, but it did not signal its demise. In the decade before the establishment of Medicean hegemony the fate of the Studio became a controversial issue in Florentine politics. While many citizens agreed with Rinaldo degli Albizzi that money appropriated for the university should be diverted to military needs,[16] others defended the school. In 1429, Pope Martin V authorized an annual levy of 1,500 florins upon the clergy in Florentine territory for the subsidy

[12] There was no official announcement of the Studio's suspension. No governors were appointed, and no money appropriated during these years (*Tratte*, 576, foll. 20ʳ-21ᵛ; *Camera, Uscita*, 355-363). The provision reestablishing the Studio (*Statuti*, p. 186) does not indicate how long the institution had been closed: "quod vacatio dicti Studii per multos annos facta extitit reprehensibilis et nociva." In June 1412 the commune appointed Giovanni Malpighini to a five-year lectureship in rhetoric, but this provision made no mention of the Studio (*Statuti*, p. 388). The Studio's closing, with incorrect dates (1404-1412), was noted by G. Zippel, *Niccolò Niccoli* (Florence, 1890), p. 28, and repeated with the same error by R. Sabbadini, *La scuola e gli studi di Guarino Guarini Veronese* (Catania, 1896), p. 18.

[13] *Statuti*, pp. 186, 191, provisions of 14 March 1413 and 16 Feb. 1415. The vote on the latter measure increasing the subsidy was 191-58 and 155-41. There is a confused and inaccurate summary of the Studio's history in these years in C. Gutkind, *Cosimo de' Medici Peter Patriae 1389-1464* (Oxford, 1938), pp. 229-231.

[14] *Statuti*, pp. 200-201, 30 March 1420. The law was passed after encountering heavy resistance in the councils. The Council of the Commune twice rejected the measure before finally acquiescing in its passage (*ASF, Libri Fabarum*, 52, foll. 31ʳ-32ᵛ). The final vote was 152-74 and 114-45. On Florence's prosperity in these years, see *Giovanni Rucellai ed il suo Zibaldone*, ed. A. Perosa (London, 1960), p. 46.

[15] *Statuti*, pp. 204, 205-207.

[16] For Rinaldo's opinion, see *CP*, 50, fol. 143ᵛ, 20 April 1434. For similar views, see *ibid.*, fol. 123ᵛ, 2 March 1434, and *Statuti*, p. 247, May 1432.

of the Studio.[17] Perhaps the most spectacular demonstration of support for higher education was the testament of the wealthy banker, Niccolò da Uzzano, who bequeathed money to build a Casa della Sapienza, to house and feed students attending the university.[18] Although the status of the Studio was still insecure in November 1434, when Cosimo de' Medici returned from exile, it appeared to enjoy substantially greater public support at that time than it had in the past.

To place Florence's expenditure on higher education in proper perspective, one must compare its subsidy with that granted by other cities to their universities. Seen in this light, Florence's fiscal commitment was very modest. Perugia, for example, had perhaps one-half of Florence's population and less than one-third of her revenue, but in 1410 the Umbrian commune spent 2,000 florins on its university.[19] The budget of Pavia's university fluctuated as sharply as did that of Florence, but it was invariably larger.[20] The republic's expenditure for the Studio was only a miniscule portion of its total budget. During the early decades of the fifteenth century the government spent approximately 50,000 florins per month, while in wartime this figure might rise to 100,000 florins monthly.[21] Thus, an annual contribution of 3,000 florins to the Studio represented approximately one-half of one percent of the commune's peacetime budget.

Florentine controversy over the Studio was revealed by administrative difficulties and disputes, as well as by the uncertainty of fiscal support. The Signoria normally delegated its authority over the uni-

[17] Since 1423 the commune had regularly appealed to Pope Martin V to grant a subsidy to the Studio, to be paid by the clergy in Florentine territory (*CP*, 45, fol. 71$^r$; *Statuti*, p. 207; *ASF, Signori, Missive*, 30, fol. 123$^v$; *ASF, Signori, Carteggi, Legazioni e Commissarie*, 5, foll. 18$^r$-18$^v$, 41$^r$-41$^v$; *ASF, Signori, Carteggi, Rapporti e Legazioni di Oratori*, 3, foll. 7$^v$-8$^r$). Florence's request for a subsidy varied in amount from 2,500 to 4,000 fl. annually, but the Pope authorized only 1,500 fl. in 1429 (*Archivio Segreto Vaticano, Reg. Vat.*, 356, foll. 29$^v$-30$^v$; *Statuti*, pp. 218-220). New sources of communal income for the Studio were also exploited (*Statuti*, pp. 210, 221-222).

[18] *Statuti*, pp. 230-239.

[19] An anonymous letter to Forese Sacchetti dated Nov. 1410 (*ASF, Conventi Soppressi*, 78 (Badià), vol. 326, no. 145).

[20] Cf. D. Zanetti, "Les salaires des professeurs de l'Université de Pavie," *Annales Economies Sociétés Civilisations*, XVII (1962), from table opposite 428. Pavia's budget for university salaries was 8200 fl. (calculated at 32 *soldi* per florin) in 1387; 12,000 in 1393; 7,900 in 1399; 4,300 in 1418; 6,600 in 1428.

[21] *Giovanni Rucellai ed il suo Zibaldone*, p. 46; *CP*, 46 foll. 76$^v$, 110$^v$. There are no accurate figures for the commune's expenditures in these years.

versity to a board of governors, elected annually. These *ufficiali dello Studio* bore the responsibility for hiring professors, establishing salary scales, and supervising instruction and examinations. But in moments of crisis the Signoria was quick to intervene in the Studio's internal affairs.

Official discontent with Studio administration was manifest by the periodic efforts to "reform" the university and its governors. A commission of eight officials was appointed to operate the fledgling university in July 1348, and these men remained in office until September 1352.[22] There are no further references to these officials in the documents until 1357. A provision enacted in that year indicated that the Signoria had taken over direct administration of the Studio.[23] After 1358, however, commissions of eight citizens were regularly appointed to govern the school with general authority over appointments, salaries, and instruction.[24] Dissatisfaction with its operation led, in 1366, to the passage of a law which prescribed the duties and responsibilities of both officials and professors.[25] But this legislation was no panacea for the Studio's difficulties, and twenty years later another reform movement culminated in the redaction of a lengthy and comprehensive statute (1387), which closely regulated the university's operation. There was some feeling that the size of the governing commission was too large and unwieldy for efficient administration, and the number of governors was reduced from eight to six, and then to five.[26] The short tenure of office was another source of difficulty, and in 1418 the Signoria appointed five governors to a three-year term.[27] But, even before their tenure expired, the Signoria abolished the office and transferred the administration of the Studio to the Calimala guild (September 1420). This experiment in guild control was not successful; three years later the officials in charge of reducing the commune's debt were given responsibility for the University's operation.[28] By the end of the decade the Signoria was again electing commissions of governors with yearly appointments to supervise the institution.[29]

[22] *Statuti*, pp. 111, 123.     [23] *Ibid.*, p. 129.

[24] The personnel of some of these commissions are identified (*Statuti*, pp. 134, 138, 140-141, 154, 157, 288).

[25] *Ibid.*, pp. 149-151.

[26] In 1406, six men were selected (*Tratte*, 576, fol. 20[r]); in 1414, the number was reduced to five (*ibid.*, foll. 20[v]-21[r]).

[27] *Tratte*, 576, fol. 22[r].

[28] *Statuti*, pp. 201-202; *ASF, Signori e Collegi, Deliberazioni, ordinaria autorità*, 35, no. pag.

[29] *Statuti*, pp. 209, 221, 241.

The office and jurisdiction of the rector was another source of communal concern. Elected annually by the community of scholars from among the senior students in law and medicine, the rectors had broad authority over instruction, examinations, and discipline. In exercising their control over student behavior, they were frequently involved in disputes with the secular courts, and the Signoria then was forced to settle their quarrels.[30] The rector's authority was not always accepted by the students; in March 1399 an assembly of scholars voted to depose the rector, one Raynaldus of Perugia, who was judged unfit for his post. But twenty years later, when another group of dissident scholars declared war on their superior, they were fined by an outraged Signoria, determined to quash this student revolt.[31]

The most dramatic case of rectorial malfeasance concerned Dino of Lucca, whose misdeeds throw some light upon Studio politics. A student in canon law and holder of a Lucca archdeaconry, Dino had been chosen rector in 1397, and in the summer of 1398 he sought to insure his reappointment to the post. After ordering the professors to refrain from lecturing, he closed the Studio doors and hid the keys in order to prevent the students from assembling to elect a new rector. When the Studio governors scrutinized his tenure of office, they discovered that he had imposed fines upon students without cause and then used the profits "to entertain several scholars, who were his henchmen, in his house, in which he permitted gambling and other dishonest activities. . . ." How badly discipline and morale had deteriorated under Dino's administration was revealed by another sentence against the university beadles. They were convicted of criticizing the orders of the governors and of divulging their secret deliberations to professors and to those citizens who were seeking to promote their candidates for Studio appointments.[32]

Normally the Signoria did not interfere with appointments of lecturers made by the governors. But in May 1367 the priors and the col-

---

[30] For an example of a jurisdictional dispute between a rector and a secular judge, see *ASF, Giudice degli Appelli*, 79, foll. 28$^r$-28$^v$, 28 June 1434. For penalties levied by rectors against students, see *ibid.*, 74, no pag., 6 March 1422; 78, fol. 278$^r$, 14 Feb. 1432; 82, fol. 196 bis, 13 May 1447. Students could also be punished by the governors (*ibid.*, 74, no pag., 28 Jan. 1417) and by the secular courts (*ASF, Atti del Podestà*, 3453, no pag., 2 Oct. 1394; *ibid.*, 3603, no pag., 8 June 1397).

[31] These two incidents are described in *Giudice degli Appelli*, 72, pt. 1, foll. 10$^r$-10$^v$, 4 March 1399, and 74, no pag., 6 May 1417.

[32] The sentences against Dino and the beadles are *ibid.*, 71, pt. 2, foll. 151$^r$-151$^v$, 181$^r$-182$^r$, 31 July and 29 Sept. 1398.

leges simply ignored the Studio's *ufficiali* and elected the full roster of professors for the succeeding year.[33] Not infrequently the Signoria made appointments on their own initiative, without consulting the governors. In 1368, for example, the priors elected Lodovico Bartoli of Gubbio to a four-year appointment as professor of medicine. The establishment of the chair in Dante studies was the result of the Signoria's initiative, and Boccaccio was elected to the post by the priors and the colleges, not by the Studio governors. Perhaps the most significant appointment in the university's history was the Signoria's election in 1396 of Manual Chrysoloras, for a five-year period, to a chair in Greek studies. In 1404 the Signoria sent a message to the governors, ordering them to appoint Filippo Villani to the Dante chair for a five-year term.[34] This sporadic interference by communal authorities in personnel matters did not contribute to academic harmony and tranquillity. Professors were aware that their contracts could be broken, or their salaries reduced, by communal fiat at any time. In November 1399, for example, the councils passed a law which cancelled all professorial contracts at the end of the school term and prohibited future appointments for more than one year.[35]

Thus, in their efforts to appoint and retain a distinguished faculty, the Studio governors were continually plagued by fiscal limitations and by the interference of their political superiors. But there were other recruiting problems, too. The *ufficiali* were hampered as well by the commune's unwillingness to appoint its own citizens to teaching positions and by the stiff competition for professorial talent from other Italian universities.

The first legislative prohibition against the holding of Studio posts by citizens was enacted in 1361. This law made a distinction between "regular" and "extraordinary" chairs in civil and canon law. Florentines were excluded entirely from "regular" professorships and could

---

[33] *Statuti*, pp. 325-326. The *ufficiali* then in office are identified in another document (pp. 154-155).

[34] For these appointments, see *Statuti*, pp. 335, 344, 367-368; *Delib. Sign. Coll.*, 29, fol. 30ʳ. Other Signoria appointments included Cristoforo di Giorgio, medicine, 1396-1397 (*Camera del Comune, Uscita*, 306); Domenico d'Arezzo, rhetoric, five years, 1398-1403 (*ibid.*, 320); Giovanni da Faenza, medicine, three years, 1397-1400; Giovanni Malpighini of Ravenna, three years, rhetoric, 1397-1400 (*ibid.*, 324).

[35] *Statuti*, pp. 178-179. A similar cancellation occurred in Dec. 1431 (pp. 240-241).

only hold the "extraordinary" posts at reduced salaries.[36] The rationale for this prohibition was obviously political: to keep the Studio out of factional quarrels and to prevent Florentine lawyers from obtaining lucrative university appointments through friends or relatives in office.[37] However laudable the provision's objectives, it did limit the search for the best qualified scholars. Whether because friends of prospective appointees exerted pressure or whether because some citizens deserved appointment on their merits, this restriction was in any event frequently relaxed. Despite periodic renewals of the prohibition and admonitions that it be enforced,[38] the faculty lists regularly contained a high proportion of native sons. In 1366 four of the six professors of law were Florentines; in 1389, six of nine.[39] Gradually the prejudice against natives tended to diminish. An enactment of 1391 stipulated that citizens be given appointments for no longer than one year, and a decade later another decree established a ceiling on salaries paid to citizens and required each faculty to have at least one foreign professor. The prohibition was entirely abolished in 1417 and apparently was never restored.[40]

Although a portion of the Studio faculty came from Florence and nearby areas, the majority were not Tuscans but Italians from other parts of the peninsula. Among the twenty-five professors appointed for the year 1388/89, ten were residents of Florence and its subject territory. Others were identified as natives of Brixen, Padua, Rome, Bologna, Ferrara, Forlì, and Montefalco.[41] It was no simple matter to induce a prominent scholar to accept a Studio appointment; doctors

[36] *Statuti*, p. 137. The salary ceiling was placed at 150 fl. per year.

[37] The problem was particularly acute in the 1360's and 1370's. Several lawyers who held university positions were embroiled in partisan politics: Lapo da Castiglionchio, Filippo Corsini, Giovanni de' Ricci, Donato Barbadori, Alessandro dell'Antella. These men were all elected to posts in 1366 (*ASF, Ufficiali dello Studio*, 2 foll. 3ʳ-4ᵛ).

[38] *Statuti*, pp. 163, 168; *CP*, 25, foll. 6ᵛ, 57ᵛ, 70ᵛ.

[39] *Ufficiali dello Studio*, 2, foll. 3ʳ-4ᵛ; R. Abbondanza, "Gli atti degli Ufficiali dello Studio fiorentino, dal maggio al settembre 1388," *Archivio storico italiano*, CXVII (1959), 85-110.

[40] These progressive relaxations of the prohibition are printed in *Statuti*, pp. 170, 182, 195-196. In 1432-1433 seven of twenty-four professors were Florentine subjects; in 1439-1440, thirteen of twenty-six (pp. 423-424, 443-445).

[41] Abbondanza, pp. 85-110. Save for two Greek scholars, Leonpilato of Thessaly (see n. 48 below) and Chrysoloras, the only non-Italian appointment to the Studio which I have noted was a German professor of medicine, Theodoric Spilinbergh, elected in 1435 (*Delib. Sign. e Coll.*, 36, fol. 50ʳ).

with Italian reputations were eagerly sought by other universities, which could frequently offer higher salaries and other lucrative perquisites.[42] In 1364 the commune engaged in diplomatic bickering with a papal legate over two law professors who had forsaken Florence for the greener pastures of the University of Bologna.[43] The Studio governors once levied heavy fines on two professors who had accepted appointments and then had broken their contracts.[44] In 1423 the refusal of the Sienese commune to permit its citizen, the physician Ugo Benzi, to accept an appointment in Florence nearly precipitated a diplomatic breach between the two states, avoided finally when Siena abandoned its opposition to the transfer.[45] By the early fifteenth century university professors had become the unwitting pawns of Italian power politics.

The extant documents have thrown considerable light upon the fiscal and administrative aspects of the Studio, but they tell us very little about the school's primary functions: teaching and learning. Only seventeen of the *rotuli* of the salaried professors have survived; of these, nine date from the years 1357-1369.[46] During this twelve-year

---

[42] Florence lost the eminent jurists, Baldo Ubaldi, to Perugia in 1364, and Angelo of Perugia, to Bologna in 1390 (*Statuti*, pp. 302, 356)—also, the medical scholar, Marsilio of S. Sophia, to Pavia in the 1390's (Abbondanza, pp. 99-100; *Statuti*, p. 354; *Codice diplomatico dell'Università di Pavia*, ed. R. Maiocchi [Pavia, 1905-1915], I, 421-422).

[43] *CP*, 6, fol. 9$^r$.

[44] *Giudice degli Appelli*, 70, foll. 51$^r$, 140$^{r-v}$. These fines were intended to persuade lecturers to return to the Studio. Florence once complained about professorial inconstancy: "Mos est fere omnium medicorum et iurisconsultorum, qui per Studia publica ad legendum conducuntur, mutare frequenter propositum, et ụt a pluribus expeti sua opera videatur, electiones alias super alias querere" (*Statuti*, p. 423).

[45] *Signori, Carteggi, Rapporti d'oratori*, 2, foll. 73$^r$, 75$^v$-76$^r$. Six years later Ugo was elected to a post in Siena but was detained by Filippo Maria Visconti, Lord of Milan (*Archivio di Stato di Siena* [henceforth cited as *ASS*], *Concistoro*, 1915, no. 35, 8 Jan. 1429). For a survey of Ugo's academic career written by his son Socino, see D. Lockwood, *Ugo Benzi, medieval philosopher and physician, 1379-1439* (Chicago, 1951), pp. 22-30. For other cases of communal rivalry over professors, see *Concistoro*, 1915, no. 14; *Missive*, 32, foll. 5$^r$, 6$^v$-7$^r$, 10$^v$-11$^r$, 147$^v$-148$^r$, 152$^r$; 33, foll. 52$^r$, 85$^r$-85$^v$.

[46] These *rotuli* are in *Camera del Comune, Uscita*, 123, fol. 42$^r$ (1357-1358); *Statuti*, pp. 288-291 (1358-1359); *Camera, Uscita*, 141, fol. 155$^r$ (1359-1360); 150, fol. 5$^r$ (1360-1361); 153, fol. 37$^r$ (1361-1362); 159, no pag. (1362-1363); 164, no pag. (1363-1364); *Studio*, 2, foll. 15$^v$-20$^r$ (1366-1367); *Camera, Uscita*, 187, no pag. (1368-1369); Abbondanza, "Ufficiali," pp. 85-110 (1388-1389); *Statuti*, p. 389 (1413-1414), p. 403 (1423-1424), pp. 405-406 (1425-1426), pp. 413-415

period the size of the faculty fluctuated from eight to eighteen, with an average complement of twelve. The two law faculties were the most favored, in terms both of size (from five to eight professors) and of salaries.[47] Two of its most famous members were the civil lawyer, Baldo Ubaldi of Perugia and Lapo da Castiglionchio, a leading scholar in canon law. The faculties of medicine and the arts were much smaller, never comprising more than three lecturers each and occasionally being reduced to a single appointment. The faculties in these disciplines were not distinguished, but they did include Francesco Bruni, later a papal *segretarius*, Leonpilato of Thessaly, who taught Greek from 1360 to 1362, and Tommaso del Garbo, a prominent Florentine physician.[48] Stipends paid to professors of law and medicine ranged from 100 to 300 florins annually, but lecturers in rhetoric and philosophy received much smaller salaries, from 30 to 100 florins. The theology faculty was tiny; it was recruited from local convents and paid minimum salaries. Professorial appointments were normally made for a single year, and few teachers held Studio posts for more than two or three years. An exception was Francesco of Arezzo, who taught civil law from 1357 to 1369 (and perhaps longer). The instructor in notarial science, Martino de Reggio, was likewise a permanent fixture on the faculty.

These were relatively lean years for the Studio; the faculty roster of 1388-1389 describes the university's curriculum in more prosperous times, with a budget of 3,000 florins.[49] Law benefited less from the

---

(1431-1432), pp. 441-442 (1435-1436), pp. 443-445 (1439-1440), pp. 461-462 (1451-1452).

[47] E.g., in 1359-1360 the salaries of the six professors (960 fl.) represented nearly 70% of the total salary budget (1, 400 fl.). In 1369 seven law professors were paid 850 fl., 60% of the total (1, 435 fl.); in 1435 nine lawyers received 975 fl., 59% of the total (1,650 fl.). The Studio faculty was divided into five colleges: theology, canon law, civil law, medicine, and the arts (*Statuti*, p. 82, rubric 74 of the 1388 statute).

[48] Bruni and Leonpilato taught from 1360 to 1362, receiving annual salaries of 80 and 100 fl., respectively (*Camera, Uscita*, 150, fol. 5[r], 153, fol. 37[r]: "Magistro Leonpilato de Tesalia eletto ad docendam grammaticam grecam et licteras grecas"). On this appointment, see P. Ricci, "La prima cattedra di Greco in Firenze," *Rinascimento*, III (1952), 159-165.

[49] Two law professors were hired in these years with very large salaries: Giovanni de S. Giorgio of Bologna (1362-1363) and Riccardo de Saliceto (1363-1365), at 800 fl. annually (*Camera, Uscita*, 159, no pag., 23 Dec. 1362; 164, no pag., 29 Dec. 1363). These were the highest recorded salaries paid in the Studio's history but see n. 55 below.

revenue increase than did the other disciplines. Among the nine professors of civil and canon law were the renowned Francesco Zabarelli of Padua (later a cardinal) and six native Florentines. The medical faculty had grown to seven; it included two highly paid instructors, Cristoforo of Bologna and Marsilio de S. Sophia of Padua. Eight men had been hired to teach courses in moral and natural philosophy, grammar and astrology, with salaries which varied from 20 to 100 florins.[50]

Yet, even during this relatively florid phase, the Florentine Studio was a pigmy by comparison with the giant on the other side of the Apennines. When Florence made twenty-four appointments in 1388, Bologna's teaching staff numbered seventy-three. The Arno city never succeeded in closing the gap, for Bologna expanded its faculty in the fifteenth century, and by 1438 it could boast of a teaching corps of ninety-four professors. Pavia's staff was also consistently larger than that of Florence. Between 1387 and 1399 the Lombard university doubled in size, from thirty-eight to seventy. Like Florence, Pavia declined in the early years of the fifteenth century, but it enjoyed a revival after 1420. Forty-seven salaried professors taught in Pavia in 1435, when only seventeen instructors were listed on Florence's payroll.[51]

Information on the quality of instruction is scanty. We may, however, assume that the lengthy service of some teachers (like the lawyer Francesco of Arezzo and the Augustinian theologian Francesco Nerli) was proof of their competence and popularity.[52] The short tenures of other scholars may have been due to the lure of better opportunities elsewhere. Did Leonpilato of Thessaly resign from his Greek professorship in 1362 to accept a more lucrative position in another school or

[50] Abbondanza, "Ufficiali," pp. 85-110. Cristoforo and Marsilio received salaries of 300 and 340 fl., respectively.

[51] For the Florentine faculty lists for these years, see above, n. 46. Bologna's *rotuli* for 1388-1389, 1407-1408, and 1438-1439 are in U. Dallari, *I rotuli dei lettori legisti e artisti dello Studio bolognese dal 1384 al 1799* (Bologna, 1888-1924), I, 6-11. For Pavia, see Zanetti's article, cited above, n. 20. In 1424, Padua had a faculty of thirty: fourteen lawyers and sixteen professors of medicine and the arts (L. Thorndike, *University Records and Life in the Middle Ages* [New York, 1944], p. 302).

[52] Other professors with long tenures were: Jacopo Folchi, decretals, 1368-1390; Lodovico di Bartolo da Gubbio, medicine, 1368-1390; Antonio Rosselli, canon law, 1422-1435; Bandino di messer Giovanni Banducci, medicine, 1422-1435; Francesco da Empoli, civil law, 1422-1432.

was he dismissed for incompetence or for lack of student interest in his lectures? A provision of September 1366 charged that "professors omit much material which they are required to cover according to the customs of the Studio" and then stipulated that offenders would forfeit part of their salary.[53] In a secret denunciation presented to the Signoria in 1368, an anonymous scholar expressed his discontent with Studio instruction. He complained that the professors did not cover one-third of the scheduled material and that they failed to hold disputations. Several doctors had only one or two students. The informer urged the authorities to interrogate the rector and the students about the quality of teaching, since the latter were afraid to denounce their masters openly. These professors, one of whom received 200 florins and another 100 florins, "rob this commune as boldly as if they were highwaymen." The disgruntled student concluded his accusation with this appeal: "Send for them and learn how they teach. Their evil habits are so numerous that I cannot describe them all to you!"[54]

Such criticism may have been unfounded, and, even if valid, it may have described a temporary situation. The fortunes of the Studio fluctuated so sharply that the documents, admittedly fragmentary, do not reveal any permanent characteristics or traditions developed over the years. The presence of famous scholars like Baldo or Chrysoloras or Guarino did attract students, but these men alone could not build a university's reputation. Their fame was personal and their residence brief; they could not transfer their charisma to the Studio, particularly since no permanent corps of distinguished scholars developed around these luminaries.[55] Within a decade of Chrysoloras's election to the Greek professorship, an appointment made with great fanfare, the Studio closed its doors. The school reopened in 1413 with a cadre of

[53] *Statuti*, pp. 149-150.

[54] This complaint is included among the *tamburazioni*, or secret denunciations, presented to a secular judge in 1368 (*ASF, Atti del Esecutore degli Ordinamenti della Giustizia*, 555, fol. 15ʳ).

[55] The dangers inherent in this policy of building a university's reputation on one or two men were demonstrated by the election, in 1432, of abbot Niccolò of Sicily to a two-year professorship in canon law with an annual salary of 1,000 fl. (*Statuti*, p. 418). Padua also bid for his services, and in a letter of protest to the Venetian doge the Signoria wrote: "Quippe cum alium doctorem nullum extimabilem habeamus, ac totum Studii fundamentum ab huius spe presentiaque dependeat, necessarium nobis esset Studium claudere si huic a nobis conducto, sub cuius fiducia stetimus, licentiam preberemus" (p. 421). Padua apparently won this contest, for the abbot was not recorded in Florence's faculty list of Nov. 1432 (pp. 423-424).

thirteen professors, but within ten years the faculty was reduced to a skeleton staff of eight poorly paid lecturers: three in law, one in notarial science, two in medicine, and two in the arts.[56] The Studio's failure to surpass Bologna and Padua is demonstrated most clearly by student choice. Not only did Italian scholars generally prefer Bologna for law and Padua for natural sciences, but large numbers of Tuscan students matriculated at Bologna, convinced that they would receive better legal training there.[57] As early as 1366 some Florentines were demanding that native students be forced to study at home.[58] But, if this prohibition was enacted into law, it remained a dead letter for thirty years. In 1396 the Studio governors decreed that, "for the augmentation and conservation of the Studio," all students resident in the city, *contado*, and district of Florence must attend the local university.[59] The exiguity of documentation on the enforcement of this decree suggests that the rule was never applied rigorously. In 1416 some thirty scholars were penalized for studying abroad. Then, after another lapse, a wave of prosecutions occurred in 1432, coinciding with the campaign to strengthen the Studio in the years before the establishment of Medicean hegemony.[60]

The one moment in its history when the Studio might have surged ahead of its Bologna rival occurred in 1429, when the Emilian city rebelled against papal rule. Political disorders seriously disrupted the academic routine and persuaded some professors and students to

[56] Salaries ranged from 150 fl. for Paolo di ser Angelo de Castro, civil law (who received 250 fl. in 1413), to 30 fl. for Luca of Perugia, logic, and Antonio in grammar (*Statuti*, pp. 403-404).

[57] Lauro Martines, *Lawyers and Statecraft in Renaissance Florence* (Princeton, 1968), pp. 481-508, contains detailed information on Florentine lawyers who received their training in Bologna and Padua. See also his book, *The Social World of the Florentine Humanists, 1390-1460* (Princeton, 1963), pp. 313, 328, 330, 332-334, 344. A recent good study of the University of Bologna is S. Stelling-Michaud's *L'Université de Bologne et la pénétration des droits romain et canonique en Suisse aux XIIIe et XIVe siècles* (Geneva, 1955).

[58] *CP*, 7, fol. 82[r], Jan. 1366, statement of Rosso de' Ricci, spokesman for the twelve *buon'uomini*.

[59] *Giudice degli Appelli*, 71, fol. 77[r], 29 Nov. 1396. Those who violated the decree were fined.

[60] For the penalties levied in 1416, see *ibid.*, 74, pt. 1, foll. 256[r]-256[v]; pt. 2, fol. 3[r], 13 Sept. and 13 Nov. 1416. The majority of those fined were natives of the *contado* and district: seven from Florence, eight from Arezzo, three from Pisa, two from Volterra, three from Pistoia. For the Nov. 1432 sentences, see *ibid.*, 77, pt. 2, foll. 25[r]-26[r], when forty students were fined 200 lire.

search for a more tranquil milieu. A few Bologna students did transfer to the Arno city,[61] but the republic was then involved in a desperate struggle with Lucca and was unable to finance major improvements in its faculty and curriculum.[62] Indeed, rival institutions were making raids upon the Florentine student body at this time. In September 1428 a Sienese ambassador reported to his government that he had persuaded five students to forsake the Florentine Studio for Siena and that another ten were disposed to transfer there.[63]

The checkered history of the Studio prior to the Medici restoration illustrates some of the factors which limited its development: fiscal exigencies, administrative interference, reservations concerning the value and utility of the university. This last element was perhaps the most crucial, if the most difficult to document. In good times and bad the Studio ranked quite low in the hierarchy of interests of the Florentine ruling class. During the crisis years around 1430, when the Studio budget was pared to the bone, the commune continued to subsidize the construction of the cathedral dome and to commission other works of art for the beautification of the city. And after 1434, when Florence had recovered some degree of tranquility and prosperity, the school did not receive a substantial budget increase, and the quality of the faculty did not improve significantly. One source of patrician indifference to the Studio's fortunes was the fact that its own educational needs were not adversely affected by the mediocre quality of university education in Florence. Sons of wealthy citizens who desired training in law, medicine, and the natural sciences could obtain an excellent education in Bologna or Padua.[64]

Equally important in shaping the patriciate's attitude toward the Studio in the Quattrocento were the new intellectual tastes for classical literature which had developed in Florence since the beginning of the century. Prior to 1430 the Studio had played a useful role in promoting the new learning, through the appointments of Chrysoloras, Guarino, Marsuppini, and Filelfo. But humanistic studies also flour-

---

[61] For these transfers, see *Statuti*, pp. 409-410.

[62] In 1431-1432 the budget for salaries of twenty professors was 1,415 fl. (*Statuti*, pp. 413-415). On the Florentine fiscal crisis in these years, see U. Procacci, "Sulla cronologia delle opere di Masaccio e di Masolino tra il 1425 et il 1428," *Rivista d'arte*, XXVIII (1953), 15-32.

[63] *ASS, Concistoro*, 1914, no. 66.

[64] In 1428 the Studio governors estimated that 250 Florentine subjects were studying in foreign universities (*Statuti*, p. 211).

235

ished beyond the confines of the university, and many of the most prominent humanists—Bruni, Niccoli, Bracciolini, Ficino—never received Studio appointments. In 1428, just a few months before the university governors had complained about the lackluster quality of their institution, Leonardo Bruni delivered a funeral eulogy for Nanni Strozzi, in which he lauded Florence as the leading center, indeed the source, of the revival of classical learning.[65] The study of the classics flourished in Florence while the Studio foundered, and this pattern continued after 1434.[66] Humanism had moved from the public university to private centers: to the homes of Palla Strozzi and Cino Rinuccini, to Traversari's convent of S. Maria degli Angeli, to palaces where tutors instructed the children of wealthy patricians. The most renowned educational institution in Florence after 1460 was not the Studio but the Platonic Academy, which had no formal curriculum, no matriculation, no salaried instructors.[67] This shift from public to private institutions of learning, from the patronage of the university to that of the academy, is one important aspect of the trend toward social and intellectual elitism in late Quattrocento Florence.

[65] H. Baron, *The Crisis of the Early Italian Renaissance* (Princeton, 1955), I, 362. It is true that the republic promoted and subsidized humanist learning through its appointment of Salutati, Bruni, and Carlo Marsuppini as chancellors.

[66] After 1430 the Studio continued to spend the major part of its revenue for law and medicine. In 1439, for example, twelve lawyers and three physicians received over 75% (1,530 fl.) of the budget. The arts faculty contained ten members, a large increase over the previous century, but they were as badly paid as ever with median salaries of 32 fl. (*Statuti*, pp. 443-445). The reputations of these scholars in the humanities were no higher than their salaries. One exception was George of Trebisond, who lectured in the Studio in 1442-1443 (A. Della Torre, *Storia dell' Accademia Platonica di Firenze* [Florence, 1902], pp. 250-252).

[67] The history of this institution, and its predecessors, is traced by Della Torre, *Storia dell'Accademia Platonica*.

# THE TEACHING OF ARGYROPULOS
# AND THE RHETORIC OF THE
# FIRST HUMANISTS

### JERROLD E. SEIGEL

ONE of the most influential of the Byzantines who settled in Italy during the fifteenth century was Joannes Argyropulos. More a philosopher than a teacher of Greek, Argyropulos helped to shape the intellectual interests of Florentines in the later Quattrocento. His own first loyalties in philosophy were to Aristotle, but his teaching also contributed to the growing enthusiasm for Plato. So large was his role in the intellectual life of Renaissance Florence that Eugenio Garin has recently found in his activity—rather than in that of Ficino—the earliest basis of the new, more strictly philosophical phase of humanist culture that emerged in the late fifteenth century. Professor Kristeller has agreed that it was with Argyropulos's arrival in 1456 that metaphysical speculation entered into the tradition of Florentine humanism.[1]

The activity of Argyropulos helped accomplish the transition from the humanism of Petrarch and his immediate followers to the philosophical culture of Florence under Lorenzo the Magnificent. His career thus offers a good vantage point from which to assess the relationship between these two stages in Renaissance thought. What was the connection between them? Were the philosophical interests encouraged by Argyropulos a continuation of the revival of ancient culture

---

[1] E. Garin, "Ricerche sulle traduzioni di Platone nella prima metà del secolo XV," in *Medioevo e Rinascimento, Studi in onore di Bruno Nardi* (Florence, 1955); idem, "La Giovinezza di Donato Acciaiuoli," *Rinascimento*, I (1950), 43-70; idem, "Il Problema Dell'Anima e dell' Immortalità . . . , 4: Influenze dell' Argiropulo," *La Cultura Filosofica del Rinascimento Italiano* (Florence, 1961), pp. 102-108; idem, "L'ambiente del Poliziano," *La Cultura Filosofica*, pp. 335-358; idem, "Platonici Bizantini e Platonici Italiani," *Studi sul Platonismo Medioevale* (Florence, 1958), esp. the "postilla argiropulea," pp. 188-190. P. O. Kristeller, "The Platonic Academy of Florence," *Renaissance News*, XIV (1961), 147-148. On Argyropulos in general, see the biography by G. Cammelli, *I Dotti Byzantini e Le Origini Dell' Umanesimo, II: Giovanni Argiropulo* (Florence, 1941); also, the relevant sections of A. Della Torre, *Storia Dell' Accademia Platonica di Firenze* (Florence, 1902); and a still useful study by G. Zippel, "Per la Biografia Dell' Argiropulo," *Giornale Storico della Letteratura Italiana*, XXVIII (1896), 92-112. There is some new information in Vito R. Giustiniani, *Alamanno Rinuccini, 1426-1499* (Cologne, 1965), *passim*.

237

championed by Petrarch, or were they part of a separate development? Historians such as Eugenio Garin who depict the main movement of ideas in the fifteenth century as a unified whole, corresponding to the novel social environment of the Renaissance and consciously opposed to medieval scholasticism, have found the teaching of Argyropulos to be quite in the spirit of the early humanists.[2] Yet there are reasons to question this view. Professor Kristeller has pointed out that the speculative philosophy of the later fifteenth century had many roots outside the humanist movement and that both Ficino and Pico owed their early philosophical education to scholastic backgrounds.[3] The conclusion of the present paper is that Argyropulos must be understood from a similar point of view. Although some uncertainties remain in the interpretation of Argyropulos's attitudes toward humanist and scholastic culture, the weight of the available evidence, supported now by a new document, indicates that his influence is better characterised by its contrasts than by its continuity with early humanist thought.

As an exemplar of the humanism of the first half of the fifteenth century we may take one of the most famous chancellors of the Flor-

[2] This is Professor Garin's most recent judgment. Earlier—in particular, before the appearance of F. Masai's *Pléthon et le Platonisme de Mistra* (Paris, 1956)— he had seen in Argyropulos's teaching the spirit which he now seems to restrict to Ficino and which viewed Aristotle "non più entro l'ambito di una stretta fedeltà allo spirito civile . . . ma con gli occhi fissi a quella finale esaltazione dell' intelletto contemplante e separato" (*L'Umanesimo Italiano* [Bari, 1958; first edn., 1951], p. 98). More recently, however, he has regarded Argyropulos from a different point of view, suggesting his approach to the "concezioni etico-politiche" of the anti-Medicean Florentine exiles (*La Cultura Filosofica*, p. 350) and, more generally, asserting that "L'Argiropulo si era inserito in pieno nella cultura filosofica fiorentina della prima metà del Quattrocento, ed aveva risposto così bene ai suoi bisogni, che le sue versioni ed il suo modo di commentare Aristotele al di fuori di ogni tradizione scolastica si imposero dovunque" (*ibid.*, p. 107).

[3] See "The Scholastic Background of Marsilio Ficino," in Kristeller's *Studies in Renaissance Thought and Letters* (Rome, 1956), pp. 35-98; "Humanism and Scholasticism in the Italian Renaissance," *ibid.*, pp. 553-583; "Florentine Platonism and its Relations with Humanism and Scholasticism," *Church History*, VIII (1939); and *The Philosophy of Marsilio Ficino*, ch. II. Kristeller has not specifically discussed Argyropulos at length in these writings, but his statement in the article cited in n. 1 above implies an interpretation of Argyropulos in line with what he has said about Ficino. For a note on the general disagreement between Garin and Kristeller, see André Chastel, *Art et Humanisme a Florence au Temps de Laurent le Magnifique* (Paris, 1961), p. 185n.

238

entine republic, a man with whose work Argyropulos came into contact during his stay in the city—Leonardo Bruni. Like other early followers of Petrarch, Bruni campaigned for the program of the *studia humanitatis* and especially for its central tenet, the combination of rhetoric and philosophy, the joining of "literary skill with the knowledge of things."[4] In opposition to the philosophy of the schools, Bruni advocated a kind of learning which he thought to be characteristic of the best minds of antiquity and which he associated especially with Cicero. "At a certain time philosophy was brought from Greece to Italy by Cicero, and it was diffused through the golden stream of his eloquence."[5] This was true philosophy, and only those who had drunk from the Ciceronian spring could have any real knowledge of it. Through his emphasis on literary skill and his insistence that philosophical knowledge depended on an acquaintance with Cicero, Bruni aided the humanist attempt to turn the axis of intellectual activity away from the dialectic of the schools and toward grammar and rhetoric. As Ernst Cassirer has observed, with Bruni "the very possibility of philosophical investigation is made to depend on the condition of education and of the literary tradition. . . . The style in which a doctrine is set forth is no longer considered an accessory and exterior element, but becomes the decisive criterion for evaluating its objective content."[6]

The question of style is basic to any understanding of early humanism. But the cultivation of style did not usually mean for the humanists what it has meant for many of their commentators. The humanistic pursuit of eloquence was not so much a search for artful beauty as it was an attempt to give to moral philosophy what was essential if it was to be effective—persuasiveness. Bruni wrote to Cosimo de' Medici with regard to ethics: "The active part [of philosophy] contains the precepts of life, to know which is a small thing, unless you make them active."[7] To make philosophy active required the eloquence of the orator. Outlining a program of studies in his treatise *De studiis et litteris*, the future chancellor said: "I also exhort you not to neglect

---

[4] *De studiis et litteris*, in Leonardo Bruni Aretino, *Humanistisch-Philosophische Schriften, Mit einer Chronologie seiner Werke und Briefe*, ed. Hans Baron (Leipzig/Berlin, 1928), p. 6.

[5] *Dialogi ad Petrum Paulum Histrum*, ed. Eugenio Garin, in *Prosatori Latini del Quattrocento* (Milan/Naples, 1952), p. 54.

[6] Ernst Cassirer, *Das Erkenntnisproblem* (Berlin, 1911), I, 121.

[7] Printed in Bruni, *Schriften*, p. 121.

to read orators. For who is wont to extoll virtue more ardently or thunder more fiercely against vice? From them we learn to praise what is well done and to execrate villainies; from them to console, to exhort, to incite, to restrain. Granted that all these things are done by philosophers, still somehow anger and pity and every excitement and restraint of the soul are in the power of the orator."[8] Thus, eloquence was necessary to moral philosophy (other kinds of philosophy were of decidedly less interest to Bruni),[9] not for producing a work which would please a refined literary palate, but for producing one which would do its work properly, which would make philosophy active.

It is in this light that we must understand the labor Bruni expended on his new translations of ancient philosophical treatises, especially those of Aristotle. Bruni's famous castigation of the medieval versions of Aristotle's writings centered upon the failure of the earlier translator to produce a Latin text which truly represented the "golden stream of eloquence" which Cicero had found in Aristotle's writings.[10] Much of Bruni's interest in Aristotle arose from the humanist's conviction that the Philosopher had been a man of eloquence himself, one who had combined philosophy with rhetoric. As Bruni wrote in the prologue to his version of the *Politics* in 1435, "Surely Aristotle filled these books with such eloquence, such variety and fullness of speech, and such a wealth of narratives and examples, that they seem to be written nearly in the style of oratory."[11] These statements are typical of Bruni's interest in ancient philosophy. What was characteristic of philosophy as practiced by the ancients was its close union with rhetoric. This was the philosophy the early fifteenth-century humanists advocated.[12] How did the teaching of Argyropulos relate to it?

Information about Argyropulos's life in the years before his appointment to the Florentine Studio is scanty. He was born around 1415.

---

[8] *De studiis, ibid.*, p. 13.

[9] Cf. *Isagogicon Moralis Disciplinae*, ed. Baron, in Bruni, *Schriften*, p. 21.

[10] See the Preface in Bruni, *Schriften*, pp. 77-81, and Jerrold E. Seigel, *Rhetoric and Philosophy in Renaissance Humanism* (Princeton, 1968), ch. IV.

[11] "Aristoteles certe tanta facundia, tanta varietate et copia, tanta historiarum exemplorumque cumulatione hos libros refersit, ut oratorio paene stilo scripti videantur" (Bruni, *Schriften*, p. 74).

[12] On this general view of humanism, see Hanna H. Gray, "Renaissance Humanism: the Pursuit of Eloquence," *Journal of the History of Ideas*, XXIV (1963), and my book, *Rhetoric and Philosophy in Renaissance Humanism*.

His own later testimony that he had dedicated himself to the study of philosophy from an early age can easily be accepted, but we have no details concerning his education. He may have been in Italy and in Florence to attend the Council presided over by Eugene IV in 1438. More definite is the information relating to his stay in Padua from 1441 to 1444 (or perhaps even somewhat longer). In Padua he lived in the house of the Florentine exile Palla Strozzi, whose grandson, Donato Acciaiuoli, was to become one of Argyropulos's most enthusiastic disciples in the city on the Arno. Argyropulos copied manuscripts for Strozzi and, according to Vespasiano, taught him Greek philosophy. Meanwhile, he seems to have been a student as well as a teacher. A decree of the University of Padua dated July 24, 1444, declared him *publica doctoratus in artibus.* After that date we have no authoritative word of Argyropulos's whereabouts until 1448, when we find him teaching in Constantinople.[13]

There is no reliable evidence that he left the Eastern Empire again before he was forced to flee when Constantinople fell to the Turks at the end of May 1453. Sometime shortly before August 1454 he visited Florence and met Donato Acciaiuoli; from that encounter date Donato's first suggestions to Argyropulos that he make his home in the Tuscan city. It does not seem that the two were acquainted before the summer of 1454, but it is likely that Acciaiuoli had heard of Argyropulos from his grandfather, Palla Strozzi. The meeting must have been a friendly one; the young Florentine's letters to, and about, the exiled Greek are full of expressions of respect and assurances of friendship. He recommended his native city as the home of civilized and humane men, not a few of whom were Argyropulos's admirers.[14]

What Donato had in mind for the Byzantine to do in Florence becomes apparent in a series of documents from the winter and spring of 1455. In February and March of that year a controversy broke out over new appointments to the Florentine Studio. On one side was a group which included the aged chancellor of the republic, Poggio Bracciolini, and which favored the appointment of a promising young man from Prato, Cristoforo Landino. On the other was a faction composed of Donato Acciaiuoli, his brother Piero, their close friend Ala-

---

[13] See the biography by Cammelli (n. 1 above), ch. I on Argyropulos's early life, ch. II on his stay in Padua.

[14] See the letter of Donato Acciaiuoli printed in Cammelli, pp. 47n-50n. Also in Ferdinandus Fossius (Fossi), *Monumenta ad Alamanni Rinuccini Vitam Contexendam* (Florence, 1791), pp. 58-60.

manno Rinuccini (in whose home the young men often gathered), Marco Parenti, Antonio Rossi, and Andrea Alamanni. They took the name "Academy" for themselves. In politics the group was usually anti-Medicean. In matters of culture they looked backward to the great days of Bruni and Carlo Marsuppini and forward to a restoration of humanistic learning which they hoped (if Donato's feelings were shared by his friends) would be led by Joannes Argyropulos.[15]

What resulted from the rivalry of these two groups seems to have been a compromise: both Landino and Argyropulos obtained posts in the Studio. On August 4, 1455, Alamanno Rinuccini wrote to the Greek informing him that his election had been "easily" obtained, and the next day an official letter from the directors of the Studio (also apparently written by Rinuccini) was dispatched, proclaiming Argyropulos's appointment.[16] Yet the Byzantine did not begin his lectures in Florence until eighteen months afterward. In November 1456 Alamanno Rinuccini wrote to his friend Donato Acciaiuoli informing him that Landino had begun his lectures, "speaking to a great crowd of listeners, and with a truly splendid and distinguished flow of words." But of Argyropulos, "who has stirred up such expectancy of his teaching, and whom we have been so eagerly waiting to hear, not a word is heard."[17] In fact, Argyropulos may have been on his way to Florence when Rinuccini wrote. We know that he went to France in May 1456, and a document of the following July attests to his presence in England. In February 1457 he began his long-awaited lectures in Florence.

Argyropulos taught in the Tuscan city until 1471.[18] The post he was

[15] On this controversy in general, see A. Della Torre, *Accademia Platonica*, ch. II, esp. pp. 364ff.; Cammelli, chs. IV-V; the document in A. Gherardi, *Statuti della università e studio fiorentino* (Florence, 1881), p. 264; the letters of Donato Acciaiuoli in Fossi, pp. 79-82; E. Garin, "La Giovinezza di D. A." (cited in n. 1 above); also, from the other side, the letter of Poggio Bracciolini in Pogii, *Epistolae*, ed. Thomas de Tonellis (Florence, 1832-1861), III, 183-188.

[16] See the letters printed in *Lettere ed Orazione di Alamanno Rinuccini*, ed. V. R. Giustiniani (Florence, 1953), pp. 12-14, 15; see also Giustiniani, *Alamanno Rinuccini, 1426-1499*, pp. 90ff. and elsewhere.

[17] *Lettere ed Orazione*, p. 18.

[18] The body of Argyropulos's philosophical writings—translations, commentaries, courses of lectures—is quite large and has never been systematically studied. For indications of the manuscript works of Argyropulos, see E. Garin, *La Cultura Filosofica del Rinascimento Italiano*, pp. 102-108. The number of works of Argyropulos in print seems to be limited to the six introductory lectures to his courses in Florence, in Karl Muellner, *Reden und Briefe Italienischer*

called to fill was a chair in rhetoric, the subject closest to the hearts of Salutati and Bruni. It was specifically to carry on the tradition of the early humanists, to uphold the glory of Florence as a center for the study of oratory, that Donato Acciaiuoli had campaigned for the appointment of Joannes Argyropulos.[19] Yet, if Donato really expected the Byzantine exile to make rhetoric his chief concern, he must have been disappointed. Joannes seems to have given no lectures on rhetorical texts, either Latin or Greek; nor did he discuss historical writings. All the available evidence indicates that his principal, perhaps his exclusive, concern (with the exception of some attention to teaching the Greek language) was with Greek philosophy. The contrast between his teaching and that of Landino is striking. The young man from Prato commented on Cicero and on Petrarch; Argyropulos lectured publicly on Aristotle and in private introduced his students to Plato. Rhetoric stood quite low on Argyropulos's own scale of intellectual values: he appears to have preferred that his disciples think of him as a metaphysician.[20] The few references to him in the published official documents of the University of Florence are further indications of this preference. On October 5, 1458, his appointment was renewed, and he was spoken of as "a most illustrious professor of the whole of philosophy." Landino, whose tenure was extended at the same time, was referred to as a teacher of oratory and poetry. Some years later a

---

*Humanisten* (Vienna, 1899), his translations of Aristotle, esp. the *Nicomachean Ethics* (printed several times during the sixteenth century), and a few of the prefaces to these translations. See Carlo Frati, "Le traduzioni Aristoteliche di G. Argiropulo e un antica legatura Medicea," *La Bibliofilia*, XIX (1917). More recently, Cesare Vasoli has edited a "Compendium de regulis et formis ratiocinandi," in *Rinascimento*, 2nd ser., IV (1964), 285-340. As has been pointed out, the short treatise published by Cammelli as an appendix to his biography of Argyropulos is not his work but that of another Greek exile, Trapezuntius. See Cesare Vasoli in *Rinascimento* (1959), pp. 157ff., and E. Garin, *La Cultura Filosofica*, pp. 60-61n.

[19] See the letter in Fossi, *Monumenta*, p. 80: "Studium orbis terrae in oratoria nobilissimum, quod iam sopitum gravi atque diuturno bello in squallore diutius iacuit, excitandum esse in lucem non autem evertendum et ad duos deferendum, qui parva mercede conducti oratoriam dedoceant, brevique tempore tantum augeant imperitorum turbam, ut Florentini, qui eloquentia et dicendi scribendique ratione ceteris non solum Italiae urbibus, sed etiam ceteris gentibus antecellunt, in summam inscitiam ignorantiamque ducantur litterarum latinarum."

[20] E. Garin, "Il Problema dell' Anima . . . ," *La Cultura Filosofica*, p. 106. See also the lecture of Argyropulos in K. Muellner, *Reden und Briefe Italienischer Humanisten*, p. 39.

similar document referred to Joannes as a teacher of "moral and natural philosophy, and poetry, both Greek and Latin."[21] What may have been meant here by poetry is uncertain; in any case, no mention of rhetoric or oratory occurs. The conclusion that Argyropulos was not a teacher of rhetoric at all is buttressed by one final document. This is a description Landino later wrote of Argyropulos's influence in Florence. Naming Alamanno Rinuccini and the two Acciaiuoli brothers as the Greek's followers, Landino said that, whereas they had previously given their attention to the study of speaking and had become men of eloquence, they now devoted themselves to philosophy under Argyropulos's direction.[22]

These considerations indicate that Joannes Argyropulos did not carry on the tradition of Salutati and Bruni. By themselves, however, they are not enough to show that he was specifically critical of the early humanists nor that he thought his own teaching contrasted with theirs. On the question of whether he felt such a contrast the evidence is conflicting, but a careful examination of it leads us to conclude that he did. Perhaps the best known of the relevant documents is the description of Argyropulos's impact which Poliziano included in his *Miscellanea*. Poliziano objected to much that the Byzantines who came to Italy said about the superiority of Greek to Latin culture, but none of their insults annoyed him more than the attack he described Argyropulos as having made on Cicero. The sting was especially sharp, Poliziano complained, since, being a very vigorous disputer and "a great slinger of words in our language," Argyropulos was able to convince his students that his slander was true. What he had said was that Cicero had been "ignorant, not only of philosophy, but also of Greek letters."[23] The import of such an assertion in fifteenth-century Flor-

---

[21] See the documents in Gherardi, *Statuti della università e studio Fiorentino*, pp. 467 and 489-492.

[22] Landino, *De vera nobilitate*, Bibl. Corsini (Accademia de' Lincei, Rome), 433 (36 E-5), fol. 8[v]: "Hunc [sc. Argyropulum] secuti sunt ex eius auditoribus viri nobiles Azaroli duo Petrus ac Donatus, Alamannus Rinuccinus qui cum iam diu dicendi artificio assiduisque declamationibus haud mediocri eloquentia ornati essent, summo deinceps studio se in philosophia Argyropylo erudiendos tradiderant: tantamque in ea re profecerant ut iam haud obscurum apud suos eorum nomen esset." A description of Donato Acciaiuoli alone in almost exactly the same terms appears in the funeral oration Landino wrote for Donato. It is published in Francesco Sansovino, *Orationi Volgarmente Scritte da Molti Huomini Illustri de' Tempi Nostri* (Venice, 1562), Pt. 1, foll. 150[v]-154[v] (see esp. 154[r]).

[23] Angeli Politiani, *Opera* (Basel, 1553), pp. 224-225.

ence would certainly have been shattering. When we consider the place given to Cicero by the partisans of the *studia humanitatis*, and especially the fundamental importance a writer like Bruni attached to Cicero's knowledge of philosophy, we can only interpret Poliziano's words as meaning that Argyropulos had conducted a direct attack on the humanism of Petrarch and Bruni. But how good was Poliziano's reporting? Eugenio Garin has recently reminded us of Poliziano's general dislike for the Byzantines and has asserted that he exaggerated Argyropulos's attitude in order to write "a bit of *bravura*."[24]

There is some evidence to support Professor Garin's point of view. In his inaugural lecture in Florence, Argyropulos specifically praised Leonardo Bruni. He referred to Bruni as "most eloquent" and particularly lauded his translation of Aristotle's *Ethics* (the text on which Joannes was lecturing). The translation had been done "most expressively," he said, and it was "worthy of Aristotle and of the Latin Language."[25] Yet, if Argyropulos belittled Cicero, it is unlikely that he could have continued to admire the author of the *Dialogi ad Petrum Histrum*. According to a letter of Francesco Filelfo, written some nine months after the Byzantine's Florentine lectures began, he did not. Filelfo referred to attacks which, he heard, Joannes had made on Leonardo and described them as "the sole thing which makes a good number of people unhappy" with Argyropulos's teaching. He urged Joannes to cease criticizing Leonardo, "if you are wise." "For Leonardo enjoys such a reputation among all the Latins that (to use the words of Homer) his glory rises to heaven."[26]

What are we to believe? The question of Argyropulos's specific attitude toward Bruni may remain somewhat obscure, but his point of view toward early fifteenth-century humanism in general is clarified by the document published in the Appendix to this essay. The importance of this document is that it was one of Argyropulos's earliest writings intended for his Florentine hosts and that he described it both here and later as serving to give "a kind of taste" of his interests and of his teaching.[27] The means he chose to give this indication to the Florentines was a Latin translation of some of Aristotle's logical

---

[24] "L'ambiente del Poliziano," *La Cultura Filosofica*, p. 347.

[25] Text in Muellner, *Reden und Briefen*, p. 18.

[26] I use the French text given by Emile Le Grand, *Cent-Dix Lettres Grecques de François Filelfe* (Paris, 1892), pp. 93-96 (Greek text, pp. 92-93).

[27] See the preface printed below and Laur. Pl. 71, 7, fol. 1, reproduced in Cammelli, *Giovanni Argiropulo*, facing p. 116.

works—the *De interpretatione* and the first part of the *Prior Analytics*. He dedicated the translation to Piero de' Medici. It is the preface he wrote to Piero in connection with these translations which gives us the information we seek about his attitude toward the culture of the early humanists. From his statements in this preface, it is clear that he would have regarded the claims made for learning in philosophy by an orator like Cicero or a humanist like Bruni with the utmost suspicion.[28]

Argyropulos gave the following reason for having chosen the two works of Aristotle to present to Piero de' Medici:

> For to translate the books of some orators into Latin and present them to you, although it would hardly seem to be a despicable gift, could never have demonstrated how great is my good will and extraordinary love toward you, nor do I think it would have preserved the dignity of either of us. For it is a thing very easily done, and as you know it is quite often done by anyone at all; and to allure your exceptional and most lofty spirit toward the opinions of the vulgar and (so to say) the serpents of the earth, would surely be too trifling and scanty and base.

The writer did not say whether anyone had actually suggested to him that he translate some Greek rhetorical works, but, given the fact that he had been called to fill a chair in rhetoric, it is not unlikely that someone had. In any case, Argyropulos went on to underline his belief in the separation between the culture of orators and the higher learning of philosophy. The writings of orators were much less useful than those of philosophers, he maintained, and were therefore much less to be prized.

> I judge that no one exists or will exist who does not go from the disregarded and unesteemed rudiments of any of the orators to the secrets of philosophy and the subtle teachings of Aristotle—when they are tastefully presented in a clear and orderly fashion—with the greatest eagerness. For it will be just as if a short and easy way to the virtues and happiness were revealed. Now just as there would then be no one who would not rather seize that path, so now hardly anyone will not take this royal and sacred way to the halls of phi-

[28] See Appendix. Professor Garin has quoted a few words from this preface (*Studi sul Platonismo Medievale*, p. 190), but I can find no indication that it has ever been published in full before.

losophy, unless perhaps someone would prefer to go through solitary and thorny places to the same goal, which no one in his right mind would ever do.

This passage breathes a spirit far removed from the early humanist insistence that true learning in philosophy could be attained only by those who united the search for it with the cultivation of eloquence. Argyropulos emphasized the contrast rather than the harmony between rhetoric and philosophy. Even on the specific question of Aristotle's style, which the early humanists had regarded in the light of Cicero's praise for his "golden stream of eloquence," Argyropulos struck a determined and jarring note. These two writings, he informed Piero, were difficult works, especially the *De interpretatione*. Moreover, the latter's difficulty stemmed "not so much from the subject matter as from the style (*dicendi modo*). In fact I do not know why the Philosopher wanted to publish a work so obscure that it appears as a very exemplar and account of difficulty itself." To be sure, Bruni had not made a translation of the *De interpretatione*, nor is it likely that he would have claimed to find Aristotle's "golden stream of eloquence" in the Philosopher's logical works. But the result was simply that Bruni showed no interest in this part of Aristotle's production. He gave his attention to those treatises which dealt with civic life and were therefore "suitable to eloquence."[29] Bruni had claimed to restore the Philosopher's eloquence in his translations of the *Ethics* and *Politics*. Argyropulos, on the contrary, told Piero that he himself gave his Latin versions of Aristotle "only as much elegance and harmony of style as philosophy, the subject matter, and the terms themselves allow. For in these things one is not allowed to roam too far afield, nor is a wide scope allowed to style." Argyropulos's attitude toward Aristotle's style certainly contrasted with Bruni's. Indeed, it recalled the attitude of one of Bruni's most vigorous scholastic opponents, who in his criticism of Bruni's version of the *Ethics* had insisted that "in philosophy words ought not be allowed to run loose without restraint, since out of the improper use of words errors of fact gradually grow up."[30]

[29] Cf. Bruni's comment on the *Politics*: "materia est civilis, et capax eloquentiae" (Leonardo Bruni Arretini, *Epistolarum Libri VIII*, ed. L. Mehus [Florence, 1741], II, 95).

[30] "Nec enim in philosophia verba sine freno laxanda sunt, cum ex improprietate verborum error ad ipsas res paulatim accrescat" (the treatise against Bruni by Alonzo Garcia of Cartagena, Bishop of Burgos, printed by Alexander Birkenmajer, "Der Streit des Alonzo von Cartagena mit Leonardo Bruni Are-

The introduction of a defender of scholasticism into a discussion of Argyropulos is not inappropriate. The Greek had received a degree from the University of Padua during his stay there in 1444, and he may well have been influenced by the scholastic curriculum. The doctorate Argyropulos received from Padua was *in artibus,* but there are indications that his studies also included medicine. Pope Calixtus III once referred to him as *magister artium et medicinae,*[31] a degree commonly held by scholastic philosophers of the day. Recalling the terms we employed with reference to Bruni, we may say that Argyropulos's teaching helped to shift the axis of philosophical learning in Florence away from the grammatical and rhetorical interests of the early humanists and back toward dialectical and speculative concerns resembling those of scholasticism. In addition to the evidence of this change already presented, several other examples are of interest.

The first has to do with Argyropulos's attitude toward Socrates. In the early fifteenth century Socrates's name had often been invoked. Some of the humanists had a fair acquaintance with Plato's Socratic dialogues, but the understanding of the historical importance of Socrates seems to have been much influenced by the description of him given by various Latin writers, especially Cicero in the *Tusculan Disputations.* There Socrates was praised as the man who called philosophy down from the heavens to its proper place on earth: he was the first moral philosopher.[32] To the early humanists, Socrates's career was an object lesson in the benefits to be gained by taking one's attention away from speculative philosophy and giving it instead to the study of ethics. A comment of Gianozzo Manetti in his *Life of Socrates* illustrates this view well. Manetti repeated the reasons for Socrates's desertion of the speculative interests of early Greek philosophy given by Diogenes Laertius and St. Augustine, and he concluded that Socrates had abandoned speculative philosophy because he considered it to be "obscure, frivolous and empty, and accordingly of no utility to human life."[33]

---

tino," in *Vermischte Untersuchungen zur Geschichte der Mittelalterlichen Philosophie: Beiträge zur Ges. der Phil. des Mittelalters,* XX [Münster, 1922] Pt. 5, p. 170).

[31] Cammelli, *Giovanni Argiropulo,* pp. 24-26 and 75.

[32] Cicero, *Tusculan Disputations,* V, 4.

[33] Manetti, *Vita Socratis,* in E. Garin, *Filosofi Italiani del Quattrocento* (Florence, 1942), p. 226.

To the humanists, Socrates's movement to moral philosophy seems to have served as a reminder of the separation of ethics from speculative philosophy, the first being of great use to men in their lives, the second of very little. Moral philosophy, separated thus from contemplation, was at the same time—as we have seen in Bruni—closely tied to eloquence. Argyropulos's attitude, however, was just the reverse. In his view, Socrates's concern for ethics implied no lessening of his interest in the other parts of philosophy; rather, the Socratic emphasis on moral philosophy was intended to free men from a culture dominated by rhetoric. "Socrates brought men to the sciences through his discussions of moral philosophy, and he is therefore called a moral philosopher even though he was an excellent speculative philosopher. He saw that at that time men were given over to forensic eloquence, from which he called them away and brought them to the study of wisdom and its perfections."[34] The parallel between this view of Socrates calling men away from eloquence to philosophy and Argyropulos's own description of the relationship between these two activities in the preface to Aristotle's *De interpretatione* is close. It may also be suggested that this image of Socrates and his relation to the rhetorical sophists is considerably closer to Plato's than was that of humanists like Manetti. It is interesting to note in this connection the relationship which both Argyropulos and the humanists envisioned as existing between rhetoric, moral philosophy, and speculative philosophy. The three disciplines formed a kind of chain, in which the study of ethics was the link between the other two. Depending on one's point of view, either the connection of moral philosophy with rhetoric or its connection with speculative philosophy could be emphasized. For the humanists of Bruni's stamp, the separation of ethics from speculation was complemented by its close tie to rhetoric, so that true learning in philosophy itself could be said to require a concern for oratory. For Argyropulos, however, the figure of Socrates suggested a view of philosophy precisely opposite to this. Through his work in moral philosophy Socrates had brought men away from their old concern for eloquence toward the true study of wisdom, a pursuit in which rhetoric was not included but in which speculative philosophy certainly was.

---

[34] "Socrates disserendo per moralem philosophiam compellebat homines ad scientias, ed ideo appellatus est moralis, quamquam speculativus summus fuerit. Videbat ea tempestate homines deditos eloquentiae forensi, a qua avocabat et compellebat deinde ad studium sapientiae et perfectiones suas." (Quoted, in a different context, by Eugenio Garin, *La Cultura Filosofica*, p. 102.)

Although Argyropulos recognized the division of philosophy into active and speculative parts, he did not draw the conclusion that the two could or should actually be kept separate. On the contrary, in his discussion of Aristotle's *De anima* he described moral philosophy as dependent on speculative knowledge. He pointed out that the consideration of man's soul and its capacities in general belonged to natural, hence, speculative philosophy. Moral philosophy required this knowledge, however, since to know what was the good for man one had to understand the nature and divisions of his soul. Argyropulos spoke here of an active as well as a higher, contemplative kind of happiness. But moral philosophy, in order to teach us about happiness of both sorts, required the *speculative* knowledge of the soul provided in *De anima*. Argyropulos would not have agreed with the early humanist assertions of the small utility of natural or speculative philosophy for man's moral life.[35]

In this connection, we may look briefly at the lecture with which Argyropulos introduced his course on Aristotle's *Physics* in November 1458. The humanists were wont to begin their courses of lectures with extravagant panegyrics to learning and especially to the subject on which they were to speak. But none of these surpasses this speech of the Byzantine, which is so grandiloquent as to seem almost a parody of the traditional introductory lectures. "At last this day—oh excellent and most distinguished sirs—this long awaited, splendid and auspicious day has arrived, which, leaving behind all cares, brings forth the greatly longed-for beginning of our studies." The day was "roseate, golden, the most beautiful of all." It was the end of winter, of confusion, of sickness; it was the beginning of spring, of stability, of health. Of course, the lecturer gave a good reason for saying all these things. "For certainly that which appears to help us toward living well and happily may rightly be called not only by the names we have used,

---

[35] Argyropulos's lecture of Nov. 5, 1460, in Muellner, *Reden und Briefe Italienischer Humanisten*, pp. 43-48: "bifariam enim dividitur philosophia, in activam et speculativam, et utraque trifariam dividitur . . . et ad omnem partem confert notitia de anima. primo ad moralem, quae inquirit duplicem felicitatem . . . quare necessario requiritur haec scientia ad cognitionem moralis [45]. redigitur autem hic liber ad philosophiam naturalem. cum enim sit pars philosophiae naturalis, redigitur ad speculativam, in eo scilicet genere in quo totum; at naturalis philosophia in speculativa: et haec igitur ad speculativam redigitur [48]."

250

but even by more excellent ones, if any more splendid and divine names could be found."[36]

Excitement about a day which promised aid to living well and happily would have been shared by the early humanists. But it is to be remembered that Argyropulos, *publica doctoratus in artibus* in the University of Padua, was here presenting a course, not on ethics, but on natural philosophy. Did he not know that Petrarch had said that medicine (in which he included the learning in natural philosophy of the Paduans) "has nothing in common with ethics, and much that is contrary to it?"[37] This is a further sign of the changed direction which Argyropulos gave to the humanistic interests of late fifteenth-century Florence. We can see its effects in the thinking of his students.

The one among Argyropulos's disciples who displays the most interesting traces of his influence is Alamanno Rinuccini.[38] In his letters we find much that is continuous with the earlier humanist tradition but, at the same time, some striking evidences of contrast with it. These latter are often quite sensitive indicators of the changing focus of late fifteenth-century Florentine culture.

Much of Rinuccini's literary activity was in the tradition of Petrarch and Bruni. He used his knowledge of Greek to translate Isocrates, whom he described as "a most agreeable orator and a man of great learning in philosophy."[39] Rinuccini's interest in Isocrates harmonized with the cultural orientation of the early humanists; moreover, his *Dialogue on Liberty* has been cited by some scholars as displaying his agreement with the political ideals of early fifteenth-century Florence.[40] In this work Alamanno also showed his sympathy for rhetoric: the form of the dialogue, as one of the participants remarked was that of oratory, not of dialectic.[41]

[36] Lecture of Nov. 3, 1458, in Muellner, pp. 31-32.

[37] Francesco Petrarca, *Invective Contra Medicum*, ed. P. G. Ricci (Rome, 1950), p. 76. Argyropulos's studies at Padua included medicine, and he was once referred to in a letter by Pope Calixtus III as *magister artium et medicinae*—see above, n. 31.

[38] On Rinuccini, see Giustiniani, *Alamanno Rinuccini, 1426-1499*.

[39] Cf. *Lettere ed Orazione di Alamanno Rinuccini*, p. 76.

[40] See, e.g., the comments of F. Adorno in his edition of the *Dialogus de Libertate*, in *Atti e Memorie della . . . Colombaria*, XXII (1957), pp. 265-267.

[41] *Ibid.*, p. 277.

The continuity of Rinuccini's interests with those of the earlier humanists is best shown in his lasting concern with the problems of education. This can be seen in the treatise on the proper education of a citizen which Rinuccini composed in the form of a letter to his son in 1474.[42] In its conception of the purpose of humanistic studies as the formation of character and in much of the curriculum proposed, this program recalls the writings on education of such humanists as Vergerio, Bruni, and Guarino. Rinuccini gave a large place in the early studies of the future citizen to Cicero, and he repeated the common humanist warning against going too far with the study of dialectic. Moreover, as models of style Rinuccini recommended not only the ancient authors whom the humanists had praised but the early humanists themselves, particularly Bruni and Poggio Bracciolini.[43]

Yet this same treatise shows that there was a wide gap between Rinuccini and these men whom he recommended as models of style. For the followers of Petrarch had claimed to be learned not only in rhetoric, poetry, and history but in moral philosophy as well. Alamanno did not grant them this claim. He remarked in several places that he owed his own training in philosophy to Argyropulos, and he attributed the order of studies he now proposed to the Byzantine, too. From his perspective, the attitude toward philosophical study diffused by the humanists left much to be desired.

So far it seems to me that I have given an account of those subjects which I have thought ought to be learned by necessity by those of our citizens who want to cultivate literary studies; and I am afraid lest, as I impose something to be included beyond that which is taught as part of rhetoric, I may be applying to those who are unwilling and reluctant, which is a special fault in those who undertake the task of teaching the young. Now since they [i.e., the teachers of letters in Florence] are ignorant even of those disciplines which I have just named [dialectic and moral philosophy]—for they do not advance beyond a certain knowledge of rhetoric and history—and even want to keep their students within the same confines, they ought the more to be urged to borrow from others what is lacking in themselves; as we are taught by Cicero, the eloquent man we seek cannot be formed without philosophy. Leaving behind these men

[42] *Lettere ed Orazioni*, pp. 86-104.

[43] On Cicero, *ibid.*, pp. 92-93; on dialectic, p. 97; on the early humanists as models of style, pp. 94-95.

with their perversity, ignorance, and negligence therefore, I exhort all those who are dear to me, and who want to cultivate humanistic studies, not to depart from this order and program of study, and let them think that whatever of extra work is required is added for the sake of true glory and perfect knowledge.[44]

Like Argyropulos, Rinuccini objected to the narrow limits imposed on the study of philosophy by men who were primarily rhetoricians. In this passage he spoke of his own contemporaries—the humanists of the later fifteenth century—but he made similar criticisms of an earlier generation of humanists in another letter.

Of philosophy, in which the knowledge of nature and of supernatural things is contained, only a short time ago few men had even a taste, thinking they had done more than enough in it if they had studied Aristotle's *Moralia*. I am speaking of our fellow citizens; notwithstanding some who gave attention to philosophy as members of a religious order or because they wanted to teach medicine, the writings of those who taught the *studia humanitatis* before our own time show that, except for Gianozzo Manetti, you will find among them the smallest number learned in philosophy.[45]

Rinuccini went on to recall his own and Donato Acciaiuoli's part in bringing Argyropulos to Florence, for it was the Greek's coming which had led to the spread of philosophic knowledge in the Tuscan city. From the treatise on education one may safely conclude that Alamanno's cultural ideal still centered on the union of wisdom with eloquence, but his understanding of what this involved differed from that of Petrarch and Bruni. In the view of the student of Argyropulos, the "philosophy" of the early humanists was no philosophy at all. Certainly he did not believe that moral philosophy was the highest pursuit. In fact, in his view, one purpose of the study of moral philosophy was to prepare the mind to comprehend the higher sciences (note the

[44] *Ibid.*, pp. 98-99.

[45] "Philosophiam vero, qua naturae tum etiam supernaturalium rerum cognitio continetur, non multo ante pauci vix summis, ut ita dicam, labiis attingebant, satis superque in ea profecisse arbitrantes, si Aristotelis *Moralia* discerent. De civibus nostris loquor; atqui religioni cuidam addicti aut medicinam profiteri volentes philosophabantur, quod illorum scripta declarant, qui ante aetatem nostram humanitatis studia profitebantur, inter quos praeter unum Iannoctium Manettum paucissimos in philosophia peritos invenies." (Letter of Rinuccini to Roberto Salviati, Nov. 24, 1489, *Lettere ed Orazioni*, pp. 188-189).

similarity with Argyropulos's description of Socrates). These, from natural philosophy to mathematics and metaphysics, were the crown of the mind's perfections, and it was in divine contemplation that the highest happiness was to be found. Whatever leisure remained after seeing to the necessities of life ought to be devoted to this. Rinuccini foresaw that some readers would think his program more apt for the retiring philosopher than for the active citizen. In reply he assured them that such an arduous program could be accomplished even by the busy citizen: nothing was too difficult for the human spirit which understood its own powers.[46]

Such attitudes as these implied a greater degree of sympathy for medieval scholastic culture than the early humanists had felt. Rinuccini explicitly affirmed the achievement of the scholastics in an account of the revival of the arts he sent to Federigo of Urbino as a preface to a translation of the Greek writer Philostratus. To be sure, he praised the humanists for the revival of true Latin eloquence and agreed that the medieval writers "wrote in a rather harsh manner." Still, he asserted, the schoolmen "attained to knowledge about many and great things."[47] In general, he did not attribute such knowledge to the humanists. Salutati, Bruni, Poggio, and Carlo Marsuppini all received credit for their eloquence, but only Manetti (as in the treatise Rinuccini sent to his son in 1474) won praise for combining wide knowledge with this ability in writing and speaking.[48] Rinuccini was proud that the men of his age had revived ancient standards, not only in grammar, rhetoric, and poetry but in painting, sculpture, and architecture as well.[49] But Alamanno did not think that a revival had been necessary in all the arts. The most important of them, he suggested, had never declined at all.

It would be a very long task to list all of the men who have been excellent in dialectic and philosophy and in knowledge of the sacred scriptures. The more necessary zeal for such studies is to living well and wisely, the more they have flourished without interruption among all peoples in every age. Wherefore it has come about that also in the time just past these studies were brought to the highest subtlety, and many men most learned in them abounded. I cannot

[46] *Lettere ed Orazioni*, pp. 99-102.
[47] *Ibid.*, pp. 107-108.     [48] *Ibid.*, p. 108.
[49] Rinuccini names, among others, Cimabue, Giotto, Masaccio; Donatello, Lucca della Robbia; Brunelleschi, Alberti (*ibid.*, pp. 106-107).

pass over in silence one most excellent man of this type, my teacher Johannes Argyropulos. . . .[50]

The achievement of the age in philosophy, however noteworthy in its own right, was not to be seen in terms of discontinuity with the Middle Ages. As a student of Argyropulos, Rinuccini learned to see the relationship between the followers of Petrarch and medieval scholastic culture from a perspective far removed from that of the early humanists themselves. Rinuccini was by no means completely alienated from the *studia humanitatis et eloquentiae,* but he set clear limits to the value of its program.

Thus, one result of Argyropulos's teaching in Florence seems to have been to foster a set of attitudes toward the relationship between rhetorical culture and learning in philosophy which contrasted sharply with the views of Petrarch and Bruni but which calls to mind a current of late fifteenth-century thinking that is becoming increasingly well known and appreciated. Notions similar to those of Argyropulos and his students appear in an early letter of Ficino's, published by Professor Kristeller, in which Ficino spoke of the need to forsake a popular style in favor of the strict language of philosophy. One thinks, too, of Pico's famous letter of 1485 to Ermolao Barbaro, in which the defense of scholastic learning leads to this statement: "The barbarians have had the god of eloquence not on the tongue, but in the heart; . . . if eloquence they lacked they did not lack wisdom; . . . eloquence should not have been joined to wisdom; only their not being joined perhaps is free from fault, so that it were wicked to join them."[51] The call for the union of eloquence and wisdom, the combination of rhetoric and

---

[50] "In dialectica autem et philosophia, tum etiam sacrarum litterarum peritia clarissimos viros enumerare longissimum esset. Talium enim disciplinarum studia, quo magis ad bene beateque vivendum sunt necessaria, eo magis apud quasque gentes quacunque aetate nunquam intermissa viguerunt, unde etiam effectum est ut superioribus quoque temporibus ad summam perducta subtilitatem, plurimis iisdemque doctissimis hominibus abundarent. In quo genere virum unum praestantissimum Iohannem Argyropylum praeceptorem meum silentio praeterire non potui. . . ." (*Ibid.,* p. 107). For other evidence of a scholastic influence in Rinuccini, see Giustiniani, *Alamanno Rinuccini,* pp. 184-186.

[51] See the letter of Ficino (ed. A. Perosa and Professor Kristeller) in Kristeller's *Studies,* p. 146; the statement of Pico in his letter to Barbaro, tr. Quirinus Breen, in *Journal of the History of Ideas,* XIII (1952), 395. Cf. also the reference to Pontano in Kristeller, *Studies,* p. 573n. Rinuccini should not be too closely associated with the circle around Ficino, however: see Giustiniani, pp. 263-264.

philosophy, was at the very heart of the humanism of the early Quattrocento. The suspicion with which men of the later fifteenth century approached this slogan is a clear indication that they felt their intellectual interests and standards to be significantly different from those of men like Bruni.

However great may have been the achievements of the Quattrocento, they did not all proceed from a single unitary spirit, nor did they all presuppose a rejection of what medieval thinkers had done. Some leaders of fifteenth-century intellectual life proclaimed their opposition to scholasticism, but other equally important representatives of Renaissance thinking found that their deepest interests led them to a rapprochement with the philosophic culture of the Middle Ages. Historians have been too eager to view Renaissance culture as a unified whole. Behind the slogan of the revival of antiquity a number of different and sometimes opposing currents can be found. We must become sensitive to these contrasts and oppositions if we are to understand the richness and complexity of Renaissance cultural life.

*Appendix*

The text of Argyropulos's preface given below is that found in a codex of the Medici Library, Florence, Laur. Plut. 71, 18. This seems to be the dedication copy of the translation. In addition, two other manuscripts of the preface have been consulted: Magb. II, ii, 52 (Biblioteca Nazionale Centrale, Florence), and Ariostea II, 138 (Biblioteca Comunale Ariostea, Ferrara). The latter two codices contain nearly identical texts, with a number of variations (for the most part quite unimportant) from that in the Laurenziana ($=L$). I have indicated in the notes all the variations in the first of the latter two ($=N$) and all those in the second ($=F$) which seem at all worth noting. I have not indicated certain variations in spelling (such as *michi* for *mihi*) or differences in paragraphing. The Milanese codex, Ambrosiana L 84 sup (noted by E. Franceschini, "L' 'Aristotele Latino' nei codici dell' Ambrosiana," *Miscellanea Giovanni Galbiati*, III [Milan, 1951], 240), does not contain this preface. I have not examined the manuscript at Naples, Biblioteca Nazionale, VII, E, 13 (described by Kristeller, *Iter Italicum*, I, 404).

PRAEFATIO IOHANNIS ARGYROPYLI CONSTANTINOPOLITANI AD CLARISSIMUM AC PRAESTANTISSIMUM VIRUM

## PETRUM MEDICEM IN LIBROS ARISTOTELIS DE INTER-PRETATIONE ET GENERATIONE RATIOCINATIONIS[1]

## IOHANNES ARGYROPYLUS[2] NOBILISSIMO ATQUE DOCTIS-SIMO VIRO PETRO MEDICI INCOLUMITATEM BONAM FORTUNAM PERPETUAM QUE FOELICITATEM.[3]

INSTITUI NOBILISSIME atque doctissime petre nonnullos aristotelis libros elegantius in latinam linguam traducere. Nam id quidem[4] et aristoteli ipsi[5] si quis est ei[6] sensus pergratum sane videbitur si qualem sese apud suos voluit esse talem et apud latinos tandem[7] viderit evasisse. Et his[8] quorum ista est lingua non inutile fuerit ut existimo quippe cum facilior illo pacto perceptio philosophie [*sic*] fieri possit atque iis tandem verbis eoque stilo que neque ab elegantia latinae linguae prorsus[9] abhorreant, et dignitatem aliquam philosophiae redoleant.

Accessit eodem et meus erga te vehementissimus amor qui me coegit ac impulit hanc[10] omnino provinciam aggredi tametsi haud[11] facilis est, neque ultro sese omnibus offerre videtur. Etenim cum saepe mecum cogitarem quidnam a me tibi gratum iocundumve fieri posset, quod ad[12] utriusque nostrum conditionem dignitatemve prope accederit,[13] id mihi in mentem venit, ut a me tibi tales aristotelis libri[14] quales iam dixeram[15] et abs te tuis civibus reliquisve[16] hominum[17] largiantur.[18] Oratorum enim quorundam libellos in latinam vertere linguam atque illos tibi largiri quanquam[19] id quidem haud despiciendum munus videtur, non tamen meam erga te benivolentiam egregiumque amorem quantus est potuisset unquam ostendere; nec utriusque nostrum ut arbitror unquam dignitatem servasset. Nam et facile admodum illud fieri potest, fitque ut scis a quibusvis saepius, et ad sententias vulgaris

---

[1] IOANNIS ARGIROPILI BISANZII AD NOBILISSIMUM ATQUE DOCTISSIMUM PETRUM MEDICEM FLORENTINUM IN LIBROS ARISTOTELIS DE INTERPETRATIONE [sic] AC DE RACIOCINATIONIS ORTU PER EUM E GRECO [E GRECO added in margin] IN LATINUM TRADUCTOS PRAEFATIO—*N.*

[2] Ioannes Argiropilus Byzantius—*N and F (with different spelling).*
[3] Felicitatem—*N and F.*          [4] Nam hoc ipsum—*N and F.*
[5] Ipsi—*missing in N and F.*        [6] Ei—*missing in N and F.*
[7] Se tandem—*N and F.*        [8] Iisce—*N and F.*
[9] Prorsus—*missing in N and F.*        [10] Hanc—*missing in N.*
[11] *N and F have* non *for* haud.
[12] *N has* quoad *for* quod ad.; *F has only* quod.
[13] Accideret—*N and F.*    [14] Libris—*N.*          [15] Dixerim—*N.*
[16] Reliquis ut—*N.*    [17] *F has* hominibus *for* hominum.
[18] Offerantur—*N and F.*    [19] Quamquam—*N.*

humique ut ita dicam[20] serpentes tuum eximium altissimumque animum invitare inepti sane parci sordidique[21] nimium esset. Praeterea illis quidem non tanta comitatur utilitas philosophiae sententiis cum auctoritate tum ipsium tum etiam aristotelis grandis eadem immo vero summa coniungitur.[22] Ex quo quid evenire possit tu te ipse considera. Neminem esse profecto foreque arbitror qui non oratorum quorumvis erudimentis neglectis atque posthabitis ad archana[23] philosophiae sententiasque persubtiles aristotelis elegantius explicatas illustratasve summa cum aviditate proficiscatur. Erit enim perinde ac si ad virtutes foelicitatemve[24] via facilis brevisque admodum patefacta fuisset. Nam uti tum nemo ferme esset qui non libentius patefactum illud arriperet iter, sic nullus[25] haud hac via regia ad aedes philosophiae sacraque perget, nisi quispiam fortasse per devia spinosaque loca ad eadem maluerit proficisci, quod quidem[26] nemo unquam sane faciet mentis. Hoc igitur tua nobilitate tuaque doctrina dignum fore arbitror a me ipso donum,[27] ex quo[28] quidem non tibi ipsi solum, sed per te etiam ipsum tuis civibus[29] pro quibus vivere cupis id quod a praeclarissimo ac sapientissimo patre quem rei totius huiusce publicae lumen splendidissimum[30] esse constat, tanquam praeclaram quandam hereditatem accipere servareque instituisti, reliquisve hominibus fructus non mediocris accedere potest.[31] Quod cum comparare[32] cepissem libellum hunc primum peractum quem[33] de interpretatione[34] consueverunt ipsi peripatetici vocitare ac primam partem priorum quam de origine compositioneque[35] ratiocinationis esse constat ad te statim tanquam degustationem quandam nostri huiusce studii laborisve misi.

---

[20] Dixerim—*F.*  [21] Sordique—*N.*

[22] *In N this sentence reads*: Praeterea illos quidem non tanta comitatur utilitas, cum philosophiae non sententiis auctoritateve tum ipsium tum etiam Aristotelis grandis eadem immo vero summa coniungitur. *In F*: Praeterea illos quidem non tanta comitatur utilitas. [¶] Cum philosophiae vero sententiis auctoritateve tum ipsius tum etiam aristotelis grandis eadem immo vero summa coniungitur. *Accepting the text in L, I would translate the sentence as follows*: Furthermore, such books have less utility than the teachings of philosophy, although both on the authority of [orators] themselves and on that of Aristotle, their utility is related to that same great—I would say highest—utility [of philosophy].

[23] Arcana—*N*; Rcana—*F.*  [24] Felicitatemve—*N and F.*
[25] Nunc nullus—*N and F.*  [26] Quidem—*missing in N.*
[27] Domum—*N.*  [28] A quo—*N and F.*  [29] Avibus—*N.*
[30] Splendidum—*N.*
[31] Fructus provenire non mediocris atque commoditas potest—*N and F.*
[32] Facere—*F.*  [33] Quem quidem—*N and F.*  [34] Interpetratione—*N.*
[35] De ortu compositioneve—*N and F.*

Hos utrosque libellos in ea qua primo conscripti sunt lingua difficiles esse cognitu scitur. Primus tamen longe difficilior est, quem de interpretatione[36] dicimus esse.[37] Nempe is[38] adeo cognitu difficilis est non tam materiei causa suae quam dicendi modo; quo quidem nescio cur in lucem hunc tam obscurum efferre philosophus voluit, ut difficultatis exemplar ipsius[39] cunctis atque ratio videatur. Hi quales in latinam linguam[40] tua causa nunc evasere legendo tu te ipse percipies. Quid enim ad te dicenda sunt singula qui non solum ea percipere per te ipsum facile sed iudicare etiam peroptime[41] potes?

Hoc scias solum tantum his attributum a me[42] concinnitatis atque[43] elegantiae esse quantum philosophia materies[44] atque ipsi termini patiuntur. Non enim his[45] in rebus pervagari[46] nimium licet, nec amplus[47] ad dicendum campus conceditur. Preterea exemplis lineamentis figuris terminis denique quibus antea prorsus[48] carebant interpuncti ac[49] illustrati admodum[50] sunt ut his etiam facilior eorum perceptio fieri possit. Tu igitur clarissime vir hosce accipe atque lege;[51] ceterosque expecta. Nullum enim mediusfidius ipse laborem unquam dehinc recusabo, modo ut aliquid[52] per illum foelicitati[53] tuae non dicam addatur (quid enim unquam addi perfectio potest?)[54] sed subministretur,[55] quo magis in actu sit,[56] ac nullo unquam fato discrimineve ab hominum memoria dilabatur. Quam cum considero[57] saepe autem id facere soleo eo mihi magis colenda observandaque videtur,[58] quo ab vulgari fucataque recedit, atque ad paternam beatitudinem propius[59] videtur accedere, quae quidem non solum civilem elegantissime[60] sed contemplativam etiam illam unquam[61] altiorem complectitur vitam. Vale perpetuo foelix atque beatus.

---

[36] Interpetratione—*N.*    [37] Esse—*missing in N.*    [38] Hic—*N and F.*

[39] Ipsius difficultatis exemplar—*N and F.*    [40] In latina lingua—*N and F.*

[41] Iudicare optime—*N;* iudicare etiam optime—*F.*

[42] A me tributum—*N and F.*    [43] Et—*N and F.*    [44] Et materies—*N and F.*

[45] Iis—*N.*    [46] Vagari—*N and F.*    [47] Amplius—*N.*

[48] Prorsus—*missing in N and F.*    [49] Atque—*N.*    [50] Adeo—*N and F.*

[51] Accipe igitur clarissime vir hosce libros et perlege—*N and F.*

[52] Aliquid modo—*N and F.*    [53] Felicitati—*N.*

[54] ? *missing in N and F; F has* potes *for* potest.    [55] Subministratur—*N.*

[56] Quo magis persistat—*N and F.*

[57] Quae quidem cum ea considero—*N and F; but F has* eam *for* ea.

[58] Colenda esse videtur—*N and F.*    [59] Proprius—*N.*

[60] Elegantissime—*missing in N and F.*    [61] Inquam—*N and F.*

IOHANNIS ARGYROPYLI CONSTANTINOPOLITANI PRAEFATIO EXPLICIT AD CLARISSIMUM AC PRAE-STANTISSIMUM VIRUM PETRUM MEDICEM IN LIBROS ARISTOTELIS DE INTERPRETATIONE ET GENERA-TIONE RACIOCINATIONIS.[62]

[62] *Colophon missing in N. F has only* Explicit prefatio.

# TALENT AND VOCATION IN HUMANIST
# AND PROTESTANT THOUGHT*

### RICHARD M. DOUGLAS

## I

THERE is a remarkable difference between the language which Erasmus used in describing the selection of his career as a scholar and the vocabulary in which Calvin recalled his vocation to the ministry at Geneva. Erasmus described the deliberate human choice of a particular way of life (*genus vitae*) and the private determination of a career consistent with his own nature, aptitude, and constitution. Calvin described a calling (*vocatio*) from God, mediated through men according to God's will, but against his own nature and inclination. Erasmus argued from the irreversibility of his own unique character, Calvin from the irresistibility of a divine command.

This contrast represents a consistent difference between humanist and Protestant attitudes toward self-definition and toward such related issues as the right understanding of human work or vocation. The difference, in its several variations, was expressed in two distinctive vocabularies: one derived from classical treatises on ethics, pedagogy, and medicine; the other derived from Scripture. Whereas the humanists tended to argue that the individual's life-style, or *genus vitae*, should be selected according to inborn aptitude, the reformers insisted that one's calling, or *vocatio*, should be understood as a divine command. The contrast therefore rests on the difference between the humanists' *eligere* and the reformers' *vocari*—between choosing and being called.

While claiming that the individual should define his work and place in the world in conformity with his inherent capacities (*ingenium, natura, indolens, solertia, aptitudo, inclinatio, facultas, complexio corporis*), the humanists implicitly defended a principle of utility resting upon the belief that the welfare of the commonweal depends upon the existence of self-determined members, each of whom

* This essay elaborates a brief article, "*Genus vitae* and *Vocatio*: Ideas of Work and Vocation in Humanist and Protestant Usage," in Comité international des sciences historiques, *XIIᵉ Congrès International des Sciences Historiques. Rapports*, vol. III: *Commissions* (Vienna, 1965), pp. 75-86.

has chosen the course of life which best suits him or which he most enjoys pursuing. The sixteenth-century reformers, on the other hand, explained vocation as the office or station in which God has placed us in the orders of creation or to which God has assigned us for the service of others through love.

The radicalism of Luther's interpretation of vocation lay in his extension of *Beruf* equally to every calling or office. Yet in denying the exclusive claim of a vocation to the clergy, he also denied the subjective choice of one's calling to the Christian layman and pastor alike. "A Christian does not select what he will do." "Regardless of the lives and examples of the saints, every one should await what is commanded of him and take heed of his calling."[1] In Luther's theological formulation of the issue, the determination of one's proper office or place belongs not to man but to God.

Calvin took the same position. In one of the few passages of autobiography which he permitted himself,[2] Calvin said that it was neither his father's will nor his own preference which finally determined the course of his life. Although he portrayed himself as a timid and retiring man who preferred privacy to the disorder and contentions of public life, his vocation—as Professor Harbison once pointed out— was inescapably to the church in Geneva, with Farel serving as God's agent at one time and Bucer at another in overcoming his natural disposition toward study:

Being by nature a bit anti-social and shy, I always loved retirement and peace, and I began to look for some hide-out where I could be away from people; but far from gaining my desire, every retreat and hide-away became like a public school to me. In short, although my aim was always to live a private life without being known, God

[1] *Kirchenpostille* (1522), Weimar edition (henceforth cited as WA), *D. Martin Luthers Werke* X:1, 1, 306; XVII:2, 37; Gustav Wingren, *Luther on Vocation*, tr. Carl C. Rasmussen (Philadelphia, 1957), p. 179; F. Edward Cranz, *An Essay on the Development of Luther's Thought on Justice, Law and Society* (Cambridge, 1959), pp. 157-158; Ruth Hinz, "Der Berufsgedanke bei Luther nach dem heutigen Stande der Forschung," *Luther. Mitteilungen der Luthergesellschaft.* (1961), Heft 2, pp. 84-94; Helmut Gatzen, *Beruf bei Martin Luther und in der industriellen Gesellschaft.* Inaugural Diss. (Westfälische Wilhelmsuniversität at Münster, 1964).

[2] Notably his *Commentary on the Book of Psalms* (1557), in *Ioannis Calvini opera quae supersunt omnia*, ed. Wilhelm Braun et al. (Brunswick/Berlin, 1863-1900), vol. 31, pp. 22-24; and his *Response to Sadoleto, ibid.*, vol. 5, pp. 386-387, 411-413.

has so taken me about and whirled me around by various vicissitudes that he has never let me rest anywhere, but in spite of my
natural inclination (*repugnante ingenio*; *maugré mon nature*), he
has thrust me into the limelight and made me "get into the game,"
as they say.[3]

Because his ministry was commanded by the calling (*vocatio*) of God,
Calvin renounced the chosen *genus vitae* of his earlier life. By necessity the adult pastor repudiated the youthful humanist: "I dared not
throw off the yoke of my calling," he admitted to Farel in 1538, "which I
was well assured had been laid on me by the Lord." "I considered myself
placed in that station [Geneva] by God, like a sentinel at his post. . . ."[4]
Temporal vocation is a command of God placed on the Christian from
the outside, to be used for the employment of God rather than for the
enjoyment of the individual. The governance of God's creation requires that each of its members occupy himself to "fulfill the occupation
to which he has been appointed," since "God has assigned to each his
station and function within the body."[5] The variety of gifts which God
has conferred is a distinction so intended that each should use his
portion, not for himself, but in reciprocity with others.[6]

This form of the organic analogy also appears from time to time in
Erasmus's treatises on education and polity. The welfare of society,
Erasmus wrote, requires that each citizen have his own place, performing his own particular duties in it.[7] Erasmus likewise described the
gifts of God as a distribution serving the good of the whole body.[8]
But, in drawing such theory to his own use, he was quick to add that,
if the commonweal is to be well served, the right use of one's distinc-

[3] E. Harris Harbison, *The Christian Scholar in the Age of the Reformation*
(New York, 1956), p. 142.
[4] *Commentary upon the Acts of the Apostles* (1552-1554), ed. Henry Beveridge
(Grand Rapids, 1957), I, 253.
[5] John Calvin, *Letters*, ed. Jules Bonnet and tr. David Constable, 2 vols. (Edinburgh, 1855-1857), I, 186, 241. Also: "Hace igitur optima vitae ratio, dum
unusquisque vocationis suae officiis intentus, exsequitur quae sibi a Domino
mandata sunt, et in iis se occupat . . ." (*Commentary on Thessalonians* 4: 11,
*Calvini opera*, vol. 52, p. 163; see also vol. 49, pp. 367, 415).
[6] *Commentary on the Epistles of Paul the Apostle to the Corinthians* (Grand
Rapids, 1948), I, 404 (I Cor. 12:12).
[7] E.g., *Institutio principis christiani*, tr. Lester K. Born (New York, 1936),
pp. 235ff.; see also pp. 110, 127.
[8] *Opus Epistolarum Des. Erasmi Roterodami*, ed. P. S. Allen and H. M. Allen,
12 vols. (Oxford, 1906-1958), III, no. 985, 611.

tive gifts or talents (*talenti*) must depend upon right knowledge of oneself and the choice of a *genus vitae* which befits one's nature and constitution. In his long and undisguised autobiographical letter to Lambertus Grunnius, in which he pleaded for papal dispensations from his youthful vows, Erasmus established that justification of his own life which became the recurrent defense of his cherished autonomy:

> For my own part I do not care to find fault with anyone's plan of life (*institutum*); neither will I defend those, who, having heedlessly thrown themselves into the ditch, turn bad into worse by taking refuge, not in liberty, but in a license of sinning. There is, however, so great a variety in men's bodies and minds (*tanta corporum et ingeniorum varietate*), that the same conditions do not suit everybody; and no more unhappy fate can befall people of signal ability, than to be inveigled or forced into a kind of life (*vitae genus*), from which they cannot extricate themselves. For human happiness depends mainly on this, that every one should apply himself to that for which he is naturally fitted (*quod natura compositus est*).[9]

The orphaned victim of the fictional account, Florentius, though "born for literature," was coerced and betrayed into a false vocation by his guardians, despite a delicate "constitution" and a "character" wholly unsuited for the monastery. Instead of being permitted to choose his own way of life, in the knowledge that Christ dwells everywhere, he was refused his liberty by oppressive superiors who tried to keep him in "servitude."

Erasmus remembered himself in his early years as one driven to literature by "some secret natural impulse," though prevented long and unjustly from achieving mastery of his own life.[10] And all that familiar fondness for children and compassion for the trials of adolescence seemed poignantly connected with his own sense of struggle for independence and for the achievement of freedom in that style of life which alone appeared to befit his temperament.[11] Equally familiar is the candor of the portrait Erasmus habitually offered of

[9] *Ibid.*, II, no. 447 (1516), 294; *The Epistles of D. Erasmus*, tr. F. M. Nichols, 3 vols. (London, 1901-1918), II, 340.

[10] *Opus Epistolarum*, I, no. 1 (1523), 1f.

[11] "Ego nullum vitae genus unquam damnavi, sed non omne vitae genus cuius convenit. Mihi certe nullum vitae genus minus conveniebat, siue corpus

himself as a cautious, obedient man—no candidate for martyrdom—
unsuited for any role of conflict, and as by nature a spectator, unable
to be or to do otherwise.[12]

Nevertheless, Erasmus claimed the right to choose for himself precisely the same kind of career which Calvin reportedly denied himself. Whereas Erasmus repudiated his vows in order to follow his own
nature, Calvin denied his own disposition in order to accept an alien
vocation. It is our fate to be at the mercy of their words. Erasmus's were
preeminently secular, at times vaguely naturalistic. His vocabulary
of self-knowledge belonged to the tradition of Cicero and the later
Stoics, certainly not to that of St. Paul. It pointed ahead to Montaigne's
statement that "My business is to shape my life," or that every life in
turn is directed by a *forme maîtresse*, a pattern all its own, since "the
greatest thing in the world is to know how to belong to oneself."[13] It
also anticipated Charron's neo-Stoic injunction: "*prendre une vocation
à laquelle on soit propre; c'est-à-dire que son naturel particulier
s'accomode, et s'applique volontiers.*"[14]

In its own time, however, Erasmus's defense of his chosen *vitae
genus* was by no means either original or idiosyncratic; his claims to
self-determination merely repeated a set of arguments and attitudes
already long established in Italian humanism. Erasmus inherited—he
certainly did not contrive or invent—a vocabulary of self-knowledge
and secular vocation at least as old as the generation of Petrarch, who
seems to have been original—once again—in his efforts to recover the
Stoic doctrine of inherent aptitude and disposition.

## II

In one of his letters to classical authors, Petrarch reminded Quintilian
that "a man's intellectual powers are not equally suited for development in all directions, but . . . will evince a special degree of qualification in one only."[15] For Petrarch, it is man's fate to accept the condi-

---

spectasses siue animum, quam hoc in quod protrussus fueram. Denique finget
me qui volet, adolescentem quaesisse libertatem quacunque via, quum servitutem
numquam ex animo probassem, cuius erat humanitatis hoc libris euulgare?"
(*Ibid.*, V, no. 1436 [1524], 430.)

[12] *Ibid.*, V, no. 1342, 221, 227.

[13] *Essais*, vol. II, ch. 17; vol. III, ch. 1; vol. I, ch. 39.

[14] *De la sagesse*, ed. Amaury Duval, 3 vols. (Paris, 1820), I, Bk. II, ch. 4, 111.

[15] *Petrarch's Letters to Classical Authors*, tr. Mario Emilio Cosenza (Chicago,
1910), Fam. XXIV, 7, p. 87. Cf. Quintilian, *Institutio oratoria*, II, viii.

tion of his own nature (*ingenii . . . sortem*), measuring his literary style to his ability and inclinations just as he measures his clothes to his body.[16] What matters most is not one's experiences of *fortuna* or the station he inherits, but rather the *ingenium* which is naturally peculiar to him. Therefore, "Let each man decide according to his preference, for it is impossible, that it should suit all men to follow a single road in life, even if they were all bound for the same ultimate destination. In this connection each man must seriously take into account the disposition with which nature has endowed him and the bent which by habit or training he has developed."[17]

In taking this position, Petrarch stood far closer to classical pedagogy than to medieval theology. This is not to say that the puzzle of human variety was ignored in medieval thought, but rather that the mode of explanation followed neither the physiology of Galenic tradition nor any of those differential psychologies to be found in Plato, Aristotle, Isocrates, Quintilian, Seneca, Plutarch, or Cicero. Paul Meissner has pointed out that medieval doctrines of human variability, like medieval pedagogies, display no real sense of childhood—an attitude not so much of hostility as of indifference toward the various stages or ages of human growth.[18] Although the idea of individual *ingenium* sometimes appears in the rare autobiographical passages of medieval literature, it is neither elaborated nor examined for its own sake. Despite the mystics' metaphors of the ladder or the road to beatitude, the medieval sense of individual life and biography limited the concept of process and growth to spiritual perfection or to Augustine's idea of progress from knowledge to wisdom. There was no serious concern with the possibility that each life has its own history, developing through time as the result of secular choices and decisions.

Abelard, in one short statement, described his early aptitude for letters and portrayed himself as one "light of heart" through "the

---

[16] Fam. XXIII, 22.

[17] ". . . nos de nobis libret unusquisque quid praeferat impossible est enim, et si unum omnes finem ultimum intendamus, ut unam omnibus vitae viam expediat sequi. Qua in re, cuique acriter cogitandum erit, qualem eum natura, qualem ipse se fecerit" (*De vita solitaria*, ed. Antonio Altamura [Naples, 1943], Bk. I, tract. 3, ch. 4).

[18] Paul Meissner, *England im Zeitalter von Humanismus, Renaissance und Reformation* (Heidelberg, 1952), p. 253. See also Philippe Ariés, *Centuries of Childhood: A Social History of Family Life*, tr. Robert Baldick (New York, 1962), pp. 10, 33-47, 128f., 262-268, and E. Garin, *L'Educazione in Europa. 1400-1600* (Bari, 1957), pp. 21-23.

nature of the soil or of my blood," recalling his decision to abandon a soldier's career for a scholar's.[19] Hugh of St. Victor condemned those who have "natural ability" for pious scholarship but fail to use it, while recognizing the problem of weighing the importance of talent (*ingenium*) and training (*exercitum*) in education.[20] By *ingenium* John of Salisbury understood "an immanent power infused into one's soul by nature," evoking the initial activity of the soul in its investigations.[21] His contemporary, Theophilus Presbyter, the Benedictine Roger of Halmarshausen, wrote a treatise *On Divers Arts* which examines the place of ingenuity (*sollertia*) in human achievement. But he warned that one who has such skill must not glorify himself "as though it had been achieved from himself and not from elsewhere. Let him know instead that such skills are the gifts of God."[22]

The theology of the seven gifts of the Holy Spirit, drawn principally from Isaiah 11:2-3,[23] was steadily built up in a number of treatises during the twelfth century, but it was Hugh of St. Victor who first related the gifts of God to the supernatural virtues. Such gifts, "differing according to the grace that is given to us," as Paul put it, are to be understood as divine inspirations infused into the creature, who is thus enabled to receive the graces of God. And all the perfections of man are to be considered divine gifts bestowed only on the righteous, even though they are perfected in the natural order.[24] As St. Thomas pointed out, both the supernatural virtues and the gifts are imparted by God to man, but the gifts differ from the virtues in that their formal reason for being is to prepare for the reception of grace.

Petrarch's interpretation of *ingenium* is as far from the theology of the seven gifts of God as it is from the organic analogy of Pauline and

[19] *The Letters of Abelard and Heloise*, tr. C. K. Scott Moncrieff (New York, 1926), p. 3.
[20] *The Didascalicon of John of Salisbury*, tr. Jerome Taylor (New York, 1961), p. 90.
[21] *Metalogicon*, vol. I, ch. 11, in Migne, *Pat. lat.*, vol. 199 (Paris, 1900), cols. 835ff. Edgar Zilsel erroneously claimed in *Die Entstehung des Geniebegriffes* (Tübingen, 1926), pp. 251-252, that *ingenium* never meant "inborn talent" or "ability" in medieval usage. But this is precisely what *natura* and *ingenium* signify in the *Metalogicon*.
[22] Theophilus, *On Divers Arts*, tr. John G. Hawthorne and Cyril Stanley Smith (Chicago, 1963), pp. 11-13.
[23] Also from Romans 12:3-6 and I Cor. 12:12-31.
[24] Theophilus, *The Various Arts*, tr. C. R. Dodwell (London, 1961), pp. x, xx-xxxiii; and A. Dardeil, "Dons du Saint-Esprit," in *Dictionnaire de Théologie catholique*, ed. A. Vacant, vol. IV, cols. 1728-81.

medieval social theory. The metaphor likening the medieval social order to the human body was used to support a corporate doctrine of commonwealth and reciprocity which emphasized the interdependence of all men and the necessity that each remain in his appointed place.[25] The social order, like the Church, was to be seen as God's design, and not as the creation of atomistic choices. Each *officium*—meaning both "office" and "duty"—was therefore defined with reference to the whole. Hence, the melancholy which Augustine found in Petrarch is treated in the *Secretum* as the spiritual anguish of one trying to live a life of his own, seeking fame instead of virtue and private good instead of his neighbor's. Augustine attempts to persuade Petrarch that happiness or beatitude comes through self-denial, and not through private strategies of self-fulfillment.[26] But to this admonition Petrarch replies, at the end of the dialogue, "I have not the strength to resist that old inclination for study altogether." The dramatic conflict of the *Secretum* develops from disagreement on how much freedom the Christian has in the pursuit or enjoyment of secular goals and whether in fact he is, or ought to be, free to select his own *genus vitae*.

Petrarch's position in the *De vita solitaria* is quite different. Here he tenaciously insisted that, although a man cannot determine his *natura*, he must discover it and then select the manner of life and work most congruent with it. Petrarch's was the familiar injunction of the later Stoics "to live according to one's nature." The defense of learned solitude in the quiet of Vaucluse was the defense of a personal choice by one without aptitude or taste for public office and by one who sought to belong to himself, honoring the counsel of the philosophers that each man cultivate "what is his own" (*quid suum sit*).[27]

[25] For discussion of the organic analogy, and the doctrine of distributive justice, see *Dictionnaire de Théologie catholique*, vol. VIII:2, cols. 2011-12; Wilhelm Schwer, *Stand und Ständeordnung im Weltbild des Mittelalters: Die geistes- und gesellschaftgeschichtlichen Grundlagen der Berufständischen Idee*, 2nd edn. (Paderborn, 1952), pp. 36, 71-72; and Ernst Troeltsch, *The Social Teaching of the Christian Churches*, tr. Olive Wyon (New York, 1931), II, 392-395.

[26] *Petrarch's Secret*, tr. William H. Draper (London, 1911), Dialogue II, p. 103.

[27] *De vita solitaria*, ed. Altamura, Bk. I, tract. 6, ch. 1; tract. 4, ch. 1. Cf. Plutarch, *De tranquilitate animae*, in *Moralia*, ed. William W. Goodwin, 6th edn. (Boston, 1898), I, ch. 13, 154-156; and Seneca, *Epistolae morales*, nos. XLI and LXXXVIII, for their treatment of *natura, indoles naturalis*, and *ingenium*. Plato's doctrine on natural gifts is in the *Republic*, II 370; V 455; VI 491; VII 519, 535. For further analysis of Greek ideas of *physis*, see A. O. Lovejoy et al., *A Documentary History of Primitivism and Related Ideas* (Baltimore, 1935), I, 104, 187, 447.

It were an excellent thing, if want of counsel, the unavoidable concomitant of youth, did not stand in the way, that each one of us at the very beginning of his maturity should give careful and earnest thought to the selection (*elegisset*) of some particular kind of life (*vitae genus*), nor ever turn aside from the path he had chosen, except for important reasons or for some grave necessity. Hercules did so on entering manhood, as is testified by Xenophon . . . and by Cicero. But because we fail to do it and live in most cases not by our own judgment but by that of the crowd, and are rushed along over tortuous paths, following the footsteps of others in the dark, we often emerge upon perilous and impassable roads and are carried so far that we have become something or other before we have had a chance to look about and consider what we wanted to be. . . . In every well-ordered plan for reforming one's life it is especially important to keep in view that we are to be guided not by idle wishes but by our character and disposition, and that we are to follow not the road which looks most attractive but the one which is most suitable (*aptissima*) to us. . . . One admonition that I have derived from the philosophers is that each man should note the relation between his own character and habits, and cultivate that which is proper to himself.[28]

The language of these passages shows a striking resemblance to the treatment of human diversity and the variability of human gifts in the *De officiis*,[29] as well as to the argument and idiom of Erasmus. "Everybody," said Cicero, "must resolutely hold fast to his own particular gifts. . . . For we must so act as not to oppose the universal laws of human nature, but, while safeguarding those, to follow the bent of our own peculiar nature." The purpose of every life should be the achievement of an inner consistency or constancy, refusing the imitation of others and of all that is alien to the self, lest inborn nature be corrupted.[30] It is, in fact, "each man's duty to weigh well what are his own peculiar traits of character" and to make a "proper estimate of his own natural ability (*ingenium*)."

Cicero was no less convinced of the duty of the individual to determine the role (*personam*) he takes by his own free and deliberate choice (*nostra voluntate*).[31] We "must decide who and what manner

[28] *De vita solitaria*, Bk. I, tract. 4, ch. 1.
[29] Cicero, *De officiis*, ed. Walter Miller (London/New York, 1921), Loeb Classical Lib., Bk. I, chs. xxx-xxxiv.
[30] *Ibid.*, p. 114.  [31] *Ibid.*, p. 116-118.

of men we wish to be and what calling (*genus vitae*) in life we would follow; and this is the most difficult decision (*deliberatio*) of all." But let it be Nature, not Fortune, which is first consulted in the choice of the individual's mode of life; let him abide by his choice, unless he has made a mistake. If he does find himself in error, as he well might, then he must choose anew. By necessity, "it is in the years of early youth, when our judgment is most immature, that each of us settles upon the manner of life he will live according to what he likes best."[32] The Latin of Petrarch, Salutati, and Erasmus, making the same point, is often identical to Cicero's.[33]

Cicero, of course, was far more concerned than Petrarch with the relation of the individual to the commonweal and with the alignment of the interest and choices of individuals with the welfare of the body politic.[34] Yet "we are not required to sacrifice our own interest and surrender to others what we need for ourselves, but each should consider his own interests, as far as he may without injury to others." We are not strangers in the world, nor is self-denial our duty in it.

For Boccaccio, however, it was not so much a matter of choosing one's place in the world as it was of discovering and accepting what Nature prescribes. In the *Genealogia deorum*, he said that "Nature . . . has produced mortal aptitudes for various offices, by whose variety she achieves the preservation of the human race . . . ," with the result that we are born for different functions determined by the will of God.[35] What we are and what we do have been established by an invincible necessity which distributes the aptitudes and duties of men in its own ultimate harmony. The argument here suggests the doctrine of distributive justice, asserting the right of each to enjoy the sphere of action which Nature marks out for him. No one may presume to do other than that for which he was born, in order that the natural medley of functions may be harmonious.

[32] *Ibid.*, p. 118. (My translation.)

[33] See e.g., Salutati to Giovanni Quartrario (1368): " . . . pubertatis ineuntis initium datum esse a natura ad eligendum quam quisque viam sit ingressus" (*Epistolario di Coluccio Salutati*, ed. F. Novati [Rome, 1891], I, 65). Cf. Petrarch, *De vita solitaria*, Bk. I, tract. 4, ch. 1; Cicero, *De officiis*, Bk. I, ch. xxxii.

[34] *De officiis*, Bk. II, 292ff. For the later reception of Cicero, see Hans Baron, "Cicero and the Roman Civic Spirit in the Middle Ages and the Early Renaissance," *Bulletin of the John Rylands Library*, XXII (1938), 72-97. See also E. Garin, *L'Umanesimo italiano. Filosofia e vita civile nel Rinascimento* (Bari, 1952).

[35] Bk. XV, ch. 10.

Speaking next of himself, Boccaccio said that he was born with a natural disposition to poetry. He remembered being driven by a powerful desire to write (*impellente natura fingendi desiderium*) even as a child,[36] turning out such inventions as his tender ability (*ingenium*) could achieve. If his father had encouraged this capacity while it was still young, "I do not doubt that I should have taken my place among poets of fame." Instead, his father—like Maffeo Vegio's[37]—tried to deflect his talents first to commerce and then to canon law, with the result that he failed as merchant, canonist, and poet alike. Nevertheless, "since I believe that I am called to this vocation by the will of God (*dei beneplacito me in hac vocatione vocatum*), I am determined to stand fast in it. . . . Let those who allow the cobbler his awl and bristles, the herdsman his flock, the sculptor his statues, leave me in peace to cultivate the poet." Like Ovid and Horace, Petrarch and Erasmus, Budé and Bembo, Boccaccio begged for leave to do what he could not avoid.[38] But the singularity of Boccaccio's defense was his willingness to describe poetry as his "vocation." This most secular poet was virtually unique in his use of a religious idiom to justify what Petrarch called his *genus vitae* and Ronsard his *mestier*.

The coercion of sons into unsuitable careers was attacked again in those humanist treatises on pedagogy which began to appear in the late fourteenth century; and in the works of Vergerio, Vittorino da Feltre, and Vegio can be found the first systematic attempts to relate nature to nurture in a general theory of education. This new humanist pedagogy—later elaborated by Vives, Ascham, Huarte, Montaigne, and Possevino—related the preliminary curriculum of liberal studies

[36] Cf. Erasmus: "a secret natural impulse (*occulta naturae vi*) compelled me to literature" (*Opus Epistolarum*, I, 2).

[37] *De educatione librorum* (1444), Bk. III, ch. 2.

[38] Ovid, *Tristia*, Bk. IV, chs. 9-10. Horace, *Satires*, Bk. II: ". . . whatever the color of my life, write I must." See also Ronsard's "A Pierre l'Escot" in *Oeuvres complètes*, ed. Prosper Blanchemain (Paris, 1886), pp. 188-189. Budé saw himself as one whose literary career had been impeded first by paternal disfavor and then by the necessity to support his family through service to Francis I as *maître des requetes* and *prevost des marchands*. The talent (*genium*) which Providence had given him, he told Erasmus, made it quite impossible either to please the king or to satisfy himself while he was attached to the court (*Opus Epistolarum*, II, 445). For other such complaints, see *Répertoire analytique et chronologique de la corréspondance de Guillaume Budé*, ed. Louis Delaruelle (Paris, 1907), nos. 26, 43, 48, 80, 87, 89, 109, 162. For Bembo's defense of his right to shape his own career, see *Lettere di M. Pietro Bembo Cardinale*, 4 vols. (Milan, 1810), I, 31, 64, 221, 250; IV, 43-49.

to the individual bent of mind and temperament in each student, so that his choice of a career might be made in harmony with his "natural disposition." Vergerio's *De ingenuis moribus* (1392) was a pedagogical manifesto to an urban aristocracy; and, although it expressed the principles of civic humanism and the *vita civile*, it also defended an ideal of education worthy of men free to make responsible choices in the selection of their places in the Italian city.[39] Vergerio examined the diversity of *ingenia*, not in the context of a preestablished system of estates, but in relation to a more fluid social order in which the world of the father was no longer assumed to be the world of the son.

Recognizing the perilous complexity of choices which the adolescent faces, in terms identical to Cicero's,[40] Vergerio was especially eager to protect those with literary promise from the vulgar and materialistic values of their families. What he especially deplored were the coercive decisions of parents who divert or ignore filial inclinations in order to impose their own. Here Vergerio juxtaposed the command (*imperium*) of parents with the choice (*electio*) or judgment (*arbitrium*) of sons,[41] praising his own father for having allowed him freely to choose a career of scholarship over the strong opposition of his kinsmen.

The dominant principle of Vergerio's theory of education in the *De ingenuis moribus et liberalibus studiis adulescentiae* is the urgency of discovering the natural capacities of children at an early age, preferably before ten, so that they may cultivate those studies and skills for which they are best suited.[42] Some minds are best able to pursue subjects requiring memory, while others incline to those more analytic and abstract; one kind of competence is most apt for natural science, another for politics, another for arms. It is significant, however, that, although Vergerio described a diversity of intelligence and tempera-

[39] E. Garin, *L'Educazione in Europa*, pp. 127-133; R. R. Bolgar, *The Classical Heritage and its Beneficiaries* (Cambridge, 1954), pp. 258-259.

[40] "Difficillima deliberatio, eademque maxime periculosa videtur michi, que in prima etate debetur homini . . ." (letter to Giovanni da Bologna, in *Epistolario di Piero Paolo Vergerio*, ed. Leonardo Smith [Rome, 1934], p. 131). Cf. Cicero: ". . . quae deliberatio est omnium dificillima. Ineunte enim adulescentia, cum est maxima imbecillitas consilii, tum id sibi quisque genus aetatis degendae constituit . . ." (*De officiis*, I, 117).

[41] *Epistolario*, p. 133. Cf. Epictetus, *Discourses*, Bk. I, ch. ii; Bk. III, ch. xv; and G. Pire, *Stoicisme et pédagogie* (Paris, 1958), pp. 132-135.

[42] William H. Woodward, *Vittorino da Feltre and Other Humanist Educators* (Cambridge, 1897), p. 202.

ment, he did not try to explain it. Although he occasionally used humoral theory to identify certain body types, such as those of soft and humid constitution which need to be "dried and hardened" by exercise, he conceded that he preferred to leave the interpretation of physiognomy to others. Vergerio, like Erasmus, was pragmatically willing to trust the recognition of natural inclinations to the intuition and experience of masters. As a teacher Vergerio was also a moralist, as scornful of the crowd as he was of the court,[43] convinced that human intelligence is the strongest resource of human freedom. It is a man's special acuity (*sollertia*), together with his free will, which makes it possible for him to control and direct his destiny. The teacher's great responsibility is to put the young in the possession of their innate powers. No doctrine could be further from the principle that each is to remain in the station to which God assigns him.

Bartolomeo Platina described Vittorino da Feltre as another accomplished *ingeniorum cultorem.*[44] As a young man of considerable promise, Vittorino abandoned the life of solitude in order to serve the commonweal as a teacher in Padua, Venice, and Mantua. Professor Woodward described him as one who "considered, almost with reverence, the tastes and bent of each of his pupils," adjusting subject and method within the curriculum to conform with demonstrated ability. Prendilacqua, also, recalled Vittorino's assertion that nature endows no one with aptitude for every kind of knowledge and withholds even several talents from all but a few; the schoolmaster's task, therefore, is not merely to instruct a boy but to discover the sources of his natural strength.[45] Thus, in the Vittorine Academy, every kind of knowledge, teaching, and skill was represented, according to Prendilacqua, for Vittorinio himself held every honorable *genus vitae* in high regard, asking only that each young student adopt the career most fitted to him, despite the fact that Vittorino himself was accomplished in every field of knowledge.

Platina praised Vittorino's Academy in the manner in which Cicero praised the school of Isocrates, from which, as from a Trojan horse, issued talented men without number.[46] Vittorino shared Isocrates's interest in impecunious scholars, as well as the curiosity of Isocrates

[43] *Epistolario*, no. LXXXXVII (1401).
[44] *Platiniae de vita Victorini Feltrensis commentariolus*, in *Il pensiero pedagogico dello umanesimo*, ed. E. Garin (Florence, 1958), p. 699.
[45] *Francesci Prendilacquae dialogus, ibid.*, p. 602; Woodward, *Vittorino*, p. 203.
[46] *Platiniae* in *Il pensiero pedagogico*, p. 693.

273

the physician about the diversity of natural dispositions. For both, as for Cicero, right education serves the common welfare of the city by cultivating the divers gifts of its members through a process which discovers the highest capacities of the man in the natural inclinations of the child. The ideals of humanist education are inseparable, as Eugenio Garin has suggested, from "a fond discovery of childhood" and of the teacher's vocation.[47] Maffeo Vegio repeated the admonition to parents and magistrates alike that they diligently direct each young citizen to the occupation to which nature inclines him, with the reminder to teachers that not all pupils are meant to be scholars; medicine, law, agriculture, arms, and the church, however, are all more honorable than trade.[48]

Behind the rhetoric of the humanist pedagogue, professor, and social critic often lies a voice of special pleading. Petrarch, Boccaccio, Vergerio, Vegio, More, Bembo, Budé, and scores of others confronted stern resistance to literary aspiration and the preference of the scholar's life in their kinsmen. General arguments from natural aptitude must be read in some measure as arguments against paternal coercion, and petitions for freedom in the choice of career as arguments against filial piety. The fact is, however, that the humanists did not stop with special pleading; beyond their rhetoric of rationalization they developed an ideal of freedom for the educated man in the art or profession most suited to his nature.

The Alberti, despite their passionate sense of family and common economic interest, did their best, according to Leon Battista, to favor the individual aptitudes of their sons and were as eager as the humanist tutors to discover the native abilities of each. They did so not only out of high-mindedness but also because they regarded proper education and *ingegno* or *virtù* as the only reliable defense against adverse fortune in defending the interests of a family.[49] In the dialogue *Della famiglia*, the pessimistic Adovardo d'Alberti recalls the solicitude of his ancestors in selecting those forms of skill and knowledge and that mode of life most appropriate to the nature of each son. Such decisions, to be sure, were also affected by other considerations, such as the good repute of the family, circumstances of time, and the expectations of other citizens. But above all, as the oracle of Apollo counseled, each young man was to be allowed to exert himself to go where his nature

[47] Garin, *ibid.*, p. xiv.     [48] *De educatione librorum*, Bk. III, ch. 1.
[49] Vittorio Lugli, *I trattatisti della famiglia nel Quattrocento* (Bologna/Milan, 1909), ch. 5.

and talent (*ingegno*) led him.[50] In this treatise *ingegno* means natural aptitude and is used along with *intelleto*, both instilled by nature, together with those *passione* and *affezione* which identify one's character. Nature also confers upon us the power of self-knowledge and a capacity to distinguish and select (*eleggere*) what befits us. So, too, can we read the signs of ability in others. By careful and steady observation a father can know what occupation is proper for his son.

Asked what attitude he would take toward a disappointing son, however, Alberti simply replies that "Every occupation (*essercizio*) which is not infamous is not evil in a gentle soul . . . I concede to you that not everyone is capable of all that his kinsmen would like, but he who achieves all of which he is capable is more pleasing to me than he who tries to do what he cannot."[51] Worse still is a lazy son who does nothing. However rich and genteel a father may be, he ought also to see to it that even his ablest sons acquire a second occupation (*mestiero non servile*) so that, if misfortune strikes, they can earn a living honorably with their hands.

However aristocratic the Alberti, it would seem that they, like Vittorino, took a long step toward imputing equal dignity to all honest occupations. Despite the common bias of humanist educators against careers in business and their praise of the life of letters, they neither express nor imply a rigid hierarchy of occupations. Fanfani appropriately cites Alberti's recognition of the arts and crafts as honorable if honorably pursued. Palmieri praised the capacity of man for action and artifact as well as for thought and lauded the artisan for putting metals and stones to our use and benefit. Tasso went out of his way to dignify the merchant, while Bruno idealized work for its own sake as a source of human excellence.[52] The *disputa delle arti*, especially the quarrel over the merits of law and medicine, was, to be sure, a frequent subject of humanist disputation in the fifteenth century.[53] Although the controversy may signify more than a rhetorical exercise, the fact

---

[50] *I libri della famiglia*, ed. Cecil Grayson (Bari, 1960), Bk. I: "De officio senum erga iuvenes et minorum erga maiores et de educationis liberis," p. 44.

[51] *Ibid.*, p. 75.

[52] Amintore Fanfani, *Le origini dello spirito capitalistico in Italia* (Milan, 1933), p. 144; Matteo Palmieri, *Della vita civile*, in *Il Pensiero pedagogico del Rinascimento*, ed. Felice Battaglia (Florence, 1960), pp. 171ff.; Torquato Tasso, *Il padre di famiglia*, in *Il pensiero pedagogico della Controriforma*, ed. Luigi Volpicelli (Florence, 1960), p. 65; Giovanni Rucellai, *Zibaldone*, ed. Alessandro Perosa (London, 1960), pp. 3, 15.

[53] *La disputa delle arti nel Quattrocento*, ed. E. Garin (Florence, 1947), p. 232.

is that the humanists themselves could not agree on the ranking even of the learned professions. And by the end of the century, having long since dignified the poet, they helped to confer new honor on the sculptor and the painter. The humanist belief that history is in some measure man-made, and that society is the achievement of human labor, contributed toward the idealization of work long before the Reformation.

What the humanists added to this kind of value was a secular ethic of work and human achievement as things good in themselves, together with the belief that the manifold labors of the laity are worthy expressions of human dignity. The same tradition of Italian humanism steadily developed a confidence not only in the possibility of usable self-knowledge but also in the capacity at least of the educated to make responsible and constructive choices in the exercise of individual freedom. Pandolfini's secular idealism defended the "natural yearning" of all men to be themselves and of each man to live in his own way, adapting *ingegno* and exertion to ends which are worthy of both the commonweal and the self.[54] Pandolfini's defense of the free individual is closely akin to Matteo Palmieri's efforts to associate the diversity of human abilities and intellect with the progressive building of the human city and the achievement of civilized life. Man fulfills himself as thinker and maker not only through the diversity of his talents but equally by the right uses of his freedom.

The same idealism, however, entailed its own contradictions and anomalies. Boccaccio, for example, prefigured one of these, which was to reappear in a variety of ways, with the argument that the individual must have freedom to pursue the goals which both God and inherent nature had determined for him. Only the very exceptional man, Boccaccio said, can overcome innate character through the exercise of free will, and Boccaccio seems to say that the good society is one in which individuals are free to make the choices which their own natures prescribe to them.[55] An immensely more complex version of this conclusion is to be found in those sections of Ficino's philosophy which systematically incorporate the determinism of Greek physiological psychology into Neo-Platonist metaphysics.

Ficino held that the three parts of the soul—*mens, ratio, idolum*—should be understood as casting their trace or shadow over the body.

[54] Angelo Pandolfini, *Tratto del governo della famiglia*, ed. F. Costero (Milan, 1937), p. 232.
[55] *Genealogia deorum*, Bk. XV, ch. 10.

To these three parts of the soul is added a quality "inherent in the living body itself," a material component which is the *complexio corporis*,[56] the body's complexion or nature consisting of the four elements of blood, phlegm, black bile, and yellow bile. Ficino therefore explained the variability of human temperament according to the ancient humoral typology of Hippocrates and Galen.[57] For Ficino, the characteristic natural affections of the sanguine, phlegmatic, choleric, and melancholic dispositions were not to be taken—as they were by Alberti[58]—as mere qualities of vice or weakness, but rather as basic differentials of human behavior and choice (*electio*).[59] Despite a common human nature, there are different appetites and affections associated with the proportion of natural elements (*complexio corporis*) which condition basic character or temperament. And although every man acquires a preestablished constancy and predetermined quality of *ingenium* from his bodily "nature," he is also at the mercy of its potential instability and imbalance.

This doctrine of organic connection between body and soul, first implied in the naturalism of the pseudo-Aristotelian *Problemata*[60] and elaborated by Galen, was applied by Ficino especially to the predicament of melancholics, "the priests of the muses."[61] What emerges from his famous treatment of melancholia in the *De vita triplica*, however, is no celebration of the autonomous and self-determining individual soul—exempt in Neo-Platonist freedom "from the disorders and the imperfections of nature"—but rather a physiological determinism by which the soul is very much the captive of the body and its humors. Even the most extraordinary qualities of genius and intellectual distinction are so explained as to make mind contingent on corporeal

---

[56] Paul Oskar Kristeller, *The Philosophy of Marsilio Ficino*, tr. Virginia Conant (New York, 1943), pp. 369ff.

[57] Rudolf and Margot Wittkower, *Born under Saturn* (New York, 1963), ch. 5; W.P.D. Wightman, *Science and the Renaissance* (Edinburgh/London, 1962), I, 210-249; Herschel Baker, *The Dignity of Man* (Cambridge, 1947), ch. 17; Lawrence Babb, *The Elizabethan Malady* (Lansing, Mich., 1951), chs. 1-2; Erwin Panofsky and F. Saxl, *Albrecht Dürer*, 2 vols. (Princeton, 1945), I, 156-169. For the Galenic antecedents, see also Richard Walzer, *Greek into Arabic. Essays on Islamic Philosophy* (Cambridge, 1962), pp. 142-157, and George Sarton, *Galen of Pergamon* (Lawrence, Kan., 1954).

[58] *I libri della famiglia*, p. 63.       [59] Kristeller, *Ficino*, p. 381.

[60] Aristotle, *Problemata*, ch. xxx, 1-3; Kristeller, p. 211.

[61] Marsilio Ficino, *De studiosorum sanitate tuenda*, in *Opera omnia*, facsimile reproduction of Basel edn. of 1576 (Turin, 1959), I, 497.

elements and these, in turn, upon the stars. "The stars determined not only the humours but also occupational interests and talent."[62] What we do and what we are, therefore, depend primarily on astrology —never on genealogy—and on the temperament it ordains.

Those born under Saturn are melancholics, madmen, or geniuses, depending upon the proportion of corporeal fluids in their bodies. "Not only must men of letters diligently take care of their bodies, but they must also carefully plot their course between phlegm and black bile, as though between Scylla and Charybdis."[63] One condition dulls and blunts *ingenium*, the other overstimulates it and inflames one's judgment. The intellectual is made to live between apathy and frenzy. Although his *ingenium* has the capacity to be less human than divine, the *melancholicus*—moody, eccentric, erratic, and solitary—is equally prone to the most barren passivities and the sloth of Petrarch's *accidie*.[64] Celestial, natural, and human causes all affect the dispositions of the atrabilious talent.

The celestial cause of melancholy is astrologically explained by the coldness and dryness induced at birth by the conjunction of Mercury and Saturn. Ficino never finally decides whether the scholar's melancholy is absolutely innate or whether in some cases it is acquired by such "natural" and "human" causes as the scholar's sedentary habits or the desiccating effects of thought on the moisture of the blood.[65] The melancholic man of letters is so either by birth or as the result of overexertion, he says; but it would seem that both inherent nature and mental exertion combine to account for the consistency of melancholy in philosophers, men of letters, and theologians.[66] The melancholic intellectual, in any event, has only the most parlous mastery of himself. His genius is threatened as much by where as by how he lives,

---

[62] Wittkower, *Born under Saturn*, p. 103. For an earlier version of the astrology of individuation, see Francesco Patrizi, *De regno et regnis institutione*, Bk. III, ch. 1, summarized in *Il Pensiero pedagogico del Rinascimento*, ed. Battaglia, p. 183.

[63] Ficino, *Opera omnia*, I, 496.

[64] Cf. Wittkower, *Born under Saturn*, pp. 101ff.; *Petrarch's Secret*, p. 84.

[65] Ficino, *Opera omnia*, I, 497; Babb, *Elizabethan Malady*, ch. 2. In the recently discovered *De moribus* of Galen, "a strongly platonizing treatise," it is clearly assumed that "the faculties of the soul follow the temperaments of the body" and that differences of character, as an inborn irrational disposition, are derived from inherent nature rather than from such external factors as education or environment. Walzer, *Greek into Arabic*, pp. 145-146.

[66] Cf. Babb, pp. 66-67; Panofsky, *Dürer*, I, 169f.

eats, drinks, and thinks. Ficino the philosopher becomes Ficino the physician, and metaphysics yields to the horoscope and the medicine cabinet:[67] *ingenium* turns out to be an inherent property of innate nature, over which in the temporal world the soul has no real powers of control.[68]

The individual's freedom and capacity for choice, like his occupation and behavior, are constrained within the limits of received physical nature. Human diversity is fixed by the variety of the humors, and human choice is so conditioned by natural disposition as to be instinctive rather than deliberate.[69] If Book I of the *De vita triplica* were all of Ficino's thought to survive, it would be impossible to associate it with Pico and Neo-Platonist mysticism. There is nothing in the *De vita triplica*, for example, which interprets the creature as one "constrained by no limits," "to have whatever he chooses, to be whatever he wills," ordaining for himself the limits of his own nature according to his own free will.[70] There is nothing in this part of Ficino's work to suggest Pico's praise of man as one who "has no semblance that is inborn," capable of becoming God-like. Yet in the *Theologia platonica* Ficino portrays man as one who "imitates all the works of divine nature" and, though of variable powers, is possessed of *ingenium* similar to that of "Him who made the heavens."[71]

Professor Panofsky has suggested that the Neo-Platonists promptly applied the Aristotelian-Galenic doctrine to supply "a scientific basis for Plato's theory of 'divine frenzy,'" so that the idea of the "*furor melancholicus* came to be synonymous with the *furor divinus*. What had been a calamity and, in its mildest form, a handicap became a privilege still dangerous but all the more exalted: the privilege of genius."[72] This was not the divine gift of sanctity or sainthood but the capacity for "divine" achievement as writer or scholar. And, by extension, what Aristotle had once described as mere pathology now became the sign and condition of rare ability: "Melancholy is the mark of genius."[73] Ficino's genius had little choice but to submit to his Satur-

---

[67] Ficino, *Opera omnia*, I, *De studiosorum sanitate tuenda*, chs. 7, 9, 10, 20.

[68] Kristeller, *Ficino*, pp. 394ff.

[69] Ficino, *Theologica platonica, Opera omnia*, I, 255.

[70] Pico, "Oration on the Dignity of Man," tr. Elizabeth Livermore Forbes, in Ernst Cassirer et al., *The Renaissance Philosophy of Man* (Chicago, 1948), p. 225.

[71] *Theologica platonica*, Bk. XIII, ch. 3.   [72] *Dürer*, I, 165.

[73] *Ibid.*, p. 166. Cf. John Donne: "But what have I done, either to *breed*, or to *breethe* these vapours? They tell me it is my *Melancholy*; did I infuse, did I drinke in Melancholly into my selfe? It is my study; doth not my *Calling* call

nian nature, yielding to self-knowledge but enabled now to speak, if he chose, with a brave new voice of self-pity and a proud new voice of self-praise.

Nowhere in any of these treatises, however, is there a celebration of versatility. The universal genius may indeed have existed as a real figure admired in Renaissance society, but he rarely appears as an abstract ideal in Renaissance theory. The humanists seem to have admired the man of a single *gran ingegno* far more than the *uomo universale*.[74]

## III

By the start of the sixteenth century, and before the Reformation, three different theories of individuation were in use among the humanists, before Luther and Calvin elaborated a fourth. One was historically biblical, elaborated in the monastery and absorbed into medieval social theory before it was codified by theologians like Hugh of St. Victor and Thomas Aquinas. Whether expressed formally as a doctrine of distributive justice or metaphorically by analogy with the human body, the divisions of human society (like the inequality of persons) were to be understood as the intention of Providence. St. Thomas explained that "This diversification of men in divers duties (*officiis*) occurs first by Divine Providence, which so distributes the conditions (*status*) of men . . . [and] second by natural causes, from which it happens that there are different inclinations to different offices in different men."[75] Such inclinations, however, though perfected in the natural order, are nonetheless the gifts of grace.

The second theory of individuation and self-knowledge was historically pre-Christian, stemming from a tradition rooted in classical ethics and pedagogy, and was largely codified by Cicero. Its humanist elaborators, from Petrarch to Erasmus and Vives, put the emphasis as much on the discovery of native character and *ingenium* as upon

for that? I have don nothing wilfully, perversely toward it, yet must suffer in it, die by it." (*Devotions upon Emergent Occasions*, ed. John Sparrow [Cambridge, 1923], p. 69.)

[74] Cf. Kristeller, "The Moral Thought of Renaissance Humanism," in *Chapters in Western Civilization*, 3rd edn. (New York, 1961), I, 311f.

[75] "Haec autem diversificatio hominum in diversis officiis contingit primo ex divina providentia, quae ita hominum status distribuit . . . secundo etiam ex causis naturalibus, ex quibus contingit, quod in diversis hominibus sunt diversae inclinationes ad diversa officia . . ." (*Quaestiones quodlibetal*, VII, Art. 17c).

the cultivation of aptitude by practice and discipline. In their view, the adolescent must be free to select the career for which nature and training have prepared him, for the advantage of society and the pursuit of his own happiness.

The third version of human variety was more consistently Greek or Hellenistic than Roman, stemming from Plato and Aristotle, Hippocrates and Galen, and transmitted to the Middle Ages and the Renaissance more through Arabic philosophy and medicine than from classical literary tradition. Codified by Ficino, it was extended into sixteenth-century physiology as much as it was into the self-picture of Elizabethan writers and artists.

Both the Ciceronian and Galenic theories concentrated on the "natural causes" of St. Thomas's distinction and on the inclinations of individuals rather than their distribution into estates. Medieval doctrine was more concerned with the justification of the latter, the individual being regarded as "inseparable" or "indivisible" from some form of corporate whole and not, therefore, as a free-standing figure whose identity is established by his inherent character or temperament[76] or by the deliberate or intuitive choices he makes in becoming himself.

These three theories were not always expressed by Erasmus's contemporaries in their pure form; each idiom sometimes showed signs of borrowing from the language or the assumptions of another. For example, Erasmus in one moment spoke of human aptitudes as the gifts of God, in another as a human endowment.[77] Although he translated several of Galen's medical essays, he never followed Galen's humoral psychology as stated in the treatises *On Temperaments* and *On Natural Faculties*.[78] He referred far more often to inborn *ingenium* and character. Yet, in his argument against false vocation, he frequently cited the unsuitability of his own physical constitution for the force in ascetic regimen.[79] He passionately spoke of himself as driven to

---

[76] Cf. Raymond Williams, *The Long Revolution* (London, 1961), pp. 73f.

[77] *Opus Epistolarum*, III, no. 985, 611; VI, no. 1596, 147.

[78] Erasmus translated the first three treatises in vol. I of the Aldine Galen in 1526. See *Opus Epistolarum*, VI, no. 1698, Introduction. He also knew Galen's *De sanitate tuenda* in Linacre's edition of 1517. Linacre also translated Galen's *De temperamentis* (1521) and *De naturalibus facultatibus* (1523). See *Galeni Pergamensis De Temperamentis*, ed. Joseph Frank Payne and tr. Thomas Linacre (London, 1881), Introduction.

[79] *Opus Epistolarum*, I, no. 296; II, no. 447. Cellini likened his achievement as artist to "a special gift lent me by the God of Nature, a temperament so healthy and well-proportioned that I could confidently carry out whatever I made up my mind to do" (*Vita*, ch. xxvi).

letters by a force in his own nature (*vi naturae*). Still, as pedagogue, he could say that "men, believe me, are not born but formed (*finguntur*)"[80] and that the unwrought shape (*rudis massa*) of the infant may be fashioned through education into the visible image of God.[81] Nevertheless, the principal theme of the *De pueris* (1529) is that the young must be observed for every sign of their natural inclinations, so that the capacities of self-knowledge and rational choice may be enlarged for the proper selection of the boy's career.[82]

Vives, who was often perplexed about his own *genus vitae*,[83] offered another example of mixed assumptions in his *De disciplinis* (1531). Natural capacities, he said, are gifts of God, and neither scholar nor artisan should think that God has any need of him in working out his plans. Yet the human order is best established when each performs the task for which he is naturally fitted. Moreover, variations of aptitude arise from constitution and temperament, of which God alone is the creator and who "alone knowest the causes."[84] It is the responsibility of schoolmasters to consider the nature of each student, reviewing his condition every three months, so that each may be placed in the work for which he is most fit.[85]

In Starkey's *Dialogue between Reginald Pole and Thomas Lupset* (ca. 1534) Pole proposes an ordinance requiring every father to "set forth" each of his children, at seven, "to letters or to a craft, according as their nature requireth . . . ," under the supervision of the curate of the parish.[86] "A certain pain must be ordered and appointed upon every man that contenteth not himself with his own mystery, craft and faculty." The organic analogy is used to enjoin each to his own "office and duty, without envy or malice to others . . . , rendering obedience to princes and lords required of their state and degree." The tranquillity of the state and the welfare of the individual are to be mat-

---

[80] *Opera* (Leiden, 1703), I, 493B.

[81] William H. Woodward, *Desiderius Erasmus concerning the Aim of Education* (Cambridge, 1904), p. 81.

[82] *De pueris statim ac liberaliter instituendis* (1529), *Opera*, I, 499C-500A; cf. also *Christiani matrimonii institutio* (1526), *Opera*, V, 722E-724B.

[83] William Sinz, "The Elaboration of Vives' Treatise on the Arts," *Studies in the Renaissance*, X (1963), 72ff., 78.

[84] *Vives: On Education*, tr. Foster Watson (Chicago, 1913), pp. 41, 76, 80, 82.

[85] *Ibid.*, p. 62. Cf. Roger Ascham, *The Scholemaster* (London, 1904), pp. 192-197.

[86] Thomas Starkey, *A Dialogue between Reginald Pole and Thomas Lupset*, ed. Kathleen M. Burton (London, 1948), pp. 124-146.

ters of public scrutiny, yet each person is somehow to pursue whatever befits his nature.

Similar contradiction is found in Juan Huarte's remarkable treatise on temperament and education, the widely influential *Examen de Ingenios* (1574).[87] Huarte, the son of a hidalgo of Navarre, was a Spanish physician, educated at Alcalà both in the arts and in medicine. No other treatise of its kind better illustrates the fusion of existing doctrines and vocabularies, despite the fact that its principal assumptions were explicitly taken from Aristotle and Galen. Huarte said that he wrote the treatise because ancient philosophers failed to explain what they meant when they attributed intellectual aptitude to nature: "none of them euer shewed in particular, what thing this nature was, nor in what ranke of causes it ought to be placed: only they affirmed, that this, wanting in him who learned," could not be created either by education or by art.[88] Vives, who influenced Huarte's thought considerably, had left the answer to God. Huarte sought it in Galen, "the groundplot" of his book. But even Galen had failed to explain "the differences of the habilities which are in men, neither as touching the sciences which euerie one requires in particular. Notwithstanding, he understood that it was necessarie to depart the sciences amongst yoong men, and to giue ech one that which to his naturall habilitie was requisit. . . ."[89] So the purpose of the *Examen* was to analyze the "varieties of natures" and to show "for what profession ech one is apt, and how far he should profit therein."

Nature provides in each individual a single quality of aptitude, determined by the ratio and temperature of the four humoral elements. The seat of intelligence is not the heart, as pre-Hippocratic philosophers believed, but the brain, whose temperature, moisture, and relative dryness determine the nature of one's intellect and ability. We know by experience that, if the brain is well-tempered for natural science, the individual needs no master to teach him. And everyone also knows

---

[87] *Examen de Ingenios. The Examination of Mens Wits*, tr. Richard Carew (1594), ed. Carmen Rogers (Gainesville, Fla., 1959). Very close to Huarte's was the position of Orazio Lombardelli (1545-1608), *Degli uffizi e costumi de' giovanni* (Florence, 1584), in L. Volpicelli, *Il Pensiero pedagogico della Controriforma*, pp. 412-414. Lombardelli classified the physiognomy of temperaments and humors and urged *elezione del fine* by the young, but he also felt that such choices must usually correspond to the *condizion di chi l'elegge*. In this respect Huarte was far bolder.

[88] Huarte, p. 5.     [89] *Ibid.*, p. 29; cf. Babb, *Elizabethan Malady*, p. 61.

that, of the four humors, "there is none so cold and dry as that of melancholie," just as everyone knows that melancholics are most suited to a life of learning. Temperature determines talent, and talent should set the task of each, who must practise "only that to which he beareth a naturall inclination."

In order to prevent mistaken choices, however, magistrates should be appointed to "discover each ones wit in his tender age, and cause him to studie that which is agreeable to him, not permitting him to make his owne election. . . ."[90] No man is without some special aptitude, but no one can alter his aptitude: "food, air, water, environment, horoscope, make the fool or wise man. . . ."[91] So Huarte, like Campanella, wanted to enter the schools in order to examine every student and place each according to his aptitude. Some children he would return to the fields, and others he would take from the fields to school.

Even though Huarte in his preface piously attributed wit to the gifts of God, humoral psychology so fully dominated the analysis of human diversity that Huarte proposed, in close clinical detail, a practical eugenics for the procreation of exceptional children. And although he urged that public officials assign each his place according to aptitude, the stated purpose of chapter VIII is to enable each man to learn his own nature, so that he may discover his own "naturall disposition" and profit from it.[92]

In its several versions, the humanist ethic of work may, therefore, be likened to a principle of utility whereby the welfare of the community depends upon the "profit" of its individual members and upon the freedom of each to derive his *genus vitae* from his natural aptitude,

[90] Huarte, p. 23. Vegio, Vives, Starkey, Bartolomeo Meduna, Campanella, and Puritans such as Richard Baxter also recommended that public officials, teachers, and pastors assist parents and sons in the selection of their careers.

[91] Otis H. Green, "The Concept of Man in the Spanish Renaissance," *The Rice Institute Pamphlet*, XLVI (Jan. 1960), no. 4, 49-50. Green suggests that Cervantes derived Don Quixote's madness from a humoral disorder. But out of his madness Don Quixote was also able to say, "I know who I am, and who I may be if I choose" (Bk. I, ch. 5).

[92] Huarte, p. 102; cf. *Antonio Possevino, Cultura ingeniorum. Ioannis Huartis expenditur*, 7th edn. (Venice, 1610). The Jesuit Possevino combined the three languages far more indiscriminately than Huarte. The doctrines of Plato, Aristotle, Galen, Cicero, and Aquinas are so mixed in Possevino's work that *intellectus* is described both as one of the seven gifts and the effect of right temperature; *ingenium* is said to be inherent but also capable of being generated in those who lack it by education and discipline.

temperament, or character. "For human happiness depends mainly on this," according to Erasmus, "that everyone should wholly apply himself to that for which he is naturally fitted."[93] As a principle of pleasure and pain, this doctrine was directed not so much against positive law, however, as against social custom. It was directed both against what the humanists regarded as false doctrines of "true nobility" and perhaps even more, at least by recurrent inference, against paternal authority (*potestas paterna*) in the determination of a son's work, profession, or vocation.[94] The coercive jurisdiction of the *potestas paterna* was said to create unhappy sons by driving them into careers for which they were unsuited by inclination or ability and, also, to deprive the commonweal of talents on which its corporate welfare depends.

## IV

Although early Protestant reformers placed an emphasis on filial obedience rarely found in humanist pedagogy or ethics,[95] Luther and Calvin were also far more pragmatic and often more radical in their proposals for the expansion and improvement of public education. Luther's idea of the school contains an egalitarianism wholly absent from the thought of Vergerio and Vittorino, and he was much more outspoken about the obligations of the state for the support of these schools.[96] Like Huarte, he insisted that the schools be opened to children of all estates and origins. He urged that the "honest crafts" be made accessible to illegitimate boys, recommended that at least an elementary education be provided for girls, and said that he saw no reason why a craftsman should not have the pleasure of learning

[93] *Opus Epistolarum*, II, no. 447 (1516), 294.

[94] Cf. Vergerio on the *parentum imperium*, *Epistolario*, ed. Leonardo Smith, pp. 133-135; Vittorio Lugli, *I trattatisti della famiglia nel Quattrocento*, pp. 1-8, 55-57; Nino Tamassia, *La famiglia italiana* (Milan, 1910), pp. 110-118, 249, 264; Lauro Martines, *The Social World of the Florentine Humanists, 1390-1460* (Princeton, 1963), pp. 50-57; P. Ariés, *Centuries of Childhood*, pp. 356ff. See also Christopher Hill, *Society and Puritanism in Pre-Revolutionary England* (New York, 1964), pp. 443-446, 461-466. The argument that true nobility rests on virtue rather than birth is made in a series of treatises *De nobilitate* by Poggio, Buonacorso da Montemagno, Platina, Landino, etc.

[95] F.V.N. Painter, *Luther on Education* (Philadelphia, 1889), pp. 114-116, 123.

[96] *An die Radherrn aller Staedte deutschen Landes*, WA XV, 27-53; tr. as *The Christian in Society*, II, ed. Walther I. Brandt, *Luther's Works* (hereafter cited as *LW*), vol. 45 (St. Louis, 1962), pp. 368-372.

Latin.[97] Luther reminded the poor that all the offices of the state and the Church—like all the professions (*Berufe*)—lay open to any candidate qualified by proper training, adding that it would surely be the children of the common people—"your son and mine"—who will have to rule the world.[98] Furthermore, he said, paternal authority is a trust which parents owe to children and society alike:

> It is again a sad evil that all live as though God gave us children for our pleasure and amusement. . . . For if we wish to have proper and excellent persons both for civil and ecclesiastical government, we must spare no difficulty, time or cost in training and educating our children, that they may serve God and the world. . . . Let everyone know, therefore, that above all things it is his duty . . . to bring up his children in the fear and knowledge of God; and if they have talents, to have them instructed and trained in a liberal education, that we may be able to have their aid in government and in whatever is necessary.[99]

In order to maintain the temporal kingdom outwardly, Luther held it to be a duty of the temporal princes to establish and maintain Christian schools, and he instructed civil authorities, in turn, to compel parents to send their children to such schools.[100] He argued that parents are also obliged to identify those sons who show special gifts of aptitude and inclination to become magistrates, jurists, pastors, teachers, lawyers, and the like and, indeed, are obligated to bring up their gifted sons for such "callings." "If one does not produce children for the sake of knowledge and for the sake of art, but rather to produce gluttons and pigs who look only for their food, where then will we take ministers . . . for clerical offices, chancellors, senators, clerks and officials?"[101] If a child is "capable and skillful" (*tüchtig und geschickt*), if he has a desire for higher education, he must be encouraged by parents and teachers, who speak as the "mouth of God" in directing him toward an office or calling ordained by God.[102] Better schools and universities are a practical necessity for undoing the devil's work.

[97] WA XXX:2, 565; Werner Elert, *Morphologie des Luthertums* (Frankfurt, 1958), II, 69-79.
[98] WA XXX:2, 577.        [99] Painter, *Luther*, p. 116.
[100] WA XV, 27; Elert, *Morphologie*, II, 73ff.; Painter, p. 264.
[101] WA XXX:2, 62; Elert, II, 72.
[102] WA XXX:2, 521. See also Hellmut Lieberg, *Amt und Ordination bei Luther und Melanchthon* (Göttingen, 1962), pp. 73ff., 162-165, for Luther's

Luther's instructions to princes and parents may seem to imply that specific callings within the orders of creation are open to human choice or subjective preference. Yet what so deeply separated Luther's theology of vocation from the humanist ethic of work was his repeated assumption that the temporal calling is to be regarded as God's command. Whereas Erasmus saw his own *genus vitae* as something he himself chose in conformity with his nature and the requirements of self-knowledge, Luther in a sermon on the *Kirchenpostille* of 1522 made it clear that one's vocation is not selected but commanded: it is an office assigned to him by God. In this sermon he used *Beruf* for the first time "as having the same meaning as occupation, class and office" and elaborated the doctrine that "each Christian, insofar as he belonged to a class or profession at all, should feel himself called to that vocation. The duties which God places upon him are indeed the commands which God Himself directs to him."[103] Luther never even vaguely suggested Petrarch's statement in the *De vita solitaria* that "there is nothing more vital than independence of judgment [on the uses of one's *ingenium*]; as I claim it for myself, I would not deny it to others."[104] It was precisely this argument in what I have called the humanist "principle of utility" that separated Luther from Petrarch and Erasmus, just as it was the absence of any "scientific" or naturalistic terminology which set Luther's doctrine of vocation apart from the theories of Ficino and Huarte. The difference is perhaps most readily apparent in what Luther had to say about vocation to the Christian ministry.

Through baptism every Christian receives the *vocatio generalis*, a spiritual or invisible vocation by which he is "born and called" to the universal priesthood. He also receives a *vocatio specialis*, an external and visible vocation beyond baptism to a concrete office, in which one is called to be a pastor, magistrate, teacher, husband, or father.[105]

---

discussion of the gifts and abilities required of the well-qualified candidate for *vocatio mediata* to the ministry.

[103] In the *Kirchenpostille* Luther developed his first definitive statement on the nature of external vocation. See Karl Holl, "Die Geschichte des Wortes Beruf," in *Gesammelte Aufsätze zur Kirchengeschichte*, III (Tübingen, 1928), 189-219, esp. 216-219, which are based largely on WA X:1, 306-311. See also Cranz, *Luther's Thought*, pp. 153-159, and Elert, *Morphologie*, II, 65-67.

[104] Petrarch, *De vita solitaria*, I, tract. 4; cf. Cardanus, *De vita propria*, ed. Jean Stoner (London, 1931), ch. 51: "Maximum in humanis est, terminum actionis invenire."

[105] Lieberg, *Amt und Ordination*, pp. 132-134; Elert, *Morphologie*, II, 65-67.

By spiritual vocation we are called through the Gospel to the *christlicher Stand* in which all men are equal; by special vocation we are called through the Law to differential offices and estates within the orders of creation by which God governs the world.[106] The realm of external vocation is temporary and temporal; it "points to the present, to the present day, to this world." It is directed through love to one's neighbor by the *lex charitatis*.[107] The external vocation of pastor, necessary to public ministration of the sacraments and the Word, is an office to which one is called by a *mandatum divinum* through a specific congregation. The ministry results from a mission (*Sendung*) into which nobody should "sneak" or "intrude"; he must be called to it by the explicit order of Christ, mediated through men, in what Luther variously described as *vocatio mediata, vocatio charitatis,* or *fraterna vocatio*—a calling in this case conveyed through the congregation and confirmed by the bishop.[108] Thus, Luther cautions pastors and rulers against false or uncalled preachers:

> ... No one should let them in or listen to them, even if they were to preach the pure Gospel, nay, even if they were angels from heaven and all Gabriels at that! For it is of God's will that nothing be done as a result of one's own choice or decision, but everything as a consequence of a command or a call. That is especially true of preaching, as St. Peter says (II Peter 1:20-21): "You should know this first: no prophecy was brought out by the will of man; the holy men of God spoke, driven by the holy spirit." ... Let everyone, then, remember this: If he wants to preach or teach, let him give proof of the call or command which drives or compels him to it, or else be silent.[109]

[106] On the orders of creation, see Martin J. Heinecken, "Luther and the 'Order of Creation' in Relation to a Doctrine of Work and Vocation," *Lutheran Quarterly*, IV (Nov. 1952), 393-414; Philip S. Watson, "Luther's Doctrine of Vocation," *Scottish Journal of Theology*, II (Dec. 1949), 364-377; Cranz, *Luther's Thought*, pp. 173-178; Lieberg, pp. 115-120.

[107] On the lex charitatis, see WA XVI, 35; WA XVII, 362; WA XX, 412; WA XXX:3, 519; Elert, *Morphologie*, I, 304-305; Johannes Heckel, "Lex charitatis, Eine juristische Untersuchung über das Recht in der Theologie Martin Luthers," *Bayerische Akademie der Wissenschaften*, Abh., Phil.-hist. Kl., NF XXXVI (1953). But see also Cranz, pp. 179-180, for a summary criticism of Heckel's methodology.

[108] Lieberg, *Amt und Ordination*, pp. 139-143, 145ff.

[109] WA XXI:1, 21; tr. C. M. Jacobs, *Selected Psalms*, II, *LW*, vol. 13 (St. Louis, 1956), p. 65. Cf. Luther's ridicule of monks and priests who claim that

Thus, "to be a pastor one must not only be a Christian and a priest but must have an office and a field of work committed to him. The call and command make pastors and preachers."[110] Although the act of calling (*Berufung*) to a concrete office is usually mediated as a "calling through man," it is ordained and intended by God.[111] Luther applied the doctrine, by way of example, to himself. "I was forced and driven into this position in the first place when I had to become a Doctor of Holy Scripture against my will." Although "God assigned this office and work to us . . . ," it is the devil who confuses our reason in the performance of it.[112] In a sermon on the Gospel of St. John, Luther said, "you should know that I do not boast of myself that I am a preacher or a prince; there is another who joins me in boasting, namely, our Lord God, who entrusted this office to me and commanded me to be a father, pastor, prince, count, nobleman, burgher or peasant."[113] Later in the same sermon he stated: "I am not a preacher

---

"they have a talent from the Lord and consequently are impelled to teach because the command of the Gospel makes it necessary for them to do so. Therefore, if they do not teach, they believe in their utterly foolish conscience that they are hiding the talent which they have from their Lord and are liable to condemnation (Matt. 25:26-30). This the devil does, in order to make them unstable in the vocation to which they have never been called. My dear brother, with a single work Christ sets you free from this complaint. Look at the Gospel, which says: 'He called his servants and entrusted to them this property' (Matt. 25: 14). 'He called,' it says; but who has called you? Wait for Him who calls. . . . If God needs you, He will call you. If he does not call you, you will not burst with your wisdom. The man who teaches without being called does so to his own harm and that of his hearers, because Christ is not with him." (WA II, 454-455; tr. in *LW*, *Lectures on Galatians* [1519], vol. 27, p. 166.)

[110] "Der beruff und befehl macht Pfarher und Prediger." (WA XXXI:1, 211.)

[111] "Haec est vocatio per hominem, sed per deum bestetiget, quod fundamentum in scriptura." (WA XVI, 34.) Cf. WA XXXVIII, 252; WA XXX:3, 521; Elert, *Morphologie*, II, 74.

[112] "But perhaps you will say to me, 'Why do you, by your books, teach throughout the world, when you are only a preacher in Wittenberg?' I answer: I have never wanted to do it and do not want to do it now." Luther explained his own career by the obligations inherent in the degree he acquired in 1512 and by his original responsibility to teach "at the command of the pope and emperor." "For what I began as a Doctor, made and called at their command, I must truly confess to the end of my life." (*LW*, vol. 13, p. 66, n. 41.)

[113] *LW*, vol. 23, *Sermons on the Gospel of St. John*, tr. Martin H. Bertram (St. Louis, 1959), p. 322. "You and I and every one must be certain of our office. We know that everybody must be able to stand on his office. He must be able

of myself or for myself in this place, as the schismatic spirits are. Nor was it by choice or daring that I took over this office. No, I have testimony that I was asked and called into the ministry here. I am preaching at the request and behest of others. . . . I am not a pastor by reason of my birth from my mother but on the strength of my call and competence for service. I was not born into this office, but I was made and ordained a preacher."[114] The prince should rule justly because he is in an office to which God "appointed" him. So, too, should those in the spiritual estate fulfill their office faithfully because God has "called and commanded" them to it.

Elert points out that

> The pastor's calling is exactly analogous to worldly callings, as Luther sets forth in his exposition of Psalms XXXII (WA 31, I, 189-218; 1530). Every performance of what a calling requires is a service to God. But only when it is actually done because of "a call and a command." Such a call and command—apart from the extraordinary instances in which God steps in directly, as in the case of the Old Testament prophets—is always given to us through men and is therefore bound up with life in a community made up of men, and is designed for the purpose of preserving and shaping this community. In such a call—one that takes place through men—we may and should see a *divine* call if those who extend the call are authorized by God to do so.[115]

One's external vocation comes about by way of God's act of calling (*Berufung*) to a concrete office (*Beruf*) through men serving as God's masks or voice—not only "worldly lords" and pastors but parents and teachers as well.[116] "Therefore," Luther cautioned, "do not follow your own counsels and desires, but do what your hand finds before it. That is, continue in the definite work given you and commanded by God. . . ."[117] Throughout his writing on vocation the master text is I

---

to tell himself: 'This is my office; this is my vocation.' Such a person is pleasing to God's will that I be a father or mother, husband or wife." (*Ibid.*, p. 323.)

[114] *Ibid.*, p. 342.

[115] Elert, *Morphologie*, I, 304; Lieberg, *Amt und Ordination*, p. 140, n. 48.

[116] WA XXX:2, 569.

[117] "Ein jeglicher bleibe in dem Beruf darinnen er berufen ist." See Watson, "Luther's Doctrine of Vocation," pp. 364-365; George Forrell, "Work and the Christian Calling," *Lutheran Quarterly*, VIII (1956), 112; and Gatzen, *Beruf bei Martin Luther*, pp. 46-48, 55-56.

Cor. 7:20: "Let everyone remain in the vocation in which he is called." "God sees no distinctions of value between the external vocations and is served alike in each of them." For not all are competent in everything. "There are varieties of service but the same Lord (I Cor. 12:5-6), who works not in one alone, but in all, not as we want, but as he wills."[118] The individual does not elect the station he will occupy in the hierarchy of estates. The "eyes of God regard not works but our obedience in them."

Gustav Wingren refers to Luther's "special emphasis on the fact that a Christian does not select what he will do, nor does he start any divisions. He contents himself with his vocation, even though it be humble and of low esteem."[119] *Vocatio externa* is given, commanded, and required.[120] As such it generates its own certainty and delivers the Christian from the fate of Cain and all those "errant and wandering people who have neither the word nor the command of God, by which the certainty of one's role is defined."[121] Vocation does not proceed in some vague way from the self, from a *vocatio interna* by which one responds to a voice of one's own. For the Christian to be certain of his vocation, he must be called to it through the independent, external fact of a calling from God, mediated to him through other men.[122]

[118] *Church and Ministry*, tr. Conrad Bergendoff, *LW*, vol. 40 (St. Louis, 1958), p. 44; also WA X:1, 1, 310-311; WA XVII:2, 37. Lieberg, *Amt und Ordination*, pp. 143ff., summarizes Luther's distinctions between *vocatio mediata* and *vocatio immediata*, which Luther sometimes refers to as the *duplex vocatio divina*.

[119] Wingren, *Luther on Vocation*, p. 179; see also pp. 195, 226, 234. "He who praises his office does not praise himself but the One who invested him with this office. He does not praise himself because of the office, but because of him who conferred the office on him and commanded him to glory in it." (*LW*, vol. 23, p. 323.) "The first thing was to give heed to what the Lord required of you, the work of whatever office he laid on you, as the Apostle Paul says, 'Everyone should remain in the state in which he was called.' " (WA I, 451; Wingren, p. ix.)

[120] WA LI, 615-616; WA X:1, 1, 307-308: "Darumb sihe drauff, wie eyn richtige strasz der weg gottis gehet; tzum ersten: er mag nit leyden menschenlere und weg oder gepott; tzum andern: er mag nit leyden eygen ersuchte oder erleszene werck; tzum dritten: er mag auch nit leyden der heyligen exempell, szondern da ist er hyn gericht, das er warttet, wie yhn gott fure, was der von yhm haben will. . . ."

[121] Elert, *Morphologie*, II, 67.

[122] "Darumb wisse ein jeder, das ehr mus gesanth sein, das ist: ehr mus wissen, das ehr beruffen sei, und night von sich selbst herein schleiche, sondern offentlich geschehe. Das heist ein Sendung von Gott und geschiecht gleichwohl durch menschen." (WA XXX:1, 211.) "War ists, Es soll sich neimant selbs unberuffen zu dem ampt dringen, Aber wenn er beruffen und gefoddert wird,

As the masks of God in the world, vocations become the means by which the "old man" is crucified and turned from self-love or self-interest to the love of his neighbor: "vocation is ordained by God to benefit not him who fulfills the vocation, but the neighbor who, standing alongside, bears his own cross for the sake of others."[123] Yet the Christian acquires a positive and constructive freedom within his vocation, once he is called to it. Having become a servant of God, he is enabled to cooperate with God.[124] Serving others in his calling, he acquires freedom to break with the Law as natural reason and objective circumstances require. Even while bearing a vocation that may weigh upon him like a cross, he obtains the "freedom to do or to leave undone," according to the varying needs of his neighbor, and thus to decide how best to fulfill God's commands in the temporal kingdom. The Christian also enjoys a further freedom to participate in God's constant re-creation of the conditions which confront men in their relations with one another. God provides each of us "with a different work, in a different place, at a different time, and before different people. . . ."[125]

Thus the command and call to external vocation take place within a diversity of offices. The Christian receives his spiritual vocation, from the outside, through baptism. He receives his temporal vocation, from the outside, through a *mandatum Dei*. There is none of the humanist's freedom of choice—*iudicii libertas, plenum arbitrium, deliberatio* or *electio*—in the alignment of the self with the secular world. Indeed, Luther warned that the devil uses every trick (*omne ingenium*) of his own to entice us from our proper callings and to lure us into vocations to which we are not called, as if God were ignorant of the vocation He intends for us.[126]

Calvin's position was essentially the same as Luther's in every important assumption. Just as Calvin described his own vocation as

---

soll er williglich hynan gehen und thun, was sein amt foddert." (WA XII, 390.) See also Elert, I, 307, 322.

[123] Wingren, *Luther on Vocation*, p. 29.

[124] WA XLIX, 610; WA XII, 130-132; Wingren, pp. 123-130. See also Lewis W. Spitz, "Ideas of Liberty in German Humanism," *Church History*, XXI, no. 3 (Sept. 1962), 3-16.

[125] WA VIII, 588; tr. Wingren, *Luther on Vocation*, p. 173. WA X:1, 1, 306f.

[126] "Sic enim diabolus omne ingenium versat, ut vocationem uniuscujusque irritam faciat et ad id sollicitet seducendo ad quod vocatus non est, quasi stultus sit Deus aut ignorans quo eum vocare voluerit." (WA, LVI, 349.)

contrary to his preference and disposition, so too did he warn that, "if a man lives by his own wit, without God's calling, he will wander and get lost all his life." The godly are called to spiritual vocation by eternal election before the creation of the world; those not elected for holiness "follow their own disposition." Calvin's basic understanding of temporal vocation is summarized thus in Book III, chapter 10 of the *Institutes*:

> Lastly, it is to be remarked, that the Lord commands every one of us, in all the actions of life, to regard his vocation. For he knows with what inquietude the human mind is inflamed, with what desultory levity it is hurried hither and thither, and how insatiable is its ambition to grasp different things at once. Therefore, to prevent universal confusion being produced by our folly and temerity, he has appointed to all their particular duties in different spheres of life. And that no one might rashly transgress the limits prescribed, he has styled such spheres of life *vocations*, or *callings*. Every individual's line of life, therefore, is, as it were, a post assigned to him by the Lord, that he may not wander about in uncertainty all his days. And so necessary is this distinction, that in his sight all our actions are estimated according to it, and often very differently from the sentence of human reason and philosophy. . . . Our life, therefore, will then be best regulated, when it is directed to this mark; since no one will be impelled by his own temerity to attempt more than is compatible with his calling, because he will know that it is unlawful to transgress the bounds assigned him. He that is in obscurity will lead a private life without discontent, so as not to desert the station in which God has placed him. It will also be no small alleviation of his cares, labours, troubles, and other burdens, when a man knows that in all these things he has God for his guide. . . . Hence also will arise peculiar consolation, since there will be no employment so mean and sordid (provided we follow our vocation) as not to appear truly respectable, and be deemed highly important in the sight of God.[127]

Calling is a gift of God, something of His election, so distributed that a different role is assigned to each of us for the benefit of all. Calvin very explicitly adapted the doctrines of distributive justice and the seven gifts to his own adopted theory of external calling, the con-

---

[127] Calvin, *Institutes*, tr. John Allen (Grand Rapids, 1949), vol. I, Bk. III, ch. 10.

nections to medieval principles being especially clear in the commentaries on Romans (1539) and I Corinthians (1546). Calvin related the variety and distinction of gifts, distributed by the Holy Spirit, to the manifold unity and concord of the church in such a way that each of the faithful surrenders himself to the portion allotted to him in his calling. Moreover, "by setting up faith in opposition to human judgment, he restrains us from our own opinions, and at the same time specifies the due measure of it. . . ." In his exegesis of Romans 12:4, Calvin likened the interdependent vocations of the faithful to the unified functions of the human body,[128] so conceived that every Christian contributes to its good according to his own faculties. But when Calvin required each "to consider what is suitable to his own nature, capacity and vocation,"[129] he did so, not to permit the choice of vocation, but rather to have each recognize and measure the obligations of the office to which he has been assigned and to prevent any man from "thrusting himself into what peculiarly belongs to others." The "difference of gifts proceeds not from the will of man, but because it has pleased the Lord to distribute his grace in this manner."[130] Calvin had in mind what is "suitable to their calling" as God intends it, and not what is suitable to personal inclination or disposition as father, son, teacher, or magistrate may read it.

The Lord requires each to be content with his own gifts and steadfast in the task conferred upon him, lest he disturb either the distinctness or the harmony which God has ordained. Each contributes his limited portion to the common stock, knowing that, since all gifts perished in the Fall, the talent of each is his own, not by personal achievement, but through grace as a gift.[131] The point is made even more severely in Calvin's preface to Olivétan's New Testament (1535). Before the Fall, "the wretched man, wanting to be somebody in himself, began incontinently to forget and misunderstand the source of his good; and by an act of outrageous ingratitude, he set out to exalt himself in pride against his Maker and the Author of all that is excel-

---

[128] *Commentaries on the Epistle of Paul the Apostle to the Romans*, ed. John Owen (Grand Rapids, 1959), p. 458; cf. Calvin on Romans 11:28: ". . . quos enim eligit Deus, vocat. . . ."

[129] ". . . quid suae naturae, quid captui, quid vocationi conveniat." (*Ibid.*, p. 458.)

[130] *Ibid.*, p. 459.

[131] *Commentary on Paul the Apostle to the Corinthians* (Grand Rapids, 1948), I, 400.

lent in him. For this reason, he went down in ruin and lost all the dignity and superiority of the state in which he was first created; he was despoiled and divested of all his glory and deprived of all the gifts which were his. . . ."[132] Hence, vocation represents less a cross than a partial restoration, by the gift of God, of man's primeval dignity. And what Adam once enjoyed as wholly his own came through sin to be redistributed in infinite variety through grace to his progeny. Those who refuse their vocations are condemned to unpurposed confusion, whereas those who accept them confirm their callings by the holiness of the lives they lead.[133]

Calvin significantly began the *Institutes* with the admonition that the "talents which we possess are not from ourselves, and that our very existence is nothing but a subsistence in God alone."[134] Moreover, "no man can arrive at true knowledge of himself, without having first contemplated the divine character, and then descended to the consideration of his own." Self-knowledge and vocation are inseparably bound to the knowledge of God and of God's intention; the whole meaning of vocation is to be found in abnegation of the self.

It is important to note, however, that this highly unified theology of vocation in its original integrity turned out to be transitory and impermanent. Although the language and the assumptions of Petrarch's *De vita solitaria* were absorbed almost undisturbed into the usage of Erasmus, Budé, and Bembo two centuries later, the basic doctrine of Luther and Calvin survived intact for scarcely two generations. Before Protestantism had entered its second century, a more secular idiom of self-knowledge and vocation began to penetrate the early orthodoxy of Luther and Calvin and to complicate its original clarity. The change is visible in several ways. First, in place of the passive voice in the idea that the individual is externally called to his vocation at God's command, treatises on vocation at the end of the sixteenth century began to include chapters on "The Good Choice of a Calling." Second, in Protestant and Puritan doctrine of the seventeenth century there was new attention paid to terms like "fitness," "natural ingenuity," "inclination," and "preference" as elements of vocational choice. Third, although vocation was still defined in later Puritan thought with relation to the good of the whole and the service of God, it was also de-

---

[132] *Calvin: Commentaries*, tr. J. Haroutunian (Philadelphia, 1958), p. 58.
[133] II Peter 1:10. Calvin, *Commentaries on the Catholic Epistles*, tr. John Owen (Grand Rapids, 1959), p. 377.
[134] Bk. I, ch. 1.

scribed with reference to the profit and advantage of individuals. And, finally, the originally stronger emphasis on the "general calling" to faith and the Word of God seems to have received less attention in seventeenth-century Puritan doctrine than the "particular calling" to one's work in the world.[135]

The addition of these new elements alongside the old is clearly apparent in *A Treatise of the Vocations* (1602) by the Cambridge Puritan, William Perkins.[136] In the beginning of this systematic little book, Perkins defined vocation as Luther had: it is "a certaine kind of life, ordained by God, for the common good." God is the source of every calling, "so he hath two actions therein. First, he ordaineth the calling itself. And secondly, he imposeth it on the man called."[137] The purpose of the "particular calling" is the common good, which is served according to the "diversitie of gifts inwardly, and distinction of order outwardly."[138] However, in the third part of the treatise, which describes the right uses of the calling, Perkins departed from Luther and Calvin to add two rules of his own. The first is "that we are to choose honest and lawfull callings to walke in." The second is that "every man must choose a fit calling to walke in; that is, every calling must be fitted to the man, and every man fitted to his calling."[139] Men outside their proper callings are like joints out of place in the body; in finding his proper place, each must examine both his "affection" and his gifts. In the same way, parents have the duty "to make choice of fitte callings" for their children. "And that they may the better judge aright, for what calling their children are fit, they must observe two things in them: first, their inclination: secondly, their natural gifts."[140] Perkins thought that every man is best off, as Professor Haller puts it, in the "vocation of his own abilities"; such is God's intention.[141] But, once again, the reasoning was like Boccaccio's when Perkins said that we must be permitted to choose what we are born—and what God has called us—to do. Vocation is in one sense imposed, but in another it is chosen according to one's gifts.

[135] Charles and Katherine George, *The Protestant Mind of the English Reformation* (Princeton, 1961), p. 169.

[136] *A Treatise of the Vocations, or Callings of Men, with the Sorts and Kinds and the Right Uses Thereof*, in *Workes* (London, 1612), I, 47-79; see also William Haller, *The Rise of Puritanism* (New York, 1957), ch. II.

[137] Perkins, p. 750.      [138] *Ibid.*, p. 753.      [139] *Ibid.*, p. 758.

[140] *Ibid.*, p. 759.      [141] Haller, *Puritanism*, p. 125.

The same willingness to derive the callings both from God's command and our own choice also appears in Steele and Baxter. For Richard Steele, a man's calling is not a condition of his birth but one which he must select for himself: "God hath given to man reason for this use, that he should first consider, then choose, then put in execution; and it is a preposterous and brutish thing to fix or fall upon any weighty business, such as a calling or condition of life, without a useful pondering of it in the balance of reason."[142] Baxter expressed Perkins's paradox by saying, in effect, that the choice of a calling must be made in obedience to God's command; it must be pleasing to him and work to his glory. Like Perkins and Steele, Baxter attempted to combine moral accountability in man with the omnipotence of God. "Choose that employment or calling (so far as you have your choice) in which you may be most serviceable to God."[143]

In chapter X of *The Christian Directory* Baxter offered "Directions for the Right Choice of our Calling and Ordinary Labour," treating the matter of choice, like Perkins, in a way which suggested Vittorino da Feltre more than Calvin: "It is not enough that you consider what Calling and Labour is most desirable, but you must also consider what you or your children are fittest for, both in mind and body. For that Calling may be one man's blessing which would be another's misery and undoing."[144] Luther's simile of vocation as a cross and a burden was clearly abandoned here. Parents must never force upon their child an inappropriate calling: "Be sure that you *first* look to the *natural ingenuity* of your children (or yourself) and then to their Grace and Piety."[145] In all cases, "you must consider, not only the *Will* of the *Child* or the *Parents* but the natural fitness of their body and mind." Magistrates, pastors, and teachers may assist and advise the young in their decisions, making certain that the choice redounds to the glory of God and conforms with the natural inclinations of children. Baxter, without irony, would have us reconcile the will of the child with the will of God in the same decision.

It matters far less whether the later Puritan vocabulary of vocation be called a version of Calvin's or a fifth language in its own right, than that it be recognized for its partial resemblance to the idiom of Vergerio and Erasmus. Robert S. Michaelson has observed "a distinct

[142] Richard Steele, *The Tradesman's Calling, being a Discourse concerning the Nature, Necessity, Choice, etc., of a Calling in General* (London, 1684), p. 35.
[143] Richard Baxter, *A Christian Directory*, 2nd edn. (London, 1678), p. 110b.
[144] *Ibid.*, p. 378b.          [145] *Ibid.*, pp. 378b-379a.

movement from a religious doctrine of vocation in early Puritanism toward the beginnings of a secular doctrine of vocation among the later Puritans." Earlier formulae of orthodoxy were repeated, but the doctrine afforded new tolerance for the natural man—not only for his gifts and talents in the biblical sense but for his aptitude and worldly aspirations.[146]

[146] Robert S. Michaelson, "Changes in the Puritan Concept of Calling or Vocation," *New England Quarterly*, XXVI (1953), 315-336.

# ERASMUS AND ALBERTO PIO, PRINCE OF CARPI

MYRON P. GILMORE

AMONG the polemics which soured the last years of Erasmus, none finally drove him to more bitter replies than the attack on him by Alberto Pio, Prince of Carpi. For many of his opponents, like Noel Beda and the Spanish monks, Erasmus had nothing but contempt; they were ignorant of "bonae litterae," and their effusions were the product of a decadent tradition. The Prince of Carpi, however, spoke from the very citadel of that Italian humanism to which Erasmus owed so much. His was an attack from within the walls, and for this reason it is of particular interest to consider how Erasmus defended himself and justified his achievement in his replies to this critic, who had so distinguished himself in his early career as an enlightened patron of Renaissance arts and letters.

The little town of Carpi lies some ten miles north of Modena on the road to Mantua. From the early fourteenth century the family of Pio, or Pius, had held the lordship of the place. Like that of many other *signorie*, the history of Carpi is filled with bitter struggles among rival members of the family, complicated also by the frequent interventions of neighboring powers, of which the most important was Ferrara under the Este. At the end of the fifteenth century these local rivalries were eclipsed in the larger tragedy of the invasions of Italy by the northern powers. By 1530 the principality of Carpi, like many other Italian city-states large and small, had lost forever its independence.

Alberto Pio was the last ruler of his inherited domain, and much of his life was spent in trying to establish his claim to be Carpi's legitimate prince, first, against other members of his family and, second, against his opponents on the national and international scene, where he sought allies strong enough to help him maintain his independence. His ultimate failure was judged by his younger contemporary, Paolo Giovio, as yet another example of the victory of fortune over virtue.[1]

Alberto's early years were occupied in the struggle with his uncle and cousin. The latter finally sold his claims to the Duke of Ferrara. Alberto then turned for aid to the French king and became the am-

---

[1] Paolo Giovio, *Elogia virorum illustrium* (Basel, 1577), pp. 154-158.

bassador of Louis XII at the papal court. He played an important role in bringing about the reconciliation between Louis XII and Maximilian and was one of the negotiators of the League of Cambrai. As a consequence of his favor with the imperial court, he persuaded Maximilian to annul the sale to the Este of his cousin's rights to Carpi. In 1510 he was sent to Rome by Louis XII to prevent Julius II from making a separate peace with the Venetians. In this mission he failed, but he was able to further his own position against the Este. As the latter were increasingly supported by the French, Alberto turned again to the Emperor and, after the French failure in the summer of 1512, received an imperial investiture declaring him to be the sole ruler of Carpi. There followed a brief period of tranquillity during which Alberto was able to divide his time between administering his principality and serving as imperial ambassador in Rome, where he enjoyed the high favor of Leo X. With the accession of Charles V he made a new and fatal reversal of his alliances and once more threw in his lot with the French. In the Hapsburg-Valois struggle he became the ally and emissary of Francis I, and, after the French defeat at Pavia and the Treaty of Madrid, he was irrevocably committed to the anti-imperial and pro-French policy of Clement VII. In the sack of Rome in 1527 he shared the Pope's captivity in the Castle of Sant' Angelo. His palace in Rome was destroyed, and the Este occupied Carpi and his other possessions. As soon as he was able to escape from Rome, Alberto fled with his family to France. There he was warmly received by Francis I, who made him a *chevalier de St. Michel* and gave him estates in Normandy. His last years were spent in Paris, where he occupied himself with his attack on Erasmus. He died on 8 January 1531 at the age of fifty-six. Three days before his death he adopted the Franciscan habit, a gesture which inspired Erasmus's colloquy, *The Seraphic Funeral*. He was buried in the Church of the Observants, and a monument was erected to him in 1535, of which the recumbent portrait statue, clad not in a Franciscan habit but in Roman ceremonial armor, may still be seen in the Louvre.[2]

[2] The most complete biography is in H. Semper, F. O. Schulze, W. Barth, *Carpi, Ein Fürstensitz der Renaissance* (Dresden, 1882), pp. 1-35, with citations from many documents. See also P. S. Allen et al., ed., *Opus Epistolarum Des. Erasmi Roterodami*, 12 vols. (Oxford, 1906-1958), VI, 200. G. Tiraboschi analyzes Alberto's career at some length in *Biblioteca Modenese* (Modena, 1783), IV, 156-201, and more briefly in *Storia della letteratura italiana* (Venice, 1796), VII, Pt. I, 265-277. Litta, *Celebri famiglie italiane* (Milan, 1819), VI, 14-16,

More fortunate in his role as a patron of arts and letters than in his diplomatic activity, the Prince of Carpi became a considerable figure in the cultural life of his generation. His mother's brother, the great Pico della Mirandola, supervised his early education and was responsible for engaging Aldus Manutius to teach him Latin. In this decision his maternal uncle, Marco Pio, concurred—perhaps from less disinterested motives—hoping that, if his nephew dedicated himself to learning, he would not take up his claim to share in the governing of the principality. In 1480 Aldus was made a citizen of Carpi and was exempted from taxes because of the zeal with which he had begun the teaching of literature to his young charge.[3] Thus began an association which was to be of critical importance to the greatest Italian printer of the Renaissance. The Prince of Carpi encouraged his teacher's ambition to publish the *editiones principes* of the Greek classics and gave financial support to the Aldine establishment in Venice. In return he received the honor of the dedication of the great edition of Aristotle's *Organon,* the first volume of which came off the press in 1495.[4]

Between 1485 and 1500 Alberto studied at Ferrara, where he became a close friend of Lodovico Ariosto, one of his fellow pupils. The poet has left two Latin poems addressed to Alberto. The first, beginning "Alberte, proles inclyta Caesarum," records their studies together under the Augustinian Gregorio of Spoleto, who had

gives the genealogy of the Pio family. A portrait of Alberto formerly in the Mond collection is now in the National Gallery in London. It has been variously attributed to Pintoricchio, Peruzzi, Bartolommeo Veneto, Grimaldi, and Loschi. See R. Longhi, *Officina ferrarese* (Florence, 1956), p. 64, and C. Gould, *The Sixteenth Century Italian Schools* (National Gallery, London, 1962), p. 85. The bronze figure in the Louvre has been attributed to Rosso Fiorentino by M. Roy, *Artistes et monuments de la Renaissance française* (Paris, 1929), pp. 138-146, but this attribution has been doubted in a recent article by Eugene A. Carroll, "Drawings by Rosso Fiorentino in the British Museum," *The Burlington Magazine,* CVIII (April 1966), 179, n. 48. On "The Seraphic Funeral," see *The Colloquies of Erasmus,* tr. Craig Thompson (Chicago, 1965), pp. 500-501. Alfonso Morselli, *Notizie e documenti sulla vita di Alberto Pio* (Carpi, 1932), contains fifty-five letters of Alberto written to relatives and friends, a notice of his library, some documents of his administration of the principality, and an account of his long betrothal to Margarita Gonzaga and of his eventual marriage to Cecilia Orsini on 13 February 1518.

[3] Semper, *Carpi,* p. 19.
[4] On the relations between Alberto and Aldus, see *ibid.,* pp. 19-20, and P. de Nolhac, "Les correspondents d'Alde Manuce," *Studi e documenti di storia e diritto* (Rome, 1887), pp. 247-289.

also taught Giovanni de' Medici, the future Leo X. The second is a lament on the death of Catarina Pico, Alberto's mother. The Prince of Carpi is also invoked in flattering terms in *Orlando Furioso*.[5] Later, however, when Ariosto had to choose between Alberto of Carpi and Alfonso of Este, loyalty to his patron caused him to break with his friend.

During the period of his studies in Ferrara, Alberto also came to know Pietro Bembo and Jacopo Sadoleto, who remained his life-long friends. One of the last letters he could have received was written to him by Sadoleto in August 1530, offering consolation on the misfortunes of ill health and political adversity. Sadoleto sends his commentary on Psalm 93 with the warmest expressions of his high opinion of Alberto's learning and character.[6]

Friendships such as these, as well as his own qualities and rank, assured Alberto of a high place at the court of Leo X. Confirmed in 1512 in his principality, he was able to devote himself to the embellishment of his city. At Rome he had before him the work of Bramante, Michelangelo, Raphael, and Peruzzi, and he determined to make of Carpi a splendid center whose architecture in the new style would illustrate his position as an enlightened patron. The portrait of Alberto by Loschi painted, according to its inscription, in 1512 shows the Prince holding a quotation from the *Aeneid*, VI, lines 724-747, where Anchises in the underworld explains the constitution of human life and the cycles of time. This passage immediately precedes the famous prophecy of the glories of Rome.[7] Without going so far as to suggest that either sitter or artist intended a comparison between Carpi and Rome, the portrait does present the image of a ruler who is a patron of the arts. Alberto intended Carpi to be as distinguished a model of a princely court as Urbino, where his cousin Emilia Pia was the companion of the Duchess whose circle was to be immortalized by Castiglione. A nearer example for emulation was provided by the Este at Ferrara.

[5] Ariosto, *Opere minori*, ed. C. Segre (Milan, 1954): "Lirica latina," IX and XIV; *Orlando Furioso*, XLVI, XLVII. See also E. G. Gardner, *The King of Court Poets: A Study of the Work, Life and Times of Lodovico Ariosto* (London, 1906), pp. 31-32.

[6] Semper, *Carpi*, pp. 21-23. The text of Sadoleto's letter is in his *Opera omnia* (Verona, 1737), I, 100-101.

[7] See n. 1 above.

In pursuit of these ideas Alberto had the castle of Carpi transformed by the addition of Renaissance portals and courtyard, the old cathedral rebuilt on a plan inspired by the work on St. Peter's in Rome, and the new collegiate church of San Niccolò (begun in 1493) enlarged and brought to completion. According to Vasari, Baldassare Peruzzi was charged with this work,[8] but there is very little documentary evidence on which to base an exact account of his contribution. Whatever architect or architects were responsible, the complex of buildings around the piazza in Carpi still remains today a splendid monument to the taste of Alberto Pio.

All the projects for the glorification of his native city came to an end with the disaster of Pavia. After 1525 Alberto was formally deprived of Carpi and his other estates by Prospero Colonna, the victorious general of Charles V. In the following years he also lost his possessions and his library at Rome. After the sack of the city he fled to Paris, where he spent the last disillusioned years of his life.

These brief indications from the biography of Alberto recall the Renaissance prince, humanist, diplomat, patron of the arts, intimate friend of the most distinguished scholars of his generation, honored counsellor of emperors, kings, and popes. It might be supposed that all his interests would have led him to be among the friends and admirers of Erasmus, dedicated to the cause of the advancement of learning and the restoration of Christian piety. Instead, he became one of Erasmus's bitterest enemies, convinced that without Erasmus there would have been no Luther.

Already in 1525 Erasmus received word that Alberto was talking against him in the highest circles in Rome. He accordingly wrote on 13 May 1525 to his Italian friend and admirer, Caelius Calcagninus, complaining with disgust that he had heard that Alberto was circulating the opinion that Erasmus was neither a philosopher nor a theologian and that there was no sound doctrine in him.[9] Calcagninus replied with regret, assuring Erasmus that he had known Alberto for many years and that there was "nihil humanius nihil modestius" than this prince, who, far from disparaging the meritorious, had even shown

---

[8] G. Vasari, *Le vite de' più eccellenti pittori, scultori ed architettori*, ed. Milanesi (Firenze, 1879), IV, 598-599 and n. 3. A letter of Alberto Pio to his agent in Rome on the building of the Duomo is printed in N. Rocca, *Lettere e documenti interessanti, la storia del Duomo e della collegiata di Carpi* (Modena, 1873), pp. 41-43. The best account of Alberto's artistic patronage is still that given in Semper, *Carpi*, pp. 37-67.

[9] *Opus Epistolarum*, VI, 77, lines 38-41.

favor to those unworthy of it. Calcagninus begged Erasmus to proceed with caution and not trust the rumors he was hearing.[10]

By October, however, Erasmus had decided to address the Prince of Carpi directly. In a letter filled with compliments and disarming politeness, Erasmus reports that he has heard that the learned Prince of Carpi has declared that Erasmus is neither a philosopher nor a theologian. Perhaps Erasmus's informants have mistaken the name; if so, Alberto should pay no attention to his letter. As to the charge, Erasmus says, it is perfectly true: he has never pretended to be either a theologian or a philosopher. Of theological subjects he has written only on free will, and that at the request of others. More serious, however, is the charge that Erasmus is the cause of the Lutheran revolt. Here Erasmus becomes ironical and notes that there is one point which Luther and the Prince of Carpi have in common, namely, the belief that Erasmus knows no theology. The fact of the matter, Erasmus goes on, is that he might have stirred up a far greater tumult than Alberto could imagine; but he preferred instead always to expose himself unarmed to the weapons of both sides, rather than raise a finger in support of a faction not recognized by the Roman Church. He frankly admits that he originally thought Luther might have been divinely sent as an instrument for correcting abuses in the Church. These abuses, not anything he himself has done or written, have in fact caused the storm. Impious priests, tyrannous monks, and ignorant and proud theologians have occasioned the Lutheran revolution. He has himself only fought the battle for a better education, which he intended to be applied to the service of Christ and the Church.[11]

This is a very characteristic epistle. Through the cautious and polite language we can sense Erasmus's desire not to get involved in a controversy with one who could be a powerful enemy in high places. The tone, however, is not cringing but courteously firm. He proclaims his entire allegiance to the *ecclesia Romana* and denies any responsibility for Luther. At the same time, he admits that he originally saw the possibility of good in Luther and shows how his own scholarship has been perverted and misunderstood.

If Erasmus hoped that his frankness would allay the suspicions of the Prince of Carpi, he was doomed to disappointment. Alberto, who probably received Erasmus's letter by November 1525, devoted a part of the winter at a highly critical moment in his affairs to composing a long

[10] *Ibid.*, pp. 121-122, lines 229-248.    [11] *Ibid.*, pp. 201-203.

reply, which is dated from Rome, 15 May 1526. It was fairly widely circulated in manuscript, and Erasmus wrote to his friend Simon Pistorius on 2 September that he had received it, together with other works written against him in Rome which he suspected to have been inspired by Aleander, his former roommate in Venice.[12]

In the following spring in a long letter to Thomas More dated 30 March 1527, Erasmus, while condemning in the strongest terms the anonymous pamphlet which he believed to be by Aleander, spoke not too disparagingly of the work of Alberto Pio. He described the Prince of Carpi as having written "summa quidem humanitate et laudibus leniens omnia" but charged that Alberto had mixed up the work of Erasmus with that of Luther and had dealt harshly with Erasmus's *Moria* and *Paraphrases*. Erasmus said he suspected that Alberto, instead of reading and studying his works, had accepted hostile opinions from others.[13]

A year after the sack of Rome, Alberto was in Paris. His reply to Erasmus continued to circulate in manuscript. Erasmus wrote on 3 April 1528 to Clement VII invoking papal protection against the unjust charge of having fomented the Lutheran heresy.[14] In the autumn he was informed by his Paris friend and disciple, Louis Berquin, that Alberto was about to publish his indictment without having received any reply from Erasmus.[15] Erasmus answered that he intended to reply, but only by letter, and now indicated a much more hostile opinion of Alberto's work than he had given to More.[16]

Alarmed at the possibility of the appearance of the attack in print, Erasmus finally again addressed the Prince of Carpi himself. On 23 December 1528 he wrote that he had not replied before because he had not known how to reach Alberto in the confusion after the sack of Rome. He now pleaded with Alberto not to publish the work or, if he did, to mitigate the severity of his charges. The letter was a mixture of appeal and threat. It is doubtful whether it would have had any effect even if it had come earlier, but it arrived too late. On 7 January, two weeks after the date of the letter, the attack was published by Badius Ascensius in Paris.[17]

---

[12] *Ibid.*, p. 403, lines 130-136.    [13] *Ibid.*, VII, 12, lines 248-256.
[14] *Ibid.*, pp. 378-379.    [15] *Ibid.*, p. 525, lines 60-65.
[16] *Ibid.*, pp. 540-541, lines 46-49.
[17] The full title is *Alberti Pii Carporum comitis illustrissimi ad Erasmi Roterodami expostulationem responsio accurata et paraenatica, Martini Lutheri et asseclarum eius haeresim vesanam magnis argumentis et iustis rationibus con-*

Albertus begins by declaring that he does not know whether Erasmus's letter has given him greater pleasure or pain—pleasure that such a great man as Erasmus, whom he had long admired, should deign to write to him, pain that the letter was occasioned by disagreement. He has hesitated to reply, he says, but it seemed rude not to do so. He has been delayed by illness and complications in his affairs. He recalls that in his youth he had seen Erasmus in the house of Aldus in Venice with Thomas Linacre.[18] Although Erasmus, he admits, has done great things for the cause of literature, he has neglected the study of moderns in theology. It is quite untrue that Alberto has spoken ill of him. He does, however, condemn Erasmus's historical ideas on the primitive Church. It is, he says, very dangerous to analyze change or development in institutions or dogma and to point out differences between the Church in apostolic times and the Church in the present. Above all—and this is the principal charge—Alberto finds many points of view common to Luther and Erasmus, so that one may say that "either Erasmus Lutherizes or Luther Erasmusizes."[19] Specifically, Erasmus has aided Luther by his writings, especially his attacks on theologians and monks, and also by his silence at a time when he, more than others, should have spoken out.

This accusation leads to an account of the Lutheran heresy and the evils it has caused. On this subject Alberto's tone becomes most violent. There are, he says, two principles of Lutheranism which are most pernicious. The first is that of the exaltation of Scripture at the expense of tradition. To say that nothing is valid unless it is found in Scripture is to make nonsense of all constituted authority. The second is the principle of private judgment. Luther maintains that he alone is capable of understanding and interpreting the Scripture. These principles are responsible for all the evil strife which has come upon Germany.

This indictment of Luther, which takes up more than a third of Alberto's reply to Erasmus, is delivered in passionate tones, and it is difficult to believe that he was motivated by anything but the deepest conviction that he was right in trying to recall Erasmus from too compromising a connection with Luther.

Turning back to Erasmus's own works, Alberto considers that the *De libero arbitrio* was too gentle. The *Moria* and the *Paraphrases* have

---

*futans*, small 4to, 95 pp. printed recto and verso. Although written in the form of a letter, it was too long to include in *opus Epistolarum*. I have used the copy in the Vatican Library.

[18] *Ibid.*, fol. 11ᵛ.　　　　　　　　[19] *Ibid.*, fol. 29ʳ.

provided material for the Lutherans. On the question of the Reuchlin controversy, Alberto takes a moderate position and admits that he had favored Reuchlin and read with pleasure the *Epistolae obscurorum virorum*. Nevertheless, he charges too exclusive a devotion to the cause of literature without the aid of philosophy and theology has been a corrupting influence.[20]

Erasmus received this publication at Basel on the 9th of February. He immediately set about to prepare a reply in order to have it ready for the spring book-fair at Frankfurt. According to his own account, he wrote eighty octavo pages in ten days when he was also busy with many other tasks. The reply was printed by Froben in March.[21] It may be doubted whether Erasmus was quite ingenuous in maintaining that a work of so considerable a length had been composed in so short a time. Berquin had written to him on 13 October 1528 in terms that indicate his knowledge that Erasmus had already drafted a reply.[22] Even if earlier material was at hand, however, it is clear that after the publication of Alberto's *Responsio* Erasmus rearranged his arguments and gave the work a more polemical tone.

Erasmus still preserves some of the amenities in addressing his high-ranking opponent. He protests, as he had done in his recent letter, that he would have replied to Alberto earlier but did not know how to reach him in the confusion that followed the sack of Rome. He has been busy and ill. He complains that his original letter of 1525 was now printed with many errors as a preface to Alberto's reply. He repudiates the rumor that he is not in favor with the Pope and cardinals. It is impossible to trust anyone, he complains, and the times are such that under every stone is found a sleeping scorpion.

After these preliminaries Erasmus turns to the heart of his argument and declares that, although he hates to be praised with Luther, he finds it still more hateful to be condemned with him and to be accused of having been the cause of Luther's attack on the Church. Erasmus supposes with disparaging irony that Alberto has collected from others arguments that do him no credit. If it comes to assessing blame, Erasmus says, he can be his own accuser. He admits that he has always been too impatient with the work of correction and revision, and some

---

[20] *Ibid.*, fol. 90ʳ.

[21] *Opus Epistolarum*, VI, 199-200. The text of Erasmus's *Responsio* is printed in his *Opera omnia*, ed. J. LeClerc, reprinted by Olms, 11 vols. (Hildesheim, 1962), vol. IX, cols. 1096-1142. (This work will hereafter be cited as LB.)

[22] *Opus Epistolarum*, VII, 525, lines 60-62.

errors no doubt are attributable to this haste. He also admits that he has undertaken occasionally at the suggestion of others works for which he was ill-prepared (the *De libero arbitrio*). He even confesses that he has written and done certain things which he would have neither written nor done could he have foreseen what has come to pass.[23]

In spite of these concessions Erasmus repudiates firmly the charge that he is the cause of the Lutheran revolt. His efforts to raise the standards of education have been perverted. To the charge that "either Erasmus Lutherizes or Luther Erasmusizes" he replies that, on re-reading his own works, he has not been able to find a single dogma which agrees with Luther and, indeed, has found many which are absolutely contrary. All men of good will have hoped for the restoration of Christian piety, Erasmus goes on. He has tried to do what he could as an individual, and the Prince of Carpi should have done the same, instead of heeding the unfounded complaints of others about Erasmus. It is astonishing, he declares, that Alberto can bring himself to repeat such false charges as that Erasmus's writings have created doubts, that he has diminished the authority of the sacraments, the sanctions of the Fathers, and the honor of the Pope, that he has vilified priests and monks and mocked the reverence due to sacred ceremonies. On each of these specific charges Erasmus protests his innocence. He has never condemned a monk as a monk, and he would himself only too gladly live the monastic life if it were not for the feebleness of his health. If the world looks more coldly on the institution of monasticism, it is not due to his writings but to the behavior of the monks. Many who now condemn Luther are not themselves good Christians, and not all who go to Rome are on Christian business. Who knows whether God has not sent this pestilent beast Luther for the correction of the morals of our age? The Church should return to its primitive sincerity and piety.[24]

Erasmus next turns to the defense of his *Moria* and the *Paraphrases*, repeating many familiar positions—on the contrast between true, inward, piety and outward conformity, on the necessity of not confusing the abuses with the true uses of institutions, on the obligation of all to read and understand the Scriptures.[25]

In the concluding portion of his *Responsio* Erasmus takes up again the accusation of guilt from silence and violently denies it. It was not

[23] LB, vol. IX, col. 1100.    [24] *Ibid.*, cols. 1102-9    [25] *Ibid.*, cols. 1105-17.

his business, he claims, to drive Luther off the stage; this task should have been undertaken by those who sat in the orchestra, of whom Alberto Pio, Prince of Carpi, was one. In language of increasing bitterness Erasmus recalls that already, eight years before, he had been charged with supporting Luther. Many pamphlets on this subject have been issued, and he has replied to them all and made his position perfectly clear. Now the Prince of Carpi, coming late to the battle, urges things which have already been done, some of them superfluous, others absurd, and all anachronistic.

Finally, Erasmus returns again—as if his conscience on the matter bothered him—to the charge of not having written to Alberto earlier. He has recently sent a letter to which he has as yet received no answer. He would like to have stopped publication of this attack upon him, but it proved to be impossible to do so. He apologizes ironically for having replied to Alberto's eloquence with "a rude Dutch letter." He has had only six days in which to compose it, days mostly filled with other occupations. Even if there had been ample time, Erasmus adds, he is not so ignorant of his own mediocrity as to aspire to contend with an opponent of such erudition and eloquence as he has always admired rather than been able to imitate.[26]

There were many things about this reply calculated to be of great irritation to the Prince of Carpi. Erasmus violently denied the charge of complicity with Luther, either through his writings or through his silence. At the same time, he courageously admitted that he had originally looked upon Luther with favor and hoped that Luther might have been divinely sent to help the cause of the restoration of true piety. The weary contempt with which Erasmus dismissed Alberto's accusations and summons to recantation must have been as wounding to the Prince's pride as the ironical modesty of the conclusion. Consequently, Alberto set about composing a serious and comprehensive reply documenting his conviction that Erasmus had prepared the way for Luther. He began work on this treatise—for a treatise it became—in March 1529, when Erasmus's *Responsio* was published, and continued writing until his death in January of 1531. His work was posthumously published by Ascensius in Paris on 9 March 1531 with the royal privilege. In the preface the printer explains to the reader that the great Prince of Carpi continued to his last day his labors for the Catholic faith. His purpose had been twofold: first, to prove conclusively his charges against Erasmus and, second, to urge

[26] *Ibid.*, cols. 1118-22.

upon Erasmus correction and retraction.[27] The Italian humanist, Franciscus Floridus Sabinus, had served as secretary to Alberto and helped to see the book through the press after his patron's death, contributing also a poem of his own in the form of a dialogue between the book and the reader, in which the book deplores the death of the author who has left it in an unpolished state.[28]

This work was devised to show the whole history of the controversy. Erasmus's original letter of 1525, together with Alberto's *Responsio* of 1526, printed in 1529, serves as the introduction. Book I consists of Erasmus's reply to the latter work, with extensive marginal comments by the Prince of Carpi. The effect is that of an animated and acrimonious conversation, which brings out vividly the differences of style and character in the participants. When, for example, Erasmus speaks with regret of his unpolished letter having been given to the world without his consent, Alberto notes, "You yourself brought about its publication, nor were you at all upset by it since it is a most elegant composition."[29] Alberto dismisses contemptuously the excuse that the lateness of Erasmus's reply was due to the confusion which resulted from the sack of Rome.[30] To the complaint of Erasmus that he is being called "Porrophagus" and "Err-asmus" at Rome, Alberto drily replies that it is unworthy of a learned man to listen to such slanders.[31] Erasmus's complaint that he hates revision is met by Alberto's retort that he has always known there are some who edit their books before they write them and write them before they are conceived.[32] Erasmus's confession that he would not have written certain books had he foreseen the outcome provokes the rejoinder, "Why then do you not recant?"[33] Occasionally, Alberto is willing to concede a point in a more disarming way than one might expect, but on the principal issues the position becomes more rigid. When Erasmus maintains

---

[27] The full title of this rare book is *Alberti Pii Carporum illustrissimi et viri longe doctissimi praeter praefationem et operis conclusionem tres et viginti libri in locos lucubrationum variarum D. Erasmi Roterodami quos censet ab eo recognoscendos et retractandos*. A second edition was printed by Giunta in Venice on 4 September 1531. (This work will hereafter be cited as *XXIII Libri*, Paris or Venice.)

[28] On Franciscus Floridus, see M. Cosenza, *A Dictionary of Italian Humanists*, 5 vols. (Boston, 1962) s.v. "Sabinus." The poem printed on fol. 1 represents the book as mourning the death of its author, which left it deprived of its finished style. The piety of the author, the poem continues, will nevertheless live.

[29] *XXIII Libri*, Paris, fol. 47ʳ.      [30] *Ibid.*, fol. 47ᵛ.

[31] *Ibid.*, fol. 48ᵛ.      [32] *Ibid.*, fol. 49ʳ.      [33] *Ibid.*, fol. 49ᵛ.

that he has always venerated ceremonies except those that are superstitious, Alberto replies that, if one begins to remove ceremonies from
the Church, religion will not long endure.[34] And so the debate continues. Erasmus: "Human institutions always degenerate." Alberto:
"How false!"[35] Erasmus (defending the *Moria*): "I have heard from
my friends that Leo X himself took pleasure in reading this work."
Alberto: "I know that he did not approve of it although he enjoyed
some of the jokes."[36] These marginalia show that Alberto devoted careful study to Erasmus's text and that he was not always motivated by
blind hatred, although he clearly had little understanding of Erasmus's
sense of humor. At the end, however, he does indulge in some irony
of his own and thanks Erasmus for his high opinion and good wishes.

The impression of seriousness and the sense of conviction in the
rightness of his cause left by these notes is confirmed by the *Praefatio*
to the twenty-three books which immediately follows and which the
author says would have preceded the Erasmian text had the latter
not been published with the marginalia.[37] This preface is, in fact,
Alberto's most serious and moving justification, written, as it was, in
the last months of his life in exile and in ill health. He begins in a
philosophical vein by recalling that he never could have imagined that
he would find himself in controversy with Erasmus. It is characteristic
of the human condition, however, that the unexpected frequently
happens. It all began, Alberto explains, with Erasmus's letter complaining that he criticized Erasmus's doctrine and made him responsible for Luther. To Alberto's considered reply, Erasmus had responded
only after a long interval of three years, and then he had given the
text to the press before Alberto had even seen it. Although it had
contained some polite expressions, it was filled with accusations of
stupidity, negligence, and malice.

Alberto now replies to the charge that he had not really read Erasmus by confessing frankly that, at the time when he first wrote, he
had indeed not read many of Erasmus's works.

"You must not think, Erasmus, that all your works are worth reading. I had read but few, not because I despised you but simply because I had no leisure. Some ten years before I had perused the
*Adages* which I judged most useful for the study of literature. Then
I read *The Praise of Folly* which I found at first lively and elegant
but which subsequently so disgusted me as to turn me away from

---

[34] *Ibid.*, fol. 51[r].    [35] *Ibid.*, fol. 51[v].    [36] *Ibid.*, fol. 55[v].    [37] *Ibid.*, fol. 66[v].

your other writings. I had read your essay on *Confession* and, naturally attracted by the title, your *Diatribe on Free Will* as well as the *New Testament* and some of the Paraphrases, but I had hardly touched anything in your other works. . . . After your last attack I have tried to get hold of as many as possible although the reading thereof is made difficult because of your many digressions."[38]

Alberto concludes his preface by protesting that he has not undertaken his reply in a spirit of contentiousness. He is, he says, well aware how great is Erasmus's reputation and how powerful his eloquence. He has been moved only by a desire for truth and his zeal for the Catholic faith. An epigram at the end of the preface hails the Prince of Carpi as the avenger of religion against both Luther and Erasmus.[39]

The result of Alberto's extensive course of reading is contained in the treatise which follows the preface. If the first exchanges between Alberto and Erasmus are counted as Book I and the preface itself as Book II, the remainder of the work is divided into twenty-one books, each devoted to a single subject on which Alberto marshalled his proofs of Erasmus's complicity with Luther.[40] The titles of the books are as follows: III, *The Moria*; IV, *Fasting*; V, *Monasticism*; VI, *Ceremonies*; VII, *Adornment of Churches*; VIII, *Images of Saints*; IX, *Relics and the Cult of the Virgin*; X, *Scholastic Theology*; XI, *Authority of Scripture*; XII, *The Trinity and Arianism*; XIII, *Priests and Bishops*; XIV, *Primacy of St. Peter and the Power of the Pope*; XV, *Ecclesiastical Constitutions and Laws*; XVI, *Chastity and other Vows*; XVII, *Celibacy*; XVIII, *Matrimony*; XIX, *The Sacrament of Confession*; XX, *Faith and Works*; XXI, *The Just War*; XXII, *Oaths*; XXIII, *Mendacity*. There is considerable difference in the amount of space devoted to each of these subjects, ranging from nineteen folios on the cult of the Virgin to only two each on matrimony and confession. This uneven coverage may well reflect the unfinished state of the work at the time of Alberto's death. His arguments are backed by copious citations from Erasmus's works as well as from traditional authorities.

The chapter on the *Moria* gives the tone of the whole work. Alberto considers that from this work dates the fall of Erasmus. How dared

---

[38] *Ibid.*, foll. 68ᵛ-69ʳ.  [39] *XXIII Libri*, Venice, fol. 56ᵛ.

[40] The twenty-three books of the original title become twenty-four if the short conclusion is counted. This explains why Le Clerc, the editor of *Opera*, adopted the title *Apologia brevis ad viginti quattuor libros* (vol. IX, col. 1123).

Erasmus write against grammarians when he owed so much to Aldus? How could he condemn mathematics and philosophy, since without them the Scriptures cannot be understood? In all his other writings Erasmus has continued the attacks on theologians, monks, good works, the cult of the Virgin and saints which he had begun in the *Praise of Folly*.[41]

The succeeding chapters amplify the indictment of the first and make of the whole work perhaps the most complete exposition of the thesis that Erasmus prepared the Reformation and shared the religious opinions of Luther. In the conclusion Alberto declares again that his apology has been undertaken only for the sake of truth and the Catholic faith. He asks pardon if he has committed any errors, submits himself to the judgment of the Church, and prays God that Erasmus will in future utter nothing save what is proper.[42]

This work immediately provoked Erasmus to another rapidly executed counterblast. It was published by Froben in Basel in June of 1531 and was by July 25 already in the hands of Augustinus Steuchus of Gubbio, who wrote Erasmus remonstrating with him for his savage attack on a man who was dead and who in his last years had been the victim of so much misfortune.[43] In this composition the amenities were, indeed, no longer observed: it is one of the most savage compositions Erasmus ever wrote.

He begins by declaring that his opponent has ingeniously escaped through death, leaving his sting behind. Alberto has produced a hodgepodge, pieced together with selections from Erasmus's writings torn out of context, scriptural quotations misunderstood, material supplied by others, including many things that the Prince probably never saw. It is, indeed, invidious to write against the dead, but what is to be done if the dead have attacked? The bee escapes, leaving the sting in the

---

[41] *XXIII Libri*, Venice, foll. 57ᵛ-65ᵛ.  [42] *Ibid.*, foll. 192ᵛ-193ʳ.

[43] *Opus Epistolarum*, IX, 305, line 684. The full title of the first edition of Erasmus's works as given in *Opus Epistolarum*, VI, 200, is *Apologia, adversus rhapsodias calumniosarum querimoniarum Alberti Pii quondam Carporum principis quem et senem et moribundum et ad quidvis potius accommodum homines quidam male auspicati ad hanc illiberalem fabulam agendam subornarunt.* I have not seen a copy of this edition. A second edition, of which there is a copy in the Vatican Library, was produced on 5 January 1532 with the title *Ultima apologia adversus rhapsodias calumnio-sarum querimoniarum Alberti Pii quondam Carporum comitis illustrissimi nuper diligentissime excusa.* The *Apology* is printed in LB, vol. IX, cols. 1123-96, under the title *Apologia brevis ad viginti quatuor libros Alberti Pii quondam Carporum comitis.* Subsequent citations are to this edition.

wound. The very fact that Alberto assumed the Franciscan habit before his death puts anyone attacking him in the position of seeming to oppose the whole Seraphic order. Alberto's work is full of lies and false citations. Those who have written against Luther, like the Bishop of Rochester, have faithfully quoted even his works, but Alberto has distorted the sense of Erasmus. His attack is not even his own. It has been undertaken at the urging of others and completed with the help of assistants, especially the Spaniard, Sepulveda.[44]

Turning to the marginalia, Erasmus describes them as not less false than the rest of the book. He takes up each comment seriatim, reiterating and elaborating his earlier positions. Against Erasmus's view of the degeneration of human institutions, Alberto had argued that Christ had restored many things to a better state. Erasmus replies: "But I indicated the nature of human affairs which is so prone to evil that even what Christ restored with such devotion deteriorates, and the best laws become the worst models."[45] To Alberto's demand "How is it possible for Erasmus to regard Luther who for ten years has brought revolution to Germany as sent by God for the correction of a corrupt age?" Erasmus answers: "It is more than ten years since we have execrated the Turks and yet we all admit that they have been imposed by God as a punishment for our sins. We accept the fact that Pharaoh was raised up by the Lord against the Hebrews but this does not mean that we approve tyranny."[46] These examples will serve to illustrate the style of spirited defense mingled with invective which Erasmus applies to Alberto's marginalia. The method of giving a particular reply to every note brings into sharp focus many details of his general position.

Next Erasmus takes up Alberto's preface. He admits that there are many fortuitous things in human affairs which could not have been foreseen.[47] One of them is the fact that, although he had treated Alberto well in his first response, Alberto had replied by charging that Erasmus was the occasion, cause, author, and beginning of the whole religious revolution. This is the accusation to which Erasmus is obviously most sensitive, and he uses every weapon of irony, ridicule, and invective in order to repudiate it.[48]

The remainder of the *Apology* is devoted to answering book by book Alberto's treatise. The most lively section is the justification of the

[44] LB, vol. IX, cols. 1123-25.      [45] *Ibid.*, col. 1128 B.
[46] *Ibid.*, col. 1128 C.      [47] *Ibid.*, col. 1134 E.      [48] *Ibid.*, col. 1138 B, C.

*Moria* and the excoriation of Alberto for not having understood how to interpret the speeches of *Folly*. What has her condemnation of sophistic and brawling theologians to do with pious and sober theologians? Interspersed in this part of the defense are also autobiographical passages of great interest, such as the description of Erasmus's association with the Greek scholars at the Aldine establishment in Venice in 1509.[49]

In the succeeding chapters Erasmus takes up—sometimes very fully, as in the case of monasticism—all the questions of institutions and doctrine which had been the subject of Alberto's twenty-three books. The margins of Erasmus's text are liberally sprinkled with charges of "lie" and "false citation" against his opponent. The peroration is a final, culminating, passionate condemnation of the Prince of Carpi.

> "Gladly do I welcome his prayer that God grant that in the future I utter only what is proper, but I in turn pray for Pio that he may find in the Lord a more equitable and clement judge than he has been toward me. . . . Now the vulgar summon me to recant. But what am I to recant?—the propositions that Pio has formulated? that *I* wished theologians done away with, that *I* despoil priests of their possessions, that *I* condemn the institution of monasticism, that *I* abrogate the authority of Scripture, that *I* condemn the ceremonies and constitutions of the church, protect the doctrine of the Arians, revive that of Priscillian and the Epicureans, and many other charges more absurd than these? Never have I thought in the way that he has interpreted me and up to now he has proved nothing of all those things to which he has so often, so strongly, and so bitterly objected. It would be a new kind of recantation if, yielding to men who are delirious with the vice of slandering, I became my own accuser. Nay, rather, let them recant who furnish us with an example of the devil, openly and shamelessly fastening libels of this kind on the undeserving, and through such sordid actions, either seek fame or promise themselves vindication and victory as if Christ were dead and had no care of His Church."[50]

If Erasmus hoped with this powerful invective to have the last word against his dead opponent, he was disappointed. The Spanish scholar Juan Gines de Sepulveda, who had been mentioned by Erasmus as having had a large part in the composition of Alberto's treatise, now

[49] *Ibid.*, col. 1137 A-F.  [50] *Ibid.*, col. 1196 B-D.

immediately took up the defense of his patron. Sepulveda, who was later to become the historiographer of Charles V and Philip II, had as a young man been sent by Cardinal Ximenes to Bologna. There in the years 1518-1523 he had come into close association with the Prince of Carpi, from whom he received financial support, and he followed the Prince to Rome, sharing his captivity in the Castle of Sant' Angelo. When Alberto went to France, however, Sepulveda remained in Italy and entered the service of one of the imperial cardinals. In March 1532 he published in Rome and Paris his *Antapologia pro Alberto Pio Principi Carpensi in Erasmum Roterodamum.*[51]

The *Antapologia,* although a defense of the Prince of Carpi, was not a severe indictment of Erasmus. Its tone is moderate and courteous. Sepulveda is grieved because Erasmus, whom he has honored, falls into a lack of that charity which he has so often urged on others.[52] Sepulveda claims that his reply has been undertaken to defend his dead friend rather than to damage the reputation of Erasmus. The latter is wrong in thinking that Alberto undertook his reply at the urging of others. Alberto wrote from conviction, and the treatise was his own work, not that of assistants. Sepulveda has no difficulty in showing that he himself was in Italy at the time when Alberto was composing the twenty-three books in Paris and, therefore, could have had no part in the writing of it. Alberto had had an extensive training in philosophy and theology and, during the period of his illness, had readers who supplied him with the necessary texts. Sepulveda particularly reproves Erasmus for some passages in the *Moria* and the *Paraphrases,* but he closes on a very "Erasmian" note. "If I agree with Alberto in disapproving some things in your books, I am still far from thinking that you are not the greatest of men. But, although you are great, you are human, and it ought not to be a cause for wonder that you can have lapses, nor that among so many books which you have written and edited, some errors may be repaired by the careful diligence of others."[53]

On 1 April 1532, Sepulveda sent a copy of the Roman edition to Erasmus, saying that he had not written it "infenso animo sed officii gratia." He had hoped, he said, to send a copy before, but the zeal of certain friends who desired to remove all cause of hostility between

---

[51] On Sepulveda, see *Opus Epistolarum,* X, 3-4, and M. Bataillon, *Erasmo y España: Estudios sobre la historia espiritual del siglo XVI,* tr. from the French (Mexico, 1950), I, 476-480.

[52] *Antapologia* in Sepulveda, *Opera omnia,* 4 vols. (Madrid, 1780), IV, 544.

[53] *Ibid.,* p. 591.

him and Erasmus had caused certain expressions to be changed; these changes were not made in the Paris edition. He now feared that Erasmus may have seen the latter edition first.[54]

It is pleasant to record that this time Erasmus reacted in a manner more worthy of what he had often preached. He replied that he had indeed seen the Paris edition before the Roman one arrived. He regrets that Sepulveda has been involved in such an argument, to which he supposes the latter has been prompted by certain affections which do credit to one who serves both the muses and Christ. "I do not see what can come of answering this except further strife of which there is already enough in the world. Therefore I think it more advisable not to reply."[55]

This mild response led to further friendly exchanges, and among the last letters received by Erasmus before his death in the summer of 1536 was one from Sepulveda discussing an interpretation of a passage in St. Mark.[56]

So came to an end the controversy which evoked from Erasmus perhaps his most comprehensive and detailed justification against his critics. Both protagonists were concerned to proclaim their orthodoxy, and it may seem that Erasmus protested too much. His sensitivity to the identification with Luther was, however, a measure of the extent to which he thought of himself, and wished others to think of him, as loyal to Rome. Again and again he insisted that the correction of abuses and the restoration of piety were not to be confused with the revolutionary rejection of tradition. His two apologies against the charges of Alberto Pio, though hastily written, constitute impressive evidence against the view that Erasmus ever favored a "third church."[57]

The personality of his opponent has always seemed in some ways enigmatic. Francesco Guicciardini, that acute and cold observer of men, although he thought the Prince of Carpi "persona di grande spirito e destrezza," was critical of Alberto's loyalty in his diplomatic maneuvering.[58] Against this charge is balanced the testimony of such high-minded friends as Aldus, Sadoleto, Bembo, and Sepulveda. Even at the end of Alberto's life we are confronted with the two images of

---

[54] *Opus Epistolarum*, X, 4, lines 1-35.

[55] *Ibid.*, p. 83, lines 1-8.          [56] *Ibid.*, pp. 283-285.

[57] The theory of the "third church" was developed by the late A. Renaudet in *Erasme et l'Italie* (Geneva, 1954), pp. 200-249.

[58] F. Guicciardini, *Storia d'Italia*, ed. C. Panigada, 5 vols. (Bari, 1929), II, 333; III, 24, 65.

the Franciscan friar preparing for the pious death which Erasmus satirized in *The Seraphic Funeral* and the recumbent figure from the tomb in the Louvre clad in the armor of a Roman conqueror. However, any former vacillations between the active and the contemplative life and between classical studies and Christian piety seem resolved when we read the pages of his last apostrophe to Erasmus. It is impossible to deny that these are the accents of deep conviction.

Beyond the personalities the interest of the controversy lies in the emergence of two contrasting views on the causes of the Reformation, both of which, partial as they were, were destined to have a long-continued fortune. For Erasmus, the Lutheran revolution was the product of abuses—immoral monks, ignorant priests, sophistic theologians, worldly prelates. For Alberto, the application of humanist scholarship to the institutions and doctrine of the Church was the root of the disaster: grammar and philology must be aided and guided by philosophy and theology. Each of these contrasting positions contained much that was paradoxical. Erasmus believed in the possibility of improvement and hoped for the assimilation of the moral inheritance of the classical world within the Christian framework. Yet he was profoundly convinced that human institutions always tend to degenerate and that the wisest provisions can lead to the worst examples. Alberto denied inevitable decline yet believed that the only way to preserve the inheritance of Christ was to take it, so to speak, out of time and allow neither criticism of institutions nor changes in doctrine. The historical view of Erasmus confronted already the rigidity of the Counter-Reformation.

# ERASMUS AND THE REFORMERS
# ON NON-CHRISTIAN RELIGIONS AND
# *SALUS EXTRA ECCLESIAM*

GEORGE HUNTSTON WILLIAMS

ALTHOUGH the religious leaders of the Age of Reformation
were seldom directly concerned with the significance of non-
Christian religions, the problem at times claimed their attention in connection, especially, with the threat presented by the Ottoman Turks or with the question of the salvation of virtuous pagans,
raised with urgency by both the recovery of classical literature and the
discovery of new peoples overseas. The discussion of these topics in
the sixteenth century was most commonly couched in terms of divine
election and the invisible Church of the elect and in terms of implicit
and explicit faith. Salvation (*salus, Seligkeit*) was understood eschato-
logically, in terms of *eternal bliss* achieved by virtue of either an immediately realized immortality of the soul, an imminent resurrection
of the body to rejoin the soul, or some combination of these acts; it
was understood only to a minimal extent experientially, in terms of a
*present blessedness* or an inner peace through faith and grace.

Despite the seriousness of the Ottoman threat and the unparalleled
discoveries overseas in that century, the interrelated theological problems of non-Christian religions and *salus extra ecclesiam* never bulked
as large in the age of the definitive Western schism as they had in
patristic antiquity and the scholastic Middle Ages. Nevertheless, it is
useful to survey the attitudes of the classical reformers, counter-reform-
ists, and radical restitutionists on this question, in order to determine
how each of these groups adapted an important patristic and medieval
legacy to their new theological positions in face of the practical problems of their own time.

Most of what has been written on this subject has dealt with the
stance taken by the reformers in the presence of the military expansion
of the Turks. Yet the attitude of Christians toward the Turks as Muslims was also a theological matter, particularly for the Protestants. It is
instructive to see to what extent Protestant theologians recast the traditional views about the existence and significance of religions other
than Christianity in the context of the theology of justification by faith

alone. What they thought belongs to the history of changing Christian attitudes toward non-Christian religiosity.[1]

Within this long history an important consideration has always been whether the Christian theorists have been thinking primarily about religions of the past, presumably superseded by Christianity, or about some contemporary religion or religio-political challenger. The theologians of the patristic age, although they had to contend as apologists with a new rabbinical orthodoxy within Judaism after the destruction of the Temple in Jerusalem and with what they considered the improper religious demands of the Roman state, nevertheless generally looked backward to biblical Judaism and to pre-Christian religious philosophies when they pondered the problem of the divine economy. Their principal categories for reflection on religion, therefore, were old and new, before and after, imperfect and perfect, lost and restored.

With the extraordinary rise of Islam, however, and the sudden overwhelming of three patriarchates by the new religion of Mohammed, Christian theologians were faced with an entirely different task, for they now had to cope at once with what, considered even in the best light, was surely divine chastisement for Christian failures and with what in any case, in the eyes of the challengers themselves (who both acknowledged Moses and Jesus and yet saw them as superseded), was a superior, more comprehensive—indeed, the definitive—revelation of the God of Adam and Abraham. Accordingly, Christian theologians alike in the vast occupied territories and in the undisturbed territories of Byzantine and Latin Christendom labored for centuries to recast the traditional patristic thinking about pre-Christian and praeter-Christian religions in the light of the contemporary martial, political, cultural, and theological challenge of Islam, which now had the advantage Christianity had once had in any debate in terms of before and after, old and new, partial and fulfilled. Christian apologists henceforth had to work more and more in the framework of truth and falsehood, divine election and chastisement, fruits rather than roots, eternity more than time.

[1] The two major comprehensive explorations of the interrelated problems of *salus extra ecclesiam* and the Christian theology of non-Christian religiosity are H. Pinard de la Boullaye, S.J., *L'Etude Comparée des Religions: Essai critique*, 3rd edn., 2 vols. and separate index (Paris, 1929-1931), and Louis Capéran, *Le Problème du Salut des Infidèles*, 1st edn., 2 vols. (Paris, 1912); 2nd edn., 2 vols. (Toulouse, 1934).

By the beginning of the Age of Discovery and the Age of Reformation Christian theologians all the way from overwhelmed Byzantium (1453) to reconquered Spain (1492) had developed a wide range of theories about contemporary religiosity whether Islamic or heathen, almost as rich and variegated as that of the Church Fathers.

Catholic thinkers in these overlapping ages of world exploration and Christian renewal and schism had the resources of both patristic antiquity and medieval experience and speculation with which to interpret alike the Protestant revolt, the renewed sway of Islam, and the diverse and often advanced religions of Asia and the New World, which were swiftly opening the minds of Europeans to dimensions of the ways of providence that their patristic or scholastic predecessors could scarcely have imagined. An awareness of new peoples and their religions, all the way from the realm of mythical "Presterjohn" in Ethiopia to the Andes and Cathay, became a part of the Catholic world view, especially of theologians under the imperial dominion of Charles V, and a great inducement to fresh thinking about dominion, natural law, morality, and religion and about the Christian theory of missions among advanced peoples overseas. The millennial elaboration of the scriptural, papal, juridical, and missionary implications of Psalm 2:8 ("I will give thee the heathen for thine inheritance and the uttermost parts of the earth for thy possession") suddenly had fresh relevance.

The Protestant theologians, in contrast, being on principle critical of the medieval religious experience—whether in the form of martial missions (the crusades), mysticism (the universalization of religious experience), or interfaith debates, parleys, and councils (Franciscan missionaries, Raymond Lull, Nicholas Cusanus)—were, theoretically, obliged to rethink the whole question of non-Christian religions and their individual devotees in terms of their new ruling principle of scriptural solafideism. But these reformers seldom came directly to grips with the problem theologically; and, whenever they came even close to undertaking the task, it was almost always in the context of an immediate religio-military crisis. Yet this contemporaneous approach was not basically congenial to Protestants. Their disposition was to look backward (*ad fontes*). At once biblicists and, to a greater or lesser extent, humanists, Protestant theologians tended to return to the stance of the apostles and the Church Fathers. They much preferred to look back of themselves in time rather than around themselves to the New World in dealing with the problem of non-Christian religiosity.

321

But their humanistic-scriptural predilection for a backward glance ran counter to the existential and even eschatological thrusts inherent in their new theological position.

For example, Protestants looked at Judaism as primarily the religion of the Law, which had arisen before Christianity with a sacred language of which they all sought now to become masters. But some Protestants, in becoming personally acquainted with Jewish rabbis in order to learn Hebrew, were thereby obliged to think also of a living and, as they commonly said, stubborn Judaism. Accordingly, some Protestants were filled with an almost apocalyptic missionary hope that their evangelical purification of Christianity would at long last commend their renewed religion to Jews, as a scholastically carapaced and coercive Christianity had not been attractive to them under the Papacy. Thus, a dispensationally oriented theology of before and after (the Law) imparted to the theology of religion of several reformers an eschatological character as well. With respect to the Turks, the reformers could not but decry the vigor of Islam as constituting a grave and common danger to Central Europe. Yet they were also freer than Catholics to descry providential purposes in the pressures exerted, apparently by God's leave, in the rise and expansion of the Ottoman Turks at a crucial moment in the process of Western religious renewal.

As the classical Protestant theologians looked backward upon the religion of the people of the Old Covenant and found there under the eternal Christ a Church and people essentially one with the people of the New Covenant, they resorted increasingly to an interpretation of other religions in terms of Gentile reprobates over against the invisible elect, the Church of Cain over against the Church of Abel, in line with the thought of their most revered Church Father, Augustine. In this way, a few of the reformers could at least conceive of the possibility that individuals chosen before and beyond the establishment of the visible Church of Jesus Christ might be included in the invisible Church of the elect from the beginning of the world. Their angle of vision, however, allowed the reformers to ignore all details of the various religious systems in which these possibly elect persons might have been nurtured.

The reformers (and with them Catholic divines) could, however, in reading the other Fathers besides Augustine, have become aware of other patristic theories about non-Christian peoples and their religions. In Christian antiquity the apologists, historians, and theologians of the new community of faith which thought of itself as a third race, neither Jew nor Gentile, neither Barbarian nor Greek, had, in fact, developed a wide range of hypotheses about the meaning of non-Christian religions in the divine economy.

Primarily concerned with the religions that had arisen prior to their own—notably, Judaism and the various Graeco-Roman religious philosophies in their cultural-mythological milieu—the Church Fathers had postulated, besides (1) the doctrine of *individual* elect persons amid the mass of fallen humanity and its numerous forms of *false religions*, the following views: (2) that Christianity was the republication of the aboriginal religion of Paradise and the Golden Age which had, here and there, survived from the beginning in the company of "the Friends of God" (the latter phrase combining both scriptural and pagan motifs); (3) that the eternal Word (*Logos*) had been guiding various groupings of humanity by means of religious philosophy and the moral law toward the plenitude of the revelation of the Word as incarnate in Jesus Christ; (4) that what was good in other religions and religious philosophies had been cravenly stolen *or* resourcefully borrowed from the Hebrews and then the Christians; (5) that other religions were Satan's tempting counterfeits of the true faith and cultus; (6) that national angels were, under God, guiding all peoples and their religious cults in various stages of obedience and disobedience on the part of both angels and men; (7) that the false religions were spiritual chastisements of various peoples for their having turned from an aboriginal universal monotheism and perfect cultus; and (8) that God intended the salvation of all men and would eventually bring about a *restitutio omnium* (Acts 2:21), including the fallen angels (universalism). These eight fairly distinct theories were also variously combined and refined. The Greek Fathers tended to be somewhat more optimistic about the divine purposes in the varieties of world religions than the Latin Fathers.

To these eight theories of the patristic age, Byzantine and Latin theologians and Arabic theologians (both Catholic and schismatic) in Muslim lands added in the course of the Middle Ages—apart from their legitimation of holy inquisition and holy warfare—three new views of non-Christian religions (notably Islam): (9) that Islam specifically was a chastisement of Christians by God for their schisms and moral defections; (10) that Mohammed (or any other heresiarch) was, contrariwise, the instrument of Satan or, more precisely, of the Antichrist, since he misappropriated the revelation in Jesus Christ; and (11) that "Allah" was merely another name for the true God and, hence, God might well deign to accord to Muslims, by virtue of their obedience to the Koran, eternal salvation in the "bosom of Abraham."[2]

Before going on to observe what several representative reformers did, or failed to do, with these eleven patristic and medieval theories and with the relevant scriptural texts, we must first take note of the position of Erasmus of Rotterdam, whose patristic editions and whose specific views on the place of the non-Christian religions in the divine economy had to be taken into consideration by Catholics and Protestants alike.

## I. *Erasmus and Non-Christian Religion*

Desiderius Erasmus, whose *philosophia Christi* stressed more the imitation of Christ than Christ's atonement and whose *Respublica Christi* stressed the virtue of charity and the cause of peace more than faith or hope, in his anti-scholastic Christian humanism slightly broadened the hope of ultimate salvation for those who had lived virtuous lives before Christ and for contemporary pagans who were still beyond the reach of evangelists. He thus helped the Catholic Church to rethink its relation to the peoples and their religions overseas. He also encouraged—indirectly, at least—the radical reformers, like the Anabaptists, to reconceive the world effect of the atonement of Christ and, in their turn, to restate the relation of "true Christians" to the devotees of other religions. At the same time, the magnanimous Christian humanism of Erasmus, with its postulate of freedom of the will in the realm of salvation, induced a reaction in most of the classical Protestant reformers toward the more severe restriction of the scope of redemption and the erection of unscalable fences on the boundaries of the invisible Church of the elect. Erasmus's views of non-Christians are, therefore, a proper introduction to the theological and ecclesiological problem of non-Christian religiosity in the sixteenth century, whether one deals with the Protestant Reformation, the Catholic Reform, or the various Radical Restitutions.

On close scrutiny, it turns out, Erasmus's views were actually not much more comprehensive than those of some of the medieval scholastic theologians (like Thomas Aquinas, who had dealt with the issue of

---

[2] The most authoritative expression of this view was that of Pope Gregory VII Hildebrand in his letter (ca. 1076) to the Moorish ruler al-Nāsir ibn Alennas (d. 1088), contained in Migne, *Patrologia Latina*, CXLVIII, cols. 450ff.; cited in *The Declaration on Non-Christian Religions* of the II Vatican Council.

*salus extra ecclesiam* in terms of election and *fides implicita*) and, indeed, not quite so inclusive as were those of some of the Church Fathers whose works Erasmus edited (for example, Irenaeus). It was natural that Erasmus, as classicist and patristic scholar, should have touched upon the theological problem of the salvation of non-Christians and the meaning of the various religions of mankind primarily in terms of pre-Christian Jews and noble Greeks and Romans; but he also had occasion to address himself formally to the contemporary threat of the Turks and to the existence of millions of inhabitants in newly discovered regions of the world who through no fault of their own had only now the bare possibility of hearing the saving Gospel proclaimed by authorized evangelists.

Erasmus first expressed himself on virtuous pagans in the oldest extant draft of his *Antibarbarorum liber*,[3] supplying us with his opinions and those of four friends and acquaintances who engaged in a colloquy (circa 1489) on the "barbarism" of the scholastics, monks, and prelates in the orchard of the summer house of the bishop of Cambray. This draft is a literary idealization and amplification of the original colloquy. Seated under the shade of an apple tree, the five discussants thought of themselves as a kind of "academy" of humanist devotees of classical literature, hence, as citizens of the abiding "republic of letters." The secretary of Bergen-op-Zoom, Jacob Batt, led the discussion. He expressed ideas which Erasmus (who allows himself to be inconspicuous in the literary version of the colloquy) also endorsed.

[3] The final version of *Antibarbarorum liber* was to be printed in Basel in 1520. The draft here discussed was copied by an unknown scribe in the library of the House of the Brethren in Gouda on empty pages of a printed work of Erasmus (his *opera* of Jerome), ca. 1495. Albert Hyma has transcribed and edited the Gouda version as Appendix B in his *The Youth of Erasmus*, University of Michigan Publications, History and Political Science, X (Ann Arbor, 1930), pp. 239-331. Rudolf Pfeiffer, critical of Hyma, identifies four stages in the evolution of *Antibarbari* and dates the Gouda text ca. 1495 as the second stage, when Erasmus resolved to turn his youthful piece of ca. 1489 into a four-part dialogue. See "Die Wandlungen der 'Antibarbari,'" *Gedenkschrift zum 400. Todestage des Erasmus von Rotterdam* (Basel, 1936), pp. 50-68. In the Gouda version one may assume that the words of the chief discussant, Batt, render for us the thoughts of Erasmus. In the original rustic colloquy his part appears to have been taken by Cornelius Gerard from Steyn. K. A. Meissinger brings out the fact that the "barbarians" were not only the scholastics but also the exponents of the New Devotion. See "Erasmus entdeckt seine Situation," *Zeitschrift für Kirchengeschichte*, XXXVII (1940), 188-198.

In the colloquy Erasmus himself, however, openly regrets that in the beginning "Christians did not know pagan literature" and that they condemned beautiful things as vile, partly because they were moved by the zeal of a faith more vehement than wise. He even alleges that primitive Christians disguised their abhorrence of human nature and their own indisposition to grasp what was being said by the most noble pagans "under the name of religion."[4] Batt in a long speech inventories and chronicles the utter dependence of Christians upon these pagans in every department of life, including the language in which they are conversing, and concludes: "[W]e Christians have nothing which was not passed on to us by pagans (*ethnicis*)."[5] Admitting that the main question before the discussants is not the much debated question of the fate of the ancient pagans "who lived before our faith," Batt nevertheless emphatically remarks in passing: "If, however, we should wish to follow surmises, I shall easily demonstrate that either those men from among the pagans are saved or else no one at all." And he asks: "Does Virgil burn in hell and Christians recite his poem?"[6] The main thrust of Batt's statement, however, is to stress the truth and beauty of classical literature without going into the question of pagan faith or conduct. By remarking that Christians profitably read Origen's theological writings even though he was condemned by the Church, Batt hopes to clear the way for arguing that moral objections are not reason enough to condemn the works of anyone who wrote effectively. He goes on, movingly, to state the view Erasmus held at this time on religions other than Christianity, though the colloquists are still thinking primarily of classical antiquity:

He [Jesus Christ] wished that all by-gone and future ages might serve the *golden age* in which it had been decreed that he should be born; and it pleased him to restore whatever there might be in the nature of things, in order that the felicity and glory of this one age might be brought to perfection, because he promised that he would perfect himself, saying [John 12:32]: "When I am lifted up from the earth, I shall draw all things to myself." Here it seems to me that the word "draw" has been used most aptly, that thou mayest understand that all things ought to be drawn—whether they be hostile, or pagan, or otherwise alien—even if they do not arrive at the worship of Christ. For where is that harmony of all things which is brought to pass, as St. Augustine testifies, lest anything evil seemed to have been

[4] Hyma, p. 250, col. A.     [5] *Ibid.*, p. 281.     [6] *Ibid.*

created in vain? To what end, from the rudimentary beginnings of the world, have there been so many emblems (*figurae*), so many prodigies, so many mysteries if not with reference to the Christian age? . . . For indeed, why all the arduous labor among the ancients in their laws, in their philosophy? To what purpose all of that? Surely not that we, having arisen therefrom, should condemn it all, but rather that the highest religion should be at once ornamented and sustained by the most beautiful studies. Whatever of the Gentiles had been bravely done, well said, ingeniously thought out, and diligently transmitted, Christ had prepared for his Kingdom (*Reipublicae*).[7]

In his *Paraclesis*, the hastily composed but moving preface to his Greek New Testament published in 1516, Erasmus spoke in his own name what we have just heard him say through Batt. This testimony to his high esteem for the virtuous pagans is all the more impressive for having appeared in a prefatory appeal to theologians to study the philosophy of Christ directly from Christ and his apostolic interpreters rather than in scholastic versions. The appeal was interspersed with an urgent invitation to scholars to make this salvific word in turn available in vernacular translation for children and the common people. After observing that theological scholars were often fascinated by recondite writings from antiquity, Erasmus asked why they were not even more engrossed by the New Testament literature, in view of the fact "that this teaching has come not from Egypt or Syria but from heaven itself." And yet precisely while proclaiming the celestial credentials of the New Testament and the extraordinary accessibility therein of the simple, saving word, Erasmus was prepared to speak very highly also of the pagan philosophers and moralists. Having expressed the hope that this kind of wisdom, which "renders foolish the entire wisdom of this world," may be translated so that it might be read "not only by Scots and Irish but also by Turks and Saracens," he wrote: "[A]lthough no one has taught this [restoration of human

---

[7] *Ibid.*, pp. 283f. There is at this point no difference in wording between ca. 1489 and 1520, except that *gentiles* becomes *ethnici*. For changes in the place of the Golden Age in Erasmus's thought, see Peter G. Bietenholz, *History and Biography in the Work of Erasmus of Rotterdam* (Geneva, 1966), pp. 35-39.

N.B. Where a passage has already been translated in readily available editions, I have used that translation and cited its source. Occasionally, I have inserted the original word or phrase in parentheses; less frequently, I have slightly modified the translation or introduced italics for emphasis. Many of the translations, of course, are my own.

nature] more perfectly and more effectively than Christ, nevertheless one may find in the books of the pagans very much which does agree with his teaching."[8] Briefly, Erasmus then characterized the views of the Stoics, Socrates, Aristotle, Epicurus, Diogenes, and Epictetus. Despite his contention that Christ presented "the same doctrine so much more fully"—which would naturally commend a primary concentration on the New Testament in all its redemptive plentitude— Erasmus nevertheless still felt obliged to add immediately: "If there are things that belong particularly to Christianity in these ancient writers, let us follow them."

In the dedicatory letter to the Benedictine Abbot Paul Volz in Alsace, which constitutes the preface of the 1518 edition of the *Enchiridion Militis Christiani,*[9] Erasmus applied his principles of Christian warfare for the Christian in the everyday world, which included the threat of Turkish invasion. It was his proposal to convert Muslims rather than to slay them. He could not see in a vainglorious or vindictive territorial expansion of Christendom an extension of the rule of Christ:

The most efficacious way of overcoming the Turks would be if they beheld that which Christ taught and exemplified shining forth in our own lives, if they perceived that we do not covet their empires nor thirst after their gold nor seek their possessions, but strive for nothing except their salvation and Christ's glory. . . . And if this be not our disposition, it will sooner come to pass that we shall degenerate into Turks rather than win the Turks to our side. And although the dice of war, ever uncertain, fall favorably, it will happen that the Pope or his cardinals perhaps may rule more widely, but not Christ, whose kingdom flourishes at last only if piety, charity, peace, and chastity thrive.[10]

Erasmus guarded himself against any charge that his injunction "to draw the Turks to religion with the help of Christ rather than by arms" might be used to sanction quiescence in the face of a Turkish attack.

Erasmus returned to his primary interest in the destiny of the virtuous pagans notably in two of the pieces of his ever expanding volume

[8] The Latin text is available in *Ausgewählte Werke,* ed. Hajo Holborn (Munich, 1933), pp. 139-149; tr. John C. Olin, *Desiderius Erasmus, Christian Humanism and the Reformation* (New York, 1965), p. 100.

[9] The critically edited text is published in *Opus Epistolarum,* ed. P. S. Allen et al. (Oxford, 1906-1958), III, 361-377; tr. Olin, pp. 107-133.

[10] Olin, p. 113.

of colloquies—*Convivium religiosum* (1522) and *Inquisitio de fide* (1524)[11]—and in the preface to his edition of Cicero's *Tusculanae Quaestiones* (1523). In both colloquies Erasmus allowed interlocutors to carry forward what the magistrate Batt had first formulated for him.

In *Convivium religiosum* a group of five discussants move back and forth between Pauline and pagan literature, reflecting on the good life and final blessedness. It is while their attention is focused on the questions of law, freedom, decorum, and expediency in connection with I Corinthians 6:12 ("all things are lawful") that Eusebius[12] makes the following generous observation: "[W]hatever is devout and contributes to good morals should not be called profane.[13] Sacred Scripture is of course the basic authority in everything; yet I sometimes run across ancient sayings or pagan writings . . . so purely and reverently and admirably expressed that I can't help believing their authors' hearts were moved by some divine power. And perhaps the spirit of Christ is more widespread than we understand and the company of saints includes many not in our calendar."[14] Another interlocutor is allowed by Erasmus—in the context of a continued comparison of Paul's views on morality with those of Cicero, Plutarch, and Cato—to ejaculate the words for which the whole colloquy has been renowned ever since: "Saint Socrates, pray for us!" And this interjection is followed im-

---

[11] The whole collection has been translated by Craig R. Thompson, *The Colloquies of Erasmus* (Chicago, 1965). Thompson earlier published, along with extensive notes, *Inquisitio de fide: A Colloquy by Desiderius Erasmus Roterodamus*, Yale Studies in Religion, XV (New Haven, 1950), one section of which (pp. 101-121) is the most extensive discussion in print of Erasmus's views on *salus extra ecclesiam*. The most recent comprehensive American study of Erasmus is the dissertation of John B. Payne, "The Sacramental Theology of Erasmus" (Harvard University, 1967). The present writer has been greatly helped by the work of both scholars, and especially by the generous personal suggestions of the latter. The most recent European study is that of Ernst Wilhelm Kohls, *Die Theologie des Erasmus* (= Die Theologische Zeitschrift, Sonderband I), (Basel, 1966).

[12] In the first edition of 1522 the discussants were a series of five, with names chosen arbitrarily in alphabetical order beginning with Adolphus. In the second edition (also of 1522) here being cited, the names have been changed to suggest the character of each, beginning with Eusebius (the pious), and four additional discussants have been included.

[13] The previous discussant had proposed to adduce Cicero in support of his view but somewhat diffidently spoke of him as being among the "profane writers."

[14] Erasmus, *Opera*, ed. J. Leclerc (Leiden, 1703-1706), vol. I, col. 681; Thompson, *Colloquies*, p. 65.

329

mediately by the comments of a third interlocutor, which bear closest upon our present theme when he remarks: "As for me, there are many times when I do not hesitate to hope confidently that the souls of Virgil and Horace are sanctified (*sanctae*)."[15]

In the epistolary preface to Cicero's *Quaestiones* (1523), Erasmus, while admitting that "where the soul of Cicero dwells is perhaps not for human judgment to decide," maintained that surely in his most noble writings Cicero was moved by Divinity; and, he added, if it be brought against Cicero that he was not without blemish, surely the same would have to be said about many an Old Testament worthy who in faith looked forward to Christ without professing the specific doctrines which after Christ would constitute "explicit faith" or would be implied in "implicit faith."[16] For Cicero to be saved, it was perhaps enough that he believed in the *Numen*, in the immortality of the soul, and in appropriate rewards and punishments in the hereafter. Surely, Erasmus argued, virtuous pagans could not be expected to have experienced as sharp an adumbration of Christian events and truth as the Jews had been able to experience with the benefit of anticipatory (prophetic) revelation; and about the salvation of righteous Jews before the advent of Christ there was generally no doubt. Erasmus's willingness here to go beyond the doctrine of "implicit [Christian] faith" (which, according to Thomas Aquinas, sufficed for salvation) toward a conception of natural religion and a pious life shows that, for a time, his view of salvation was more comprehensive than that of most scholastics.[17]

In the colloquy *De fide*, which is a commentary on the Apostles' Creed in the form of a dialogue between Aulus and Barbatius, the latter an idealized "heretic" with some of the traits of Luther, Erasmus had to take up directly the question of the outer limits of the Holy Catholic Church and the Communion of Saints and, in the simplest terms, the

---

[15] *Opera*, vol. I, col. 683; Thompson, *Colloquies*, p. 68.

[16] Letter to John Vlatten (Basel, ca. Oct. 1523); *Opus Epistolarum*, V, pp. 339f.; noted by Thompson, *De fide*, p. 116.

[17] This is the view of Hans Baron in his review essay of Thompson's *De fide*, esp. in the second section, entitled "Der Humanismus und die Thomistische Lehre von den *gentiles salvati*," *Archiv für Reformationsgeschichte* (henceforth cited as *ARG*), XLIII (1952), 254-263. For what Baron considers the Italian humanist strain in Erasmus' thought on non-Christians, see, with special reference to Colucci Salutati and Francesco da Fiano (Florence, ca. 1400), "Classicism and Ancient Religion," *The Crisis of the Early Italian Renaissance*, 2 vols. (Princeton, 1955), I, ch. 14, 270-284.

questions of salvation *extra ecclesiam* and of virtue *extra fidem*. Here we see Erasmus, as heir of the medieval tradition in which Augustine's views bulked large, expressing himself as magnanimously as he could in the person of Barbatius, at a time when he was already well on his way to rejecting the real Luther, whose views concerning the bondage of the will unto salvation, the predestinarian confines of the invisible Church, and the essentially anti-Christian character of the Papacy had profoundly alienated the Catholic evangelical humanist. This idealized heretic is encouraged to say to the interlocutor, Aulus, what perhaps Erasmus wished that the reformer of Wittenberg had been content to say about the Church and salvation: that Christ, on the cross "with his limbs stretched to every quarter of the world" called "all the nations to salvation"; that his invisible Church as a spiritual body is "a communion of all goods among all godly people from the beginning of the world even to the end"; but that "outside this fellowship not even a man's good deeds bring him to salvation unless he be reconciled (*nisi reconcilietur*)[18] with the holy congregation" "because outside the Church there is no remission of sins, however much a man may torment himself with penance or perform works of mercy"; and, finally, that at the end of history before Christ's "judgment seat all men will be forced to stand, of whatever rank, whether kings or commoners, Greeks or Scythians."[19]

Any survey of Erasmus's life-long views of the eternal destiny of virtuous pagans, ancient and contemporary, and of the providential meaning of virtue, faith, and cultus outside Christendom must take seriously the foregoing relatively conservative statement made midway in his public career on an issue of paramount importance to the theologians propounding salvation by faith alone. Although, to be sure, the latter would have stressed justification of the elect few, Erasmus also, by stressing "the remission of sins," seemed here in his own idiom to have limited the membership in the Church—in this case, to those within the range of its sacramental ministry. Moreover, by not bringing in divine election, which with Augustine, for example, allowed for a

---

[18] In the definitive translation of the *Colloquies*, Thompson has at this point "unless he is *reunited*." I have gone back to Thompson's preliminary translation in *De fide*, p. 71, which literally renders the Latin original and which might allow for some relationship to the invisible Church analogous to baptismal regeneration and penitential readmission.

[19] Thompson, *Colloquies*, pp. 183, 187, 185. All these phrases belong to Barbitius, and Aulus professes to agree with him.

theoretical inclusion of saints in the invisible Church before the advent of Christ, Erasmus himself in *De fide* actually offered no theological basis for his disposition to include "godly people from the beginning of the world even to the end," like the virtuous pagans, about whose salvation in earlier pieces already cited he had been sanguine.

When in 1530 Erasmus was approached both by Philip Melanchthon for the evangelicals and by the Catholic party to express himself on the Turkish problem on the occasion of the Diet of Augsburg, he had a good opportunity to take up again the contemporary implications of our question; but, though his response was humane, he could go no further in his understanding of Islam as a religious and moral system than to hope for irenic conversion. His answer took the form of a letter addressed to the jurist Johannes Rinck, entitled *Ultissima consultatio de bello Turcis inferendo*, which was printed successively in Basel, Vienna, Paris, Cologne, and Antwerp, in 1530.[20] Erasmus now acknowledged the necessity of defense against the menacing Turks. He was criticizing Luther (actually, the Luther of an earlier phase) when he argued that, just because the body of Christendom was ailing through its own misbehavior, it would be wrong to resist God's normal punishment for unhealthy living; instead, chastened Christians should resort to the services of a physician or surgeon—in other words, war against the Turks. But Erasmus felt also that the princes of Europe should secure the approval for such a war from the cities and lands concerned[21]—and only after every conceivable effort had been made to avoid the horrible remedy of mutual slaughter and destruction (invocation of the canons of the just war vs the crusade).

Erasmus described Islam as an incoherent amalgam of paganism, Judaism, and aberrant Christianity (notably Arianism). He deplored the reduction of Christ in this perverted religion to the level of a prophet considered the equal of Mohammed, who was "but a ruffian." Yet Erasmus acknowledged also that even this limited Christology and the general respect of Muslims for the sacred revelations of the Jews and Christians made them semi-Christians—and that, after all, was no mean status, in view of the fact that the majority of Christians were morally less Christian than many Turks! The Turks themselves, as distinguished from the Arab bearers of the faith of Mohammed, Eras-

[20] *Opera*, vol. V, cols. 345-368. For the early editions, see Carl Göllner, *Turcica: Die europäischen Türkendrucke des XVI. Jahrhunderts*, vol. I (Bucharest/Berlin, 1961), items 371-375.
[21] *Opera*, vol. V, col. 354.

mus characterized as originally a barbarian people without any particular gifts, who owed their extraordinary triumph over Greek Christians and others to the lamentable failings of the latter. But Erasmus was unprepared to go along with a common cynical appraisal of the situation which held that ordinary Christians had little to lose in passing from under the government of Christian princes to the control of Turks.[22] Deploring the wickedness of his age, Erasmus recognized in the Turk God's avenger (*ultor*) for the defections from Christendom, and, calling upon Christians to repent and to better exemplify Christian virtues, he reproduced several of the arguments and, indeed, phrases of his letter to Paul Volz. Although he justified purely military defense against the Turks, he elaborated a quite extensive program for attracting Turks, with all Europeans becoming winsome Christians.

Toward the end of his life Erasmus in some five writings dealt, at least in passing, with religious contemporaries besides the Muslims and with *salus extra ecclesiam et Christum*, in most cases more conservatively than during his early career.

However, in the first of these works, *Explanatio Symboli Apostolorum* (1533), Erasmus expressly extended the outer limits of the *una sancta Ecclesia* and the *communio sanctorum*. Speaking in the guise of a catechist addressing his catechuman, Erasmus remarked:

No one is obliged to know whether this one or that one is a member of the Church. It is enough to believe that there is on earth such a *society of those predestined to* [*eternal*] *life* which Christ by his spirit adhered to himself whether among the Indians, the inhabitants of Cádiz (*Gaditanos* = in general Moors), Hyperboreans, or Africans. It may well be that there are lands somewhere on the earth either islands or continents which have never been discovered by sailors or geographers in which nevertheless the Christian faith might flourish. It is for God alone to examine the recesses of the heart, whence it be that the judgments of many men are uncertain.[23]

Erasmus in referring to the *societas ad vitam praedestinatorum* meant, of course, an invisible Church of the elect in the Nominalist (Semi-Pelagian) sense of all those in whom God in his prescience has foreseen a meritorious use of his grace (predestination *post praevisa merita*). Such foreknown merits in virtuous pagans beyond the reach of the

---

[22] *Ibid.*, cols. 349f., 358, 364.    [23] *Ibid.*, col. 1175 A. (Italics mine.)

Gospel might well appear similar to the ethical implementations of the *philosophia Christi* among those who had received the Gospel. It is of interest in this connection, therefore, that in the *Explanatio Symboli* Erasmus suggested that the sacraments are the ordinary but not the only means of grace.[24]

In his *Purgatio adversus epistolam non sobriam Martini Lutheri* (1534), Erasmus defended himself spiritedly against Luther's charge that he, the great humanist and patrologist, really "abhorred all religions, especially the Christian," that his Christ was at best but a great teacher and he himself probably an Epicurean.[25] With intensity Erasmus stressed the visible Church from which Luther had withdrawn and avowed that, although he had indeed held to a *preparatio evangelii* among Jews and Gentiles for the restoration of all mankind in Christ, he had never regarded Christianity itself as anything but the true religion and "the cultus of the one true God."[26] Similarly, in his commentary on Psalm 83(84) *De amabili ecclesiae concordia* (1533),[27] discussing the third verse on the birds which have nests for their fledglings, Erasmus, while recognizing the virtues of admired pagans, held that *extra Christum* their offspring have no proper nest;[28] that the exponents of the religions of the different nations are strangely discordant; that, even where they might conserve a vestigial or groping faith, *saving* faith is a gift of God; and that only by such explicit faith, attended by rebirth in Christ and sealed in baptism, is salvation effected.[29] In commenting on verse 10 ("For a day in thy courts is better than a thousand [elsewhere]"), Erasmus referred to the Light of

---

[24] *Ibid.*, col. 1140 B: "Utrumque quum aliis modis, tum vero praecipue per Ecclesiae sacramenta suggerit gratia Dei." In an earlier treatise, *Matrimonii institutio* (Basel, 1526), Erasmus, in passing, went beyond Jean Gerson, whom he cites and who held the opinion that the infants of godly parents through no fault of their own deprived of baptism would not be given over to eternal punishment; for, said Erasmus, just as baptism is not denied to anyone, so, in case of necessity, it cannot be said to be not given by anyone. *Opera*, vol. V, col. 622 C. The reference to Gerson is *Sermo de nativitate Mariae virginis; Opera omnia*, ed. L. E. DuPin (Paris, 1706), vol. III, col. 1350 A-B. For other passages suggesting a concordance of the *philosophia Christi* and the law of nature, see Payne, "Sacramental Theology," p. 53, nn. 3-5, and p. 54, n. 1.

[25] *Opera*, vol. X, cols. 1537-58, esp. cols. 1551f.

[26] *Ibid.*, cols. 1551 D, 1556 F.

[27] Also called *De sarcienda ecclesiae concordia; Opera*, vol. V, cols. 469-506; last portion tr. P. S. Allen, *Erasmus: Lectures and Wayfaring Sketches* (Oxford, 1934), pp. 87-96.

[28] *Opera*, vol. V, col. 485 E.  [29] *Ibid.*, cols. 475 C, 489 C, 493 F.

redemptive day in Revelation 21:23 and adduced as the prophetic allusions therein both Zechariah 14:6 and Isaiah 60:2, contending on the authority of these two prophecies that at the End all peoples without the Light of Christ, and therefore *extra ecclesiam*, will be covered by "thick darkness" and that for them, without the Sun of righteousness, there will be "cold and frost."[30]

In *Ecclesiastes, sive de ratione concionandi* (1535)[31] Erasmus assembled a lifetime's disparate and often "dirty and torn" notes on the office of the preacher in a Christendom now completely riven by several major forms of reformation. In passing, Erasmus also expressly turned his attention from preaching in Christendom to evangelizing beyond it and therewith touched upon the meaning for Christianity of diverse peoples in the overseas realm of Charles V and in Asia and Africa.[32] One might wish that in this fairly extensive section on Christian missions Erasmus would have indicated in what ways the moral aspirations of these distant peoples and their religions could be construed as a possible preparation for the fuller Gospel of Catholic missionaries; but he chose to limit his ebbing energies to exhorting men to go out as evangelists, to simplify the Gospel, to extricate themselves and their mission from every worldly consideration and thus exemplify the Gospel in their pure lives, so that infidels the world over would be drawn to Christ in ever increasing numbers. In this connection Erasmus took note of schismatic allies like the head of the Ethiopian Church and nation, "Presterjohn," and regretted that the idealized priest-king, in temporarily "submitting" through his emissaries to the Pope, had found so much to deplore about the worldly aspects of papal behavior.[33]

Erasmus was prepared in his *Ecclesiastes* to acknowledge the Muslim conquests of Palestine and Greece, "the homelands of the Evangelists and the best of the Church Fathers," as divine punishment for Christian failures in the distant past and to confess with sorrow the nominal and even hypocritical character of much that passed for Christian in contemporary Europe. He then gently cajoled monks, friars, and canons into giving up the easier tasks of splitting theological hairs to follow the apostles in becoming exemplary and self-sacrificial missionaries, prepared to adapt Christianity to the needs and expectations of all races and conditions of men, and, with the same resourcefulness with which the trainers of elephants and lions toil to win over their

---

[30] *Ibid.*, cols. 494 D - 495 B.  [31] Ed. Friedrich A. Klein (Jena, 1820).
[32] Bk. I, chs. 41-47 and pp. 104-113.  [33] *Ibid.*, p. 105.

charges to please their earthly princes, to "dress the inhabitants" of the world beyond old Christendom and to train them as obedient, loving children in order to please the heavenly Prince of Peace. Erasmus did not go on expressly to say that the eternal Word, at work at one time among the virtuous pagans of classical antiquity, had prepared the hearts of natives overseas for the coming of the seed to be sown by Catholic missionaries.

At the very end of his final work, however—*Enarratio Psalmi XIV* (1536), where he took the opening verse 14 (15):1 ("Who shall dwell in thy tabernacle?") as his subtitle ("De puritate tabernaculi sive Ecclesiae christianae")—it is evident that the patristically and humanistically formed exegete expressly recognized the role of the eternal Christ as *Logos* in preparing everywhere in the world for man's salvation. At the same time, he clearly stated that the requisite response of the pre-Christian and praeter-Christian virtuous pagan had to be something more than the intuition of moral monotheism in a Cicero[34] or "the crude and confused belief in divine things" in the pre-Christian Jew.[35] Salvation was possible only for him "who puts his whole trust (*fiduciam*) in the gracious mercy of God offered to all through Christ" and in "the divinely revealed remission of sins." With this proviso it was possible for Erasmus to assert that "some have been saved under the law of nations, many under the law of Moses, and very many under evangelical law. From the beginnings of the world there was the Church of the just, the Body of Christ, there was the Gospel...."[36]

We may conclude this sampling of Erasmus's views on salvation outside the visible Church and on the role of non-Christian religions in the providence of God by observing that, over a lifetime of musing on these two interrelated themes, Erasmus scarcely surpassed the schoolmen and, for the most part, failed to make very much of the eight soteriological themes in writings of the Church Fathers. However, in his doctrinal simplification of Christianity, aimed at making it both more comprehensible to the common man and to the unconverted and

---

[34] Cf. Erasmus on the faith behind the Tusculan *Quaestiones*, above at n. 16.

[35] Prefatory letter to *Tusculanae Quaestiones*, p. 339, lines 66f. The Jews at the time of the crucifixion, Erasmus thought, deserved and received mercy because they were in ignorance. But Jews after the resurrection were considered by him to have willfully rejected salvation. *Opera*, vol. VII, cols. 462 B, 703 B, 522 F - 523 A.

[36] *Opera*, vol. V, col. 293 F.

more attractive to them morally, he greatly reduced the distinctions between explicit and implicit Christian faith, between explicit faith and pre- or praeter-Christian moral theistic *fiducia*, with the consequence that the boundary between the *philosophia Christi* and natural law morality without benefit of an external revelation was obscured to the prospective advantage of contemporary devout pagans.[37] Moreover, the fact that Erasmus recoiled from the more severe and consequent formulations of the doctrine of predestination in the cause of defending free will meant that, in preserving the Augustinian concept of the invisible Church (without its predestinarian rationale), he had to resort to upright behavior and simple piety as marks of adhesion to the true Church. Despite the formal conservatism of his theology of salvation, Erasmus by his policy of simplification and humane vacillation effectively extended the outer boundaries of the invisible Church in space and time.

## II. *Luther and Melanchthon on Muslims and Pagans*

Martin Luther went through a number of phases in his thinking about Islam. He had relatively little to say about other religions besides Judaism and was only vaguely aware of the theological implications of the discovery of pagans "on a few islands" across the Atlantic.[38]

With respect to the eternal destiny of individuals, whether within or beyond Christendom, who die without faith in Christ, Luther expressed himself as early as 1522.[39] Alluding to the view of Origen

---

[37] This is also the view of Thompson (*De fide*, p. 118) and, much more emphatically, of Baron (". . . *gentiles salvati*," esp. p. 262).

[38] Herbert Vossberg, *Luthers Kritik aller Religion: Eine theologiegeschichtliche Untersuchung zu einem systematischen Hauptproblem* (Erlangen, 1922); Walter Holsten, *Christentum und nichtchristliche Religion nach der Auffassung Luthers* (Gütersloh, 1932); *idem*, "Reformation und Mission," *ARG*, XL (1953), 1-32. I have not been able to consult Holsten, ed. [*Luthers Gesammelte*] *Schriften wider Juden und Türken* (suppressed and replaced in the postwar series), *Ausgewählte Werke*, ed. H. H. Borchardt and Georg Merz, Ergänzungsband III (Munich, 1936). The literature on Luther and the Jews, a theme inextricably bound up with his theological concern about justification by faith alone, is too complex and enormous to be cited here. For the relation to Islam, see George W. Forell, "Luther and the War against the Turks," *Church History*, XIV (1945), 256-271; Harvey Buchanan, "Luther and the Turks, 1519-1529," *ARG*, XLVII (1956), 145-160; and, most comprehensively and substantially, Kenneth M. Setton, "Lutheranism and the Turkish Peril," *Balkan Studies*, III (1962), 133-168.

[39] *Ein Sendbrief über die Frage, ob auch jemand, ohne Glauben verstorben,*

that all men, angels, and devils would one day be saved, he roundly rejected universalism. Taking up several scriptural texts that might be construed in support of the more comprehensive view of salvation *extra ecclesiam*, if not *extra Christum*, such as I Timothy 2:4 on God's desire that "all men be saved," Luther restricted the application of these texts by placing them alongside more exacting prerequisites, namely, God's election and man's utter faith (in the sufficiency of the proffer of Christ's righteousness).

With special reference to pre-Christian noble pagans, Luther, against Erasmus in the controversy on the will in 1524, expressly excluded them from eternal salvation, mentioning Cicero; and, quite apart from virtue, he programmatically restricted the possibility of election to an invisible Church thought of always as consisting of but a minority within Old Israel and Christendom: "Since the world began, there have always been superior talents, greater learning, and a more intense earnestness among pagans than among Christians and the people of God. It is as Christ Himself acknowledges: 'the sons of this world are wiser than the sons of light' (Luke 16:8). . . . Who dare say that not one among them pursued truth with all his heart? Yet we are bound to maintain that *not one of them reached it*."[40] Later, Luther would refute Zwingli's very inclusive view of the salvation of virtuous pagans, showing it to be, in effect, "non-Christian," and excoriating him "for becoming himself a heathen."[41]

Luther's persisting conviction of the insufficiency of all religions apart from divine election, revelation in Christ, and clarification through the Holy Spirit was very well expressed in his *Commentary on Jonah* (1526). In connection with the verse 1:5 ("Then the mariners were afraid, and each cried to his god"), Luther observed that among all peoples there survives, from the primordial revelation in Paradise, a vague "light and reason" with regard to the existence of God (Epicureans and other skeptics to the contrary) but that, outside of Christianity, they cannot know for certain either that God is beneficent toward them or just where and who He is—namely, the Father as revealed by the Son through the Holy Spirit. In the same commen-

---

*selig werden möge*, Weimar Edition (henceforth cited as WA), *D. Martin Luthers Werke, Kritische Gesamtausgabe* (1883-    ), X:2, 318-326.

[40] *De servo arbitrio* (1524), WA, XVIII, 651; tr. J. I. Packer and O. R. Johnson, *The Bondage of the Will* (Westwood, N.J., 1957), p. 121. (Italics mine.)

[41] *Kurzes Bekenntnis vom heiligen Sakrament* (1544), WA, LIV, 143f.

tary he went so far as to say that even among Christians (the Papists) a worship of their own fanatical piety and darkness can become the idolatrous service of Satan.[42]

Of Islam, Luther first made significant mention in 1518 in connection with his defense of the fifth thesis of the *XCV Theses* (1517) about the Pope's alleged power of remitting penalties. This was in his *Resolutiones*, where, arguing that guilt could only be removed by inner repentance, he placed his thesis in the broad scriptural context of the repentance of the people of Nineveh whose remorse alone saved them from punishment. Then, with specific reference to the Turks, Tartars, and other infidels, Luther, quoting Isaiah 10:5 ("Ah, Assyria, rod of my fury and the staff itself in his hands my indignation"), went on to speak against any anti-Turkish crusade under the Pope, as though the mere bishop of Rome could, by external indulgences, make up for that inner repentance which would alone turn God from his fury toward a wayward Christendom: "To make war against the rod of iniquity is nothing else than to strive against God who is saying that through the rod he is visiting upon us our iniquities the more so that we do not punish them ourselves."[43]

To Leo X the whole of Luther's behavior was execrable and his asseveration about the Turks treasonable to Christendom. The Pope responded to the reformer with a warning of excommunication (*Exsurge Domine*, 15 June 1520) in which he had summarized Luther's position as sharply as possible: "To fight against the Turks is to resist God's visitation upon our iniquities."[44] Luther, in his third in a series of refutations, *An Argument in Defense of all Articles . . . Wrongly Condemned by the Roman Bull* (composed as a Mock New Year's greeting to the Pope in 1521), advanced theological, historical, and moral reasons why the Pope had done Christendom more harm than good by his efforts to mount a crusade and encourage Catholic rulers to break their treaties with certain Muslim powers. In the Latin version he insisted that true Christians must with prophetic discernment recognize that God was punishing them in body and soul for their

[42] *Der Prophet Jona ausgelegt* (1526), WA, XIX, esp. 206.
[43] *Resolutiones disputationum de indulgentiarum virtute* (1518), Conclusion V, WA, I, 535; tr. Carl W. Folkemer, "Explanations," *Luther's Works*, ed. Harold J. Grimm (Philadelphia), XXXI (1957), 92. Luther expressed the same view more fully in his letter to George Spalatin, 21 Dec. 1518, WA, *Briefwechsel* (1930-1948), I, 282.
[44] *Bullarum Romanum* (Turin, 1860), V, 151.

sins "per hos *Romanos* Turicissimos Turcas." In the German version he went on to say: "Now I set up this article [in 1518] not meaning to say that we are not to make war against the Turk, as that holy heresy-hunter, the Pope . . . charges me, but to say that we should first make ourselves better and cause God to be gracious to us. The Pope does nothing more, with his crusading indulgences and his promises of heaven, than lead Christians' lives into death, and their souls in a great crowd to hell, as befits the true Antichrist."[45] Luther opposed the Pope's mingling the sacred and secular, much like a caliph, financing "sacred" warfare with sacramental indulgences and involving the clergy in a task appropriate solely to the martial estate.

By the following year, 1522, Luther had become even clearer about his main position, that it was not the Sultan but the Pope who was alone the Antichrist. The enraged reformer rendered the Pope's Maundy Thursday *Bulla de Coena Domini* into German with glosses and commentary; and, addressing Rome in gross and ironic language, he remarked that the vicar of Christ might better preach the Gospel than a crusade:

He [the Pope] anathematizes those who ship iron and wood to the Turks and Saracens, that one may see that it is his earnest desire to do good for Christendom. If, however, he was the vicar of Christ, he would follow his footsteps, and go and preach the Gospel to the Turks, giving himself to the task body and soul. That would be a Christian way to oppose the Turk, and to enlarge and protect Christendom. Because what purpose does it serve to hold back the Turk physically? What evil does the Turk do? He takes land and rules temporally. But must we not suffer the same from the Pope, who skins us of both body and soul, which at least the Turk doesn't do! Besides the Turk lets everyone remain in his own belief. That the Pope doesn't. . . .[46]

Luther had yet to live through the common terror of Central Europe as the Sultan Suleiman defeated King Louis II of Hungary at the battle of Mohács in 1526. While all Germany awaited the return of the new

[45] *Assertio omnium articulorum* (1520), WA, VII, 94-151; German version, 308-457, specif. 443; tr. C. M. Jacobs, *Works of Martin Luther* (Philadelphia), III (1930), 105f.

[46] *Bulla coenae domini, das ist, die Bulla vom Abendfressen* (1522), WA, VIII, comment on item 6, pp. 697f. Luther first identified the Antichrist with the Pope in his exposition of Psalms 10:12 in 1519.

King Ferdinand's envoys from Istanbul, hoping against hope that the Sultan would not insist on extending any farther the boundary of Ottoman suzerainty, Luther became more explicit about the distinction between the Ottoman Turks as a military threat and as Muslims, although he continued to use "Turk" in speaking of the foe under both aspects, even when, on his own side, he distinguished between German and Christian. With his distinctions in mind, Luther dedicated to Landgrave Philip of Hesse in October a major religio-political tract, which appeared in the following April of 1529, entitled *On War Against the Turk*.[47] He insisted that the Christian *qua* believer would never fight against the Turk but would rather suffer. At the same time, he argued, both the ruler (even when Christian, but *qua* ruler) and his subject (though a Christian believer), in obedience to temporal necessity, might properly fight in a just war against Turks, as against any other enemies; but they should no longer invoke Christ's name or involve ordained clerics in battle. That was the monstrous confusion of the Pope, who presumed to sanction war with the name of the cross when the only truly Christian warfare, in keeping with Christ's mandate, would be an inward and outward suffering for his sake (John 18:36 and Matthew 26:52). Luther realized, of course, that with Europe in peril his earlier statements about the Turkish army as the rod of God's anger might well seem seditious, and hence he desired to explain clearly to a representative Protestant prince just what he intended. He stuck to his earlier view, arguing with the courageous self-confidence of an Old Testament prophet that the Turkish onslaughts were God's only way of making clear the validity of the point he had made back in 1518 against the Pope: "[T]he Turk comes ravaging on at his leisure and ruins Germany without trouble and without resistance. Why does this happen? Because my article, which Pope Leo condemned, remains uncondemned and in full force. Because the Papists reject it, arbitrarily and without Scripture, *the Turk must take its part and prove it with the fist and with deeds. If we will not learn out of the Scriptures, we must learn out of the Turk's scabbard*, until we find in our hurt that Christians [*qua* Christians] are not to make war or resist evil."[48] Convinced that the Turk was at once "God's rod and the devil's servant" and that God had, accordingly, justly given an unreformed and unrepentant Christendom "into the hands of the devil and the

---

[47] *Von Krieg wider die Türken* (1529), WA, XXX:2, 107-148; tr. C. M. Jacobs, *Works of Martin Luther*, V (1931), 79-123.

[48] WA, p. 113; Jacobs, *Works*, pp. 85f.

Turk," Luther nevertheless gave a very clear and helpful answer to the princes of Christendom in telling them how to face the common enemy. They should all fight under the Emperor but not call their defense a "crusade"; and, when any true Christian among the defenders happened to be captured and not slain, he should testify to his faith in Christ and perhaps by his suffering valor even convert a few Turkish guards and jailers, as the apostles once did.

Luther's practical counsel, with its distinction between the Turk as enemy and as non-Christian, was based upon his religio-political distinction between the Kingdom of Christ and the kingdoms of this world and upon his theological distinction between God and Allah. Said Luther, "if the Turk's god, the devil, is not first beaten, there is reason to fear that the Turk will not be easy to beat."[49] In this sharp phrasing Luther departed from the highest achievement of some medieval divines and dialoguists, West and East. Calling the deity of the Turks a devil was a more serious charge than calling Mohammed the Antichrist, as the Catholics did. Yet, in reserving the latter designation strictly for the Pope, Luther was intending to make clear that he regarded Islam as merely one more religious aberration common to human history, but that papalized Christianity was a monstrous turpitude of cosmic proportions. The basis of Luther's characterization of Islam at this stage was what he could say, over and above common opinion in university circles, on the basis of "some pieces of Mohammed's Koran . . . of the kind we call Pope's decretals." He remarked that, if he could get a whole copy, he would like to do it into German for every man to see "what a foul and shameful book it is."[50]

At this point in *On War Against the Turk* Luther embarked upon a three-fold criticism of Islam for its deceit, its murder, and its disregard of marriage. We shall restrict our discussion to the charge of deceit. Luther held that the Koran was a tissue of lies and misrepresentations which Mohammed tendentiously "patched together out of the faith of Jews, Christians, and heathens": "He gets it from the Christians when he praises Christ and Mary and the apostles and other saints. He gets it from the Jews that people are not to drink wine, are to fast certain times of the year, wash like the Nazarites, and eat off the ground, and go on with such holy works as part of our monks do and hope for everlasting life at the Judgment Day; for, holy people that they are, they believe in the resurrection of the dead, though few of the papists believe in it."[51] Indeed, one article of faith conspicuously

[49] *Ibid.*, p. 89.  [50] *Ibid.*, p. 94.  [51] *Ibid.*, p. 95.

common to Christian and Muslim was this expectation of the resurrection and the Last Judgment. For the rest, Luther was vexed both by the amount of the Christian ingredient in Islam and by the extent of its adulteration:

In the first place, he [Mohammed] praises Christ and Mary very much as those who alone were without sin, and yet he believes nothing more of Christ than that he is a holy prophet. . . . On the other hand, he praises and exalts himself highly and boasts that he has talked with God and the angels, and that since Christ's office of prophet is now complete, it has been commanded to him to bring the world to his faith and if the world is not willing, to compel it or punish it with the sword; and there is much glorification of the sword in it. Therefore, the Turks think their Mohammed much higher and greater than Christ, for the office of Christ has ended and Mohammed's office is still in force. . . .[52]

Here, of course, Luther was being unfair to Mohammed who, claiming for himself no virgin birth nor other miracle, regarded himself as *muslim*, submitting himself to God in exactly the way his followers did. But, having charged Mohammed with lying, Luther went on to observe that the ruthless power of Islam had its indubitable fascination for men, "that people even submit to it willingly."

Later in the same year, 1529, as the military situation in the East became ever more frightening with the siege of Vienna and accounts came back of the cruelty of the Turkish soldiery, Luther was, despite himself, moved to turn his thoughts almost into a kind of Protestant crusade sermon, although he still steadfastly refused to identify either the Sultan or Mohammed with the Antichrist. The *Army Sermon against the Turks*[53] was shaped in part by the prophecies of the Franciscan Johannes Hilten (based on Daniel), who influenced both Luther and Melanchthon. In a letter to a friend at this time Luther declared: "I am a battler against the Turks and the god of the Turks to the death."[54] He saw in the four beasts of Daniel 7 (as traditionally also in the four parts of the statue in Daniel 2) the four great empires in the history of mankind, the last being the Roman Empire (continued in the person of Charles V). There is some fascination in following

[52] *Ibid.*     [53] *Heerpredigt wider den Türken*, WA, XXX:2, 149-197.
[54] To Nicholas Hausmann, 26 Oct. 1529; WA, *Briefwechsel*, V, 166. Luther was perhaps more directly influenced by the recent publications of Melanchthon and Justus Jonas, for which see below at n. 72.

Luther into the details, because here a great translator and exegete was at work, seeking the inner meaning of history as he prophesied in his turn the impending travail of the Latter Days.

Luther easily identified the ten horns on the head of the last of the four beasts with some ten major parts of the ancient Roman Empire, as Luther thought of it. In Daniel's vision (7:8) there came up among the ten horns "a little one, before which three of the first horns were plucked up by the roots; and behold, in this horn were eyes like a man, and a mouth speaking great things." This verse is immediately followed by the vision of the throne of the Ancient of Days. Luther recognized at once in the little horn Mohammed and in the crowding out of three horns the expansion of Islam. Thus far Luther was wholly within the medieval apocalyptic interpretation of Islam. The novelty was in recognizing that, in a sense, the Turk in Constantinople since 1453, having conquered "three kingdoms—Egypt, Greece and Asia"— was the embodiment of Rome, pagan, Christian, now Muslim; and, since there could, according to Daniel, never be a fifth mundane empire, therefore the Sultan's realm would never outgrow the geographical limits of the ancient Roman Empire, "or Daniel would be a liar, which is not possible."[55] Luther went on to identify the human eyes in the little horn as a clear reference to Mohammed's merely human wisdom in assembling his Koran, while its mouth speaking great things could be none other than a clear reference to Mohammed's pretentious claim to being greater than Christ. Luther drew on the imagery of Gog and Magog in Ezekiel and the Apocalypse, interpreting Gog as the political enemy of Christ, Islam, and Magog as the spiritual foe, the Papacy.[56] Confident that Gog would be defeated, Luther thought of a perhaps prolonged war as a culmination of history in the battle of Armageddon, ushering in the Last Judgment.[57]

Luther's refusal to countenance a crusade (as distinguished from a defensive just war) against the Turks in 1529 is all the more remarkable in that, on his analysis, the Turkish assault was itself a combination of both an unjust war (unprovoked aggression) and, as it were, an anti-crusade (a religio-political war under an authority at once religious and military). Luther, vexed, nevertheless called only the army,

[55] *Heerpredigt*, p. 166.
[56] See also his earlier letter to Hausmann, 10 Nov. 1529, WA, *Briefwechsel*, V, 176.
[57] *Ibid.*, pp. 171, 194ff.

not the religion, of the Sultan the instrument of the devil (and also the rod of an angry God).

When the military danger subsided and Suleiman lifted the siege of Vienna, Luther fell back into his earlier mood of greater tolerance of Islam as a religion. The time had come, he now thought, to publish a *Libellus* on the rites and customs of the Turks composed by one (Georg von Mühlbach) who had been held a prisoner for twenty-two years in Transylvania after the fall of Constantinople. For this book, which brought out the good and bad in Islam as fairly as possible, Luther wrote a preface in 1530. He commended the author of the *Libellus* for his fairness. He remarked further that the Papists had generally sought to avoid allowing authentic Muslim material to get into the hands of the Christians, lest in contrasting the morals of the infidels with those of their fellow Catholics they be tempted to follow Mohammed! But the main point for all to bear in mind, said Luther, is that true Christianity is not a matter of morals but of salvation through Christ. Therefore, it is good to have the mirror of sober morality according to a fairly easy code held up in order by comparison to see what true Christianity is not—though Islam may indeed be superior to the fraudulent piety of many a Carthusian or Benedictine, not to say a Pope: "For in all these things [ethics] the Turks are far surpassing, who nevertheless both deny Christ and passionately persecute him, no less than do our Papists deny and persecute him! Besides let them [the Papists] feel this to be the truth, namely, that the Christian religion is far other than good behavior and good works. For in these things this book [thus introduced] shows that the Turks are far superior to us."[58] Like Ambrose of Milan with his *De Brachmanorum moribus* and Thomas More with his *Utopia*, partly inspired by it, Luther with his introduction to a *Libellus* on the morals of the Muslims bestowed praise upon another religion in order to shame the practitioners of his own—but with this important and unusual, distinctively Lutheran turn: with respect to plain morality, he claimed, the Muslims are perhaps better than Roman Catholic Christians, especially since their visible head is none other than the Antichrist, and better also than Evangelicals; but true (i.e., Evangelical) Christianity is not a matter of morality or rites but of faith, through the power of the Holy Spirit,

[58] *Libellus de ritu et moribus Turcorum* (1530), WA XXX:2, 206. The first European edition of the Koran in Arabic was published by Paganini in Venice, also in 1530.

in Christ, the Son of God, who died for sins. Muslims have Christ the Teacher, but they lack the Creator *Logos* and Christ the eschatological Judge, hence both the Alpha and Omega of true religion.

In 1541 Luther printed his third major tract on the Turkish threat, *Admonition to Prayer against the Turk*. It was occasioned by Suleiman's annexation of central Hungary and the resulting transformation of the cathedral of Buda-Pest into a mosque. Luther's *Admonition* reveals more about his understanding of divided Christendom than of Islam. The tract moves ambiguously between a prophetic reproof of Germany for having failed to live righteously and an exhortation to prayer on the part of the Evangelical remnant who were being punished conjointly by Papists and Turks for their steadfastness in cleaving to God's Word. Seldom was Luther so detailed and comprehensive in his rebuke of all classes, from princes to peasants, from Anabaptists to Zwinglians; and he willingly recognized the Turk as at once the tyrant who dooms and the schoolmaster who flogs Christendom,[59] because of its rampant social evils. Styling himself a prophet, he was certain that neither the Pope nor the Sultan had much more time to act before the Last Judgment. At the same time, Luther was unequivocal in his identification of his word as God's will, of the Evangelical cause as divine. Although at one point he wondered whether it could be considered proper to pray at all in face of the Turkish threat, he finally made bold to set forth the following prayer for the "little [Evangelical] flock": "Thou knowest, Almighty God our Father, that we have not sinned against the devil, the Pope, or the Turk, and that they have no right or power to chastise us, but rather that thou canst and mayest use them as thy stern rod against us, who have sinned against thee and have deserved all this misfortune."[60]

Further development of Luther's views of Islam was prompted by his translation into German in 1542 of the *Confutatio Alcorani* (1320) by the Florentine Dominican Ricoldo da Montecroce. The translation was selective and summary. Luther preceded it with a preface and followed it with his own refutation, brought up to date in the spirit of his own reformation. In the preface Luther said that he had long ago (1530) read the *Confutatio* but that he had not then agreed with it. He had wanted in fairness to read the Koran for himself. On Shrove Tuesday, 1542, the Latin translation of the Koran came into his hands;

[59] *Vermahnung zum Gebet wider den Türken* (1541), WA, LI, esp. 594f. The MS and printed version are set one above the other.

[60] *Ibid.*, p. 608.

he then realized "how bad it was." In his preface he restated his general view that the Muslims were too hardhearted ever to be converted to Christianity but that, at the same time, they should never be opposed as though they were the Antichrist; instead, he said, repentant evangelical Christians should try to avert God's wrath by reforming Christendom against the Antichrist at its heart: "We must therefore let the Turks and Saracens with their Mohammed work their will, as they on whom the wrath of God has come to the very end" (I Thessalonians 2:16).[61] Luther readily acknowledged the laudable work of a number of Muslim philosophers, beginning with Avicenna; but he felt that they themselves probably did not even believe in the Koran and were in any case but men of reason who considered themselves above Jews, Christians, and Muslims, being devoted solely "to Reason and *Philosophia*."[62] On philosophical grounds there probably was not too much difference between Latin humanists and Muslim seekers of unrevealed philosophical truth. On moral grounds, indeed, the Muslim philosophers might be said to have a slight advantage, since at least they laid no claim to having the Christian revelation, with its exacting moral code with respect to love of neighbor, to suffering (rather than inflicting) pain, and to holy matrimony. With gruffness and some humor, Luther claimed that on the battlefield he would, with God, probably favor the true rather than the counterfeit Turk (!):

> Now if there were two Turkish armies drawn up against each other, one of them called Mohammedan, the other calling itself Christian, for goodness' sake, give our Lord God good counsel . . . which of the Turks He ought to help and give a chance to. I for one of His least among counsellors would nevertheless give the advice that He should give the chance to the Mohammedan Turks against the Christian Turks which in any case He has long since done without our counsel and despite our cry and petition! Now the reason for this [judgment] is that the Mohammedan Turks do not have God's Word, nor preachers of the same; they are gross filthy sows, and they do not know why they live or what they believe. To be sure, if they had preachers of the divine Word, they would—a few of them anyway—from being sows become human beings. But now our Christian Turks already have God's Word and preachers, not wishing however to hear it, and from being human beings become plain sows. . . .[63]

[61] *Verlegung des Alcoran Bruder Richardi* (1542), WA, LIII, 276.
[62] *Ibid.*, pp. 389f.          [63] *Ibid.*, p. 391.

347

In his own refutation, going much beyond Ricoldo, Luther characterized the Romanization of Christianity as, in effect, the Islamization of Christendom. After estimating three-fourths of the Koran and, hence, Islam to be a tissue of lies, he continued: "And indeed it's not been much better among us. For there are surely so many lies in our alkorans, decretals, *lie*gends, *summae*, and innumerable books, that no one knows where they all come from, when they were written and who their authors were. . . ."[64] Following this strong indictment of the Romanizing, papalizing, and canonicizing of Latin Christendom, Luther restated with mounting mordancy his basic theme:

> And I do not hold Mohammed for the Antichrist. He is too gross and has a recognizable black devil [in him] who cannot deceive either faith or reason and is like a pagan, who outwardly persecutes the Church as did the Romans and other pagans. . . . But the Pope is for us the real Antichrist who has the high, subtle, nice, slithery devil [in him, and] who sits in the midst of Christendom, letting stand the Holy Scripture, baptism, eucharist, the keys, catechism, and matrimony . . . and yet he so masterfully rules that, alongside these, he raises his own "dirtycals" (*Drecktal*), his Koran, his man-made doctrine, all above God's Word. . . .[65]

The East, Luther went on, has its Mohammed, the West its Pope, its own false prophet.

Luther contrasted Muslim and Christian marriage, and here his verdict was especially sharp. Mohammed had so many women that he really had no wives, Luther wrote, while the "lily-white, chaste, modest, self-disciplined" Supreme Pontiff had any number of wives and virgins. In sarcastic invective he pointed out that, in comparison with what went on under the name of Christ, "Mohammed might well appear before the world as a sheer saint," concluding: "If we are going to have now any luck against Mohammed . . . we must first renounce the inner foe, Antichrist with his devil, by means of a goodly penance."[66] And with a few more words of evangelical fervor he finally cried out: "God grant us His grace and may He punish both Pope and Mohammed along with their respective devils. I have done what I could as a true prophet and preacher! Whoever will not hear it, let it go. I am henceforth discharged of my duty for the day [of Judgment] and for eternity."

[64] *Ibid.*, pp. 391f.  [65] *Ibid.*, pp. 394f.  [66] *Ibid.*, p. 396.

At this point in his career, 1542, Luther had almost completed his thinking on Islam. He had recognized in the Turk the rod of God's anger, he had justified war against the Turk, but not as a crusade, and he had distinguished between one's duty as a subject of the lords temporal and as a subject of Christ's inner Kingdom of love and suffering. He had pilloried the Pope as the Antichrist. While legitimating political self-defense against the Turk as a marauding and ruthless foe, he had at the same time urged an inner reformation and renewal and a repudiation of the Antichrist as the ultimate defense against the staff of God's indignation. But that staff, he was sure, God would never permit to lay waste more than three-tenths of the area once covered by the ancient Roman Empire, and then after the Last Judgment would follow the Fifth Monarchy or the abiding Realm of Christ. In the meantime, the residual morality, hospitality, and other natural virtues of the Muslim—functioning albeit within a kingdom of unparalleled rapine and murderousness in time of war—could serve as a mirror to evangelical Christians to make clear to them what true Christianity is not.

Luther had still one further step to take. Theodor Bibliander, professor of theology at Zurich, had prepared a classicized Latin version of Peter the Venerable's Koran. The Basel authorities sought to imprison the printer for making Islam thus freshly accessible to Christians; but Luther defended the project in a letter, saving the printer and editor, and also supplied the new imprint with a Latin preface in 1543. Luther did not make reference therein to the fact that Bibliander on the title page referred to Mohammed as Satan's messenger, the Antichrist. But Luther did take a new tack, defending the publication of secrets of the Koran for the same good reason that had prompted other humanists and reformers to edit a number of Jewish books, namely, in order to disclose to the evangelical public the perversities of the alien religion. Taxing the Jews with stubbornness and the Muslims with innovation, Luther urged Evangelicals to be faithful to the Word of God which was handed down by prophets and apostles. Then remembering also his principal foe, the Papists, Luther wrote: "Thus if we in this last age of the world are oppressed by a huge multitude of Jewish, Muslim, and Papist idols, let us nevertheless sound the voice of the Gospel and testify to Jesus Christ crucified and resurrected."[67] "Indeed," he went on, "it is disgraceful and impious laziness if [evan-

---

[67] *Vorrede zu Biblianders Koranausgabe*, WA, LIII, p. 570.

gelical Christians] do not daily in their progress admonish themselves on this point, separate themselves from Jews, Turks, and Gentiles in their prayers, that is, if they really do consider that it is alone God eternal, creator and sustainer of all things, who hears our prayers and is ready to give us eternal life, who revealed himself in the prophetic and apostolic scriptures, and who sent his Son and wished him to be a sacrifice for us." Never before had Luther made it so explicit that he regarded his God as utterly different from that not only of Muslims and Jews but also of Papists, Anabaptists, and other heretics. It was with reference to these reactionaries and radicals that Luther closed his preface, noting that, like them, Mohammed did not fulfill any sayings of the prophets but rather boasted "that he had thought up *new opinion*, dissenting from the prophets and apostles."[68]

Luther did not live to write the fuller refutation of the Koran which he said in his preface he would have liked to undertake, the basic (Latin) text now being at hand. His final word on the Turks seems to have been in his letter to Justus Jonas, 16 July 1545, in which he both called for God's malediction on the council about to convene at Trent and denounced Kings Francis and Ferdinand for sending envoys of peace to Istanbul. Although Lutheranism was the principal beneficiary of the Turkish threat, Luther himself seems to have been oblivious of any connection between his theological achievements and the Muslim conquests. He closed his letter: "Let us rejoice . . . , the end of the world is nigh!"[69]

It is interesting to note that toward the end of his life, in his protracted lectures on Genesis, Luther, adopting for his purposes the traditional tripartite schematization of world history, ascribed greater perfection to the pre-Noachites than to Christians in the third age, rapidly coming to an end in fire, as the first age had with the flood, and the second with the destruction of Jerusalem. Luther at this point,

---

[68] *Ibid.*, p. 571.

[69] WA, *Briefwechsel*, XI, 142. In a forthcoming book, *The Infidel Scourge of God: The Turkish Menace as Seen by German Pamphleteers of the Reformation Era*, John W. Bohnstedt ranges Luther's several tracts against the Turks in the larger context of a genre of literature, the *Türkenbüchlein*, pamphlets and tracts for a time of crisis composed in considerable quantity by both Catholics and Protestants. He shows that, apart from confessional bias on the question whether Lutheranism or Papalism was the doctrinal aberration calling down the divine wrath, these tracts had much in common—except that, as in Luther's last word on the subject, the imminence of the Last Judgment figured only in the Lutheran tracts.

like some of the Church Fathers (Lactantius, for instance), identified the age of the pre-Noachites, described in the first five chapters of Genesis, as "the Golden Age, which even the [ancient, pagan] poets recalled without doubt from the tradition and the words of the patriarchs."[70] This is one of the few instances of Luther's use of a patristic theme in speaking of non-Christian religions.

To other patristic themes, it may be noted in passing, Luther's son Johannes alluded (negatively) as a university student in a doctoral disputation presided over by his father in 1545. Respectfully conforming to his father's views, he asked the candidate a *quaestio doctoralis* on the possibility of salvation for ancient and modern non-Christians of virtuous life, guarding against anything that would make "the religions of all peoples equal." He may have had in mind the generous intimations of his Greek professor Melanchthon about certain virtuous pagans.[70a]

Philip Melanchthon (d. 1560), usually more generous in his humanistic leanings than Luther, was on the matter of Islam much harsher and even less concerned to get at the theological and religious reality of the opposing religion.[71] Melanchthon did join Luther in the final effort to get the Basel authorities to permit the sale of Bibliander's new Latin version of the Koran, but for the most part the two Wittenberg colleagues seem seldom to have conferred with each other on the meaning of Islam. Like Luther, however, it was in a commentary on Daniel (1529/1543) that Melanchthon expressed his eschatological view of Islam.[72] Unlike Luther, Melanchthon, using roughly the same traditional texts, events, images, and persons, interpreted *both* Islam and the Papacy as the Antichrist,[73] even though with Luther and medieval interpreters the Turk remained also the rod of God's anger against Christendom.[74] Melanchthon thought of the Turks as

[70] *Vorlesungen über I. Mose* (1535-1545), WA, XLII, 263.

[70a] The *quaestio* directed to candidate Peter Hegemon in the disputation *De homine* is printed in *Corpus Reformatorum*, X (Halle, 1842), cols. 761f. Cf. WA, XXXIX:2, 338. For Melanchthon on virtuous pagans in 1543, see below, n. 81.

[71] See Manfred Köhler, *Melanchthon und der Islam: Ein Beitrag zur Klärung des Verhältnisses zwischen Christentum und Fremdreligionen in der Reformationszeit* (Leipzig, 1938), p. 164.

[72] The edition of 1529 is entitled *Ennaratio Danielis*; an expanded edition entitled *In Danielem Prophetam Commentarius* (1543) is edited by Karl Bretschneider, *Melanchthonis opera omnia*, 28 vols. (Halle, 1834-1860) = *Corpus Reformatorum*, vol. XIII (Halle, 1846), cols. 823-1003.

[73] "Nomine *Antichristi comprehenduntur ambo regna, Mahometicum* [regnum] et pontificatus Romanus," *Commentarius*, col. 871.

[74] The image of the four animals and the quadripartite statue in Daniel 2,

"Red Jews" and supplied the etymological and genealogical explanation for this common designation by tracing the derivation of the Muslims from Edom (Esau), Jacob's elder brother. ("Edom" signifies "red.")

Melanchthon went further than Luther in detailing historically the way in which Islam was being used by God as a punishment of Christendom for its departure from revealed truth. He specified the basic grievance of God against his people as the papal doctrine of transubstantiation and sought to correlate the promulgation of this doctrine at the IV Lateran Council in 1215 with the rise of Ottoman Turkish power shortly thereafter as God's condign chastisement for idolatrous aberration.[75] Melanchthon was moved to make of Daniel both a warning and a consolation to the Evangelicals in the face of the prolonged Turkish threat. On a small scale Melanchthon, in effect, rehearsed the history of the Two Cities and brought the recital up to date by including the Turks and Saracens as the last representatives of the Fourth Monarchy.

As for the immediate future, Melanchthon, turning for substantiation from Daniel to Ezekiel and the Apocalypse, interpreted the Turk and the Pope as respectively Gog and Magog, hence as the Beast and as "the Pseudoprophet, that is, the pontiff defending idols."[75] Melanchthon assured his Evangelical readers that the Turks would never take the whole of Europe and that the Papists would never prevail.

Noting the intrepidity of Daniel in scorning the false and fabricated religions of the Chaldees, the Magi, and the Egyptians, and particularly Daniel's prayer (cf. 9:16) "non propter iusticiam nostram, sed propter Dominum," Melanchthon declared that prayers to God on the part of Mohammedans and heathens are not efficacious—for they know not the Lord Jesus Christ. He even suggested that for the same reason Catholic prayer was invalid(!): "Indeed let us execrate Mohammedan and pagan invocations, which do not acknowledge the Son of God and are in effect contumelies. Depraved also even among our adver-

---

7, 12, the prophecy of Zechariah 5:9 about two Babylonian women, and Kedar in Psalm 120:5 are all in the discussion. See Köhler, p. 65.

[75] *Commentarius*, col. 864.

[76] *Ibid.*, col. 871. Elsewhere in the commentary, as later in a prefatory letter to a book published in 1556, Melanchthon was content to identify the Turks alone as Gog and Magog (*Opera omnia*, XIII, col. 663).

saries who have suffocated the doctrine on faith [alone] . . . is their prayer which differs not at all from pagan invocation."[77]

Harsh on Papists and heretics, Melanchthon persevered in a humanistic concern for ancient virtuous pagans. It is of interest that he differed from Luther in holding to a literal hell and to a purgatory or limbo for pre-Christian worthies. Although he showed traces of the mystical *descensus-resignatio* theme,[78] Melanchthon was actually instrumental (despite Luther)[79] in perpetuating within Lutheranism the medieval view of a *limbus patrum*. Melanchthon even wrote of Christ as *triumphator*, who during the descent had "shown himself resurrected (*resuscitatum*!) to the devils, striking terror in them."[80] In this passage, Melanchthon eschewed the occasion to specify the ancient worthies retained in Sheol, and then liberated by Christ; but in a letter of 1543 he casually mentioned it to be plausible that during the descent "Christ aroused many of the dead and perhaps the most distinguished men from all nations, as for example, Scipio, Fabius, and others," citing I Peter 3:19.[81]

---

[77] *Commentarius*, col. 901. Melanchthon says much the same in his commentary on John 20 (*Opera omnia*, vol. XXIV, col. 763).

[78] Erich Vogelsang, "Weltbild und Kreuzestheologie in den Höllenfahrtsstreitigkeiten der Reformationszeit," *ARG*, XXXVII (1940), 90-132.

[79] Luther was emphatic in his allegorical interpretation of the article in the Apostles' Creed. In face of the very literalistic imagery of I Peter 3:19, Luther remained noncommittal but incredulous. He had taken over the mystical *descensus* as *resignatio*, and, interpreting the descent in his *theologia crucis* as the bitter anguish of suffering under the law before justification by faith alone, he virtually eliminated the whole realm of a literal hell and purgatory under the alleged control of the papacy with its indulgence system and stressed, instead, the resurrection and the Last Judgment—one further indication of Luther's disposition to narrow the scope of salvation *extra ecclesiam* and *extra fidem*. Luther spoke thus of the believers' prison of hell before the ascension through justification (1527): "What is the prison which took Christ captive? Some have construed 'prison' in the sense that Christ before his ascent into heaven, saved the holy fathers from the *limbus patrum*. . . . [But] this prison which takes us captive is the law, sin, death, devil, and hell" (WA, XXIII, 706, lines 5-13).

[80] *Postilla* on Psalm 16:10; *Opera omnia*, vol. XXIV, col. 742; noted by Vogelsang, p. 106.

[81] Letter to Anthony Musa, 12 March 1543; *Opera omnia*, vol. V, col. 58. In both this letter and the Postil quoted above, Melanchthon said that he had discussed the difficult article with Luther and that they were in essential agreement. Vogelsang adduces clear evidence that Melanchthon was mistaken (esp. p. 105).

### III. *Bucer, Zwingli, and Calvin on Muslims and Pagans*

Moving on from Luther and Melanchthon, we may in the Reformed tradition include for convenience not only Ulrich Zwingli (d. 1531) and John Calvin (d. 1564) but also the sometime Dominican Martin Bucer (d. 1551), primarily of Strassburg but active from Bern to Marburg, from Augsburg to Cambridge.

Like Melanchthon, Bucer[82] was theologically quite prepared to identify Islam with the Antichrist. Like Melanchthon also, he traced the derivation of the Muslims, not according to their own pedigree from the elder son of Abraham, Ishmael, but rather from the elder son of Isaac, namely, Esau. The patriarchal rejection of Esau (Edom) because of a huntsman's hunger that lost him his patrimony was, for Bucer, a divine judgment that sanctioned an identification of the Edomite Mohammed as a son of perdition.[83]

In an epoch when Jews were being driven from most Germanic lands and towns, Bucer developed another plan. Theocratically oriented, much more like Zwingli than Luther, Bucer advocated a coercive but pedagogically gradual and thorough conversion of the Jews not only in Strassburg but also in Hesse, where Gypsies and "other heathen" had been obliged to leave the territory (1524) but where Landgrave Philip had more magnanimous views about reordering the laws concerning Jews. Many Protestant advisers counseled the Landgrave to exile Jews also. Bucer in his *Judenratschlag* (1538) proposed that Jews be allowed to remain but that they be subjected to severe restraints and concerted efforts toward their conversion, with the consequence that Jews in Hesse were never to dispute with Christians, never to use passages from the Talmud to weaken the testimony of the Old Testament for Christians, were not to build any new synagogues, and were required to attend upon the divine services of

---

[82] See, on our subject, Walter Holsten, "Christentum und Nichtchristliche Religion nach der Auffassung Bucers," *Theologische Studien und Kritiken*, CVII (1936), 105-194. Holsten is comphrehensive and systematic, taking as his point of departure Bucer's conception of the divine law at various stages. Under strong Barthian influence, Holsten finds Bucer judging matters in this area *coram hominibus* rather than with Luther *coram Deo* and, consequently, considers him both more open to the possibilities of an acceptable universal theism beyond Christianity and more harsh in his actual judgment, for example, of Islam (p. 189). See further Henri Strohl, *Bucer humaniste Chrétien*, Cahiers de la Revue d'Histoire et de Philosophie Religieuses (Paris, 1939), no. 29, esp. pp. 17-27.

[83] *Evangelien-Kommentar* (Strassburg, 1533), 456f.; *Psalmorum libri v* (Strassburg, 1554), pp. 25, 147; noted by Holsten, "Christentum . . . ," p. 186.

the established church.[84] The theological bases for Bucer's view were his theocratic ideal of a Christian magistrate protecting the true Church and his biblicistic identification of his true Church with the Israel of the Old Covenant, which permitted him not only to consider living and, therefore by definition, "stubborn" Jews as in effect *ethnici* but also—here going much beyond Old Testament precept and practice— to use coercion and even humiliation to convert the "infidel" sojourners.[85]

One of Bucer's close associates in Strassburg, Wolfgang Capito (d. 1541), developed in the interstices between Bucer's comparatively tolerant theocracy and the sectarian underworld of that crossroads city an unusual view of the Jews, which should be mentioned here. In his *Commentary on Hosea* (Strassburg, 1528), Capito gave expression to the hope that Jews might be restored to Palestine in a *regnun corporale* of their own in order to hasten the Second Advent of Christ.[86] The lost *Commentary* was annotated by Martin Cellarius, a friend of Melanchthon's from Tübingen days. Apparently, Cellarius was the source of the eschatological plan for the Jews. In his own *De operibus Dei* (Strassburg, 1527) with an introduction by Capito, Cellarius declared within the high Protestant predestinarian context that God "has also among Jews, Greeks, Romans, yea and Scythians and among all the peoples of the earth made his elective choice of certain ones and given his blessing to them in their mother's womb."[87]

Bucer did not go so far on ancient religions and religious philosophies as Capito and Cellarius. But, by virtue of his recognition of a primordial revelation and the survival of the *semen* or *lumen naturae*, Bucer was not nearly so negative as Luther about the achievements and permanent contributions of non-Christian religiosity and contemplation. Bucer worked with the patristic theories both of an aboriginal revelation and of a borrowing from the Hebrews, but he rejected the Fathers' literal view of Christ's *descensus ad inferos* to save the virtuous

---

[84] *Die hessische Juden-Ordnung* (1539), ed. Robert Stupperich, *Martin Bucers Deutsche Schriften*, VII (Gütersloh/Paris, 1964), 391, items 1-4. See an earlier treatment by Hastings Eells, "Bucer's Plan for the Jews," *Church History*, VI (1937), 127-135.

[85] *Judenratschlag*, ed. Stupperich, *op.cit.*, esp. pp. 335-337.

[86] Indicated in a letter of Konrad Pellikan to Capito, 28 June 1528; *Elsass, Stadt Strassburg 1522-1532*, Quellen zur Geschichte der Täufer, ed., Manfred Krebs and Jean Rott (Gütersloh, 1959), VII:1, 164. Zwingli, on being informed of this, was scandalized.

[87] *Judenratschlag*, pp. 336f.

pre-Christian worthies. In one context or another, he could find something good to say about the Magi of the Persians, the gymnosophists among the Hindus, the "Chaldeans" among the Babylonians—all likened to Moses among the Hebrews as proclaimers of divine oracles and authors of holy scriptures.[88] Bucer, seeing anticipations of Christian usage and sacraments in both the ceremonial law of the Jews and in the institutions of the more aspiring pagans, found in Plato's dictum about goods and wives in common, for example, an anticipation of the Dominical injunction to let kith and kindred go, while in primitive initiation rites and various ablutions he saw Christian baptism foreshadowed.[89] Bucer tended to construe the survival of the *lumen naturae* or *internum lumen Dei* in non-Christian traditions as evidence of divine election, but not always.[90] Bucer was also less reserved than Luther about actual identification of the elect, was less reticent than Luther on the ultimate mystery of the division between the *electi* and *reprobati*.[91]

It was Bucer's view of the persistence of the internal light in individual pagans (whether because of primordial election or because of the gift of God in continuously strengthening the original *lumen* with philosophical light) that encouraged him, in contrast to all the other Protestant reformers, to become interested in missions to the new peoples overseas. Like Erasmus, Bucer had an explicit concern for sustained missionary activity—as distinguished from proselytizing or from a Christian's merely witnessing to Christ among non-Christians in case of shipwreck, of captivity through war or piracy, or of commercial and colonizing contacts. He first expressed himself on missions, conceived theocratically as being primarily under the aegis of Christian rulers, in *The True Cure of Souls* (1538).[92] Like Erasmus, he deplored the grossly selfish motives that impelled not only Catholic princes but even clerics to exploit and even destroy distant aborigines under the guise of a "Christian" mission, which was at its very best, said Bucer, but the imposition of one superstition on another. In the Catholic mission he could see only the wrath of God being visited

---

[88] *Evangelien-Kommentar*; noted by Holsten, "Christentum . . . Bucers," p. 169.
[89] Holsten, *ibid.*, p. 170.
[90] Strohl (*Bucer*, p. 25) notes that Bucer sometimes eliminated the Augustinian restriction that a virtuous life among pagans is that of the (few) elect only.
[91] Noted by Holsten, "Christentum . . . Bucers," pp. 148f.
[92] *Von der waren Seelsorge* (Strassburg, 1538), critically edited by Stupperich, *op.cit.*, pp. 67-245, esp. pp. 151-153.

upon the infidels: "Thus there is also [as with the Turkish onslaught upon Christendom] manifest the strong wrath of God in the discovery of new lands and islands, about which some feel so triumphant as if Christendom were thereby greatly extended; for nothing else is accomplished out there than that after first depriving those poor people of their bodily freedom and their goods, they are undone in their souls by the false faith which they are taught by the mendicants."[93] Theocrat and magisterial reformer, Bucer then called upon the Lord "to give our princes and magistrates the understanding and the will to enlarge Christendom properly and to improve it." In this spirit Bucer thought not only of Jews and Muslims and the inhabitants of lands overseas but also of communalized Christians living as ethnic *millets* under Muslim rule and of Papists as the proper objects of evangelical missionary effort.

Having, in connection with Bucer, allowed the huge issue of the Protestant attitude toward Judaism to surface, the author cannot forebear to mention alongside him (with Capito and Cellarius) also the Nuremberg and Königsberg reformer, Andreas Osiander (d. 1552). An accomplished Hebraist, he became in 1540 in print the first impassioned Christian defender of German Jews against the charge of child murder.[94]

In Zurich, Zwingli, a Hebraist mostly concerned with the creation of an Alpine Israel of Reformed cantons in renewed covenant, construed the doctrines of predestination and the people of election also as an overall theological sanction for his humanistic impulse to include virtuous pagans, especially of antiquity, in the company of the redeemed, interpreting their virtue as *signa electionis*.[95] Although Zwingli took issue with Erasmus on free will (even before Luther), he nevertheless found it plausible to propose the inclusion of virtuous pagans in the comprehensive work of Christ, perhaps because he did not share Luther's view of the gravity and totality of the original sin of the first Adam. Zwingli distinguished, in fact, between Adam's sin (*Erbsünde*) and guilt (*Erbschuld*) from the contagion or disposition to sin in his offspring (*Erbbresten, contagio originalis, morbus*). Sin

---

[93] *Ibid.*, p. 152. Cf. Edgar Prestage, *Portugal: A Pioneer of Christianity*, 2nd edn. (Lisbon, 1945).

[94] See the forthcoming book by Carl Cohen, *The Protestant Reformation in Its Relation to the Jews*, ch. 7, and Gottfried Seebass, *Das reformatorische Werk des Andreas Osiander* (Nuremberg, 1967).

[95] See Rudolf Pfister, *Die Seligkeit erwählter Heiden bei Zwingli* (Zurich, 1952).

(*peccatum*), according to Zwingli, is in each person the willful self-conscious implementation of the latent impulse (*Erbbresten*).

All this, and much more, Zwingli set forth in his theological epistle to Urbanus Rhegius, *De peccato originali declaratio* (15 August 1526).[96] There he raised the question whether Christ as the obedient Second Adam and Restorer had not made good (*sanando*) for *all* mankind what had been undone by Adam's disobedience (*peccando*).[97] If he had, then Christ could be said to have restored the whole human race (*genus universum*), and not just the Church of the faithful (elect). But, while Zwingli could not be at all sure of this point on the basis of Scripture, he insisted that it was certainly no more a derogation of the work of Christ to surmise that he intended to save the elect from all mankind than it was to hold that he is able to save only those infants within the Christian community who are actually baptized. Zwingli was, in any event, positive that "original sin cannot condemn infants of Christians" and that, quite possibly, "the [elect] infants of the Gentiles" are likewise saved "by the benefit of Christ," also without baptism. With regard to these infant *gentiles*, on their becoming responsibly sinful adults, Zwingli pointed out that there was biblical precedent (Jethro in Exodus 18:19ff. and Cornelius in Acts 10:4) to support the view that their good works and faith would suffice to bring about their inclusion in the benefits of election: "For where there are works done worthy of God, there surely there has long since been a pious covenant with God."[98] Zwingli's biblicist-humanist conflation of Israelite and classical virtues had the consequence that he could even identify redemptive membership in the Church and virtuous citizenship in the state. This point comes out notably in his epistolary preface to his Latin translation of, and commentary on, Jeremiah (11 March 1531). Here amid abundant references to Zeus, Minerva, Hercules, and Circe, and with the God of Jeremiah and the Father of Jesus Christ called *Numen*, Zwingli declared: "To be a Christian is nothing other than to be a faithful and good citizen, a Christian city nothing other than a Christian Church."[99]

[96] Zwingli, *Sämtliche Werke*, V (Leipzig, 1934), 359-396.

[97] *Ibid.*, p. 388. See also *Commentary on the True and False Religion* (1525), esp. sections "On Religion" and "Conclusion," not yet in *Sämtliche Werke; Opera omnia*, ed. Melchior Schuler and Johann Schultheiss, 8 vols. (Zurich, 1828-1842), III, esp. 173-179, 322-325.

[98] *Ibid.*, p. 389, lines 7f.

[99] *Complanatio Jeremiae prophetae foetura prima; Werke*, XIV (Zurich, 1959), 417ff.; *Opera*, V: 1, 1ff.

In his *Exposition of the Faith* (1531) Zwingli sought to make the whole Reformed version of Christianity, as he had worked it out, attractive to Francis I. Near the end of his *Exposition* Zwingli came to the subject of eternal life. Defining it in juxtaposition to the doctrine of the Anabaptists, most of whom believed in the sleep of the soul along with the body until the Resurrection, Zwingli stated his view of eternal blessedness thus: "Finally, we believe that after this existence, which is captivity and death rather than life, there is for saints and believers an everlasting life of joy and felicity, but for the wicked and unbelieving, of misery and wretchedness."[100] After going into this matter in more detail, he addressed the Catholic monarch in the following oft-cited passage:

After that you may expect [immediately upon your death] to see the communion and fellowship of all the saints and sages and believers and the steadfast and brave and the good who have ever lived since the world began. You will see the two Adams, the redeemed and the Redeemer, Abel, Enoch, Noah, Abraham, Isaac, Jacob, Elisha, Isaiah, and the Virgin Mother of God of whom he prophesied, David, Hezekiah, Josiah, the Baptist, Peter, Paul; *Hercules too and Theseus, Socrates, Aristides, Antigonus, Numa, Camillus, the Catos and Scipios*; Louis the Pious and your predecessors the Louis, Philips, Pepins and all your ancestors who have departed this life in faith. In short there has not lived a single good man, there has not been a single pious heart or believing soul from the beginning of the world to the end, which you will not see there in the presence of God.[101]

Elsewhere, Zwingli identified other righteous pagans who were to be found with Christ in heaven, among them Plato, Cicero, and Seneca. Such an inclusive view of eternal salvation, though it could be found in several of the universal theists of humanist training in Renaissance Italy, is striking in its specificity, all the more so because it came from the pen of one of the major Protestant reformers. Like Augustine, Zwingli could ascribe salvation of pre-Christian worthies to the eternal Christ.[102] New was Zwingli's willingness to name specific elect persons

[100] *Opera*, ed. Schuler, IV, 49; G. W. Bromiley, *Zwingli and Bullinger*, Library of Christian Classics, XXIV (Philadelphia, 1953), p. 273.

[101] *Opera*, VI, 51; *Zwingli and Bullinger*, pp. 275ff. (Italics mine.)

[102] *Enarratio in Evangelium Johannis* (Strassburg, 1528), pp. 264f. We have found a less exuberant list in Melanchthon—but there on the basis of a literal *descensus ad inferos* rather than as here on the basis of primordial election, n. 81.

born after Christ.[103] That Zwingli was inconsistently scriptural and classical, predestinarian and humanistic, and that he separated Word and Spirit more readily than Luther were not clear to him. More research is needed to fit his comprehensive predestinarianism into the late medieval and humanistic stream of universal theism.[104]

When Heinrich Bullinger, Zwingli's successor as chief pastor in Zurich, edited the above passage for publication, he saw fit to remove the names of the Catholic king's royal predecessors! Luther, as we noted, repudiated Zwingli's idea of elect *religio* evidenced in *pietas* as pagan. But Theodor Bibliander (d. 1564), Zwingli's professorial successor, whom we have already met as the courageous translator of the Koran, *Apologia pro editione Alcorani* (1543),[105] was much concerned not only with Islam but also, in *De legitima vindicatione christianismi* (1553), with other religions and with the world mission to them of Reformed Christianity as the *vera religio*. Modifying predestinarianism, Bibliander, on the basis of a humanistic universal theism (as aboriginal) combined with his strong eschatological conviction, held that God had revealed himself partially to all peoples, but that their piety and aspiration could never be satisfied except in the fuller revelation of Christ as the Son of God. He ranged Islam alongside the *pre*-Christian religions, using precisely the Christian ingredients in the Koran as evidence of a *preparatio evangelii*(!) among Arabs and other peoples in the Islamic stage of religiosity and ethics. Bibliander attached great importance to the mastery of the major religious languages, including Arabic, in order to facilitate the reestablishment of rational relations among the families of mankind, confused since the dispersion at Babel. He saw the ultimate unity of *humanitas* in the Reformed

[103] The Catholic Church had traditionally included a few pagans in heaven by name, e.g., Statius, on the basis of certain legends in which they were accorded special revelation. Also, there is a long history of the effort to interpret Aristotle on the basis of two spurious writings as a Christian before the fullness of time and, therefore, as redeemed. For the literature, see Baron in *The Crisis of the Early Italian Renaissance*; Martin Grabmann, "Aristoteles im Werturteil des Mittelalters," *Mittelalterliches Geistesleben*, II (Munich, 1936), 92-100.

[104] Pfister (*Die Seligkeit . . .*) ruled out a humanistic-Renaissance strand in Zwingli's vision of salvation and saw it grounded wholly in election; but see, besides Baron, Rudolf Stadelmann, "Der religiös-universale Theismus und die Toleranzidee," *Vom Geist des ausgehenden Mittelalters* (Halle, 1929), IV: 2, 146-187.

[105] See above at n. 67. Emil Egli, *Analecta Reformatoria*, II (Zurich, 1901), 1-144; Holsten, "Reformation und Mission," pp. 22-31.

Church but hoped that the precious elements in all religions (which he regarded as gifts of the common heavenly Father to priests, bards, and philosophers among all nations and not, in the manner of some of the Church Fathers, as thefts or borrowings from revealed religion) would, like good grain, be garnered by scholars and evangelists and gathered into the granary of Christ.

John Calvin, influenced by Bucer's view of the Jews, was in the end pilloried as *Calvinus judaizans*.[106] On the whole, Calvin, more merciful toward the Jews than toward Christian heretics, nevertheless reinforced the general thrust of Protestantism, beginning with Luther, to narrow the scope of effectual calling and to inhibit missionary zeal.

With respect to the Muslims, Calvin, like Luther, was rather mild when he made his first recorded observation about them. Thus, in the first edition of the *Institutes of the Christian Religion* (1536), we find Calvin calling for moderation in dealing with born Saracens (also heretics and schismatics under Turkish sway).[107] The attitude in France toward the Turkish threat to the German Empire was, in any event, different from that in Germany. Calvin, whose life span almost coincides with that of Suleiman, remained reserved about the Turkish menace. He never became involved in the eschatological speculation about the Muslims,[108] as did both Luther and Melanchthon.

[106] This sobriquet is, indeed, the title of a work (1593) by the Lutheran Marburg professor, Aegidius Hunnius (d. 1603), who figured in the Lutheran struggle against crypto-Calvinism. For a recent study, with the literature, see Salo W. Baron, "John Calvin and the Jews," *Harry Austryn Wolfson Jubilee*, ed. Saul Lieberman, 3 vols. (Jerusalem, 1965), I, 141-163. I have not been able to consult the doctoral dissertation by Pierre Lechot, "La pensée de Luther et de Calvin relative aux religions non-chrétiennes" (Neuchâtel, 1944).

[107] *Institutes* (1536), ch. 4 ("De fide"); ed. Jacques Pannier (Paris, 1936), II, 145; referred to by *idem*, "Calvin et les Turcs," *Revue Historique*, CLXXX (1937), 268-286. At about the same point in the definitive edition of the *Institutes* (1559), Bk. 4, ch. 1, Calvin completely ecclesiasticized the eternal *Logos*-Pedagogue of Clement of Alexandria, characterizing the Pedagogue as inwardly effecting faith in the presence of the written Word.

[108] The printer of Bibliander's Koran, John Operin, who was threatened with imprisonment in Basel and who was saved from this fate by the intercession of Luther, was Calvin's printer for the *Institutes*; when Operin was in financial straits with his contested publication, he wrote to Calvin, asking him to invest in the hazardous printing at six per cent. We do not have Calvin's reply, which would surely have been very interesting. The letter from the editor, Operin, is in Calvin's *Opera*, XI, 464; Herminjard, *Correspondance des Réformateurs*, VIII, 188.

When Calvin received in 1555 a French translation of Luther's and Melanchthon's commentaries on Daniel, he read these pages of eschatological fervor and exegetical confidence carefully but concluded that neither the common Protestant interpretation that the Pope was the little horn nor the specifically Lutheran view that Daniel and the Seer of Revelation referred to Mohammed seemed to him probable.[109] But Calvin did, like Luther, refuse to identify Mohammed with the Antichrist. Mohammed was an "apostate," the Papacy alone the Antichrist.[110] Although Calvin was involved in the charge brought against Michael Servetus, that the latter's doctrine tended to favor Muslims (and Jews), for the most part we must conclude that Calvin was not much interested either in the historic phenomenon or in the current military threat of Islam and apparently never found time even to leaf through the Latin edition of the Koran put out by his own publishing house in Basel.

As for religions other than Islam, Calvin retained the barest remnants of a natural theology and held that any original perception of the unity of God was of little avail, "for religion was commonly adulterated throughout almost all ages" and "all the heathen to a man slipped back into false inventions." He ascribed the aberrations in part to man's perversity and in part to Satan's deceptions.[111] Moreover, after his revelation to his elect people, God "condemned as falsehood and lying whatever of divinity had formerly been celebrated among the heathen." Even the pagan philosophers had failed to glimpse anything but "fleeting unrealities." He observed that, with the advent of Christ, even the Samaritans, "the *pagans* [who] . . . seemed to come closest to true piety," knew not what they worshiped (John 4:22).[112] Perhaps Calvin's soteriologically most restrictive thought was to consider the Holy Spirit (often in patristic thinking held to be the expression of the divine omnipotence, prevenience, and omnipresence) as limited to the things of Christ and the visible Church: "It is . . . no wonder that the Holy Spirit rejects as base all cults contrived through the will of

---

[109] He expressed this judgment in *Praelectiones in librum prophetarum Danielis* (Geneva, 1561); *Opera*, XLI, col. 517; *Commentary*, II, 26; noted by Pannier, p. 284, n. 2.

[110] Commentary on II Thessalonians 2:3; Ross Mackenzie, tr., *Epistles of Paul to the Romans and to the Thessalonians* (Edinburgh/London, 1961), pp. 398f.

[111] *Institutes*, i, x, 3.    [112] *Ibid.*, v, 13.

men. . . . And though nothing more harmful [than error] may result, yet to worship an unknown God by chance is no light fault."[113]

## IV. *Some Radical Reformers:*
### *Carlstadt, Hofmann, Ziegler, Schwenckfeld*[114]

The radicals of the sixteenth century (Anabaptists, Spiritualists, and others) fanned out in utter disregard of territorial boundaries and local laws, thinking themselves to be emissaries and exemplars of a Gospel at once new and old, to be shared by the whole world. With imaginations excited by the vistas opened before them in Bible study and amid apocalyptic rumor, a number of these radicals pondered what might be the providential and redemptive significance of the persistence of the Jews, the military successes of the Turks, and the opening up of whole continents of aborigines who had never heard either of Adam and his fall or of the Second Adam and a provisional redemption of all the children of men. Characteristic of many radicals was an eschatological interpretation of the mission to the Jews, the prophetic interpretation of the current military successes of the Turks, and an ambivalent mystical-primitivist-missionary interpretation of the aboriginal pagans overseas, as well as of the virtuous pagans in antiquity.

In discussing the relationship with Jews, the radical reformers displayed a considerable range of attitudes, from gross anti-Semitism to either programmatic Judaizing or interfaith solidarity.

The Muslims they regarded variously and sometimes interchangeably: (a) as the instrument of God's wrath because of the insufficiency of the Reformation; (b) as the instrument of his redemption, Suleiman being the new Cyrus; (c) as the object (along with the Jews) of a special missionary proclamation in the Latter Days; (d) as already constitutive of an interfaith church of spiritual Semites in three covenants; and (e) as, along with Jews and virtuous pagans, already a part of the *Ecclesia spiritualis* insofar as they conformed to the inner Word. Whatever the stress, whether tutelary chastisement or missionary conversion or interfaith concord, the radicals differed from most of the classical Protestants in minimizing the territorial aspects

---

[113] *Ibid.*, 13; ed. John T. McNeill, tr. Ford Lewis Battles (Philadelphia, 1960), I, 67. See the same restriction in n. 107.

[114] The author has written more fully than here on the subject in *Radical Reformation* (Philadelphia, 1962), ch. 32, sect. 2, and in "Sectarian Ecumenicity: Reflections on a Little Noticed Aspect of the Radical Reformation," *Review and Expositor*, LXIV (1967), 141-160.

of the Muslim challenge in an effort to make a religious accommodation.

As for the third grouping—ancient and contemporary pagans—many radicals, even though not strategically located or equipped to carry out a world mission, were, more than most Protestant reformers, concerned about their salvation.

One of their ways of providing for non-Christians was the apostolic, patristic, and medieval view about the harrowing of hell, supported not only by I Peter 3:19 but also, for the radicals, by the apocryphal Gospel of Nicodemus. As we noted, some of the classical Protestants, under the influence of a mystical tradition, interpreted the credal *descensus ad inferos* non-literally as referring to the intensity of Christ's suffering (Luther consistently, Calvin in part) while others (Bucer and Zwingli) simply construed *infernum* as the sepulcher, in either case eliminating a major provision for pre-Christian worthies. Many of the radicals shared the mystical interpretation of the *descensus* as the utter anguish of Jesus's dereliction; but several of them retained alongside it the traditional Catholic view as well and even sought to enlarge the scope of the presumed work of Christ among the shades.

The most notable development of the *descensus* among the radicals was with Andreas Bodenstein von Carlstadt (d. 1541), especially in the first phase of his thinking. Although under the same mystical influence as Luther of the *resignatio* theme (*Gelassenheit*), he did not allow the spiritualization of the *descensus* to inhibit his belief in a real hell and purgatory. Indeed, under the influence of the late medieval pietist Wessel Gansfort, Carlstadt, in his *Sermon on Purgatory* (1523),[115] specified two places beyond the tomb prior to the general resurrection, namely, hell for the wicked and purgatory for the majority of "Christ-believing souls." He thought of purgatory as the realm of progressive purgation and supplementary instruction. After insisting that during the *descensus* it was "right and fitting that Christ preached to those who were dead," he went on to suggest that tutelage in purgatory was possible for those who died since the advent and *descensus* of Christ: "Now if God does not want to judge [unjustly?] and says that the dead in their graves will hear God's voice, it follows that it is not contrary to Scripture to say that the souls must then study

[115] *Ein Sermon vom stand der Christglaubigen seelen von Abrahams schosz und fegfeuer der abgeschidnen seelen* (Wittenberg, 1523). See John Kleiner, "Andreas Bodenstein von Karlstadt's Eschatology as illustrated by Two Major Writings of 1523 and 1529" (Harvard S.T.M. thesis, 1967).

(*studirn*) what they have here missed (*versaumpt*)."[116] Now, although Carlstadt here did not go so far as Melanchthon to mention specific virtuous pagans in purgatory and, indeed, for the moment concerned himself only with "Christ-believing souls," still the very concept of studious progress and thoughtful purgation in spiritual flame and light was so prominent in his thought that he vigorously excoriated the Pope for presuming to grant indulgences to cut short this benign process; and one must conclude that it was not far from this singular *Schwärmer* to suppose that those who died without Christian faith, distant from the centers of evangelical proclamation, might also pass into purgatory, under the eternal Christ's tutelage, to "study" what had here been "missed."[117]

Besides the expansion and reapplication of the patristic article on a literal *descensus*, some of the radicals worked with the idea of the universal application of the work of Christ, taking literally the scriptural asseveration that Christ died for the sins of the whole world. In this matter some were possibly following a surmise of Zwingli, but without his stark predestinarianism.[118] Taking seriously what Zwingli had conjectured concerning the restorative work of Christ, the Second Adam, the Anabaptists held that baptism was in fact *not necessary* for already redeemed infants. They adopted believers' or confessional baptism for the function discharged by penance (plus the eucharist) in Catholic practice. Christ as Restorer had made possible for all the children of men everywhere the implementation of a free will which Adam had lost in Paradise through voluntary disobedience. In the Second Adam God had truly fulfilled his promise to Abraham that in his seed *all* the nations of the earth would be blessed.

This universalizing note was most clearly struck by Melchior Hofmann (d. 1543), sometime Lutheran lay evangelist, forerunner of both the Münsterites and the Mennonites, after he had broken away from Luther's conception of the bondage of the will of fallen man. In *On*

---

[116] *Ein Sermon* . . . , p. Cii$^r$; noted by Kleiner, p. 32.

[117] Marsilio Ficino, mindful of the Thomist requirement of at least an implicit (Christian) faith on the part of pre-Christian Jews and Gentiles, conjectured that the prophets, like Isaiah, also in limbo awaiting the foretold Messiah, instructed the virtuous pagans there with their prophecies. Thus Pythagoras, Socrates, Plato, and other worthies (in limbo because of their virtues) were prepared to receive the grace of Christ at his *descensus*. "Epistola de salute philosophorum," *Opera* (Basel, 1561), I, 806; cf. also 459; noted by Baron, ". . . gentiles salvati," pp. 259f.

[118] For the hint from Zwingli, see above on p. 358.

*the Will in Bondage and Free* (ca. 1531) Hofmann explained the basis of his confidence. He interpreted the children of Israel in bondage to Pharaoh as paradigmatic of all mankind. Only the liberating act of God had made it possible for the Israelites to depart from bondage in Egypt and, in the wilderness of Sinai, to choose freely to be loyal (or disloyal) to the covenant. By hermeneutical analogy Hofmann held that God's liberating act on Calvary was valid for the whole human race (not only for the elect Jews), whether peoples in lands remote from Christendom (or even at its center) knew this to be true or not! They had long since been freed from bondage to the Pharaoh of world and self by the once-and-for-all act of redemptively obedient *justitia* of the Second Adam: "God says to his Son [Psalm 2:8]: I will give to thee the heathen for an inheritance and the ends of the world for a possession.... For, it is not a part of mankind that was given to Christ as Redeemer, as some suppose, but rather *all peoples* were given to him by his Father, *both the heathen and the Jews*, as God said elsewhere to the holy patriarch Abraham.... He made man from the beginning, that is, he 'has born' him again from out the first death of Adam through his Word, Christ Jesus, unto life so that (John 8: [36]) man has become now a truly free creature."[119] Hofmann connected the exercise of this Christ-won freedom of the will with the resolution to accept believers' or confessional baptism.

Clement Ziegler, garden preacher in Strassburg, gave voice to another universalizing concern. Deeply convinced in 1525 that he was living in the age of Elijah's return (Malachi 4:5f.), he strove to eliminate the "eucharistic idolatry" of Christianity in order "to turn the hearts of fathers to their children"—that is, the Jews to Christianity—by stressing the eternal Christ in glory rather than the Jesus, son of Mary, according to the flesh. He hoped, indeed, that not only Jews but "also Turks, Tartars, Greeks, and pagans," all of whom had direct access to the glorified Lord "through faith," would on their own turn to Christ because, with the Last Days impending, even the Jews, "like the other peoples, are ready to receive the true Messiah, Christ the High Priest unto eternity."[120] Ziegler, concerned with the implementa-

[119] *Van den geuangenen ende vrien wil; Bibliotheca Reformatoria Neerlandica,* V (The Hague, 1909), 188, 194. (Italics mine.)

[120] *Ein fast schon büchlin* (Strassburg, 1525), foll. 24b, 25a, 27b. Portions of this book are printed in Rott and Krebs, *Elsass,* I, 30-36, esp. 35; Rudolphe Peter, "Le maraîcher Clément Ziegler," *Revue d'Histoire et de Philosophie Religieuses,* XXXIV (1954), esp. 270.

tion of the Dominical command to preach the Gospel "to all creatures" (Mark 16:15), also universalistically referred to Origen, if not expressly to his *apokatastasis* or *restoratio omnium* (Acts 2:21), in support of his conviction that distant pagans and devils, even without their knowledge of the redeeming work of Christ, might be saved before the Last Judgment.[121]

Similarly, the mystical-humanist Anabaptist Hans Denck (d. 1527), alluding to the Lord's Supper, wrote: "Whoever is so minded and drinks from the *invisible* chalice the *invisible* wine, which God from the beginning of the world mixed through his Son, through the Word ... he will be completely divinized through the love of God; and God in him will be humanized (*vermenscht*)."[122] If Denck seemed to minimize the atoning suffering of the *historic Logos* incarnate, it was only because, as a universalist, he was moved to maximize and, as it were, universalize the redeeming role of the royal and high priestly *Logos*, not only from the beginning of the world but also in the world, growing ever larger in an age of vast exploration and discovery.

Caspar Schwenckfeld (d. 1561), who suggested a eucharistic action of Christ in the *descensus ad inferos* and who suspended the practice of liturgical communion among his followers in the sufficiency of the celestial flesh or manna, may be cited also as an exponent in our period of the classical, scriptural, patristic, and mystical idea of the abiding company of a circle of elect Friends of God: "Thus did the Church of Christ begin soon after the creation of the world (though in a hidden manner); and Adam, Abel, Enoch, Noah, and all the elect faithful fathers were members of the Church and were true Christians; for the Church of Christ is much older than that of the Jews ...; Abraham was faithful and righteous, which is to say that he was a Christian before he was circumcised." Therefore, Schwenckfeld continued, all "the holy fathers, patriarchs, and prophets were Christians and the children of God and Friends."[123]

---

[121] Rott and Krebs, I, 13. Ziegler probably got his reference to Origen from Luther's "Sendbrief," cited above at n. 39; for it was accessible, having been republished at Strassburg in 1523. Ziegler was pleased to find in Origen what Luther rejected.

[122] *Bekenntnis* (1525); *Schriften*, ed. Georg Baring and Walter Fellmann, *Täuferquellen*, VI (Gütersloh, 1955, 1956, 1960), Pt. II, 25.

[123] *Judicium* (1542), a criticism of an Anabaptist treatise from the circle of Pilgram Marpeck; *Corpus Schwenckfeldianorum*, VII (Leipzig, 1927), 197, lines 33-38; 158, lines 1-7, 28-29.

## *Conclusion*

In the Age of Discovery and Reformation the initial forces of Christian renewal were also by and large the forces which tended to restrict rather than enlarge the scope of salvation. The Protestant attack upon the indulgence system (and its extension into the realm of purgatory) and their proclamation of justification *sola fide* as grounded in the divine decree of election (authoritatively set forth *sola scriptura*) brought into prominence the fewness of those who could be considered saved even within nominal Christendom and *a fortiori* contracted for non-Christians the hope of salvation on the basis of morality *extra fidem*, of piety *extra ecclesiam*, and of religion *extra Christum*.

With most of the classical Protestant reformers, the patristic provision for the pre-Christian worthies in the *descensus ad inferos* became either a metaphor for mystical anguish or simply the grave, whereupon hell and purgatory dissolved as physical realms. To be sure, Melanchthon and several radical reformers were exceptions. Almost unique was the theory of Carlstadt that purgatory, far from being a realm of deferred penance, was actually a realm for progressive purification and even "study" on the part of all who had missed the full teaching of Christ during their earthly sojourn.

The doctrine of eternal election, which for Augustine had allowed for an inclusion of saints in an invisible Church from the beginning of the world, served most of the classical Protestant reformers in further limiting the scope of Christ's atonement. Here, however, Erasmus, Zwingli, and Cellarius were exceptions, construing the virtues of pagans as *praevisa merita* or *signa electionis*.

The patristic *preparatio evangelii* through the *Logos* operating in the philosophies and higher religions and moral systems of mankind was contracted in most of the classical Protestant reformers into a non-functioning relic. Bucer, however, with his *lumen naturale* and Bibliander with his provisional revelations were exceptions. With the radical reformers, natural theology reappeared primarily in the quite new form of a theology of a fallen and groaning nature awaiting the redemption of the sons of men.

In some respects the radicals were the most exclusive reformers of their age, because of their stress on the exacting moral qualifications of the righteous remnant. Yet, beyond their sectarian ecclesiology, they suggested avenues of salvation for other peoples, even through other religions. One is reminded, indeed, of comparable utterances from the patristic age, especially from the period before Christianity became the established religion of the Roman Empire. The recognition, among some of the radicals, of interfaith elect Friends of God, for example, belongs not only to the world of the medieval mystics but also to that of the ancient philosophers and Church Fathers. Similar to the views of the Greek Fathers in particular, too, was the conviction of some Anabaptists that Christ on Calvary in a cosmic victory over Satan freed man everywhere from the grip of determinism in body and soul and restored to him that freedom of choice lost by Adam's disobedience, restoring to all a new moral accountability.

Apart from holding to the universal application of the work of Christ to all mankind as a first stage toward ultimate salvation, certain radicals adopted one particular patristic view of universal salvation, that of Origen, the *restoratio omnium*. There was also the interesting view of Schwenckfeld and Ziegler that the redemptive eucharistic element, the celestial flesh of Christ, was available like manna directly through prayer to men everywhere in the wilderness of the world.

Of the three medieval addenda to the patristic theories of non-Christian religiosity (largely connected with the rise of Islam), two theories remained alive among Protestants: namely, that Islam was the Antichrist and that Islam was a chastisement for Christian failures. Profoundly theological was Luther's exclusive espousal of the latter theme, with his insistence that the Antichrist was an institution, not a person, and precisely a Christian institution, or whatever else in Christianity might presume to interpose itself between man and his Redeemer. Luther was undeviatingly determined to identify heresy and ecclesiastical pretension as more truly the embodiment of the Antichrist than a non-Christian religion like Islam, however terrifying the latter might appear for the moment. Astounding, but not without patristic precedent, was the unwillingness of Luther and some other reformers to regard the God of Islam, and even of their schismatic and heretical opponents, as one with their own. New, in application, was the radical sectarian view that Suleiman might be a deliverer of the righteous (Anabaptist) remnant within Christendom, as Cyrus was once an instrument of the Almighty under the old dispensation. Quite new was the view among several radical theorists that Judaism, Christianity, and Islam might be three successive and equally valid covenants of God with peoples of different temperaments and aptitudes. Its counterpart within the main line of Protestant development was Bibliander's evaluation of Islam for Arabs and Turks as preparatory for the plenitude of Christ.

Although concern for the salvation of peoples beyond the hearing of Christian missionaries and an interest in contemporary and superseded religions must be put down as on the whole only a small facet of theology in the Age of Reformation, it should be remarked in conclusion that it was in part the sensitivity and openness of Erasmus, Bucer, Bibliander, and many of the radicals to the problem of *salus extra ecclesiam* and *fides extra Christum* that, working its way into the main Protestant bodies in the course of the seventeenth and eighteenth centuries, made it possible for Protestantism belatedly to undertake a world mission (as distinguished from Protestant colonization), an assignment which Catholics had felt laid upon them already in the Age of Discovery.

# INFLATION AND WITCHCRAFT:
## THE CASE OF JEAN BODIN

### E. WILLIAM MONTER

MANY problems becloud the scholarly evaluation of Jean Bodin, who was surely one of the finest and most original thinkers of the late sixteenth century. He has always been something of a puzzle to subsequent generations. The opinion that Bodin's genius displayed itself unequally in his works—that the *République* was an undoubted masterpiece but that some of his other works ought to be consigned to decent oblivion—was expressed only a generation after his death by such erudite libertines as Guy Patin and Gabriel Naudé.[1] Bayle's *Dictionnaire historique et critique* expressed similar judgments in its article on Bodin, and in a general way these opinions about the unevenness of Bodin's works have been shared by nineteenth- and twentieth-century scholars. The modern version of Bodin's fame was crystallized over a century ago by Henri Baudrillart, who praised him as a philosopher of history, of law, and of political economy but passed impatiently and with obvious embarrassment over his other writings.[2]

Today most important students of Bodin continue to concentrate on his political theories and on their connections to his essays in history and jurisprudence. Fifty years ago there appeared a Sorbonne thesis, which remains the fullest biography of Bodin: Roger Chauviré's *Jean Bodin, auteur de la République*. Since then the leading Bodinist has been Pierre Mesnard, who is justly famous for his work in the history of political philosophy.[3]

[1] Naudé is given primary responsibility for this opinion by Harold Mantz, "Jean Bodin and the Sorcerers," *Romanic Review*, XV (1924), 155, n. 7; Platin, by F. von Bezold, "Jean Bodin als Okkultist und seine *Démonomanie*," *Historische Zeitschrift*, CV (1910), 3.

[2] See his *Jean Bodin et son temps* (Paris, 1853), pp. v-viii. Baudrillart introduces a brief discussion of the *Démonomanie* and the *Theatrum* by remarking (p. 183), "Voici un bizarre et ridicule chapitre qui vient s'ajouter à l'histoire des contradictions de l'esprit humain."

[3] Mesnard has written several articles on Bodin and has naturally discussed him at length in his chief work, *L'essor de la philosophie politique au XVIe siècle*, 2nd edn. (Paris, 1951). His most recent general appraisal may be found in *Jean Bodin en la storia del pensamiento* (Madrid, 1962). The newest study in English, Julian Franklin's *Jean Bodin and the Sixteenth-Century Revolution*

The reasons behind this modern consensus are not hard to find. Bodin was a prolific author, and his immortal *République* of 1576 is only the bulkiest of his many published works. However, Bodin's other writings are less remarkable for their number than for the variety of their subject matter. He composed a *Methodus* "for the easy understanding of history" in 1565; the *Response à M. de Malestroit*, explaining the recent rise in prices, in 1568; the *Démonomanie des sorciers*, a guide to witchcraft, in 1580; the *Heptaplomeres*, an essay (long unpublished) on the comparative merits of seven major religions and philosophies, in 1593; and the *Theatrum Naturale Universarum*, a guide to the physical universe, in 1596. Bodin wrote many other things, including a short treatise on the nature of universal jurisprudence (1578), an annotated Latin edition of an ancient treatise on hunting (1555), and minor polemics during the days of the Holy League. In other words, Bodin's total corpus is a potpourri which rebuffs efforts at simple classification or arrangement from a single common denominator.

In the eyes of the twentieth century, there are flagrant contradictions between the Bodin of some treatises and the Bodin of others. Not long ago a historian of sixteenth-century rationalism observed that "there are two men in Bodin," one a conventional lawyer and the other a boldly skeptical religious relativist, an "achriste":[4] Jekyll-Bodin, the author of the *République* and Hyde-Bodin, the author of the *Heptaplomeres*. A different variation on this theme has been offered by a distinguished historian of science. This time the opposition is between the Bodin of the *République* and the Bodin of the *Démonomanie*, one a remarkably shrewd analyst of human society and the other a naive fool as an investigator of physical phenomena. Bodin, he grumbled, deserved to be as infamous for the latter as he was famous for the former. This most renowned of lawyers, master of evidence and organization, produced a treatise on witchcraft which "may be described as a formless screed and a dribbling mess."[5]

A good contemporary summary of opinions about Bodin was offered in 1951 by M. Mesnard. While eschewing the more flagrant paradoxes

---

*in the Methodology of Law and History* (New York, 1964), is broadly in the same vein.

[4] Henri Busson, *Le rationalisme dans la littérature française de la Renaissance*, 2nd edn. (Paris, 1957), pp. 541ff.

[5] Lynn Thorndike, *A History of Magic and Experimental Science*, 8 vols. (New York, 1923-1958), VI, 525f.

of the type described above, he does recognize several important difficulties in the path toward a comprehensive evaluation of Bodin's thought. Documentary evidence about Bodin is scanty, confusing, and ambiguous. Much ink has been shed, pro and con, on whether or not he lived in Calvin's Geneva in the early 1550's and whether or not he supported the Holy League against the French monarchy (and thus against his own theory of sovereignty) after 1590. Mesnard concludes his survey of Bodin's career in politics and literature by describing him as a "brilliant example of a generation seeking a synthesis of law, literature, government, and religion."[6] What has been omitted from this summary, and also from the first thick quarto of Bodin's *Oeuvres philosophiques* which it introduces, is mention of Bodin's interest in natural science, which increasingly occupied him in his later years. Even here it seems that Bodin is a difficult subject to synthesize and to explain satisfactorily to a contemporary audience.

Yet, despite the wide variety of his subjects and despite the apparent paradoxes or inconsistencies in his treatment of these subjects, there is an obvious fact which any serious student of Bodin must immediately recognize: this man was a remarkably organic thinker. His works overlap—or rather interlock—with each other at several points, and sometimes Bodin himself will supply his reader with the appropriate cross-reference. The *République* is partly an expanded recapitulation of his earlier works, especially the *Methodus*. In particular, the sixth book of the *Methodus* ("The Type of Government in States," which fills over two-fifths of the entire treatise) serves as the point of departure for Bodin's masterpiece of political theory.[7] The sixth book of the *République* repeats and expands the ideas on economics first developed in the *Response à M. de Malestroit.*[8] A short digression in the *République* on state control of education repeats the phrases of Bodin's first public oration at the University of Toulouse in 1559.[9] Similar arguments, which frequently extend down to fine points of detail,[10] link the *République* to Bodin's earlier writings.

[6] P. Mesnard, ed., *Oeuvres philosophiques de Jean Bodin*, I (Paris, 1951), xv.
[7] All major students of Bodin (Baudrillart, Chauviré, Mesnard, Franklin) have recognized this fact, and the connections have been studied at length.
[8] This point is admirably discussed by Henri Hauser in his very complete introduction to *La response de Jean Bodin à M. de Malestroit* (Paris, 1932), pp. lix-lx. The *Response* looks backward as well as forward, for at one point (p. 25) it cites the *Methodus*.
[9] R. Chauviré, *Jean Bodin, auteur de la République* (Paris, 1914), p. 113.
[10] See, e.g., Bodin's description of the aristocracy of the Republic of Ragusa

Turning in the opposite direction, one sees that Bodin continued to repeat ideas from the *République* in his later works. General theories about the influence of climate on human behavior and on the ideal form of government can be found in later works. His refutation of some theories of Copernicus reappears in the *Theatrum*, virtually unchanged from the *République*.[11] In the *Démonomanie* Bodin refutes a minor contention of Aristotle by referring his reader to the sixth book of the *Methodus*.[12] In the *Heptaplomeres* he refutes the arguments of the Manichaeans with the same reasoning he has used in the *République*.[13] Not only are Bodin's works on witchcraft, religion, and physics consistent with the *République*, but they are also consistent with each other. The argument that witches can only cure evils which are of demoniacal rather than natural origin appears in the *Heptaplomeres*, summarized from the *Démonomanie*.[14] Bodin uses the phenomenon of ecstasy in both the *Theatrum* and the *Démonomanie* to show how the spirit can leave the body without causing death.[15] He tells the same story in the *Heptaplomeres* and in the *Démonomanie* about the god Mopsus and diabolical advice of oracles,[16] and he gives the same explanations for the physical substance of demons in the *Theatrum* that he gives in the *Démonomanie*.[17] The most thorough student of Bodin's thought has underlined the "almost immobile fixity of his mind across thirty years" and has observed that one of Bodin's

---

in the *Methodus*, tr. B. Reynolds (New York, 1945), p. 245, and in the *République*, Bk. II, ch. 7 (*The Six Bookes of a Commonweale*, ed. K. D. McRae [Cambridge, 1962], pp. 235f.); or his preference for "harmonic" over either arithmetic or geometric justice (*Methodus*, 286f.; *Rép.*, Bk. VI, ch. 6 [McRae, pp. 756f.]).

[11] See Chauviré, *Bodin*, p. 113.

[12] *Démonomanie des sorciers* (Paris: J. Dupuys, 1580), Bk. I, ch. 5, fol. 29ᵛ. All page numbers are cited from the earliest editions.

[13] Cf. R. Chauviré, *Le colloque de Jean Bodin des secrets cachez des choses sublimes entre sept scavans qui sont de differens sentimens* (Paris, 1914), p. 30 (all further notes refer to the book and folio number of Bibliothèque Nationale, MS fr. 1923, from which Chauviré translated and summarized the *Heptaplomeres*: as, in this case, *Hept.*, Bk. III, foll. 156-159), with *Rép.*, Bk. II, ch. 2 (McRae, *Six Bookes*, p. 199).

[14] Cf. *Hept.* Bk. II, fol. 66, with *Dém.*, Bk. III, ch. 2, foll. 127ᵛ-132.

[15] Cf. *Theatrum*, Bk. IV, ch. 15, with *Dém.*, Bk. II, ch. 5.

[16] Noticed by Chauviré, *Bodin*, p. 113 (*Hept.*, Bk. IV, fol. 259, and *Dém.*, Bk. I, ch. 5, in the later editions after 1587).

[17] Cf. *Theatrum*, Bk. IV, ch. 14, and *Dém.*, Bk. I, ch. 1, fol. 6ᵛ.

characteristics "seems to be an invariable fixity in his ideas."[18] With his mind well trained by the philosophers of Paris and the jurists of Toulouse and with his memory thoroughly stocked by continuous and varied reading (including a remarkable quantity of Jewish and Protestant authors), Bodin confronts us as an intellectual monolith. His interests may have shifted slightly as he grew older, but he seldom changed his opinions. The paradox of two or more Bodins—political scientist and witch-hunter, pioneer economist and reactionary physicist, religious skeptic and earnest calculator of the speed of angels whirling through the eighth heaven, a Bodin of dazzling inconsistencies— is a paradox created by us and not by him.

In his own eyes Bodin was not only consistent; he was also methodical. Considering the extent to which his works overlap, is it possible to discern some master plan, some grandiose structure in which each treatise would have its appointed place? If there is an answer to these questions, it should be sought from the clues provided in the introduction to his first important work, written at the age of thirty-five:[19]

Of history, that is, the true narration of things, there are three kinds: human, natural, and divine. The first concerns man; the second, nature; the third, the Father of nature. One depicts the acts of man while leading his life in the midst of society. The second reveals causes hidden in nature and explains their development from earliest beginnings. The last records the strength and power of Almighty God and of the immortal souls, set apart from all else. . . . It shall come about that from thinking first about ourselves, then about our family, then about our society, we are led to examine nature, and finally to the true history of Immortal God.

If anyone does not wish to include mathematics with the natural sciences, then he will make four divisions of history: human, of course, uncertain and confused; natural, which is definite, but sometimes uncertain on account of contact with matter or an evil deity, and therefore inconsistent; mathematical, more certain, because it is free from the admixture of matter . . . ; finally, divine, most uncertain and by its very nature changeless.

A certain simple, three-level program may be constructed from this outline. Long ago Chauviré suggested a schema in which Bodin was

[18] Chauviré, *Bodin*, pp. 112, 113.
[19] *Methodus*, Bk. I (Reynolds, pp. 15, 16, 19).

regarded as having revealed his general goals in the *Methodus,* accomplished the first part in the *République,* accomplished the second part with the *Theatrum,* and began the final part with his unpublished dialogue, the *Heptaplomeres.*[20] If the whole of human wisdom consists of knowledge of man, nature, and God, then Bodin explored them all in a truly encyclopedic program of a sort rarely undertaken in his troubled age.

Yet something is wrong with this schema. Chauviré himself admitted that "J'excepte le *Démonomanie des sorciers,* parce qu'elle gêne mon propos sans doute,"[21] although it is certain that this was one of Bodin's more important books. Except for the *République,* it was the most popular and widely read of his works. It was his only other full-length book to be composed in the vernacular, and it was the only other book to be translated into a foreign vernacular.[22] It seems that his discourse on witchcraft is the most important stumbling block in the road to a unified and systematic interpretation of Bodin's writings and thought. This is the ultimate pill which his numerous admirers cannot swallow and which they cannot ignore. This is the principal reason for the ambiguity of Bodin's posthumous reputation from the seventeenth to the twentieth century—from Guy Patin, who considered it hypocritical, to the late Lynn Thorndike, who considered it detestable.

Is it possible to remove these logical (and psychological) difficulties and to integrate the *Démonomanie* with Bodin's other works? We already know that several ideas found in it are repeated elsewhere in Bodin's writings, that it bears the authentic stamp of his inflexible mind. We know that the *Démonomanie* was a popular book, that its author regarded it as an important and timely book. Perhaps the first clue toward a correct evaluation of this book comes from the circumstances which prompted its publication. In large measure the *Démonomanie* was a polemic directed against a clear and present danger: the skepticism in regard to witchcraft expressed by prominent jurists like Alciati and, more recently, in the notorious books of the Rhine-

---

[20] Chauviré, *Bodin,* p. 114-115.    [21] *Ibid.,* p. 114, n. 2.

[22] The best bibliography of the *République* (McRae, *Six Bookes,* pp. A 78-83) lists nineteen French editions by 1608, plus five Latin editions and Italian, Spanish, German, and English translations. The *Démonomanie* (Chauviré, *Bodin,* pp. 518-519) saw nine French editions by 1604, plus three Latin editions and an Italian translation (Venice: Aldus, 1587). Both books were originally printed by the same *libraire,* Jacques Dupuys of Paris. None of Bodin's other books went through more than five editions before 1604.

land physician Johann Weyer. In all editions of the *Démonomanie* there is a lengthy appendix of at least seventy pages which refutes Weyer's opinions. This polemic with a single opponent was a sport in which Bodin, unlike many other authors of his age, seldom engaged. I know of only one other case in all his writings where a single opponent is refuted at such length and with such devastating skill (for Bodin never felt the need to answer his rivals or their spokesmen more than once). The lone parallel is the *Response à M. de Malestroit,* composed twelve years earlier.

The parallel between these two polemics may seem at first glance to be superficial and capricious, but they do have other common features. Of course, it must be noted that the historical fate of Bodin's polemic with Malestroit about inflation was exactly the reverse of his polemic with Weyer about witchcraft. Three centuries later Bodin had become a precursor of the quantity theory of money and a precursor of historical research in economics from his first polemic; but he had become an opponent of justice and reason, as well as a gullible consumer of the worst kind of old wives' tales, from his second polemic. Yet, after a bit of reflection, one begins to see a common pattern of concern underlying both polemics, endowing them with a common purpose and even at times with a common method. To Bodin, the respective errors of Malestroit and Weyer sprang from their common love of artificial and illusory paradoxes which went against the grain of common sense. Each man attempted to demonstrate, by a form of sophistry which Bodin found infuriating, that what was so was not. One man denied the reality of inflation, the other the reality of witchcraft. And both could be refuted, earnestly and convincingly, by common and reliable weapons. Bodin preferred to smother his opponents under the accumulated weight of ancient and modern evidence, of personal and recorded experience. Then, after lining up his authorities, he proceeded to reveal the hollowness of his opponents' reasoning by skillful and precise analysis.

Let us consider Bodin's means of persuasion, point by point. In both polemics he undergirds his arguments at each and every point with a wealth of ancient and modern evidence which he draws from a huge fund of sources, including unpublished financial and legal records and testimony from many different countries, both past and present. Bodin seems to have tried to strike some rough balance between ancient and modern testimony in his arrangement of evidence, so that his case rested precisely on their agreement. We know that he generally occupied a position of neutrality with regard to the relative merits of the ancients and the moderns. If, at thirty-five, he had said that "they are mistaken who think that the race of men always deteriorates; when old men err in this respect, it is understandable," by the time he was sixty-three he had changed his mind; he observed then that the world was becoming decrepit, slowly but surely, and bemoaned that the men of old were giants compared with the men of his day.[23] But the important point was not who was superior to whom as a witness: it was whether or not they agreed. Bodin skillfully selected a cosmopolitan array of evidence which he draped like a protective shield around each of his assertions. The *Response à M. de Malestroit* is, in fact, so stuffed with evidence that it has little space for assertions. Throughout this pamphlet runs a basic parallel between the rapid Roman conquest of the ancient world and the equally rapid Spanish conquest of the New World, both of which brought a sudden sharp rise in prices.[24] Bodin compares the price of pearls in the age of Cleopatra with the price in Francis I's time to support his hypothesis that an abundant supply of anything leads to a fall in its price.[25] He compares the rapid depreciation of Rome's coinage after the Punic wars with that of France's money after the Hundred Years' War to show the catastrophic effects of tampering.[26]

The most curious case of Bodin's use of ancient and modern evidence, however, comes in a fascinating and little-noticed passage near the end of the *Response*. Here he marshals bits of evidence from Herodotus, Livy, Pliny, and contemporary Europe to show that the value of gold relative to silver had never varied farther than from 1:10 to 1:15 and that their ratio naturally stabilized around a "just price" of 1:12. Money, concludes Bodin in a typical piece of his reasoning, is literally a law unto itself: "even the Greeks called money and law by the same word, as we say *loy* and *aloy*. And just as the law is a sacred thing, which should not be violated, so money is a holy thing which should not be altered, once given its just weight and worth."[27] The

---

[23] Cf. *Methodus*, Bk. VII (Reynolds, p. 302), with *Hept.*, Bk. II, fol. 51. Because Hans Baron misses Bodin's change of opinion, his discussion of this point in "The Querelle of the Ancients and the Moderns as a Problem for Renaissance Scholarship," *Journal of the History of Ideas*, XX (1959), pp. 10-11, is misleading.

[24] *La response à M. de Malestroit*, pp. 10, 13, 22-25.

[25] *Ibid.*, p. 19.          [26] *Ibid.*, p. 47.

[27] *Ibid.*, p. 52f. When Bodin discusses this point in the *République*, Bk. VI, ch. 3 (McRae, *Six Bookes*, p. 691f.), he does not refer to money as "une chose sainte."

essentially sacred nature of money and the peculiarity of the nearly constant ratio of gold to silver have been noticed by some modern authors, who connect their relative values to the 1:12+ ratio between the cycles of the golden sun and the silvery moon around the earth.[28] One wonders what Bodin would have thought of this theory; I feel sure he would have welcomed it as one more proof of the harmonies of the universe.

The same balance and concordance between ancient and modern evidence is equally obvious in the *Démonomanie*. Bodin's preface[29] notes that, according to St. Augustine, all ancient sects except the Epicureans punished sorcery. The Pythagoreans, he adds, wondered if there had ever existed a man who had *not* seen a demon. He gives a lengthy review of the history of necromancy and witchcraft in Homer and Orpheus, in early Jewish history, and in Greco-Roman antiquity down to St. Augustine, who reported in the *City of God* that demons surely did copulate with women. Bodin continues with an array of modern witnesses, including Pico della Mirandola, who once saw two sorcerers (disguised as priests) meeting with several demons (disguised as women). Bodin himself, of course, had seen confessed sorcerers on several occasions. He points out the remarkable unanimity between ancient and modern witnesses on the subject of witchcraft: for example, everyone agrees that demons are black and that they are either giants or dwarfs, but never normal-sized. We have known about sorcerers and their *maleficia* for three thousand years, he concludes, and our sources have told us substantially the same story. To doubt it is to doubt ancient and modern history and Holy Scripture—hence, to doubt God himself.

In the refutation of Weyer which concludes the *Démonomanie* Bodin repeats part of this array of evidence, occasionally to expose Weyer's shallow scholarship, his obvious twisting of scriptural texts, or his fraudulent confusion of sorcery with poisoning in antiquity (they were distinct, argues Bodin, and it most assuredly was sorcery which the laws punished).[30] Later he amasses ancient and modern evidence on the unnatural and evil deeds wrought by sorcerers. Bodin cleverly cites Weyer himself in this list, for his opponent admitted to having seen a case of triple levitation exactly like those reported by

[28] See N. O. Brown, *Life Against Death*, paper edn. (New York, 1964), p. 247, esp. nn. 39, 40.

[29] Unpaginated in all editions. Bodin resumes many of these arguments at the start of Book III of the *Démonomanie*.

[30] *Dém.*, foll. 220-224[v].

confessed witches.[31] Bodin also deals with one important piece of evidence used by Weyer: the *Canon Episcopi*, a clerical forgery, supposedly from the fourth century, which denied that sorcerers had any real power. Here Bodin simply notes that none of the Fathers of the Church mentioned the *Canon*, and he compiles a list of the "very best theologians" (Augustine, Aquinas, Bonaventure) who affirmed the contrary.[32] History was on Bodin's side in both polemics, and he used his well-stocked arsenal of unimpeachable authorities with devastating effect. No one dared use a historical argument against him for a very long time. Even in regard to witchcraft, the ultimate refutation of Bodin's arguments had to come from new *a priori* reasoning, from a will to disbelieve, rather than from *a posteriori* appeals to "the facts."[33]

Having disposed of the facts, Bodin proceeded to the second part of his polemic, namely, his insistence on precise reasoning. To a modern observer, this appears to be the weaker part of Bodin's strategy, partly because it tends to slide into mere quibbling about Aristotle's definitions and logic. It has recently been suggested that this "carping and often unfair criticism of Aristotle which runs like a continuous thread through the whole of Bodin's writings" should be understood in the light of his Ramist background.[34] Yet this quibbling with Aristotle, although frequently encountered in the *République*, is of minor importance in Bodin's polemics on witchcraft and inflation. The explanation is simple. Aristotle wrote a treatise on *Oeconomica*, but his subject was household management rather than gold and silver coinage, which was the object of dispute between Bodin and Malestroit. Aristotle also wrote nothing about witchcraft, yet Bodin could not let the matter rest. He argues in the preface to the *Démonomanie* that Aristotle's silence about demons and things supernatural proves nothing, because "most natural things were not known by him either." Weyer had been rash enough to make use of Aristotle's silence in his treatises, and Bodin returns to this point in his refutation, explaining why Aris-

[31] *Ibid.*, fol. 241ᵛ. Weyer had also seen wild beasts stopped by a mere word (fol. 239).

[32] *Ibid.*, fol. 249; Bodin had already made this point in his text (Bk. II, ch. 4, fol. 81).

[33] This point was made a century ago by one of the great champions of Victorian rationalism, who was no friend to the witch-hunters. See W.E.H. Lecky, *History of the Rise and Progress of Rationalism in Europe* (London, 1865), I, 34-37, 88.

[34] K. D. McRae, "Ramist Tendencies in the Thought of Jean Bodin," *Journal of the History of Ideas*, XVI (1955), p. 320.

totle never wrote about spirits and why his arguments about incorporeal things were contradictory.[35]

In general, we can see a clear difference with regard to this question of reasoning between Bodin's earlier and later polemics. Malestroit's paradoxes were inductively demonstrated, based on fact alone; a clearer and broader array of facts, which Bodin provided in his *Response*, sufficed to dissolve them. Weyer's arguments, on the other hand, were based both on incorrect facts and on flawed reasoning, and Bodin's refutation needed to be both inductive and deductive. Consider the problem of defining witchcraft. Bodin lampoons Weyer's attempt to define a *lamia* as a person "who is believed to be in league with Demons, and by their aid to do that which she cannot do." This definition is dialectically poor, says Bodin, because it contains no fewer than six disjunctions and because it describes something which is supposed to be but is not. A good definition would "point right at the thing and show at a glance its true essence."[36] He, Bodin, had begun his treatise with the first clear definition of a witch (reprinted with admiration by the late Montague Summers at the start of his *History of Witchcraft*): "A witch is a person who knowingly tries to accomplish something by Diabolical methods."[37]

Weyer's shabby definition, however, was among his lesser sins. Bodin was more angered by his opponent's contradictions. For example, Weyer admitted that in antiquity a sorcerer like Simon Magus could fly through the air but denied that modern sorcerers had this ability— a contradiction which showed his "extreme folly."[38] Bodin fills whole pages listing supernatural occurrences whose reality Weyer did admit, both in ancient and modern times. Weyer merely maintained that such deeds were due solely to demons and never to the witches who invoked the demons. This, said Bodin, was to deny the whole relation-

---

[35] *Dém.*, foll. 246-246ᵛ. Bodin was much less ingenious in this matter than the famous Italian naturalist Cesalpino, who in 1580 constructed an "Aristotelian" explanation for the physical reality of demons (see Thorndike, *History of Magic and Science*, VI, 335ff.).

[36] *Dém.*, fol. 229.

[37] *Ibid.*, Bk. I, ch. 1 ("Sorcier est celuy qui par moyens Diaboliques sciemment s'efforce de parvenir à quelque chose"). Summers's *History of Witchcraft*, reprint (New York, 1956), observes (p. 1) that "it would be, I imagine, hardly possible to discover a more concise, exact, comprehensive, and intelligent definition of a Witch." Bodin thought so too; he refers to his definition at several different places in the *Démonomanie*.

[38] *Dém.*, fol. 238.

ship between cause and effect in a "capricious and sophistic" attempt to absolve witches of responsibility for their *maleficia*.[39]

Weyer's whole line of reasoning, Bodin observes, must have come either from wickedness or from ignorance. Obviously Weyer was not ignorant. How else could he have learned all the words and diagrams used by practitioners of black magic in order to summon demons? How else could he have learned the constitutional structure of the Diabolic Monarchy, with its 72 princes (each with his own special attributes) and its legions of 6,666 lesser demons, adding up to 7,405,926 demons "sauf erreur de calcul"?[40] Worse yet, what reason did he have to reveal all those incantations and all those names and attributes in print? Even Weyer's master, Cornelius Agrippa, "the greatest sorcerer of his age," never dared go this far in the fourth book of his *De Occulta Philosophia*, as Bodin had already noted.[41] Since Weyer was not ignorant, his actions could only be explained on the hypothesis that he was trying to *teach* black magic while claiming to combat it and that he was truly in league with the devil. This line of reasoning, I believe, best explains the towering wrath which Bodin displayed toward his opponent, particularly at the end of his refutation.

Bodin made many other attacks upon Weyer, including one interesting foray into his rival's professional corner to demonstrate that he was a poor physician. Weyer had explained that most women accused of witchcraft were really suffering from melancholia. Bodin, relying on Galen, said that this was a disease peculiar to men (at least in its acute form) and prevalent in warmer climates than Germany.[42] His refutation of Weyer, whose sophistries sprang from wickedness rather than ignorance (which was the source of Malestroit's errors), was appropriately thorough and pulverizing. His answer to Malestroit had been based on fuller evidence and on personal experience;[43] ultimately Bodin ringed his facts around a few simply hypotheses, of which the most important was that a greatly increased supply of gold and silver automatically caused a rapid rise in prices. In his later quarrel with

[39] *Ibid.*, fol. 218ᵛ.    [40] *Ibid.*, fol. 219.    [41] *Ibid.*, Bk. II, ch. 1, foll. 54-54ᵛ.
[42] *Ibid.*, foll. 225ᵛ-226ᵛ; same point made earlier (Bk. II, ch. 5, fol. 90ᵛ).
[43] In the *Response* (p. 44) Bodin refers to his personal experience in diminishing gold in a furnace, which freed him from a common error. He had also experimented with dissolving silver by aquafortis. Later, in the *Theatrum* (Bk. II, ch. 9), Bodin called experience "the master of all certitude." There is a good discussion of his empiricism in Chauviré, *Bodin*, pp. 118ff. Of course, the *Démonomanie* is stuffed with the fruit of Bodin's personal experiences.

Weyer the facts were not in doubt so much as their explanation; here the argument really turned on matters of cause and effect, since both sides agreed that supernatural effects exist. As Bodin said in his preface to the *Démonomanie*, skeptics "should not obstinately deny the truth if they can perceive only the effects but not the cause." In these polemics, as in all his writings, Bodin imagines himself as a man who knows both theory and practice, who has acquired all the important evidence and has at the same time unraveled its network of causes and effects. It should also be noted that Bodin presents himself as a layman in both polemics. He has, he says, no intimate acquaintance with the royal treasury (as had Malestroit), nor is he a merchant like many other writers on monetary questions; moreover, he has been only marginally involved in witchcraft trials, never engineering giant witch-hunts like many other demonologists, and he is not a magician like Weyer. In other words, he has no immediate personal interest, beyond that of the concerned citizen, in either inflation or witchcraft.

In our study of Bodin's polemical procedures, his massive use of diversified evidence and his criticism of his opponent's logic, we have left aside some of his more curious attitudes. The most interesting of these is Bodin's fascination with mathematical relationships in nature. This loyal follower of Pythagoras had proclaimed in his *Methodus* that "Immortal God arranged all things in numbers, order, and marvellous measure," and demonstrations of these harmonious relationships appear in all his important works. Not only was Bodin intrigued by the importance of numbers in human and natural affairs, but he was also highly interested by the possibility of a reformed and purified astrology—a hope which he shared with such other prominent neo-Pythagoreans as Kepler.[44] Yet Bodin's fascination with numbers plays only a marginal role in his polemics. Only elementary calculations are involved in his answer to Malestroit, on such questions as the rate of inflation during the past sixty years in France, or on Guillaume Budé's evaluation of Roman weights and measures.[45] In the *Démonomanie* Bodin's calculations are primarily decorative and digressive. There is one passage in which he discusses the relative speeds of celestial

[44] *Methodus*, Bk. VI (Reynolds, p. 223). The importance of numbers fills a long chapter of the *République* (Bk. IV, ch. 2). Remarks on the purification of astrology, similar to those in the *République* but somewhat fuller, occur in *Dém.*, Bk. I, ch. 5 (foll. 30ᵛ-34ᵛ). Cf. Kepler's remarks on the reformation of astrology, summarized by Max Caspar, *Kepler*, tr. C. D. Hellman, paper edn. (New York, 1962), pp. 190ff.

[45] *Response*, pp. 9, 30f., 49f.

and demonic motion in order to prove that angels guiding the eighth sphere of heaven move much faster than demons transporting witches,[46] but this demonstration is not central to his purpose. If Bodin really did agree with the ancients who considered mathematics to be "the bridge between physics and metaphysics,"[47] he postponed its most extensive use for his most important syntheses, such as the *République* or the *Theatrum*.

After discussing the strength and variety of Bodin's polemical techniques, we should not be surprised to find that he generally did convince his readers that the skeptics who doubted the reality of inflation and witchcraft were wrong. This is not to suggest that Bodin's solutions to these problems were universally accepted; they were not. But discussions of these issues in the early 1600's had to begin where Bodin had left the problems, not where Malestroit or Weyer had left them. Pamphlets dealing with inflation were not terribly numerous between 1580 and 1620, perhaps because the problem itself was not quite so acute as it had been earlier. Bodin's conclusions were sometimes repeated or refuted by important pamphleteers, especially by Malynes in England in 1603.[48] But, in general, inflation was a far less lively issue for the next generation than witchcraft, and it is here that Bodin's analysis of his subject received the most attention.

Because the history of witchcraft theory is a great deal less well known and less well organized than the history of monetary theory, it may be helpful to review the former as it developed after 1580. Within thirty years of the publication of the *Démonomanie*, a sizable number of important tracts on witchcraft were composed by lawyers and theologians in many European countries. The largest single contingent came from the Germans, who tended to agree with some of Bodin's main contentions (and almost none of Weyer's) but to disagree with him on matters of detail. The famous Bishop Peter Binsfeld, whose *De confessionibus maleficarum et sagarum* appeared in 1589, offers a good example of such learned German comment.[49] Demonologists in other

---

[46] *Dém.*, foll. 248-248ᵛ. Bodin calculated 1,706,155 leagues per minute for the angels vs. 200 leagues "in a short time" for the demons.

[47] *Dém.*, Preface.

[48] Bodin's influence is carefully discussed by Hauser, *Response*, pp. lxviii-lxxv. One French pamphleteer, who wrote from 1609-1614, totally ignored Bodin's quantity theory and apparently considered Malestroit's theories to be unrefuted (pp. lxxi-lxxii).

[49] Thorndike, *History of Magic and Science*, VI, 538. See pp. 534f., 539, 240, for other German discussions of Bodin.

lands—such as the transplanted Spanish Jesuit Martin Delrio, whose *Disquisitionum magicarum* appeared at Louvain in 1599, the Italian Francesco Maria Guazzo, whose *Compendium maleficarum* appeared in 1608, or King James VI of Scotland, whose *Demonologie* appeared in 1597—seldom discussed Bodin's opinions as carefully as Binsfeld.

The French-speaking world also saw a rapid increase in demonologies after 1580. "By a typical paradox of history," writes the most recent and intelligent historian of witchcraft, "France, the home of reason and critical sense, seems to have been plagued more than the rest of Europe by this kind of book, often written by secular judges, and even by men who in other spheres of life were very distinguished. . . . Thanks to men such as Bodin, Grégoire, Remy, Boguet, DeLancre, and others less well known, the crime of witchcraft was taking on a more uniform appearance."[50] Like Bodin, the other French demonologists were lawyers; but, unlike him, they were generally men who had personally instigated large-scale witch-hunts in lands on the periphery of French civilization (Bodin lived and worked after 1576 in the Île-de-France). Remy based his *Demonolatry* of 1595 on his experiences as a judge in the imperial and bilingual territory of Lorraine; Boguet based his *Discours des sorciers* of 1602 on experiences in the Hapsburg Free County of Burgundy; DeLancre, judge of the Parlement of Bordeaux and husband of Montaigne's grand-niece, hunted the witches he described in the *Tableau de l'inconstance des mauvaises anges et démons* of 1612 in the Basque lands. All three were famous and useful legal guides in their day. Boguet's work was particularly valuable for its appendix, which codified existing statutes and court practices in witchcraft cases, but the others were more erudite.

Although Bodin's *Démonomanie* clearly belongs with this latter group insofar as it is a lawyer's approach to witchcraft, it is different from them in some important ways. Bodin had never had practical experience in uprooting whole communities of witches. He was, of course, aware that witches gathered in assemblies called Sabbats and that demons carried them through the air to such assemblies;[51] but he was not obsessed with the fine points of the Sabbat, as were the three other demonologists. In other words, he was less concerned with

---

[50] Julio Caro Baroja, *The World of the Witches*, tr. O.N.V. Glendenning (Chicago, 1964), p. 112; see also Robert Mandrou, *Magistrats et sorciers en France au XVII^e siècle* (Paris, 1968), pp. 137-143.

[51] *Dém.*, Bk. I, ch. 6, fol. 47; Bk. II, ch. 4, foll. 81ff. Remy, Boguet, and De-Lancre all devote at least seven chapters to the minutiae of the Sabbat.

witches as an organized sect of devil-worshippers. But he was more concerned than they were with occult phenomena in general, and the whole first book of the *Démonomanie* is directed toward such questions as separating angelic from demonic advice and useful from harmful magic.[52]

Whereas both these features separate Bodin's work from that of many of the later French demonologists, other features help link it to an earlier demonology which he may have been trying to modernize and update. The similarities between the *Démonomanie* and the *Malleus Maleficarum*, composed almost a full century earlier, are striking. Except for their first sections, these books share a common organization. Bodin's second book consists of eight long chapters on the *maleficia* of witches, and his third book consists of six chapters telling how to combat their magic. The second book of the *Malleus* is split into two parts which treat these two problems in the same order and almost in the same proportions as Bodin's work. The fourth and final book of the *Démonomanie* corresponds especially closely, both in form and in spirit, with the third and final book of the *Malleus*; both deal with the legal problems raised by witch-trials. Although other demonologies obviously treat many of these same questions, they do not have the same neat and symmetrically organized discussion as the *Démonomanie* and the *Malleus*.[53]

It seems probable that Bodin in his *Démonomanie* was constructing a new handbook—partly a philosophical examination of the subject, partly a practical guide to the detection and punishment of witches— to replace the *Malleus*. In an age when the investigation and punishment of witchcraft had long since been transferred from the Inquisition to lay judges, Bodin's book filled a real need. By the late sixteenth century the scholastic shell of *quaestiones* in which the *Malleus* en-

---

[52] See an excellent discussion by F. von Bezold, "Jean Bodin als Okkultist und seine *Démonomanie*," *Historische Zeitschrift*, CV (1910), pp. 1-64; also D. P. Walker, *Spiritual and Demonic Magic from Ficino to Campanella* (London, 1958), pp. 171-177.

[53] In other words, precisely because the *Démonomanie* is *not* a "formless screed and a dribbling mess," as Thorndike described it (*supra*, p. 372), it is superior to such later rivals as the works of Remy or Boguet. A thorough comparison between the *Démonomanie* and the *Malleus* would be a highly useful effort. Bodin cites the *Malleus*, of course (see Bk. II, ch. 5, fol. 93; Bk. III, ch. 2, foll. 129, 130$^v$; Bk. III, ch. 4, fol. 141$^v$; Bk. III, ch. 5, foll. 146$^v$, 151$^v$; Bk. III, ch. 6, foll. 155, 155$^v$, 157, 160; Bk. IV, ch. 1, fol. 171; etc.), but no more than some other eminent authorities, such as Pico, Grillandus, or Daneau.

cased its discussion of witchcraft was badly antiquated. The whole subject needed to be updated. Yet the *Malleus renovatus* which Bodin constructed in 1580 still had to serve the same dual purpose for the secular court which its predecessor had filled for the ecclesiastical court. It had to refute skeptics who scoffed at the deeds of witches or objected to the severity of the prosecution (for witchcraft was *crimen exceptum* in both kinds of courts), and it had to instruct the judge as fully as possible concerning his duties in such cases. The measure of Bodin's success was the popularity of the *Démonomanie*, which soon spawned several inferior rivals (none of which, with the possible exception of Boguet's work, was as successful). If imitation truly is the sincerest form of flattery, then the fact that the *Démonomanie* virtually began a literary genre speaks eloquently for its timeliness. These considerations may also help explain why this was Bodin's only major literary effort, except for the *République*, to be composed in French. Like its illustrious predecessor, the *Démonomanie* discussed a clear and present danger, and its author had particular cause to address it to the widest possible audience.

Let us now return to the question asked much earlier and see if we can arrange the *Démonomanie* within the total corpus of Bodin's writings, so that it need not "gêner mon propos" as it did Chauviré's. To begin with, we can consider the *Démonomanie* as the first indication of Bodin's shift of interest from human history to natural history—from a type of history which the *Methodus* called "uncertain and confused" to one which was "definite, but sometimes uncertain on account of contact with matter on an evil deity." It was his first step[54] after the great synthesis of human history in the *République* toward the great synthesis of natural history in the *Theatrum*, which he completed on his deathbed in 1596. Admittedly, the *Démonomanie* is a halting and halfway transition between human and natural history. Its subject matter is unusual precisely insofar as it involves elements of both kinds of history. This makes it a particularly interesting topic for a professional lawyer who was also widely read in the occult and natural sciences. Continuing this line of thought, we can suggest that the role which the *Démonomanie* played in Bodin's later syntheses corresponds very roughly to the role which a lengthy pamphlet like the *Response* of 1568 eventually played in his grand synthesis of human history. Of

---

[54] If we except the *Juris universi distributio*, published in 1578 but written at least twelve years earlier (see McRae, "Ramist Tendencies in Bodin," p. 310).

course, demons and witches play a somewhat greater role in natural and divine history than do monetary factors in human history. But Bodin's polemic on witchcraft could be gracefully absorbed into his later treatment of a larger subject in much the same way as his polemic on inflation was absorbed into the *République*. It seems, upon preliminary investigation, that Bodin's use of his information about witches was more important in divine than in natural history; it is the second book of the *Heptaplomeres*, his "notoriously radical" essay in comparative religion, which most fully incorporates the results of the *Démonomanie*, rather than the more "reactionary" *Theatrum*.[55]

A provisional arrangement of this sort has several advantages. It is not offered as a desperate attempt to make order out of chaos in the wide variety of writings which Bodin offered to the world. Neither is it offered as an attempt to whitewash Bodin on the issues of witchcraft. Its main assets are that it will remove a few of the artificial paradoxes about Jean Bodin. It will reestablish a minimum of consistency and logic in our evaluation of this man of inflexible and virtually unchanging opinions. Bodin believed he was logical—even if his logic was often that of Petrus Ramus, difficult to understand today and not always followed by Bodin himself, who was incurably fond of digressions.[56] One must therefore examine his thought as a unit, in which the subject matter changes often, while the methods and prejudices remain fixed. In the *Démonomanie*, as in his other writings, whether polemics or encyclopedic syntheses, Bodin utilized the same basic procedures. He was always fundamentally empirical, fascinated by the problem of collecting and comparing bits of evidence from widely scattered authorities. His empiricism was very crude, because his critical apparatus was superficial. He could never distinguish hearsay from genuine eyewitness reporting, either among the ancients or among the moderns; this shortcoming led him to accept tales which told of men with skin like cows and men who had eyes like owls, being able to see better by night than by day.[57] But, though Bodin was gullible, he tried hard; whenever possible, he tried to experience things himself, to see strange

---

[55] I repeat that this is a preliminary observation. It seems that *Hept.*, Bk. II, esp. foll. 58-67, 88-91, 114-117, contains more material on witchcraft than all of the *Theatrum*. Demons, of course, are very important in both books, though here, too, Books II and III of the *Hept.* seem to contain more material than the *Theatrum*, IV and V.

[56] McRae, "Ramist Tendencies in Bodin," esp. pp. 316, 319f.

[57] *Rép.*, Bk. V. ch. 1 (McRae, *Six Bookes*, p. 548).

beasts like crocodiles and ostriches.[58] If we conceive of Bodin as an empiricist, albeit a blindfolded empiricist, we can dissolve many of the paradoxes surrounding him, such as that between Bodin the "pragmatic" economic historian and Bodin the "gullible" demonologist. In his lifetime nobody possessed any truly accurate guide for separating fact from fiction.[59]

The only other immortal figure among the lawyers and *politiques* of Bodin's generation, Michel de Montaigne, is often set up as his rival, particularly in such questions of gross superstitution as witchcraft. Yet Montaigne's systematic skepticism, as displayed in the *Essais*, was in no way superior to Bodin's systematic credulity in the *Démonomanie*; it was merely its reverse. Montaigne was once confronted with a dozen confessed witches, all medically examined and found to be possessed with the devil's mark, by a well-meaning nobleman who intended to cure his doubts about witchcraft—but to no avail.[60] The man who refuses to believe what he has seen is no better off than the man who all too readily believes what he has not seen, and the first position is psychologically much harder to sustain.

[58] *Theatrum*, Bk. III, chs. 11, 14.

[59] Cf. the remarks in Robert Mandrou, *Introduction à la France moderne (1500-1640): essai de psychologie historique* (Paris, 1961), pp. 258-260: the later 1500's saw "men of experience—but of few experiments—and of tradition. . . . Experience, at this time, must be understood not as the art of demonstrating a fact by repeating it, but as a fact purely and simply noted down, or carefully observed; an apparition, a flaming star in the sky, a dream which proved prophetic are facts of experience."

[60] Busson, *Rationalisme dans la littérature française*, pp. 452ff.; see also A. M. Boase, "Montaigne et la sorcellerie," *Humanisme et renaissance*, no. 2 (1935), pp. 402-421.

# HISTORY AND POLITICS:
## THE CONTROVERSY OVER THE SALE OF OFFICES IN EARLY SEVENTEENTH-CENTURY FRANCE

DAVIS BITTON

NOT until the beginning of the seventeenth century did the sale of offices become the subject of a full-blown public controversy in France. *Vénalité* had been practiced long before this, of course, and had been frequently denounced. But there had been no genuine controversy. At the Estates-General of 1560, and again in 1576 and 1588, when the practice was denounced by clergy, nobility, and Third Estate alike, the response of the king was not to defend venality as a permanent feature of the government. Instead, ordinances supposedly curtailing venality were promulgated in 1560 and 1579, and in 1588, while addressing the opening session of the Estates-General of that year, Henry III promised to abolish the practice altogether.[1] If this promise remained unfulfilled, if the ordinances forbidding venality were not enforced, if the practice was in some respects even extended, the explanation was simple: it was a regrettable expedient due to the financial exigencies of the religious wars. Once peace was restored, it was assumed, the sale of offices would be quickly eradicated. With such an apparent consensus there could be complaints but, on the subject of venality, no real clash of views, no debate.

The situation changed markedly in 1604, when Henry IV issued an edict attempting to regulate some features of the sale of offices. He too had indicated his dislike for the system of venality, and its early demise had seemed likely. The edict of 1604, however, seemed to represent a "hardening" of the system. Known as the edict of "la Paulette," it allowed officeholders to insure the patrimonial status of their charge by the payment of a modest annual tax (the *droit annuel*). If it is an exaggeration to say that this edict created an officeholding class, it was

[1] Examples of ordinances on the subject of venality are in Isambert, *Recueil général des anciennes lois françaises* (Paris, 1822-1827), XIV, 380, 484, 517. The early growth of the practice, the complaints enunciated in the late sixteenth century, and the indecisive responses of the king are summarized in the standard work by Roland Mousnier, *La vénalité des offices sous Henri IV et Louis XIII* (Rouen, n.d.), Bk. I, ch. 2, esp. pp. 66-69.

at least a significant further step in the direction of a hereditary office-holding aristocracy.[2] Not surprisingly, strong opposition was expressed. A bitter argument broke out in the royal council itself. Although the edict finally "passed" by a vote of seven to five, it was even then implemented only over the strong protest of the chancellor, Bellièvre.[3]

During the next few years arguments were heard on both sides. By the beginning of the Estates-General of 1614, where venality was one of the central issues, the controversy had culminated in a swirl of pamphlets, cahiers, and vibrant speeches. Quite often, of course, the discussion centered on the specific question of *droit annuel,* but the larger question of venality itself was always in the background. It was a central issue, having to do with the power of the crown, the structure of government, and the nature of public power. By examining some of the pamphlets, cahiers, and treatises published during the early years of the seventeenth century, we can discover the arguments, ranging from the selfish and practical to the theoretical and historical, most frequently used on both sides.[4] It is an instructive case study of political rhetoric in early modern Europe.

# I

Arguments for and against the sale of offices were often couched in terms of practical advantage or disadvantage. At the lowest level the argument was an appeal to group interests, attempting to show how a given class would suffer or benefit from the revocation of venality. An obvious example of such an argument from class interest emanated from the old nobility. Frustrated by their own exclusion from many public charges, noble pamphleteers denounced the whole system of venality, ridiculing the practice of filling positions on the basis of money rather than merit. "True gentlemen," said one writer, "can no longer hope to arrive at any charge by reason of either birth or merit; but the children of the *officiers* of justice and finance, with their relatives or their connections, can hope to possess everything, since they have money in their hands."[5] In the words of another pamphleteer:

---

[2] Mousnier, pp. 208-209. The significance of the 1604 edict in its effects on the "rising" judicial aristocracy is discussed by Franklin L. Ford, *Robe and Sword* (Cambridge, Mass., 1953).

[3] Mousnier, pp. 208-216.

[4] Mousnier, pp. 576ff., provides a concise summary of some of the arguments, but he does not consider them as an example of political controversy.

[5] *Discours d'un gentilhomme françois à la noblesse de France* (n.p., n.d.), p. 10.

"It is well known that not one out of a thousand nobles can afford to buy an office for his son without selling his lands."[6] In such pamphlets, as well as in their various *cahiers de doléances*, the nobility vigorously denounced the system of venality which had grown up. Although they seemed at times to be advocating some system of *places aux mérites*, their class interest was usually apparent, as in the specific proposal that certain important charges be reserved for members of the old nobility.[7]

Not wishing to oppose merit as such, the officeholders ridiculed the assumption that the nobles were somehow possessed of superior merit. It was not the cost which prevented nobles from filling offices, said Savaron, but their lack of education and professional competence.[8] Money might not be equivalent to personal merit, others said, but it did not preclude genuine ability.[9] In fact, men coming from families of wealth would be more likely to have the proper background, including education, to equip them for positions of public trust.[10] To counter the nobility's complaints of unfair treatment, the officeholders could point out that they had purchased their charges in good faith, often at great sacrifice, and that a revocation of venality, a reduction in the number of offices, or even the abolition of the *droit annuel* would lead to their financial ruin.[11] In putting forward such arguments, most notably in the Estates-General of 1614, the officeholders showed a remarkable capacity to work together as a *corps* conscious of its own interests.[12]

Yet, even if such arguments by the two sides could rally support within each group and perhaps garner some sympathy by appealing to a general sense of "fair play," they would not have wide persuasive power unless they could appear as something more than self-serving. Thus the nobles did not usually demand outright preferential treatment. They preferred to denounce the whole outrageous system of venality of offices, to point out the obvious absurdity of neglecting to make appointments on the basis of merit, and to urge that a designation of certain offices for the noble class would be in keeping with a more

[6] *Utile et salutaire advis au Roy, pour bien regner,* (n.p., n.d.), pp. 49-50.
[7] The effort of the old nobility to regain public functions is described in my *The French Nobility in Crisis, 1560-1630* (Stanford University Press, 1969).
[8] Jean Savaron, *Chronologie des Estats Généraux* (Paris, 1615). Cf. *Discours à Messieurs les Deputez aux Estats Généraux de France* (n.p., n.d.), p. 59.
[9] *Utile et salutaire advis,* pp. 59-61.  [10] *Ibid.*
[11] *L'Officier et Catholique royal sur le droict annuel* (1615), p. 14.
[12] *Ibid.,* pp. 1-8.

equitable approach to the whole problem. Similarly, the officeholders did not stop by mentioning their own interests. Abolition or curtailment of the present system would not only lead them to bankruptcy, they alleged, but would also ruin their creditors.[13] And they noted that the costs of redemption would fall, not on the privileged orders who were calling for the end of venality, but on the common people who paid the *taille*.[14]

It was not at all clear, however, whether the interest of the common people, or of the nation as a whole, would be better served by continuing the existing practice or by abolishing it. Frequently the "horde" or "mob" of *officiers* was described as a "burden," but seldom was it made clear whether this was due to the inferior brand of justice administered by incompetent persons or to the heavy financial costs which they imposed in an effort to make good their investment.[15] Or, since many offices enjoyed exemption from the *taille*, it could be argued that the officeholders represented an increased burden on those who remained on the tax rolls.[16] Occasionally critics of venality pointed out that money invested in offices could not be invested in commerce; thus the system worked to the detriment of national economic prosperity.[17] On the other hand, the *officiers* could readily demonstrate that a certain percentage of the government's revenue came from the traffic in offices; to gain an equivalent amount from the *taille* or other imposts, they said, would scarcely decrease the tax burden.[18]

Besides claiming to represent the best interest of the country as a whole, both sides in the controversy were anxious to associate their own objectives with strengthening the power of the king. The opponents

[13] *Ibid.*                    [14] *Ibid.*

[15] The burden of the *officiers* was a common theme in the cahiers. See *Recueil des cahiers généraux des trois ordres aux Etats généraux*, ed. Lalourcé and Duval, 4 vols. (Paris, 1789). Cf. Mousnier, *Vénalité*, p. 119.

[16] Other aspects of the sensitivity to the relationship between numbers of exemptions and the tax burden of those who paid are discussed in my *The French Nobility in Crisis*, ch. 1.

[17] Bellièvre was only one of those who pointed out the economic consequences of venality "La marchandise est délaissée . . . le commerce souffre, le pays s'appauvrit, sa capacité contributive diminue . . ." (Mousnier, *Vénalité*, pp. 119, 221).

[18] The suppression of the *droit annuel* alone would have meant a loss of an annual income of some 1,600,000 livres for the king. The nobles did not respond favorably to the suggestion that one way to compensate for such a loss without increasing taxes would be to abolish pensions at the same time. (Mousnier, p. 571.)

of venality argued, for example, that the king's power was weakened by selling offices which, for all their theoretical ties with the crown, were actually in private hands and could be transferred at will. In effect, they said, the king lost his power of appointment, since the charges were sold or transferred, as purely financial transactions, through the Bureau des Parties Casuelles. When posts on the royal council or departments of the central government could be purchased, what was to prevent a foreign power from providing financial backing for individuals in these key positions? Then, surrounded by advisors who had purchased their offices, the king could at almost any time be assassinated.[19] Possibilities of such conspiracy and intrigue did not seem so remote in an age just emerging from the religious wars, especially when we remember that the last two kings of France, Henry III and Henry IV, had both been assassinated.

Again, the tenuousness of the king's control over *officiers* was obvious in the border provinces, where Frenchmen who purchased charges naturally came to regard them as property. Private persons thus usurped regalia, said the opponents of venality, and began to behave as "kinglets," and France was on the verge of breaking up into "cantons."[20] This picture did not seem overdrawn during the aftermath of the religious wars and during the instability of the regency. To be sure, the *officiers* who thus endangered the monarchy were a rather special group: princes of the blood, royal governors, families of the high nobility with ducal titles and the power to appoint *officiers* themselves. These were the *grands,* the magnates, who were quite unlike the average officeholder.[21] But, for some opponents of venality, it was all part of the same system of allowing public charges to be regarded as private property. Once an office was subject to purchase, it could become part of a network of obligations and family connections which, to say the least, weakened the control of the king.[22] This seemed all the more true when it was suggested, once again, that foreign money could in theory control the border provinces by providing funds for the purchase of key charges.[23]

[19] *Utile et salutaire advis,* p. 19; *Discours à messieurs les deputez, passim.*

[20] *Discours à messieurs les deputez,* pp. 15-16, 27. When the office is purchased, said this *Discours,* the *officier* thinks of the province as his and refuses to be dislodged. The king then is under pressure to bestow titles on such provincial magnates "et d'en faire les Roytelets."

[21] On the rise of governors during the religious wars, see Roger Doucet, *Les institutions de la France au XVIe siècle,* 2 vols. (Paris, 1948), I, 229-244.

[22] Mousnier, *Vénalité,* pp. 64ff.    [23] *Ibid.,* p. 309.

In the face of such considerations the officeholders had somehow to make a case that venality, as it had grown up, enhanced the power of the king. The purchase of an office was said to establish an identity of interest between the *officier* and the state. He would scarcely work to undermine the state in which he had, so to speak, invested his private fortune. The *droit annuel* made it necessary for all officeholders, even those who might have gained their charge through a provincial magnate, to pay an annual tax to the central government if they wished to insure their right to transmit or bequeath their offices. Again, it was not to their interest to alienate or undermine the state.[24] The consequences of abolishing the system, moreover, would not be a strengthening of the royal power but civil disorder and uprisings. On 4 January 1615 the president of the Parlement of Paris addressed the king, expressing his fear that efforts to deprive officeholders of a possession which they had enjoyed for several years would force them to seek support elsewhere. He spoke of the "common discontent" which would spread among "the infinite number affected by this matter" and expressed his fear that the "public tranquillity" would suffer.[25] It was a thinly disguised threat, declaring that the stability of the monarchy would not be improved by the overthrow of a system on which so many persons had come to depend.

To show that the venality of offices diminished or enhanced the power of the king served an important function in linking one's own cause, more or less convincingly, to that of the crown. From the point of view of the king, however, the immediate financial effects of venality were crucial. In 1613 the Trésor des Parties Casuelles (in charge of the sale and transfer of offices) took in 4,797,286 livres, about eighteen percent of the total government revenue. During the first half of the seventeenth century this relationship varied considerably. Sometimes the income from offices constituted only nine or ten percent of the national revenue, but on occasion, as in 1633, it was as high as fifty-two percent.[26] Even if the possibility of violence by dispossessed officeholders were ignored, the system could scarcely be abolished without providing a practical means for reimbursing officeholders for their investment and bringing an equivalent annual income into the treas-

[24] These arguments in favor of the existing system of venality are eloquently expressed in *L'Officier et Catholique royal*, pp. 1-8.

[25] Mousnier, *Vénalité*, pp. 576-577.

[26] Mousnier, pp. 391-392. This entire chapter deals with "Le Role joué par les offices dans les finances royales."

ury. Most demands for the end of venality or of the *droit annuel* made no effort to suggest alternative sources of income, and it was virtually impossible to find sources without alienating other classes.[27] Richelieu was not the only one to discover that denouncing the sale of offices in theory was easier than abolishing the system in practice.

## II

Since self-interest and practical needs were obviously central features of the controversy over venality, it is significant how frequently participants on both sides included as part of their argument some kind of appeal to history. Not that historical evidence was likely to be decisive in forming opinions. But at the beginning of the seventeenth century any controversy, especially if it dealt with any aspect of "constitutional thought," was likely to have a historical dimension.[28] And the controversy over offices, with its many ramifications, was no exception.

The most obvious tactic was to cite past experience as evidence of the wisdom or the fatuity of venality. The conception of history as a storehouse of didactic examples, inherited from the humanists of previous generations, was readily applied in controversies such as this. The Greeks, the Persians, the Assyrians, the Cathaginians, the Egyptians were all cited as examples of the effects of venality.[29] More familiar, of course, was the history of Rome. Opponents of venality praised the Roman Republic for its practice of rotating offices. They admired Julius Caesar for his prohibition of nepotism, plurality of charges, and tenure of more than one year.[30] And they often quoted a statement of the Emperor Alexander Severus: "I will not permit during my time

[27] If the revocation of the edict of "la Paulette" is for the common good, "comme les deputez du Clergé et de la Noblesse le chantent, qu'ils contribuent avec le tiers-estat au payement du prix que vallent les offices" (*L'Officier et Catholique royal*, p. 14). For the strategy of the Third Estate and the response of the nobles, see Mousnier, pp. 571-572.

[28] See J.G.A. Pocock, "The Nature of Constitutional Thought in Early Modern Europe," *Colloquium*, no. 5 (Spring, 1966), pp. 1-9.

[29] E.g., in order to prove that venality of offices had always existed, defenders of the practice "invoquaient les Romains, les Carthaginois, les Vénitiens, les rois de France depuis les Mérovingiens, Louis XII et Henri IV" (Mousnier, *Vénalité*, p. 577).

[30] *Utile et salutaire advis*, p. 19; *Harangue de l'amateur de justice aux trois estats* (1615), *passim*.

that offices, dignities, and powers be sold and placed in commerce."[31] Thus presented, Roman history seemed to teach the "lesson" that offices should not be sold. Besides, Roman law contained clear prohibitions against the sale of judicial charges.[32]

But Roman history was not so simple as to allow of only one interpretation. It was useless to demand, as did one pamphleteer, a simple return to the ancient Roman practice.[33] The historical school of Roman law, which became prominent in sixteenth-century France, had brought about an acute awareness that the Roman experience was not monolithic, that law could not be understood apart from its political and social environment, and that there had been significant change and development in Roman institutions.[34] The classical past still had sufficient cultural prestige to make it worthwhile for writers on both sides of the controversy over offices to refer to it. But practically no one considered the Roman experience to be decisive, and some writers were emphatic in insisting that the only relevant historical arguments were those drawn from the history of France.[35]

Not surprisingly, the "lesson" of French history could also be read in different ways. Cited as model kings who disdained the venality of offices were Louis IX, Charles V, and Louis XII.[36] But it was easy to cite examples of rulers, including those of the sixteenth century, who had allowed or even extended the practice. Which, then, represented the norm? The effort of Charles V to reduce the number of offices was mentioned as an example of statesmanship; it was also offered as proof that attempts to reduce or abolish venality aroused dis-

[31] *Utile et salutaire advis*, pp. 25-26.
[32] Cited, e.g., in Charles Loyseau, *Cinq livres du droict des offices* (1610), Bk. III, ch. 1, para. 42.
[33] *Discours à messieurs les deputez*, p. 45.
[34] Julian H. Franklin, *Jean Bodin and the Sixteenth-Century Revolution in the Methodology of Law and History* (New York, 1963), chs. 1-3; Myron P. Gilmore, *Argument from Roman Law in Political Thought, 1200-1600* (Cambridge, Mass., 1941), ch. 2.
[35] On the often misunderstood application of Roman law in France, see F. Olivier-Martin, *Histoire du droit français* (Paris, 1948), pp. 427-432. The contrast between Roman institutions and French practice was emphasized repeatedly in the works of Loyseau.
[36] Presenting Louis IX as a model for kings was *Le miroir royal des Louis* (Paris, 1614). On the other kings, see *Libre discours et véritable jugement sur l'hérédité des offices insinuée en France, dans le doux venim du droict annuel* (Paris, 1615), pp. 6-10.

content and sedition.[37] Louis XII was known fondly as the "father" of his people. Was he so honored because he had allowed offices to be sold or because he had done so reluctantly, as a last resort, with the clear understanding that the practice was to be temporary?[38] Similarly, Henry IV had continued the practice and had attempted to regularize it by the edict of 1604. But did he do so gladly or, as some said, reluctantly and with the intention of abolishing the whole system in the near future?[39] Not only the politics of the individual rulers but also their motivation and intentions thus became grist for the mills of the controversialists.

Those who opposed the system of offices often demanded a return to the standards of an earlier age. They sought "the re-establishment of justice in its original and ancient brilliance," wishing it to be as thorough, prompt, and complete as it was "in the time of our ancestors."[40] The idea of returning to the purity of an earlier age had wide appeal and had entered into other controversies, both political and religious.[41] But it was typical of such primitivism to become entangled in defining the nature of the "return." In the controversy over venality, for example, there was no agreement whether the "return" should be to the practice of Henry IV (before 1604), Henry III, Henry II, Francis I, or Louis XII, all of whom were suggested.[42] The desire to go back to an earlier standard collided with the interests of those who had purchased or transferred offices under the more recent programs. Offices going back to the time of Francis I or of Henry II were claimed by prescriptive right. More surprisingly, a similar argument was used in defense of the *droit annuel* a mere ten years after it was established,

---

[37] *L'Officier et Catholique royal*, p. 12.

[38] Some had argued that Louis XII was loved by his people because of his willingness to sell offices. "O quelle imposture," responded the *Libre discours*, p. 34.

[39] *Ibid.*, p. 9.

[40] *Harangue de Turlupin le Soufreteux* (1615), in *Variétés historiques et littéraires*, ed. E. Fournier (Paris, 1856), VI, 80.

[41] The prominence of the idea of "return" in the religious thought of the sixteenth century is now obvious. For an example of the same approach to problems of political reform a century earlier, see Felix Gilbert, *Machiavelli and Guicciardini* (Princeton, 1965), p. 35.

[42] These goals changed with the passing of time. By 1614 there were still hopes of returning to the practice of Francis I, but 1576 was more often mentioned. Those who wished to abolish only the *droit annuel* were even less ambitious—and more realistic.

thus illustrating the impossibility of finding a moment in the past which everyone would accept as a realistic standard for the present.[43]

Doubtless it was pleasant to believe that history was on one's side, confirming the salutary (or the noxious) effects of the system of venality. To think that one's struggle for (or against) venality was on behalf of the *mos maiorum* was probably reassuring. To satisfy this psychological need pamphlets on both sides pointed to isolated examples, made sweeping claims about the "lessons" of history, and carefully ignored contrary instances or alternative interpretations. Yet, whatever their emotional impact, such appeals to the past could have no probative force as long as there was no accepted criterion for identifying the norm. Jurists, after all, had long recognized that there were "bad" as well as "good" customs.[44]

In some respects it was the very lack of a single tradition, the awareness of multiplicity and discontinuity in the country's experience, that facilitated an approach to the past more properly historical.[45] It is not in political controversy, of course, that one would expect to see historical explanation at its best, but there were some examples of such explanation even in the pamphlets. For instance, there were efforts to explain how the system of venality had evolved in France. Sometimes the explanation was pursued all the way back to Merovingian times, but more typically it was limited to a survey of the expansion of venality under the kings of the sixteenth century. One pamphlet, for example, described the sale of offices as allowed by Charles VIII, Louis XII, Francis I, and Henry IV, citing as sources of information the histories of France by Gilles and by Gaugin. There is no need to point out the "slanting" which such material would receive in a polemical pamphlet, for it is apparent that there was at least some desire to provide a historical explanation for the existing state of affairs.[46]

---

[43] An attempt to defend the *droit annuel* on the basis of prescriptive right is found in *Utile et salutaire advis*, p. 13. A brief discussion of long usage as "sufficient legal basis for any right not specifically regalian" is in W. F. Church, *Constitutional Thought in Sixteenth-Century France* (Cambridge, Mass., 1941), p. 101.

[44] On "good" and "bad" customs, see Church, p. 104.

[45] See J. G. A. Pocock, "The Origins of the Study of the Past: A Comparative Approach," *Comparative Studies in Society and History*, IV (1962), 237.

[46] *Libre discours*, pp. 6-10. An approach to the problem of offices from the more distant perspective of Merovingian times is in Jean Savaron, *Traicté de l'annuel et vénalité des offices* (Paris, 1615), pp. 3-7.

There were also efforts to draw parallels between the present and the past. Such an approach was liable to abuse, of course, but it did represent a concern for interpretation. The process by which dukes and counts of the early Middle Ages had transformed their holdings into hereditary patrimonies—the rise of feudalism described in textbooks —was compared to the expansion of the venality of offices in the sixteenth century. Purchased or inherited offices were compared to fiefs; their proliferation was said to have created a "new feudality."[47] Proponents of venality, on the other hand, argued that the supposed historical parallel was faulty, that modern officeholders were far more closely dependent on the king than Merovingian dukes and counts had been, and that it was precisely the abolition of venality which would weaken the king, strengthen the provincial magnates, and create factions comparable to those of the past.[48] Neither side in the controversy over offices wished to be identified with the centrifugal tendencies of feudalism in earlier centuries. But the very fact that they were thinking in such terms meant that at least a few of the writers were grappling with problems of historical explanation.

One of the best examples of a writer whose discussion of venality often included a historical dimension is Charles Loyseau, a lawyer at the Parlement of Paris who in 1610 published a monumental treatise on offices.[49] His writing was obviously on a higher level than the cloud of pamphlets stirred up by the Estates-General of 1614. As a jurisconsult he gave careful attention to distinctions which could have legal importance. He was anxious to define the powers of officeholders and to determine the extent to which offices were truly patrimonial.[50] Taking a practical view of the problem, he recognized that the system was undesirable in theory but could not be quickly abolished.[51] And permeating his lengthy discussion of the problem, even on rather

---

[47] *Libre discours*, pp. 10-11, 36-37.     [48] *L'Officier et Catholique royal*, p. 30.

[49] The standard study of Loyseau, inadequate in many ways, is Jean Lelong, *La vie et les oeuvres de Loyseau* (Paris, 1909). Useful treatments of certain aspects of Loyseau's thought can be found in W. F. Church, *Constitutional Thought*, pp. 315-332, and in Gilmore, *Argument from Roman Law*, pp. 113-126. Loyseau's works were produced almost entirely during the first decade of the seventeenth century. The great *Cinq livres du droict des offices* was first published in 1610. In order to facilitate reference to the various later editions of his collected works, I am using chapter and paragraph numbers.

[50] *Offices*, Bk. II, ch. 1. Cf. Gilmore, pp. 117-123.

[51] See, e.g., *Offices*, Bk. III, ch. 1, para. 200-201.

technical issues, was his concern for the relationship of the present to the past.

Loyseau's interest in the historical aspect of venality was not limited to the relatively recent developments of the sixteenth century. He presented a compelling survey of venality in the ancient world, replete with legal and moral maxims as well as examples of the untoward consequences of allowing public charges to become subject to purchase.[52] Loyseau was well versed in Roman law and constantly cited relevant passages from Justinian's collection. But over and over again he was constrained to contrast the practice in France to "bonne Jurisprudence." The Roman institutions could provide guidelines or suggest what was proper, but Loyseau was acutely aware that France had a history of its own.[53]

He pointed out the specific steps by which France had been led into allowing venality of offices and the succeeding steps by which the practice had been extended and regularized. He was cognizant of circumstances and alert to the difference between theory and practice, between intention and actual policy.[54] But there is little doubt of his general disapproval of what had happened during the past century and a half. After tracing the historical development, he said: "That is how the bad counsel of our recent kings found the means, not only to expose the people to the mercy of the *officiers*, but also . . . to alienate almost all the lawful financial reserves of the king, against the laws of the State."[55]

Besides tracing venality in France from the High Middle Ages to his own time, Loyseau frequently drew parallels between the rise of venal offices and the rise of feudalism in Merovingian and Carolingian times. He described the increasing independence of the ancient dukes and counts as the "usurpation" of sovereign rights. Probably no single word was used more frequently in his treatment of early feudalism

[52] *Ibid.*, para. 14-59.
[53] "Voilà pour les Romains, & quant à nous . . ." (*ibid.*, para. 60). Such a contrast appears repeatedly in Loyseau's work.
[54] See, e.g., his sympathetic analysis of Charles XII (*ibid.*, para. 86-90). Also noteworthy is his description of historical practice by such words as "abuse" or "usurpation."
[55] *Ibid.*, para. 100. By "contre les loix de l'Estat" Loyseau doubtless means that "fundamental law" which forbade alienation of the royal domain, which some had interpreted to include public power or sovereignty in general. See W. F. Church, *Constitutional Thought*, pp. 27, 49, 81, 145-147.

401

than "usurp," which meant essentially "illegal seizure."[56] Thus the fragmentation and decentralization of public power in the early Middle Ages rested not on law but on force. He was equally outspoken in describing the tendency of venal offices to slip out of the king's control. The offices were compared to fiefs. About all that some persons owe to the kings for their offices, he said, was faith and homage, "as with true fiefs." Only this "feudal" relationship, or "cest féodalité," prevented complete expropriation by the officeholders.[57] But, never one to oversimplify, Loyseau recognized one crucial difference in the modern "feudal" fragmentation. The modern *officiers*, including even *baillis* and dukes, did not have the territorial base that the ancient dukes and counts had possessed. It would be more difficult, therefore, for the modern *officiers* to bring about a "cantonization" of the country. Nevertheless, there were dangers in the fragmentation of the "public power," and the country was experiencing a kind of "infeudation."[58]

There is infinitely more sophistication in Loyseau's approach to history than in that of the pamphleteers. It was not that he pretended to be "objective" or to be disinterested in implications for the present. Rather, it was that he demonstrated an awareness of development, of changing circumstances, of differences between cultures and between periods, and of the "plurality of tradition."[59] At the same time, he recognized the possibilities of a comparative approach, which he brought off with remarkable finesse. He borrowed without shame from previous historians, of course, and his entire conceptualization of the problem owed almost everything to those predecessors, especially Jean Bodin, who had developed the concept of sovereignty. But, utilizing such tools as were near at hand, Loyseau was unsurpassed in his powers of analysis and his recognition of the complexity of history. The combination of practical interests with an appeal to the past was characteristic of Loyseau's work. The same combination, with less real historical consciousness and less concern for scholarship, characterized the controversy over offices as a whole.

[56] In the first four pages of Loyseau's small treatise *De l'abus de la justice seigneuriale* the term "usurp" (or an equivalent phrase) is used no less than nineteen times.

[57] *Offices*, Bk. I, ch. 1.      [58] *Ibid.*, Bk. II, chs. 1-2.

[59] I have borrowed this phrase from J.G.A. Pocock, "The Origins of the Study of the Past," p. 237.

# III

It would be absurd to maintain that the references to history were the most persuasive arguments in deciding the outcome of the debate. It seems unlikely that the king was deeply moved by the plea of one pamphleteer that he abolish the *droit annuel* in order to avoid the blame "that all historians are preparing for him."[60] Yet, even if one concedes that the financial needs of the government were paramount, the fact remains that a verbal battle raged for several years and that it included frequent glances at history. No one was comfortable with a purely rational argument, disregarding tradition and experience. Nor was it usually considered sufficient to appeal to the absolute power of the king. Both opponents and defenders of venality were clearly anxious to find some kind of historical sanction. An appeal to precedent, to tradition, or to an "ancient constitution" would help them escape from arguments based on self-interest or power or unprincipled pragmatism. But the idea of tradition, like that of an "ancient constitution," had grown dim in France. The variety of customary laws, the influence of Roman law, the innovations brought about by crisis, and even the diverse perspectives of different elements of the population combined to prevent a consensus on the meaning of the country's history. In short, the modes of continuity with the past were several and confused. But such a complex relationship to history can foster, as the controversy over offices demonstrates, a desire to explain apparent discrepancies, to trace historical change, and thus to reach out for a deeper understanding of the relationship of the present to the past.

[60] *Libre discours*, p. 48.

# REASON AND GRACE:
## CHRISTIAN EPISTEMOLOGY IN DANTE, LANGLAND, AND MILTON

ROLAND MUSHAT FRYE

### I. *The Place of Reason*

THE great mainstream of Christian thought has sought to employ reason to the full extent of its natural usefulness without overextending it and giving it authority beyond the bounds of its nature. Christianity has also maintained the supremacy of divine revelation which does not obliterate and destroy reason. The consensus has been that within the province of effective natural inquiry reason should control but that it should be suspected when it operates beyond its own domain, unless it is illumined by grace when it enters the field of divine revelation. Christianity has thus attempted to preserve a delicate and sometimes precarious balance between overextending reason and repudiating it. This has been the general rule, and, though there have been notable exceptions to it in theological theory and even more numerous failures to implement it intelligently in practice, the rule itself still provides the most useful basis for understanding the central attitudes toward reason which characterize classical Christianity, and especially those which formed the bases for Christian humanism.

The purpose of this essay is to outline the doctrinal and critical consensus on the relations between reason and grace, with the clear recognition that no consensus on a matter of this complexity, especially in a historical community as varied as the Christian, can have been unanimous. The clarification of this consensus will have value in itself, and it should also help us to understand and appraise the various modifications of the central position which we encounter as we study intellectual history.

Basically, the Christian view of reason has held it to be capable of absorbing supernatural truths, but not capable of arriving at such truths by itself. Man's natural reason can attain tremendous heights within the range of worldly knowledge and skill but cannot penetrate the sphere of the supernatural truths which the Christian finds rooted in the mind of God. To these truths, which the Christian regards as ultimate, the mind cannot lift itself. Here we have a theological counter-

404

part to the physical law according to which man cannot lift himself by his own bootstraps: natural reason by itself cannot with assurance reach beyond the realm of nature.

At the same time, reason can be lifted by an outside power, so that it can assimilate for its own needs an extension of its knowledge. This extension is the product of revelation, the free gift of God to man for his guidance and salvation. Without it man can have no sure knowledge of his human destiny, as conceived by his Creator. Once the revelation has been opened and once man has received the grace of God, which further prepares his understanding for the acceptance of revelation, he is ready to make a new use of his reason. What was natural reason now reemerges as reason under grace, under the free gift of God's love.

Some fifteen hundred years ago St. Augustine clearly expressed the position when he wrote that, unless one believes, one will not understand. Reason alone and unaided can deal with many terrestrial and temporal affairs, but it stops short at the ultimate questions of human life in terms of which all terrestrial and temporal affairs must be ordered. Faced with this impasse, Augustine enunciated the principle "I believe in order to understand."[1] In so doing, Augustine was developing the teaching of the Apostle Paul, who had declared that every thought should be brought into the service of Christ (II Cor. 10:5). The point again is clear, for the Son of God is not made captive by thought; rather, thought is made captive by Christ. Thought is not thereby suppressed, in the Christian's perspective, but is enfranchised for the fullest comprehension of life. Just as the Christian, by entering the service of Christ, is freed from that most restrictive of all bondages, the bondage to himself, so the mind is freed from the strictest limits of its own nature.

From these basic interpretations it is usually expected that further development will move in the general direction of systematic theology or of philosophy and logic, but that is not the direction in which we shall move. Our concern is primarily with the great Christian poets, who express a full vision of Christianity operating in the fullness of life. The poets with whom we shall deal—Dante, Langland, and Milton—wrote of the whole of human experience, placing the Christian squarely in the midst of all the challenges and tensions of human existence, where he must express his salvation in the face of problems

[1] Saint Augustine, *In Iohannis Evangelium Tractatus*, CXXIV, in *Corpus Christianorum*, Series Latina, XXXVI (Turnholti, 1954), 287.

both rational and irrational. The situation of man, for these poets, is fully "existential," in the sense that it is involved with every facet of existence and every trial and triumph of man. It is here, rather than in the cool element of abstraction, that the Christian's reason under grace must validate itself as being in fact the highest reach of the human mind, the most efficacious operation of human intelligence.[2]

Despite the many historical, theological, and personal contrasts which may readily be drawn between Dante, Langland, and Milton and despite the three centuries of change in religious thought, including the Reformation, which separated them, there is evident in their poetry an essential agreement on the relations between reason and revelation. Had they been systematic theologians, they might perhaps have developed more explicit and idiosyncratic variations upon our central theme, but the fact that they wrote as theologically astute Christian poets addressing general readers in poetically universal terms allowed them to be far more effective in expressing the central consensus of classical Christianity on the relations between reason and revelation.

## II. *Reason and Love*

Human intelligence must extend beyond the mere possession of proper information if it is, according to the Christian view, to carry man to his highest destiny. It cannot be stated too strongly that, apart from the love of God, merely correct information about God is not sufficient for the *salvation* of man. Belief alone is not enough to carry man to the fulfillment of life everlasting, even though the belief itself may be correct. "You believe that God is one," writes the author of the Epistle of James (Jas. 2:19). "You do well. Even the devils believe —and shudder." Belief alone, no matter how correct, may lead only to a shudder.

John Milton writes of heretics in the truth—men who hold rigidly and with the utmost formal correctness to true statements about God

---

[2] For a fuller analysis of explicitly Christian works of literature (Milton's *Paradise Lost* and Bunyan's *Pilgrim's Progress*), see my *God, Man, and Satan* (Princeton, 1960). A more general analysis of the relations between Christianity and literature may be found in my *Perspective on Man* (Philadelphia, 1961). The relations between Christianity and explicitly "secular" literature are explored in my *Shakespeare and Christian Doctrine* (Princeton, 1963). Literarily oriented comments on the Bible may be found in my edition of *The Bible* (Boston, 1965). Reference is made here to these longer works, for they contain qualifications and extensions of the partial analysis of literary and theological concerns presented here.

but who are nonetheless heretical. Among such heretics are the fallen angels, now demonic, whose natural reason exceeds that of men, who know God with factual accuracy, and who yet are debased before the reality of which they possess the most precise information. At one point, however, Milton presents even Satan as being in doubt—in doubt concerning the nature of the sonship of Jesus. This particular ignorance furnishes a motive for Satan's wilderness temptation of Christ in *Paradise Regained*,[3] and from the words of Satan himself we learn that he regards it as a prime necessity to determine the true nature of Christ. Thus, throughout the four parts of Milton's short epic, Satan persistently investigates the Messiah, repeatedly seeking an answer to his own eager curiosity. At the end of the poem he gets his information, knows fully that Jesus is the Son of the living God sent on a mission of redemption. His intellectual knowledge is complete, accurate, unassailable. It is the knowledge which many have sought as the key to life, but this knowledge as such is not enough to put Satan in command of life. Rather, it relegates him inescapably to the realm of death:

> But Satan smitten with amazement fell . . .
>
> . . . . . . . . . . . . . . . . . . . . .
> . . . as that Theban Monster that propos'd
> Her riddle, and him, who solv'd it not, devour'd;
> That once found out and solv'd, for grief and spite
> Cast herself headlong from th' Ismenian steep,
> So strook with dread and anguish fell the Fiend,
> And to his crew, that sat consulting, brought
> Joyless triumphals of his hop't success,
> Ruin, and desperation, and dismay,
> Who durst so proudly tempt the Son of God.
> So Satan fell. . . .
>
> (*PR* IV, 562-581.)

Milton's treatment of Satan's inquisition of Christ in the wilderness clearly embodies the perennial Christian teaching that, even if the Incarnation could be made rationally convincing beyond all doubt, the key to salvation would still be lacking.

[3] Citations from John Milton's poems in my text are to *Paradise Regained, The Minor Poems and Samson Agonistes*, ed. Merritt Y. Hughes (New York, 1937), and *Paradise Lost*, ed. Merritt Y. Hughes (New York, 1935). References to *Paradise Regained* are henceforth abbreviated as *PR*, and to *Paradise Lost* as *PL*.

Martin Luther, and the reformers generally, marked the difference between two types of faith, the one being a faith which is really a form of knowledge, a belief in correct doctrine. This is not saving faith, in the Reformation sense. Saving faith, the second and centrally important type, is a relationship with God. It is what Luther called a lively, reckless confidence in the grace of God.[4] Such faith is not merely intellectual—though it will involve the intellect—but is a relationship of trust and love. In formulations such as this, the reformers were merely giving sixteenth-century expression to very ancient Christian doctrine.

The major subject for the Christian's study, then, is neither theology, nor philosophy, nor sacred poetry, but charity. In his great allegorical poem, *Piers Plowman*,[5] William Langland asks the counsel of Nature as to what science it is best to study, and is told at once, "Learn to love" (XX, 205). Conscience joins with Nature to advise that "nothing shall fail you/ If you will leave logic and learn loving" (XX, 246-247). Even the personification of Study herself is quite clear on this point and says of Theology, the queen of science, that "I should hold it idleness if love were not in it" (X, 190).

Love, then, is superior to reason in the Christian understanding of life, and reason without love is a moribund thing. Man's primary obligation is to love God, not to rationalize about Him, and from this primary obligation comes the second great commandment of love toward one's neighbor. Love is dominant, and its first object is God. The synoptic gospels all carry the commandment of Christ that men should love the Lord their God with all heart, soul, mind, and strength (Mark 12:30, Matt. 22:37, Luke 10:27). Now the mind is one of the principal channels for expressing the love of God, and yet, to the Christian, reason is ancillary to love as an avenue to divine truth. By mind alone man cannot comprehend God—how can the finite comprehend the infinite? But love offers access to God and to the ultimate Truth of the universe.

The point may be illustrated by the experience of Milton's angels in *Paradise Lost*, for whom reason is also related to love and yet subordinate to it. Thus Satan's hosts are the angels who repudiate reason—in Milton's words, they "reason for their law refuse,/ Right reason for

[4] Martin Luther, "Scholien zum 118. Psalm," *Werke*, XXXI (Wiemar, 1913), 176f.

[5] Citations from Langland in my text are to *The Vision of Piers Plowman*, tr. Henry W. Wells (London, 1938).

their law, and for their king/ Messiah" (*PL* VI, 41-43). But, as Archbishop William Temple has written in our time, the Christian conception of reason is indissolubly linked to love. "The Principle of Reason which governs the world," Temple writes in summarizing this position, "is the eternal victory of Love over selfishness at the cost of sacrifice."[6] So Raphael says of the faithful angels, that "Freely we serve,/ Because we freely love" (*PL* V, 538-539). For reason to attain its fullest potential, merely natural reason must be purged and ennobled by love.

### III. *The Extent of Reason*

The limits of natural reason are similar to the limits of other natural powers. The eye sees only so far, no further, and the recognition of the extent of vision is no more a repudiation of sight than the recognition of the extent of thought is a repudiation of mind. This is Dante's point when, in the *Paradise*,[7] he compares the potential of the human intellect to the power of the human eye to discern the bottom of the sea:

> Wherefore the sight that your world liveth by
> Penetrates not the eternal justice more
> Than into the ocean penetrates the eye;
> For though it sees the bottom from the shore,
> On the open sea it cannot: none the less
> It is there; but the depth conceals the floor.
> *(Par.* XIX, 58-63.)

The image is an apt one, treating the vision as effective at closer range, less so as the distance increases, while the object observed does not fail to exist simply because it fails to appear.

But, although reason cannot take man to his fullest realization of God, it can put him on the way. Dante embodies this understanding in the central structure of his *Divine Comedy.* Virgil, the pre-Christian sage, is Dante's first guide, representing the highest extent of man's natural mind. As such, he is delegated by heavenly spirits to rescue Dante in his lostness. Natural reason is thus appointed to be the first

---

[6] William Temple, "The Divinity of Christ," *Foundations: A Statement of Christian Belief in Terms of Modern Thought* (London, 1913), pp. 221-222.

[7] Citations from Dante in my text are to *The Divine Comedy*, tr. Laurence Binyon, in *The Portable Dante*, ed. Paolo Milano (New York, 1947). References to *Inferno* are henceforth abbreviated as *Inf.*, to *Purgatory* as *Purg.*, and to *Paradise* as *Par.*

vehicle of heavenly grace for the salvation of Dante, and, although it cannot convey him into the presence of God, it is able to lead him to the point where the very emissary of heaven will take him in charge. Virgil, as symbol of the limited revelation which can come from natural reason, shows Dante both hell and purgatory, representing, respectively, the everlasting dwelling place of man's sin and the continuing process of man's purgation. Hell, within this conception, confronts Dante with the realization of sin in its true proportions as separation from man's greatest good, the communion with God. Purgatory, further, clearly indicates man's need to be cleansed of defilement before he can enter upon that communion. These two revelations can be imparted through Virgil, who acts under the orders of heaven. Dante is thus given a knowledge of himself (allegorically represented by one of the steps to purgatory) and a knowledge of his human need, as prerequisite to the redemption of the *Paradise*.

Dante can be led into heaven only by Beatrice, who is, among other things, the bearer of divine revelation and grace. When Dante has emerged from purgatory, Virgil, his guide by human reason, disappears and is replaced by Beatrice, who first conducts Dante through the earthly paradise which is possible for the souls of men who are regenerate and then introduces him to heaven itself. Beatrice guides her lover well into the realm of the blessed, but even she cannot convey him into the very presence of God, where he can, as it were, contemplate deity face to face. Beatrice is therefore succeeded by the mystic St. Bernard, who, as a contemplative soul on earth, had enjoyed a direct vision of God even before his entrance into heaven. It is appropriate now that he, as a figure of direct communion with God, should replace Beatrice, the figure of revelation, just as she had earlier replaced her humanist messenger, Virgil, a development which may be traced to the declaration of the apostle Paul (I Cor. 13:12) that "now we see through a glass darkly, but then face to face. Now I know in part; but then shall I know even as also I am known." This statement implies the rationality of admitting the limits of reason, and immediately following upon it is Paul's enthronement of love: "So faith, hope, love abide; but the greatest of these is love." So, too, Dante goes on to the direct vision of "the Love that moves the sun and the other stars," the Love which binds together "in one volume the scattered leaves of all the universe" (*Par.* XXXIII, 145, 85-87).[8]

[8] The latter phrase is taken from *The Paradise of Dante Alighieri* in the J. M.

Here we must pause for a moment to consider the last image cited from Dante. It is an image of synthesis—the binding together "in one volume the scattered leaves of all the universe." The result of Dante's pilgrimage, then, is a vision which joins together all the fragments of life into one great meaningful volume, which renders existence totally intelligible, in the circle of the divine trinity in unity, represented by a "sublime light, which in itself is true." All that is "within its pale/ Is perfect, which, without, hath some defect" (*Par.* XXXIII, 54, 104-105). Here, then, is the ultimate key to life, the final synthesis which men seek—but which they cannot find apart from the loving grace of God. The scattered leaves of all the universe are bound together, not by reason, but by love. Again we see the Christian economy of reason and love. Man's search may begin under the guidance of reason, but, if it is to reach its destination of ultimate concern, it must submit to the primacy of love and the grace of God.

The primary issues with which man is faced are issues of love and hate, not of reason and unreason, and his understanding of life must be ordered in these terms if it is to be a rational understanding. Milton treats reason as choice which accords with the scale of values established by God:

> . . . what obeys
> Reason is free, and Reason he [God] made right,
> But bid her well beware, and still erect,
> Lest by some fair appearing good surpris'd
> She dictate false. . . .
>
> (*PL* IX, 351-355.)

One such deceptively "appearing good" is a false view of the potential of reason itself, which subverts rationality by deluding it as to its own powers, just as Satan subverted Eve by deluding her as to her own potential. Man's attempt to deny the scale of values established by God comes first, of course, through the primary sin, the attempt by the creature to usurp upon the Godhead and to become "as god." Of Satan, the prince of rebellious angels, Milton writes in *Paradise Lost* that "he trusted to have equall'd the most High" (I, 40), while Moloch, another chieftain among the fallen angels, attempted

---

Dent edition (London, 1946), where in this instance the translation seems both more pleasing and more faithful.

> ... with th' Eternal to be deem'd
> Equal in strength, and rather than be less
> Car'd not to be at all.
>
> (II, 46-48.)

In tempting Eve, Satan leads her to repeat his own sin, promising her that, if she will yield to his temptation, she may become "a goddess among gods, ador'd and serv'd," and God the Father refers to man's basic sin as "affecting Godhead, and so losing all" (*PL* IX, 547, and III, 206). The Fall, then, is the violation of that reason which we have already defined as judgment in accord with the scale of values incorporated by the Creator into creation. Thus, of the Fall of man, Milton writes that "Understanding rul'd not, and the Will/ Heard not her lore." Similarly, the rebellious angels were, as we have seen, those who "reason for their Law refuse,/ Right reason for their Law, and for their King/ Messiah" (*PL* IX, 1127-28, and VI, 41-43). Reason subverts itself when it violates its own limitations as established in the order of creation.

### I V. *The Perversion of Speculation*

There are at least two important ways in which thought can destroy its own usefulness: one way is through futile speculation and the other is through the endless pursuit of knowledge, both taken as paths to salvation. Let us first examine the perversion of speculation, which is essentially the attempt to convert an ivory tower into the kingdom of heaven. Dante places adherents of futile speculation neither in heaven nor in hell but in an anteroom of hell, apart from the main structure. So concerned with the joys of the dilettante mind were these men that they refused to side either with good or with evil, with the powers of light or with the powers of darkness, so that they were found unworthy not only of the company of the blessed but even of the company of the damned. Having maintained a studied "academic" neutrality and having made the great refusal implicit in the perpetual suspension of value judgments, they find themselves despised by God and Satan alike:

> Heaven chased them forth, lest their allegiance cloud
> Its beauty, and the deep Hell refuses them,
> For, beside such, the sinner would be proud.
>
> (*Inf.* III, 40-42.)

Because they refused both heaven and hell in life, these unbiased spirits find themselves everlastingly repudiated by both realms after death, as they endlessly and aimlessly speed in dizzy circles like sand blown by a whirlwind. Dante appropriately describes them as "scum, who never lived" (*Inf.* III, 64).

Milton is not surpassed by Dante in his ridicule of those whose joy it is to keep their minds permanently unsettled regarding basic issues, and with magnificent irony he presents in hell a company of demons who depart to "a Hill retir'd" to carry on endless reasonings about final misery and damnation even while they are enduring it (*PL* II, 555-561).

Again, however, just as both Milton and Dante repudiate speculation which never commits itself on crucial issues, so too they join in repudiating that speculation which concludes too rashly on the minutiae. Like the Scottish theologian who advised his students against becoming concerned over the furniture of heaven and the temperature of hell, Milton has Adam warned that

> Heaven is for thee too high
> To know what passes there; be lowly wise:
> Think only what concerns thee and thy being.
> (PL, VIII, 172-174.)

Dante, too, warns that men should, in view of their own earthly capacities, "move slow . . . both to yea and nay" in difficult disputes,

> Since oft it haps that rashness of surmise
>> Leadeth the judgment on false roads to start;
>> Then fond desire the understanding ties.
> On voyage worse than vain doth he depart
>> (Since he returns not such as he sets out),
>> Who fishes for the truth and lacks the art.
> (Par. XIII, 114, 118-123.)

It is Thomas Aquinas who speaks this warning against rash judgment, particularly in accusing others of heresy, and he concludes with an image which graphically portrays the danger of presumptuous condemnation of other men:

> Let not the people be too self-assured
>> In judging early, as who should count the rows
>> Of green blades in the field ere they matured.

For I have seen how first the wild-brier shows
Her sprays, all winter through, thorny and stark,
And then upon the topmost bears the rose.

*(Par.* XIII, 130-135.)

Man's primary fear of erring opinion must, then, be for himself, and he must maintain a charitable and reserved judgment of others, not presuming to usurp the prerogatives of God's judgment.

As a striking embodiment of this rebuke of intolerant condemnation, Dante places among the great doctors of the church in the fourth circle of paradise a man whose writings had actually been condemned as heretical—Sigier of Brabant. As a professor in the University of Paris, he was a vigorous opponent of St. Thomas Aquinas's teachings. But in paradise it is Thomas himself who points Sigier out to Dante as an "illumined spirit" who was the author of "grave thought."

Tis Sigier's eternal light, who taught
In the Straw Street, and there for all to hear
Syllogized truths that hatred on him brought.

*(Par.* X, 136-138.)

In the partial light of earth the "truths" taught by Thomas and Sigier had seemed irreconcilable, but not so in heaven, where all truth is orthodox. Even Gregory the Great had been guilty of earthly error, though not of heresy, and ". . . at himself he smiled when all things were/ In heaven to his enlightened eyes unbarred" *(Par.* XXVIII, 134-135).

Speculation is thus attacked both for the dilettantism which refuses to conclude upon fundamental issues and for the intolerant rashness which too readily dogmatizes about the inconsequential and too readily condemns others who disagree. In either of these ways speculation may be dangerous, and in both the danger is again a product of the absence of love—the lack of concern for God and for man.

## V. *The Perversion of Knowledge*

A too great concern for knowledge, for information, may also exclude love and delude man as to his highest good. Knowledge can be sought as an escape from thought, and the pursuit of knowledge can so fascinate man that the mind never moves on to evaluation. Keeping busy, as Pascal observed, is a sure way to evade the really significant problems of human existence, and one of the best ways to keep busy is to be forever engaged in the amassing of knowledge. This particular escape mechanism is especially effective, for it involves some use of mind so that man intent upon the amassing of information may even be able to indulge the happy delusion that he is a thinker.

According to the Christian view that life is not merely mortal but also has an everlasting possibility, the mind must be attuned to the widest horizons of existence, here and hereafter. The Christian's life is not a shattered fragment of time but in God's grace is linked through the resurrection with eternity. Within such a context natural knowledge is not repudiated, but natural knowledge which regards itself as an end in itself is deemed a blind guide, able only to divert attention from the ultimate concerns of human existence. The fault is not in natural knowledge itself but rather in those who treat such knowledge as the chief end of man. Within the created order man's place is such that he cannot exist by bread alone, whether the bread be food for the body or for the mind. In *Piers Plowman*, Langland cogently points up the difficulty:

> Man have marked [nature's] ways and mused upon them,
> Have seen strange sights and so taught their children,
> And held their wisdom as an high science.
> But alas, through this science no soul was delivered,
> Nor have their books brought them to bliss and happiness—
> Natural knowledge is but numberless observation.
>
> (XII, 134-139.)

From any point of view it would surely be folly to jettison the results of such numberless observation. It would be as great folly to stop short at the collections themselves. "Scholarship is material; it is not life," wrote Professor Woodrow Wilson of Princeton. "It becomes immortal only when it is worked upon by conviction, by schooled and chastened imagination, by thought that runs alive out of the inner fountains of individual insight and purpose. Colorless, or without suffusion of light from some source of light, it is dead."[9]

Wilson's emphasis upon imagination—"schooled and chastened imagination"—is significant, for here the Christian poets, too, have seen a preservative for knowledge. In Langland's allegory of the life of man, the central character, Will, has been separated from Reason because he had gone beyond his rational limits, had "blamed and praised" beyond his powers of judgment. He is rescued by Imagina-

[9] Woodrow Wilson, *Mere Literature and Other Essays* (Boston, 1896), p. 20.

tion, who comes to correct and instruct him. That the doctrine taught by Imagination is not obscurantist and is not opposed to learning is clear from this advice to Will: "You will never blame logic nor law nor their habits/ Nor ever oppose learning, if you believe me truly" (XII, 99-100). So Imagination does not seek to destroy natural knowledge but rather to illuminate it. Imagination is simply a more advanced means for understanding the ultimate goals of life and for instructing man in his nature and destiny. Imagination further develops its case:

> A man with natural knowledge and no more may never
> Come into Christendom and gain salvation;
> He is a blind man in a battle who bears a weapon
> But has no hope that his axe will hit his enemy.
>
> (XII, 107-110.)

Natural knowledge is in itself good and useful, but it is limited. A good weapon in its own right, it cannot achieve victory in the holy war for salvation when wielded by a blind man who can have "no hope that his axe will hit his enemy." The image is a powerful one and conveys better than logic alone could the limits of mere learning. Knowledge is power, and, although power is surely not immoral, it is amoral until seasoned by something apart from itself. It needs to be worked upon by another substance, and transmuted, if it is to contribute to the highest potentials of human life.

But knowledge has a fascination all her own, a charm, a magnetic attractiveness, even a hypnotic quality. So pleasant is the acquisition of knowledge to some men that it can completely envelop them in its own delights. Knowledge is so like wisdom in its appearance that it can indeed be confused with wisdom. The pedantic hunger for knowledge alone and the humane hunger for wisdom are related as gluttony is related to a healthful appetite—at times confusingly similar, but in essence quite different. The comparison is implicit in John Milton's development of the usurpation of knowledge over wisdom in *Paradise Lost*:

> ... Knowledge is as food, and needs no less
> Her Temperance over Appetite, to know
> In measure what the mind may well contain,
> Oppresses else with Surfeit, and soon turns
> Wisdom to Folly, as Nourishment to Wind.
>
> (VII, 126-130.)

So knowledge, which should be the servant of wisdom, may become its enemy and turn wisdom to folly.

## V I. *Man's Wisdom*

Within the Christian perspective, then, what is human wisdom? It is a trained and judicious capacity for the fullest ordering of life—where by "life" is meant a full existence broadening out of the transitory into the everlasting. Upon this capacity of wisdom natural knowledge—numberless observation—infringes when man persuades himself that the quality of his life is determined by the abundance of the things which he possesses intellectually. The greed for information may be as disastrous for the individual as greed for material possessions. It is at its worst a more subtle form of the same temptation.

This understanding comes out clearly in *Paradise Regained* when Milton's Satan is tempting Christ in the wilderness. Satan's first temptations of Christ are for the satisfaction of appetite, for worldly renown and temporal power; upon failing to win over Christ with these lures, Satan turns to the temptation of knowledge, for Milton interprets the vision of the kingdoms of the world as including enticement to a life of learning. Satan thus offers Christ the alluring prospect of deep study, the amassing of a universal knowledge. And the subtlety of this appeal is that such knowledge is presented as being wisdom itself:

> ... Be famous then
> By wisdom; as thy Empire must extend,
> So let extend thy mind o'er all the world.
> In knowledge, all things in it comprehend.
> *(PR* IV, 221-224.)

So, again, knowledge would usurp upon wisdom, and the final subtlety of the demonic strategy rests here upon the false identification of wide-ranging knowledge with wisdom. This is the danger against which Milton warned in *Paradise Lost*, as we have seen. Christ's reply to Satan underscores the fact that he who reads incessantly, without a "spirit and judgment equal or superior" to his learning, will remain

> Deep verst in books and shallow in himself,
> Crude or intoxicate, collecting toys,
> And trifles for choice matters, worth a sponge;
> As children gathering pebbles on the shore.
> *(PR* IV, 327-330.)

The inordinate pursuit of knowledge, then, may furnish blinders to wisdom, and the gluttony for information may inhibit the fullest digestion of life. When the psalmist writes that the fear of the Lord is the beginning of wisdom (Ps. 111:10), he is speaking of a wisdom which transcends common sense, prudence, knowledge, and speculation. He is concerned with that form of thought which aligns immediate decision in a living harmony with the will of God: it is the application of grace to temporal choice.

Thinkers of every kind have realized that one essential mark of wisdom is the recognition of its own limitations, and in the Christian conception this recognition is deepened by viewing man's situation in terms of the divine will. Thus, the beginning of wisdom is the fear of the Lord, but fear here is not terror, is not fright. Most of all, it is not anxiety. It is rather an awareness of the purity and wisdom of God which fills man with a recognition of his own finiteness and with adoration of his Creator. Every other anxiety is dissolved in the presence of this single "fear," which as a contact with ultimate reality tends to destroy petty vanity, self-assertion, and self-concern. At this point begins wisdom: the reverence for God brings the divine dimension into the human, replacing man's smaller conceptions with a larger order.

## V I I. *God's Accommodation*

The divine cannot be understood by the human, however, in its full eternal verity. Man, the creature, can only understand the Creator in terms of dimensions established by the Creator, so that the truth of God is translated into terms which man can assimilate. God does not yet appear to man face to face but as in a glass darkly, and revelation is accommodated to man's perception. The result in Scripture is language which is symbolic and parabolic rather than abstract and propositional. The quality of true humanity is realized through the encounter with God and is presented through concretion and embodied in narratives which involve the total life of man. Whereas mere learning may lead only to the integration of information and mere intellect only to the integration of thought, true wisdom leads to that integration of life which is man's ultimate concern. Divine accommodation to man in revelation, therefore, concerns itself with the large, the inclusive matters. Man does not primarily need information about God, although this is a part of what he needs; his greater need is rather for harmony with God. Therefore, God does not give a definition of Himself but gives instead the Incarnation. So in *Piers Plowman* the passion of Christ is dramatically presented as the central experience of the life of every Christian, which must be seized upon and assimilated into each individual existence. In this way man's existence becomes truly centered, and all his lesser concerns assume their proper places and proportions.

Just as the supreme accommodation of God's wisdom to man's limitation comes in the Incarnation, so lesser accommodations come in other regards. The great Christian poets consciously endeavor to maintain in their teaching of others the methods of the revelation which has taught them. In *Paradise* Dante points to the necessity for accommodation in his memorable treatment of God's "infinite excess":

> Each lesser nature, than, if thou perpend,
> Is a too scant receptacle for that Good
> Which is its own measure, and hath no end.
> *(Par.* XIX, 45, 49-51.)

Words are convenient vehicles for communication, but words cannot circumscribe the Almighty; for the finite cannot set bounds to the infinite, and definition here is impossible. The most that is possible is suggestion, and suggestion comes by way of symbol, parable, and example:

> The passing beyond bounds of human sense
> Words cannot tell; let then the example sate
> Him for whom grace reserves the experience.
> *(Par.* I, 70-72.)

In the concluding canto of his epic Dante tells of the beatific vision of God, in which his sight

> Deeper and deeper entered through the beam
> Of sublime light, which in itself is true,

and yet his speech is as inadequate as an infant's to communicate what he saw and felt:

> Thenceforth my vision was too great for theme
> Of our speech, that such glory overbears,
> And memory faints at such assault extreme.
> *(Par.* XXXIII, 52-57.)

So, too, the apostle Paul, when he was "caught up into paradise," had

419

"heard things that cannot be told, which man may not utter," (II Cor. 12:3-4) and had recognized that man's weakness, though redeemed by God, still cannot put into words the perfection of God.

The revelation of God's truth must be accommodated to man's capacity, and Beatrice, as the figure of revelation in the *Divine Comedy,* teaches Dante through accommodation, expressing reality, not as it is, but as he can best understand it. The concept of teaching by accommodation is important in the history of Christian thought, and it was given a significant place both in the Church of the Middle Ages and in the Church of the Reformation. We can scarcely find a better statement of the doctrine than Beatrice's counsel to Dante:

> Speech to your wit must needs be tempered so,
> Since but from things of sense it apprehends
> What it makes apt for the intellect to know.
> Scripture to your capacity condescends
> For this cause, and a foot and hand will feign
> For God, yet something other it intends.
>
> *(Par.* IV, 40-45.)

Revelation must, therefore, be transmitted in terms of man's life and, if it is to communicate, must be in good measure anthropomorphic.

The Christian thinker does not really regard God as having hands and feet but recognizes that such descriptions convey best to our limited capacities that understanding of an active divine personality which we are most concerned to have. Our surest road to understanding is thus to think in terms of those accommodations of the Creator to the creature which the Creator has regarded as most representative. The point was important for Aquinas, was repeatedly emphasized by Calvin, and was as central for Milton as for Dante. In a prose work Milton has developed it in a passage which reads like a pastiche of Calvin's expressions:

> Our safest way is to form in our minds such a conception of God, as shall correspond with his own delineation and representation of himself in the sacred writings. For granting that both in the literal and figurative descriptions of God, he is exhibited not as he really is, but in such a manner as may be within the scope of our comprehensions, yet we ought to entertain such a conception of him, as he, in condescending to accommodate himself to our capacities, has

420

shewn that he desires we should conceive. For it is on this very account that he has lowered himself to our level, lest in our flights above the reach of human understanding, and beyond the written words of Scripture, we should be tempted to indulge in vague cogitations and subtleties.[10]

God is thus conceived as presenting himself "within the scope of our comprehension," for "flights above the reach of human understanding" are futile. So in *Paradise Lost* Milton follows the method of concretion rather than the method of abstraction, since concretion is a more generally adequate vehicle for conveying superhuman truth to the human understanding:

> ... what surmounts the reach
> Of human sense, I shall delineate so,
> By lik'ning spiritual to corporal forms,
> As may express them best, though what if Earth
> Be but the shadow of Heav'n, and things therein
> Each to other like, more than on earth is thought?
>
> (*PL* V, 571-576.)

Accommodation is regarded by the Christian thinker as one of the primary methods given by God for bringing man's powers of understanding into the widest and most efficacious use. The method is not to override, to cancel out, or to destroy reason but rather to illuminate and complete it.

## VIII. *Right Reason*

Reason under grace, then, is a reason fulfilled and extended. It is what Milton and the Christian humanists called right reason—reason which has been lifted up to stand erect and to go no longer on all fours. It is a reason which repudiates dilettantism and bigotry and which realizes that the greed for knowledge apart from wisdom is a bypassing of life. Right reason, along with wisdom, recognizes its limitations and knows that the mere acceptance of correct doctrine is not enough to bring man into accord with the will of God. It perceives that the opposition of heaven and hell is in part the opposition of reason against unreason but that, even more profoundly, it is the conflict of love and

---

[10] John Milton, *The Christian Doctrine*, tr. Charles R. Sumner, in *The Works of John Milton*, ed. Frank Allen Patterson, XIV (New York, 1933), 31-33.

hate. The divine victory will not come as the winning of an argument but, as Milton puts it, when "Heav'nly love shall outdo Hellish hate" (*PL* III, 298). As thus understood by the great epic poets of the Christian tradition, reason under grace appraises and guides the life of man with a sense of charity and harmonious proportion.

# JOHN LOCKE AND THE NEW LOGIC*

WILBUR SAMUEL HOWELL

THE lasting significance of John Locke's greatest work, *An Essay concerning Human Understanding*, lies in its having outlined more influentially than any previous work the modern method by which knowledge is to be sought, validated, and understood. It did not set forth a system of beliefs that people should accept in regard to the substance of the sciences and the scholarly disciplines; rather, it defined the program to be followed in order that inquiries in those fields would yield dependable results. What should a man do when he sets out to obtain valid knowledge about himself and his world? This was the question which Locke's *Essay* raised, and his reply turned out to be the right answer at the right time.

The tradition which Locke demolished, as interpreted by John Sergeant, for example, had said that man obtains valid knowledge about himself and his world by examining propositions previously established in connection with all of the subjects of human concern and by treating those propositions as alone capable of yielding complete certainty in all sciences.[1] This tradition meant on the simplest level that, if a man wanted knowledge about the realities of his environment, he examined the opinions and beliefs which he had been taught to regard as the proper interpretation of those realities and by examining them he derived fresh truths to guide his beliefs and actions. Locke believed

---

* The following essay is an abridged version of a part of my forthcoming work on eighteenth-century British logic and rhetoric. For a preliminary exploration of the essential differences between the old logic and the new in Great Britain during the 1700's, see my essay, "The Plough and the Flail: The Ordeal of Eighteenth-Century Logic," *Huntington Library Quarterly*, vol. 28 (1964-65), pp. 63-78. The seventeenth-century antecedents of the new logic are discussed in my book, *Logic and Rhetoric in England, 1500-1700* (Princeton, 1956).

[1] During the decade in which Locke's *Essay* appeared, John Sergeant, identifying himself as "J. S.," published at London two attacks upon the new methods for arriving at truth in the sciences. The earlier of these, entitled *The Method to Science* (London, 1696), assailed the investigative procedures recommended by Bacon and Descartes and reaffirmed the belief that the deductive investigation of self-evident axioms was the only way to scientific certainty. The later one, called *Solid Philosophy Asserted, Against the Fancies of the Ideists* (London, 1697), broadened the attack to include Locke's *Essay*, which, according to Sergeant's preface, had already become very influential among dons and students at Oxford and Cambridge to the detriment of true learning.

423

profoundly that the method of the past confined men not only to past truths transmitted in a spirit of indifference but also to past errors that could not be put to death. He saw that past truths could be appreciated as living present truths only if the present undertook to examine them afresh in the light of the realities behind them and to recognize again how accurately they interpreted those realities. He also saw that errors could be detected as errors and avoided as dangers only if the present undertook to eliminate them after taking another look at the facts behind them and after seeing that the facts did not support them.

The chief difference between the twentieth century and the seventeenth century in regard to the benefits to be derived from reading Locke's *Essay* is that we today are taught the lesson of Locke in every one of the sciences and the arts to have been influenced by him, and thus we know him even when we have not read him at first hand, whereas the seventeenth century was taught only to respect the tradition that Locke was to demolish, and had little inclination to doubt that tradition, although Bacon and Descartes had flung the heaviest of challenges against it, in what turned out to be the prelude to Locke's success in transforming it at last into a minority voice in modern culture. Thus, the seventeenth century was shocked by Locke's *Essay* into realizing that it had been blindly groping along the trails of the past and listening only to the past, at a moment when the new science was following Bacon in making many of the beliefs of that past obsolete. If Locke's *Essay* is seen today largely through eyes which have been already taught its essential lesson, it may appear to the unwary to have lost its uniqueness as a shaper of the modern mind. He who turns to it today, however, will be benefited as by a lesson which teaches new things in being reviewed again.

If a work can be called classic when it is accepted into the universities as part of the undergraduate program, Locke's *Essay* became a classic almost at once. It was first published at London in 1690, and it was incorporated into the curriculum of Trinity College, Dublin, before 22 December 1692. Earlier in that year the new provost, Dr. St. George Ashe, ordered the undergraduates of Trinity to make the *Essay* one of their required books, and he stipulated that they would be strictly examined during their progress through it. The authority for this statement is William Molyneux, a scientist and philosopher who resided in Dublin and carried on a scholarly correspondence with Locke. In a letter dated from Dublin 22 December 1692, Molyneux said that he was the first to have recommended and lent the *Essay* to Dr. Ashe and that Dr. Ashe was so wonderfully pleased and satisfied with it that he took steps to have his students make it part of their formal program.[2] Molyneux said one other highly significant thing in that letter: Locke's next work, he observed, "should be of a model wholly new, and that is by way of logick; something accommodated to the usual forms, together with the consideration of extension, solidity, mobility, thinking, existence, duration, number, &c. and of the mind of man, and its powers, as may make up a complete body of what the schools call logicks and metaphysicks."[3] A large discourse upon these matters, added Molyneux, would be attractive in all universities, "wherein youths do not satisfie themselves to have the breeding or business of the place, unless they are ingaged in something that bears the name and form of logick." This recommendation did not mean, however, that Molyneux had no regard for the *Essay* itself as an important contribution to logical theory. In a letter dated eight months later than the one just quoted, he chided Locke gently for having failed in *Some Thoughts concerning Education* to name specific authors whom he would advise gentlemen to read in the various parts of learning. "Had you done this," said Molyneux, "I know no *logick* that deserves to be named, but the *Essay of Humane Understanding*. So that I fear you would rather have left that head open, than recommended your own work."[4]

Not long after Dr. Ashe's pioneering step at Dublin, Oxford began to show interest in Locke's *Essay* as a treatise on logic. In a letter to his Dublin admirer on 26 April 1695, Locke wrote that Molyneux, in view of his expressed wish to have Locke compose a work on logical theory, might be pleased to hear of an abridgment of the *Essay* then being prepared by an Oxford don, who had already written two letters to Locke in connection with his undertaking and who seemed in Locke's judgment to be an ingenious man and to write sensibly about what he was doing.[5] The abridgment, said Locke, was being planned to take the place "of an ordinary system of logick" in the education of young scholars at Oxford. "From the acquaintance I had of the temper of that place," Locke tartly commented, as he no doubt thought

---

[2] *Some Familiar Letters between Mr. Locke, and Several of his Friends* (London, 1708), p. 17. Dr. Ashe gave the *Essay* an abridgment for the use of students, but no copy of it appears to have survived. See H. O. Christophersen, *A Bibliographical Introduction to the Study of John Locke* (Oslo, 1930), p. 28.

[3] *Some Familiar Letters*, p. 16.

[4] *Ibid.*, p. 54. This letter is dated 12 Aug. 1693.     [5] *Ibid.*, pp. 109-110.

of the reception of his *Essay* in an Oxford dominated by Aristotelians, "I did not expect to have it get much footing there." Molyneux, who had become a veteran admirer of the *Essay* and had confessed on 23 December 1693 to having already given it a third reading,[6] rejoiced in the prospect of an abridgment of it "from a judicious hand in *Oxford*" and added, " 'tis what I always thought might be of good use in the universities, where we yet want another sort of language, than what has hitherto prevail'd there, to the great hindrance of science."[7] On 2 July 1695 Locke wrote again to Molyneux:

> The abridgment of my *Essay* is quite finish'd. It is done by a very ingenious man of *Oxford*, a master of arts, very considerable for his learning and virtue, who has a great many pupils. It is done with the same design you had in view, when you mention'd it. He has generally (as far as I could remember) made use of my words; he very civilly sent it me when it was done, and, upon looking it over, I guess you will approve of it, and think it well done.[8]

"I am mightily pleased that your *Essay* is abridg'd," replied Molyneux on 24 August of that year, "tho', for my own reading, I would not part with a syllable of it." " 'Tis to me," he went on, "no small argument of the curious genius of the english nation, that a work, so abstract as yours, should now suffer three impressions in so short a time."[9]

In fact, however, the abridgment of the *Essay* did not finally appear in print until the following spring. Its compiler was John Wynne of Jesus College, who dedicated the work "To the much Esteemed *Mr. John Locke*" and who remarked in the dedicatory epistle that, although his epitome could not take the place of the complete *Essay*, it would nevertheless serve "to make the way to Knowledge somewhat more plain and easie; and afford such Helps for the improvement of Reason, as are perhaps in vain sought after in those Books, which profess to Teach the *Art of Reasoning*."[10] These words aim the abridgment squarely at the target which Molyneux had wanted it to hit.

[6] *Ibid.*, p. 66.    [7] *Ibid.*, p. 112.    [8] *Ibid.*, p. 116.
[9] *Ibid.*, p. 123. (The word "english" is not capitalized in the printed text.)
[10] [John Wynne], *An Abridgment of Mr. Locke's Essay concerning Humane Understanding* (London, Printed for *A.* and *J. Churchill* at the *Black Swan* in *Pater-noster-Row*, and *Edw. Castle* next *Scotland-Yard-Gate*, near *Whiiehall* [sic], 1696), sig. A3ᵛ. (I reverse the style of the original quotations in respect to the use of roman and italic type.)

But, when Molyneux received a copy of the abridgment from its London publisher at the request of Locke himself,[11] he was no longer mightily pleased, nor did he think it well done. He wrote to Locke on 6 June 1696:

> I have read over Mr. *Wynne's* abridgment of your *Essay*. But I must confess to you, I was never more satisfy'd with the length of your *Essay*, than since I have seen this abridgment; which, tho' done justly enough, yet falls so short of that spirit which every where shews it self in the original, that nothing can be more different. To one already vers'd in the *Essay*, the abridgment serves as a good remembrancer; but, I believe, let a man wholly unacquainted with the former, begin to read the latter, and he will not so well relish it. So that how desirous soever I might have formerly been of seeing your *Essay* put into the form of a logick for the schools, I am now fully satisfy'd I was in an error; and must freely confess to you, that I wish Mr. *Wynne's* abridgment had been yet undone.[12]

When he answered these complimentary words in a letter to Molyneux on 2 July 1696, Locke did not enter into a dispute with his friend on the merits of Wynne's abridgment. In fact, he could with justice have felt that Molyneux's opinion of it was not open to serious question. What interested him, rather, was that the undergraduates at Cambridge seemed suddenly to be reading the *Essay*, as they had not previously done, and that Wynne's abridgment might have played a part in that development. Thus he wrote to Molyneux:

> 'Tis your pre-occupation, in favour of me, that makes you say what you do of Mr. *Wynne's* abridgment; I know not whether it be that, or any thing else, that has occasion'd it; but I was told, some time since, that my *Essay* began to get some credit in *Cambridge*, where, I think for some years after it was published, it was scarce so much as looked into. But now, I have some reason to think it is a little more favourably received there, by these two questions held there this last commencement; *viz. Probabile est animam non semper cogitare:* And, *Idea dei non est innata.*[13]

Locke did not live to see the abridgment succeed in winning the *Essay* an audience of undergraduates in Scottish universities, nor did

---

[11] *Some Familiar Letters*, p. 145.     [12] *Ibid.*, p. 149.
[13] *Ibid.*, pp. 156-157.

he have an early admirer in Scotland to recommend the full *Essay* to Aberdeen or Edinburgh or Glasgow or St. Andrews, as Molyneux had recommended it to Dublin. But the abridgment and its original were certainly influential in the schools of Scotland from the late 1720's to the end of the century. One of the graduation theses at Aberdeen in 1730 proposed that "omnis idea, aut oritur a sensibus aut a reflectione,"[14] and thus was Locke's doctrine of the origin of ideas made evident in Scottish educational circles some twenty-six years after his death. At the University of Edinburgh the story of his early influence is connected with John Stevenson, who was appointed to the chair of logic and metaphysics on 25 February 1730 as successor to Colin Drummond. In *The Scots Magazine* for August 1741, in an article entitled "A short account of the University of Edinburgh, the present Professors in it, and the several parts of Learning taught by them," we read that Stevenson was discharging his duties in respect to logic by lecturing "upon *Heineccii Elementa Philosophiae rationalis,* and the abridgment of Mr Locke's *Essay on Human Understanding.*" Sir Alexander Grant, classical scholar and historian, observed that Stevenson substituted Heinecke and Locke for Aristotle and Ramus with such success as to cause a principal of Edinburgh to remark in 1826 upon the extreme scarcity of lectures at that institution on Aristotle's logic after the year 1730.[15] In the same connection it might be noticed that during the eighteenth century there were ten editions of Wynne's abridgment and that two of these appeared at Edinburgh, the earlier in 1767 and the other in 1770, both obviously printed to meet the needs of undergraduates in their course in logic.[16] No doubt to perform a similar service for students at the University of Glasgow, Wynne's

---

[14] See William L. Davidson, "The University's Contribution to Philosophy," in *Studies in the History and Development of the University of Aberdeen,* ed. Peter J. Anderson (Aberdeen, 1906), p. 75.

[15] Sir Alexander Grant, *The Story of the University of Edinburgh* (London, 1884), II, 328-329. For a full account of Stevenson's career as professor of logic at Edinburgh, see Alexander Bower, *The History of the University of Edinburgh* (Edinburgh, 1817-1830), II, 269-281. See also James McCosh, *The Scottish Philosophy, Biographical, Expository, Critical, From Hutcheson to Hamilton* (New York, 1875), pp. 107-108.

[16] As I indicated above, the first edition appeared at London in 1696. There was a second edition at London in 1700; a fourth at London in 1731; a fifth at London in 1737; a seventh at Glasgow in 1752; a new edition at Edinburgh in 1767, at Edinburgh in 1770, and at Boston in 1794. I have been unable to locate copies of the third or the sixth editions.

abridgment was published in that city in 1752 by Robert and Andrew Foulis, university printers. Similar evidence that it was used at St. Andrews seems not to exist, although Henry Rymer, professor of logic, rhetoric, and metaphysics at that university between 1747 and 1756, is said to have replaced the old system of Aristotle and Ramus with the new logic of Bacon and Locke, and his example was clearly followed by his immediate successor, Robert Watson, between 1756 and 1778, and by Watson's successor, William Barron, between 1778 and 1803.[17]

Perhaps Molyneux's warm admiration of Locke's *Essay* as a new and effective logic for the mature philosopher and his desire to have Locke write something himself on that subject for university students were instrumental in shaping events, once Wynne's abridgment had not satisfied Molyneux's expectations. At any rate, Locke embarked upon a new project just as Wynne's abridgment was celebrating its first anniversay as a printed book, and the project can certainly be construed as having reference to what Molyneux had proposed almost five years before. As if, indeed, to suggest Molyneux's part in it, Locke announced the new project to Molyneux himself in a letter dated 10 April 1697:

> I have lately got a little leisure to think of some additions to my book, against the next edition, and within these few days have fallen upon a subject that I know not how far it will lead me. I have written several pages on it, but the matter, the farther I go, opens the more upon me, and I cannot yet get sight of any end of it. The title of the chapter will be *Of the Conduct of the Understanding*, which, if I shall pursue, as far as I imagine it will reach, and as it deserves, will, I conclude, make the largest chapter of my *Essay*.[18]

Molyneux died a year and a half after he had received this letter from his friend, and Locke's new project had not yet been published. But Molyneux might have seen some part of it in manuscript during his visit to England in the summer of 1698, when he met Locke for the first and only time of his life. Progress upon the rest of it might have been slow. At any rate, it was not incorporated in the fourth edition of

---

[17] See Robert Blakey, *Historical Sketch of Logic, from the Earliest Times to the Present Day* (London, 1851), pp. 436-438. Barron's logical theory, which was completely in the spirit of the new logic of Bacon, Descartes, and Locke, has been preserved in his *Lectures on Belles Lettres and Logic* (London, 1806), II, 357-597. See below, n. 62. Barron gave fourteen lectures on the second of his two main topics.

[18] *Some Familiar Letters*, p. 194.

the *Essay*, printed "with large Additions" in 1700; nor did it ever appear within that work in subsequent editions. Its first printing, in fact, occurred in 1706, two years after Locke's death, when it was included in a collection of his hitherto unpublished writings bearing the general title, *Posthumous Works of Mr. John Locke.*[19] At that time, and not until that time, did it become a matter of public knowledge that Locke had made another contribution to logic, as Molyneux had wanted him to do all along.

This contribution, the title of which may for convenience be shortened to *The Conduct of the Understanding,*[20] establishes itself in its introductory paragraphs as a timely substitute for the logical theory then being studied in universities.

> The Logick now in use has so long possessed the Chair, as the only Art taught in the Schools for the Direction of the Mind in the Study of the Arts and Sciences, that it would perhaps be thought an affectation of Novelty to suspect, that Rules that have served the learned World these two or three thousand Years, and which without any complaint of Defects the Learned have rested in, are not sufficient to guide the Understanding. And I should not doubt but this Attempt would be censured as Vanity or Presumption, did not the great Lord *Verulam's* Authority justifie it; who not servilely thinking Learning could not be advanced beyond what it was, because for many Ages it had not been, did not rest in the lazy Approbation and Applause of what was, because it was; but enlarged his Mind to what might be.[21]

Locke supported his reference to Bacon's authority by quoting next a Latin passage from the *Novum Organum* and by translating it at once into English. The translation ascribes the following sentiments to Bacon:

> *They . . . who attributed so much to Logick, perceived very well and truly, that it was not safe to trust the Understanding to it self, without the Guard of any Rules. But the Remedy reach'd not the*

[19] Its imprint reads: "London, Printed by *W. B.* for *A.* and *J. Churchill* at the *Black Swan* in *Pater-Noster-Row.* 1706."

[20] It has repeatedly been published not only under the title originally assigned to it by Locke but also under the slightly shorter title which I am using. Moreover, it has appeared as *Some Thoughts on the Conduct of the Understanding in the Search of Truth* and as *A Treatise on the Conduct of the Understanding.*

[21] *Posthumous Works of Mr. John Locke* (London, 1706), p. 4.

*Evil, but became a part of it: For the Logick which took place, though it might do well enough in civil Affairs, and the Arts which consisted in Talk and Opinion, yet comes very far short of Subtilty in the real Performances of Nature, and catching at what it cannot reach, has served to confirm and establish Errors, rather than to open a way to Truth.*[22]

In line with these opening words, *The Conduct of the Understanding* devotes itself to procedures calculated to guide the inquirer seeking an accurate understanding of the performances of nature. It is not a closely organized work. It does not follow Molyneux's original suggestion that it be accommodated to the usual forms of logic. But it has an adequate degree of order, and it may perhaps best be described as a logic for the guidance of the mental states which the inquirer should achieve if he is ever to succeed in establishing truth of any sort.

Thus, it deals first with the "three Miscarriages that Men are guilty of in reference to their Reason, whereby this Faculty is hindred in them from that Service it might do and was design'd for."[23] One of these miscarriages occurs to those who do not use their reason at all but merely follow the thinking of their parents, their neighbors, or their spiritual advisors. Another miscarriage occurs to those who put passion in the place of reason and who hearken to their own or other people's thinking only so far as it suits their humor, interest, or party to do so. The third miscarriage, to which Locke devotes a considerable amount of space, occurs to those who readily and honestly follow reason "but for want of having that which one may call *large, sound, round about Sense,* have not a full view of all that relates to the question, and may be of moment to decide it."[24] In his subsequent discussion of this part of his subject, Locke pointed to a human faculty which, if properly used, will make the rules of formal logic unnecessary. "Every Man carries about him a Touchstone, if he will make use of it to distinguish substantial Gold from superficial Glitterings, Truth from Appearances. And indeed the Use and Benefit of this Touchstone, which is natural Reason, is spoil'd and lost only by assumed Prejudices, overweening Presumption, and narrowing our Minds."[25]

[22] *Ibid.*, p. 5. (My quotation follows Locke's original in respect to the use of italics.)

[23] *Ibid.*, p. 7.  [24] *Ibid.*, p. 8.  [25] *Ibid.*, p. 12.

The next and only other major topic of this work concerns "several Weaknesses and Defects in the Understanding, either from the natural Temper of the Mind, or ill Habits taken up, which hinder it in its progress to Knowledge."[26] The tendency to be too forward or too slow in making observations on the particular facts which constitute the foundations of our civil and natural knowledge; the tendency to cram the mind with particular facts without digesting them; the tendency to draw general conclusions and raise axioms from every particular fact which one encounters; the tendency to resist "the proper business of the Understanding," which is "to think of every thing just as it is in itself," and instead, in open defiance of common sense, to do the exact contrary;[27] the tendency to hunt arguments "to make good one side of a Question, and wholly to neglect and refuse those which favour the other side"[28]—these are a few of the imposing number of just weaknesses and defects which Locke wanted the searcher of truth to be aware of and to correct in the process of making himself capable of basing his knowledge upon accurate ideas of things as they are.

*The Conduct of the Understanding* and its parent work, *An Essay concerning Human Understanding*, were without question the most popular, the most widely read, the most frequently reprinted, and the most influential of all English books of the eighteenth century. Between 1700 and 1800 Wynne's abridgment went through a total of nine editions, and these, as we have seen, greatly contributed to the influence of the *Essay* in academic circles, where the leaders of eighteenth-century thought were being educated. Thanks to the assistance which it received from the popularity of the abridgment and thanks, above all, to its own capacity to attract readers and admirers, the *Essay* flourished in the eighteenth century as no other English work did. If Molyneux found it a mark of the curious genius of the English nation that a work as abstract as the *Essay* could have gone through three editions between 1690 and 1695, the admirers of Locke in the year 1805 should have been even more complimentary toward the genius of Great Britain and Europe, for in that year the *Essay* went into its twenty-first edition at London. Moreover, those who valued the *Essay* could take added pride in the fact that it had been included in each one of the ten editions of Locke's complete works which had been published by that date and, also, that it could claim not only to have had four editions in a Latin translation prepared by an Irish friend of

---

[26] *Ibid.*, p. 47.　　　[27] *Ibid.*, p. 50.　　　[28] *Ibid.*, p. 51.

Molyneux's, Richard Burridge, for circulation in the learned world but also to have made nine appearances in the French translation by Pierre Coste and at least three appearances in German translations.[29] As for *The Conduct of the Understanding*, it had made twenty appearances in print by the year 1805. These included its first printing in 1706 among hitherto unpublished writings of Locke, its later presence, of course, in each of the first ten editions of Locke's complete works, its appearance on seven occasions as a separate volume, and its publication once in company with the full *Essay* and once in company with an abstract of the *Essay* prepared by Sir Geoffrey Gilbert.[30] Blakey says that *The Conduct of the Understanding* was often used in British universities as a textbook on logic.[31] Doubtless his remark applies especially to the work in its separate editions, which, so far as the period between 1700 and 1805 is concerned, appeared at Glasgow in 1741, 1754, and 1763, at London in 1762, 1800, and 1802, and at Dublin in 1782. Such printings all have the character of the textbook about them, and in the hundred years that followed 1805 the work went through many other editions of similar character, including eleven in company with Bacon's *Essays Moral, Economical, and Political*. But these latter publications are part of the story of the long duration of Locke's influence. Our present concern is to emphasize that the eighteenth century was the century of his special greatness and that his famous *Essay* and its supplement, *The Conduct of the Understanding,* contributed more than his other works did toward making his influence dominant.

[29] See Christophersen, *Bibliographical Introduction to Locke*, pp. 26-28, 92-99. See also H. R. Fox Bourne, *The Life of John Locke in Two Volumes* (London, 1876), II, 440-441. The British Museum holds three different copies of eighteenth-century German translations of Locke's *Essay*, one published at Altenburg in 1757, one at Mannheim in 1795, and one at Jena and Leipzig in 1795-1797. Bourne states (II, 441) that the first German translation of the *Essay* appeared at Königsberg in 1755, but no copy of it seems to have survived. See Christophersen, p. 97.

[30] See Christophersen, pp. 71-73. *The Conduct of the Understanding*, Christophersen notes, also had eighteenth-century German and French translations. Christophersen's list of appearances of this work fails to include the edition published in the year 1741, supposed to have been printed by R. Foulis at Glasgow, a copy of which is in the Princeton University Library. This copy represents the first separate edition of the work. See below, n. 34. Christophersen also fails to mention the edition published at Dublin by W. Wilson, the printer, in 1782, a copy of which is listed in *Bibliotheca Lindesiana*.

[31] *Historical Sketch of Logic*, p. 281.

Now that the *Essay* and *The Conduct of the Understanding* have been delineated as contributions to logical theory in the eyes of Locke's contemporaries and have been established as having offered an increasingly influential alternative to conventional logic in British universities and throughout the community of European learning during the eighteenth century, we need next to comment upon the precise nature of the revolution wrought by these two works in supplying the schools with a new logic containing what Molyneux called "another sort of language, than what has hitherto prevail'd there, to the great hindrance of science."[32] We need next, in short, to describe Locke's contribution to the kind of new logic which was fully to emerge in the late eighteenth century. Perhaps the best way to describe that contribution is to say bluntly that Locke founded the new logic in respect to each of seven characteristics which it possessed in its fully developed form. No one would want to deny, of course, that Bacon and Descartes had prepared the way toward the new logic, and that without them Locke's achievement might have been substantially diminished in importance or might have been prevented altogether. But it must always be remembered that Locke's *Essay* was gaining its first readers at the very moment in history when Henry Aldrich in his Aristotelian treatise, *Artis Logicae Compendium*, was denying to Bacon and Descartes the right to be considered as true logicians, and that under Aldrich's guidance the old logic seemed to have withstood successfully the assaults of its two most formidable early seventeenth-century adversaries and to be no longer in danger from them for the indefinite future.[33] Thus, without the appearance of Locke's *Essay*,

[32] See above, n. 7.

[33] Henry Aldrich (1648-1710), churchman, scholar, composer, and architect, attended Christ Church, Oxford, and took the degree of bachelor of arts in 1666. His *Artis Logicae Compendium* (Oxford, 1691) was an enormously popular work in the eighteenth and early nineteenth centuries. Inspired itself by Robert Sanderson's *Logicae Artis Compendium* (1615), it became the chief influence upon Whately's *Elements of Logic* (1826). Its determined opposition to the new logic of the late seventeenth century is proclaimed in the *Conclusio* appended to the shorter of the two versions of its first edition. That *Conclusio* says in part (translation mine): "Among the founders of the New Logic Gassendi numbers Verulam and Descartes, each of whom the *Logicae Compendium* wishes also to notice. But yet, Descartes did not plan upon the restoration of logic even in his dreams; he rather seems to attempt a philosophy which does not use the art of logic at all, perhaps in the same spirit in which he considered that geometry ought to be extended so far as to embrace all demonstration. As for Verulam, he had quite another intention in a distant sphere. His *Organon* has nothing in

Bacon and Descartes might have had to wait another century or two for full recognition in the field of logical theory, whereas with its appearance an improved form of their views began at once to get a fresh scrutiny. That is to say, the *Essay* gave their views a fully modern treatment and stripped them of the backward-looking vocabulary in which Bacon and Descartes had expressed them. Such achievements would entitle any work to a place in the history of logic. But the *Essay* possesses one other excellence that gave it special influence in its own time—an excellence at once curious, puzzling, inexplicable, wonderful. For, in addition to being a good, helpful, timely, and useful book, it had the luck to be a masterpiece as well. In that capacity it gave the new logic of the eighteenth century an auspicious beginning indeed.

In their ultimate influence upon logical doctrine *The Conduct of the Understanding* and the *Essay* may be said to have given the new logic the first of its important characteristics—that of emphasizing the connection between logic and the theory of scientific inquiry and of dissociating logic from the theory of learned communication. These two works, in short, tied logic to the inductive sciences and freed it from its traditional association with the humanistic enterprise of transmitting ideas. When *The Conduct of the Understanding* was first given a separate identity of its own through being published by itself, it received a new title consisting of thirteen words, only five of which had been part of Locke's own original title; and the thirteen words identified the work as containing "some thoughts on the conduct of the understanding in the search of truth."[34] The accuracy of the final phrase

---

common with that of Aristotle save the title alone." (*Artis Logicae Compendium,* sig. G3ᵛ.)

[34] As I indicated above, n. 30, there is a copy of this first edition in the Princeton University Library. Its title page reads in part as follows: "Some Thoughts On the Conduct of the Understanding In the Search of Truth. . . . By John Locke Esq; *Quid tam temerarium . . . defendere?* Cic. de Natura Deorum, lib. I. Printed in the Year M DCC XLI." Written by hand above the date of the edition are the following words: "Glasgovv Printed by R. Foulis." I do not find this work listed in the "Catalogue of Books Printed by Robert and Andrew Foulis," in *Notices and Documents Illustrative of the Literary History of Glasgow, During the Greater Part of Last Century* (Glasgow, 1831), pp. 49-78. Nor for that matter is it listed among the works published by the other prominent eighteenth-century Glasgow printer, Robert Urie. See *Records of the Glasgow Bibliographical Society* (Glasgow, 1915), III, 98-108. It is quite probable, however, that the Princeton bibliographer is correct in saying that Foulis printed it. The fact that its imprint omits the name of its publisher explains why it was not listed among works known to have been put out by Foulis.

in this title is obvious to all who examine what the work discusses. And the same phrase could equally well be used to designate Locke's paramount interest in writing the *Essay*, as that work reveals throughout its full extent and, in particular, in the winning terms of its "Epistle to the Reader," where Locke stated:

> I shall always have the satisfaction to have aimed sincerely at Truth and Usefulness, though in one of the meanest ways. The Commonwealth of Learning, is not at this time without Master-Builders, whose mighty Designs, in advancing the Sciences, will leave lasting Monuments to the Admiration of Posterity; But every one must not hope to be a *Boyle*, or a *Sydenham*; and in an Age that produces such Masters, as The Great—*Huygenius*, and the incomparable Mr. *Newton*, with some other of that Strain; 'tis Ambition enough to be employed as an Under-Labourer in clearing Ground a little, and removing some of the Rubbish, that lies in the way to Knowledge; which certainly had been very much more advanced in the World, if the Endeavours of ingenious and industrious Men had not been much cumbred with the learned but frivolous use of uncouth, affected, or unintelligible Terms, introduced into the Sciences, and there made an Art of, to that Degree, that Philosophy, which is nothing but the true Knowledge of Things, was thought unfit, or uncapable to be brought into well-bred Company, and polite Conversation.[35]

It must be emphasized that Locke's *Essay*, in associating itself with the method of inquiring into the true knowledge of things, did not disparage the enterprise associated with the communication of truth to others. Locke felt, however, that the method of acquiring knowledge and the method of communicating it should not be allowed to dictate to each other in such a way as to impair the functioning of either one. The method of communicating knowledge from specialist to specialist or from specialist to student, for example, had not only been a part of Ramistic logic and of early post-Ramistic Aristotelianism but had also tended to create in the old logic as a whole a false sense of values in respect to scientific inquiry. Thus, the citing of maxims at the beginning of a learned discourse and the subsequent reference to them in

---

[35] *An Essay concerning Humane Understanding, In Four Books*, The Fourth Edition, with large Additions (London, 1700), sig. b3ʳ-b4ʳ. (In this particular quotation I reverse the style of the original in respect to the use of roman and italic type.)

order to demonstrate the truth of a relevant but less familiar statement were standard parts of the procedures recommended by the old logic for teaching truths to others; but, at the same time, these very procedures tended to make truth appear to be issuing from maxims rather than from the facts of experience, with the result that maxims were regarded as being the highest of the objects of study while the facts of experience were deemed to be lower objects and were often dismissed contemptuously for producing merely probable knowledge, as distinguished from the certainty to be derived from maxims syllogistically examined. Locke had in mind this unfortunate impact of learned communication upon learned inquiry when he condemned the use of maxims as follows:

> Would those who have this Traditional Admiration of these Propositions, that they think no Step can be made in Knowledge without the support of an *Axiom*, no Stone laid in the building of the Sciences without a general *Maxim*, but distinguish between the Method of acquiring Knowledge, and of communicating it; between the Method of raising any Science, and that of teaching it to others as far as it is advanced, they would see that those general *Maxims* were not the Foundations on which the first Discoverers raised their admirable Structures, nor the Keys that unlocked and opened those Secrets of Knowledge. Though afterwards, when Schools were erected, and Sciences had their Professors to teach what others had found out, they often made use of *Maxims, i.e.* laid down certain Propositions which were self-evident, or to be received for true, which being setled in the Minds of their Scholars as unquestionable Verities, they on occasion made use of, to convince them of Truths in particular Instances, that were not so familiar to their Minds as those general *Axioms* which had before been inculcated to them and carefully setled in their Minds. Though these particular Instances, when well reflected on, are no less self-evident to the Understanding than the general *Maxims* brought to confirm them: And it was in those particular Instances, that the first Discoverer found the Truth, without the help of the general *Maxims*: And so may any one else do, who with Attention considers them.[36]

As in this passage, so in the *Essay* in general, Locke kept clearly in mind the distinction between the method of learned inquiry and the method of learned communication, and it was toward the former

[36] *Ibid.*, p. 360.

437

method, I repeat, that he directed his thought. If he had been asked to speculate upon the future of the latter method in a world in which logic no longer administered it, he might, I believe, have expressed the hope that it would identify itself with the concerns of the emerging new rhetoric and that the new rhetoric would accordingly provide the theory and doctrine for learned communication as it had historically provided the theory and doctrine for popular communication between the orator and the public. This is not the place, however, for an analysis of Locke's view of rhetoric. I need only mention here that the *Essay* contains not only Locke's memorable attack upon the accepted stylistic rhetoric of his time but also his prophetic indication of the direction in which a reconstructed rhetoric might develop out of the necessity to recognize that language is abused or deficient when it fails to convey with ease and quickness a true knowledge of things between one man and another. It was in part Locke's idea of the new rhetoric that Adam Smith and George Campbell fulfilled in the middle years of the eighteenth century, and thus Locke helped found the new rhetoric as well as the new logic.

The long passage last quoted indicates another main characteristic of the new logic, namely, its assertion that the discoverers of the truths of science find those truths in particular instances, not in general maxims. "For in particulars," said Locke in another passage, "our Knowledge begins, and so spreads its self, by degrees, to generals."[37] At still another place Locke devoted himself to a criticism of the syllogism, the central implement of the old logic, and in the course of that criticism, after citing the rule "That no Syllogistical Reasoning can be right and conclusive, but what has, at least, one general Proposition in it," he remarked with some firmness: "As if we could not *reason*, and have Knowledge *about Particulars*. Whereas, in truth, the Matter rightly considered, the immediate Object of all our Reasoning and Knowledge, is nothing but Particulars."[38] Statements like this turned the old theory of scientific inquiry upside down. For had not the old theory—as understood, for example, by John Sergeant—insisted that true science addresses itself to general principles supplied by metaphysics and that it considers its true task to be one of extracting from those principles the whole range of particular truths which could be shown to be consistent with them? It was Locke's attack upon this assumption that not only led Sergeant to write *Solid Philosophy As-*

[37] *Ibid.*, p. 362.　[38] *Ibid.*, p. 412. (Italics are those of the original passage.)

*serted* but also led the new logic of the eighteenth century to place particular things above traditional generalizations in its theory regarding the proper objects of scientific inquiry.

Locke did not address himself to the problem of constructing an inductive logic, as Dugald Stewart and John Stuart Mill were later to do with great authority and perceptiveness. But his *Essay* had certain things to say against the syllogism, in addition to the criticism noted above; and the sum of his objections to this great instrument of the old logic gave the new school of logicians of the eighteenth century still another of their distinguishing characteristics. His objections are set forth in the famous seventeenth chapter of Book IV, at which point the *Essay* is closer to the history of logical theory than it could claim to be in any other of its parts. In the first edition of the *Essay* this chapter did not contain seven subsections which were to appear in later editions as supplements in section IV. And the second edition of Wynne's abridgment gave this part of the *Essay* more space than the first edition had done. Thus, there can be no doubt that Locke's unfavorable attitude toward syllogistic logic grew stronger during his own lifetime and that the abridgment gave the unfavorable attitude an increasing amount of attention. Small wonder, then, that the new logicians became increasingly disposed to think of the syllogism with disfavor and disrespect.

The seventeenth chapter of Book IV is entitled "Of Reason." This word has various meanings in English, but, as he would use the term, said Locke, it would stand "for a Faculty in Man, That Faculty, whereby Man is supposed to be distinguished from Beasts, and wherein it is evident he much surpasses them."[39] There are four degrees in reason, he declared: "the first and highest, is the discovering, and finding out of Proofs; the second, the regular and methodical Disposition of them, and laying them in a clear and fit Order, to make their Connexion and Force be plainly and easily perceived; the third is the perceiving their Connexion; and the fourth, the making a right conclusion."[40] It is with such a vision of the full scope of reason and its several aspects that Locke proceeded to consider whether the syllogism is or is not the proper instrument and the most useful exercise of this faculty. Four considerations led him to conclude that it is not.

"*First,*" he argued, "Because Syllogism serves our Reason, but in one only of the forementioned parts of it; and that is, to shew the con-

[39] *Ibid.*, p. 404.    [40] *Ibid.*, p. 405.

nexion of the Proofs in any one instance, and no more: but in this, it is of no great use, since the Mind can perceive such Connexion where it really is, as easily, nay, perhaps, better without it."[41] When Locke made this statement, he wanted it to indicate that the syllogism applies solely to the third of the four degrees of reason and that it applies there, not as the primary means of establishing a connection among the truths under inspection, but as a device for confirming the connection seen in a previous flash of insight. He also wanted this statement to make very clear the lack of value of the syllogism even in that one capacity. His elaboration of these lines of argument contains many trenchant and memorable observations, some of which were of special significance in cutting the syllogism down to a new unimportance. If we will observe the way in which our own minds behave, he remarked, we shall find ourselves reasoning best and most clearly when we pay attention, not to the rule of the syllogism, but to the actual connection of the proof. "If Syllogisms must be taken for the only proper instrument of reason and means of Knowledge," he remarked, "it will follow, that before *Aristotle* there was not one Man that did or could know any thing by Reason; and that since the invention of Syllogisms, there is not one of Ten Thousand that doth."[42] But God had been more bountiful to man, Locke continued, than to give him two legs while leaving it to Aristotle to make him rational. In other words, God had given man a mind that can reason "without being instructed in Methods of Syllogizing: The Understanding is not taught to reason by these Rules; it has a native Faculty to perceive the Coherence, or Incoherence of its *Ideas*, and can range them right, without any such perplexing Repetitions."[43] "For the natural order of the connecting *Ideas*," Locke added somewhat later, "must direct the order of the *Syllogisms*, and a Man must see the connexion of each intermediate *Idea* with those that it connects, before he can with Reason make use of it in a *Syllogism*. And when all those Syllogisms are made, neither those that are, nor those that are not Logicians will see the force of the Argumentation. [*sic*] *i. e.* the connexion of the Extremes one jot the better."[44] Indeed, said Locke with mounting sarcasm as he concluded this first phase of his objections to formal syllogistic logic, the chief use of syllogisms in or out of the schools is to allow men "without shame to deny the connexion of *Ideas*, which even to themselves is visible."[45] By contrast, he observes, the ingenuous inquirers, having

---

[41] *Ibid.*    [42] *Ibid.*, p. 406.    [43] *Ibid.*

[44] *Ibid.*, p. 408.    [45] *Ibid.*

no aim but to find truth, "must see the connexion, that is between the intermediate *Idea*, and the two other *Ideas* it is set between, and applied to, to shew their Agreement, and when they see that, they see whether the inference be good or no, and so *Syllogism* comes too late to settle it.'[46] And if the lovers of truth allow themselves to think syllogisms useful in detecting the fallacies that are hidden in florid, witty, involved, or rhetorical discourses, they would be better advised, said Locke, "to lay the naked *Ideas* on which the force of the Argumentation depends, in their due order, in which Position the Mind taking a view of them, sees what connexion they have, and so is able to judge of the Inference, without any need of a Syllogism at all."[47]

"Secondly," Locke declared, "Another reason that makes me doubt whether Syllogism be the only proper Instrument of Reason in the discovery of Truth, is, that of whatever use *Mode* and *Figure* is pretended to be in the laying open of Fallacy (which has been above consider'd) those scholastique Forms of Discourse, are not less liable to Fallacies, than the plainer ways of Argumentation: And for this I appeal to common observation, which has always found these artificial Methods of reasoning more adapted to catch and intangle the Mind, than to instruct and inform the Understanding."[48] In supporting this argument, Locke pointed to the fact that men might be silenced by a chain of formal syllogisms and might even admire the virtuosity of the one who used them but that they would, nevertheless, not be truly convinced by such a means. "And therefore," said Locke, "Syllogism has been thought more proper for the attaining Victory in dispute, than for the Discovery or Confirmation of Truth, in fair Enquiries."[49] For those, however, who might feel the syllogism genuinely useful in their own quest for knowledge, Locke had a word of comfort. They ought, of course, to continue to employ whatever they found really helpful, and syllogisms were no exception to this rule. "All that I aim at," said Locke, "is, that they should not ascribe more to these Forms than belongs to them; And think that Men have no use, or not so full a use of their reasoning Faculty without them."[50] With these mollifying sentiments he turned to his third argument against the syllogism.

This argument consisted in the brief observation that, however lacking in utility the syllogism might be in respect to the processes by which true knowledge is established, it is of even less use in dealing with probabilities. The mind, Locke argued, judges whether a proposi-

---

[46] *Ibid.*        [47] *Ibid.*, p. 409.        [48] *Ibid.*, p. 410.
[49] *Ibid.*                 [50] *Ibid.*

tion is probable or not by weighing all the proofs and all the circumstances on both sides and by deciding where the preponderance of weight lies. Such a process requires that the mind have freedom to move wherever it feels it needs to move, whereas the syllogistic process dictates that it examine one assumed probability so exhaustively as to lose sight of the real question at issue. Locke's imagery at this point strongly reinforces his philosophical opinion. Thus, he spoke of the mind as being held "fast," "intangled perhaps, and as it were, manacled in the Chain of Syllogisms," instead of being at liberty to show "on which side, all Things considered, is the greater Probability."[51] Since in traditional rhetorical doctrine probabilities were regarded as the chief materials of rhetorical proof, the force of this argument tells ultimately against the theory that rhetorical syllogisms or enthymemes are indispensable instruments for deciding which argument is the more probable or the more weighty for deliberative speeches, debates, and popular controversies. Thus, Locke's disparagement of the syllogistic process implies a necessary reappraisal of the value of the enthymeme in rhetoric.

Locke's fourth and final objection to the syllogism was that it has no value whatever in directing the reason toward the making of new discoveries in science and scholarship. Since these discoveries are the object of the reason in its hardest task, as Locke had himself indicated, this objection tells not only against the syllogism but also against continuing the affiliations between scholastic logic and scientific inquiry. Locke's words upon these matters have lasting significance, and they should be quoted at some length:

> The Rules of *Syllogism* serve not to furnish the Mind with those intermediate *Ideas*, that may shew the connexion of remote ones. This way of reasoning discovers no new Proofs, but is the Art of marshalling, and ranging the old ones we have already. The 47th. Proposition of the First Book of *Euclid* is very true; but the discovery of it, I think, not owing to any Rules of common Logick. A Man knows first, and then he is able to prove syllogistically. So that *Syllogism* comes after Knowledge, and then a Man has little or no need of it. But 'tis chiefly by the finding out those *Ideas* that shew the connexion of distant ones, that our stock of Knowledge is increased, and that useful Arts and Sciences are advanced. *Syllogism*, at best,

[51] *Ibid.*, p. 411.

is but the Art of fencing with the little Knowledge we have, without making any Addition to it.[52]

Somewhat before Locke uttered these words, he had described in terms of two practical illustrations what he considered to be the natural way of arriving at knowledge. This natural way consists in the process which the human reason would follow by itself in forming ideas that are in agreement with the realities which the human being has to interpret. Locke called this process inference. "To infer," he declared, "is nothing but by virtue of one Proposition laid down as true, to draw in another as true, *i. e.* to see or suppose such a connexion of the two *Ideas*, of the inferr'd Proposition."[53] Locke's first illustration of this process indicates that he considered it an instantaneous action of the rational faculty in its environment of sensation and reflection. "Tell a Country Gentlewoman," he said, "that the Wind is South-West, and the Weather louring, and like to rain, and she will easily understand, 'tis not safe for her to go abroad thin clad, in such a day, after a Fever: she clearly sees the probable Connexion of all these, *viz.* South-West-Wind, and Clouds, Rain, wetting, taking Cold, Relapse, and danger of Death, without tying them together in those artificial and cumbersome Fetters of several Syllogisms, that clog and hinder the Mind, which proceeds from one part to another quicker and clearer without them: and the Probability which she easily perceives in Things thus in their native State, would be quite lost, if this Argument were managed learnedly, and proposed in Mode and Figure."[54] Locke's other illustration of the natural process of inference applies, not primarily to the conclusions of everyday life, but to the world of philosophical argument.[55] And yet this example, too, is close to familiar experience: "Let this be the Proposition laid down, *Men shall be punished in another World*, and from thence be inferred this other, *then Men can determine themselves*. The Question now is to know, whether the Mind has made this Inference right or no; if it has made it by finding out the intermediate *Ideas*, and taking a view of the connexion of them, placed in a due order, it has proceeded rationally, and made a right Inference." After a precise denial that the mind would in the first instance resort to syllogisms in determining whether there is a rational connection between the idea of men's punishment in another world and the idea of men's freedom and self-determination, Locke went on:

[52] *Ibid.*   [53] *Ibid.*, p. 407.   [54] *Ibid.*, p. 406.   [55] *Ibid.*, p. 407.

In the instance above mentioned, what is it shews the force of the Inference, and consequently the reasonableness of it, but a view of the connexion of all the intermediate *Ideas* that draw in the Conclusion, or Proposition inferr'd. *v. g. Men shall be punished,—God the punisher,—just Punishment,—the Punished guilty—could have done otherwise—Freedom—self-determination*, by which Chain of *Ideas* thus visibly link'd together in train, *i. e.* each intermediate *Idea* agreeing on each side with those two it is immediately placed between, the *Ideas* of Men and self-determination appear to be connected. *i. e.* this Proposition *Men can determine themselves* is drawn in, or inferr'd from this *that they shall be punished in the other World.*

Those who deny the belief in freedom of the will might be disposed to quarrel with the content of the passage just quoted, but they should not allow such a doctrinal consideration to cloud their awareness that Locke's two illustrations present a revolutionary picture of the human mind at work upon the facts of its environment. Locke saw the mind engaged with such concrete realities as the southwest wind, the clouds, the likelihood of rain, the thought of getting wet and catching cold, the recollection of a recent fever, and the sense of danger in a relapse and death. He saw the mind proceed from its own conviction that it would face punishment in the other world to its sense of God and justice and guilt and innocence and freedom. To Locke, these were the sequences which began with things and ended in knowledge. These were the sequences which the old logic called an imperfect form of the syllogism but which were in reality the perfect form of inference. Moreover, these were the sequences which would give learned discourse a new pattern of organization and a new theory of method, in contrast to the scholastic theory of arranging ideas in a strict descending order of generality or in a syllogistic or enthymematic formulation. The new rhetoric, so far as it would seek to describe the method of communication to be used in the world of scholarship and science, could be expected to recommend the natural movement of discourse from a factual statement to its successive logical consequents and to find completely unusable the methods that had been dictated by Ramus, Sanderson, and Aldrich. It could be expected to do so, that is to say, wherever it had the courage to follow Locke into the modern world.

In his evaluation of the syllogism Locke did not discuss the *dictum de omni et nullo*, even though traditional logicians had considered it to be the principle from which the whole impressive structure of syllogistic logic had been deduced. Nevertheless, when the new logicians of the eighteenth century began to disparage the *dictum*, they were reflecting an attitude that can be traced to implications in Locke's *Essay*, and thus Locke may also be supposed to have supplied the new logic with this particular characteristic. In a very real sense, of course, Locke's whole theory of the origin of human knowledge tells against what the *dictum* took for granted—that the foundation of our understanding of the individual case rests upon our previous understanding of the whole class to which the individual case belongs. This assumption, indeed, was not only at odds with the concepts which Locke evolved to explain the actions of the human mind in the quest for truth; it was also contrary to his view of the generating forces behind the development of any given science. "There is, I know," said he, "a great deal of Talk, propagated from Scholastick Men, of Sciences and the *Maxims* on which they are built: But it has been my ill luck, never to meet with any such Sciences; much less any one built upon these two *Maxims, What is, is*; and *It is impossible for the same thing to be and not to be*." "And I would be glad to be shewn," he continued, "where any such Science erected upon these, or any other general *Axioms* is to be found: and should be obliged to any one who would lay before me the Frame and System of any Science so built on these, or any such like *Maxims*, that could not be shewn to stand as firm without any Consideration of them."[56] If these words cannot be construed to suggest that Locke had no regard for the *dictum* considered as the main source of the principles of logic, then the new logicians of the eighteenth century may be assumed to have acquired their own disrespect for the *dictum* from some other source than the *Essay*. But the chances in favor of this latter eventuality are not numerous or convincing.

The chances are excellent, however, that Locke's distaste for the disputation as an effective instrument in the establishment and propagation of truth was a direct influence in providing the new logic with the same attitude and, hence, with another of its major characteristics. From the quotations which I have used to clarify Locke's adverse opinion of the syllogism, it can be seen that he regarded disputation more as an exercise in entangling the mind of an opponent in fallacies,

---

[56] *Ibid.*, p. 359.

in achieving a victory over him in debate, or in fencing against him with what little knowledge one may have than as an instrument for discovering or confirming truth in fair inquiries. This selfsame unfavorable attitude toward disputation appears in other parts of the *Essay*.

For example, in chapter X of Book III, in speaking of the deliberate resort to obscure words as one of the abuses of language, Locke said:

> To this abuse, and the mischiefs of confounding the Signification of Words, Logick, and the liberal Sciences, as they have been handled in the Schools, have given Reputation; and the admired Art of Disputing, hath added much to the natural imperfection of Languages, whilst it has been made use of, and fitted, to perplex the signification of Words, more than to discover the Knowledge and Truth of Things: And he that will look into that sort of learned Writings, will find the Words there much more obscure, uncertain, and undetermined in their Meaning, than they are in ordinary Conversation.[57]

Locke disparaged disputation again in his chapter on maxims, where he speculated that these were used in debate, not as the true originals and sources of knowledge, but as conventions which, on being invoked by a disputant, required his opponent as a matter of ritual to admit the force of the argument to which they were tied and thus concede defeat. But why were such rituals acceptable? Because, said Locke, the schools, "having made Disputation the Touchstone of Mens Abilities, and the *Criterion* of Knowledge, adjudg'd Victory to him that kept the Field: and he that had the last Word was concluded to have the better of the Argument, if not of the Cause."[58] Certainly, these opinions show little of the respect lavished by the old logic upon maxims and much of the disrespect which Locke cherished toward the philosophical disputes of his own day.[59] But, of course, it must be remembered that his disapproval was directed less against the dispute as a preparatory academic exercise than against its presumption in claiming for itself a crucial role in the search for the true knowledge of things.

The new logic of eighteenth-century Britain was to question the propriety of using the ancient machinery of topics as a means of arriving at scientific proofs for propositions under investigation, and ulti-

---

[57] *Ibid.*, p. 291.          [58] *Ibid.*, p. 360.
[59] For further confirmation of Locke's disapproval of disputation, see his *Some Thoughts, concerning Education*, in *The Works of John Locke in Four Volumes*, 7th ed. (London, 1768), IV, 116-117.

mately that machinery was to disappear as a subject of attention in logical theory. Locke encouraged this development, and thus his work may be said to be connected with another of the characteristics of the new school. But, so far as his logical writings are concerned, he did not condemn the topics in any detail, no doubt because their use was directly contrary to his whole theory that true understanding originates in the study of things rather than in the manipulation of words and, also, because the topics had been so severely questioned by *The Port-Royal Logic* and by Bernard Lamy's *The Art of Speaking* that little remained to be said against them.[60] Nevertheless, Locke did speak directly upon this matter, and I shall indicate his attitude by pointing to one set of remarks concerning it in *The Conduct of the Understanding*.

These remarks fall in the final pages, where he emphasized once more that in any question under scrutiny the most important thing is "to examine and find out upon what it bottoms."[61] Here he delivered a broader and more devastating condemnation of topical argument than he had previously done:

> Most of the Difficulties that come in our way, when well consider'd and trac'd, lead us to some Proposition, which known to be true, clears the Doubt, and gives an easie Solution of the Question, whilst Topical and Superficial Arguments, of which there is store to be found on both sides, filling the Head with variety of Thoughts, and the Mouth with copious Discourse, serve only to amuse the Understanding, and entertain Company without coming to the bottom of the Question, the only place of Rest and Stability for an inquisitive Mind, whose tendency is only to Truth and Knowledge.

Locke did not concede that the topics might be useful in teaching youngsters to write Latin compositions in support of propositions which, on the one hand, were deemed true in the eyes of the learned and, on the other, were considered difficult to handle when the student was not allowed to discuss them in his native tongue. Indeed, the chief use of the topics had historically been to encourage fluency in Latin within a culture which regarded the acquisition of that language as a necessary part of learning and religion; and within such a context

---

[60] See my *Logic and Rhetoric in England, 1500-1700*, pp. 355-357, 380-381.

[61] *Posthumous Works of Mr. John Locke*, p. 127; see also pp. 31, 54, for Locke's previous disparagements of the topics. My present discussion of Locke's attitude toward topical arguments borrows wording from a paragraph of my recently published essay, "John Locke and the New Rhetoric," *Quarterly Journal of Speech*, vol. 53 (1967), p. 324.

the topics possessed a real but limited value. Even there, however, they encouraged the idea that the verbal copiousness which they sought to produce was a desirable end in itself, when as a matter of fact it is a desirable end only when it is coupled with the highest regard for accuracy and consistency of verbal statement. Since Locke's whole emphasis was upon the need to develop in students a true respect for these two latter qualities, it is understandable that he would not think highly of an educational machinery which overlooked them in order to give undue stress to some lesser goal.

The final characteristic of the new British logic of the eighteenth century was its belief that truth is achieved when verbal statements correspond to the factual states with which they are dealing. William Barron, professor of logic, rhetoric, and metaphysics at St. Andrews between 1778 and 1803, was one of the new logicians who defined this belief with great clarity and directness. "Truth," he said, "relates to the enunciation of knowledge, and is the agreement of ideas with words. If I assert that the British is a free government, and that the English are more industrious than any other nation in Europe, I maintain truth, because my words actually correspond to accurate ideas of the facts."[62] There can be no doubt that Barron had Locke's *Essay* in mind when he defined truth in this way, inasmuch as his defintion bears a striking resemblance to Locke's own as set forth in chapter V of Book IV. That chapter, which is entitled "Of Truth in general," begins by remarking that, since truth is what all men search for or, at least, pretend to search for, its exact nature is something that requires careful examination, so that we may understand in what it consists and how the mind may distinguish it from falsehood. At this point Locke defined truth as follows:

> *Truth* then seems to me, in the proper import of the Word, to signify nothing but *the joining or separating of Signs, as the Things signified by them, do agree or disagree one with another.* The *joining* or *separating* of signs here meant is what by another name, we call Proposition. So that Truth properly belongs only to Propositions: whereof there are two sorts, *viz.*, Mental and Verbal; as there are two sorts of Signs commonly made use of, *viz. Ideas* and Words.[63]

This definition led Locke to speak of two aspects of truth: truth of thought, in which our ideas of things correspond to the things them-

---

[62] *Lectures on Belles Lettres and Logic,* II, 412.
[63] *Essay concerning Humane Understanding,* p. 344.

selves, and truth of words, in which our ideas of things and our words about those ideas also correspond. Having discussed various troublesome questions connected with the understanding of these aspects, Locke returned once more to his main subject, and once more he spoke of the nature of the concept of truth.

> *Truth* is the marking down in Words, the agreement or disagreement of *Ideas* as it is. *Falshood* is the marking down in Words, the agreement or disagreement of *Ideas* otherwise than it is. And so far as these *Ideas*, thus marked by Sounds, agree to their Archetypes, so far only is the *Truth real*. The knowledge of this Truth, consists in knowing what *Ideas* the Words stand for, and the perception of the agreement or disagreement of those *Ideas*, according as it is marked by those Words.[64]

In the old logic, too, truth was acknowledged to be the accurate correspondence between verbal propositions and factual states. But this acknowledgment tended always to be obscured or supplanted by the more attractive belief that truth is achieved when a particular statement can be shown to have issued from a preexisting self-evident axiom. In other words, the old logic was prevailingly interested in defining truth in terms of consistency, whereas Locke and his school preferred to define it in terms of accuracy. It is instructive at this point to remind ourselves that the syllogism is the most efficient instrument ever perfected for testing the consistency of verbal propositions—a fact which helps to explain the enduring popularity of deductive logic. Moreover, in historical periods characterized by an unswerving belief in a body of theological revelations or metaphysical first principles, the chief business of man is to establish consistency between the particulars of his daily conduct and the truths to which he subscribes, and at such times the syllogism seems to provide perfect guidance in the quest for certainty. Bacon and Descartes had not questioned the efficacy of this function of the syllogism. But they had been disturbed by the indifference of the old logic to the factual inaccuracy of many of the standard propositions cited to illustrate syllogistic major premises, and they had rightly questioned whether those propositions were entitled to guarantee the truth of any conclusion drawn from them in conformity to rule. Their desire to protect reason against supposing that consistency alone is the test of truth led them to disparage the old logic, and Locke added his powerful authority to theirs. Nowhere

---

[64] *Ibid.*, p. 346.

is the difference between the old logic and the new more significant and more interesting than it is on this particular issue.

Locke's formula for the new logic was more impressively stated in his own works than in any of the early logics claiming to have been influenced by him.[65] In fact, his first acknowledged followers were inclined to borrow from his discussion of ideas and of words but to remain loyal to traditional doctrine when they spoke of the forms of reasoning. This tendency began in Jean Le Clerc's *Logica*, published in 1692 in London and in Amsterdam. Not only was this work indebted to Locke's *Essay*, as Molyneux pointed out at once,[66] but it was also the earliest European work to view the *Essay* as a contribution to logic. Even so, it is not conspicuous for its boldness or novelty. As editor of a monthly periodical, the *Bibliothèque Universelle et Historique*, Le Clerc prevailed upon Locke to write an English epitome of his projected *Essay* and to allow Le Clerc to translate it into French and include it in one of his issues. The epitome was accordingly published in January 1688, two years before the full *Essay* appeared. It is obvious, of course, that the epitome could do no more than indicate what the main subjects of the *Essay* would be and how each subject looked in preliminary outline. It could not be expected to do full justice to anything. Thus, it was not the sort of document that would be likely to revolutionize logical theory, and, indeed, it was able to do scant justice to what would ultimately become Locke's criticism of syllogistic logic.[67] Le Clerc in his *Logica* acknowledged his indebted-

---

[65] For other studies of Locke's contribution to logic, see the following: Blakey, *Historical Sketch of Logic*, pp. 271-282; Eduard Martinak, *Zur Logik Lockes: John Lockes Lehre von den Vorstellungen aus dem Essay concerning Human Understanding* (Graz, 1887); Walther Küppers, *John Locke und die Scholastik* (Berlin, 1895); A. Tellkamp, *Das Verhältnis John Locke's zur Scholastik* (Münster in Westfalen, 1927), pp. 34-45; W. and M. Kneale, *The Development of Logic* (Oxford, 1962), pp. 312-313.

The anonymous treatise, *Lectures on Locke: or, the Principles of Logic: designed for the Use of Students in the University* (London, 1840), I have not seen. Nor have I examined William Knighton, *The Utility of the Aristotelian Logic; or the Remarks of Bacon, Locke, Reid and Stewart on that Subject considered; being the Substance of Three Lectures delivered to the Senior Students of the Hindu College, Calcutta* (Calcutta, 1847).

[66] See *Some Familiar Letters*, pp. 16-17.

[67] See *Bibliothèque Universelle et Historique*, VIII (Jan. 1688), 136-137. The epitome devoted thirty lines of type to Locke's much longer discussion of syllogistic logic in the *Essay*, Bk. IV, ch. XVII.

ness to the epitome, not to the *Essay* as a whole.[68] Small wonder, then, that his treatment of the syllogism was fully conventional, his indebtedness to the *Essay* being confined to his discussion of perception and ideas. The same sort of comment is applicable to Jean-Pierre de Crousaz's *Logique*. When Crousaz translated it finally into Latin and published it as the *Logicae Systema*, he avowed in his preface that "the most famous and most justly celebrated *De Intellectu Humano*, by Mr. Locke, is a distinguished work, the best thing that we have from him, and it will always be numbered among the most useful of logics."[69] But it was clear to English readers from John Henley's translation of the French text of this work that Crousaz was traditional in his explanation of the syllogism and that he was influenced by Locke's *Essay* only when he spoke of perceptions.[70] So, too, Isaac Watts's *Logick*, which was enormously popular in England and America throughout the period from 1725 to 1825, reflected its author's knowledge of Locke's *Essay* and *The Conduct of the Understanding*, while hewing to the traditional line in dealing with syllogisms.[71] Its chief rival in popularity between 1748 and 1825 was William Duncan's *Elements of Logick*, a work of great merit and of undoubted influence in suggesting to Thomas Jefferson the organizing principle of the Declaration of Independence.[72] But even Duncan, the most sensitive interpreter of Locke's logical doctrine to appear on the scene before 1750, did not respond to Locke's criticism of the syllogism, although he did recognize promising alternatives to it in the fields of natural science and history.

[68] See Joannes Clericus, *Logica: sive, Ars Ratiocinandi* (London, 1692), sig. *3ᵛ.

[69] See Ioh. Petrus De Crosa, *Logicae Systema, Juxta Principia ab ipso in Gallico Opere posita* (Geneva, 1724), sig. †7ʳ. (Translation mine.)

[70] See Jean-Pierre de Crousaz, *A New Treatise of the Art of Thinking. . . . In Two Volumes* (London, 1724), I, 9-292; II, 191-295. See also Jacqueline E. de La Harpe, *Jean-Pierre de Crousaz (1663-1750)*, University of California Publications in Modern Philology, vol. 47 (Berkeley/Los Angeles, 1955), p. 207. John Henley declared himself to be the translator of Crousaz's *Logique* in his pamphlet, *Books Written, and Publish'd, By the Reverend John Henley, M.A.* (London, 1724), p. 12; also in his periodical, *Oratory Transactions*, No. I, p. 12. Professor La Harpe, pp. 29, 270, attributes this translation to Benjamin Hoadly, I know not on what grounds.

[71] See Isaac Watts, *Logick* (London, 1725), pp. 20-21, 42, 47, 68, 177-179, 421-504.

[72] See "The Declaration of Independence and Eighteenth-Century Logic," *William and Mary Quarterly*, 3rd ser., no. 18 (Oct. 1961), pp. 463-484.

Indeed, the new logic did not begin to reach maturity until 1774. That was the year when Thomas Reid contributed to Lord Kames's *Sketches of the History of Man,* upon the invitation of Kames himself, an essay entitled "A Brief Account of Aristotle's Logic. With Remarks." Reid's achievement consisted in his subjecting syllogistic logic to a withering analysis and inductive logic to a challenging and enthusiastic summons to battle. Then, within the next twenty-four months, George Campbell's *Philosophy of Rhetoric* came out with its memorable attack upon the syllogism as, in effect, a *petitio principii,* a question-begging device, a self-defeating effort to use a proposition to prove itself.[73] Campbell developed Locke's criticism of the syllogism so far as to remove that historic implement altogether from Campbell's own theory of proof and to replace it by natural logic. After Reid and Campbell came Dugald Stewart. His lectures on moral philosophy at the University of Edinburgh between 1785 and 1809 contained the most brilliant analysis of inductive logic before the time of John Stuart Mill.[74] I cannot discuss those lectures here for reasons of space. But it seems fair to remark that Stewart, Campbell, and Reid succeeded in giving the new logic the effective endorsement and interpretation that Locke would have accepted as a major step toward the fulfillment of his own vision. The actual fulfillment of that vision would come, of course, with the publication of John Stuart Mill's *A System of Logic, Ratiocinative and Inductive* at London in 1843.

[73] See George Campbell, *The Philosophy of Rhetoric In Two Volumes* (London, 1776), I, 163-185.

[74] Stewart's lectures on the new logic were published in his *Elements of the Philosophy of the Human Mind.* They can be found in *The Collected Works of Dugald Stewart,* ed. Sir William Hamilton, Bart. (Edinburgh, 1854-1860), III, 70-365.

# INDEX*

* NOTE: In general, footnotes have not been indexed.

453